# Diversity IN EDUCATION

## Diversity in Education Faculty Committee

Grand Valley State University
**School of Education**

Cover photo © 1996 by Silver Burdett Ginn.

Excerpts taken from:

*Teaching in a Diverse Society,*
by Herbert Grossman
Copyright © 1995 by Allyn & Bacon
A Pearson Education Company
Upper Saddle River, New Jersey 07458

*Teaching Exceptional, Diverse, and At-Risk Students in
the General Education Classroom,* Second Edition,
by Sharon Vaughn, Candace S. Bos, and Jeanne Shay Schumm
Copyright © 2000, 1997 by Allyn & Bacon

This copyright covers material written expressly for this volume by the editor/s as well as the compilation itself. It does not cover the individual selections herein that first appeared elsewhere. Permission to reprint these has been obtained by Pearson Custom Publishing for this edition only. Further reproduction by any means, electronic or mechanical, including photocopying and recording, or by any information storage or retrieval system, must be arranged with the individual copyright holders noted.

This publication has been printed using selections as they appeared in their original format. Layout and appearance will vary accordingly.

Printed in the United States of America

10 9 8 7 6 5 4 3 2 1

*Please visit our website at www.pearsoncustom.com*

ISBN 0-536-60323-5

BA 990709

PEARSON CUSTOM PUBLISHING
160 Gould Street/Needham Heights, MA 02494
A Pearson Education Company

# Acknowledgments

I would like to thank the following School of Education faculty for their contributions toward the completion of this textbook:

Mary Antony Bair
Edward Birch
Ram Chattulani
Patsy Fox
Diane Hollums
Marty Lithedand
Linda McCrea
Allan Ten Eyck
Connie Widdis

Their devotion to this course and constant efforts to serve our students creates a dynamic learning and teaching environment for us all.
-David E. Bair, Diversity in Education course coordinator

# Contents

**PART I: TEACHING IN A DIVERSE SOCIETY**
*HERBERT GROSSMAN*

CHAPTER 1
SCHOOL RELATED DIFFICULTIES .................................................3

CHAPTER 2
INTRINSIC CAUSES OF ETHNIC AND SOCIOECONOMIC DISPARITIES ..........17

CHAPTER 3
EXTRINSIC CAUSES OF ETHNIC AND SOCIOECONOMIC DISPARITIES ..........55

CHAPTER 4
COMMUNICATIVELY APPROPRIATE EDUCATION .........................89

CHAPTER 5
CAUSES OF GENDER DISPARITIES ....................................119

CHAPTER 6
GENDER APPROPRIATE EDUCATION ..................................139

CHAPTER 7
ASSESSMENT IN A DIVERSE SOCIETY .................................153

CHAPTER 8
INSTRUCTION IN A DIVERSE SOCIETY ................................179

**PART II: TEACHING EXCEPTIONAL, DIVERSE, AND AT-RISK STUDENTS IN THE GENERAL EDUCATION CLASSROOM**
*SHARON VAUGHN, CANDACE S. BOS, JEANNE SHAY SCHUMM*

CHAPTER 9
PLANNING AND GROUPING STRATEGIES FOR SPECIAL LEARNERS ..........225

CHAPTER 10
TEACHING STUDENTS WITH LEARNING DISABILITIES
OR ATTENTION DEFICIT DISORDERS ..................................257

CHAPTER 11
TEACHING STUDENTS WITH COMMUNICATION DISORDERS . . . . . . . . . . . . . . . .289

CHAPTER 12
TEACHING STUDENTS WITH EMOTIONAL AND BEHAVIORAL DISORDERS . . . . . .319

CHAPTER 13
TEACHING STUDENTS WITH MENTAL RETARDATION
AND SEVERE DISABILITIES . . . . . . . . . . . . . . . . . . . . . . . . . . . . . . . . . . . . . . . .343

CHAPTER 14
TEACHING STUDENTS WITH VISUAL IMPAIRMENTS, HEARING LOSS
PHYSICAL DISABILITIES, OR HEALTH IMPAIRMENTS . . . . . . . . . . . . . . . . . . . . .373

CHAPTER 15
TEACHING CULTURALLY AND LINGUISTICALLY DIVERSE STUDENTS . . . . . . . . . .403

## PART III: JOURNAL ARTICLES

**CHAPTER 16**
THE SILENCED DIALOGUE: POWER AND PEDAGOGY
IN EDUCATING OTHER PEOPLE'S CHILDREN . . . . . . . . . . . . . . . . . . . . . . . . . . .439

CHAPTER 17
EMPOWERING MINORITY STUDENTS: A FRAMEWORK FOR INTERVENTION . . . . .458

CHAPTER 18
SOCIAL CLASS AND THE HIDDEN CURRICULUM OF WORK . . . . . . . . . . . . . . . .478

CHAPTER 19
CHALLENGES FOR EDUCATORS: LESBIAN, GAY, AND BISEXUAL FAMILIES . . . . . .502

**APPENDIX**
**MAKING A DIFFERENCE THROUGH ACTION LEARNING:**
**TEACHING STUDY SKILLS, LEARNING STRATEGIES, AND SELF-ADVOCACY** . . . . .527

DIMENSIONS OF MULTICULTURAL EDUCATION . . . . . . . . . . . . . . . . . . . . . . . .545

# PART 1: Teaching in a Diverse Society

## Herbert Grossman

# Chapter 1

# School Related Difficulties

To be truly just, society should guarantee that all students have an equal opportunity to succeed in school regardless of their ethnic and socioeconomic background, their gender, living conditions (the contextual aspects of their lives), and English proficiency or dialect. Unfortunately, many students are poorly served by and fail to succeed in the American education system. Among these are students from non-European ethnic backgrounds, especially African American, Native American, and Hispanic American students; students from employed and unemployed poor families; rural students; immigrant and refugee students; limited English proficient students and those who speak a nonstandard English dialect; homeless students; and students whose school experiences are adversely affected by gender biases. This introductory chapter describes the many school-related problems of such students.

## *Ethnic and Socioeconomic Disparities*

The population of the United States is rapidly becoming less European American (1–5). By the year 2000, non-European Americans are expected to comprise one third of the U. S. population. The three fastest growing groups are Hispanic Americans, African Americans, and Southeast Asian Americans. The two largest minority groups, 30 million African Americans and 20 million Hispanic Americans, will comprise almost a third of the total school enrollment. Currently, non-European American students are the majority in the 25 largest school districts in the country. The number of children and youth living in poverty is also continuing to rise. Between 1979 and 1989, the numbers of Hispanic American, European American, and African American children living in poverty increased by 29%, 25%, and 6%, respectively, leading to an overall increase of 19%.

Many non-European American students and students from employed and unemployed poor families do very well in school. However, as the following statistics indicate the lack of educational success that characterizes these students as a whole is a national disaster:

1. The average achievement of African American, Native American, Hispanic American, and poor students is consistently lower than that of middle- and upper-class European American students at every grade level (6–17). By the eleventh and twelfth grades only 25.7% of European American students have repeated at least one grade level; the corresponding figures for African American and Hispanic American students are 39.0% and 40.8%, and for Hispanic American males, 54.2% (16).

2. A smaller percentage of African American, Hispanic American, and Native American students graduate high school (7, 18–28). Although the dropout rate of African American students has improved dramatically in recent years, in large cities where the vast majority of African American students are poor more than half of them drop out (7). On a nationwide basis, Native Americans have the highest dropout rate. In Alaska and California, their dropout rate has been estimated at 90% and 70%, respectively (25, 28). The Hispanic American dropout rate is almost as high. In some areas, such as New York City, the rate has been as high as 80%. As a group, Asian and Pacific Americans have a low dropout rate; however, combining the statistics for all Asian and Pacific Americans is misleading. Those immigrant and refugee students who come from developing countries where they and their families had little access to formal education have very high dropout rates.

3. African American students, especially males, are also more likely to get into trouble in school and to be suspended (14, 29-34).

4. Although many non–European American high school students perform very well during their high school years, the average achievement level of these graduates leaves much to be desired. In comparison to European American students, African American, Hispanic American, and Native American students who graduate from high school are less likely to be computer literate or to have enrolled in high-level academic courses such as algebra, geometry, trigonometry, chemistry, physics, biology, and foreign languages. They are also more likely to have taken remedial math and science classes (9, 16).

The results for students who are poor and have either an African American or Hispanic American background are especially discouraging. In comparison to middle-class African American and Hispanic American students, they are even more likely to drop out of school, to achieve less while in school, and to earn lower grades. They are also more likely to be enrolled in general and vocational programs than academic programs and remedial rather than advanced or honors classes.

## *Gender Disparities*

Although students' performance and participation in school cannot be predicted on the basis of their gender alone, on the average, males and females have somewhat different experiences in the American education system. These differences are discussed next.

When students are given the opportunity to select their courses and activities, males and females make somewhat different choices (35–45). Females tend to enroll in fewer advanced math courses, especially intermediate algebra and calculus, computer courses, and science courses—the courses that are important for college admission and for success in many technological and scientific fields. This generalization characterizes females from many Asian and Pacific American backgrounds, those who are Native Americans, and European American and Hispanic American females from poor backgrounds. It is not true for African American females in general or for females from European American, Filipino American, and Vietnamese American middle-class backgrounds.

There is considerable evidence that males and females choose very different vocational education courses and aspire to different careers (46–60). Females comprise more than 90% of the students in cosmetology, clerical, home economics, and health courses, and less than 10% of the students in courses that deal with agriculture, electrical technology, electronics, appliance repair, auto mechanics, carpentry, welding, and small engine repair. In general, Hispanic American, Southeast Asian American, and poor European American males are more likely than females to plan to work outside the home and to aspire to professional careers that require at least a bachelor's degree. These gender differences do not apply to the same extent to middle-class European American, Vietnamese American, Filipino American, and African American students.

Although the gender gap on standardized achievement tests and school grades has narrowed in recent years (61–66), male and female students still have different success rates in many academic subjects and skills (67–101). However, many of these differentials do not apply to all ethnic groups and socioeconomic classes. African American, Hispanic American, European American, and Native American females receive higher grades than males on tests of verbal skills in both elementary and secondary school. In elementary school, females, with the exception of Native Americans, tend to score higher than males on mathematics skills tests. Beginning in high school, females, again with the exception of Native Americans, score better than males on tests of basic computational skills. However, with the exception of African American females and some Asian groups, they score less adequately than males on mathematics tests involving complex mathematical skills, word problems, and visual-spatial tasks.

In elementary school there are few, if any, gender differences in students' science achievement. In secondary school, males tend to score higher than females on tests of physical and earth science information, but not on tests of health science information. Poor and African American males are exception to this generalization.

Females are less likely to get into trouble for behavioral problems, and they are less likely to be disciplined by their teachers or suspended from school (14, 102–105).

In comparison to males, European American and Hispanic American females are more fearful and anxious in courses such as science and math, traditionally thought to be in the male domain (108, 109). African American females are no more and perhaps even less anxious than African American males in these courses (107). Recently, females have become less anxious in these courses, perhaps because they are less likely to be perceived to be in the male domain (106).

With the exception of African American students, females tend to be less self-confident about school than males, especially in courses that are considered to be in the male domain such as mathematics and science courses, in competitive situations, and when they lack objective information about how well they have done or can do (110–118). They react less positively than males to difficult and challenging situations and are less likely to take risks in school (119, 120). Females are less persistent and perform less adequately than males following failure or the threat of failure (116, 121). Finally, female students tend to seek the assistance and approval of adults more than males do (122–125).

These characterizations do not apply to all females. They are more likely to apply to poor females and to Hispanic American and Asian and Pacific American females who are brought up in families that adhere to traditional ideas about sex roles, rather than to European American middle-class females and African American females (50, 126, 127). However, these characteristics do apply to other ethnic groups and to many females regardless of their ethnic or socioeconomic backgrounds.

## *Contextual Disparities*

The contextual aspects, or living conditions, of many students affect their achievement in school. Migrant students' dropout rate, which has been estimated at between 45% and 57%, is the highest rate of any group in the United States (130–132). Even while they are attending school these students often fail to actualize their potential for learning. The dropout rate for rural students, between 40% and 50%, is more than twice the national average (see Chapter 5).

Between 1,000,000 and 1,500,000 children and youth run away from home each year (133). Because they attend school erratically, move from place to place, do not have the documents required by schools, and lack parents or guardians to speak and sign for them, they are unlikely to receive the education services they require. Estimates of the number of homeless children range from 272,773 to 1,600,000 (128, 129). The problems that confront homeless children interfere with their schooling to the point that many of them do not even attend school.

## *Communicative Disparities*

The limited English proficient (LEP) population is the fastest-growing in the United States. Although estimates of how many LEP children and adolescents are now in the schools vary, it is probable that almost 8 million American youngsters have a non-English background, either because they were born elsewhere or because they grew up in a home in which another language was spoken. More than 3 million of these students scored in the lowest 20% on tests of English proficiency. More than 5 million scored in the lower 40%. Whichever of these two figures one uses, it is clear that millions of students are not proficient enough in English to function in English-only classes without considerable difficulty (134, 135). Unfortunately, many LEP students do poorly in school because they are taught by monolingual English-speaking teachers. The problems of students who speak nonstandard English or who use non–European American non–middle-class communication styles are similar but not nearly as severe (see Chapter 6).

## *Research-Based Approach*

This text emphasizes research findings. Enough is known about the role of ethnic, socioeconomic, gender, and contextual factors in education for teachers to take these factors into account when they assess, instruct, and manage their students. The following are two examples of how knowledge of these factors can help educators.

Some educators employ competitive instructional techniques because they believe such techniques bring out the best in students. Other educators stress cooperative approaches because they think these improve relationships among students, prepare them to function in a democratic society, and lead to higher levels of achievement. However, research indicates that, with exceptions, males, in general, and European Americans and certain Asian and Pacific Americans perform better in competitive learning situations, whereas females, in general, and other ethnic groups such as African Americans, Hispanic Americans, and Hawaiian Americans perform better in cooperative learning situations.

Educators who act on their preference for competitive or cooperative learning without considering their students' preferred learning styles will only meet some students' needs. Educators who are aware of differences in students' learning styles can make reasonable choices. If they want to maximize students' academic achievement, they can use cooperative techniques with some students and competitive ones with others. However, if their goal is to help students to act competitively when competition is required and cooperatively when cooperation is required, the educators might employ techniques designed to expand students' behavioral repertoires. In either case, a knowledge of gender and ethnic differences in preferences for competitive and cooperative learning environments would certainly help.

Some primary-grade teachers tend to use material reinforcers, such as food, toys, and time to use especially desirable classroom equipment, or symbolic rewards, such as gold stars, checks, and points that can be converted into material rewards to motivate students. Others prefer to use interpersonal motivational techniques, such as praising students, telling students they are proud of them, patting them on the back, sending home a note, and so on. Research indicates that females, Hispanic Americans, African Americans, and certain other groups are more receptive to personal rewards. Males and European Americans are more responsive to impersonal rewards, especially in the lower grades. A knowledge of students' ethnic- and gender-influenced preferences can help an educator select effective reinforcers.

Some words of caution about research-based teaching are in order. Although we know a considerable amount about some topics, many important issues remain to be studied. What we do know is sometimes obsolete. What was true of group a few years ago may not be true today and even less so tomorrow. For example, generalizations that characterized the Southeast Asian students who were brought to the United States by their well-educated, middle- and upper-class, urban parents in the early 1970s do not describe the children of the uneducated, poor, rural, boat people who came here in the 1980s and 1990s. The first group of children may have had considerable difficulty adjusting to American schools; however, the second group of children, most of whom have never attended school and who have had to survive the trauma of running blockades, avoiding pirates, and confinement in detention camps for many years, typically have much more serious academic and emotional problems.

Many researchers fail to consider socioeconomic differences when they study the cognitive skills, learning styles, and so on of different ethnic groups of students. Since a smaller percentage of European American children currently live below the poverty level than Hispanic American and African American children, differences that are observed among uncontrolled samples of these groups cannot be attributed solely to ethnicity. Conclusions about educationally relevant differences between African American and European American students based on comparisons between African American poor students and European American middle-class students should have no influence on educational policy and practices. Unfortunately, this is not the case.

## *Avoiding Stereotypes and Overgeneralizations*

Educators who wish to take their students' ethnic, socioeconomic, and gender characteristics into consideration must avoid misleading stereotypes and overgeneralizations about these groups. All students do not conform to the stereotypic behavior patterns of the gender, ethnic, and socioeconomic groups they belong to. Even when people behave in stereotypic ways, they all do not behave the same. For example, subgroups within larger ethnic groups differ. Although not all Mexican American students fit the following generalizations, they tend to be exposed to much more traditional values and role models than the Nicaraguan American students, who were exposed to values that were encouraged by the Sandinistas after their assumption of power. Filipino females tend to grow up in a society in which the roles that the genders fulfill are much more similar than in Vietnam. Chinese American, Japanese American, Samoan American, Vietnamese American, and Hmong American students have very different experiences and cultural backgrounds. Native Americans who maintain their traditional life-styles live differently than those who have assimilated to the mainstream European American culture.

There are important differences among students raised in families with similar ethnic backgrounds. Parents who want their children to maintain their ethnic identities may pressure them to follow traditional values, attitudes, and behavior patterns to a much greater degree than parents who wish to assimilate into the mainstream culture. Migrant workers and their children who plan to return to Mexico may be less apt to adopt European American values and behavior patterns than those who plan to settle in the United States permanently. Native American students who plan to continue to live on their reservations may be less motivated to adapt to European American ways than those who plan to leave the reservations. Similar differences occur between African Americans who want to integrate fully into European American society and those who want to maintain their African American identities.

Although students from poor backgrounds are more likely to fulfill traditional roles than middle-class students, this may be less true for students in upwardly mobile families and students who identify with and wish to join or emulate the middle class than for those who are content with their life-style. This may also be less important for poor students growing up in Appalachia than for poor students from New York City, who have somewhat different life experiences and much more exposure to middle-class values and behavior patterns.

Students from different socioeconomic backgrounds are also influenced by dissimilar cultural experiences. Students from the same socioeconomic class may not be equally motivated to maintain their cultural heritages. Students in upwardly mobile low-income families and those who identify with and wish to join or emulate the middle class may be less likely to accept traditional values or roles than students who are content with their economic situation.

Regional differences create diversity among ethnic and socioeconomic groups. For example, Mexican American students who live in "border towns" in Texas, New Mexico, and Arizona, and Cuban Americans who live in areas with large Hispanic American populations such as Miami are much more likely to be exposed to the traditional Latino cultural life-styles and attitudes than Mexican American and Cuban American students who live in other parts of the United States. Likewise, students from low-income families in Appalachia have somewhat different experiences and exposure to middle-class values and behavior patterns than students from cities such as New York, Detroit, or Atlanta, and they may be more likely to behave in traditional ways than urban students.

It is extremely important to avoid stereotypic overgeneralizations about all non–European American, poor, immigrant, or refugee students. Therefore, research is included on the various subgroups of these large groups.

For these and other reasons, generalizations about gender, ethnic, and socioeconomic differences among students can be very misleading. Despite these cautions, however, it is important to recognize that some descriptions of socioeconomic or ethnic groups tend to apply to the majority of their members, and some gender differences cut across socioeconomic, ethnic, and geographic boundaries.

Such generalizations can be helpful. They can sensitize educators to the *possibility* that students may have certain stereotypic attitudes, preferences, values, learning styles, and behavior patterns. However, educators should never assume that students will *necessarily* think and behave in these ways. It is as important to avoid relating to students on the basis of incorrect stereotypes as it is to avoid being insensitive to the role ethnic-, socioeconomic-, or gender-influenced attitudes and behavior may play in some students' lives. As long as educators keep these limitations in mind, they will be more effective with students, especially with those groups who traditionally have not performed well in today's diverse society.

## *Summary*

There are great ethnic, socioeconomic, gender, contextual, and communicative disparities in the extent to which students succeed in American schools. This text examines their causes and includes much of the information teachers need in order to provide students with the nonbiased/nonsexist assessment, instructional, and classroom management approaches necessary to reduce these disparities.

## *Activities*

1. Compare the ethnic composition of the classes and program in which you are studying to the ethnic composition of the community your college or university serves. If there are disparities, determine whether they fit the patterns described in this chapter.

2. Ask the administrators of one of the local school districts in your area about the success rates of their LEP students and their students with contextual problems.

## *References*

These references discuss population trends.

1. Bureau of the Census. (1988a). *Hispanic Population in the United States: Current Population Reports, Series P-20, No. 438.* U.S. Department of Commerce, Washington, DC: U.S. Government Printing Office.
2. Bureau of the Census. (1988b). *Money, Income and Poverty Status in the United States: (Advance Data from the March 1989 Current Population Survey). Current Population Reports, Series P-60, No. 166.* U.S. Department of Commerce, Washington, DC: U.S. Government Printing Office.
3. Bureau of the Census. (1988c). *The Black Population in the United States. Current Population Reports, Series P-20, No. 442.* U.S. Department of Commerce, Washington, DC: U.S. Government Printing Office.
4. National Information Center for Children and Youth with Handicaps. (1988). *Minority Issues in Special Education: A Portrait of the Future.* Washington, DC: Author.
5. Puente, T. (1991). Latino child poverty ranks swell. *Hispanic Link Weekly Report, 9*(35), 1, 2, 8.

The following references deal with the low success rates of non–European American and poor students.

6. Educational Testing Service. (1989). *Who Reads Best?* Princeton, NJ: Author.
7. Individuals with Disabilities Education Act. (20 USC., Sections 1400–1485; Education of the Handicapped Act Amendments of 1990).
8. Johnson, M. L. (1984). Blacks in mathematics: A status report. *Journal for Research in Mathematics Education, 15*(2), 145–153.
9. National Assessment of Education Progress. (1988a). *Computer Competence: The First National Assessment.* Princeton, NJ: Educational Testing Service.
10. National Assessment of Education Progress. (1988b). *The Mathematics Report Card: Are We Measuring Up?* Princeton, NJ: Educational Testing Service.
11. National Assessment of Education Progress. (1988c). *The Science Report Card: Elements of Risk and Recovery.* Princeton, NJ: Educational Testing Service.
12. National Assessment of Education Progress. (1990a). *The Reading Report Card, 1971–1978: Trends from the Nation's Report Card.* Princeton, NJ: Educational Testing Service.
13. National Assessment of Education Progress. (1990b). *The Writing Report Card, 1984–1988: Findings from the Nation's Report Card.* Princeton, NJ: Educational Testing Service.
14. National Black Child Development Institute. (1990). *The Status of African American Children: Twentieth Anniversary Report.* Washington, DC: Author.
15. National Center for Educational Statistics. (1989). 1987 High school transcript study. In *National Center for Educational Statistics. Digest of Educational Statistics 1989.* Washington, DC: U.S. Department of Education.
16. National Council of La Raza. (1990). *Hispanic Education: A Statistical Report.* Washington, DC: Author.
17. Office of Educational Research and Improvement, National Center for Educational Research. (1990). *National Education Longitudinal Study. A Profile of the American Eighth Grader: NELS: 88 Student Descriptive Summary.* Washington, DC: U.S. Department of Education.

The high dropout rates of non–European American and poor students are the focus of the following references.

18. American Council on Education, Office of Minority Concerns. (1989). *Minorities in Higher Education: Eighth Annual Status Report,* 1989. Washington, DC: Author.
19. Arciniega, T. A., & Moray, A. I. (1985). *Hispanics and Higher Education: A CSU Imperative. Final Report of the Commission on Hispanic Underrepresentation.* Long Beach, CA: California State University, Office of the Chancellor.
20. Aspira. (1983). *Racial and Ethnic High School Dropout Rates in New York City.* ERIC ED 254–600.
21. Astin, A. (1982). *Minorities in American Higher Education.* San Francisco, CA: Jossey-Bass.
22. Bureau of Indian Affairs. (1988, March). *Report on B. I. A. Education: Final Review Draft.* Washington, DC: Department of the Interior.
23. Hirano-Nakanishi, M. J., & Diaz, R. L. (1982). *Differential Educational Attainment Among "At-Risk" Youth: A Case Study of Language Minority Youth of Mexican Descent and Low Socioeconomic Status.* Los Alamitos, CA: National Center for Bilingual Research.
24. Illinois State General Assembly. (1985). *A Generation Too Precious to Waste.* ERIC ED 268–198.
25. National Public Radio Broadcast. (1990, September). *On the Alaskan Native American.* Washington, DC: All Things Considered.
26. New York Alliance for Public Schools. (1985). *A Study of the Identification, Monitoring, and Tracking of Potential High School Student Dropouts for the New York City Board of Education: Executive Summary. Final Report.* ERIC ED 273–720.
27. Rumberger, R. W. (1983). Dropping out of high school: The influence of race, sex, and family background. *American Education Research Journal, 20,* 199–220.
28. Steinberg, L., Blinde, P. L., & Chan, K. S. (1984). Dropping out among language minority youth. *Review of Educational Research, 54,* 113–132.

The following references document that African Americans and poor Americans get into more trouble in school and are more likely to be suspended for misbehaving.

29. Bennett, C., & Harris, J. J. (1982). Suspension and expulsion of male and black students: A

case study of the causes of disproportionality. *Urban Education, 16*(4), 399–423.
30. Bickel, F., & Qualls, R. (1981). *The Impact of School Climate on Suspension Rates in the Jefferson County Public Schools.* Paper presented at the annual meeting of the American Educational Research Association, Boston.
31. Grossman, H., & Grossman, S. (1994). *Gender Issues in Education.* Needham, MA: Allyn and Bacon.
32. Moore, W. L., & Cooper, H. (1984). Correlations between teacher and student background and teacher perception of discipline problems and disciplinary techniques. *Psychology in the Schools, 21,* 386–392.
33. Stevens, L. B. (1983). *Suspension and Corporal Punishment of Students in the Cleveland Public Schools, 1981–1982.* Cleveland, OH: Office of School Monitoring and Community Relations.
34. Woolridge, P., & Richman, C. (1985). Teachers' choice of punishment as a function of a student's gender, age, race and I. Q. level. *Journal of School Psychology, 23,* 19–29.

The following references deal with gender differences in academic interests and activities.

35. Alspach, P. A. (1988). *Inequities in the Computer Classroom: An Analysis of Two Computer Courses.* ERIC ED 301–180.
36. Chen, M. (1986). Gender and computers: The beneficial effects of experience on attitudes. *Journal of Educational Computing Research, 2*(3), 265–282.
37. Goertz, M. (1989). *Course Taking Patterns in the 1980's.* Princeton, NJ: Educational Testing Service.
38. Klinzing, D. G. (1985). *A Study of the Behavior of Children in a Preschool Equipped with Computers.* ERIC ED 255–320.
39. Lee, V. E., & Ware, N. C. (1986). *When and Why Girls "Leak" Out of High School Mathematics: A Closer Look.* Paper presented at the annual meeting of the American Educational Research Association, San Francisco.
40. Linn, M. C. (1983). *Fostering Equitable Consequences from Computer Learning Environments.* ERIC ED 242–626.
41. Lockheed, M., & Frakt, S. (1984). Sex equity: Increasing girls use of computers. *The Computing Teacher, 11*(8), 16–18.
42. Parsons, J. E. (1984). Sex differences in mathematics participation. In M. W. Steinkamp & M. L. Meehr (Eds.), *Women in Science: Advances in Motivation and Achievement,* Vol. 2. Greenwich, CT: JAI Press.
43. Rampy, L. (1984). *We Teach Children: Computer Literacy as a Feminist Issue.* ERIC ED 240–028.
44. Silvern, S. B., Countermine, T. M., & Williamson, P. A. C. (1982). *Young Children Interacting with a Computer.* Paper presented at the annual meeting of the American Educational Research Association, New York.
45. Stage, E. K., & Kreinberg, N. (1982). *Equal Access to Computers.* Paper presented at the semiannual meeting of the American Educational Research Association Special Interest Group, Research on Women in Education, Philadelphia.

These references are concerned with gender differences in vocational training and career aspirations.

46. American College Testing Program. (1989). *State and National Trend Data for Students Who Take the ACT Assessment.* Iowa City: Author.
47. Dao, M. (1987). *From Vietnamese to Vietnamese American.* Unpublished manuscript. San Jose, CA: San Jose State University, Department of Special Education.
48. Falkowski, C. K., & Falk, W. W. (1983). Homemaking as an occupational plan: Evidence from a national longitudinal study. *Journal of Vocational Behavior, 22*(2), 227–242.
49. Farmer, H. S., & Sidney J. S. (1985). Sex equity in career and vocational education. In S. Klein (Ed.), *Handbook for Achieving Sex Equity Through Education.* Baltimore: The Johns Hopkins University Press.
50. Grossman, H. (1984). *Educating Hispanic Students: Cultural Implications for Instruction, Classroom Management, Counseling and Assessment.* Springfield, IL: Charles C. Thomas.
51. Gupta, N. (1982). *The Influence of Sex Roles on the Life Plans of Low-SES Adolescents.* ERIC ED 235–434.
52. Hannah, J. S., & Kahn, S. E. (1989). The relationship of socioeconomic status and gender to occupational choices of grade 12 students. *Journal of Vocational Behavior, 34*(2), 161–178.
53. Holmes, B. L., & Esses, L. M. (1988). Factors influencing Canadian high school girls' career motivation. *Psychology of Women Quarterly, 12*(3), 313–328.
54. Jensen, E. L., & Hovey, S. Y. (1982). Bridging the gap from high school to college for tal-

ented females. *Peabody Journal of Education, 59*(3), 153–159.
55. Kelly, K. R., & Cobb, S. J. (1991). A profile of the career development characteristics of young gifted adolescents: Examining gender and multicultural differences. *Roeper Review, 13*(4), 202–206.
56. Odell, K. S. (1989). Gender differences in the educational and occupational expectations of rural Ohio youth. *Research in Rural Education, 5*(3), 37–41.
57. Pido, A. J. A. (1978). *A Cross-Cultural Change of Gender Roles: The Case of Pilipino Women Immigrants in Midwest City, U.S.A.* ERIC ED 159–244.
58. Smith, E. J. (1982). The black female adolescent: A review of the educational, career, and psychological literature. *Psychology of Women Quarterly, 6*, 261–288.
59. Vasquez, M.J. T. (1982). Confronting barriers to the participation of Mexican American women in higher education. *Hispanic Journal of Behavioral Sciences, 4*(2), 147–165.
60. Wells, J. (1983). *Statement of the National Coalition for Women and Girls in Education.* Washington, DC: National Coalition for Women and Girls in Education.

References that deal with the narrowing of the gender gap in academic ability and achievement are listed next.

61. Becker, C., & Forsyth, R. (1990). *Gender Differences in Grades 3 Through 12: A Longitudinal Analysis.* Paper presented at the annual meeting of the American Educational Research Association, Boston.
62. Coladarci, T., & Lancaster, L. N. (1989). *Gender and Mathematics Achievement: Data from High School and Beyond.* ERIC ED 308–207.
63. Feingold, A. (1988). Cognitive gender differences are disappearing. *American Psychologist, 43*, 95–103.
64. Halpern, D. F. (1989). The disappearance of cognitive gender differences: What you see depends on where you look. *American Psychologist, 44*, 455–464.
65. Hyde, J. S., & Linn, M. C. (1988). Gender differences in verbal abilities: A meta-analysis. *Psychological Bulletin, 104*(1), 53–69.
66. Mullin, I., & Jenkins, L. (1988). *The Science Report Card: Elements of Risk and Recovery.* Princeton, NJ: Educational Testing Service.

The following references discuss gender differences in verbal and mathematics achievement.

67. Allred, R. A. (1990). Gender differences in spelling achievement in grades 1 through 6. *Journal of Educational Research, 83*(4), 187–193.
68. Armstrong, J. M. (1981). Achievement and participation of women in mathematics. *Journal for Research in Mathematics Education, 12*, 356–372.
69. Benbow, C. P., & Stanley, J. C. (1982). Consequences in high school and college of sex differences in mathematical reasoning ability: A longitudinal perspective. *American Educational Research Journal, 19*(4), 598–622.
70. Benbow, C. P., & Stanley, J. C. (1983). Sex differences in mathematical reasoning ability: More facts. *Science, 222*, 1029–1031.
71. Brandon P. R., Newton, B. J., & Hammond, O. W. (1987). Children's mathematics achievement in Hawaii: Sex differences favor girls. *American Educational Research Journal, 24*(3), 437–461.
72. Conner, J. M., & Serbin, L. A. (1980). *Mathematics, Visual-Spatial Ability, and Sex Roles* (final report). Washington, DC: National Institute of Education.
73. Eastman, S. T., & Kendrl, K. (1987). Computer and gender: Differential effects of electronic search on students' achievement and attitudes. *Journal of Research and Development in Education, 20*(3), 41–48.
74. Fennema, E., & Carpenter, T. (1981). Sex-related differences in mathematics: Results from the national assessment. *Mathematics Teacher, 74*(7), 554–559.
75. Fox, L., Brody, L. A., & Tobin, D. (Eds.). (1980). *Women and the Mathematical Mystique.* Baltimore: The Johns Hopkins University Press.
76. Fox, L., & Cohn, S. (1980). Sex differences in the development of precocious mathematical talent. In L. Fox, L. A. Brody, & D. Tobin (Eds.), *Women and the Mathematical Mystique.* Baltimore: The Johns Hopkins University Press.
77. Harris, C. S. (1986). *A Summary of the Language Arts Achievement of Students in a Phase-Elective Mini-Course System as Compared to the Language Arts Achievement of Students in a Traditional Program.* ERIC ED 280–064.

78. Hyde, J. S. (1981). How large are cognitive gender differences? A meta-analysis using w and d. *American Psychologist, 36,* 892–901.
79. Marshall, S. P. (1984). Sex differences in students' mathematics achievement: Solving computations and story problems. *Journal of Educational Psychology, 76*(2), 194–204.
80. Midgley, C. (1983). Expectations, values, and academic behaviors. In J. T. Spence (Ed.), *Achievement and Achievement Motivation.* San Francisco: W. H. Freeman.
81. Scott-Jones, D., & Clark, M. L. (1986). The school experience of black girls: The interaction of gender, race, and socioeconomic status. *Phi Delta Kappan, 67*(7), 520–526.
82. Sharp, L. M. (1989). *The SAT-M Gap: Looking at Micro Level Data.* ERIC ED 307–292.
83. Sherman, J. (1981). Girls' and boys' enrollment in theoretical math courses: A longitudinal study. *Psychology of Women Quarterly, 5,* 681–689.
84. Simmons, W. (1990). *Black Male Achievement: Strategies for Ensuring Success in School.* Paper presented at the annual meeting of the National Black Child Development Institute, Washington, DC.

The following references relate to gender differences on visual-spatial tasks.

85. Burnett, S. A., & Lane, D. M. (1980). Effects of academic instruction on spatial visualization. *Intelligence, 4,* 233–242.
86. Fennema, E. H., & Carpenter, T. P. (1981). Sex-related differences in mathematics: Results from national assessment. *Mathematics Teacher, 74,* 554–559.
87. Harris. L. J. (1981). Sex-related variations in spatial skill. In L. S. Liben, A. H. Patterson, & N. Newcombe (Eds.), *Spatial Representation and Behavior Across the Life Span.* New York: Academic Press.
88. Linn, M. C., & Petersen, A. C. (1985). Emergence and characterization of sex differences in spatial ability: A meta-analysis. *Child Development, 56,* 1479–1498.
89. Linn, M. C., & Petersen, A. C. (1986). Gender differences in spatial ability. In J. S. Hyde & M. C. Linn (Eds.), *The Psychology of Gender: Advances Through Meta-Analysis.* Baltimore: The Johns Hopkins University Press.
90. McGee, M. G. (1979). Human spatial abilities: Psychometric studies and environmental, genetic, hormonal, and neurological influences. *Psychological Bulletin, 86,* 889–918.
91. Nash, S. C. (1979). Sex-role as a mediator of intellectual functioning. In M. A. Witting & A. C. Petersen (Eds.), *Sex-Related Differences in Cognitive Functioning: Developmental Issues.* New York: Academic Press.
92. Petersen, A. G. (1979). Hormones and cognitive functioning in normal development. In M. A. Witting & A. C. Petersen (Eds.), *Sex-Related Differences in Cognitive Functioning: Developmental Issues.* New York: Academic Press.
93. Richmond, P. G. (1980). A limited sex difference in spatial test scores with a preadolescent sample. *Child Development, 51,* 601–602.

Gender differences on science achievement are the focus of the references listed as follows.

94. Becker, B. J. (1989). Gender and science achievement: A reanalysis of studies from two meta-analyses. *Journal of Research in Science Teaching, 26*(2), 141–169.
95. Hueftle, S. J., Rakow, S. J., & Welch, W. W. (1983). *Images of Science.* Minneapolis: University of Minnesota Press.
96. Hyde, J. S., & Linn, M. C. (1986). *The Psychology of Gender: Advances Through Meta-Analysis.* Baltimore: The Johns Hopkins University Press.
97. Maehr, M. L., & Steinkamp, M. (1983). *A Synthesis of Findings on Sex Differences in Science Education Research.* ERIC ED 229–226.
98. Malone, M. R., & Fleming, M. L. (1983). The relationship of student characteristics and student performance in science as viewed by meta-analysis research. *Journal of Research in Science Teaching, 20,* 481–495.
99. Shaw, E. L., Jr., & Doan, R. L. (1990). An investigation of the differences in attitude and achievement between male and female second and fifth grade science students. *Journal of Elementary Science Education, 2*(1), 10–15.
100. Steinkamp, M. W., & Maehr, M. L. (1983). Affect, ability, and science achievement: A quantitative synthesis of correlational research. *Review of Educational Research, 53,* 369–396.
101. Steinkamp, M. W., & Maehr, M. L. (1984). Gender differences in motivational orientations toward achievement in school science: A quantitative synthesis. *American Educational Research Journal, 21*(1), 39–59.

The following references indicate that females are less likely to get into trouble for behavior problems, be disciplined by their teachers, or be suspended from school.

102. Center, D. B., & Wascom, A. M. (1987). Teacher perceptions of social behavior in behaviorally disordered and socially normal children and youth. *Behavioral Disorders, 12*(3), 200–206.
103. Duke, D. L. (1978). Why don't girls misbehave more than boys in school? *Journal of Youth and Adolescence, 7*(2), 141–157.
104. Epstein, M. H., Cullinan, D., & Bursuck, W. D. (1985). Prevalence of behavior problems among learning disabled and nonhandicapped students. *Mental Retardation and Learning Disability Bulletin, 213*, 30–39.
105. Ludwig, G., & Cullinan, D. (1984). Behavior problems of gifted and nongifted elementary school girls and boys. *Gifted Child Quarterly, 28*(1), 37–39.

The following references describe gender differences in emotional reactions in school.

106. Hadfield, O. D., & Maddux, C. D. (1988). Cognitive style and mathematics anxiety among high school students. *Psychology in the Schools, 25*, 75–83.
107. Haynes, N. M., Comer, J. P., & Hamilton-Lee, M. (1988). Gender and achievement status differences on learning factors among black high school students. *Journal of Educational Research, 81*(4), 233–237.
108. Marsh, H. W. (1987). *The Content Specificity of Math and English Anxieties: The High School and Beyond Study.* ERIC ED 300–402.
109. Wynstra, S., & Cummings, C. (1990). *Science Anxiety: Relation with Gender, Year in Chemistry Class, Achievement, and Test Anxiety.* ERIC ED 331–837.

Gender differences in self-confidence are discussed in the following references.

110. Armstrong, J. M., & Kahl, S. (1980). *A National Assessment of Performance and Participation of Women in Mathematics* (final report). Washington, DC: National Institute of Education.
111. Brush, L. (1980). *Encouraging Girls in Mathematics: The Problem and the Solution.* Boston: Abt.
112. Eccles (Parsons), J., Adler, T. F., Futterman, R., Goff, S. B., Kaczala, C. M., Meece, J., & Midgley, C. (1983). Expectations, values, and academic behaviors. In J. T. Spence (Ed.), *Perspective on Achievement and Achievement Motivation.* San Francisco: W. H. Freeman.
113. Fox, L. H., Brody, L., & Tobin, D. (Eds.). (1980). *Women and the Mathematical Mystique.* Baltimore: The Johns Hopkins University Press.
114. Hyde, J., & Fennema, E. (1990). *Gender Differences in Mathematics Performance and Affect: Results of Two Meta-Analyses.* Paper presented at the annual meeting of the American Educational Research Association, Boston.
115. Levine, B. (1990). *Arithmetic Development: Where Are the Gender Differences?* Paper presented at the annual meeting of the American Educational Research Association, Boston.
116. Reyes, L. H. (1984). Affective variables and mathematics education. *Elementary School Journal, 84*(5), 558–581.
117. Sherman, J. (1980). Mathematics, spatial visualization, and related factors: Changes in girls and boys, grades 8–11. *Journal of Educational Psychology, 72*, 476–482.
118. Stevenson, H. W., & Newman, R. S. (1986). Long-term prediction of achievement and attitudes in mathematics and reading. *Child Development, 57*, 646–659.

The focus of the references listed below is gender differences in risk taking and reaction to failure.

119. Ginsburg, H. J., & Miller, S. M. (1982). Sex differences in children's risk-taking behavior. *Child Development, 53* (2), 426–428.
120. Licht, B. G., Linden, T. A., Brown, D. A., & Sexton, M. (1984). *Sex Differences in Achievement Orientation: An "A" Student Phenomenon.* ERIC ED 252–783.
121. Miller, A. (1986). Performance impairment after failure: Mechanisms and sex differences. *Journal of Educational Psychology, 78*(6), 486–491.

Gender differences in seeking teacher feedback, support, and help is the focus of these references.

122. Brutsaert, H. (1990). Changing sources of self-esteem among girls and boys in secondary school. *Urban Education, 24*(40), 432–439.
123. Nelson-LeGall, S., & Glor-Scheib, S. (1983). *Help-Seeking in Elementary Classrooms: An Observational Study.* ERIC ED 230–286.
124. Stewart, M. J., & Corbin, C. B. (1988). Feedback dependence among low confidence preadolescent boys and girls. *Research Quarterly for Exercise and Sport, 59*(2), 160–164.

125. Sullivan, H. J. (1986). Factors that influence continuing motivation. *Journal of Educational Research, 80*(2), 86–92.

These references deal with ethnic differences in female roles.

126. Dao, M. (1987). *From Vietnamese to Vietnamese American.* Unpublished manuscript. San Jose, CA: San Jose State University.
127. Simpson, G. (1984). The daughters of Charlotte Ray: The career development process during the exploratory and establishment stages of Black women attorneys. *Sex Roles, 11*(1/2), 113–139.

Contextual disparities are the focus of the following references.

128. Burns, S. (Ed.). (1991). Homelessness demographics, causes and trends. *Homewords, 3*(4), 1–3.
129. Cavazos, L. F. (1990). *U.S. Department of Education Report to Congress on the Education for Homeless Children and Youth Program for the Period October 1, 1988 through September 30, 1989.* Washington, DC: U.S. Department of Education.
130. Henderson, A. (1987). *The Evidence Continues to Grow: Parent Involvement Improves Student Achievement.* ERIC ED 315–199.
131. Interstate Migrant Education Council. (1987). *Migrant Education: A Consolidated View.* ERIC ED 285–701.
132. Lawless, K. (1986). *Neediest of the Needy: Special Education for Migrants. Harvesting the Harvesters. Book 8.* ERIC ED 279–473.
133. Powers, J. L., Eckenrode, J., & Jaklitsch, G. (1988). *Running Away from Home: A Response to Adolescent Maltreatment.* ERIC ED 296–228.

These references document the prevalence of LEP students.

134. Individuals with Disabilities Education Act. Education of the Handicapped Act Amendments of 1990. (20 USC, Sections 1400–1485).
135. Woodrow, K. A. (1988). *Measuring Net Immigration to the United States: The Emigrant Population and Recent Emigration Flows.* Paper presented at the annual meeting of the Population Association of America, New Orleans.

# Chapter 2

# Intrinsic Causes of Ethnic and Socioeconomic Disparities

Educators do not agree about the causes of the ethnic and socioeconomic disparities in school. Some educators believe that many non–European American and poor students are predisposed to have problems in school because they are exposed to more biomedical problems, are less intelligent, and come from disadvantaged cultural backgrounds that do not prepare them to learn effectively. Other educators consider these explanations to be examples of blaming the victims for problems inflicted on them by others. These educators blame the schools and society at large for these ethnic and socioeconomic inequities.

Educators who locate the causes of these disparities within students themselves tend to favor solutions that change students or accommodate educational approaches to their assumed differences or inadequacies. For example, educators who believe that some students are brought up in disadvantaged cultures that do not prepare them to succeed in school usually favor modifying the students' culturally influenced attitudes and behavior. Examples of these are encouraging students to work at a faster pace and encouraging them to function more independently. Educators who believe there are genetic differences among students from different ethnic and socioeconomic backgrounds that make it difficult for them to use higher-level cognitive processes typically suggest that teachers should reduce the goals they hope to achieve with these students and should adapt their methods for achieving them to these students' assumed limitations.

Educators who hold the school system responsible for these disparities want the schools and the teachers who staff them to improve so that all students can realize their full potential. By and large they support multicultural education as a way of combatting cultural insensitivity and prejudice in schools. Many of them favor a redistribution of the educational pie—with more money spent on educating non–European American and poor students, and economic reforms that will provide poor parents with the financial means to assist their children to succeed in school.

This chapter and Chapter 3 examine these different points of view. In particular, this chapter discusses explanations that locate the cause within the students; Chapter 3 deals with causes that exist in the educational system and society at large.

## *Biomedical Problems*

The living conditions of many poor African American, European American, Hispanic American, and Native American students place them at greater risk for biomedical problems. Poor health care and nutrition can cause neurological problems, which in turn can cause them to do poorly in school. Most poor parents do not abuse drugs while the mothers are pregnant. However, some people believe that in comparison to middle-class European American children, children of poor parents are more likely to suffer the results of exposure to harmful substances because their mothers abuse drugs and alcohol while they are pregnant. (Whether this is actually true is discussed later.) If current trends continue, poor African American, European American, Hispanic American, and Native American students may also suffer the unfortunate effects of being born HIV positive in greater relative numbers than their European American middle-class peers.

### *Health Care and Nutrition*

As a group, poor families, especially the millions of families whose incomes fall below the poverty line, do not have adequate access to prenatal and postnatal health care (7, 10). In fact, the percentage of poor mothers who receive prenatal care has actually decreased in recent years (1). As a result, poor children are more likely to suffer the consequences of complications of pregnancy and delivery, prematurity, and low birth weight, and the learning, emotional, and behavior problems these conditions can cause (2, 3, 6, 7, 13, 14–16). Six to 8% of children who are born with a moderately low birth weight will have developmental problems. Among those born with severely low birth weight the percentage is twice as large (5, 8). As the mortality rate from these complications has declined and more infants who are born with these risky conditions survive, the number of poor children who experience the learning and behavior problems caused by these conditions has increased.

Poor parents are also less able to provide their children with the same nutrition and medical care that their more advantaged peers receive. This can also cause their children to develop learning and behavior problems (11, 12). Thus, because of inadequate medical care and nutrition, poor children may experience a higher incidence of learning and behavior problems (4, 9). Because African American and Hispanic American children are more likely than European Americans to be born poor, they are at greater risk to experience these problems.

Fortunately, the deleterious effects of low birth weight and other perinatal problems can be counteracted in many cases by providing youngsters with proper care. In addition, the harmful effects of malnutrition appear to occur primarily when severe malnutrition is present, which is typically not the case with most American students from poor or poverty backgrounds. And these effects may also be reversible.

We do not know the exact effects of limited access to medical care and poor nutrition on students' school careers. When considered as a whole, it seems reasonable to expect that the disproportionately small share of the medical and nutritional benefits received by the families who earn the least in our society contributes at least to some degree to these students' problems in school. However, whether these problems are a very significant factor is a point that can only be answered by more research.

### Substance Abuse

Some individuals believe that parental substance abuse contributes to the lack of academic success of African American, Native American, and poor students. They claim that African American, Native American, and poor parents abuse substances such as alcohol, marijuana, cocaine, and so on, during pregnancy more frequently than middle-class European American parents, and that as a result their children perform less adequately in school.

Substance abuse does cause both severe and subtle birth defects and a variety of learning and behavior problems (17–19, 22, 26–28, 30, 32–35, 38, 39, 41, 43–46, 52, 53). Even supposedly less severe forms of substance abuse, such as smoking cigarettes during pregnancy, can cause children to develop learning, social adjustment, and behavior problems (24, 30).

Fortunately, only some substance-exposed children actually develop the difficulties these dangerous substances may cause (49, 53). The reasons for this are largely unknown. However, one has been identified—good prenatal care reduces the likelihood that substance-exposed children will actually suffer the potential problems for which they are at risk (32, 41).

Substance-exposed children do not suffer all of the possible problems that their exposure can cause (27, 32, 41, 49). The problems children of substance-abusing parents can experience vary. Approximately 2% to 17% suffer from severe congenital defects, developmental disabilities, cerebral palsy, seizure disorders, and so on (23, 49). Many others develop normally at first, then demonstrate learning and behavior problems as they approach school age.

Substance-exposed students often function adequately under adult guidance and in structured learning and play situations. However, they have great difficulty in adjusting to situations that require them to provide their own structure, initiative, or organization. They do much better in one-to-one situations or when they have to cope with only one individual, task, or toy. When they have to deal with group situations or multiple activities, materials, tasks, or people, they quickly become overstimulated, overwhelmed, and disorganized.

Many, but not all, substance-exposed children suffer additional insults and injuries (21, 23, 29, 31, 32, 34, 42, 43). Their parents tend to have a host of additional medical and social problems. Mothers who are unable to stop abusing drugs for their children's sake during their pregnancy are often unable to care for them after they have been born. (The fact that mothers abuse drugs during pregnancy is often an indication that their children will receive inadequate care.) Those who are poor tend to abandon their children in the hospital, which often leads to eventual foster care placement. Mothers who do decide to care for their children often provide inadequate care for them because of their drug problems.

> *Growing numbers of crack babies simply are being abandoned in hospitals by their crack-smoking mothers. As for those babies who are discharged, the vast majority go from the hospital nursery to chaotic home environments characterized by deep poverty and little physical or emotional nurturing. With one strike already against them, these babies are at high risk for the second strike—neglect and abuse by crack-using adults. (43, p. 19)*

Presently we are unable to determine when and to what extent exposed children's problems are caused by physiological factors or the environmental disadvantages often associated with substance-abusing parents. For now, the prudent position is that these students' learning and behavior problems can best be understood as resulting from the interaction of both biological and environmental factors.

The actual number of mothers who abuse drugs while they are pregnant and the number of drug-exposed infants is unknown. Surveys of the percentage of parents who expose their unborn infants to harmful substances have yielded results that range from 0.4% to 27% of the parents tested or questioned, depending on the hospital and the neighborhood surveyed (21, 25, 37, 48, 51), and their number is growing at an alarming rate (36). Estimates of the number of infants that may be affected yearly by crack alone range from 48,000 to 375,000 (20, 21, 43, 47, 51).

There appears to be evidence that poor, African American, Native American, and inner city mothers in general abuse these substances while they are pregnant more frequently than other mothers (40, 43, 49, 50). However, some researchers believe that the difference between these mothers' rates of drug abuse and those of European American middle-class mothers is overstated because European American middle-class mothers are better able to hide their substance-abusing behavior from the authorities (24, 43).

> *A minority woman who uses drugs or alcohol during pregnancy is almost ten times more likely to be reported to child-abuse authorities than is a white woman. White middle-class mothers—along with other white middle-class cocaine users—find it easier to hide their substance abuse than do poor, minority women. (43, p. 21)*

Even if the difference is overstated, there is evidence that substance-abusing poor parents in general, and non-European poor parents in particular, are less able to obtain the good prenatal care that reduces the likelihood that substance-exposed children will actually suffer the potential problems for which they are at risk. Thus, it may be that their children are at even greater risk than European American middle-class children.

Although African American, Native American, and poor students are currently more likely to suffer from such problems than European American middle-class students, it is unclear what proportion of their school problems is caused by their parents' substance abuse during pregnancy. It may well turn out to be too small to account for much of the disparity between the educational experiences of different ethnic groups and socioeconomic classes.

*The media have painted a dire picture of infants who were exposed to alcohol and other drugs in utero. . . . Children who were prenatally exposed to substances are unique, but as a whole they are more like than different from other children. . . . There is a danger in this label in that it can engender a self-fulfilling prophecy: Children will become what their parents and teachers expect them to become. Given the current view of drug exposure this would be an unfair prophecy. (49, p. 1, 24)*

### Acquired Immune Deficiency Syndrome

The dramatic increase in the number of AIDS-exposed infants who are born HIV positive is adding to the number of children who demonstrate problems similar to those who are drug exposed (54–56). As better methods of prolonging their lives are developed, more and more HIV-positive students will experience difficulty in school.

Non–European American poor children are disproportionately affected by AIDS (57–58). In one national study, African Americans and Hispanic Americans represented 53% and 23% of the reported cases (58). Although the number of students affected by AIDS is still small, their numbers continue to grow.

## Genetic Differences/Inferiority

In the not-too-distant past, it was both acceptable and commonplace to justify colonialism, slavery, gross economic inequality, the inferior status of women, racial segregation, immigration restriction, sterilization of the poor, unequal educational opportunities, and a host of other inequities on the basis of imagined genetic differences (59, 61, 69, 72). Abraham Lincoln was not immune to the point of view prevalent during his time. Despite his emancipation proclamation, he maintained that

*There is a physical difference between the white and black races which I believe will forever forbid the two races living together on terms of social and political equality. And inasmuch as they cannot so live, while they do remain together*

*there must be the position of superior and inferior, and I as much as any other man am in favor of having the superior position assigned to the white race. (63, p. 35)*

Most of these conditions are no longer acceptable in our society. However, some individuals still believe that certain groups of students, most notably African American, Hispanic American, and poor students, are less successful in school because they inherit different amounts or kinds of intelligence (62, 64–76). The following quotes by Shockley and Jensen are representative of this position.

*Nature has color-coded groups of individuals so that statistically reliable predictions of their adaptability to intellectually rewarding and effective lives can easily be made and profitably be used by the pragmatic man-in-the-street. (70, p. 375)*

*The most parsimonious hypothesis—one that would comprehend virtually all the established facts about the white-black IQ difference without the need to postulate any environmental factors besides those that are known to affect IQ and on which blacks in general are less advantaged—is that something between one-half and three-fourths of the average IQ difference is attributable to genetic factors, and the remainder to environmental factors and their interaction with genetic differences. (67, p. 227)*

Currently, there are two major theories of how genetic differences operate to create presumed ethnic- and socioeconomic-based intellectual differences. These theories and the evidence regarding them follow.

## *Meritocracy Theory*

The meritocracy theory offers an explanation for why poor students, especially those that come from poverty backgrounds, tend to have lower IQ scores than middle- and upper-class students. According to the theory, our society is a meritocracy in which all people have an equal opportunity to succeed. Those who do not succeed lack either the ability or motivation to do so. Thus, it is to be expected that those who remain in the working class, especially those who are below the poverty level and those who do poorly in school, lack either the motivation or the intelligence to do better. In other words, proponents of this theory offer a simple explanation for poor students' lack of achievement in school. If their parents were smarter, they would learn more and earn more. As Herrenstein puts it:

*1. If differences in mental abilities are inherited, and 2. if success requires these abilities, and 3. if earnings and prestige depend on success, 4. then social standing (which reflects earnings and prestige) will be based to some extent on inherited differences among people. (64, pp. 58–59)*

Various authors (60, 65, 68) have suggested that there are many millions of people in the working class, especially among those that fall below the poverty level, with what they call cultural familial retardation. They believe that these individuals suffer from two related problems. They inherit limited intellectual potential from their parents. And they are brought up by their parents in

> *families which are unable—due to their own lack of intellectual ability—to provide their children with the support that they need to acquire and maintain a reasonable standard of living. . . . Having low mental ability, exacerbated by a lack of parental encouragement, support, and proper modeling, the cultural familial retarded settle permanently into the lowest of the lower socioeconomic strata of society, become life-long clients of welfare programs, drift from job to job, are easily exploited, and reproduce an inordinately large posterity that will perpetuate this grim circumstance. (68, pp. 3, 4, 8)*

### Levels of Cognitive Ability

For many years, educators and others who believed that different ethnic groups and socioeconomic classes inherited dissimilar intellectual potentials claimed the groups inherited varying *amounts* of intelligence. Since 1969 however, many of them have accepted a theory of intelligence, first proposed by Jensen, that states that poor and African American students tend to inherit different *types* or *levels* of intelligence rather than different amounts of intellectual ability. According to Jensen, there are two types of intelligence, which he calls Level I and Level II.

> *Level I ability consists of rote learning and primary memory; it is the capacity to register and retrieve information with fidelity and is characterized essentially by a relative lack of transformation, conceptual coding, or other mental manipulation intervening between information input and output. Level II ability, in contrast, is characterized by mental manipulation of inputs, conceptualization, reasoning, and problem solving: it is essentially the general intelligence (g) factor common to most complex tests of intelligence. (66, p. 99)*

Although all individuals and groups supposedly inherit the ability to use Level I (rote learning and associative learning) to solve problems more or less to the same degree, they supposedly inherit different capacities to use Level II (conceptual ability). Jensen and others claim that African Americans and poor students do not score as high as European American and middle- and upper-class students on "intelligence tests" because they tend to be endowed with a diminished capacity for Level II intellectual functioning. "The hypothesis in its most simple and extreme form states that low and middle socioeconomic-status groups differ in Level II but not Level I ability" (66, p. 104).

### Implications

Individuals who believe that genetics play a role in causing socioeconomic and ethnic differences in school outcomes do not agree about how educators should handle these differences. Educators who believe the influence of genetic differences can be mitigated typically recommend that schools provide students with experiences and training that will counteract the effects of genetic differences.

Those who think the effects of genetics are unmodifiable suggest that teachers should accommodate their goals for students, their instructional approaches, and their classroom management techniques to the intellectual differences among their students, and they have provided suggestions for adapting instructional approaches to the different kinds of operations characteristic of Level I and Level II intellectual functioning. Believing that ethnic groups and socioeconomic classes require different educational approaches, these individuals are not troubled by the fact that European American middle- and upper-class students are more likely to be assigned to courses of study (tracks) for high-potential students in which teachers stress independent study and higher-level cognitive skills, whereas Hispanic Americans, African American, and poor students are overrepresented in tracks for low-potential students, in which teachers stress instructional techniques that involve concrete repetitive drill and practice, and in special education programs for students of limited intellectual potential, and are underrepresented in programs for gifted and talented students.

## Criticisms

The claim that different ethnic groups and socioeconomic classes inherit different kinds or amounts of intelligence is based on four assumptions. (1) American society is a meritocracy. (2) Individuals from different ethnic and socioeconomic backgrounds inherit different amounts of intelligence or learning potential. (3) Ethnic groups and socioeconomic classes differ in their abilities to use Level I or Level II types of intellectual operations when solving problems. (4) Level I and Level II differences are genetically determined. These assumptions and the arguments against them offered by their critics are now discussed.

**1.** *American society is a meritocracy.* Many people have argued that the United States is not a meritocracy (73–76). They claim that schools do not provide a level playing field that enables all students to achieve up to their potential. Instead of being designed to provide all students the knowledge and skills they need to succeed in life regardless of their ethnic and socioeconomic backgrounds, schools are biased against the very groups that do so poorly. In fact, some individuals propose that myths about the democratizing influences of schools are propaganda used to legitimize the privileged positions of middle and upper socioeconomic classes by convincing poor and non–European American students and parents that they are not capable of profiting from the education offered them. In this way, poor and non–European American students and their parents will blame their lack of success in school on themselves and will believe that they merit their eventual inferior positions in society because they did not take advantage of the opportunities afforded them in school. (See the section on structured reproduction in Chapter 3.)

The evidence presented throughout this book confirms that schools are not a level playing field. Schools that serve primarily middle- and upper-class European American students have many more resources than schools that serve primarily non-European and poor students (see Chapter 3). The United States is far from a perfect meritocracy. For example, even when certain groups of students do well in school, the amount of money they earn is not commensurate with their educational attainment. It is true that European American males who have earned a high school diploma obtain higher-paying jobs than those who have not graduated high school. However, research indicates that non–European American students, especially African Americans and Hispanics who graduate from high school, do not earn significantly more than those of their peers who do not complete high school. Given the same level of education, students' earnings depend more on how high up the socioeconomic ladder their parents are (75, 76). Moreover, despite the corrective effects that affirmative action has had, middle- and upper-class European American job seekers still receive preference over their non-European and poor competitors in certain sectors. (See the section on structured reproduction in Chapter 3.) Thus, there is no justification for believing that poor students who do not do well in school and families that remain poor or below the poverty level are responsible for the state of affairs they find themselves in.

**2.** *Individuals from different ethnic and socioeconomic class backgrounds inherit different amounts of intelligence or learning potential.* There are a number of reasons for questioning this assumption. Supporters of the genetic explanation base their conclusion that intelligence is inherited primarily on the results of research that studies twins. They claim these studies indicate that

- Intelligence test scores of identical twins are more similar than those of fraternal twins.
- Identical twins reared apart have very similar intelligence test scores despite being brought up in different environments.
- The IQ scores of adopted children resemble those of their natural parents to a greater degree than expected.

However, these studies have been criticized on a number of grounds (77–87). Researchers who are critical of the theory claim that the studies were flawed methodologically. They suggest that because identical twins are treated more similarly by their parents than fraternal twins, the greater similarity in their test scores could be caused by the similar treatment they receive. They point out that the twins in the adoption studies tended to be placed in homes of families with the same socioeconomic backgrounds as their natural parents, thereby introducing the possibility that environmental factors accounted for the similarity between their scores and those of their natural parents. They note that African American children adopted by European American families score much higher on intelligence tests than one would expect if they had inherited a fixed amount of intelligence from their biological parents.

Another reason for doubting that some non–European American groups such as African Americans inherit less intelligence than European Americans is the fact that environmental factors are the more likely explanation of the difference in scores between African American and European American students. For example, within each socioeconomic class African American students who grow up in racially mixed neighborhoods score higher on intelligence tests because they are exposed to the contents of tests that reflect the experiences of European Americans (83). In addition, almost without exception, studies of African American children's performance on tests that purport to measure their intellectual functioning indicate that poor students do not perform as well as their middle-class peers and that socioeconomic class is a more powerful predictor of how children will perform than ethnic background (78, 88–92).

**3.** *Ethnic groups and socioeconomic classes differ in their abilities to use Level I or Level II types of intellectual operations when solving problems.* Research on Jensen's two-level theory has indicated that poor, African American, and Hispanic American students do score lower than middle-class and European American students on tests that purport to measure Level II abilities (78, 87, 93, 99–103, 105, 107), but a number of researchers (94–98, 104, 106, 108, 109) have criticized the results of these studies for the following reasons.

- The differences obtained in these studies are not as strong or as consistent as those originally reported by Jensen. Some studies have found relationships between Level II scores and ethnicity but not socioeconomic status, for one ethnic group but not another, or for socioeconomic status but not for ethnicity, and contrary to Jensen's theory, most studies have found differences between ethnic groups and socioeconomic classes on tests that purport to measure Level I abilities.
- The differences observed between the scores of European American middle-class students and African American, Hispanic American, and poor students on so-called intelligence tests are more likely to be due to test bias than to real differences in intellectual ability (see Chapter 9).
- There is also evidence that the difference between the scores of European American and middle-class students and African American, Hispanic American, and poor students on tests of Level II abilities is greater than the differences between their scores on tests of Level I abilities because tests of Level II abilities are even more biased against these groups than tests of Level I abilities. Finally, because training students on the use of specific strategies for solving Level II–type problems has been shown to raise the low scores of poor, African American, and Native American students, it appears that the difference in scores on these tests are due to exposure rather than heredity (95, 106, 108).
- Tests of intelligence, including those used to study students' Level I and Level II abilities, are poor predictors of scholastic achievement and therefore are invalid measures of "intelligence." There is no reason to look for explanations for why groups of students have different Level I and Level II intellec-

tual abilities because the tests used to measure these intellectual abilities neither measure intelligence nor predict how students will perform in school (see Chapter 9).

As will be seen in Chapter 9, the results of studies that appear to support the levels theory are based on invalid assessment instruments that cannot be used to measure or evaluate students' intelligence. The content, language, and format of standardized tests that purport to measure intelligence are neither culture-free nor culture-fair; assessors employ them in a biased manner; and they are poor predictors of non-European and poor students' academic achievement or their learning potentials. Comparisons of the assumed intelligence of different groups based on the results of biased instruments and assessors are invalid, misleading, and harmful. They do not explain or justify ethnic or socioeconomic differences in students' achievement.

**4.** *Level I and Level II differences are genetically determined.* Some educators grant the possibility that the differences between ethnic groups and socioeconomic classes on intelligence tests reflect real differences in intellectual ability but disagree that their cause is genetic. They argue that there have been no studies to investigate why some students do poorer on problems that involve conceptual learning (Level II) than on tasks requiring associative and rote learning (Level I), and they claim that because there is no evidence that these differences are inherited, there is no reason to attribute them to genetic factors rather than to such environmental factors as different exposure at home to the kinds of mental operations measured by the tests, inadequate preparation for the tasks on the tests in biased and prejudiced school systems, and so on.

## *Conclusions*

There is no evidence that genetically determined differences in intellectual ability contribute significantly to ethnic and socioeconomic educational disparities or that ethnic groups and socioeconomic classes inherit different intellectual potentials. Differences that have been observed occur because current methods of evaluating intelligence are biased against the groups who perform least adequately on them and because our imperfect society has not yet achieved the assumptions underlying the meritocracy theory.

## *Cultural Deprivation/Educational Disadvantage*

In the 1960s, at the same time that the genetic explanation of the low rates of success among non–European American and poor students was rejected by increasing numbers of educators, the theory of cultural deprivation gained a great deal of acceptance (110–123). According to this theory, certain non–European American students—especially African Americans, Hispanic Americans, and the children of poor parents—are brought up in inferior cultural environments that deprive them of the skills, attitudes, and acceptable behaviors that are transmitted to students who grow up in the superior European American middle-class culture. As a result, they are ill-prepared to succeed in school either academically or behaviorally. As Bloom described them, culturally deprived students have "experiences in homes which do not transmit the cultural patterns necessary for the type of learning characteristics of the schools and the larger society" (112, p. 4).

The term used to label such students has undergone a number of modifications since the 1960s. First it was changed from "culturally deprived" to "culturally disadvantaged" to signify that these students were not cultureless—deprived of a culture—but brought up in a culture that placed them at a disadvantage. Then "culturally disadvantaged" was replaced by "educationally disadvantaged" to indicate that the whole of students' cultures were not being indicted, merely the way they prepared students to function in school. Today, although few educators would publicly proclaim that certain non–European American and poor students are brought up in inferior cultures, numerous educators are on record as believing that some students are ill-prepared to succeed in school because their culture places them at an educational disadvantage. In fact, the U.S. Department of Education spends millions of dollars on educational programs for "educationally disadvantaged students."

## *Characteristics*

According to the theory, disadvantaged and advantaged students differ in terms of their cognitive and linguistic ability, self-concept, level of aspiration, locus of control, and social behavior.

### *Cognitive Skills*

Educationally disadvantaged students are assumed to have "special difficulty in developing concepts of an abstract nature and generalizing" (112, p. 71). They are also considered to be deficient in the "semiautonomous essential processes demanded for adequate skill in the use of linguistic and mathematical symbols and for the analysis of causal relationships" (117, p. 236). In other words, their thinking processes are concrete and convergent/conforming, rather than abstract and creative.

According to the theory, these cognitive deficits occur because educationally disadvantaged students' parents do not interact sufficiently with them; stimulate them intellectually through conversation, field trips, books, magazines, encyclopedias; correct their misperceptions; or encourage their curiosity. As McCloskey put it,

> *Intellectual stimulation between adult and child is relatively slight. Adults seldom talk with children. Parents who work at physical tasks for long hours, often during evening hours, are too tired or inaccessible for conversation with children . . . .*

> *Disadvantaged children have not developed sufficient cognitive and reasoning skills essential for typical rates and dimensions of school progress. These deficiencies accumulate partly from prolonged restriction to the limited experiences of culturally and intellectually impoverished homes and neighborhoods. . . . Disadvantaged children's communication capabilities are elementary. Analytic conversations with adults at home are limited. There, children learn, think, and speak largely about concrete matters of immediate import. Generalities and long-range goals are seldom discussed or recognized. (121, pp. 6, 16)*

Katz stated it this way:

> *In crowded lower-class homes, where mothers often are away at work during the day and both parents lack intellectual sophistication, the child's early efforts at verbal and cognitive mastery are less likely to be favorably reinforced than in middle-class homes, resulting in lower expectations of reward for intellectual effort. (138, p. 19)*

### *Linguistic Ability*

The language of educationally disadvantaged students is supposedly deficient for two reasons. First, it is perceived to be structurally deficient. It is full of grammatical errors, lacks prepositions and other forms that are necessary to perceive and express logical relationships, uses tenses incorrectly, and is repetitive, dull, and colorless.

> *Language in the lower class is not as flexible a means of communication as in the middle class. It is not as readily adapted to the subtleties of the particular situation, but consists more of a relatively small repertoire of stereotyped phrases and expressions which are used rather loosely without much effort to achieve a subtle correspondence between perception and verbal expression. Much of lower class language consists of a kind of incidental "emotional" accompaniment to action here and now. In contrast, middle-class language, rather than being a mere accompaniment to ongoing activity serves more to represent things and events not immediately present. Thus middle-class language is more abstract and necessarily somewhat more flexible, detailed and subtle in its descriptive aspects. (118, pp. 118–119)*

Second, educationally disadvantaged students' use of language is supposedly inadequate because the environments in which they grow up "offered inadequate opportunities to use language in cognitively complex ways" (158, p. 303). These deficits are attributed to parents who provide children poor language models and spend insufficient time communicating with children (112, 114, 116, 167). "In the deprived home, language usage is more limited. Much communication is through gestures and other non-verbal means. When language is used, it is likely to be terse and not necessarily grammatically correct" (112, pp. 70–71).

> *Compared with other children whose families provide them with adequate or extensive spoken language stimulation, children from lower socioeconomic families may be less fortunate. . . . For example, often missing is an atmosphere of family conversation where a child's questions are answered—extending his vocabulary and giving him a right to stand up for and explain his point of view. Also missing in some homes of this type is a family environment which sets an example for acceptable speech and reading patterns. And, children from meager family situations are too often not exposed to a variety of toys and play materials of different colors, shapes, and sizes which challenge the child's ingenuity with his hands and mind, and learn only "restricted" types of language. (167, pp. 332–333)*

### Self-Concept and Self-Esteem

Non–European American students, especially those from African American, Native American, Hispanic American, and poor backgrounds, are thought to have poor self-concepts and low self-esteem. This is attributed to a variety of causes. They are supposed to lack successful role models in their families and communities with whom to identify; repeated failure in school and other competitive situations is assumed to lower their self-image; and they are believed to suffer a loss of self-esteem when they compare their lives and living conditions with those of their middle-class and European American peers. "Disadvantaged children have relatively impoverished self-concepts. From quite realistic appraisals of their experiences, these children have acquired the attitude that they cannot achieve as much as their middle- or upper-class counterparts" (127, p. 5).

### Educational Aspirations

Disadvantaged students are assumed to have low educational and career aspirations. "Their expectations and aspirations are correspondingly low. Many have learned to '*not hope for too much*'. As a result, they are less motivated by goals that fuel the efforts of pupils who have acquired larger aspirations from richer experiences" (121, p. 5).

Disadvantaged students' supposed low level of aspirations are attributed to four factors.

- Their parents do not expect them to do well in school.
- They perceive that their culture and environment does not prepare them to compete successfully with their more advantaged peers.
- Their life experiences, and those of their parents, quickly teach them that it is unrealistic to expect that they will accomplish very much.
- Many of them, especially African American males, lack role models because of the absence of fathers in the house. Because the male parent represents the external world and serves as a role model for dealing with life outside the family while the female parent represents the internal/family world, students without fathers are not motivated to succeed because they do not see that model at home (115, 120, 123).

*Locus of Control*
Theoretically, disadvantaged students have little faith that they are in control of their own lives. Their fatalistic, pessimistic, and dependent attitude amounts to an external locus of control. Their poor performance in school is assumed to be caused in part by the fact that they attribute their poor performance to fate, chance, and various circumstances beyond their control, and do not believe they can determine whether they will succeed.

Disadvantaged students' presumed external locus of control is attributed to three factors. They are as follows:

- Parents of disadvantaged students do not train their children to function independently or praise them for doing so.
- These parents are too harsh and authoritarian and as a result fail to encourage autonomy or positive self-expectations.
- The very conditions of being poor and powerless convinces students that they and their parents cannot exercise control over their lives. "Deprivation impels a child to adopt fatalistic attitudes about the probability that he can meet even his most basic physical needs, let alone his emotional and social needs" (121, p. 24).

*Behavior*
Disadvantaged students are described as misbehaving more often and presenting more discipline problems in school than other students. The theory of cultural deprivation also offers a number of explanations for why this is so (110, 113, 115, 120–122).

- The environment in which disadvantaged students grow up does not encourage acceptable behavior because much of the behavior they observe in their neighborhoods would be unacceptable in school.
- Because their parents stop supervising them at an early age, they are socialized by peer groups that model socially unacceptable values and behavior.
- The lack of fathers at home leaves many of them, especially African American students, without models of appropriate behavior for them to emulate.
- Raising males in a matriarchal setting causes them to overcompensate in exaggeratedly aggressive, masculine ways and leads to

*"desperate efforts of males in lower class culture to rebel against their early overprotective, feminizing environments and to find a masculine identity" (113, p. 9).*

## Implications

Some educators who subscribe to the theory of cultural/educational disadvantage are pessimistic about the possibilities that schools can overcome its presumed effects. This was especially true in the 1960s and 1970s.

> *Class-cultural factors largely account for the conspicuous differences between the slum and the suburban school. Each school has a class character imposed upon it by the social setting in which it exists; this, and not staff inefficiency, racial discrimination, or inequitable provisions of resources, is the main reason for the virtues of one and the defects of the other. The implication is one that reformers find hard to accept—to wit, that no matter how able, dedicated, and hard-working the teachers, no matter how ample the facilities of the school or how well designed its curriculum, no matter how free the atmosphere of the school from racial or other prejudice, the performance of pupils at the lower end of the class-cultural scale will always fall short not only of pupils at the upper end of the scale, but also of what is necessary to make them educated workers. (124, p. 142)*

Educators who do not believe that the effects of cultural disadvantage can be reversed tend to favor lowering expectations for educationally disadvantaged students, modifying their curriculum, using alternative instructional strategies that involve concrete teaching techniques, and segregating them from the mainstream by placing them in separate tracks. Many other supporters of the theory believe that it is possible to combat the characteristics they attribute to the educationally disadvantaged. They tend to support additional funding to schools that serve educationally disadvantaged students; programs such as Head Start and Upward Bound to compensate for students' educational disadvantage; school integration to expose non–European American students to the influence of the more positive, advantaged culture of majority students; affirmative action to provide students with the added resources they are thought to require in order to compete successfully with their more advantaged peers; and parent education programs to help parents prepare children to succeed in school.

> *The litany of past and present innovation, strategies, and acronyms is endless—Parent Child Centers, Upward Bound, Chapter 1, Head Start, Job Corps, Follow Through, Home Start. These programs, including their predecessors and progenitors, are primarily the Great Society's compensatory efforts based on beliefs and assumptions that if only the appropriate method, environment, parenting style, money, program, materials, and personnel were implemented, underachieving minority students would catch up with white children. This deficit view assumes that black children, because of cultural, biological, environmental, and social differences lack the adaptations and knowledge necessary for school achievement. (136, pp. 1–2)*

## *Criticisms*

These beliefs concerning the supposed impact of cultural disadvantages have been criticized on a number of grounds since the 1960s (125–152). In general, critics claim the descriptions of so-called disadvantaged students and the cultural/familial factors these characteristics are attributed to are incorrect, unscientific, and prejudiced. "These terms carry the weight of authority and scholarship instead of the label of ignorant prejudice" (133, p. 63).

Some of their specific criticisms include:

- Many of the characteristics that are attributed to cultural disadvantage are actually the result of poor people's inability to afford and obtain the resources available to the middle and upper classes and the disadvantages many poor immigrants experience because of their limited English proficiency (126, 145–150). Since many more non–European American students than European American students come from lower-class backgrounds, many of the apparent cultural differences between them are actually the result of financial factors. Although poor parents want their children to do well in school, many of them are unemployed, underemployed, underpaid, and undereducated. Thus, they are unable to provide their children with the childhood experiences needed to prepare them for school or the educational and financial support they require to assist their youngsters during their educational careers. The following comments by educators about the poor parents of the Hispanic students with whom they worked illustrate this point of view.

*Spanish-speaking parents believe in the educational system but do not know how to help their youngsters. . . . How can a man with a second grade level of education help his son figure out an algebra equation? (134, p. 169)*

*Among poor families, the necessities of the day-to-day existence such as trips to the grocery store or laundromat, emergency health needs, car trouble, etc. are of primary importance. . . . It is not uncommon for a 7- or 8-year-old girl to stay home from school to baby sit for younger siblings so that Mother can go to work, for a bilingual child to be taken along as "translator" when monolingual parents have medical or legal appointments, or for ten-year-olds to take major responsibility for preparing meals at home for working family members. (134, p. 72)*

Critics complain that society spends less on the economically disadvantaged. They believe that local and state governments should spend more, not less, on schools that serve predominantly poor students. They favor programs, such as day care and preschool programs, designed to assist and supplement poor parents' efforts, programs that train parents to participate in their children's education, and equal opportunity, open admissions, and affirmative action programs that provide students with access to educational programs and the added resources they require to compete successfully with their more economically advantaged peers. They believe such programs are necessary for poor European American and non–European American students to achieve their potential in school; they maintain that educators should have a realistic picture of both the kinds of educational support and assistance parents can provide their children, and how their financial situation impacts on their children's functioning in school; and they advise educators to adapt their educational approaches to these realities. They believe that until this happens, many children of poor parents will continue to fail in school.

- Because students with similar socioeconomic and ethnic backgrounds (for example African American poor students) are actually exposed to very different living conditions, the theory offers misleading overgeneralizations. Within the same socioeconomic class or ethnic group, there are great differences in terms of such factors as parents' educational aspirations for their children; family size; housing conditions; frequency of parent-child cultural activities such as trips to the zoo, library, museums, and movies; frequency and type of adult-child conversation; preschool and kindergarten attendance; and so on. Students with similar socioeconomic and ethnic backgrounds often grow up to be very dissimilar, and many of them do not conform to cultural stereotypes (146, 151, 152).

*There are substantial variations in children's outcomes across families that are identical in parents' education and work history, family income, family size, and other standard measures of social and economic well-being . . . differences in family behavior and attitudes have large and important long-term effects on children's academic performance. (131, pp. 528, 543)*

*A broad rubric such as "educationally deprived" does little if anything toward defining characteristics and educational needs of children. . . . Defining children by social economic level and then designing educational programs for this group will not suffice. . . . The terms "educationally deprived" or "disadvantaged" therefore are of little or no use for educators seriously concerned with providing meaningful educational experiences for Afro-American children, in particular, and for all children in general. (143, pp. 127, 133)*

- The theory has a harmful effect on students because the curriculum offered educationally disadvantaged students is based on lowering standards, modifying content, utilizing less effective instructional strategies, and placing the students in separate tracks (125, 128, 132, 139, 140). (See the section on structured reproduction in Chapter 3.)

*The development of compensatory education programs has traditionally been informed by the belief that disadvantaged students can benefit most from a less challenging curriculum and limited achievement goals. Thus, Chapter 1 services, provided through the Federal Education Consolidation and Improvement Act, comprise curricula stressing basic skills in reading and mathematics, vocational rather than academic programs, and a slower instructional pace. . . . Students receive more instruction in factual and lower-level skills—drill and practice—and less in higher-order skills. [This] hampers the ability of low achieving students to develop thinking skills, lowers their learning expectations and stigmatizes them as inferior. (140, p. 1)*

*The cultural deprivation explanation has provided the substance for the educational self-fulling prophecy which shackles the lives of these low-status children. Because they are "culturally deprived," low-status children are not expected to perform academically up to the norms of other children—the curriculum is watered down and they are placed, for the most part, in slow-learning classes or slow tracks. And because they are treated that way and, at times, told that they are intellectually slow and culturally deprived, they are not motivated to learn and they do not learn. (129, p. 7)*

- The theory blames the victim and diverts people's attention away from the school's contribution to students' problems (127, 130).

*Since both the academic opportunity structure and the occupational opportunity structure of the larger society are assumed to be open and accessible, failure becomes the fault of the individual, his family, his environment, or his culture. Since the cream rises to the top, it is implied that the people who remain at the bottom are either low in ability or psycho-motivationally defective. Further, if whole groups remain at the bottom, it follows that something must be wrong with their particular form of social organization or culture. . . . The cultural deprivation theory, because its focus is on the family and individual personality traits, subtly calls attention away from the schools themselves as precipitators of school success and failure. (130, pp. 340, 341)*

## Research

### Cognitive Ability

*Poor parents' and some non–European American parents' communication, teaching, and parenting styles impede their children's cognitive development and academic achievement.*

The evidence does not support this claim. First, as discussed previously, there is no evidence that students from different socioeconomic and ethnic backgrounds differ in cognitive (intellectual) ability (discussed earlier and in Chapter 9). Second, there is little reason to accept the claim that poor parents impede their children's cognitive development by providing them with an impoverished language environment (154, 155). Early researchers believed that poor parents restrict the development of thought in their children because they "use a restricted language code, in which messages are short, are not made explicit, and are bound to the context in which the message occurs. Middle-class speakers, in contrast, use an elaborated code in which messages are made explicit and context-free." Middle-class mothers also differ from working class parents on the "quality of speech, sentence length, syntactic complexity, use of abstract nouns and verbs, and adjective-verb-ratio" (174, p. 280).

However, the studies this claim was based on were typically not conducted in natural settings such as children's homes, but in laboratory settings, which have been shown to make poor parents anxious and less fluent (144, 168, 178). Research in naturalistic settings indicates that poor parents do not use a restricted language code with their children (162, 163). In addition, there is no evidence that complex linguistic forms are superior to simplistic forms or that complex linguistic forms are necessary for adequate development of children's cognitive skills, reading ability or academic achievement (161, 174, 175). In the absence of such evidence, there is little reason to assume the type of language employed by students' parents affects their cognitive development.

Third, as was noted in the previous section, parenting/teaching styles do not affect students' cognitive development.

Fourth, although parenting and teaching styles do contribute to students' school success (165, 169, 177, 181) there is no evidence that the styles used by different ethnic groups and socioeconomic classes affect children's academic achievement. The early studies that appeared to demonstrate that African American and poor people's parenting styles impeded their children's success in school were poorly controlled. Like the studies on communication styles referred to earlier, the studies did not take into account the fact that poor parents behave differently in experimental settings such as laboratories and in more natural settings such as their own homes and apartments, and they did not control for the fact that parents use different teaching techniques for the real-life tasks and those involved in laboratory experiments.

Later studies that better controlled for these factors found fewer and often no class differences in parenting/teaching styles (153, 156, 159, 164, 172). As a result, researchers concluded that earlier researchers who claimed that ethnic and socioeconomic differences in parental teaching styles cause differences in cognitive development and academic achievement and asserted that the teaching style of poor parents is less efficient than the style employed by middle-class parents were merely expressing their biases and preferences for middle-class norms (174).

### Linguistic Proficiency
*Non-European and poor students do not have the linguistic skills necessary to succeed in school.*

Many studies of students' linguistic proficiency have affirmed the existence of socioeconomic-class and ethnic group differences in oral language (167), vocabulary (166, 180), and syntactic usage (170). To some educators these differences indicate that middle-class and European American students have acquired a higher level of linguistic skills than poor and African American students. Other educators, however, interpret these results in terms of linguistic differences rather than linguistic deficiencies. They feel that certain groups of linguistically able students *appear* to have poorly developed linguistic skills because of a mismatch between the way they and their teachers use language. For example, Slaughter and Epps state that

> *Lower income Black children are quite "verbal," but . . . the norms governing when and how they should speak are different from middle-class norms. To be effective educators, teachers need to know some of these norms, to adapt them to their own classroom behaviors, and, conversely, to point out the differences between in-school and out-of-school speech to the students. (176, p. 9)*

A number of studies have documented the poor match between how teachers engage African American students in conversations and how these students use language in their homes and communities. For example, African American adults seldom ask questions that require children to state something that the children realize adults already know. Rather, they are asked to talk about things about which adults are unaware. Teachers, however, often ask questions about things that they obviously know more about than their students. Thus, in the early grades African American students are often puzzled why teachers are asking them for information that they already know. African American adults ask about things related to children's experiences, whereas teachers often ask questions about things outside their students' life experiences. As a result, students are unprepared to discuss things about which they have no direct experience or understanding. African American parents issue direct orders to students such as "do such and such" whereas European American teachers are often more indirect and say things such as "Why don't you do such and such?" or "You might want to do such and such." Therefore, African American students are not always aware that their teachers have required them to do something and not merely made a suggestion that they can choose to accept or reject (157, 163).

The use of nonstandard speech by African American and Hispanic American students does have an effect on students' academic achievement. But this effect is the result of the way teachers react to their speech patterns, not the speech patterns themselves. Teachers of nonstandard English speakers, especially those who believe standard English to be a more preferable/correct version of English, tend to spend too much time correcting students' "grammatical and dialectic pronunciation errors" instead of teaching them the skills they need to acquire (158, 171). In addition, teachers think that students who do not speak standard English are less intelligent, they have lower academic expectations for them, and they evaluate both their oral and written work to be lower than comparable work of standard-English–speaking students (160, 179), and they are also more likely to disapprove of them (169). (Also see the section on teacher prejudice in Chapter 3.)

### Auditory Discrimination
*Disadvantaged students have poor auditory discrimination skills.*

Although there is a modest relationship between auditory discrimination and reading achievement, there is little evidence that African American, Hispanic American, or poor students have poor auditory discrimination skills. During the 1960s a number of researchers reported that these students scored lower on tests of auditory discrimination (182, 185, 190, 191). However, these differences were actually the result of biased assessment procedures.

Many African American, Hispanic American, and poor students speak nonstandard forms of English that utilize somewhat different sounds. As a result, when they are required to discriminate between unfamiliar sounds that are included in standard English but not in their dialects and languages, they are unable to do so. On the other hand, when they are given auditory discrimination tests in their own languages or dialects, African American, Hispanic American, and poor students do not demonstrate any auditory discrimination problems (183, 184, 186–189, 192).

### Self-Concept
*Educationally disadvantaged students' poor self-concepts interfere with their achievement in school.*

Research reveals that students' self-concepts, the characteristics they attribute to themselves, have a significant effect on the way they behave both in and out of school. Positive self-concepts have been shown to enhance learning and encourage acceptable behavior; poor self-concepts impede achievement and lead to emotional and behavioral problems. However, there is little evidence that poor, African American, and Hispanic American students have poorer self-concepts than their European American middle-class peers.

Some studies, primarily those done in the 1960s, found weak, but statistically significant relationships between students' self-concepts and their ethnic and socioeconomic backgrounds. In general, poor, African American, Native American, and Hispanic American students had lower self-concepts than European American middle-class students (196, 198, 199, 201, 203, 204, 208, 213, 216).

More recent studies of Native American students completed since the 1960s confirmed these earlier findings. Many Native American students, especially those with the greatest exposure to the European American culture and school system, have lower self-esteem than European Americans (207). Most studies of Hispanic American students' self-concepts done since the 1960s indicate that they do not have lower self-concepts (202, 206, 209, 217), and the vast majority of studies, especially those done after the 1960s, have revealed that poor and African American students' self-concepts are at least as high as, if not higher than, those of middle-class European Americans (193–195, 200, 202, 205, 208, 210–212, 214, 215, 218).

Following are four of the common explanations for why African American and Hispanic American students, including those from poor backgrounds, do not have low self-concepts despite their poor neighborhoods, the discrimination they experience, and their low academic success rates.

**1.** The prevailing view that African Americans and other non–European American groups suffer from poor self-concepts is a product of a European American–centric perspective. European American researchers and commentators do not realize that most non–European American children and their parents do not accept the dominant society's view that they are inferior and incapable. They are not aware that African American, Native American, Hispanic American, and other non–European American families have always attempted to counteract the messages students receive about their "inferiority" and have done so with increasing success since the black, brown, and red power movement of the late 1960s and 1970s (197, 210, 212).

*To act as if the only influence upon the formation of self-concepts is that of the dominant culture negates the idea of the child having any other culture or a socialization process that might counteract such a negative view. Such conclusions assume that all a Black or Indian child will get from his family socialization is a carbon copy of the negative stereotyping and evaluation of the white racist culture. . . . Either from ethnocentric distortion or from the negation of the culture of the minority group, researchers leave only psychopathological explana-*

*tions for observed behavior (i.e., academic failure due to "poor self-concept.")* (210, p. 17)

*Blacks have not really believed that white equals goodness and purity. Their self-concept has never entirely been controlled by whites. . . . Blacks have struggled to show their children that the white view of blacks as inferior is incorrect as well as immoral.* (212, p. 139)

*The supposed negative self-image of the Mexican-American is, in reality, our own stereotype projected onto him. "Anglos" tend to think of Mexican-Americans in negative ways, and conclude they see themselves in the same light.* (197, p. 218)

**2.** Many non–European American poor students grow up and attend schools in their neighborhood primarily with students like themselves and are not actually exposed to the more advantaged groups or to the prejudice many have against them.

**3.** Many poor non–European American students do not have poor self-concepts because they experience less stress and tension than middle-class European American students. Unlike middle-class students, they are not trying to live up to high expectations because family's, teachers', and self-expectations for them are not as high.

**4.** Non–European American and poor students who believe that discrimination, not lack of effort or ability, is the cause of many of their problems, do not accept blame for not doing well and do not lose self-respect. Middle-class students tend to blame themselves for their lack of success and thus experience a loss of self-esteem.

### Academic and Vocational Aspirations and Expectations

*Disadvantaged students, especially males, do not aspire or expect to do well in school because their parents do not have high aspirations for them, do not expect them to do well, and do not provide them with acceptable male role models.*

Research offers little support for this supposition. The most telling argument against it comes from studies of students' academic and vocational aspirations done in the 1960s, 1970s, and 1980s, which have consistently indicated that African Americans' aspirations are as high as, if not higher than, those of their European American peers (219–222). The difference between the groups is not their aspirations, but the extent to which they believe they will achieve their aspirations.

African American students start off placing even greater value on education than European American students. However, after attending school for a few years they often expect that they will not achieve the level of education to which they aspire.

Parents' aspirations and expectations for their children in school and their evaluations of their children's academic ability do affect students' confidence about their academic abilities, their academic and occupational aspirations, and the courses they choose to enroll in school. However, research about ethnic and socioeconomic differences in these parental characteristics is inconsistent. Some studies have found that poor, African American, and Hispanic American parents expect their children to do less well in school and do not encourage them as much as European American middle-class parents (126, 223–225). Other studies indicate that African American and poor parents have as high if not higher *aspirations* for children than European American middle-class parents. Again, the difference lies in the fact that African American and poor parents do not expect their children's academic or vocational achievement to fulfill their aspirations for them, so they are willing to accept lower levels of achievement than European American middle-class parents (135, 141, 142, 226–228).

Research that appears to indicate that African American students do not have high educational aspirations and are not encouraged to set high goals for themselves is often culturally insensitive, biased, and invalid (135, 137, 142). European American researchers do not consider the role of the African American community. Through individuals such as teachers, trusted adults, neighbors, community groups and agencies, and so on, outside the family, the community encourages African American students to set high achievement goals for themselves. Therefore, research that only includes the influence of students' families does not present a true picture of the encouragement African American students receive within their culture. Researchers also focus too exclusively on individual achievement. Because African American students are more cooperative and interested in group goals, researchers who do not take include students' desire to contribute to the advancement of African Americans as a group underestimate their achievement orientation.

*Locus of Control*
*Many disadvantaged students have an external locus of control, which has a negative effect on their academic and vocational achievement.*

The research evidence used to support this claim is questionable for two reasons.

**1.** Research about the locus of control of poor, African American, and Hispanic American students has produced mixed results. Some studies have found that they have an external locus of control (177, 229); others have found they do not (126, 231, 233, 234).

**2.** It is unclear whether or not the research that shows that students with an internal locus of control tend to achieve more in school than those whose locus of control is external applies equally to middle-class European American students and to poor and non–European American students (181, 231). Studying locus of control from a European American point of view, researchers failed to recognize the special circumstances of many poor and non–European American students. These researchers mistakenly thought that all students with an internal locus of control attributed their successes and failures to their own ability and effort, whereas all students with an external locus of control attributed their successes and failures to fate and chance. In so doing, they did not realize that many non–European American students with an external locus of control believe, often correctly, that the environment they encounter both in and out of school is so hostile and prejudiced that despite their best efforts, skills, and abilities they will not be able to accomplish their goals (138, 230, 232).

In a society that is fair, as it tends to be for most middle-class European Americans, students with an internal locus of control should do better in school. This is because they will try harder to succeed and to improve when they do poorly. However, in the case of poor students, African Americans, Native Americans, and Hispanic Americans, who exist in a racist and prejudiced environment, an internal locus of control may be self-destructive because it may lead students to blame themselves or hold themselves responsible for failure caused by unfairness, prejudice, and economic injustice. Students with an internal locus of control who are not doing well because of discrimination may blame themselves and give up, but students who correctly understand that external factors are to blame may strive to change them, especially if they are supported by others who hold similar beliefs and have similar characteristics.

> *"Feelings of fate control" may in fact be valid perceptions of institutional barriers (for example tracking and negative teacher attitudes) which prevent black students from actually exercising any significant and meaningful control over their own lives. . . . The way to solve the learning difficulties encountered by black students is to remove the institutional barriers which prevent them from exercising any significant and meaningful control over their intellectual and personal destinies rather than blaming the black family for something over which it has no control. (232 p. 75)*

### Father Absence
*Many of the educational and behavior problems of poor students, especially African American males, are caused at least in part by the absence of a father in the family.*

During the 1960s and 1970s a number of studies found that students, particularly African American males growing up in one-parent families headed by females, performed less adequately on tests purported to measure intelligence and moral development, had lower academic and vocational aspirations, achieved less, were more aggressive in school, and were less well-adjusted (115, 165, 235, 237, 239, 240, 242, 243, 246, 249). However, these early studies have been justly criticized.

Most of them failed to control for socioeconomic differences. This is a very important omission because families that are deprived of the income of fathers were and are more likely to fall into the poor or poverty groups. Currently, 46% of European American, 66% of Hispanic American and 67% of African American children living in single-parent female-headed families live in poverty (256). In the 1960s and early 1970s fewer women were in the work force, the discrepancy between what working women and men earned was even greater than today, and there were fewer resources such as day care centers and other supports available to single-parent families. Thus, the differences observed in these studies could well have been due to socioeconomic factors.

Most subsequent studies that were better controlled, and a number of studies done in the 1960s and 1970s reported results that contradict the findings of the early studies (173, 181, 219, 236, 241, 242, 247, 250, 253). They typically found either no relationship between the presence of students' fathers at home and their adjustment in or out of school, or a relationship that was so small that it accounted for very little of the differences observed between successful and unsuccessful students. In addition, the relationship tended to be confined to poor students. These facts suggest that the small relationship between children's adjustment and the presence or absence of their fathers is primarily the result of the loss of income poor families experience rather than the absence of a male role model.

The early studies misunderstand and misrepresent the nature of poor and African American families (238, 244, 245, 251, 252, 254). Culturally insensitive European American researchers underestimated the strength of black families. They designed studies and interpreted the results of these studies while unaware of the role the African American extended family, teachers, trusted adults, neighbors, community groups and agencies, and churches play in encouraging, guiding, and supporting African American students. It is also incorrect to assume that fathers who are legally not a part of the family are actually absent. Many males who are separated or divorced from the children's mothers, or pretend to be absent and uninvolved so their families can qualify for welfare and other forms of assistance, often play significant roles in the children's lives.

Researchers may have also projected their sexist points of view on the African American family (137, 238, 248, 255). African American families are much more egalitarian and nonsexist than many European American families. Gender roles are much less stereotyped; mothers can be role models for activities and functions that are usually reserved for males in the European American culture. So even when males are absent, females can often provide the necessary role models.

## *Conclusions*

The validity of the cultural deprivation/educational disadvantage theory can be evaluated in terms of three questions.

**1.** *Do the characteristics attributed to educationally disadvantaged students negatively affect educational outcomes?* Research indicates that students' auditory discrimination skills, locus of control, level of aspiration and self-concept do affect their achievement in school. The assumed negative influence of students' use of nonstandard English, parental teaching styles, and father absence are not supported by research.

**2.** *Do African American, Hispanic American, and poor students have these characteristics to a greater degree than European American and middle-class students?* There is no evidence that poor, African American, and Hispanic American students have poor auditory skills. Research on their locus of control is mixed. However, it is likely that even when these students appear to have an external locus of control, they may be accurately perceiving the obstacles they face in a society rife with prejudice rather than attributing their successes and failure to fate, luck, or chance. Contrary to what the theory predicts, these students have aspirations and self-concepts as high as, if not higher than, middle-class European American students.

*3. If African American, Hispanic American, and poor students have these characteristics to a greater degree than European American and middle-class students, are the differences caused by cultural/familial factors rather than racism, economic disadvantage, and so on?* The few differences observed between African American, Hispanic American, and poor and European American and middle-class students and their families that have been confirmed by research are more likely to be caused by the prejudiced and hostile environment they face and the limited opportunities their lack of financial resources impose of them than by cultural differences.

## *Summary*

Some educators believe that many poor, African American, Native American, and Hispanic American students are more likely to suffer biomedical problems, to inherit less intellectual potential than their peers, and to come from culturally deprived or disadvantaged backgrounds. They attribute the high percentage of failure among these students to the educational problems these conditions can create.

Although poor, African American, Native American, and Hispanic American students are more likely to suffer biomedical problems, it is unlikely that these problems are a major cause of their lack of achievement. Research does not support the contention that they inherit less intellectual potential than others. The early research on cultural deprivation/disadvantage was done from a European American point of view. Better controlled, more culturally sensitive studies refute the idea that poor, African American, and Hispanic American students are brought up in deprived or disadvantaged cultures.

## *Activities*

1. The following are the major contentions of those who believe that cultural disadvantage is an important cause of the educational problems of many students. Ask some of your European American middle-class friends or fellow students to tell you their opinion about which, if any, of these assumptions are characteristic of African American, Hispanic American, or poor students. Ask some of your African American or Hispanic American friends or fellow students from poor backgrounds if they were ever told or believed any of these assumptions.

Parents' communication, teaching, and parenting styles impede children's cognitive development and academic achievement. Their children do not have the linguistic skills necessary to succeed in school. Disadvantaged students have poor auditory discrimination skills. Their poor self-concepts interfere with their achievement in school. They do not aspire or expect to do well in school because their parents do not have high aspirations for them, do not expect them to do well, and do not provide them with acceptable male role models. They have an external locus of control, which has a negative effect on their academic and vocational achievement. Many of their educational and behavior problems are caused at least in part by the absence of a father in the family.

2. Improve your understanding of the problems of children born addicted to substances such as alcohol and drugs by visiting a program that serves them.

## References

The following references deal with the effects of poor nutrition and health care on students' behavior and school success.

1. Baumeister, A. A., Kupstas, F., & Klindworth, L. M. (1990). New morbidity: Implications for prevention of children's disabilities. *Exceptionality, 1*, 1–16.
2. Escalona, S. K. (1982). Babies at double hazard: Early development of infants at biological and social risk. *Pediatrics, 70*, 670–675.
3. Food Research and Action Center. (1984). *The Widening Gap: The Incidence and Distribution of Infant Mortality and Low Birthweight in the United States—1978–1982*. Washington, DC: Author.
4. Galler, J. R. (Ed.). (1984). *Human Nutrition: A Comprehensive Treatise: Vol. 5. Nutrition and Behavior*. New York: Plenum Press.
5. Hoy, E. A., Bill, J. M., & Sykes, D. H. (1988). Very low birthweight: A long-term developmental impairment? *International Journal of Behavioral Development, 11*, 37–67.
6. Hughes, D., Johnson, K., Rosenbaum, S., Butler, W., & Simons, J. (1988). *The Health of America's Children: Maternal and Child Health Data Book*. Washington, DC: Children's Defense Fund.
7. Institute of Medicine. (1985). *Preventing Low Birthweight*. Washington, DC: National Academy Press.
8. Kopp, C. B., & Kaler, S. R. (1989). Risk in infancy: Origins and implications. *American Psychologist, 44*(2), 224–230.
9. Lane, J. M., & Johnson, C. L. (1981). Prevalence of iron deficiency. In *Report of the Eighty-Second Ross Conference on Pediatric Research*. Columbus, OH: Ross Laboratories.
10. Lieberman, E., Ryan, K., Monson, R., & Schoenbaum, S. (1987). Risk factors accounting for racial differences in the rate of premature birth. *New England Journal of Medicine, 317*, 743–748.
11. Lozoff, B. (1988). Behavioral alterations in iron deficiency. *Advances in Pediatrics, 35*, 331–360.
12. Lozoff, B. (1989). Nutrition and behavior. *American Psychologist, 44*(2), 231–236.
13. National Center for Clinical Infant Programs. (1986). *Infants Can't Wait: The Numbers*. Washington, DC: Author.
14. National Center for Health Statistics. (1987). *Advance Report of Final Natality Statistics, 1985*. (Monthly vital statistics report, Vol. 36). Washington, DC.
15. R. W. Johnson Foundation. (1983). *A National Collaborative Study*. Princeton, NJ.
16. Shapiro, S., McCormick, M. C., Starfield, B. H., & Crawley, B. (1983). Changes in infant morbidity associated with decreases in neonatal mortality. *Pediatrics, 72*, 408–415.

The following references discuss the prevalence and effects of prenatal substance abuse.

17. Adler, T. (1989). Cocaine babies face behavior deficits. *American Psychological Association Monitor, 20*(7), 14.

18. Archer, L. D. (1987). *Program Strategies for Preventing Fetal Alcohol Syndrome and Alcohol Related Birth Defects.* DHHS Publication No. (ADM) 87–1482.
19. Aronson, M., Kyllerman, M., Sobel, J. G., Sandin, B., & Olegard, R. (1985). Children of alcoholic mothers: Developmental, perceptual, and behavioral characteristics as compared to matched controls. *Acta Paediatrica Scandinavica, 74,* 27–35.
20. Besharov, D. J. (1989). The children of crack, will we protect them? *Public Welfare, 47*(4), 6–11.
21. Besharov, D. J. (1990). Crack children in foster care. *Children Today, 19,* 21–35.
22. Brooks-Gunn, J., & McCarton, C. (1991). *Effects of Drugs In-Utero on Infant Development.* (Report to Congress). Washington, DC: National Institute of Child Health and Human Development.
23. Burkett, B., Yasin, S., & Palow, D. (1990). Perinatal implications of cocaine exposure. *Journal of Reproductive Medicine, 35*(1), 35–42.
24. Chasnoff, I., Landress, H., & Barrett, M. (1990). The prevalence of illicit drug and or alcohol use during pregnancy and discrepancies in mandatory reporting in Pinellas County, Florida. *New England Journal of Medicine, 322,* 1202–1206.
25. Chavin, W., & Kandall, S. R. (1990). Between a rock and a hard place: Perinatal drug abuse. *Pediatrics, 85,* 223–225.
26. Cohen, S. (1985). *The Substance Abuse Problems, Vol II. New Issues for the 1980s.* Redding, CA: Hawthorn Press.
27. Cole, C., Ferara, V., Johnson, D., Jones, M., Schoenbaum, M., Tyler, R., Wallace, V., & Poulsen, M. (1989). *Today's Challenge: Teaching Strategies for Working with Young Children Pre-natally Exposed to Drugs/Alcohol.* Los Angeles: Los Angeles Unified School District.
28. Dow-Edwards, D. L. (1988). Developmental effects of cocaine. *National Institute of Drug Abuse Research Monographs, 88,* 290–303.
29. Finnegan, L. (1989). *Drug Dependency in Pregnancy: Clinical Management of Mother and Child.* Washington, DC: National Institute of Drug Abuse Service Research Monograph Service, U.S. Government Printing Office.
30. Fried, P. A., & O'Connell, C. M. (1987). A comparison of the effects of prenatal exposure to tobacco, alcohol, cannabis, and caffeine on birthsize and subsequent growth. *Neurotoxicology and Teratology, 9,* 79–85.
31. Gittler, J., & McPherson, M. (1990). Prenatal substance abuse. *Children Today, 19,* 3–7.
32. Griffith, D. (1991, May). *Intervention Needs of Children Prenatally Exposed to Drugs.* Congressional testimony before the House Select Committee on Special Education. Washington, DC.
33. Haflon, N. (1989). *Hearing: Born Hooked, Confronting the Impact of Perinatal Substance Abuse.* Select Committee on Children, Youth and Families, U.S. House of Representatives. April 27.
34. Howard, J., Beckwith, L., Rodning, C., & Kropenske, V. (1989). Development of young children of substance-abusing parents: Insights from seven years of intervention and research. *Zero to Three, 9,* 8–12.
35. Kronstadt, D. (1989). *Pregnancy and Cocaine Addiction: An Overview of Impact and Treatment.* San Francisco: Far West Laboratory for Educational Research and Development.
36. Miller, G. (1989). *Hearing: Born Hooked, Confronting the Impact of Perinatal Substance Abuse.* Select Committee on Children, Youth and Families, U.S. House of Representatives. April 27.
37. New York City HRA Office of Management Analysis. (1990). *Report Issued on January 31, 1990.* New York: Author.
38. The New York Times. (1989). *Crack's Toll Among Babies: A Joyless View of Even Toys.* September 17.
39. Petitti, D. B., & Coleman, C. (1990). Cocaine and the risk of low birth weight. *American Journal of Public Health, 80*(1), 25–28.
40. Phillipson, R. (1988). The fetal alcohol syndrome: Recent international statistics. *Australia and New Zealand Journal of Developmental Psychology, 14*(3/4), 211–221.
41. Poulsen, M. (1991). *Schools Meet the Challenge: Educational Needs of Children at Risk Due to Substance Exposure.* Sacramento, CA: Resources in Special Education.
42. Reed, B. (1987). Developing women sensitive drug dependent treatment services: Why so difficult? *Journal of Psychoactive Drugs, 19*(2), 151–164.
43. Rist, M. C. (1990). The shadow children. *American School Board Journal, 177*(1), 19–24.
44. Straus, A. (1981). Neonatal manifestations of maternal phencyclidine (PCP) abuse. *Pediatrics, 66,* 4.
45. Streissguth, A. P. (1989). *Prenatal Alcohol Exposure and Child IQ, Achievement and Class-*

*room Behavior at Age 7*. Paper presented at the annual conference of the Society for Research in Child Development, Kansas City, MO.
46. Streisstguth, A. P., Clarren, S. K., & Jones, K. L. (1985). Natural history of the fetal alcohol syndrome: A 10-year follow-up of eleven patients. *Lancet, 2*(8446), 85–91.
47. U.S. Department of Health and Human Services, Office of Inspector General. (1990). *Crack Babies*. Washington, DC: Author.
48. U.S. National Center for Health Statistics. (1989). *Advance Report of Final Natality Statistics, 1987*. Vol. 38, No. 3, Supplement, June 29. Washington, DC: U.S. Department of Health and Human Services.
49. Vincent, L. J., Poulsen, M. K., Cole, C. K., Woodruff, G., & Griffith, D. R. (1991). *Born Substance Exposed, Educationally Vulnerable*. Reston, VA: Council for Exceptional Children.
50. Wescott, S. M. (1990). Time to address a preventable tragedy. *Winds of Change, 5*(3), 30–34.
51. Weston, R. R., Ivins, B., Zuckerman, B., Jones, C., & Lopez, R. (1989). Drug-exposed babies: Research and clinical issues. *Zero to Three, 9*, 1–7.
52. Wilson, G. S. (1989). Clinical studies of infants and children exposed prenatally to heroin. *Annals of The New York Academy of Sciences, 562*, 183–194.
53. Zuckerman, B. (1991). Drug-exposed infants: Understanding the medical risk. *The Future of Children, 1*(1), 26–35.

The prevalence and effects of pediatric autoimmune deficiency syndrome is the focus of the following references.

54. Belman, A. L., Diamond, G., Dickson, D., Horoupian, D., Llena, J., Lantos, G., & Rubinstein, A. (1988). Calcification of the basal ganglia in infants and children with acquires immuno-deficiency syndrome. *American Journal of Diseases of Children, 36*, 1192–1199.
55. Belman, A. L., Ultmann, M. H., Horouopian, D., Novick, B. D., Spiro, A. J., Rubinstein, A., Kurtzberg, D., & Cone-Wesson, B. (1985). Neurological implications in infants with acquired immunodeficiency syndrome. *Annals of Neurology, 18*, 560–566.
56. Epstein, L. G., Sharer, L. R., Oleske, J. M., Cannon, E. M., Gouldsmit, J., Bagdon, L., Robert-Guroff, M., & Koenigsberger, M. R. (1986). Neurological manifestations of HIV infection in children. *Pediatrics, 78*, 678–688.
57. Mays, V. M. (1987). *Epidemiology of AIDS among Ethnic Minorities*. Paper presented at the annual meeting of the American Psychological Association, New York.
58. Task Force on Pediatric AIDS. (1989). Pediatric AIDS and human immunodeficiency virus infection. *American Psychologist, 44*(2), 258–264.

Genetic explanations of ethnic and socioeconomic differences in school outcomes are presented in the references listed next.

59. Agassiz, L. (1850). The diversity of origin of the human races. *Christian Examiner, 49*, 110–145.
60. Blatt, B. (1981). *In and Out of Mental Retardation*. Baltimore: University Park Press.
61. Davenport, C. B. (1911). *Heredity in Relation to Eugenics*. New York: Holt.
62. Eysenck, H. J., (1973). *The Inequality of Man*. London: Temple Smith.
63. Gould, S. J. (1981). *The Mismeasure of Man*. New York: W. W. Norton.
64. Herrnstein, R. J. (1973). *IQ in the Meritocracy*. Boston: Little, Brown.
65. Jensen, A. R. (1971). *A Two-Factor Theory of Familial Mental Retardation*. ERIC ED 060–577.
66. Jensen, A. R. (1974). Interaction of Level I and Level II abilities with race and socioeconomic status. *Journal of Educational Psychology, 66*(1), 99–111.
67. Jensen, A. R. (1981). *Straight Talk about Mental Tests*. New York: Free Press.
68. Latham, G. L. (1987). *Breeding Poverty? Great Issues Lecture*. ERIC ED 293–232.
69. Popenoe P., & Johnson, R. H. (1918). *Applied Eugenics*. New York: Macmillan.
70. Shockley, W. (1971). Models, mathematics, and the moral obligation to diagnose the origins of Negro IQ deficits. *Review of Educational Research, 41*(4), 369–377.
71. Spuhler, J. N., & Lindzey, G. (1967). Racial differences in behavior. In J. Hirsch (Ed.), *Behavior-Genetic Analysis*. New York: McGraw-Hill.
72. Thorndike, E. L. (1931). *Human Learning*. New York: Century.

The fallacy of the meritocracy theory is the subject of these references.

73. Goldberg, A. S. (1974a). *Mystery of the Meritocracy.* Madison, WI: Institute for Research on Poverty, University of Wisconsin.
74. Goldberg, A. S. (1974b). *Professor Jensen, Meet Miss Burks.* Madison, WI: Institute for Research on Poverty, University of Wisconsin.
75. Jencks, C., Smith, M., Acland, H., Bane, M. J., Cohen, D., Gintis, H., Heyns, G., & Michelson, S. (1972). *Inequality: A Reassessment of the Effect of Family and Schooling in America.* New York: Harper & Row.
76. Rumberger, R. W. (1983). The influence of family background on education, learnings, and wealth. *Social Forces, 3,* 755–773.

Arguments and evidence against the genetic explanation of educational disparities are included in the following references.

77. Bronfenbrenner, U. (1972). Is 80% of intelligence genetically determined? In U. Bronfenbrenner (Ed.), *Influence on Human Development.* Hinsdale IL: Dryden.
78. Green, R. B., & Rohwer, W. D. Jr. (1971). SES differences on learning and ability tests in black children. *American Journal of Educational Research, 8*(4), 601–609.
79. Kamin, L. J. (1973). Text of Dr. Kamin's presentation denying that proof exists that IQ test scores are hereditary. *South Today, 4*(8), 1–5.
80. Kamin, L. J. (1974). *The Science and Politics of I. Q.* Hillsdale, NJ: Lawrence Erlbaum.
81. Mensh, E., & Mensh, H. (1991). *The IQ Mythology: Class, Race, Gender, and Inequality.* Carbondale, IL: Southern Illinois University Press.
82. Moore, E. G. J. (1986). Family socialization and the IQ test performance of traditionally and transracially adopted black children. *Developmental Psychology, 22,* 317–326.
83. Moore, E. G. J. (1987). Ethnic social milieu and black children's intelligence achievement. *Journal of Negro Education, 56*(1), 44–52.
84. Persell, C. H. (1981). Genetic and cultural deficit theories: Two sides of the same racist coin. *Journal of Black Studies, 12*(1), 19–37.
85. Scarr, S. (1968). Environment bias in twin studies, *Eugenics Quarterly, 15,* 34–40.
86. Scarr, S. (1971). Race, social class and IQ. *Science, 174,* 1285–1295.
87. Vernon, P. E., & Mitchell, M. C. (1974). Social-class differences in associative learning. *Journal of Special Education, 8*(4), 297–311.

The role of socioeconomic factors in predicting differences in scores on tests of intellectual functioning within ethnic groups is discussed in the following references.

88. Bardouille-Crema, A., Black, K. N., & Feldhusen, J. (1986). Performance on Piagetian tasks of black children of differing socioeconomic levels. *Developmental Psychology, 22*(6), 841–844.
89. Blau, Z. S. (1981). *Black Children/White Children.* New York: Free Press.
90. Hall, V. C., & Kaye, D. B. (1980). Early patterns of cognitive development. With commentary by Sandra W. Scarr. *Monographs of the Society for Research in Child Development, 45*(2), Serial No. 184.
91. Scarr, S. (1981). *Race, Social Class, and Individual Differences in I. Q.* Hillsdale, NJ: Erlbaum.
92. Yando, R., Seitz, V., & Zigler, W. (1979). *Intellectual and Personality Characteristics of Children.* Hillsdale, NJ: Erlbaum.

Research regarding and discussion of the theory of genetically determined ethnic group and socioeconomic differences in Level I and Level II abilities is included in the following references.

93. Bee, H., Barnard, K., Eyres, S., Gray, C., Hammond, M., Speitz, A., Snyder, C., & Clark, B. (1982). Prediction of IQ and language skills from perinatal status, child performance, family characteristics, and mother-infant interaction. *Child Development, 53,* 44–75.
94. Borkowski, J. G., & Krause, A. (1983). Racial differences in intelligence: The importance of the executive system. *Intelligence, 7,* 379–395.
95. Bridgeman, B., & Buttram, J. (1975). Race differences on nonverbal analogy test performance as a function of verbal strategy training. *Journal of Educational Psychology, 67*(4), 586–590.
96. Butcher, H. J. (1972). Comments on Arthur Jensen's "Do schools cheat minority children". *Educational Research, 14*(2), 87–100.
97. Humphreys, L. G., & Dachler, P. (1969a). Jensen's theory of intelligence. *Journal of Educational Psychology, 60,* 419–426.
98. Humphreys, L. G., & Dachler, P. (1969b). Jensen's theory of intelligence: A rebuttal. *Journal of Educational Psychology, 60,* 432–433.
99. Jensen, A. R. (1969). How much can we boost IQ and scholastic achievement? *Harvard Educational Review, 39,* 1–123.

100. Jensen, A. R. (1971). The role of verbal mediation in development. *Journal of Genetic Psychology, 118,* 39–70.
101. Jensen, A. R. (1973a). *Genetics and Education.* New York: Harper & Row.
102. Jensen, A. R. (1973b). *Level I and Level II Abilities in Three Ethnic Groups.* ERIC ED 080–646.
103. Jensen, A. R., & Inouye, A. R. (1980). Level I and Level II abilities in Asian, white, and black children. *Intelligence, 4,* 41–49.
104. Nisbet, J. (1972). Comments on Arthur Jensen's "Do schools cheat minority children?" *Experimental Research, 14*(2), 87–100.
105. Orn, D. E., & Das, J. P. (1972). IQ, socioeconomic status, and short-term memory. *Journal of Educational Psychology, 63,* 327–333.
106. Schubert, J., & Cropley, A. (1972). Verbal regulation of behavior and IQ in Canadian Indian and white children. *Developmental Psychology, 7,* 295–301.
107. Sigel, I. (1982). The relationship between parental distancing strategies and the child's cognitive behavior. In L. Laosa & I. Sigel (Eds.), *Families as Learning Environments for Children.* New York: Plenum.
108. Skanes, G. R., Sullivan, A. M., Rowe, E. J., & Shannon, E. (1974). Intelligence and transfer: Aptitude by treatment interactions. *Journal of Educational Psychology, 66,* 563–568.
109. Vernon, P. (1972). Comments on Arthur Jensen's "Do schools cheat minority children?" *Experimental Education, 14*(2), 87–100.

Publications by proponents of the cultural deprivation theory are listed below.

110. Bacon, M. K., Child, I. L., & Barry, H. (1963). A cross cultural study of correlates of crime. *Journal of Abnormal and Social Psychology, 66,* 291–300.
111. Bandura, A., & Walters, R. H. (1959). *Adolescent Aggression.* New York: Ronald.
112. Bloom, B. S., Davis, A., & Hess, R. (1965). *Compensatory Education for Cultural Deprivation.* New York: Holt, Rinehart & Winston.
113. Bronfenbrenner, U. (1967). *The Psychological Costs to Quality and Equality in Education.* ERIC ED 113–405.
114. Deutsch, C. P. (1964). Auditory discrimination and learning: Social factors. *Merrill-Palmer Quarterly, 10,* 277–296.
115. Deutsch, M. (1960). Minority group and class status as related to social and personality factors in scholastic achievement. *Society for Applied Anthropology,* Monograph No. 2. Ithaca, NY: Cornell University Press.
116. Hess, R. (1970). Social class and ethnic influences on socialization. In P. Hussen (Ed.), *Manual of Child Psychology,* Vol. 2. New York: Wiley.
117. Hunt, J. (1964). The psychological basis for using pre-school environment as an antidote for cultural deprivation. *Merrill-Palmer Quarterly, 10,* 209–248.
118. Jensen, A. R. (1968). Social class and verbal learning. In M. Deutsch, I. Katz, & A. R. Jensen (Eds.), *Social Class, Race and Psychological Development.* New York: Holt, Rinehart & Winston.
119. Lewis, O. (1966). The culture of poverty. *Scientific American, 215,* 19–25.
120. McClelland, D. C. (1961). *The Achieving Society.* New York: Van Nostrand.
121. McCloskey, E. F. (1967). *Urban Disadvantaged Pupils; Characteristics, Environments, Potentials.* Portland, OR: Northwest Regional Educational Laboratory.
122. Miller, W. B., (1958). Lower class culture as a generating milieu of gang delinquency. *Journal of Social Issues, 14*(30), 5–19.
123. Pettigrew, T. F. (1964). *A Profile of the Negro American.* Princeton: Van Nostrand.

The implications of the cultural deprivation theory is the focus of the reference listed below.

124. Banfield, E. (1970). *The Unheavenly City.* Boston: Little, Brown and Company.

Criticism of the concepts culturally deprived, culturally disadvantaged, and educationally disadvantaged and the procedures used with students with these labels is contained in the following references.

125. Adams, M. J. (1986). Teaching thinking to Chapter 1 students. In B. I. Williams, P. A. Richmond, & B. J. Mason (Eds.), *Designs for Compensatory Education: Conference Proceedings and Papers.* ERIC ED 293–913.
126. Bender, P. S., & Ruiz, R. A. (1974). Race and class as differential determiners of underachievement and underaspiration among Mexican-Americans and Anglos. *Journal of Educational Research, 68*(2), 51–55.
127. Bowles, S., & Gintis, H. (1976). *Schooling in Capitalist America: Educational Reform and the Contradictions of Economic Life.* New York: Basic Books.

128. Calfee, R. (1986). Curriculum and instruction: Reading. In B. I. Williams, P. A. Richmond, & B. J. Mason (Eds.), *Designs for Compensatory Education: Conference Proceedings and Papers.* ERIC ED 293–912.
129. Clark, K. B., Deutsch, M., Gartner, A., Keppel, G., Lewis, H., Pettigrew, T., Plotkin, L., & Reissman, F. (1972). *The Educationally Deprived: The Potential for Change.* New York: Metropolitan Applied Research Center.
130. Cummings, S. (1977). Explaining poor academic performance among black children. *Educational Forum, 41*(3), 335–346.
131. Datcher-Loury, L. (1989). Family background and school achievement among low income blacks. *Journal of Human Resources, 24*(3), 528–544.
132. Dolye, W. (1986). Vision and Reality: A reaction to issues in curriculum and instruction for compensatory education. In B. I. Williams, P. A. Richmond, & B. J. Mason (Eds.), *Designs for Compensatory Education: Conference Proceedings and Papers.* ERIC ED 293–918.
133. Goodman, Y. T. (1969). The culturally deprived child: A study in stereotyping. *Integrated Education, 7*(4), 58–63.
134. Grossman, H. (1984). *Educating Hispanic Students: Cultural Implications for Instruction, Classroom Management, Counseling and Assessment.* Springfield, IL: Charles C Thomas.
135. Gurin, P., & Epps, E. (1975). *Black Consciousness, Identity and Achievement.* New York: Wiley.
136. Irvine, J. J. (1991). *Black Students and School Failure*: Policies, Practices, and Prescriptions. New York: Praeger.
137. Irvine, R. W. (1978). The black family and community: Some problems in the development of achievement values. *Negro Educational Review, 29*(3–4), 249–254.
138. Katz, I. (1969). A critique of personality approaches to negro performance, with research suggestions. *Journal of Social Issues, 25*(3), 13–27.
139. Levin, H. M. (1987). *New Schools for the Disadvantaged.* Unpublished manuscript. Stanford, CA: Stanford University.
140. Passow, A. H. (1990). *Enriching Compensatory Education Curriculum for Disadvantaged Students.* New York: ERIC Clearinghouse on Urban Education, Teachers College, Columbia University.
141. Sowell, T. (1976). Patterns of black excellence. *The Public Interest, 43*, 26–58.
142. Staples, R. (1976). *Introduction to Black Sociology.* New York: McGraw-Hill.
143. Sullivan, A. R. (1972). The influence of social processes on the learning abilities of Afro-American School Children: Some educational implications. *Journal of Negro Education, 41*(2), 127–136.
144. Tulkin, S. (1972). An analysis of the concept of cultural deprivation. *Developmental Psychology, 6*, 326–339.

The relative influences of cultural, linguistic, and socioeconomic factors on school achievement are discussed in the following references.

145. Laosa, L. M. (1982). School, occupation, culture, and family: The impact of parental schooling on the parent-child relationship. *Journal of Educational Psychology, 74*(6), 791–827.
146. Laosa, L. M. (1984). Ethnic, socioeconomic, and home language influences upon early performance on measures of abilities. *Journal of Educational Psychology, 76*(6), 1178–1198.
147. Macias, R. F. (1979). *Mexicano/Chicano Sociolinguistic Behavior and Language Policy in the United States.* Unpublished doctoral dissertation. Georgetown University, Washington, DC.
148. Rosenthal, A. S., Milne, A., Ginsburg, A., & Baker, K. A. (1981). *A Comparison of the Effects of Language Background and Socioeconomic Status on Achievement Status among Elementary School Students.* Draft final report, subcontract #b43601 from System Development Corporation under contract #300–75–0332. Washington, DC: U.S. Department of Education.
149. So, A. Y., & Chan, K. S. (1982). *What Matters? The Relative Impact of Language Background and Socioeconomic Status on Reading Achievement.* Los Alamitos, CA: National Center for Bilingual Research.
150. Valencia, R. R., Henderson, R. W., & Rankin, R. J. (1981). Relationship of family constellation and schooling to intellectual performance of Mexican American children. *Journal of Educational Psychology, 73*(4), 524–532.

The following references deal with the low validity of ethnic and socioeconomic profiles in identifying students who do not fit their ethnic and socioeconomic stereotypes.

151. Stodolosky, S. S., & Lesser, G. (1967). Learning patterns in the disadvantaged. *Harvard Educational Review, 37,* 546–593.
152. Trotman, F. K. (1977). Race, IQ, and the middle class. *Journal of Educational Psychology, 69*(3), 266–273.

The following references deal with ethnic and socioeconomic differences in cognitive verbal skills.

153. Adams, J. L., & Ramey, C. T. (1980). Structural aspects of maternal speech to infants reared in poverty. *Child Development, 51,* 1280–1284.
154. Bee, H., Van Egeren, L., Striessguth, A. P., Nyman, B. A., & Leckie, M. S. (1969). Social class differences in maternal teaching strategies and speech patterns. *Developmental Psychology, 1*(6), 726–734.
155. Bernstein, B. (1961). Social class and linguistic development. In A. Halsey, J. Floud, & C. Anderson (Eds.), *Education, Economy and Society.* Glencoe, IL: Free Press.
156. Borduin, C. M., Henggeler, S. W., Sanders-Walls, M., & Harbin, F. (1986). An evaluation of social class differences in verbal and nonverbal maternal controls, maternal sensitivity and child compliance. *Child Study Journal, 16*(2), 95–112.
157. Brice-Heath, S. (1982). Questioning at home and at school: A comparative study. In G. Spindler (Ed.), *Doing Ethnography: Educational Anthropology in Action.* New York: Holt, Rinehart & Winston.
158. Collins, J. (1988). Language and class in minority education. *Anthropology and Education Quarterly, 19*(4), 299–326.
159. Farron, D. C., & Ramey, C. T. (1980). Social class differences in dyadic involvement during infancy. *Child Development, 51,* 254–257.
160. Ford, C. E. (1984). The influence of speech variety on teachers' evaluation of students with comparable academic ability. *TESOL Quarterly, 18*(1), 25–40.
161. Gibson, E., & Levin, H. (1975). *The Psychology of Reading.* Cambridge, MA: MIT Press.
162. Hall, W., & Dore, J. (1980). *Lexical Sharing in Mother-Child Interaction.* Technical Report No. 161. Urbana, IL: University of Illinois at Urbana-Champaign, Center for the Study of Reading.
163. Hall, W., & Tire, W. (1979). *The Communicative Environment of Young Children: Social Class, Ethnic, and Situational Differences.* Technical Report No. 125. Champaign, IL: University of Illinois at Urbana-Champaign, Center for the Study of Reading.
164. Henggeler, S. W., & Tavormina, J. B. (1980). Social class and race differences in family interaction: Pathological, normative, or confounding methodological factors? *Journal of Genetic Psychology, 137,* 211–222.
165. Hess, R. D., & Shipman, V. (1968). Maternal influences upon early learning: The cognitive environment of urban preschool children. In R. D. Hess & R. M. Bear (Eds.), *Early Education.* Chicago: Aldine.
166. Hill, E. H., & Giammatto, M. C. (1963). Social economic status and its relationship to school achievement in elementary school. *Elementary English, 40,* 465–470.
167. Howard, M. J. Jr., Hoops, H. R., & McKinnon, A. J. (1970). Language abilities of children with different socioeconomic backgrounds. *Journal of Learning Disabilities, 3*(6), 328–335.
168. Labov, W. (1972). Academic ignorance and black intelligence. *Atlantic Monthly, 229,* 59–67.
169. Laosa, L. M. (1979). Inequality in the classroom: Observational research on teacher-student interactions. *Aztlan, 8,* 51–66.
170. Loban, W. D. (1963). *The Language of Elementary School Children.* Research Report No. 1. Champaign, IL: National Council of Teachers of English.
171. Piestrup, A. (1973). *Black Dialect Interference and the Accommodation of Reading Instruction in First Grade.* Monograph No. 4. Berkeley, CA: University of California—Berkeley, Language-Behavior Research Laboratory.
172. Rogoff, B., & Gardner, W. (1984). Adult guidance of everyday cognition. In B. Rogoff & J. Lave (Eds.), *Everyday Cognition: Its Development in Social Context.* Cambridge, MA: Harvard University Press.
173. Scheinfeld, D. R. (1983). Family relationships and school achievement among boys of lower-income urban black families. *American Journal of Orthopsychiatry, 53*(1), 127–143.
174. Scott-Jones, D. (1984). Family influences on cognitive development and school achievement. *Review of Research in Education, 11,* 259–304.
175. Simon, H. (n. d.). *Black Dialect Interference and Classroom Interaction.* Unpublished manuscript, University of California—Berkeley, School of Education.

176. Slaughter, D. T., & Epps, W. G. (1987). The home environment and academic achievement of black American children and youth: An overview. *Journal of Negro Education, 56*(1), 3–20.
177. Solomon, D., Hirsch, J. G., Scheinfeld, D. R., & Jackson, J. C. (1972). Family characteristics and elementary school achievement in an urban ghetto. *Journal of Consulting and Clinical Psychology, 39*(3), 462–466.
178. Sroufe, L. A. (1970). A methodological and philosophical critique of intervention-oriented research. *Developmental Psychology, 2,* 140–145.
179. Taylor, J. B. (1983). Influence of speech variety on teachers' evaluation of reading comprehension. *Journal of Educational Psychology, 75*(5), 662–667.
180. Templin, M. C. (1957). *Certain Language Skills in Children: Their Development and Interrelationships.* Minneapolis: University of Minnesota Press.
181. Wilson, K. R., & Allen, W. R. (1987). Explaining the educational attainment of young black adults: Critical familial and extra-familial influences. *Journal of Negro Education, 56*(1), 64–76.

Research on ethnic and socioeconomic differences in auditory discrimination is found in the following references.

182. Baratz, J. A. (1969). A bidialectic task for determining language proficiency in economically disadvantaged Negro Children. *Child Development, 40,* 889–901.
183. Bartel, N. R., Grill, J. J., & Bryen, D. N. (1973). Language characteristics of black children: Implications for assessment. *Journal of School Psychology, 11*(4), 351–364.
184. Bryen, D. N. (1976). Speech-sound discrimination ability on linguistically unbiased tests. *Exceptional Children, 42*(4), 95–201.
185. Clark, A. D., & Richards, C. J. (1964). Auditory discrimination among economically disadvantaged and nondisadvantaged preschool children. *Exceptional Children, 33,* 259–262.
186. Evans, J. S. (1974). Word-pair discrimination and imitation abilities of preschool Spanish-speaking children. *Journal of Learning Disabilities, 7*(9), 49–56.
187. Fowles, B. R., & Kimple, J. A. (1972). Language tests and the "disadvantaged" reader. *Reading World, 11*(3), 183–195.
188. Karger, G. (1970). *The Effect of Black English on the Performance of Lower Class Black Children on the Wepman Auditory Discrimination Test.* Unpublished manuscript. Cambridge, MA: School of Education, Harvard University.
189. Mathewson, G. C., & Pereyra-Suarez, D. M. (1975). Spanish language interference with acoustic-phonetic skills and reading. *Journal of Reading Behavior, 7*(2), 187–196.
190. Oakland, T. D. (1969). Auditory discrimination and socioeconomic status as correlates of reading ability. *Journal of Learning Disabilities, 2,* 32–39.
191. Ralph, J. B. (1965). Language development in socially disadvantaged children. *Review of Educational Research, 35,* 389–400.
192. Ross, H. W. (1979). Wepman Test of Auditory Discrimination: What does it discriminate? *Journal of School Psychology, 17*(1), 47–54.

The relationship between ethnic and socioeconomic background and self-concept is the focus of the references listed below.

193. Arnez, N. (1972). Enhancing the black self-concept through literature. In J. Banks (Ed.), *Black Self-Concept: Implications for Education and Social Science.* New York: McGraw Hill.
194. Banks, J. A., & Grambs, D. (Eds.). (1972). *Black Self-Concept: Implications for Education and Social Sciences.* New York: McGraw-Hill.
195. Baughman, E. E. (1971). *Black Americans: A Psychological Analysis.* New York: Academic Press.
196. Braroe, N. W. (1975). *Indian and White: Self Image and Interaction in a Canadian Plains Community.* Stanford, CA: Stanford University Press.
197. Carter, T. P. (1968). Negative self-concept of Mexican-American students. *School and Society, 96,* 217–219.
198. Coopersmith, S. (1967). *The Antecedents of Self-Esteem.* San Francisco: W. H. Freeman.
199. Deutsch, M. (1960). *Minority Group and Class Status as Related to Social and Personality Factors in Scholastic Achievement.* Society for Applied Anthropology, Monograph 2. Ithaca, NY: Cornell University Press.
200. Douglas, L. A. (1970). Comparative analysis of the relationships between self-esteem and certain selected variables among youth from

diverse racial groups. *Dissertation Abstracts, 31*(2A), 641.
201. Evans, F. B., & Anderson, J. G. (1973). The psychocultural origins of achievement and achievement motivation: The Mexican-American family. *Sociology of Education, 46*, 396–416.
202. Healy, G. W., & DeBlassie, R. R. (1974). A comparison of Negro, Anglo, and Spanish American adolescents' self concepts. *Adolescence, 33*, 15–24.
203. Heaps, R. A., & Morrill, S. G. (1979). Comparing the self-concepts of Navajo and white high school students. *Journal of American Indian Education, 18*(3), 12–14.
204. Hishiki, P. (1969). The self-concepts of sixth grade girls of Mexican-American descent. *California Journal of Educational Research, 20*, 56–62.
205. Ladner, J. (1973). The urban poor. In R. P. Rothman & W. Wilson (Eds.), *Through Different Eyes: Black and White Perspectives on American Race Relations.* New York: Oxford University Press.
206. Larned, D. T., & Muller, D. (1979). Development of self-concept in Mexican American and Anglo students. *Hispanic Journal of Behavioral Sciences. 1*(2), 179–185.
207. Luftig, R. L. (1982), *The Effects of Schooling on the Self-Concept of Native American Students.* ERIC ED 220–227.
208. McDaniel, E. L. (1967). *Relationship between Self-Concept and Specific Variables in a Low-Income Culturally Different Population.* ERIC ED 019–124.
209. Muller, D., & Leonetti, R. (1974). Self-concepts of primary level Chicano and Anglo students. *California Journal of Educational Research, 25*, 57–60.
210. Parry, R. (1982). Poor self-concept and differential academic achievement: An inadequate explanation of school performance of black and Native American children. *Canadian Journal of Native Education, 10*(1), 11–24.
211. Patton, S. M., Walberg, H. J., & Yeh, E. G. (1973). Ethnicity, environmental control, and academic self-concept in Chicago. *American Educational Research Journal, 10*, 85–91.
212. Poussaint, A. R. (1974). Building a strong self-image in the black child. *Ebony*, August, 136–143.
213. Schwartz, A. J. (1969). *Comparative Values and Achievement of Mexican-American and Anglo Pupils.* Occasional Report No. 37. Los Angeles: Center for the Study of Evaluation, University of California—Los Angeles.
214. Trowbridge, N. T. (1973). Self-concept and socioeconomic status in elementary-school children. *American Educational Research Journal, 9*, 525–537.
215. Wells, E. E. (1978). *The Mythical Negative Black Self Concept.* San Francisco: R & E Research Associates.
216. Ziller, R. C., Hagey, J., Smith, M. D. C., & Long, B. H. (1969). Self-esteem: A self-social construct. *Journal of Consulting and Clinical Psychology, 33*(1), 84–95.
217. Zirkel, P. A. (1973). Self-concept and the "disadvantage" of ethnic group membership and mixture. *Review of Educational Research, 41*, 211–225.
218. Zirkel, P. A., & Moses, E. G. (1971). Self-concept and ethnic group membership among public school students. *American Educational Research Journal, 8*, 253–265.

Research that deals with students' level of aspiration is discussed in the following references.

219. Bales, K. B. (1979). The single parent family aspirations and academic achievement. *Southern Journal of Educational Research, 13*(4), 145–160.
220. Castenell, l. A. (1983). Achievement motivation: An investigation of adolescents' achievement patterns. *American Educational Research Journal, 20*(4), 503–510.
221. DeBord, L. W., Griffin, L. J., Clark, M. (1977). Race and sex influences in the schooling processes of rural and small town youth. *Sociology of Education, 42*, 85–102.
222. George, V. D. (1981). Occupational aspirations of talented black and white adolescent females. *Journal of Non-White Concerns in Personnel and Guidance, 9*(4), 137–145.

The following references found that middle-class parents have higher aspirations for their children, and expect and encourage them to attain more education.

223. Baker, D. P., & Entwisle, D. R. (1987). The influence of mothers on the academic expectations of young children: A longitudinal study of how gender differences arise. *Social Forces, 65*(3), 670–694.
224. Brooks, J. S., Whiteman, M., Lukoff, I. F., & Gordon, A. S. (1979). Maternal and adolescent expectations and aspirations as related

to sex, ethnicity, and socioeconomic status. *Journal of Genetic Psychology, 135,* 209–216.
225. Lareau, A. (1987). Social class differences in family school relationships: The importance of cultural capital. *Sociology of Education, 60,* 73–85.

References that found that poor and African-American parents have as high if not higher aspirations for their children are listed next.

226. Goodwin, L. (1976). A critical comment on success-value research. *American Journal of Sociology, 81,* 1151–1155.
227. Kandel, D. B. (1971). Race, maternal authority, and adolescent aspiration. *American Journal of Sociology, 76*(6) 999–1020.
228. Rodman, H., & Voydanoff, P. (1978). Social class and parents' range of aspirations for their children. *Social Problems, 25,* 333–344.

Students' locus of control is the focus of the references listed below.

229. Brown, D., Fulkerson, K. F., Furr, S., & Ware, W. B. (1984). Locus of control, sex role orientation, and self-concept in black and white third- and sixth-grade male and female leaders in a rural community. *Developmental Psychology, 20*(4), 717–721.
230. Cummings, S. (1977). Family socialization and fatalism among black adolescents. *Journal of Negro Education, 46*(1), 62–75.
231. Epps, E. G. (1969). Negro academic motivation and performance: An overview. *Journal of Social Issues, 25*(3), 5–11.
232. Gurin, P., Gurin, G., Lao, R. C., & Beattie, M. (1969). Internal-external control in the motivational dynamics of negro youth. *Journal of Social Issues, 25*(3), 29–53.
233. Knight, G. P., Kagan, S., Nelson, W., & Gumbiner, J. (1978). Acculturation of second- and third-generation Mexican American children: Field independence, locus of control, self esteem, and school achievement. *Journal of Cross-Cultural Psychology, 9*(1), 87–97.
234. Willig, A. C., Harnisch, D. L., Hill, K. T., & Maehr, M. L. (1983). Sociocultural and educational correlates of success-failure attributions and evaluation anxiety in the school setting for black, Hispanic and anglo children. *American Educational Research Journal, 20*(3), 385–410.

The following references discuss the effects of father absence on students' cognitive development and school achievement.

235. Collins, M. A. (1970). Achievement, intelligence, personality, and selected school-related variables in Negro children from intact and broken families attending parochial schools in central Harlem. *Dissertation Abstracts International, 30,* 5280A–5281A.
236. Fowler, P. C., & Richards, H. C. (1978). Father absence, educational preparedness, and academic achievement: A test of the confluence model. *Journal of Educational Psychology, 70*(4), 595–601.
237. Havinghurst, R. J., & Neugarten, B. L. (1967). *Society and Education.* Boston: Allyn & Bacon.
238. Hill, R. (1972). *Strengths of Black Families.* New York: National Urban League.
239. Hoffman, M. L. (1971). Father absence and conscience development. *Developmental Psychology, 4*(3), 400–406.
240. Jaffe, B. D. (1966). The relationship between two aspects of socioeconomic disadvantage and the school success of 8th grade Negro students in a Detroit junior high school. *Dissertation Abstracts International, 27,* 1546A.
241. Kukuk, C. R., Levine, D. U., & Meyer, J. K. (1978). Neighborhood predictors of reading achievement in six big city school districts: A path analysis. *Multiple Linear Regression Viewpoints, 8*(3), 27–43.
242. LeCorgne, L. L., & Laosa, L. M. (1976). Father absence in low-income Mexican-American families: Children's social adjustment and conceptual differentiation of sex role attributes. *Developmental Psychology, 12*(5), 470–471.
243. Lessing, E. E., Zagorin, S. W., & Nelson, D. (1973). WISC subtest and IQ score correlates of father absence. *Journal of Genetic Psychology, 117,* 181–195.
244. Liebow, E. (1967). *Tally's Corner.* Boston: Little, Brown.
245. McAdoo, H. (1977). Family therapy in the black community. *American Journal of Orthopsychiatry, 47*(1), 75–79.
246. Peterson, R. A., DeBord, L., Peterson, C. L., & Livingston, S. K. (1966). *Educational Supportiveness of the Home and Academic Performance of Disadvantaged Boys.* Nashville: Institute on Mental Retardation and Academic Development, George Peabody College for Teachers.
247. Prom-Jackson, S., Johnson, S. T., & Wallace, M. G. (1987). Home environment, talented minority youth and school achievement. *Journal of Negro Education, 56*(1), 111–121.
248. Scanzoni, J. (1971). *The Black Family in Modern*

*Society: Patterns of Stability and Security*. Chicago: University of Chicago Press.
249. Sciara, F. J. (1975). Effects of father absence on the educational achievement of urban black children. *Child Study Journal, 5,* 45–55.
250. Scott-Jones, D. (1984). Family influences on cognitive development and school achievement. *Review of Research in Education, 11,* 254–304.
251. Solomon, B. (1976). *Black Empowerment*. New York: Columbia University Press.
252. Stack, C. (1975). *All Our Kin: Strategies for Survival in a Black Community*. New York: Harper & Row.
253. Svanum, S., Bringle, R., & McLaughlin, J. E. (1982). Father absence and cognitive performance in a large sample of six-to-eleven-year-old children. *Child Development, 83,* 136–143.
254. Williams, M. (1974). *Community in a Black Pentecostal Church*. Pittsburgh: University of Pittsburgh Press.
255. Willie, C. (Ed.) (1976). *The Family of Black People*. Columbus, OH: Merrill.

The following reference discusses ethnic differences in poverty rates.

256. Baumeister, A. A., Kupstas, F., & Klindworth, L. M. (1990). New Morbidity: Implications for prevention of children's disabilities. *Exceptionality, 1,* 1–16.

# Chapter 3

# Extrinsic Causes of Ethnic and Socioeconomic Disparities

The previous chapter dealt with the ideas of those who attribute some non–European American and poor students' lack of success in school to the students themselves. Actually, the research described in this and subsequent chapters indicates that many of the causes of their problems in school lie outside of the students. This chapter describes how, with the exception of some excellent bilingual and multicultural education programs, the American educational system provides these students with contextually and culturally inappropriate instruction, and classroom management, counseling and assessment services that do not suit their educational and psychological needs. Many teachers, psychologists, and administrators are prejudiced against non–European American and poor students. School officials have attempted to maintain segregated educational settings by assigning non–European American and poor students to low-ability tracks and groups, and misplacing them in special education programs. When these students realize that both schools and society in general are structured in ways that reproduce ethnic and socioeconomic inequality, many of them become alienated and angry, and they resist the prejudice and hostility they experience by refusing to do their homework, truanting, and dropping out of school.

## Contextually Inappropriate Educational Approaches

The educational approaches that predominate in most schools are ill-suited to the context or living conditions of many poor and non–European American students' lives. For example, immigrant and refugee students are especially unlikely to receive the education services they require and likely to do poorly in school (1–7) (see Chapter 5). Too often they do not receive the assistance they require to overcome the culture shock they experience upon entering a new and strange environment. As a result, they may react angrily and aggressively toward teachers and systems they do not understand and cannot easily adjust to, or they may become sullen, depressed, and withdrawn. This is especially true of students who have never attended school because they come from rural areas or internment camps, or grew up in cultures that have no written languages.

Even when their culture shock passes, they need more help than they typically receive to learn how to learn in classes taught in foreign languages and unfamiliar teaching styles. This, too, can interfere with their learning.

Refugee students who suffer the psychological effects of the war, famine, and persecution they experienced at home or in internment camps are most likely to lack the assistance they need to overcome their problems. Educators who work with refugee and immigrant students need skills in instructing students with special needs and managing the special problems these students bring to school, and they need to maintain a high degree of tolerance for behavior that students cannot control while adjusting to their new educational environments.

Like foreign-born students, Native American students who live on reservations live in a region separate from mainstream America where they speak a language other than English. They, too, are ill-prepared to adjust to and profit from the curriculum typically offered in mainstream schools, which encourages beliefs and values which conflict with their communities, and is often taught in a language they do not understand by teachers who are unprepared to succeed with them in schools (8, 9). Like immigrant students, they are susceptible to experiencing culture shock, identity conflicts, and feelings of alienation, confusion, and frustration.

Contextual problems make it difficult for poor non–European American migrant students to actualize their potential for learning (10–16). Attending school irregularly, losing considerable time traveling with their families from job to job, enrolling in numerous schools during the academic year—all contribute to their poor achievement. Lack of a stable home base, inadequate medical care, poverty, and prejudice are examples of other contextual problems that complicate their lives. In addition, although migrant students can be helped by educational programs geared to their needs, school systems that have been designed for students who are permanent members of the community often add to their problems rather than contribute to solving them.

Rural students face many contextual problems (17–27). Those from rural families that rely on seasonal activities such as fishing, agriculture, timber, and so on, may not be able to attend school during certain times of the year. In addition, it is difficult for school systems to provide services to small numbers of students scattered over vast land areas with major transportation problems.

The contextual problems that confront poor homeless students are horrendous (28–45). Many do not have their basic food, clothing, and shelter needs met. They have four times as many health problems and twice as many chronic diseases, but they have less access to medical care and are less able to follow the health regimes prescribed by physicians. They move from place to place and shelter to shelter and attend school erratically.

When one considers the numbers of poor urban, rural, homeless, and migrant students and the large numbers of immigrant and refugee students whose contextual needs are not met by the American educational system, it becomes clear that many students are not receiving an appropriate education. Thus, contextually inappropriate educational approaches contribute significantly to the problems of poor and non–European American students.

## *Culturally Inappropriate Educational Approaches*

In the past, and especially in recent years, an increasing number of individuals have come to believe that schools have not adapted their educational approaches to the cultural needs of their non-European and poor students (46–49, also see Chapter 4). They tend to claim that schools in the United States, like many other aspects of life, have historically served the needs of the European American middle-class majority. They argue that once the European Americans succeeded in wresting control of the territory that presently comprises the United States from the Native Americans and Hispanics who shared it with them, they installed their approach to life from the Atlantic to the Pacific, to Alaska and Hawaii.

That is not to say that other cultures did not continue to survive. However, they survived in a powerless state. Most Native Americans were confined to their reservations, African Americans were subjected to stringent restrictions—first slavery and then segregation—and the Hispanic Americans who inhabited the lands taken from Mexico were considered to be inferior and treated as second-class citizens. For many years, therefore, the European American way of life, including the educational system that developed to serve the needs of the upper-class and middle-class European Americans who had the power and influence to shape it, reigned supreme with no effective challenges to it.

Over the years many events contributed to a change in the status quo. Immigration from Mexico, Puerto Rico, other Latin American countries, China, Japan, the Philippines, and Eastern Europe increased the numbers of persons who were not prepared for or able to adapt easily to the established educational system. Segregation was ended in most areas of American life, including education. The American working class unionized and gained political power. Large numbers of African Americans and Hispanic Americans gained the right to vote. With all of these developments, the demand for educational reform grew louder and louder.

One of these demands was for the modification and elimination of biased programs and programs such as Head Start that some reformers believed attempted to compensate for unreal deprivations or to change students' socioeconomically or culturally determined behavior or learning styles.

*Child rearing practices not in accord with mainstream values have generally been seen. . . . as unfortunate personal practices that indicate a lack of information or training. Black families in particular have been labelled "pathological", black mothers deficient, and black children deprived.*

*Since the problem is seen to rest with individuals, it is assumed that it is individuals who need to change. Millions of dollars have been expended both to provide poor, frequently non–European American, children with educational experiences that their own homes "lack" or to provide poor and minority parents with training that would enable them to raise children "properly." (49, pp. 46–47)*

*The entire intervention model of Head Start rests on an assumption of linguistic and cognitive deficits which must be remedied if the child is to succeed in school. . . . The theoretical base of the deficit model employed by Head Start programs denies obvious strengths within the Negro community and may inadvertently advocate the annihilation of a cultural system which is barely considered or understood by most social scientists. . . . Education for culturally different children should not attempt to destroy functionally viable processes of the subculture. . . . Head Start has failed because its goal is to correct a deficit that simply does not exist. (46, p. 112, 116, 124, 125)*

A second demand was to make education more culturally relevant. Many reformers insisted that school personnel should be sensitized to the importance of educationally relevant ethnic and socioeconomic cultural differences and the special challenges and problems poor students have to deal with because of their economic situations. They wanted educators to be trained to take such differences into consideration when planning school programs and selecting instructional, classroom management, counseling, and assessment techniques for non–European American and poor students.

This belief is still current. It is clearly reflected in the following quotation, which summarizes the results of a national survey of the opinions of experts and parents about the state of the educational services for non–European American students.

*The current educational system has a mainstream cultural bias which adversely affects the education of students from minority backgrounds. This bias is manifested in preconceived expectations about children from diverse cultures that are limiting and inaccurate. In addition, lack of awareness, sensitivity and understanding of diverse cultures by school personnel interfere with the education of students and the development of productive relationships with parents. . . . In general, the current instruction curricula, materials/methods and service delivery models are inadequate for meeting the educational needs of children from minority backgrounds. . . . Existing methods are not adequate to correctly assess/ identify students from diverse backgrounds and determine appropriate educational services. (47, pp. 5–7)*

The opinion of these experts is supported by a great deal of research evidence. This research is discussed in detail in Chapters 6, 9, 10, and 11. The following two examples illustrate these research findings.

Students from different cultural backgrounds have different learning styles (see Chapter 10). When educators do not adapt their educational approaches to these differences, mismatches between teachers' culturally determined teaching style and students' culturally determined learning styles occur. This can cause students to do poorly in school and to be referred to and accepted into programs for students with learning disabilities and/or cognitive disabilities.

Students from different cultures also have different *behavioral* styles (see Chapter 11). Students who come from different ethnic or socioeconomic backgrounds than their teachers may be viewed as troublesome if they behave in ways that are acceptable in their homes and communities, but not in school (50). (See Chapter 11.)

## *Prejudice and Discrimination in the Educational System*

It has been clear for many years that the behavior of teachers, psychologists, and school administrators toward poor and certain non-European students reflects the biases that exist in the larger society. As a result, these students often fall behind in school and misbehave. In the 1960s, 1970s, and 1980s, research repeatedly documented the prejudice and discrimination that non–European American students experienced in America's schools. To a considerable degree the groups that bore the brunt of this biased approach were those that populated the particular school or school system. For example, Stein reported that in an area with substantial numbers of African American and Puerto Rican American students,

> *At every grade level the curriculum is "modified" to the teacher's image of what the child can be expected to do—even in kindergarten where Black and Puerto Rican children are taught to hang up their clothes and "take turns," while white children are taught "numbers and letters." (55, pp. 168–169)*

Bennet and Harris cite the following results of their survey of the attitudes of a group of European American teachers to support their conclusion that the European American faculty of the school they studied was rife with prejudice against Black students.

> *Many of the teachers would not live in a desegregated neighborhood, did not favor mandatory school desegregation, felt the civil rights movement had done more harm than good, and felt that the problems of prejudice were exaggerated. One-third believed that Blacks and whites should not be allowed to intermarry. Furthermore, the majority of the teachers perceived their white students to be superior intellectually, socially, and in other characteristics related to school achievement. (52, pp. 420–421)*

Becker described the attitude of teachers toward the Portuguese American students in a Rhode Island community as follows:

> *Teachers' attitudes and behavior reflected stereotypes of the Portuguese student as intellectually inferior, noneducationally oriented, socially backward.... The teachers expressed feelings of alienation from their students.... When the teach-*

*ers' feelings about the Portuguese were examined closely, many revealed patterns of racism, ethnocentrism and cultural superiority. . . . There was definite resistance to cultural diversity. (51, p. 4)*

Working-class non-European students often are treated in an even more discriminatory manner than their middle-class peers. For example, in his classical study comparing the way teachers treated African American students from different socioeconomic backgrounds, Rist documented how teachers acted out their prejudices against poor students.

*When a teacher bases her expectations of performance on the social status of the student and assumes that the higher the social status, the higher the potential of the child, those children of low social status suffer a stigmatization outside of their own choice or will. Yet there is a greater tragedy than being labeled as a slow learner, and that is being treated as one. The differential amounts of control-oriented behavior, the lack of interaction with the teacher, the ridicule from one's peers, and the caste aspects of being placed in lower reading groups all have implications for the future life style and value of education for the child. . . . Given the treatment of poor children from the beginning of their kindergarten experience, for what class strata are they being prepared other than that of the lower class? It appears that the public school system not only mirrors the configurations of the larger society, but also significantly contributes to maintaining them. Thus the system of public education in reality perpetuates what it is ideologically committed to eradicate—class barriers which result in inequality in the social and economic life of the citizenry. (54, pp. 107–108)*

Reviews of the educational system done in the 1990s indicate that prejudice and discrimination are very much alive and well. For example, The National Black Child Development Institute described the educational conditions for African Americans in Selma, Alabama, twenty years after the school system was supposedly desegregated as follows:

*Selma schools are desegregated, although African American children largely remain in separate classes due to a racially discriminatory tracking system. Children are tracked into three levels, with level I designated as the college preparatory track. . . . Ninety-seven percent of African American children were placed in levels II and III, and African American faculty were not assigned to teach at the higher levels. [One student reported] "In sixth grade I was next to the top of my class. Yet my sixth grade teacher referred me to level III classes." (53, p. 12)*

Anecdotal evidence suggests that most educators believe that they are not biased against non–European American and poor students, and many researchers have found little or no prejudice or discrimination among the educators they studied (56–63). However, as the research summarized in the next section indicates, many teachers were and continue to be biased.

## Biased Expectations

Although a few studies (discussed earlier) failed to find significant ethnic and class differences in educators' expectations for their students, most studies have found such bias. Beginning in preschool and continuing through their college careers, educators and education students tend to expect the European American middle-class students in their classes to do better academically than non–European American and poor students. In addition, they expect European American middle-class students to be more intelligent, even when students' achievement test scores, grades, and school histories would predict otherwise. In experiments in which educators are given the exact same information about students except for their ethnic or socioeconomic backgrounds, they attribute higher academic and intellectual potential to European American students than African American students (64, 65, 68, 69, 71, 76, 79) and Hispanic students (66, 70, 72, 79). They have the same prejudicial expectations for middle-class students in comparison to poor students (65, 73, 75, 76).

All too often teachers have overly optimistic expectations for Asian and Pacific American students (67, 74, 77, 78). Dao offers the following observation.

*There is an assumption that Asian-Americans, in general, are a model minority. This notion is related to the stereotypic perception that Asian-American families place high priority on education and push their children to succeed in school. . . . Although there have been impressive occupational and educational achievements by Asian-Americans in the past, these achievements should not obscure the changes now occurring in the Asian-American population. . . . The growing and changing Asian-American student population includes many children from families with life and educational experiences vastly different from children from established Asian-American families. Among the Mein and Hmong refugees, for example, the unemployment rate is 90%. Recent immigrant or refugee children from these families face the triple burden of simultaneously learning English and the new school curriculum, adjusting to a new culture, and surviving an impoverished environment. (67, p. 594)*

Educators also maintain prejudicial behavior expectations for non–European American students, especially African Americans, whom they expect to be more disruptive and deviant than European Americans (see Chapter 11).

## Biased Evaluation

Although a few studies have not found teacher bias (57, 61), most studies done in the 1970s and 1980s indicate that teachers tend to evaluate African American, Hispanic and poor students' academic performance and behavior in a biased manner (80–85, 88–91). For example, although neither ethnicity nor social class is ever the sole criterion educators use when assigning students to ability groups, teachers often assign non–European American and poor students to lower ability groups than objective data such as test scores would warrant.

Teachers also evaluate African American students' behavior in a biased manner. When teachers evaluate the severity or deviancy of students' behavior problems, they judge the exact same transgressions as more severe or deviant when they are committed by African American male students. They evaluate European American females higher than they evaluate African American females in the areas of responsibility, compliance, persistence, performance, ability, and relationships with others. And African American students who are seen as fun-loving, happy, cooperative, energetic and ambitious by African American teachers are viewed as talkative, lazy, fun-loving, high-strung, and frivolous by their European American teachers.

Teachers also tend to allow their judgments about students' work to be influenced by whether students express themselves in Black English (the English dialect many African Americans speak—especially, but not exclusively, those from poor backgrounds), a working-class dialect (a variety of nonstandard dialects spoken by individuals from poor backgrounds), an Hispanic accent, or standard English (the English used in textbooks, newspapers, television news programs, found in grammar books, and typically used by most middle- and upper-class European Americans). In general teachers incorrectly rate the quality and accuracy of the English of speakers of standard English higher than nonstandard English. More important, even when students' work is identical or of equal quality, teachers judge the oral and written work of students who speak in a black English, Hispanic, or a working-class accent to be poorer than students who speak standard English. African American students who speak "Black English" are also rated lower than those who speak more standard English (58, 60, 61, 63, 64, 66, 68, 69).

As is noted in Chapters 2 and 9, at one time many educators may not have perceived this as a biased approach to evaluation. In the 1960s and early 1970s, researchers typically used European American middle-class students' scores on tests prepared in standard English as the norm to which they compared the scores of students who spoke nonstandard English. As a result, they concluded that Black English and working-class English were inferior to standard English. By the mid-1970s, the results of research studies that did not make that methodological error led most authors to conclude that these varieties of English are actually equally effective and valid forms of communication, and many scholars, especially those from African American backgrounds, were encouraging schools to incorporate Black English into the curriculum rather than attempt to eradicate it.

*Black children must be educated to learn and believe that deviation from the normative pattern of standard English is not an indication that they are abnormal. . . . Whites should not become reference points for how Black children are to speak and behave. One's family and community and how one measures up to one's peers should provide some of these reference points. Black children's encounters with the white world should be filtered through a Black frame of reference, which includes the use of Black English. (59, p. 215)*

Apparently, many teachers still believe that standard English is superior to other forms of English. That is, instead of correctly viewing Black English, Hispanic, and working-class dialects and accents as different, they view them as deficient, and they continue to allow their beliefs to prejudice their evaluations of students.

There is no reason to assume that the biases found in the studies reported earlier have disappeared. Because they were done in the 1970s and mid- 1980s, however, additional research is needed to determine whether the situation has improved significantly in recent years.

There is also evidence that teachers evaluate Asian and Pacific American students in a biased manner (86, 92, 93). There appear to be three reasons for this. First, believing that all of them are good students, they fail to notice their academic problems (93). As Yao puts it: "Many school teachers share a myth: that all Asian American youngsters are diligent, respectful, intelligent, good students. But teachers should not be dismayed if they find the opposite is true in their classrooms." (93, p. 82).

Second, Asian American students tend to internalize their emotional problems rather than act them out. Even though they may be experiencing serious emotional problems, their suffering is less obvious and less disruptive than that of students who act out their problems. As a result, they are less likely to be noticed by teachers (86). For example, Kim reports that many troubled Asian and Pacific American students

> *resort to passivity and conformity. . . . Their quietness, inconspicuousness, withdrawal, and non-threatening stance in the classroom tend to make them less noticeable. A teacher might not recognize a certain behavioral manifestation of passivity as a sign of poor adjustment. [In addition] Teachers tend to perceive passive Asian American children as being better adjusted to the classroom as compared to passive Caucasian children. (87, pp. 83–84)*

Third, because teachers welcome the quiet unobtrusive behavior of many Asian and Pacific Americans, they often fail to recognize when it may be a sign of problems. Takeuchi points out that "the quiet passive behavior of Asian American students should not be unquestionly encouraged. Rather, it often signifies problems in verbalization needing attention" (78, p. 2).

**Teachers' Perceptions of Asian American and European American Students**

| European Americans | Asian Americans |
| --- | --- |
| More extroverted | Less extroverted |
| Less cheerful | More cheerful |
| Less emotionally stable | More emotionally stable |
| Less kind | More kind |
| Less obedient | More obedient |

*Continued*

**Teachers' Perceptions of Asian
American and European American Students** *(Continued)*

| European Americans | Asian Americans |
|---|---|
| Less disciplined | More disciplined |
| Less cooperative | More cooperative |
| Less patient | More patient |
| More prone to anger | Less prone to anger |
| Less academically competent | More academically competent |
| Less able to concentrate | More able to concentrate |
| Less organized | More organized |
| Less persevering | More persevering |
| Less adequate memory | More adequate memory |

## *Biased Treatment*

Most, but not all, studies indicate that, in addition to having biased expectations for non–European American and poor students and evaluating them in a discriminatory manner, many teachers also treat them unfairly. The following are some of the discriminatory ways many educators treat African American, Native American, and Hispanic American students (52, 53, 71, 95–97, 99–102, 104–112).

In comparison to European American students, teachers praise African Americans less and criticize them more. The praise teachers give these students is more likely to be routine, rather than feedback for a particular achievement or behavior, and when teachers praise them for a specific behavior, it is more likely to be qualified ("Your work is almost good enough to be put on the board.") or, in the case of females, more likely to be for good behavior than for academic work.

Teachers interact more with European American students than with African Americans, especially males, and give the latter less attention. In comparison to European American students, educators are less likely to respond to African American male students' questions or to direct questions to them. Unlike the preferential treatment many teachers give their brightest European American students, they give bright African American students, especially females, the least attention and criticize them the most. Although European American teachers typically demonstrate considerable concern and interest in European American females' academic work, they pay less attention to African American female students' academic work than to their social behavior. Teachers encourage European American female students in intellectual and academic areas, whereas they encourage and praise African American females in areas involving social skills. In addition, European American females are more likely to receive trusted lieutenant duties and special high-prestige assignments; African American female students' duties typically involve social responsibilities.

Educators tend to use different classroom management techniques with African American and European American students. In general, teachers of classes with high percentages of African American students are more likely to be authoritarian and less likely to use an open classroom approach. Teachers spend more time on the lookout for possible misbehavior by African American students, especially males. When male students misbehave, educators are especially prone to criticize the behavior of African American males and to use more severe punishments, including corporal punishment and suspension, with them, and when females misbehave, teachers treat African Americans more harshly than European Americans.

Grant describes the effect this can have on African American females' perception of the role that is most suitable for them in the following way:

*The emphasis on black girls' social rather than academic skills, which occurs particularly in white-teacher classrooms, might point to a hidden cost of desegregation for black girls.... While such skills assuredly are helpful in high-status adult roles, the lesser attention to black girls' work might diminish motivation for gaining credentials to enter such positions. Black girls' everyday schooling experiences seem more likely to nudge them toward stereotypical roles of black women than toward alternatives. (71, p. 109)*

Teachers relate to Hispanic American students in much the same way as they treat African American students. Although Hispanic American students tend to prefer more positive reinforcement and feedback from their teachers than most European American students (see Chapters 10 and 11), teachers praise them less often and give them less positive feedback when they answer correctly or perform well. Teachers are also less likely to encourage them when they need encouragement, to accept their ideas, and to direct questions to them.

Research about how teachers treat Native Americans is sparse. There is some evidence that teachers and their aides tend to speak to and attend to them less than European American students (102). However, this may be partly the result of the teachers' failure to recognize the nonverbal ways in which Native American students ask for help and attention.

Poor students also receive unfair treatment in school (94, 98, 103, 106). Beginning in primary school, teachers give them less attention and fewer rewards. Educators provide poor students, especially males, fewer social and instructional contacts, but more disciplinary and control contacts. And when they discipline students, teachers in schools that serve predominantly poor students are more likely to endorse or use corporal punishments, verbal punishments, or suspension than teachers in middle-class schools.

## *Apparent and Real Lack of Bias*

Bias against non–European American students and poor students is not quite as pervasive as the preceding summary suggests. African American teachers tend to be less prejudiced than European American teachers toward African American students (71, 108); only some European Americans are biased against non–European American students and poor students; and there is some evidence that the ratio of non–European American to European American teachers on the staff of a school district has an effect on the discriminatory treatment students receive. For example, in one study, a high percentage of African American teachers in a school district was associated with a decrease in the overrepresentation of African American students among students who were disciplined by corporal punishment, suspended, or expelled. There also was a decrease in their dropout rates and their underrepresentation in programs for gifted and talented students, and an increase in their high school graduation rates (114).

At least in some cases, however, the apparent lack of bias against students who belong to a different ethnic group may not be real (108, 110, 113). Many European American and African American teachers are not aware of their biases against students from ethnic backgrounds different from their own. In order to hide their true feelings and attitudes from themselves, some European American and African American teachers may give students a double message without realizing it. They consciously praise students who belong to a different ethnic group more than they do students who share their ethnic background, but they unknowingly treat them negatively by giving them less nonverbal positive attention, maintaining a greater distance from them, and touching them less often.

European American teachers exhibit more unconscious discrimination than African American teachers do. In addition to the negative, nonverbal communication mentioned earlier, they also give African American students less positive feedback when they answer questions correctly and fewer helpful hints when they call on them to answer questions. Simpson and Erickson report:

*Naturalistic observational studies in the classroom may show overcompensatory behavior on the part of black and white teachers. However, the nonverbal behaviors may indicate a natural preference or comfortableness with students of one's own race. (108, p. 185)*

## Implications

Many educators believe that much of the disruptive behavior, inadequate motivation, lack of participation in school, and poor achievement that many poor, and non–European American students demonstrate is caused, at least in part, by the biased evaluations, expectations, and treatment they receive in school. Thus, these problems will not be solved until teachers correct their biased attitudes, beliefs, and treatment of non–European American and poor students.

These educators also believe that teacher bias contributes to the unnecessary suspension of many African American, Hispanic American, and poor students, and their overrepresentation in special education programs for the behaviorally disordered and emotionally disturbed (53, 115–117). They feel that non–European American and poor students will not receive the kind of educational services they deserve until educators behave more democratically and serve the needs of the population as a whole. To their way of thinking, the elimination of teacher prejudice and discrimination is the first and most important step educators can take to ensure that students receive culturally appropriate education services.

## Conclusions

Prejudice and discrimination against non–European American and poor students is still rampant. Not all teachers are biased. As was noted earlier, a few studies have found that ethnic and class differences do not influence how educators perceive, judge, and relate to students; those that have uncovered bias did not find that all teachers behaved in a biased manner; and a few studies found that some teachers evaluate and treat opposite-race students better than same-race students. However, when the evidence is considered as a whole, it is clear that teachers' conscious and unconscious prejudice against certain non–European American and poor students influences their relationships with them, their expectations for them, their evaluation of their work, and their choices of which instructional and classroom management techniques to use with them. In turn, these biases affect their students' performance in and attitudes toward school.

---

**SELF-QUIZ: Students' Responses to Prejudice**

What is your opinion about the following statement? "In a prejudiced society, students' assertive behavior in school that is aimed at correcting injustices may be positive and acceptable even though teachers and others may find it disruptive, be uncomfortable with it and threatened by it."

---

## Structured Reproduction

As was noted at the beginning of this chapter, schools reproduce the inequalities found in society at large. One of the schools' many missions is to perpetuate the values, ideas, and attitudes of the societies they serve. Because American society does not completely live up to the high ideals it espouses, much of what is transmitted from generation to generation is what actually is, rather than what should be. This applies to ethnic and socioeconomic issues as well as to many other aspects of American life. Because many of the prevailing societal views and values about ethnicity and socioeconomic class are biased, students are exposed to an educational structure that reproduces the ethnic and socioeconomic disparities in outcomes.

Some educators with a neo-Marxist perspective see purpose behind the bias in the schools' structure. They believe it is only one of many biased structures that the European American middle and upper classes, especially males, have set up throughout society to maintain their economic and social power and position. That is, they believe that those who exercise control and power in our society—middle- and upper-class European American males—structure its institutions, including schools, to maintain their special position by reproducing the inequality that serves their interests (118–131). Thus, they use schools to maintain an ethnic, class, and gender division of labor. According to these theorists, schools provide non–European American, poor, and female students with the kinds of educational experiences that maintain them as a source of cheap, though well-prepared, labor, whereas more affluent European males are trained to be the leaders of society. At the same time, schools teach poor, non–European American, and female students to accept the status quo—their economic and social inferiority.

Giroux has described three ways in which schools could be said to reproduce inequality:

*First, schools provided different classes and social groups with knowledge and skills they needed to occupy their respective places in a labor force stratified by class, race, and gender. Second, schools were seen as reproductive in the cultural sense, functioning in part to distribute and legitimate forms of knowledge, value, language, and modes of style that constitute the dominant culture and its interests. Third, schools were viewed as part of a state apparatus that produced and legitimated the economic and ideological imperatives that underlie the state's political power. (123, p. 258)*

Grant and Sleeter claim that

*School plays a major role in the culture students develop. Like the family and neighborhood, school affects how students understand and pursue their life chances. It provides an institutional ideology, socializing agents, and an experiential context within which students define and shape the way they think about their personal dreams. The school context, containing social relations defined by race, social class, and gender, can produce a student culture in which young people accept and live out their parents' place in a stratified society, in spite of the school's espoused mission as equalizer and escalator to a better life. (125, p. 19)*

Reproduction theorists criticize the schools for the disparity between the lower level of funding for schools that serve students from poor and non–European American neighborhoods, the use of tracking and ability grouping to separate European American middle-class students from other students, and the use of the community college system to prevent working-class and minority students from enrolling in four-year colleges. They claim that females, especially minority and poor females, are exposed to two separate but related forces in the schools—those designed to maintain middle- and upper-class hegemony over the poor and those designed to maintain male hegemony over females. The following quotation is an example of their point of view. Although it focuses on Native American females' educational experiences in government run schools, it exemplifies what they think about the education many non-European women receive.

*The government's master plan for Indian women has been to generate an endless stream of domestics, and to a lesser extent, secretaries. The vocational choices for native children in boarding schools have always been sexist: boys do woodworking, car repair, house painting or farmwork; while girls do domestic or secretarial work.... When we look at the occupations of native women in this country today, it should come as no surprise to find us locked into the nations' female work ghetto employees; it was designed that way. (115, pp. 47–48)*

## Resistance, Production, and Transformation

Neo-Marxist reproduction theorists also suggest that although students are being exposed to ethnic, socioeconomic, and gender biases in school and society at large, they are also being exposed to ideas and experiences that contradict these biases. These theorists note that egalitarian ideas are available in the media and in the materials students read in school. In addition, many teachers do not believe in the current class, ethnic, and gender biases. Thus, bombarded by conflicting messages, students do not passively accept the biases presented to them. Instead, they are constantly involved in a process of accommodating to some messages and resisting others (132–159).

According to reproduction theorists, especially those with a neo-Marxist perspective, students are alienated, distrustful, angry, and disillusioned about the problems inherent in attending schools that are structured to maintain inequality, but many of them also realize that schools are merely one aspect of a society structured against them. These theorists believe that many students also know that even if they do well in school, a society stratified along class, ethnic, and gender lines will not afford them the same benefits that European American upper-class males receive from succeeding in school. Therefore, instead of acquiescing to the educational system for payoffs they do not believe will be forthcoming, they battle against the system to maintain their own sense of identity.

There are significant ethnic, socioeconomic, and gender differences in how students resolve these contradictions (132, 140, 154). This makes sense when one considers the fact that students from different ethnic, socioeconomic, and gender backgrounds have somewhat different options available to them for resolving the contradictory pressures they experience.

Some students accommodate more than they resist; others actively resist the biased education they receive and the inferior position it threatens to place them in. Some defy schools' ethnic, socioeconomic, and gender biases in nonconstructive ways. They purposefully misbehave in aggressive or sexual ways, tune out their teachers, refuse to do their homework, come late to school, drop out before graduating, decide not to participate in higher education, and so on (133, 134, 146–148, 150, 154).

Other students battle the same forces in constructive ways. They reject the biased ideas they are exposed to. Instead, they assert their own experiences, heighten their own sense of self-identity, and leave school transformed into a new person with a new understanding of their ethnicity, gender, and class and with the knowledge, skills, value, and self-awareness they require to contribute to transforming society (129, 140, 141, 143). Thus, for some students, schools reproduce the stereotypes prevalent in society, whereas in other cases schools actually help students to reject these stereotypes.

Some theorists believe that society and schools are not equally biased against all non-European students. They believe that the European American dominant class differentiates between voluntary immigrants and involuntary, subordinated caste-like groups such as African Americans, Native Americans, Puerto Rican Americans, and Mexican Americans. Voluntary immigrants, according to their way of thinking, are those who chose to come to the United States. Involuntary immigrants are those who were brought here as slaves (e.g., African Americans) or who were incorporated into the United States against their will by conquest (e.g., Native Americans and Mexican Americans). Voluntary immigrants are likely to be accepted into society as equals once they have assimilated, and they tend to be the preferred non–European Americans because they most resemble the original northern European American settlers of the continent. Involuntary groups, however, are unlikely to be accepted as equals, regardless of what they do, for three reasons: the history of their relationship with the dominant European Americans; the myths European Americans have created about their innate inferiority in order to justify the conquest of their land, the eradication of their culture, and the enslavement of their ancestors; and the fact that they do not resemble European Americans in either looks or behavior.

European Americans are willing to accept voluntary immigrants into their country clubs and into some high-status positions, and school personnel are willing to tolerate their cultural differences at least to some degree. Involuntary caste-like groups are not treated as well socially or vocationally, and in school, the cultural differences between them and European Americans are devalued, disliked, and squashed because these groups have been deemed inferior for hundreds of years.

According to these theorists, students from the subordinated groups are less willing to play the educational game according to the rules established by their oppressors. They reject and resist school because of the prejudicial treatment they receive no matter how much they accomplish academically. Their point of view is aptly expressed by Ogbu.

*All minority children encounter social adjustment and academic learning problems, at least initially. For some minority groups these tend to diminish over time, so that they eventually learn more or less successfully. For some other minority groups the problems tend to persist and may even increase in magnitude and seriousness.... The main factor differentiating the more successful from the less successful minorities appears to be the nature of the history, subordination, and exploitation of the minorities, and the nature of the minorities' own instrumental and expressive responses to their treatment which enter in the process of their schooling.*

*[These subordinate minorities] develop a new sense of social identity in opposition to the social identity of the dominant group after they have become subordinated and they do so in reaction to the way that dominant-group members treat them in social, political, economic, and psychological domains. [They] do not really believe that they have an equal chance with white Americans to get ahead through education. They tend to reject or attack the criteria by which aca-*

*demic achievement is measured and also the use of educational qualifications or measures as a criterion for employment in some situations.*

*The relationship between involuntary minorities and white Americans, who control the public schools, characterized by conflict and distrust, contributes to the minorities' social adjustment and academic performance problems. . . . Involuntary minorities do not necessarily accept or interpret school rules of behavior and standard practices in the same way that white people and immigrants do. The latter seem to endorse the rules and standard practices as necessary. . . . Involuntary minorities appear, on the other hand, to interpret the same rules and standard practices as an imposition of the white frame of reference, which does not necessarily meet their educational needs.*

*[As a result, those involuntary minorities students who are rebelling against the schools] do not work hard, and spend limited time on academic tasks; they avoid taking "hard"/"difficult"/"white" courses; they tend to be satisfied with average grades; although the children may do their homework, they do not routinely study; they do not usually separate academic tasks from their activities; they seem to prefer peer solidarity to schoolwork and easily submit to peer pressures that take them away from their schoolwork; they distrust school authorities with whom they are frequently in conflict; and they have a tendency to resist following school rules and standard practices. (148, pp. 317, 323, 324, 333, 334)*

Like those who believe in the cultural difference explanation, those who share Ogbu's point of view want schools to offer culturally relevant and culturally appropriate educational experiences to minorities. However, they also believe that society as a whole must be reformed in ways that give non–European American students confidence that if they succeed in school they will reap the benefits of their success.

## Implications

Although neo-Marxist reproduction theorists believe that it is important to eliminate class, cultural, and gender inequities in the schools, their ultimate goal is to transform the very nature of the public schools. Neo-Marxists want teachers to prepare students to resist the reproductive forces of society in more constructive ways and above all to change both the schools and the social and economic structure of the society they serve instead of preparing students to fit into the capitalist status quo (129, 155, 156).

*The ultimate purpose of radical pedagogy is not simply one of changing people's consciousness or restructuring schools along more democratic principles; the latter aims are important but are reformist in nature and incomplete when viewed within a radical problematic. At the core of any radical pedagogy must be the aim of empowering people to recognize and work for a change in the social, political, and economic structure that constitutes the ultimate source of class-based power and domination. (122, p. 427)*

## Criticisms

Many educators are critical of the major assumptions underlying the theory of structured reproduction. Some critics question whether schools are actually structured in ways that reproduce the inequalities found in society at large; many more believe that even if schools do help to reproduce inequality there is no evidence that this is part of a purposeful plan by those in power to maintain the status quo; and many do not agree with the distinction between voluntary immigrants and caste-like groups. For example, Treuba challenges the claim that Mexican Americans are a caste-like group.

> *Ogbu has described "caste-like" groups, and Mexican Americans in particular, as being composed of individuals who live involuntarily in this country, occupy menial positions, and remain at the bottom of the educational and economic ladder, failing to incorporate into mainstream American society. . . . In the case of Mexicans, classified by Ogbu as an exemplary caste-like group, we have obtained recent empirical evidence from studies showing that there is educational progress, an increase in English language proficiency, and upward mobility taking place among the Mexican families in California and Arizona, and that the improvement is incremental across generations over a period of time. (157, pp. 276–277)*

Treuba goes on to explain that the apparent lack of progress of many Mexican Americans in such states as California is not due to their caste-like condition but to the large numbers of recent immigrants who have not had time to be incorporated into the American educational economic and social systems.

> *The overwhelming majority of people who recognize themselves as Mexicans (85%) are either foreign born or first generation U.S. born. . . . High dropout rates are much more characteristic of the Mexican born, who constitute a large proportion of the current Latino population in the state. Dropout rates among the U.S. born Latinos are not much higher than those of all Californians. Comparing the occupational profiles of Mexican born with those of U.S. born, and both with that of all Californians, we find the following distribution: Highly skilled jobs, professional, teacher, manager, technician, sales clerk, account for 5% of Mexican born, 12% of U.S. born Mexican origin, and 27% of all Californians. Service jobs account for 14%, 33%, and 34% respectively. Semi-skilled jobs represent respectively 21%, 20%, and 19%. Farm jobs, 15%, 6%, and 3%. Unskilled, 45%, 29%, and 17%. (157, p. 277)*

## Research

There is a great deal of evidence to support the contention that the structure of American schools contributes to the reproduction of ethnic and socioeconomic inequality. Examples of the relevant research follow.

*Financing*

Local and state governments spend less money on educating poor and non–European American students and provide them with less adequate instructional materials and equipment, especially in the areas of computer technology and science (158–170). Per-pupil expenditures for schools serving students in poor and non–European communities are considerably below those for European American middle-class students. For example, in Kentucky the per-pupil cost ranged from a low of $1,800 to a high of $4,200. In Texas the per capita expenditure on education in the 100 poorest school districts was less than $3,000 compared to the more than $7,000 spent on pupils attending the 100 richest school districts. In New Jersey the gap between the amount of money spent per pupil by the richest and poorest districts was more than $10,000 (165). The per-pupil expenditure for students in New York City, a predominantly non–European American poor student population, was $4,351 compared to $6,605, $6,539, and $5,852 in the three surrounding suburban counties (168). The results of these disparities are reflected in the availability of equipment and materials, especially computers and science laboratory equipment, for academic courses, the availability of nonacademic course offerings, the quality of the educational staff, and so on. Karp describes the effects of the disparities in spending for education in these three states in the following way:

> *These numbers translate into daily injustices for school kids. Princeton's high school science students study in seven modern, well-equipped labs and student athletes can play golf, field hockey and lacrosse in addition to baseball, basketball and football. In Jersey City, middle-school science students have no labs at all while in East Orange, NJ, the track team practices in a second floor corridor. In rural Kentucky, elementary schools have done without music and art teachers. In one poor Texas district students study computer science by pretending to type on an artificial paper replica of a computer keyboard. (165, p. 1, 14)*

Even programs specifically designed to serve poor students are underfinanced. At the height of their financial support in 1980, compensatory educational programs only served 57% of the 9,000,000 eligible students. Since then the program has experienced repeated cutbacks. Even Head Start only reaches 18% of eligible students (159).

*Tracking and Ability Grouping*

As reported earlier, research confirms that poor and non–European American students are much more likely to be placed in low-track and low-ability groups than are European American middle-class students. Tracking and ability grouping has been justified on the grounds that

> *students learn better when they are grouped with other students who are similar to them academically; that the placement process used to sort students into groups is accurate and fair and, in addition, reflects past achievements and*

*innate abilities; that slower students develop more positive attitudes in relation to themselves and their schools if they are not sorted into groups with students who are more capable; that it is easier for teachers to accommodate individual differences in homogeneous groups; that similar students are easier to manage. (172, p. 94)*

However, research on these approaches indicates that they typically do more harm than good (169, pp. 171–182). Students placed in low-ability groups do not learn better. After reviewing the research, Lake concluded:

*Once in a low track, students rarely switch tracks after grade three. Schools do not help them to move into a higher track. By the end of the primary grades students are set into rigid ability tracks correlating to their race and socioeconomic status. The effects last even longer than the school years. (176, abstract)*

In a similar vein, Oakes reported:

*The typical ways elementary schools respond to students' performance may help to "fix" students' perceptions of their ability to learn and, over time, may actually exaggerate initial differences among them. . . . At the high school level, whether a student is enrolled in an academic (college-preparatory) or non-academic program has an independent effect on achievement. Students who are initially similar in background and aptitude exhibit increased achievement differences resulting from their placements in higher and lower tracks. . . . Students placed in low-ability groups in elementary school are likely to continue in these tracks in middle schools and junior highs; in senior high they typically are found in non-college-preparatory tracks.*

*In the data about curriculum paths, course offerings, and track-related classroom differences, we find that the differentiated structure of schools often throws up barriers to achievement and participation of poor and minority students. Measures of ability work against them, which leads to minimal course offerings at their schools and these students' disproportionate placement in groups identified as "slow." Once in these classes, their success seems to be further inhibited by the type of knowledge they are taught and by the quality of the learning experiences that are afforded. (179, pp. 115–116, 118–119)*

Students in low tracks and ability groups do not improve their self-esteem. On the contrary, they experience a loss of self-esteem and a worsening of their attitudes towards school.

Students do not receive the instructional approaches and attention they require. In fact, research clearly demonstrates the opposite. Schools spend less money on students in low-ability groups. They are counseled less often. They are exposed to a watered-down curriculum and treated poorly by their teachers, who call on them less often, criticize them more often, praise them less frequently, give them less help and feedback, expect less from them, and so on.

Management problems are typically increased rather than diminished by grouping students into low-ability groups and tracks because students tend to be more disruptive and teachers tend to interrupt the academic work more often to deal with discipline problems. After studying the effects of ability grouping, Eder concluded:

> *Students in low groups were instructed in an environment characterized by disruptions from the teacher as well as from other members. In other words, those students who were likely to have more difficulty learning were inadvertently assigned to groups whose social contexts were much less conducive for learning. (173, p. 159)*

Finally, students are not placed in ability groups in an accurate and fair manner. On the contrary, as noted earlier, non–European American and poor students are often assigned to low-ability groups in a biased manner when objective evaluation of their academic functioning would not justify their placement, and in some cases, ability grouping is used to resegregate students, not to enhance their learning. This topic will be discussed later in this chapter.

Community colleges serve to track students rather than to provide them with the opportunity to achieve their potential (183–187). Research reveals that non-European and poor students are grossly overrepresented in the two-year college system. Many of the programs in which they enroll do not lead to viable occupations. The majority of students drop out before completing their programs. Of those that graduate, few go on to earn degrees at four-year colleges. As a result, the community/two-year college system serves to segregate non–European American students in an educational system that does not typically lead to the completion of a four-year college degree or the attainment of sufficient vocational skills to obtain a high-paying or prestigious job. The following quotations are representative of the conclusions of many of the critics of the community college system.

> *The rise of two year systems in some cities raises the unmistakable impression that such systems were established in order to preserve the status quo and to enable senior institutions to remain inaccessible to minority students. (186, pp. XIII–XIV)*
>
> *The two year college system in the United States is a system of whites, it is controlled and operated by whites, and reserves its major rewards for whites. (184, p. 42)*
>
> *Hispanics have made few appreciable gains in either their participation or achievement in community colleges. The fact remains that few Hispanics earn college credentials, graduate, or transfer to senior institutions. (185, p. 139)*

### Socioeconomic-Class Differences in School Structure

A study comparing two comprehensive high schools serving students in both a poor and an affluent neighborhood in the same city, discovered the following differences (166).

| | Poor Neighborhood | Middle-Class Neighborhood |
|---|---|---|
| Campus | Fenced in, security guards | Open, no security guards |
| Selection of courses | Students select courses | No choice of courses |
| Dress code | No dress code | Dress code |
| Teacher resources invested in | Vocational and general tracks | Academic track |
| Courses emphasized | Physical education, home economics, industrial arts, business education, special education | Science, math, language arts, fine arts, and foreign languages |
| Program for mentally gifted minors | Available | None available |
| Academic courses | Restricted to basic level | Many advanced courses offered |
| Industrial arts course and apprenticeship programs geared to | Blue-collar jobs | White-collar jobs |
| Graduates advised to attend | Two-year colleges | Four-year colleges |

*Resistance, Production, and Transformation*

Although there has not been a great deal of research on the topic, the available evidence suggests that many non-European and poor students are alienated, distrustful, angry, and disillusioned about the schools they attend and believe that even if they do well in school, they will not obtain the same benefits that European American upper-class males receive from succeeding in school (188–192). Studies indicate that African American middle school and high school students feel alienated and distrustful about their teachers, the schools they attend, and the American political system (187, 191, 192). Research also suggests that although African American students think that getting a good education is important, many of them do not believe that education necessarily leads to a good job (189, 190). In one study, over 50% of 10- to 15-year-old African American students did not believe that a high school diploma led to a good job (189). Although they did not report specific percentages, the authors of another study observed that many African American male high school students had similar doubts and speculated:

> If African American male youth feel that racism hampers the "cashing in of their educational check," it is probably valid to assume that they will not take full advantage of the educational opportunities that their schools have to offer. (190, p. 12)

There is also evidence that Native American and African American high school graduates do not reap the benefits a high school diploma affords European American students. For example, a recent study indicated that with rare exceptions Native American students who graduated from high school obtained the same "menial or service-industry positions" as dropouts (193).

## Conclusions

One may believe that schools *simply reflect* the biases that permeate society, that "education does not create the sexual division of labour, nor the kinds of work available in the labour market, nor the class relationships of society, but it rarely does anything to undermine them" (121, p. 20). Or one may agree that European American middle and upper-class males *purposely* structured schools in ways that reproduce their power in society, that "schools provided different classes and social groups with knowledge and skills they needed to occupy their respective places in a labor force stratified by class, race, and gender" (122, p. 258). Whether the current situation is purposeful or not, it is clear that despite the progress that has occurred in providing equal educational opportunities to all students, the educational systems perpetuate inequality both in school and in the larger society, and cause many students to misbehave, tune out, and drop out.

We currently lack the knowledge to predict which students will accept the prevailing biases more than they resist them and which will resist more than succumb, and we certainly cannot predict the manner in which they will resist.

## School Resegregation

Some individuals claim that strict disciplinary measures and ability grouping and tracking are often employed to resegregate desegregated school systems and to reinstitute the unequal educational opportunity that accompanies segregation rather than to improve instruction and classroom management,

> *Many school systems remain segregated "even after a court ordered desegregation plan has been fully implemented." Through such practices as unequal application of disciplinary measures, ability grouping and educational placement, minority students continue to receive uneven and unfair treatment. They have been, in effect, resegregated. (194, p. 184)*

There is considerable evidence to support this contention (187–210). The use of more severe forms of discipline, ability grouping, and tracking was increased significantly in desegregated school systems, especially in the South during the late 1960s and 1970s (114, 195, 197, 206, 208, 210). Desegregation has also been accompanied by a tendency toward the inflexible administration of strict disciplinary codes and an increased use of corporal punishment and suspensions with African American students (202, 203). For example, during the first year of the desegregation of the Milwaukee school system, of the 22 schools who increased their African American student enrollment, 16 had increases in their suspension rates, and of the 11 schools that experienced a decline in African American student enrollment, 8 also experienced a decrease in their suspension rates (203).

## *Summary*

A number of factors contribute to the poor academic achievement of many non–European American students. Their education is often contextually, culturally, and linguistically inappropriate. Too often teachers, psychologists, and administrators are prejudiced against them. In some cases they are assigned to low-ability tracks and groups in order to maintain segregation. When they realize that both schools and society in general are structured in ways that reproduce ethnic and socioeconomic inequality, many of them resist the prejudice and hostility they experience in nonconstructive ways.

## *Activities*

1. Interview students from different ethnic and socioeconomic backgrounds in the courses you are taking about some of the issues discussed in this chapter. Do their opinions vary with their ethnic or socioeconomic backgrounds?

2. Review the textbooks and other materials your professors assign in the courses you are taking. Do they deal with the diversity issues inherent in the topics they cover? Do they focus exclusively or primarily on European Americans to the exclusion of other ethnic groups?

3. Compare your professors in terms the time they devote to the diversity issues inherent in the courses they teach. Do you find that some professors are more sensitive to and interested in diversity issues than others?

## *References*

The special problems of immigrant and refugee students that are not met by the educational system are discussed in the following references.

1. Cervantes, R. C., Salgado de Snyder, V. N., & Padilla, A. M. (1988). *Post Traumatic Stress Disorder among Immigrants from Central America and Mexico.* Los Angeles: University of California, Spanish Speaking Mental Health Resource Center.

2. Juffer, K. A. (1983). Culture shock: A theoretical framework for understanding adaptation. In J. Bransford (Ed.), *Monograph Series: BUENO Center for Multicultural Education, 4,* 136–149.

3. National Coalition of Advocates for Students. (1988). *New Voices: Immigrant Students in the Public Schools.* Boston: Author.

4. Nguyen, T. P. (1987). Positive self-concept in the Vietnamese bilingual child. In M. Dao (Ed.), *From Vietnamese to Vietnamese American: Selected Articles.* San Jose, CA: Division of Special Education and Rehabilitative Services, San Jose State University.

5. Olsen, L. (1988). *Crossing the Schoolhouse Border: Immigrant Students and the California Public Schools.* San Francisco: California Tomorrow.

6. Padilla, A. M., Lindholm, K. J., Alvarez, M., & Wagatsuma, Y. (1985). *Acculturative Stress in Immigrant Students: Three Papers*. Los Angeles: University of California, Spanish Speaking Mental Health Resource Center.
7. Wei, T. T. D. (1980). *Vietnamese Refugee Students: A Handbook for School Personnel.*, (2nd ed.). ERIC ED 208–109.

These references discuss the unmet educational needs of Native American students.

8. Bureau of Indian Affairs. (1988, March). *Report on B. I. A. Education: Final Review Draft*. Washington, DC: Department of the Interior.
9. Chavez, R. C., Belkin, L. D., Hornback, J. G., & Adams, K. (1991). Dropping out of school: Issues affecting culturally, ethnically, and linguistically distinct student groups. *Journal of Educational Issues of Language Minority Students*, 8, 1–21.

The contextual problems of migrant students are discussed in the following references.

10. Center for Educational Planning. (1989). *Migrant Education Dropout Prevention Project Final Report*. ERIC ED 321–951.
11. Interstate Migrant Education Council. (1987). *Migrant Education: A Consolidated View*. ERIC ED 285–701.
12. Interstate Migrant Secondary Services Program. (1985). *Survey Analysis: Responses of 1070 Students in High School Equivalency Programs, 1984–1985*. ERIC ED 264–070.
13. Johnson, F., Levy, R., Morales, J., Morse, S., & Prokop, M. (1986). *Migrant Students at the Secondary Level: Issues and Opportunities for Change*. ERIC ED 270–242.
14. Lawless, K. (1986). *Neediest of the Needy: Special Education for Migrants. Harvesting the Harvesters*, Book 8. ERIC ED 279–473.
15. Migrant Attrition Project. (1987). *Migrant Attrition Project: Abstract of Findings*. Oneonta, NY: State University of New York at Oneonta.
16. Rasmussen, L. (1988). *Migrant Students at the Secondary Level: Issues and Opportunities for Change*. Las Cruces: New Mexico State University, ERIC/CRESS.

The special problems of rural students are described in the following references.

17. Berkeley, T. R., & Ludlow, B. L. (1991). Meeting the needs of special student populations in rural areas. In A. J. DeYoung (Ed.), *Rural Education: Issues and Practices*. New York: Garland.
18. Brown, D. L. (1989). Demographic trends relevant to education in nonmetropolitan America. In *Rural Education—A Changing Landscape*. Washington, DC: U.S. Department of Education.
19. Helge, D. (1984). The state of the art of rural special education. *Exceptional Children*, 50, 294–305.
20. Helge, D. (1989). *Rural Family-Community Partnerships: Resources*. ERIC ED 320–736.
21. Helge, D. (1991). *Rural, Exceptional, At Risk*. Reston, VA: Council for Exceptional Children.
22. Leadership for Special Education. A Conversation with Robert R. Davila. (1989). *Education of the Handicapped*, September 13, 28.
23. National Council on Disabilities. (1989). *The Education of Students with Disabilities: Where Do We Stand?* Washington, DC: Author.
24. Students at Risk. (1990). *Education Week*, October 19, 26.
25. O'Connor, C., Murr, A., & Wingert, P. (1986). Affluent America's forgotten children, *Newsweek*, 107(22), 20–21.
26. Pollard, K. M., & O'Hare, W. P. (1990). *Beyond High School: The Experience of Rural and Urban Youth in the 1980's*. ERIC ED 326–363.
27. Phelps, M. S., & Prock, G. A. (1991). Equality of educational opportunity in rural America. In A. DeYoung (Ed.), *Rural Education Issues and Practice*. New York: Garland.

These references concern the contextual problems of homeless children and adolescents.

28. Bass, J. L., Brennan, P., Mehta, K. A., & Kodzis, S. (1990). Pediatric problems in a suburban shelter for homeless families. *Pediatrics*, 85(1), 33–38.
29. Bassuk, E. L., & Gallagher, E. M. (1990). The impact of homelessness on children. In N. A. Boxill (Ed.), *Homeless Children: The Watchers and the Waiters*. Binghamton, NY: Haworth.
30. Bassuk, F., & Rubin, L. (1987). Homeless children: A neglected population. *American Journal of Orthopsychiatry*, 57(2), 279–286.
31. Bowen, J. M., Purrington, G. S., Layton, D. H., & O'Brien, K. (1989). *Educating Homeless Children and Youth: A Policy Analysis*. Paper presented at the annual conference of the American Educational Research Association, San Francisco.

32. Eddowes, A., & Hranitz., J. R. (1989). Education children of the homeless. *Childhood Education: Infancy through Early Adolescence, 65*(4), 197–200.
33. Friedman, L., & Christiansen, G. (1990). *Shut Out: Denial of Education to Homeless Children.* ERIC ED 320–987.
34. Heflin, L. J., & Rudy, K. (1991). *Homeless and in Need of Special Education.* Reston, VA: Council for Exceptional Children.
35. Miller, D. S., & Linn, E. H. B. (1988). Children in sheltered homeless families: Reported health status and use of health services. *Pediatrics, 81,* 668–673.
36. Rafferty, Y., & Rollins, N. (1989a). *Learning in Limbo: The Educational Deprivation of Homeless Children.* Long Island City: Advocates for Children of New York.
37. Rafferty, Y., & Rollins, N. (1989b). *Homeless Children: Educational Challenges for the 1990's.* ERIC ED 325–589.
38. Rescoria, L., Parker, R., & Stolley, P. (1991). Ability, achievement and adjustment in homeless children. *American Journal of Orthopsychiatry, 61*(2), 210–220.
39. Rivlin, L. G. (1990). Home and homelessness in the lives of children. In N. A. Boxill (Ed.), *Homeless Children: The Watchers and the Waiters.* Binghamton, NY: Haworth.
40. Rosenman, M., & Stein, M. L. (1990). Homeless children: A new vulnerability. In N. A. Boxill (Ed.), *Homeless Children: The Watchers and the Waiters.* Binghamton, NY: Haworth.
41. Russell, S. C., & Williams, E. U. (1988). Homeless handicapped children: A special education perspective. *Children's Environments Quarterly, 5*(1), 3–7.
42. Schumack, S. (Ed.). (1987). *The Educational Rights of Homeless Children.* ERIC ED 288–915.
43. Stronge, J. H., & Helm, V. M. (1990). *Residency and Guardianship Requirements as Barriers to the Education of Homeless Children and Youth.* ERIC ED 319–845.
44. Stronge, J. H., & Tenhouse, C. (1990). *Educating Homeless Children: Issues and Answers.* Bloomington, IN: Phi Delta Kappa Educational Foundation.
45. Wright, J. D. (1990). Homelessness is not healthy for children and other living things. In N. A. Boxill (Ed.), *Homeless Children: The Watchers and the Waiters.* Binghamton, NY: Haworth.

The effects of cultural differences is dealt with in the following references.

46. Baratz, S. S., & Baratz, J. C. (1975). Early childhood intervention: The social science basis of institutional racism. In *Challenging the Myth: The Schools, the Blacks, and the Poor.* Cambridge, MA: *Harvard Educational Review,* Reprint Series No. 5, pp. 111–132.
47. Federal Regional Resource Center. (1991). *Exploring the Education Issues of Cultural Diversity.* Lexington, KY: Interdisciplinary Human Development Institute, University of Kentucky.
48. Hurn, C. J. (1985). *The Limits and Possibilities of Schooling: An Introduction to the Sociology of Education,* (2nd ed.). Boston: Allyn and Bacon.
49. Lubeck, S. (1988). Nested contexts. In L. Weis, *Class, Race, and Gender in American Education.* Albany, NY: State University of New York Press, pp. 46–47.

The following reference discusses reasons why students may get into trouble in school for behaving in ways that are acceptable in their communities.

50. Grossman, H. (1984). *Educating Hispanic Students: Cultural Implications for Instruction, Classroom Management, Counseling and Assessment.* Springfield, IL: Charles C Thomas.

Examples of the opinions of writers in the 1970s, 1980s, and 1990s about prejudice in schools are found in the following references.

51. Becker, A. (1980). *The Role of the School in the Maintenance and Change of Ethnic Group Affiliation.* ERIC ED 259–052.
52. Bennett, C., & Harris, J. J. (1982). Suspension and expulsion of male and black students: A case study of the causes of disproportionality. *Urban Education, 16*(4), 399–423.
53. National Black Child Development Institute. (1990). *The Status of African American Children: Twentieth Anniversary Report.* Washington, DC.
54. Rist, R. C. (1971). Student social class and teacher expectations: The self fulfilling prophecy in ghetto education. In *Challenging the Myths: The Schools The Blacks and the Poor.* Cambridge, MA: *Harvard Educational Review.* Reprint Series No. 5.
55. Stein, A. (1971), Strategies for failure. In *Challenging the Myths: The Schools The Blacks and*

*the Poor*. Cambridge, MA: *Harvard Educational Review*. Reprint Series No. 5.

The following references describe studies that did not find teacher bias.

56. Flynn, T. M. (1983). IQ tests and placement. *Integrated Education, 21*, 124–126.
57. Heller, E. J. (1985). Pupil race and elementary school ability grouping: Are teachers biased against black children? *American Educational Research Journal, 22*(4), 465–483.
58. Huebner, E. S., & Cummings, J. A. (1986). Influence of race and test data ambiguity upon school psychologists' decisions. *School Psychology Review, 15*(3), 410–417.
59. Jaeger, R., & Freijo. T. (1975). Race and sex as concomitants of composite halo in teachers' evaluative ratings of pupils. *Journal of Educational Psychology, 67*(2), 226–237.
60. Matuszek, P., & Oakland, T. (1979). Factors influencing teachers' and psychologists' recommendations regarding special class placement. *Journal of School Psychology, 17*(2), 116–125.
61. Moacdieh, C. (1981). *Grouping for Reading in the Primary Grades: Evidence on the Revisionist Theory*. ERIC ED 200–938.
62. Tobias, S., Zibrin, M., & Menell, D. (1983). *Special Education Referrals: Failure to Replicate Student—Teacher Ethnicity Interaction*. ERIC ED 224–221.
63. Wiley, M., & Eskilson, A. (1978). Why did you learn in school today? Teachers' perceptions of causality. *Sociology of Education, 51*, 261–269.

The references listed below describe teachers' biased expectations for students.

64. Beady, C. H., & Hansell, S. (1980). *Teacher Race and Expectations for Student Achievement*. ERIC ED 200–695.
65. Bennet, C. I. (1979). The effects of student characteristics and task performance on teacher expectations and attributions. *Dissertation Abstracts International, 40*, 979–980-B.
66. Campos F. (1983). *The Attitudes and Expectations of Student Teachers and Cooperating Teachers Toward Students in Predominantly Mexican American Schools: A Qualitative Data Perspective*. ERIC ED 234–026.
67. Dao, M. (1991). Designing assessment procedures for educationally at-risk Southeast Asian-American students. *Journal of Learning Disabilities, 24*(10), 594–601, 629.
68. Derlega, V., Wang, P., & Colson, W. (1981). *Racial Bias in Expectancies and Performance Attributions*. Unpublished manuscript. Norfolk, VA: Old Dominion University.
69. Dusek, J. B., & Joseph, G. (1983). The bases of teacher expectancies: A meta-analysis. *Journal of Educational Psychology, 75*,(3), 327–346.
70. Figueroa, R. A., & Gallegos, E. A. (1978). Ethnic differences in school behavior. *Sociology of Education, 51*, 289–298.
71. Grant, L. (1984). Black females' "place" in desegregated classrooms. *Sociology of Education, 57*, 98–110.
72. Matute-Bianchi, M. E. (1986). Ethnic identities and patterns of school success and failure among Mexican-descent and Japanese-American students in a California high school: An ethnographic analysis. *American Journal of Education, 95*(1), 233–255.
73. Metheny, W. (1979). *The Influences of Grade and Pupil Ability Levels on Teachers' Conceptions of Reading*. ERIC ED 182–713.
74. Mizokawa, D. T., & Morishima, J. K. (1979). *Education for, by, and of Asian/Pacific Americans. I*. ERIC ED 199–355.
75. Ogbu, J. U. (1978). *Minority Education and Caste: The American in Cross-Cultural Perspective*. New York: Academic Press.
76. Smith, J. A. (1979). Ascribed and achieved student characteristics in teacher expectancy: Relationship of socioeconomic status to academic achievement, academic self-concept, and vocational aspirations. *Dissertation Abstracts International, 40*, 959–960-B.
77. Sue, S., & Kitano, H. H. L. (1973). Stereotypes as a measure of success. *Journal of Social Issues, 29*(3), 83–98.
78. Takeuchi, S. M. (1972). *Verbal Skills and the Asian American Student*. ERIC ED 097–395.
79. Wilkerson, M. A. (1980). The effects of sex and ethnicity upon teachers' expectations of students. *Dissertation Abstracts International, 41*, 637-A.

The following references discuss bias in teachers' evaluations of students.

80. Davis, S. A. (1974). *Students' SES as Related to Teachers' Perceptions and Ability Grouping Decisions*. ERIC ED 090–487.
81. DeMeis, D., & Turner, R. (1978). Effects of students' race, physical attractiveness, and dialect on teachers' evaluations. *Contemporary Educational Psychology, 3*, 77–86.

82. Eaves, R. (1975). Teacher race, student race, and the behavior problem checklist. *Journal of Abnormal Child Psychology, 3*(1), 1–9.
83. Elliot, S. N., & Argulewicz, E. N. (1983). The influence of student ethnicity on teachers' behavior ratings of normal and learning disabled children. *Hispanic Journal of Behavioral Sciences, 5*(3), 337–345.
84. Granger, R. E., Mathews, M., Quay, L. C., & Verner, R. (1977). Teacher judgements of communication effectiveness of children using different speech patterns. *Journal of Educational Psychology, 69*(6), 793–796.
85. Haller, E. J., & Davis, S. A. (1980). Does socioeconomic status bias the assignment of elementary school students to reading groups? *American Educational Research Journal, 17*(40), 409–418.
86. Ishi-Jordan, S. (1992). *Effects of Students' Racial or Ethnic Background on Teacher Expectations and Intervention Selection for Problem Behaviors.* Paper presented at the Topical Conference on Cultural and Linguistically Diverse Exceptional Children. Minneapolis, MN.
87. Kim, Y. J. (1983). Problems in the delivery of the school-based psycho-educational services to the Asian immigrant children. *Journal of Children in Contemporary Society, 15*(3), 81–89.
88. Marwit, K., Marwit, S., & Walker, E. (1978). Effects of student race and physical attractiveness on teachers' judgements of transgressions. *Journal of Educational Psychology, 70*, 911–915.
89. Scheinfeld, D. R. (1983). Family relationships and school achievement among boys of lower-income urban black families. *American Journal of Orthopsychiatry, 53*(1), 127–143.
90. Taylor, J. B. (1983). Influence of speech variety on teachers' evaluation of reading comprehension. *Journal of Educational Psychology, 75*(5), 662–667.
91. Tobias, S., Cole, C., Zibrin, M., & Bodlakova, V. (1981). *Bias in the Referral of Children to Special Services.* ERIC ED 208–637.
92. Wong, M. G. (1980). Model students? Teachers' perceptions and expectations of their Asian and white students. *Sociology of Education, 53*, 236–246.
93. Yao, E. L. (1987). Asian-immigrants students—Unique problems that hamper learning. *NASSP Bulletin, 71*(503), 82–88.

Bias in teacher-student interactions is the focus of the following references.

94. Appleford, B., Fralick, P., & Ryan, T. J. (1976). *Teacher-Child Interactions as Related to Sex, Socio-Economic Status and Physical Attractiveness.* ERIC ED 138–869.
95. Barba, L. (1979). *A Survey of the Literature on the Attitudes Toward the Administration of Corporal Punishment in Schools.* ERIC ED 186–538.
96. Bickel, F., & Qualls, R. (1981). *The Impact of School Climate on Suspension Rates in the Jefferson County Public Schools.* Paper presented at the annual meeting of the American Educational Research Association, Boston.
97. Buriel, R. (1983). Teacher-student interactions and their relationship to student achievement: A comparison of Mexican-American children. *Journal of Educational Psychology, 75*(60), 889–897.
98. Friedman, P. (1976). Comparison of teacher reinforcement schedules for students with different social class backgrounds. *Journal of Educational Psychology, 68*, 286–293.
99. Glackman, T., Martin, R., Hyman, I., McDowell, E., Berv, V., & Spino, P. (1980). *Corporal Punishment in the Schools As It Relates to Race, Sex, Grade Level and Suspensions.* Philadelphia: Temple University, National Center for the Study of Corporal Punishment in the Schools.
100. Grant, L. (1985). Race-gender status, classroom interaction, and children's socialization in elementary school. In L. C. Wilkinson & C. B. Marrett (Eds.), *Gender Influences in Classroom Interaction.* New York: Academic Press.
101. Grossman, H., & Grossman, S. (1994). *Gender Issues in Education.* Needham, MA: Allyn and Bacon.
102. Guilmet, G. M. (1979). Instructor reaction to verbal and nonverbal styles: An example of Navajo and Caucasian children. *Anthropology and Education Quarterly, 10*, 254–266.
103. Hamilton, S. (1983). The social side of schooling. *Elementary School Journal, 83*, 313–334.
104. McGhan, B. R. (1978). *Teachers' Use of Authority and Its Relationship to Socioeconomic Status, Race, Teacher Characteristics, and Educational Outcomes.* ERIC ED 151–329.
105. Moody, C. D., Williams, J., & Vergon, C. B. (1978). *Student Rights and Discipline: Policies, Programs and Procedures.* ERIC ED 160–926.
106. Moore, W. L., & Cooper, H. (1984). Correlations between teacher and student back-

ground and teacher perception of discipline problems and disciplinary techniques. *Psychology in the Schools, 21,* 386–392.
107. Richardson, R. C., & Evans, E. T. (1991). *Empowering Teachers to Eliminate Corporal Punishment in the Schools.* Paper presented at the annual conference of the National Black Child Developmental Institute. Washington, DC.
108. Simpson, A. W., & Erickson, M. T. (1983). Teachers' verbal and nonverbal communication patterns as a function of teacher race, student gender and student race. *American Educational Research Journal, 20*(2), 183–198.
109. Stevens, L. B. (1983). *Suspension and Corporal Punishment of Students in the Cleveland Public Schools, 1981–1982.* Cleveland, OH: Office of School Monitoring and Community Relations.
110. Taylor, M. (1979). Race, sex and the expression of self-fulfilling prophecies in a laboratory teaching situation. *Journal of Personality and Social Psychology, 37*(6), 897–912.
111. Washington, V. (1982). Racial differences in teacher perception of first and fourth grade pupils on selected characteristics. *Journal of Negro Education, 51,* 60–72.
112. Woolridge, P., & Richman, C. (1985). Teachers' choice of punishment as a function of a student's gender, age, race and I.Q. level. *Journal of School Psychology, 23,* 19–29.

Apparent and real lack of bias and their effects are the focus of the following references.

113. Feldman, R., & Donohoe, L. (1978). Nonverbal communication of affect in interracial dyads. *Journal of Educational Psychology, 70*(6), 979–986.
114. Meier, K. J., Stewart, J. Jr., & England, R. E. (1989). *Race, Class, and Education: The Politics of Second-Generation Discrimination.* Madison, WI: University of Wisconsin Press.
115. Office for Civil Rights. (1982). *1980 Elementary and Secondary School Civil Rights Surveys.* Washington, DC: U.S. Department of Education.
116. Office of Civil Rights. (1987). *Elementary and Secondary School Civil Rights Survey, 1986. National Summaries.* ERIC ED 304–485.
117. Plata, M., & Chinn, P. C. (1989). Students with handicaps who have cultural and language differences. In R. Gaylord-Ross (Ed.), *Integration Strategies for Students with Handicaps.* Baltimore: Brookes.

References that discuss the role of schools in the reproduction of inequities in society are listed here.

118. Apple, M., & Weis, L. (Eds.). (1983). *Ideology and Practice in Schools.* Philadelphia: Temple University Press.
119. Bowles, S., & Gintes, H. (1977). *Schooling in Capitalist America.* New York: Basic Books.
120. Connell, R. W. (1989). Curriculum politics, hegemony, and strategies of social change. In H. A. Giroux & R. I. Simon (Eds.), *Popular Culture, Schooling and Everyday Life.* Granby, MA: Bergin & Garvey.
121. Deem, R. (1978). *Women and Schooling.* Boston: Routledge Kegan Paul.
122. Giroux, H. A. (1981). Hegemony, resistance, and the paradox of educational reform. In H. A. Giroux, A. N. Penna, & W. F. Pinar, *Curriculum & Instruction: Alternatives in Education.* Berkeley, CA: McCutchan.
123. Giroux, H. A. (1983). Theories of reproduction and resistance in the new sociology of education: A critical analysis. *Harvard Educational Review, 53*(3), 257–293.
124. Giroux, H. A., & Penna, A. N. (1988). Social education in the classroom: The dynamics of the hidden curriculum. In H. A. Giroux (Ed.), *Teachers as Intellectuals: Toward a Critical Pedagogy of Learning.* Granby, MA: Bergin & Garvey.
125. Grant, C. A., & Sleeter, C. E. (1988). Race, class, and gender and abandoned dreams. *Teachers College Record, 90*(1), 19–40.
126. Irvine, J. J. (1989). *Black Students and School Achievement: A Process Model of Relationships among Significant Variables.* ERIC ED 310–220.
127. Kelly, G., & Nihlen, A. (1982). Schooling and the reproduction of patriarchy: Unequal workloads, unequal rewards. In M. Apple (Ed.), *Culture and Economic Reproduction in Education.* Boston: Routledge Kegan Paul.
128. Valli, L. (1986). *Becoming Clerical Workers.* Boston: Routledge Kegan Paul.
129. Weiler, K. (1988). *Women Teaching for Change: Gender, Class & Power.* Granby, MA: Bergin & Garvey.
130. Witt, S. H. (1979). Native women in the world of work. In T. Constantino (Ed.), *Women of Color Forum: A Collection of Readings.* ERIC ED 191–975.
131. Wolpe, A. (1981). The official ideology of education for girls. In M. McDonald, R. Dale, G. Esland, & R. Fergusson, (Eds.), *Politics,*

*Patriarchy and Practice*. New York: Falmer Press.

The following references deal with student resistance to school.

132. Anyon, J. (1984). Intersections of gender and class: Accommodation and resistance by working class and affluent females to contradictory sex-role ideologies. *Journal of Education, 166*(1), 25–48.
133. Arnot, M. (1982). Male hegemony, social class and women's education. *Journal of Education, 164*(1), 64–89.
134. Bouie, A. (1981). *Student Perceptions of Behavior and Misbehavior in the School Setting: An Exploratory Study and Discussion*. San Francisco: Far West Laboratory for Educational Research and Development.
135. Comer, J. P. (1990). What makes the new generation tick? *Ebony*, October, 34–38.
136. Ford, D. Y. (1991). *Self-Perceptions of Social, Psychological, and Cultural Determinants of Achievement among Gifted Black Students: A Paradox of Underachievement*. Unpublished doctoral dissertation, Cleveland: Cleveland State University.
137. Ford, D. Y. (1992). The American achievement ideology and achievement differentials among preadolescent gifted and nongifted African American males and females. *Journal of Negro Education, 61*(1), 45–64.
138. Fordham, S. (1988). Racelessness as a strategy in Black students' school success: Coping with the burden of "acting White." *Urban Review, 20*, 176–207.
139. Fordham, S., & Ogbu, J. U. (1986). Black students' school success: Coping with the "burden of acting white." *Urban Review, 18*(3), 176–203.
140. Fuller, M. (1980). Black girls in a London comprehensive school. In R. Deem (Ed.), *Schooling for Women's Work*. Boston: Routledge and Kegan Paul.
141. Gaskell, J. (1985). Course enrollment in high school: The perspective of working class females. *Sociology of Education, 58*(1), 48–59.
142. Gibson, M. A. (1987). The school performance of immigrant minorities: A comparative view. *Anthropology and Education Quarterly, 18*(4), 262–275.
143. Kessler, S., Ashenden, R., Connell, R., & Dowsett, G. (1985). Gender relations in secondary schooling. *Sociology of Education, 58*(1), 34–48.
144. Matute-Bianchi, M. E. (1986). Ethnic identities and patterns of school success and failure among Mexican-descent and Japanese-American students in a California high school: An ethnographic analysis. *American Journal of Education, 95*(1), 233–255.
145. MacLeod, J. (1987). *Ain't No Makin' It: Leveled Aspirations in a Low-Income Neighborhood*. Boulder, CO: Westview.
146. Nieto, S. (1992). *Affirming Diversity: The Sociopolitical Context of Multicultural Education*. New York: Longman.
147. Ogbu, J. U. (1986). The consequences of the American caste system. In U. Meisser (Ed.), *The School Achievement of Minority Children: New Perspectives*. Hillsdale, NJ: Erlbaum.
148. Ogbu, J. U. (1987). Variability in minority school performance: A problem in search of an explanation. *Anthropology & Education Quarterly, 18*(4), 312–334.
149. Ogbu, J. U. (1990). Minority education in comparative perspective. *Journal of Negro Education, 59*, 45–57.
150. Simon, R. (1983). But who will let you do it? Counter-hegemonic possibilities for work education. *Journal of Education, 165*(3), 235–256.
151. Suarez-Orozco, M. M. (1987). Becoming somebody: Central American immigrants in the United States. *Anthropology and Education Quarterly, 18*(4), 287–299.
152. Weis, L. (1985). *Between Two Worlds: Black Students in an Urban Community College*. Boston: Routledge and Kegan Paul.
153. Weis, L. (1985). Excellence and student class, race and gender cultures. In P. Altbach, G. Kelly, & L. Weis (Eds.), *Excellence in Education: Perspective on Policy and Practice*. Buffalo: Prometheus Press.
154. Willis, P. (1981). Cultural production is different from cultural reproduction is different from social reproduction is different from production. *Interchange, 12*(2/3), 48–68.

The references listed below include suggestions for preparing students to change both schools and society.

155. Hartsock, N. (1979). Feminist theory and the development of revolutionary strategy. In Z. Eisenstein (Ed.), *Capitalist Patriarchy and the Case for Socialist Feminism*. New York: Monthly Review Press.

156. Lather, P. (1984). Critical theory, curricular transformation and feminist mainstreaming. *Journal of Education, 166*(1), 49–62.

The following author criticizes the theory that there are voluntary and caste-like groups in the United States.

157. Treuba, H. T. (1988). Culturally based explanations of minority students' academic achievement. *Anthropology and Education Quarterly, 19*(3), 270–287.

The following References deal with the inadequate educational services provided to non-European middle-class students.

158. Ascher, C. (1989). *Urban School Finance: The Quest for Equal Educational Opportunity*. New York: ERIC Clearinghouse on Urban Education.
159. Bastian, A., Fruchter, N., Gittell, M., Greer, C., & Haskins, K. (1986). *Choosing Equality*. Philadelphia: Temple University Press.
160. Becker, H. J. (1986). *Computer Survey Newsletter*. Baltimore: The Johns Hopkins University, Center for the Social Organization of Schools.
161. Center for Social Organization of School. (1983). *School Uses of Microcomputers: Reports from a National Survey*, No. 3. Author.
162. Darling-Hammond, L. (1985). *Equality and Excellence: The Status of Black American Education*. New York: College Entrance Examination Board.
163. Furr, J. D., & Davis, T. M. (1984). Equity Issues and microcomputers: Are educators meeting the challenges? *Journal of Educational Equity and Leadership, 4*, 93–97.
164. Hood, J. F. (1984). *Update on the School Market for Microcomputers*. Westport, CT: Market Data Retrieval.
165. Karp, S. (1991). Rich schools, poor schools & the courts. *Rethinking Schools, 5*(2), 1–15.
166. Mickelson, R. A. (1980). Social stratification processes in secondary schools: A comparison of Beverly Hills High School and Morningside High School. *Journal of Education, 162*(4), 83–112.
167. National Assessment of Education Progress. (1988). *Computer Competence: The First National Assessment*. Princeton: Educational Testing Service.
168. New York City Board of Education (1989). *A New Direction: 1989–1990 Budget Request*. New York.
169. Oakes, J. (1983). Limiting Opportunity: Student race and curricular differences in secondary vocational education. *American Journal of Education*, May, 328–355.
170. O'Brien, E. M. (1989). Texas legislators impatient to solve unfairness of school financing system. *Black Issues in Higher Education, 6*(16), 23.

These references are concerned with the effects of tracking and ability grouping.

171. Brophy, J. (1983). Research on the self-fulfilling prophecy and teacher expectation. *Journal of Educational Psychology, 75*(5), 631–661.
172. Chun, E. W. (1988). Sorting black students for success and failure: The inequity of ability grouping and tracking. *Urban League Review, 11*(1–2), 93–106.
173. Eder, D. (1981). Ability grouping as a self-fulfilling prophecy: A micro-analysis of teacher-student interaction. *Sociology of Education, 54*, 151–162.
174. Gamoran, A. (1986). *The Stratification of High School Learning Opportunities*. Paper presented at the annual meeting of the American Educational Research Association, San Francisco.
175. Goodlad, J. (1984). *A Place Called School*. New York: McGraw-Hill.
176. Lake, S. (1985). *Update on Tracking and Ability Grouping*. ERIC ED 274–708.
177. Lee, V. (1986). *The Effect of Tracking on the Social Distribution of Achievement in Catholic and Public Secondary Schools*. Paper presented at the annual meeting of the American Educational Research Association, San Francisco.
178. Oakes, J. (1985). *Keeping Track: How Schools Structure Inequality*. New Haven: Yale University Press.
179. Oakes, J. (1988). Tracking in mathematics and science education: A structural contribution to unequal schooling. In L. Weis, *Class, Race, and Gender in American Education*. Albany, NY: State University of New York Press.
180. Rosenbaum, J. E. (1980). Track misperceptions and frustrated college plans: An analysis of the effects of tracks and track perceptions in the National Longitudinal Survey. *Sociology of Education, 53*(2), 74–88.
181. Simpson, W. (1990). *Black Male Achievement: Strategies for Ensuring Success in School*. Paper presented at the annual meeting of the National Black Child Development Institute. Washington, DC.

182. Slavin, R. (1986). *Ability Grouping in Elementary Schools: A Best Evidence Synthesis*. Baltimore: The Johns Hopkins University Press.

The results of community colleges are discussed in the following references.

183. Astin, A. W. (1982). *Minorities in American Higher Education*. San Francisco: Jossey-Bass.
184. Moore, W. (1976). Black knight/white college. *Community and Junior College Journal, 6*(7), 18–20, 40–43.
185. Nora, A., & Rendon, L. (1988). Hispanic student retention in community colleges: Reconciling access with outcomes. In L. Weis, *Class, Race, and Gender in American Education*. Albany, NY: State University of New York Press.
186. Olivas, M. A. (1979). *The Dilemma of Access: Minorities in Two Year Colleges*. Washington, DC: Howard University Press.
187. Weis, L. (1983). Schooling and cultural production: A comparison of black and white lived cultures. In M. A. Apple & L. Weis (Eds.), *Ideology and Practice in Schooling*. Philadelphia: Temple University Press.

Alienation among African American students is the focus of the following references.

188. Fisher, S. (1981). Race, class, anomie, and academic achievement: A study at the high school level. *Urban Education, 16*(2), 149–173.
189. Ginsberg, E., Berliner, H. S., & Ostow, M. (1988). *Young People at Risk: Is Prevention Possible?* Boulder, CO: Westview Press.
190. Harris, W. G., & Blanchard, R. (1990). *A Select Group of African American Males' Perceptions of Barriers to Successfully Achieving the Typical Male Familial Role—Implications for Educators*. Paper presented at the annual meeting of the National Association for Multicultural Education, New Orleans.
191. Hirsch, B. J., & Rapkin, B. D. (1987). The transition to junior high school: A longitudinal study of self-esteem, psychological symptomatology, school life, and social support. *Child Development, 58*, 1235–1243.
192. Long, S. (1980). Personality and political revenge: Psychopolitical adaptation among black and white youth. *Journal of Black Studies, 11*(1), 77–104.
193. (1992). Utah researcher blames discrimination for Native American high school dropout rate. *Black Issues in Higher Education, 9*(9), 3.

Techniques for resegregating schools are discussed in the following references.

194. Carter, D. G. (1982). Second-generation school integration problems for blacks. *Journal of Black Studies, 13*(2), 175–188.
195. Children's Defense Fund (1974). *Children Out of School*. Washington, DC: Children's Defense Fund of the Washington Research Project.
196. Cross, D. E., Long, M. A., & Ziajka, A. (1978). Minority cultures and education in the United States. *Education and Urban Society, 10*(3), 263–276.
197. Eyler, J., Cook, B. J., & Ward, L. E. (1983). Resegregation: Segregation within desegregated schools. In C. H. Rossell & W. D. Hawley (Eds.), *The Consequences of School Desegregation*. Philadelphia: Temple University Press.
198. Finn, J. D. (1982). Patterns in special education placement as revealed by the ORC surveys. In K. A. Heller, W. H. Holtzman, & S. Messick (Eds.), *Placing Children in Special Education*. Washington, DC: National Academy Press.
199. Gelb, S. A. (1983). *Special Education and Linguistic Minority Students: The Historical Bases of Discriminatory Practices*. ERIC ED 232–401.
200. Goodale, R., & Soden, M. (1981). *Disproportionate Placement of Black and Hispanic Students in Special Education Programs*. ERIC ED 204–873.
201. Johnson, J. L. (1969). Special Education and the Inner City: A challenge for the future of another means for cooling the mark out? *Journal of Special Education, 3*(3), 241–251.
202. Kritek, W. J. (1979). Teacher's concerns in a desegregated school in Milwaukee. *Integrated Education, 17*(1), 19–24.
203. Larkin, J. (1979). School desegregation and student suspension: A look at one school system. *Education and Urban Society, 11*(4), 485–495.
204. Network of Regional Desegregation Assistance Centers. (1989). *Resegregation of Public Schools: The Third Generation*. Author.
205. Richardson, J. G. (1979). The case of special education and minority misclassification in California. *Educational Research Quarterly, 4*(1), 25–40.
206. Rogers, H. R., & Bullock, C. S. III (1972). *Law and Social Change*. New York: McGraw Hill.

207. Smith, G. R. (1983). Desegregation and assignment for children to classes for the mildly retarded and learning disabled. *Integrated Education*, *21*(1–6), 208–211.
208. Smith, M., & Dziuban, C. D. (1977). The gap between desegregation research and remedy. *Integrated Education*, *15*, 51–55.
209. Tillman, J. (1991). Wake up! Please don't let your children become special education students. *Black Issues in Higher Education*, *8*(16), 31.
210. Trent, W. T. (1981). Expert opinion on school desegregation issues. In W. D. Hawley (Ed.), *Assessment of Current Knowledge about the Effectiveness of School Desegregation Strategies*. Nashville, TN: Institute for Public Policy Studies, Vanderbilt University.

# Chapter 4

# Communicatively Appropriate Education

In a pluralistic society such as ours, students come to school speaking different languages and dialects and using different verbal and nonverbal communication styles. This chapter discusses how educators can take these differences into account when they instruct and assess students.

## *Limited English Proficiency*

As was noted in Chapter 1, the limited English proficient (LEP) population is the fastest growing in the United States. It is probable that almost 8 million American youngsters have a non-English background, either because they were born elsewhere or because they grew up in the United States in a home where another language was spoken. More than 3 million of these students scored in the lowest 20% on tests of English proficiency. More than 5 million scored in the lower 40%. Whichever of these two figures one uses, it is clear that millions of students are not proficient enough in English to function in English-only classes without considerable difficulty (1).

The appropriate instructional services required by LEP students has been the subject of a number of court decisions and federal laws. In 1974, in Lau v. Nichols, the Supreme Court unanimously decided that schools must provide special assistance to LEP students in the form of linguistically appropriate educational services (3).

The Bilingual Education Act defines these services (2). Schools may satisfy the requirement that LEP students receive linguistically appropriate services by providing students with instruction in their native language (bilingual education), English as a second language (ESL), sheltered English (also called structured English), or a combination of these approaches. These alternate ways of providing linguistically appropriate education services are discussed in this section. However, it should be noted that many LEP students are not being taught by any of these approaches.

## *Bilingual Education*

In the not too distant past, many people argued that the best way to work with LEP students was to immerse them in English as quickly and as completely as possible. Now we know from research that English immersion programs are less desirable than teaching students subject matter in their native languages (bilingual education) while they are also learning English as a second language (4, 6, 8). There are three main reasons for this.

**1.** Although it takes only a year or two for students to become proficient enough in a second language to carry on everyday conversations—basic interpersonal communication skills (BICS)—it usually takes at least five years to reach the level of proficiency in a second language that is required to learn subject matter—cognitive academic learning proficiency (CALP) (5). Thus, if students are instructed in subject matter too soon in a second language they will not be able to benefit optimally from such instruction.

A bilingual educator put it this way:

*The fact is, it takes time to learn English. But we cannot forgo learning other content areas while they're in the process of acquiring English. Put a child in a class for a year or two to learn English and meanwhile forget learning math, forget art, forget social studies. I don't think we can do that. (7, p. 57)*

A principal of a school designed to prepare immigrant students for the regular school in their area stated:

*We know that the kind of English we are talking about is not just fluency, being able to converse, being able to make small talk. We are talking about academic English . . . the English you need to evaluate, criticize, voice your opinion. That kind of English requires a lot of study and requires a certain amount of cultural literacy in the American context. It takes time to acquire it. We know for a fact that what these kids most need is time—time in the school system. (7, p. 64)*

**2.** There is considerable evidence that switching students from their native language to a new language before they have acquired CALP can stunt their language development in either language. However, once students have acquired CALP in one language they are able to transfer their understanding of the logic and rules of language to the learning of a second language (5, 7). Thus, students taught in their native language until they have developed "languageness" read better and learn more in school than those who are immediately taught in second language.

**3.** Rejecting students' native languages can alienate students and lead them to develop poor self-concepts.

Although bilingual education is the preferable approach, it is not a practical alternative for many school districts because they lack bilingual education personnel and/or are faced with providing services to LEP students in many different languages. This is an especially difficult problem for school districts that serve a linguistically diverse population—such as the Los Angeles School District, which serves students who speak over one hundred different languages. As a result, a number of school districts have opted for ESL or sheltered English programs for their LEP students.

## *English as a Second Language*

In recent years the art of teaching students a second language has become much more of a science. As a result, educators are now achieving a great deal of success in ESL programs. Unfortunately, only a limited number of teacher preparation programs train teachers to use ESL techniques. Therefore, this option is not readily available to many students and school districts.

## *Sheltered English/Structured Immersion*

In a sheltered English/structured English approach students are taught subject matter in a modified/controlled English vocabulary at their level of English comprehension. Teachers omit difficult words and forms, explain new vocabulary words, often in students' native languages, and employ as many nonverbal gestures, audiovisual aids, and other materials as possible. Gersten and Woodward describe the approach in the following manner.

> *With structured immersion all instruction is done in the commonly used language of the school . . . However, all instruction is conducted at a level understood by students. Superficially, structured immersion may seem similar to what the U.S. court outlawed in 1974; that is, a sink-or-swim approach for those not proficient in the language of the dominant culture. But there is a critical difference: teachers do not assume that the children understand English. Difficult new words are pretaught, sometimes using the child's native language. (11, p. 75)*

Research indicated that students improve their second language proficiency and learn subject matter in well-planned sheltered English programs staffed by trained teachers (9–12). However, very few LEP students are enrolled in sheltered English programs.

## *English Submergence*

As was noted earlier, many LEP students are not in bilingual education, ESL, or sheltered English programs. Thus, many LEP students without CALP, and often BICS, English fluency are submerged in the regular classes and are taught in English without regard to their linguistic needs. Submerged in English without the skills necessary to profit from the instruction they receive, they are at risk for

> **ESL Programs Versus Submergence Programs**
>
> Compare the experiences of the following three students. A student in an English submergence program reported:
>
> *I just sat in my classes and didn't understand anything. Sometimes I would try to look like I knew what was going on, sometimes I would just try to think about a happy time when I didn't feel stupid. My teachers never called on me or talked to me. I think either they forgot I was there or else wished I wasn't. I waited and I waited, thinking someday I will know English. (7, p. 62)*
>
> Two other students made the following comparison between their experiences in ESL and a regular class taught in English.
>
> *My ESL teacher helped me a lot in my first year here. I could relax there. I wasn't afraid.... In my other classes I was always confused and lost and I didn't want to ask anything because of my bad English. (7, p. 62)*
>
> *My first school I didn't want to go, just to stay home. When I went I just sat there and didn't understand anything.... No one talked to me and I couldn't say anything. I didn't know what was going on. My second school had an ESL teacher who taught me from the ABC's and helped me learn many more things. (7, p. 62)*

joining the ranks of students who tune out their teachers, cut classes, and drop out before graduating from high school.

## *Dialectal Differences*

In the past, many educators believed that the English dialect spoken by many poor African American students (Black English/Ebonics), the dialects spoken by Native Americans, Hispanic Americans, Hawaiian Americans, and certain regional dialects spoken by poor European Americans such as the ones spoken in Appalachia (mountain English) and in the greater New York City Metropolitan Area (New Yorkese) interfered with learning to read and write standard English correctly. Critics of nonstandard dialects also believed that many of them were inferior forms of English and should be eradicated. Today, as was noted in Chapter 2, experts tend to consider dialect variations to be linguistic differences rather than linguistic deficiencies. Nevertheless, they still disagree about how to handle them in school.

### *Legal Aspects*

Since the 1970s schools have had to provide students with linguistically appropriate educational services that take into account the students' nonstandard English dialects. In 1972, the Equal Educational Opportunities Act stated that

> **Standard English**
>
> Although the term "standard English" is used in this text, some people question whether there is a such a thing as standard English. They point out that so-called standard English is not the English dialect spoken in many regions of the United States or by many ethnic groups or poor people. They suggest that the term be replaced by one that avoids the connotation that it is the standard by which other dialects should be judged and the implication that it should be the preferred dialect. The term "American English" has been offered as a substitute. However, it too has many problems.

*No state shall deny equal educational opportunity to an individual by . . . the failure by an educational agency to take appropriate action to overcome language barriers that impede equal participation by its students in its instructional program. (13)*

In 1979 a U.S. District Court judge ruled in favor of 15 African American students who claimed that they were denied an equal education because their school did not take their nonstandard English dialect into account. Although this ruling only affected schools within the jurisdiction of the court, it has set a national tone. Judge Joiner, the presiding judge reflected the knowledge of the day in his ruling.

*The court does not believe that language differences between "Black English" and standard English to be a language barrier in and of itself.*

*The unconscious but evident attitude of teachers toward the home language of the plaintiffs causes a psychological barrier to learning by the student. . . . The child who comes to school using the "Black English" system of communication and who is taught that this is wrong loses a sense of values related to mother and close friends and siblings, and may rebel at efforts by his teacher to teach reading in a different language.*

*If a barrier exists because of the language used by the children in this case, it exists not because the teachers and students cannot understand each other, but because in the process of attempting to teach the students how to speak standard English the students are made somehow to feel inferior and are thereby turned off from the learning process. (14, pp. 18, 26, 36, 41–42)*

The court required the school district to help the teachers of the plaintiff children at the King School to identify children speaking "Black English" and the language spoken as a home or community language in order to use that knowledge in teaching such students how to read standard English. However, the court did not provide guidelines for how teachers should use their knowledge of Black English to teach students. As a result, two very different educational approaches are being employed in schools to deal with mismatches between the English dialects spoken by many students and the oral and written English used by their teachers and found in almost all textbooks and curriculum materials: bidialectalism and appreciation.

## Speaking

### Bidialectalism

Many individuals believe that speakers of nonstandard dialects should be taught to express themselves in standard English as well as their nonstandard dialects and to use each form when it is appropriate for a given situation. The objectives of bidialectal programs, although expressed in various ways, usually include the following:

1. *To create an awareness of the need for "functional flexibility"' in oral communication (i.e., the ability to use language for varying purposes)*
2. *To develop an understanding of the education, social and economic ramifications of unproductive communication skills, and*
3. *To provide opportunities to develop and practice the alternative style of communication (i.e., mainstream English) while not eradicating the importance and function of "home language." (22, p. 211)*

Three reasons are typically cited in support of bidialectalism.

1. *Although nonstandard English dialects are not substandard, they interfere with students' academic progress* (15, 22). The evidence regarding this contention is mixed. Most studies have found that speakers of nonstandard dialects do not have difficulty learning to read (18, 30–40, 43, 44). Some researchers have reported findings that indicate that Black English and Native American English dialect speakers have difficulty learning to read standard English (34, 45). However, the cause of the relationship between reading difficulty and nonstandard dialect usage that has been observed in some studies is unclear. Although some educators believe that these results indicate that nonstandard dialects interfere with learning, three other explanations have been offered.

Students of nonstandard English dialects tend to be from poor backgrounds. It is the many factors associated with having a poor background, not the students' nonstandard dialects, that account for their lack of progress in reading. Support for this hypothesis lies in the fact that within the various groups that speak nonstandard dialects (such as African Americans, Hawaiian Americans, and so on), nonstandard dialects are much more prevalent among poor than middle-class students.

Educators' prejudiced attitudes against certain nonstandard English dialects interfere with students' learning. As was noted in Chapters 2 and 3, teachers of nonstandard English speakers, especially those who believe standard English to be a more desirable or correct version of English, tend to believe that students do not understand something if they cannot explain it in standard English. They think that students who do not speak standard English are less intelligent; they have lower academic expectations for them; they evaluate both their oral and written work to be worse than comparable work of students speaking standard English; and they are more likely to disapprove of them.

Teachers spend too much time correcting students' dialectal vocabulary, grammatical, and pronunciation "errors." There is considerable evidence that many teachers focus on dialect differences that are not true errors, rather than concentrating their efforts on improving students higher-level skills, and relate to them in unproductive ways (36, 37, 41, 42, 46). The following description illustrates how insistence on standard English speech can interfere with good teaching.

*A sixth-grade math teacher was quite disturbed because his students referred to the concept of lowest common denominator as "breaking it down more smaller." The students obviously understood the concept and had demonstrated, on the chalk board and in class and homework papers, that they could apply the concept to solve math problems. The teacher kept correcting the students because his perception was, "These kids obviously don't know how to arrive at lowest common denominators." When queried as to how, then, were the students able to solve problems involving the concept, his explanation was, "You can't do anything if you don't know the right word for it."*

*The teacher's solution was to waste the next few days drilling his students on the spelling and textbook terminology of various mathematical operations that they already knew how to perform! (41, p. 89)*

On balance the evidence does not support the contention that students' nonstandard dialects interfere with their learning. As Padak has commented, "one need not speak a dialect in order to understand it" (27, p. 150).

**2.** *Competency in oral standard English is necessary for students to learn to write standard English.* Although it is true that nonstandard forms of English intrude in students' writing when they are first learning to write standard English, most experts in the field agree that it is not necessary for students to be able to speak standard English in order to write standard English. They point out that many nonstandard English speakers can write standard English; they note that the longer students remain in school, the fewer nonstandard English forms intrude in their writing (21); and they remind us that writing is not speech written down.

*Learning to write standard English does not mean first learning to speak it. . . . Forcing Chicanos to change their way of speaking English in order to learn to write makes no more sense than forcing an east Texas child or a child from Boston or the Bronx to drop their speech peculiarities and replace them with midwestern English so that they can learn to write. (62, p. 25)*

**3.** *Standard English is necessary for vocational success and in other areas in which nonstandard dialect speakers are branded as uneducated and ill-prepared (19, 23, 29).* The following quotation typifies this line of thinking.

> *There are many dialects in every language, but the standard form is that which is acceptable for purposes of state, business, or other everyday transactions. It is the official language of the country, and anyone who is successful in that country uses it. Those who use the nonstandard language are forever relegated to the most menial jobs and stations in life. . . . If blacks are prepared to accept the hypothesis of "Black English," then they ought to be prepared to accept the relegation to "Black" jobs. If their preparation is second class, their lives will be second class. (30, pp. 318, 320)*

It is true, as was noted in Chapter 3, that many members of our society are prejudiced against certain nonstandard English dialects. However, many educators believe the solution to the problem is to combat discrimination, not accommodate and acquiesce to it. As Dean and Fowler suggested quite some time ago:

> *Previously, people who have applied for a job have been judged on clothing and hair styles. These discriminations have been lessened by change of public opinion. Then, people were judged on the color of their skin or their sex. These prejudices, while still present, are being lessened with the "help" of legislation. . . . Yet proponents of bidialectalism state that a person must speak standard English to be hired for a "good job". . . . White middle-class society has reexamined its values in the previously mentioned areas of hair style, clothing, race and sex. Surely that society can have its eyes opened once again. (17, pp. 305–306)*

Moreover, many individuals believe that schools have an important role to play in correcting discrimination against nonstandard English dialects. On the other hand, many individuals have pointed out that community attitudes are difficult if not impossible to change quickly, and they argue that schools should prepare students to succeed in the meantime.

Those who believe that students should be taught to be able to communicate in standard English in appropriate situations have offered the following guidelines and principles (22, 42, 47–51, 53, 55–57, 59, 64).

- Motivate students to want to become bidialectal. Employ age-appropriate motivational techniques. The older students are, the more they can appreciate the advantages, value, and importance of becoming bidialectal.
- Correct students' misperceptions that standard English is the "white man's" language
- Avoid creating resistance among students. For example, do not correct students. Instead, discuss alternative acceptable ways of saying the same things in different situations.

- Concentrate on those dialect characteristics that are most stigmatized by the community and most hamper success. For example, nonstandard grammar (double negatives, nonagreement of subject and verb, "them" for "those") is viewed much more negatively than nonstandard pronunciation (51).

Many techniques have been employed to help students become bidialectal. Techniques vary depending on the point of view of the educators.

The most common approach is the method of contrastive analysis. In this method students are taught to use both standard and nonstandard forms for expressing same ideas in both dialects and to identify when to use each one (22, 31, 42, 47, 53, 57, 59, 64). In some cases audio- and videotaping has been used to help students experience the difference in their language. Typically this approach involves seven steps.

**1.** Identify nonstandard dialect speakers. This is usually done informally, but some instruments are available (59).
**2.** Explain that there are different dialects.
**3.** Contrast and teach the differences. Lists and descriptions of dialect differences for a number of dialects are available (69–74). Very young children may not be mature enough to recognize, label, and contrast dialect differences.
**4.** Teach students to distinguish between home English and school and work English and to use the most appropriate one for a given situation.
**5.** Drill them in substituting standard forms for nonstandard ones.
**6.** Provide students with opportunities to practice standard forms in class.
**7.** Evaluate the results. This last step can be done informally or by using a formal instrument (67).

Research indicates that contrastive analysis increases students' use of standard English in the classroom; little data is available about its effects on students' language usage outside of school.

Some educators use the ESL instructional techniques that were developed to assist limited English proficient students to teach nonstandard dialect speakers to speak standard English (66). However, many educators object to the use of a method designed to teach non-English speakers with students who speak English, albeit in a nonstandard dialect.

*English as a second language is a must for those who have just entered this country; however, I find it distressing when the term is applied to English for my Black brethren who have been in this English-speaking country for generations. (30, p. 318)*

Many educators stress the importance of helping students to resolve their ambivalence and resistance to standard English and increasing their motivation to learn and use it (54, 63, 68). Unlike limited English proficient students, who need to learn English in order to survive in the United States, nonstandard English speakers already speak English. They often have no felt need to learn a second English dialect that is different from the English spoken and accepted by their family, friends, and neighbors, and they often resent teachers' attempts to make them do so.

Educators have used discussions about the advantages of using standard English on the job to increase students' understanding of the economic importance and value of speaking standard English. Role-playing job interviews in which students speak standard and nonstandard English and the class is asked to judge which applicant would be hired have also been tried. Exposing students to the speech of celebrities from their background who speak standard English, and inviting successful non-European business persons who speak standard English to deliver the message that Black English does not open many doors in our society have all been used in this endeavor. An African American female teacher has described how she used herself as a model for her Black English dialect speakers. Her rationale for doing so follows.

*As the students' teacher, I assumed the students perceived me to be competent with status and having control over the learning resources. As a Black person, I assumed these Black students would view me as being similar and would identify with me. As a seemingly successful person, I assumed the students would view my success, in part, the result of my being able to speak standard English. (63, p. 106)*

Changing the attitude of all of the students in a class so that they are no longer resistant to and support a bidialectal approach and then having students engage in cooperative learning activities designed to improve their bidialectal skills can be effective (54). Another technique is to expose students to the example of people who changed their way of speaking and profited from the change. Reading *Pygmalion* or *My Fair Lady*, or watching the movies made from these plays and discussing the lessons they teach, illustrate this approach.

Some individuals believe that exposing students to public criticism by correcting their dialects in front of others and teaching standard English are too confronting to students and create unnecessary resistance. They believe less confrontational methods such as reading literature in standard English aloud to students and including works by non–European American writers are more effective means for increasing students' understanding of and ability to use standard English.

Despite the fact that many teachers are currently trying to make students bidialectal, research suggests that attempts to teach nonstandard English speakers to speak standard English have backfired.

*The teaching of standard English to all learners is an implicitly and explicitly stated goal of the American school. Yet the national performance of the American school in teaching standard English to nonstandard speakers is dismal. On almost every reported measure at the national or state level, children from non-*

*standard English speaking communities achieve lower competency levels in the language of education than children who come from standard English speaking communities. The result has been an overplacement of nonstandard English speaking children in special education classes, speech-language pathology clinical services, and compensatory education classes, and an underplacement of these children in classes for talented and gifted students.... In addition this failure has contributed to diminished student self-esteem, lowered teacher expectations, and discipline problems. (29, p. 156)*

In addition, the limited research available leaves a number of urgent questions unanswered.

- Is there any value to teaching students to speak standard English besides avoiding discrimination in the community?
- Does encouraging students to speak standard English also encourage the community to continue to discriminate against nonstandard English speakers?
- Should school officials or the students themselves decide whether they should become bidialectal?
- Can all students learn a second dialect through the approaches offered in school?
- What student characteristics foster or impede second dialect learning?
- Which are the most effective approaches to second dialect teaching?
- Which techniques work best with which students?
- What negative side effects accompany schools' attempts to make students bidialectal?
- What are the best ways to avoid these unwanted effects?

*Appreciation*

Many educators reject the bidialectal approach. They believe that as long as students can understand spoken and written standard English, they should be allowed or even encouraged to express themselves in their own dialects in any and all situations (17, 53). The appreciation approach has been described as follows:

*Teachers who employ this approach accept the fact of linguistic equality of the two dialects (standard and Black) and believe that the Black dialect is a competent form of communication. There are no drills to bring out contrasts or comparison between Black and standard English. Teachers, instead, look for additional techniques to bring out the verbal facility that is already present—not merely the potential of verbal ability.... This requires special consideration in the language arts—allowing students to use their own dialects or accents without correction in reading, by the teachers dictating oral spelling tests in both dialects if found helpful ... by accepting Black dialect grammar in written composition, etc. (17, p. 305)*

Proponents of the appreciation approach to dialect differences offer the following reasons for their position.

**1.** *Efforts to teach students to speak standard English do not work.* There is considerable evidence that although highly motivated individuals can learn standard English if they are given intensive instruction and interact on a frequent basis with standard English speakers, the way students are taught to speak standard English in school does not produce an increase in the frequency or correctness of students use of standard English in the classroom, much less outside of school (16, 20, 25; also discussed earlier). As Labov and Harris state it,

> *Underlying grammatical patterns of standard English are apparently learned through "meaningful" and intensive interaction with those who already use standard English grammar, not simply by exposure in the mass media or in schools. (25, p. 22)*

**2.** *Dialect speakers who are required to speak standard English become less fluent and have difficulty expressing themselves.* The proposition has not been researched very well. However, there is some evidence to support it (29).

**3.** *Teaching students standard English before they are completely fluent in their original dialects stunts their language development.* In the words of Kochman, switching from one dialect to another "does not develop the child's ability to use language beyond what he is already capable of doing.... It is concerned with *how* the child says something rather than *how well* he says it." (24, p. 91)

There is no research regarding this supposition.

**4.** *It is not possible to encourage students to learn a second dialect without also communicating that their way of speaking is less desirable.* As an English teacher put it:

> *No matter how carefully I explained my purpose and assured them that I was not judging their parents, grandparents, race, or culture ... my students still resented my correcting them although most of the time they accepted my corrections in good humor. (28, p. 49)*

**5.** *Acceptance and appreciation of nonstandard dialects by schools and teachers improves students' self-esteem.*

> *Black children must be educated to learn and believe that deviation from the normative pattern of standard English is not an indication that they are abnormal. They must be helped to understand that these negative social and psychological views have resulted and can continue to result in low self-esteem, identity crisis, and self-hatred. An appreciation of Black habits, values, and goals is essential for Black children to develop a positive Black self-identity. The issue of Black English is a "good" place to start. Whites should not become reference points for how Black children are to speak and behave. (53, p. 215)*

**6.** *Teaching standard English to nonstandard dialect speakers is a form of political and cultural subjugation.* Non-standard English-speaking students and their teachers often have different perceptions of the implications of standard English. Teachers tend to view it as a way to learn more effectively and get ahead in the real world; students often view it as talking white, denying their heritage, and giving in to the European American power structure (26, 41). These individuals tend to believe that the solution to dialectal inequality can only be achieved by eliminating the power differential in society.

> *If one culture possesses hegemony over the other, the less-powerful culture generally adopts the language of the more powerful but not without serious consequences for and potential danger to the harmonious relationship between the two groups. For even as the less-powerful speech community is expanding its linguistic repertoire to incorporate the language of the predominant group, simultaneously its loyalty to the mother tongue and native culture is intensified. . . . In the school setting, the linguistic norms and cultural context of white America prevail and the speech norms and cultural identity of the Black community are forced to give sway to those of the more powerful cultural group. (41, pp. 88–89)*

Proponents of appreciation favor activities that instill pride in students about their language and further their language development. High on the list of recommended activities are studying audio and video tapes of well-known nonstandard dialect speakers, reading plays and novels written in nonstandard dialects, and encouraging students to write nonstandard dialect fiction.

## *Writing*

Teaching dialect speakers to write standard English has been the focus of considerable research and discussion. Anecdotal evidence suggests that few people believe that it is unnecessary to teach nonstandard dialect speakers to write standard English. In fact, many educators who favor the appreciation approach to oral language support a bidialectal approach to written language. They believe students should be encouraged to speak any way they prefer, but they should be taught to write in standard English.

Anecdotal evidence suggests that most teachers currently follow this approach. However, research is needed to determine whether this is actually the case.

Some authors have advised teachers to use written English rather than oral English to teach standard English skills because it does not subject students to public scrutiny and it is more effective (26, 51).

> *Writing provides the means through which black students can experience language and develop alternative mechanisms for using it effectively. . . . Unlike speech, the writing process is slow paced and requires deliberate thinking and planning. Extensive revision and editing allows the student to focus on vocabulary, grammar, and syntactical problems as well as those in content and organization. Because there are no gestures or other nonverbal expressions to help communicate ideas, the written language must be shaped and fashioned so that it alone can convey the intended message. (26, p. 168)*

The references at the end of the chapter provide additional information about techniques for teaching standard English writing skills to nonstandard dialect speakers (18, 50, 52, 57, 58, 60, 61). However, research indicates that the instructional techniques used to teach standard English writing skills are no more effective than those used to teach oral skills (18, 54). This is probably because in most schools students do not write enough to learn the necessary skills; writing a few sentences or filling out blank spaces in work books is insufficient.

---

**SELF-QUIZ**

What is your opinion about the following statement? Do you believe that students should be encouraged to speak and/or write in standard English because of the prejudices of society, especially employers? Or do you feel that it is society's obligation to clean up its act?

*Language is personal and private; therefore, offering instruction to "improve" speech indicates criticism not only of the language but also of the person. However, since the "real world" is judgmental and critical, we do students a great disservice by continuing to ignore this serious issue. (65, pp. 22–23)*

---

## Communication Style

Mismatches between students' and teachers' communication styles can impair students' learning in much the same way as mismatches between students' and teachers' language proficiency. They make it difficult for educators to understand what their students are telling them about how the students feel or think, and sometimes they lead to misunderstandings. For example, teachers who are unaware of students' culturally influenced communication styles may mistakenly believe that the students are shy, insecure, disrespectful, and so on, and students who are unfamiliar with their teachers' communication styles may not be able to distinguish when their teachers are serious and when they are joking. Therefore, to communicate effectively with students, educators should be aware of the communication style differences between them and their students. The following are some examples of typical communication style differences. The references at the end of the chapter provide more in-depth information (75–93).

### Formal Versus Informal Communication

Although all cultures have rules that people are expected to follow when they communicate with each other, the expectations of some cultures are much more flexible than others. Some groups expect strict adherence to communication conventions in certain situations—such as when children are addressing parents and other adults or when subordinates are communicating with those who have more status and/or power. Other cultures are much more relaxed and informal about communication codes. Strict codes of communication may be designed to show respect for others, to avoid open demonstrations of conflict and disagreement, or to avoid causing individuals to "lose face."

The communication styles of Hispanic Americans and some Asian and Pacific American groups tend to be much more formal than either the African American or European American communication styles.

> *Because one of the ways in which Hispanics demonstrate their respect for each other is through the maintenance of certain formal conventions like the use of the formal usted rather than the informal tu in conversation, Hispanics may mistake an Anglo's less formal approach to interpersonal relationships as a sign of disrespect. (81, p. 130)*

> *In Asian cultures the communication interaction is very structured and predictable.... The individual's status in the situation will define the role that he or she is expected to play in communication. These roles are usually defined by tradition and are often highly formalized. For communication to proceed smoothly, each participant must behave in the expected manner by using verbal and nonverbal behaviors appropriate to one's role. (88, p. 46)*

### *Emotional Versus Subdued Communication*

When people communicate, are they expected to be considerate of other people's sensibilities—their reactions to what is communicated to them and how it is communicated? Or are the right of individuals to express their feelings, regardless of how it might affect others, considered more paramount? Some cultures protect individuals' rights to express their feelings and require their members to learn to tolerate, accept, and deal with the expression of intense feelings. Cultures that are more concerned with protecting people's sensibilities expect feelings to be communicated in a subdued way. African Americans and European Americans tend to be very different in this regard.

> *Whites want social interaction to operate at an emotionally subdued level. To realize this goal they first establish the rule that expressive behavior shall be subdued, which develops sensibilities capable of tolerating only relatively subdued outputs.... Black cultural norms desire levels of public interaction that are more emotionally intense. Consequently they allow individuals to express themselves at the level at which feelings are felt. (86, p. 117)*

Although students are allowed to protest the decisions of their teachers, they are expected to do so in an acceptable manner. Because of communication style differences, when African American students express their positions passionately, European American teachers who tend to value cool-headed reasoning may perceive these expressions as being beyond the bounds of acceptability (86).

## Direct Versus Indirect Communication

Do people express themselves directly, openly, and frankly, or do they speak indirectly and politely in order to maintain smooth interpersonal relationships? Should teachers be indirect or frank when they have to criticize students' work or behavior?

As the following quotes about Southeast Asian Americans and Filipino Americans indicate, many Asian and Pacific American groups shun European American frankness.

> *American straightforwardness is considered at best impolite if not brutal. In Indochina, one does not come directly to the point. To do so is, for an American, a mark of honesty and forthrightness while a person from Indochina sees it as a lack of intelligence or courtesy. (90, p. 6)*

> *The (Filipino) student will sometimes employ a mediator in communicating with the teacher. While this procedure may appear strange to the Anglo teacher, the child may have had numerous experiences at home with difficult-to-approach adults which have required the services of a mediator. This may be especially true if the teacher is held in high esteem. (82, p. 19)*

If educators use an indirect approach in order to tell students when they want them to do something, will the students who are accustomed to a more direct approach understand that they are actually expected to comply? For example, African American students and students from poor backgrounds who are accustomed to being told directly what they should and should not do may not understand just how serious their teachers are when they are spoken to in an indirect manner (75).

## Poetic and Analogous Communication

Some groups use a more poetic communication style or explain things by means of analogies rather than clear and concise terms and relationships. When teachers and students use different communication styles, there is the real possibility of miscommunication between them. Educators who prefer direct expression may also mistakenly think that some African American and Hispanic American students who use a more poetic and analogous speech pattern are "beating around the bush," that they cannot think straight, or that they have communication problems (81).

## Honesty

Cultures have very different ideas about exactly what is honest communication and even whether honest communication is desirable. No culture expects people to be completely honest. Other issues besides honesty, such as the relative importance placed by the culture on maintaining one's honor or one's face, avoiding disagreement and conflict, avoiding personal responsibility, and so on, influence a group's opinion about how honest communication should be. In fact, in some cultures when people communicate it is more important to maintain smooth interpersonal relationships than to tell the truth. For example,

> *Falsehood carries no moral stricture for a Cambodian, Laotian, or Vietnamese. The essential question is not whether a statement is true or false, but what the intention of the statement is. Does it facilitate interpersonal harmony? Does it indicate a wish to change the subject? Hence, one must learn the "heart" of the speaker through his/her words. (90, pp. 6, 7)*

Even within cultures, subgroups have different attitudes about honest communication. In the European American culture, although some individuals feel that people should take responsibility for, pay the price for, and stand up for one's actions, many politicians believe that it is appropriate to use such techniques as damage control, spin control, and plausible deniability to color the truth and even hide it from the voters.

In some cultures, a promise to do something or to comply with an expectation may not be meant literally. If a refusal would lead to an awkward or uncomfortable interpersonal moment or insult a person, especially someone in a position of authority, a promise may be little more than a way of maintaining smooth interpersonal relationships. Thus, some students do not have the slightest intention of complying with a behavior plan they have agreed to or a contract they have signed.

## *Responses to Guilt and Accusations*

When individuals are accused of doing the wrong thing, how do they express guilt and remorse or proclaim their innocence? European American students tend to express guilt by lowering their eyes and avoiding eye contact. When they are falsely accused, they may issue vigorous denials. Kochman describes the European American reaction in the following way: "If they are innocent, they issue a vigorous and defensive denial—especially if the charge is serious. If they are guilty and are not trying to pretend otherwise, their response is subdued and embarrassed" (86, p. 93).

As was noted earlier, African American students lower their eyes as a sign of respect, not as an admission of guilt, and they do not experience the same need to proclaim their innocence by emotional statements when they are not guilty. Because European Americans and African Americans respond differently when they admit or deny guilt, they can each assume the other has communicated guilt when he or she has not.

Educators who do not know that African American students tend to avoid direct eye contact with authority figures or elders as a sign of respect and submission, may judge their students' behavior by their own standards—which is exemplified by the expression, "Look me in the eye, and tell me the truth." When

African American students avert their eyes while being confronted about their behavior, teachers may misinterpret their lack of eye contact as indicating insincerity and guilt.

> *When whites . . . issue a vigorous and defensive denial—the kind that whites often use when they feel falsely accused—blacks consider this a confirmation of guilt since they believe only the truth would have been able to produce a protest of such intensity. (86, p. 92)*

## Themes Discussed

All cultures have unwritten rules about what should or should not be talked about and with whom. Because teachers and students may have culturally determined different expectations about what students should be willing to discuss with their teachers or their peers, it is important to know what students are and are not comfortable discussing. Here are some examples of themes that some students may be reluctant to discuss with teachers.

### Needs

In some cultures people are so sensitive to others' needs that it is unnecessary for individuals to be open and direct about their needs. Thus, it is important to ask whether individuals from a student's cultural background express their needs openly or expect others to be sensitive to their feelings and problems. This is especially true for Hispanics.

> *Mexican American children seldom ask for help. Their socialization has accustomed them to the expectation that their needs will be noticed and help provided without its having to be asked for. This type of socialization results in children learning to be sensitive to the needs and feelings of others. (91, p. 15)*

> *Educators should be tuned into these subtle expressions of need. They should not assume that because Hispanic students have not expressed a need for help or understanding in a direct and forthright manner, they do not need special attention or consideration. (81, p. 96)*

### Admission of Errors and Mistakes

Do people admit when they are wrong or have made a mistake? Students who have difficulty accepting responsibility for their errors and mistakes or apologizing to others for cultural reasons may be misperceived as defiant or stubborn.

In Spanish-speaking countries, language forms make it easy for people to avoid accepting responsibility for their mistakes. An Hispanic American educator explained it this way:

> *Let's pretend I missed the plane which brought me to this conference. Maybe it was my fault, and maybe not. Perhaps my husband turned off the alarm. Or perhaps my car would not start. But whatever rationalization I use, if I express*

*myself in English it is my fault. The only way I can express what happened in English is to say "I missed the plane." So I think it would be better to express myself in Spanish. That way I don't have to feel guilty about what happened. I simply say, "El avion me dejó."' That means the plane left me.... If I were to drop this glass, some of you would say to yourselves, "She dropped the glass," implying that I'm clumsy. Others of you would say, "se cayo el vaso." Somehow the glass managed to slide out of my hand and break itself. (84, pp. 6–7)*

Should students be required to admit that they made a mistake or to apologize for something they did? Would that make students lose face? Perhaps students should learn to verbally accept both responsibility for and the consequences of their behavior, but some students may be willing to accept the consequences of their behavior whereas they resist admitting their responsibility to others. In such cases, it may be more effective to permit them to avoid having to admit their errors and mistakes.

*Disagreement, Unwillingness, and Inability*
Are people expected to say when they are unwilling or unable to do something? Are they likely to express disagreement? When people say they, too, feel or believe as others do or that they will do something, do they mean it? Or is this just their way of avoiding an unpleasant moment?

> *In the midst of a great cultural emphasis on harmony and respect in Japan one speaker will rarely directly contradict another or even answer a question with a direct "no." Even in situations in which Americans can perceive "nothing personal" to be conveyed by a "no" answer, the Japanese will usually find one of at least 16 different ways of saying "no" without using the literal equivalent. (79, p. 47)*

> *Hispanics often find themselves in difficulty if they disagree with an Anglo's point of view. To them, direct argument or contradiction appears rude and disrespectful. On the surface they seem agreeable, manners dictating that they do not reveal their genuine opinion openly unless they can take time to tactfully differ. (81, p. 131)*

Can teachers count on students to do the things they commit themselves to do? Some students are brought up to believe that not following through on promises and saying something that is not so are acceptable behavior when doing so contributes to interpersonal harmony or helps someone save face. When students do not fulfill a contract, do they think of it as lying or irresponsible behavior? Or do they believe that their behavior is appropriate?

> *An American who is not familiar with the Filipino culture might become annoyed when a Pilipino speaker says he or she will "try to come" and does not appear for the appointment.... The American probably does not know that when the Pilipino speaker says "I'll try" he or she usually means one of the following:*

*1. "I cannot do it, but I do not want to hurt feeling by saying no." 2. "I would like to, but I am not sure you really want me to come. Please insist that I do." 3. "I will probably come, but I will not say yes because something may prevent me from coming. I have no control over what may happen." (77, pp. 32–33)*

Will students be able to ask questions or request help when they do not understand something?

*A Japanese youth.... Will not insult the teacher's efforts by saying, "I don't understand." Will nod politely even while not understanding and attribute the difficulty to his or her own lack of diligence. (75, p. 19)*

### Facts Versus Feelings

Many cultural groups frown on displays and discussions of feelings but expect their members to discuss matters of fact. For this reason, when students have problems it is important to know whether they are as comfortable discussing feelings such as resentment, anger, shame, guilt and the like, as facts.

*In the USA as well as in northern European cultures and many oriental groups, the expression of emotion is limited. Southern European cultures and some Latin American groups seem to permit the incredible in this matter of expressing emotions. (87, p. 4)*

### Sensitive and Controversial Topics

What are the sensitive subjects that people shy away from? Depending on the group, topics such as politics, sex, religion, finances, and so on, may be acceptable or unacceptable topics of conversation.

*East Indian American students would not respond or give opinions about the existence of god because they are afraid of being rude and offensive to anyone (maybe even the teacher) with their opinions. They are taught not to be this way.... On the other hand European American students felt totally comfortable discussing this question.... As a matter of fact, they felt they were being totally honest and straightforward in letting everyone know how they felt about the issue. (93, p. 2)*

How well do individuals have to know each other and what kind of relationship do they have to have in order to be able to discuss sensitive or intimate topics? When and under what circumstances will students be willing to discuss sensitive topics with their teachers? In some cultures people will discuss sensitive issues only with family members and extremely close friends.

### Affection

Do people demonstrate affection easily? Do they do so verbally or physically? Would students welcome or reject their teachers' display of affection? What are the acceptable ways teachers can express their affection for students? Is a pat on the back, an arm on the shoulder, and so on, acceptable, or are displays of affection limited to verbal statements? Although many students welcome physical touching, it is "taboo" behavior in some cultures. For example, the Hispanic American culture encourages more physical displays of affection than the European American culture does.

> *Hispanics tend to show affection and acceptance through touching. Friends are likely to kiss when they meet. Males are likely to hug each other or pat each other on the back as well as shake hands. And it is not unusual for people to hold others by the arm or place their hands on their shoulders when conversing. Therefore, educators should utilize physical contact when expressing approval and acceptance of their Hispanic students, especially the young ones. (81, p. 97)*

## *Group Processes*

How do groups arrive at decisions and resolve disagreements? Do groups have leaders? Do leaders make decisions or lead the group to arrive at their own decisions? Are differences of opinion discussed openly, or are they side-stepped? Would students be comfortable participating in the decision-making process, or would they prefer to have decisions made by their teachers? Would they feel comfortable expressing opinions and feelings that differ from others in the group? Would they be able to participate in discussions of controversial issues or feel comfortable about deciding group issues by a public vote? Students who have been trained to avoid public conflicts and disagreements may be unable to participate in discussions of controversial issues, express opinions that are different from a previous speaker, or even vote on what the group should or should not do.

The following quotes describe ways in which group process as practiced in Asian American and Hispanic American groups can often differ from the typical European American approach.

> *Because being a member of a group is so important, the ability to work harmoniously with a group is highly valued. . . . The goal of group problem solving is to reach consensus, not to compete for acceptance and approval of one's idea or position at the expense of others in the group. Directness and forthrightness are not valued, and people who display these traits are considered to be rude and impolite. (87, p. 47)*

> *When a group of Hispanics disagree they may resolve the issue by continuing to discuss it until it becomes apparent that a consensus has been reached without polling the group or calling for a vote . . .*

> *This is much better than bringing out the differences of opinion among people by requiring them to take a stand—stand up and be counted, show which side you're on, etc. This can increase conflict and often does. (81, pp. 100–101)*

How many people speak at a time? European Americans expect that even in group situations only one person will speak and the others will wait their turn and listen. This is not true of all cultures.

*In Arab countries and in many Latin American ones, conversations are invitations for everybody to join. (87, p. 4)*

*In a heated discussion, blacks frequently make their points whenever they can enter the discussion. Deference is given to the person who considers his or her point most urgent. Turn-taking is the style of whites, who usually raise their hands to be recognized. Teachers find Black students impolite, aggressive, and boisterous when they cut off another student or fail to restrain themselves so that every student can have a turn to talk. (83, p. 29)*

Many European Americans expect groups to function quietly. However, African Americans, Mediterranean Americans, and Hispanic Americans are comfortable with much higher levels of what may seem like noise to European Americans.

## *Conflict Resolution*

Are conflicts faced and dealt with in a straightforward manner or swept under the table? Should teachers bring conflicts between students into the open to resolve them? At home, are youngsters who disagree allowed or encouraged to argue and/or fight it out, or are they required to settle their differences peacefully and shake hands and make up? Is it better to intervene when students have conflicts or permit them to settle their conflicts themselves? Should students be required to shake hands and "make friends"? African American students are brought up to settle their conflicts in a much more open manner than many European American middle-class students and teachers. Teachers' intolerance of their behavior contributes to their being mislabelled behavior disordered.

### *Turn Taking*

The length of time a person must wait to begin to respond or to introduce a new topic after another person has completed a statement varies with different cultures. Students from cultures that require longer pauses may feel left out or blocked out of classroom discussions because others who are used to shorter pauses take the floor before they do (75).

## *Nonverbal Communication*

Nonverbal and verbal communication are different in a number of important respects. Unlike verbal communication, some of the ways people communicate nonverbally are universal. Frowns, smiles, and grimaces, for example, tend to mean the same thing in all groups. Other nonverbal communications—such as

> **SELF-QUIZ: Communication Style**
>
> People are not always comfortable with the way others communicate. For example, some individuals feel uncomfortable when people speak their mind in an emotional or frank manner; others find subdued or indirect expression difficult to understand and overly polite. State your preferences, if you have any, about the following aspects of people's communication styles. Do you feel more comfortable with one than the other? Do you think one is preferable to the other. Would you attempt to change those aspects of students' communication styles that you feel are less desirable or acceptable?
>
> In general, are you more comfortable when students speak their minds in an emotional, passionate, excited, spontaneous manner or in a subdued, calm, controlled manner?
>
> Do you prefer direct, open, and frank communication with students or indirect, polite communication?
>
> Would you rather students communicate their feelings, opinions, values, judgments, and so on, directly, factually, and frankly, or indirectly in order to protect people's face or honor or to maintain smooth interpersonal relationships?
>
> Do you prefer that students express their needs directly and openly or would you rather that they do so indirectly?
>
> Would you rather that students admit their mistakes, accept responsibility for their actions, and apologize when they have wronged someone, or would you be satisfied if they are contrite and sorry without admitting so to others?
>
> When students disagree with others or are unwilling or unable to do something, would you rather that they say so directly or indirectly?
>
> Are you more comfortable with confronting and resolving conflicts directly, or do you prefer to avoid them as much as possible?

how people signal agreement, disagreement, disapproval, come here, and goodbye—are specific to a particular group.

People have much more conscious control over their verbal than their nonverbal communication. As a result, at times individuals who choose to hide their real feelings, attitudes, opinions, and so on, by verbal miscommunication actually communicate their true reactions nonverbally, often without realizing that they are doing so.

When people make decisions about how another person feels or thinks through her or his verbal messages, they usually can tell you what exactly it was that the individual said that led them to the conclusions they reached. When they arrive at such decisions because of an individual's nonverbal communication, however, they are often unaware of the nonverbal messages on which they based their conclusions.

Although dictionaries are available for almost every verbal language, there are no dictionaries of nonverbal communication that people can turn to when they are unsure of what another person is communicating. This is unfortunate, because people's nonverbal communication can be an even more important clue to their thoughts, feelings, and attitudes than their actual words.

Because of the differences between verbal and nonverbal communication, lack of familiarity with an individual's nonverbal communication can lead to many miscommunication problems. The first step in avoiding such miscommunication is to become sensitive to the differences in people's nonverbal styles. Unfortunately, many educators are unaware of the cultural differences in students' nonverbal communication styles. This section provides some examples of these differences and how they influence teacher–student relationships. More detailed discussions of the topic are found in the references.

### *Emotion*

Cultures differ in how people are expected to express their emotions. In some Asian and Pacific cultures, students laugh or giggle when they are embarrassed. Some cultures bring up males and females to express their feelings differently. For example, in some groups only males can express anger: Females never talk sharply or snap at others. When they are angry, they smile, and their voices becomes softer.

Because cultures differ in how they express emotions and feelings, educators cannot always judge what students are feeling by referring to how they themselves behave when they are upset, embarrassed, angry, and so on. To understand their students' feelings, they need to be sensitive to the subtle, and often not so subtle, clues that are obvious to those who are able to recognize them.

### *Defiance*

European Americans typically express anger and defiance by silent stares. African Americans roll their eyes, and many Asian and Pacific Americans force a smile when they are angry. As Johnson explains, among African Americans, especially females,

> *Rolling the eyes is a non-verbal way of expressing impudence and disapproval of the person who is in the authority role and of communicating every negative label that can be applied to the dominant person. . . . Often white teachers (who are in an authority role and who have contact with Black children) will miss the message communicated by Black children when they roll their eyes. (85, pp. 18, 57)*

African American (and Hispanic American) females will also stand with their hand or hands on their hips when they are angry or defiant. Johnson advises that "Most Black people know to 'cool it' when Black women take this stance. The non-verbal message communicated when a Black female takes this stance is: 'I'm really mad, now. You better quit messing with me.'" (85, p. 57).

### *Submissiveness*

How do students express their respect for authority? In some cultures, looking an adult in the eye is a sign of respect and submission. In other cultures, avoiding eye contact communicates the same message. As a result, teachers may misinterpret the nonverbal messages communicated by students from other cultural backgrounds. The ways African American, Asian and Pacific American, Hispanic American, and other non–European American students are taught to show respect and submission typically differ from how European American students are expected to behave. As a result, European Americans often misinterpret the lack of eye contact among their non–European American students. For example,

> *Asians generally tend to use repeated head nodding, avoidance of direct eye contact, and minimal spontaneous verbalization, and to refrain from making critical comments, as a way of showing deference toward an authority figure. (88, p. 49)*

> *Occasional avoidance of eye contact by Oriental children may be classified as submissive behavior . . . such avoidance of eye contact provides others with a distorted image of an Oriental child—as being timid, shy, insecure, suspicious, undependable, and lacking self confidence. (93, p. 69)*

> *Avoidance of eye contact by a Black person communicates "I am in a subordinate role and I respect your authority over me," while the dominant culture member may interpret avoidance of eye contact as "Here is a shifty, unreliable person I'm dealing with." (85, p. 18)*

The way some African American males walk away from a reprimand can also reveal whether they have accepted it or not.

> *If the young Black male walks away in a natural manner then the reprimand was received positively; if he walks away with a "pimp strut" it means that the young Black male has rejected the reprimand and in fact is non-verbally telling the authority person to "go to hell." (85, p. 19)*

In some cultures a youngster may behave submissively, but grumble about the fact that they have to comply; in other cultures grumbling would be a sign of severe disrespect (80).

## *Physical Contact*

In comparison to European Americans, non–European American groups are more likely to touch each other in many different situations. Differences between European Americans and Haitian and Hawaiian Americans and their implications are described in the following quotations.

> *Haitian children are very physical . . . we use our hands. . . . If a child wants to speak, instead of saying: "Hi, Johnny," he will touch the other child automatically. (Olga Bzdyk, Director, Head Start Program, Homestead, Florida) (89, p. 62)*

> *Children will often simply lay a friendly hand on an adult they are trying to reach, rather than make a verbal approach. For Western teachers such touching on the part of Hawaiian youngsters can cause discomfort and is often not under-*

*stood, leaving the teacher with a vague sensation of being pawed at or hung on, and the child with a feeling of having been ignored.*

*One part of the body not commonly touched by Hawaiians is the head, which is considered tabu throughout Polynesia.... By contrast, one of the few touching gestures which is natural and comfortable for Westerners is a friendly pat on the head or tousling a youngster's hair.... Although not on a conscious level, Hawaiians react quite negatively to such behavior, with emotions ranging from a vague feeling of discomfort to resentment and anger and a feeling of physical violation. (76, p. 2)*

### Agreement and Disagreement

How do people communicate yes and no, agreement and disagreement, willingness and unwillingness, and so on?

*There is a marked tendency on the part of Westerners to feel that the meaning of head-nods are universal, up-and-down to mean "yes" and side-to-side to mean "no." ... Hawaiians raise their eyebrows to say "yes", sometimes simultaneously jerking the head back slightly and lowering the corners of the mouth. (76, p. 4)*

### Beckoning

European Americans call others with their finger or upturned palms. In some cultures this is a sign of disrespect or is used only for dogs. For example, among Hawaiian Americans,

*In beckoning someone, the finger is never used nor the upright hand. Both these gestures to the Hawaiians are extremely abrupt and rude. People are called to come by placing the hand sideways, palm facing the center of the body, and beckoning with the hand in that position. (76, p. 4)*

A similar problem can occur with Filipino American students.

*The familiar "come here" gesture made by curling the forefinger in an upward manner becomes a frightening "you have done something wrong" signal to the Pilipino child. Pilipinos, as well as some other Asian groups, use a palm down sign to indicate "come here," which is often confused with the Anglo gesture "go back." (82, p. 19)*

## Summary

Students speak many different languages and dialects and use different communication styles. Linguistically appropriate education services for LEP students should include bilingual education, ESL, or sheltered English approaches. Unfortunately, a great many LEP students are placed in English submersion programs. Although students who speak nonstandard dialects can learn to read and write standard English without learning to speak standard English, many educators insist on teaching standard speech to them. Educators who understand their students' communication styles can communicate effectively with them.

## *Activities*

1. Observe and listen to your peers in class. Do you notice any of the dialect and communication style differences described in this chapter? How sensitive are you to these differences?

2. Interview some nonstandard English dialect speakers about their experiences in school. Did/do their dialects interfere with their learning? How did/do their teachers and/or professors react to their dialects?

3. Ask some of your friends or fellow students from different ethnic and socioeconomic backgrounds to describe their communication styles in terms of the characteristics included in this chapter. To what extent do their communication styles conform to the stereotypes reported earlier? Ask them to rate their acculturation to the European American middle-class mainstream culture. Is there a relationship between their type and level of acculturation and their communication style preferences?

## *References*

This reference discusses the large number of limited English proficient students in the United States.

1. Woodrow, K. A. (1988). *Measuring Net Immigration to the United States: The Emigrant Population and Recent Emigration Flows.* Paper presented at the annual meeting of the Population Association of American, New Orleans.

The following references deal with the legal definition of linguistically appropriate education for LEP students.

2. Bilingual Education Act of 1968.
3. Lau *v.* Nichols (1974). 414 U.S. 563.

Bilingual education approaches are the focus of the following references.

4. Crawford, W. (1991). *Bilingual Education: History, Politics, Theory, and Practice.* Trenton, NJ: Crane.

5. Cummins, J. (1984). *Bilingualism and Special Education: Issues in Assessment and Pedagogy.* San Diego, CA: College Hill Press.
6. Cummins, J. (1989). *Empowering Minority Students.* Sacramento, CA: California Association for Bilingual Education.
7. Olsen, L. (1988). *Crossing the Schoolhouse Border: Immigrant Students and the California Public Schools.* San Francisco: California Tomorrow.
8. Willig, A. (1985). A meta-analysis of selected studies on the effectiveness of bilingual education. *Review of Educational Research, 55,* 269–317.

References that discuss sheltered English approaches and their effectiveness are listed next.

9. Chamot, A. U., & O'Malley, J. M. (1986). *A Cognitive Academic Language Learning Approach: An ESL Content-Based Curriculum.* Rosslyn, VA: National Clearinghouse for Bilingual Education.

10. Crandall, J. (Ed.). (1987). ESL *Through Content Area Instruction: Mathematics, Science, Social Studies*. Englewood Cliffs, NJ: Prentice Hall.
11. Gersten, R., & Woodward, J. (1985). A case for structured immersion. *Educational Leadership, 43*(1), 75–79.
12. Northcutt, M., & Watson, D. (1986). *Sheltered English Teaching Handbook*. San Marcos, CA: AM Graphics & Printing.

Legal requirements regarding nonstandard English dialects is the focus of the following references.

13. Equal Educational Opportunities Act of 1972.
14. Martin Luther King Junior Elementary School Children *v.* Ann Arbor School District Board of Education, 451 F. Supplement 1324 (Michigan 1978); 463 F. Supplement 1027 (Michigan 1978); No. 7–71861, Slip Op. (Michigan, July 12, 1979).

Various approaches to dialect differences are the focus of the following references.

15. Adler, S. (1987). Bidialectalism: Mandatory or elective? *Asha, 29*(1), 41–44.
16. Ash, S., & Myhill, J. (1983). *Linguistic Correlates of Interethnic Conflict*. Philadelphia: University of Pennsylvania, Linguistics Laboratory.
17. Dean, M. B., & Fowler, E. D. (1974). An argument for appreciation of dialect differences in the classroom. *Journal of Negro Education, 43*(3), 302–309.
18. Farr, M. (1986). Language, culture, and writing: Sociolinguistic foundations of research on writing. In E. Z. Rothkopf (Ed.), *Review of Research on Education*, No. 13, 195–223.
19. Ferguson, A. M. (1982). A case for teaching standard English to Black students. *English Journal, 71*(3), 38–40.
20. Graff, D., Labov, W., & Harris, W. (1983). *Testing Listeners' Reactions to Phonological Markers of Ethnic Identity: A New Method for Sociolinguistic Research*. Paper presented at the annual meeting of the New Ways of Analyzing Variations in English, Montreal.
21. Groff, P. (1980). Black English and the teaching of spelling. In J. Schwartz (Ed.), *Teaching the Linguistically Diverse*. New York: New York State English Council.
22. Harris-Wright, K. (1987). The challenge of educational coalescence: Teaching nonmainstream English-speaking students. *Journal of Childhood Communication Disorders, 11*(1), 209–215.
23. Hochel, S. S. (1983). *A Position Paper on Teaching the Acquisition of the Mainstream Dialect in Kindergarten and Elementary School*. ERIC ED 238–060.
24. Kochman, T. (1969). Culture and communication: Implications for Black English in the classroom. *Florida Foreign Language Reporter*, Spring/Summer, 89–92, 172–174.
25. Labov, W., & Harris, W. (1983). *De facto Segregation of Black and White Vernacular*. Paper presented at the annual meeting of the New Ways of Analyzing Variations in English, Montreal.
26. Lipscomb, D. (1978). Perspectives on dialects in Black students' writing. *Curriculum Review, 17*(3), 167–169.
27. Padak, N. D. (1981). The language and educational needs of children who speak Black English. *Reading Teacher, 35*(2), 144–151.
28. Simmons, E. A. (1991). Ain't we never gonna study no grammar? *English Journal, 80*(8), 48–51.
29. Taylor, O. L. (1986). A cultural and communicative approach to teaching standard English as a second dialect. In O. L. Taylor (Ed.), *Treatment of Communication Disorders in Culturally and Linguistically Diverse Populations*. San Diego, CA: College Hill Press.
30. Thomas, E. W. (1978). English as a second language—For whom? *The Crisis, 85*(9), 318–320.
31. Wolfram, W., Detwyler, J., & Adger, C. T. (1992). *All About Dialects: Instructors Manual*. Washington, DC: Center for Applied Linguistics.
32. Wood, B. S., & Curry, J. (1969). Everyday talk and school talk of the city Black child. *Speech Teacher, 18*(4), 282–296.

The following references shed light on the relationship between nonstandard dialects and reading.

33. Anastasiow, N. J., Levine-Hanes, M., & Hanes, M. L. (1982). *Language & Reading Strategies for Poverty Children*. Baltimore: University Park Press.
34. Barth, J. L. (1979). Nonstandard English and native students: When is a difference a disability? *British Columbia Journal of Special Education, 3*(4), 357–363.

35. Bougere, M. B. (1981). Dialect and reading disabilities. *Journal of Research and Development in Education, 14*(4), 67–73.
36. Collins, J. (1988). Language and class in minority education. *Anthropology and Education Quarterly, 19*(4), 299–326.
37. Dandy, E. B. (1988). *Dialect Differences: Do They Interfere?* ERIC ED 294–240.
38. Gibson, E., & Levin, H. (1975). *The Psychology of Reading*. Cambridge, MA: MIT Press.
39. Lass, B. (1980). Improving reading skills: The relationship between the oral language of Black English speakers and their reading achievement. *Urban Education, 14*(4), 437–447.
40. Levine-Hanes, M., & Hanes, M. L. (1979). *Developmental Differences in Dialect, Function Word Acquisition and Reading*. Paper presented at the annual meeting of the International Reading Association, Atlanta.
41. McGinnis, J., & Smitherman, G. (1978). Sociolinguistic conflict in the schools. *Journal of Non-White Concerns in Personnel and Guidance, 6*(2), 87–95.
42. Pflaum, S. W. (1978). Minority student language and reading acquisition. In S. E. Pflaum-Connor (Ed.), *Aspects of Reading Education*. Berkeley, CA: McCutchan.
43. Simons, H. (n.d.). *Black Dialect Interference and Classroom Interaction*. Berkeley, CA: School of Education, University of California.
44. Sims, R. (1976). What we know about dialects and reading. In P. D. Allen & D. J. Watson (Eds.), *Findings of Research in Miscue Analysis: Classroom Implications*. Urbana, IL: National Council of Teachers of English.
45. Strand, C. M. (1979). *Bidialectalism and Learning to Read*. Unpublished doctoral dissertation. Ann Arbor: University of Michigan.
46. Washington, V. M., & Miller-Jones, D. (1989). Teacher interaction with nonstandard English speakers during reading instruction. *Contemporary Educational Psychology, 14*(3), 280–312.

Techniques for helping students acquire bidialectal skills are described in the following references.

47. Adler, S. (1979). *Poverty Children and Their Language*. New York: Grune & Stratton.
48. Anderson, E. (1989). *Students' Language Rights*. ERIC ED 311–959.
49. British Columbia Department of Education. (1981). *English as a Second Language/Dialect Resource Book for K-12*. Victoria BC: Author.
50. Brooks, C. (Ed.). (1985). *Tapping Potential: English Language Arts for the Black Learner*. Urbana, IL: National Council of Teachers of English.
51. Christian, D. (1987). *Vernacular Dialects in U.S. Schools*. ERIC Digest. ERIC ED 289–364.
52. Cronnell, B., (Ed.). (1981). *The Writing Needs of Linguistically Different Students. Proceedings of a Research Practice Conference Held at the Southwest Regional Laboratory for Educational Research and Development*. ERIC ED 210–932.
53. Davis, B. G., & Armstrong, H. (1981). The impact of teaching Black English on self-image and achievement. *Western Journal of Black Studies, 5*(3), 208–218.
54. Eubanks, I. M. (1991). Nonstandard dialect speakers and collaborative learning. *Writing Instructor, 10*(3), 143–148.
55. Farr, M., & Daniels, H. (1986). *Language Diversity and Writing Instruction*. New York: ERIC Clearinghouse on Urban Education, Institute for Urban and Minority Education.
56. Kizza, I. (1991). *Black or Standard English: An African American Student's False Dilemma*. ERIC ED 342–008.
57. Koenig, L. A., & Biel, C. D. (1989). A delivery system of comprehensive language services in a school district. *Language, Speech, and Hearing Services in Schools, 20*(4), 338–365.
58. Larson, D. A. (1989). "Snow White" and Language Awareness. *Journal of Teaching Writing, 6*(1), 171–179.
59. Love, T. A. (1991). *A Guide for Teaching Standard English to Black Dialect Speakers*. ERIC ED 340–248.
60. Morris, R. W., & Louis, C. N. (1983). *"A Writing of Our Own." Improving the Functional Writing of Urban Secondary Students*. Final Report. ERIC ED 241–668.
61. Nembhard, J. P. (1983). A Perspective on teaching Black dialect speaking students to write standard English. *Journal of Negro Education, 52*(1), 75–82.
62. Penfield, J. (1982). *Chicano English: Implications for Assessment and Literary Development*. ERIC ED 255–050.
63. Reed, D. F. (1983). Helping Black high school students speak standard English. *English Journal, 72*(2), 105–108.
64. Reynoso, W. D. (1984). *Standard English Acquisition*. ERIC ED 246–693.
65. Robbins, J. F. (1988). Employers' language expectations and nonstandard dialect speakers. *English Journal, 77*(6), 22–24.

66. Schierloh, J. M. (1991). Teaching standard English usage: A dialect-based approach. *Adult Learning, 2*(5), 20–22.
67. Shipley, K. G., Stone, T. A., & Sue, M. B. (1983). *Test for Examining Expressive Morphology*. Tucson, AZ: Communication Skill Builders.
68. Taylor, H. (1991). Ambivalence toward Black English: Some tentative solutions. *Writing Instructor, 10*(3), 121–135.

The following references provide descriptions of differences between standard English and some nonstandard dialects.

69. Owens, R. E. (1988). *Language Development*. Columbus, OH: Merrill.
70. Hemingway, B. L., Montague J. C. Jr., & Bradley, R. H. (1981). Preliminary data on revision of a sentence repetition test for language screening with Black first grade children. *Language, Speech, and Hearing Services in Schools, 12*, 145–152.
71. Labov, W. (1972). *Language in the Inner City: Studies in Black English Vernacular*. Philadelphia: University of Pennsylvania Press.
72. Labov, W. (1974). *The Study of Nonstandard English*. Urbana, IL: National Council of Teachers of English.
73. Wolfram, W. A., & Christian, D. (1975). *Sociolinguistic Variables in Appalachian Dialects*. Arlington, VA: Center for Applied Linguistics.
74. Wolfram, W. A., & Fasold, R. W. (1974). *The Study of Social Dialects in American English*. Englewood Cliffs, NJ: Prentice Hall.

These references describe differences in verbal and nonverbal communication styles.

75. Wolfram, W., & Adger, C. T. (1993). *Language Differences Across Dialects*. Baltimore: Baltimore City Public Schools.
76. Anthony, A. P. (n.d.). *Hawaiian Nonverbal Communication: Two Classroom Applications*. Honolulu: University of Hawaii at Manoa, Department of Indo-Pacific Languages.
77. Boseker, B. J., & Gordon, S. L. (1983). What Native Americans have taught us as teacher educators. *Journal of American Indian Studies, 22*(3), 20–24.
78. California State Department of Education. (1986). *Handbook for Teaching Pilipino-Speaking Students*. Sacramento: Author.
79. California State Department of Education. (1987). *Handbook for Teaching Japanese-Speaking Students*. Sacramento: Author.
80. Goodwin, M. H. (1990). *He-Said-She-Said: Talk as Social Organization Among Black Children*. Bloomington, IN: Indiana University Press.
81. Grossman, H. (1984). *Educating Hispanic Students: Cultural Implications for Instruction, Classroom Management, Counseling, and Assessment*. Springfield, IL: Charles C Thomas.
82. Howells, G. N., & Sarabia, I. B. (1978). Education and the Pilipino Child. *Integrated Education, 16*(2), 17–20.
83. Irvine, J. J. (1991). *Black Students and School Failure: Policies, Practices, and Prescriptions*. New York: Praeger.
84. Jaramillo, M. L. (1973). *Cautions When Working with the Culturally Different Child*. ERIC ED 115–622.
85. Johnson, K. R. (1971). Black kinetics: Some nonverbal communication patterns in the Black culture. *Florida Reporter*, Spring/Fall, 17–20, 57.
86. Kochman, T. (1981). *Black and White Styles in Conflict*. Chicago: University of Chicago Press.
87. Leggio, P. (n.d.). *Contrastive Patterns in Nonverbal Communication Among Different Cultures*. Trenton: Office of Equal Opportunity, New Jersey State Department of Education.
88. Matsuda, M. (1989). Working with Asian parents: Some communication strategies. *Topics in Language Disorders, 9*(3), 45–53.
89. National Coalition of Advocates for Students. (1988). *New Voices: Immigrant Students in U.S. Public Schools*. Boston: Author.
90. Nguyen, L. D. (1986). Indochinese cross-cultural adjustment and communication. In M. Dao & H. Grossman (Eds.), *Identifying, Instructing and Rehabilitating Southeast Asian Students with Special Needs and Counseling Their Parents*. ERIC ED 273–068.
91. Rodriguez, J. (n.d.). *An In-Service Rationale for Educators Working with Mexican American Students*. Stanford, CA: Chicano Fellow, Stanford University.
92. Sra, D. (1992). *A Comparison of East Indian American and European American Students*. San Jose, CA: Unpublished manuscript, San Jose State University, Division of Special Education.
93. Yao, E. L. (1979). Implications of biculturalism for the learning process of middle-class Asian children in the United States. *Journal of Education, 16*(4), 61–72.

# Chapter 5

# Causes of Gender Disparities

As was noted in Chapter 1, males and females have very different experiences in school. Depending on their ethnic and socioeconomic background, they choose different courses, participate in different extracurricular activities, aspire to different careers and occupations, and earn different scores on standardized achievement tests. Male students tend to score higher than females in the upper ranges of tests of advanced mathematics skills, but they do not perform as well as females in language arts and basic computational skills.

Depending on their ethnic background, girls tend to be less self-confident than boys in situations that are in the "male domain" (such as mathematics and physics courses), in competitive situations, and when they lack objective information about how well they have done or can do. They react less positively than boys to difficult and challenging situations; they are less likely to take risks and perform less adequately than boys following failure or the threat of failure; they are more likely to attribute their poor performance to lack of ability rather than lack of effort or motivation; and they tend to seek the assistance and approval of adults more than boys do. Males are more likely to get into trouble for behavior problems, to be disciplined by their teachers, and to be suspended from school.

This chapter examines the causes of gender differences in students' academic achievement, school participation, and behavior. Chapter 8 discusses techniques educators can employ to solve these problems.

## *Biological Predispositions*

Many people believe that biology is a major cause of the gender differences observed in school. Physiological factors that are thought to contribute to these differences include dissimilarities in females' and males' hormonal systems and the lateralization and specialization of their right and left brains.

### *Hormonal Differences*

Some researchers have proposed that the higher levels of male hormones such as testosterone make males more active, assertive, and aggressive (1, 4–6, 11–13, 16,

21). They suggest that teachers are intolerant of the male behavior patterns these hormonal differences create and overreact to their students' behavior.

It is true that males exhibit more behavior problems and get into more trouble in school than females (22–26). There also is evidence that teachers, especially females, tend to be less tolerant of male behavior patterns (27–29), and use more punitive management techniques with males (30, 31). However, these facts do not answer the question of whether teachers should be more tolerant of male behavior patterns or whether males' aggressive, assertive, and active behavior is caused by hormonal rather than cultural differences.

Research indicates that males and females do have different levels of testosterone and that this does affect their levels of activity and aggression and their emotional reactions (1, 4–6, 11–13, 16). It is not clear, however, whether the higher levels of testosterone observed in males *cause* them to behave more assertively and aggressively than females or merely *predispose* them to do so when environmental conditions encourage them to behave in these ways.

## *Lateralization and Specialization*

A number of researchers believe that male-female differences in verbal achievement are largely due to differences in the age at which and the extent to which their brain's right and left hemispheres become specialized in mathematical and verbal functioning (3, 11). Although there are many different theories about exactly how cerebral specialization may cause gender differences, one that is more widely accepted than others is based on the fact that hemispheric specialization in certain functions such as verbal, visual-spatial, and mathematical reasoning occurs earlier in females than in males. This theory proposes that early development of females' brains and their greater hemispheric specialization provides them with a head start that improves their verbal functioning.

Research results regarding gender differences in hemispheric specialization are not entirely consistent. On balance, considerable evidence of differences in cerebral lateralization between males and females exists (3, 7–10, 14, 15, 17–20). Researchers have found that hemispheric specialization in females begins earlier, perhaps as early as three months of age, and develops to a greater degree. However, research has not yet established a direct causal relationship between these physiological differences and the ages at which the genders acquire initial language skills or their scores on tests on verbal skills (3). More research is needed before we can consider the biological explanation for this gender disparity to be proven.

## *Predisposition Versus Determinism*

Educators disagree about the extent to which hormonal and lateralization/specialization differences make gender disparities inevitable. Some think that they cause definite gender differences in behavior and learning; many others view them not as a complete determiner of how individuals behave, but as one of several interacting influences. In this view, aptly expressed by Maccoby and Jacklin in 1974, behavior differences that have a biological base can still be modified by environmental events.

> *We suggest that societies have the option of minimizing, rather than maximizing, sex differences through their socialization practices. A society could, for example, devote its energies more toward moderating male aggression than toward preparing women to submit to male aggression, or toward encouraging rather than discouraging male nurturance activities. In our view, social institutions and social practices are not merely reflections of the biologically inevitable. A variety of social institutions are viable within the framework set by biology. It is up to human beings to select those that foster the life styles they most value. (11, p. 374)*

Although research since 1974 has provided considerable information about the possible biological bases of gender differences, we still are relatively ignorant about which gender differences have a biological component. In addition, very little research has been conducted to determine the extent to which biological factors cause versus merely predispose males and females to function differently, whether some biological predispositions are more resistant to change than others, and the psychological costs, if any, people pay when they behave in ways that contradict their biological predispositions.

## *Conclusions*

The possibility that male-female differences in hormonal levels and brain specialization and lateralization contribute significantly to differences in their academic success and behavior is basically unsubstantiated. It is also possible that as society and the education it provides students become less sexist, male-female differences in students' attitudes, behavior, academic achievement, and so on, will decrease, and as we learn more about non–European American and non-middle-class students we will find that many of the male-female differences observed among European American middle-class students do not apply to other ethnic groups and socioeconomic classes. As a result, the need to question whether biological factors contribute to gender differences will diminish.

We do not know whether some physiological predispositions are more resistant to change than others, nor do we know the psychological costs, if any, people pay when they behave in ways that contradict their physiological predispositions. Therefore, when educators react to students' gender-specific behaviors that may have a physiological component, they have little to guide them regarding either the extent to which such behavior can be changed or the possible costs involved in attempting to eliminate the behavior completely rather than modify it.

## Differential Reinforcement

Everyday life experiences confirm that males and females learn gender-stereotypic roles in part because they tend to be rewarded for behaving differently (playing with different toys, communicating in different styles, settling arguments differently, enrolling in different courses, participating in different sports, and so on) and negatively reinforced for behaving similarly (boys crying about bruises and scrapes, girls playing in an active, boisterous manner, and the like). In addition, considerable research evidence supports this explanation. Although different ethnic and socioeconomic groups may not all share the same ideas about the sex roles children should learn, parents tend to reward their children for behaving in ways that they feel are gender-appropriate and punish them for behaving in ways that they feel are gender-inappropriate (11, 32–35). Teachers also use rewards and punishments to modify their students' behavior, although they differ about the kinds of behavior they want students to exhibit.

Children, even toddlers and preschoolers, also reinforce each other for behaving in gender-stereotypical fashion (36–39). Children in general and males in particular reward each other for playing with the right toys, in the right way, and with the right sex, and for relating to each of the sexes in acceptable ways.

Differential reinforcement affects students' behavior, but only to a limited degree. Students' parents, teachers, and peers cannot decide for them what they will think and how they will behave.

## Constructivism: Cognitive Awareness and Modeling

Children voluntarily adopt some gender-stereotypical ways of behaving without having to be rewarded (11, 40–47). They become aware of and identify with their gender, and then copy behavior they believe is gender-appropriate. In fact, as their conceptual abilities develop, they construct increasingly more elaborate schemes of gender-appropriate behavior and proceed to match their behavior to their constructs.

Maccoby and Jacklin describe the process in the following way:

*A child gradually develops concepts of "masculinity" and "femininity," and when he has understood what his own sex is, he attempts to match his behavior to his conceptions. His ideas may be drawn only very minimally from observing his own parents. The generalizations he constructs do not represent acts of imitation, but are organizations of information distilled from a wide variety of sources. (11, pp. 365–366)*

There is ample evidence that adults, including parents, model gender-specific behavior and communicate gender-specific expectations to children and youth, which children tend to copy (16, 40–58). Considerable evidence also suggests that children as young as two and three years of age develop constructs of appropriate male and female behavior and tend to bring their behavior into line with these constructs (37, 40).

## *Structured Reproduction*

As was noted in the previous chapter, reproduction theorists claim that schools purposely perpetuate the values, ideas, and attitudes European American middle- and upper-class males have set up throughout society to maintain their economic and social power and position. That is, they believe that those who exercise control and power in our society—middle and upper-class European American males—structure its institutions, including schools, to maintain their special positions by reproducing the inequality that serves their interests (59–65). According to these theorists, schools provide females and others with the kinds of educational experiences that maintain them as a source of cheap, though well-prepared, labor while more affluent male students are trained to be the leaders of society. At the same time, schools teach females and others to accept the status quo—their economic and social inferiority.

## *Resistance, Production, and Transformation*

Although students are exposed to gender and class biases in school and society at large, they are also exposed to ideas and experiences that contradict these biases (66–75). Nonsexist ideas have become more frequent in the media and in the materials students read in school. Many teachers and parents do not adhere to society's stereotypic gender, ethnic, and socioeconomic expectations for children and adolescents. Since they are given conflicting messages, students accept some and resist others.

Some students accept most of the stereotypic messages they receive. Many others do not. They understand that schools are structured to maintain gender inequality, and they know that even if they do well in school, a society stratified along gender lines will not afford them the same benefits that males, especially European American upper-class males, receive from succeeding in school. Therefore, instead of acquiescing to the educational system for payoffs they do not believe will be forthcoming, they strive to maintain their own sense of identity.

As was noted in Chapter 3, some students accommodate more than they resist; others actively resist the biased education they receive and the inferior position it threatens to place them in. Some defy schools' gender and socioeconomic biases in nonconstructive ways (67, 68, 72–75). Other students battle the same forces in constructive ways. They reject the biased ideas to which they are exposed. Instead, they gain a sense of self-identity and a better understanding of their gender and class, and begin to contribute to transforming society (63, 69–71).

## Conclusions

Biology, differential reinforcement, modeling, cognitive awareness, and structured reproduction all interact in undetermined ways to lead a given individual to behave in a particular way in a specific situation. These factors can contribute to gender differences; however, they do not make male and female students behave differently. Physiological factors only predispose or incline the genders to act in dissimilar ways. Students can modify and channel their biological predispositions. Differential reinforcement, cognitive awareness and modeling, and educational structures reproduce gender stereotypes, but they can also produce students with new perspectives on gender issues.

## The School's Role

This section examines the school's role in the creation and maintenance of gender differences in students' achievement and participation in school.

### Administrative Imbalance

Although females comprise the majority of classroom teachers, they are grossly underrepresented in administrative positions (76–79). In 1990 eighty-three percent of the nation's school principals and superintendents were male and the majority of these, 75%, were European American males (79). Thus, the current situation, especially in elementary schools, is no different than the situation described by Frazier and Sadker in 1973: "Elementary school is a woman's world, but a male captain heads the ship" (77, p. 96).

What message does this situation communicate to students? Many authors believe that it teaches them that males, especially European American males, are and should be the authorities (76–79).

### Curriculum Materials

Although curriculum materials such as textbooks, readers, and biographies that students currently use are not as sexist as the materials used in classes in the 1960s and 1970s, they continue to introduce society's gender biases into the school's structure (80–91). The disparity in the number of pictures of males and females has been reduced. The stereotypic portrayal of females as nurses and secretaries has been largely eliminated, and working females are engaged in many more occupations. The preponderance of male characters in basal readers has been reduced by eliminating male characters from many stories and replacing them with nonhuman characters such as talking trees or animals without sex roles.

However, many problems still exist. For example, authors and publishers still use male pronouns to describe individuals whose gender is unknown and man for all people. The use of nonhuman characters in basal readers avoids the appearance of sexism, but it does not increase the number of female characters or stories about females. In fact, stories about males still greatly outnumber stories about females in students' readers in the higher grades and in the biographies found in school libraries. In most of the material students read, fathers still work and mothers still stay home. At home, mothers do domestic chores such as taking care of children and cooking; fathers build and repair things. When parents work outside the home, they are still described as involved in gender-stereotypic jobs, but to a lesser degree. Males are depicted as engaged in three times as many different occupations as females, and fathers are the executives, professionals, scientists, firefighters, and police officers. Males participate in a variety of different athletic activities; females are involved primarily in sports that have traditionally been considered female sports.

Females are described as overemotional, dependent, concerned about their appearance, and watching others do things. Males are depicted as actively involved in solving problems and doing adventurous things. Females are still portrayed as receiving help and males as helping them.

In math books, boys learn to count by driving cars, flying planes, and engineering trains, but girls learn to count by jumping rope, measuring cloth, and following cooking recipes. Males are still the scientists in science materials. Although the number of pictures of males and females is about equal in history textbooks, only 5% of their text deals with female experiences, and when females' roles in history are included in the 5% of the text devoted to female experiences, women whose contributions fulfill the more acceptable traditional female role are described almost to the exclusion of feminists or those who were involved in feminist issues.

Computer software is also biased against females. As Woodill puts it: "Much of computer software has been designed by males for males, as shown by the predominance of male figures in programs, computer ads, and on the software packaging" (91, p. 55). Although changes have occurred, curriculum materials are in general still quite sexist.

## *Teacher Attention, Feedback, Evaluation, and Expectations*

Teachers tend to create and maintain gender differences in school through the attention and feedback they give students, how they evaluate them, and the expectations they communicate to them. Chapter 3 described the adverse effects of teachers' biased expectations and evaluations. This section focuses on the harm done to students by gender bias in teacher attention and feedback.

Beginning in preschool, boys receive more attention from their teachers (11, 92–109). One reason boys receive more attention is that teachers spend more time disciplining them for misbehavior (103, 109, 124). Much of the difference, however, is due to the fact that teachers demonstrate a clear bias in favor of male participation in their classes. Teachers are more likely to call on males when students volunteer to recite and when they call on nonvolunteers. When students recite, teachers are also more likely to listen to and talk to males. They also use more of their ideas in classroom discussions and respond to them in more helpful ways (105).

The pattern of giving more attention to males is especially clear in science and mathematics classes. Beginning in preschool grades, teachers ask males more questions and give them more individual instruction, acknowledgment, praise, encouragement, corrective feedback, opportunities to answer questions correctly, and social interaction (92, 100–102, 108). In mathematics classes, they wait longer for males to answer questions before calling on someone else. They reward females for performing computational skills and males for higher-level cognitive skills, demonstrate more concern about giving males remedial help, and expect males to be more interested in math and better at solving math problems (137).

Gender differences do not favor males in all subjects. In reading, a course traditionally seen as in the female domain, teachers tend to spend more time instructing and attending to females (102, 107).

How do females interpret their teachers' apparent disinterest in them? No one knows for sure. However, Boudreau's conclusion about the probable interpretation students put on the message teachers give them may be correct: "The idea conveyed to girls is, although subtle, quite clear. What boys do matters more to teachers than what girls do" (94, p. 68).

Teachers also provide males and females different kinds of attention. Again the differential treatment favors males. Teachers give boys more praise and attention for high levels of achievement and correct responses (95–97, 99, 111). In fact, teachers give high-achieving girls the least amount of attention, praise, and supportive feedback and the largest number of disparaging statements compared to low-achieving girls and all boys (86, 111). They praise girls more for neatness, following instructions exactly, and raising their hands. Even when they give the wrong answer, girls are often praised for raising their hands and volunteering (110, 114). Many teachers avoid criticizing girls' responses even when they are wrong (114). This is unfortunate because girls learn better when they receive corrective feedback (112).

There is some evidence that these biases are more characteristic of European American teachers than African Americans (115). This may be one more example of the fact that "Blacks are less gender-typed and more egalitarian than whites" (113, p. 61).

What are teachers telling their female students by relating to them in these ways? Are they communicating that they do not expect their female students to be able to perform well in academic areas? Are they implying that they do not believe the females can respond correctly? Are they saying that they feel females are too fragile to be criticized? Any and all of these explanations are possible in the absence of research data.

How do female students interpret their teachers' behavior? A probable answer is that, with the exception of courses in the "female domain," they are still getting the message that teachers do not expect them to do as well as boys.

Research, which needs updating, suggests that teachers have different academic expectations for females and males (93, 116–122). Although they do not expect males and females to have different achievement levels in school, they view high achievement as a masculine characteristic and low achievement as feminine. They believe that courses such as physics are more appropriate for students with masculine characteristics. In mathematics classes they assign females to lower ability groups than their achievement would warrant. These differences can affect students' self-confidence about their academic ability and their motivation to succeed in school.

As was noted in Chapter 3, the message African American females receive is even more destructive (123–126). Teachers, especially European American teachers, perceive and treat African American females in an even more biased manner than European American females (123, 125, 126). Their teachers seem to be telling them that all they are good for is the stereotypic roles such as housekeepers, maids, child care providers, and so on, that European Americans have historically assigned to African American females.

Gender and ethnic differences in teacher attention, feedback, expectations, and evaluations can have other negative effects on students (127–130). These differences may help to explain why girls are more likely than boys to react poorly to failure or the threat of failure and to attribute their poor performance to lack of ability rather than lack of effort. They may also contribute to females' high anxiety during testing situations, and they may be one reason why European American females think such subjects as mathematics and science are less important to them and enroll in fewer math and science courses.

## *Courses and Activities*

Many teachers believe that some courses belong in the male domain and others in the female domain (134). For example, teachers and counselors tend to reward boys more than girls for learning math. They encourage boys to enroll in math and science-related courses and discourage girls from taking advanced courses such as calculus and physics, and boys from enrolling in such "feminine" courses as languages and home economics. Many teachers and counselors believe that higher education and certain careers and occupations are more appropriate for one sex or another, and vocational education teachers often harass female students enrolled in nontraditional vocational courses (131–133, 136).

Students receive sexist messages about participation in physical education activities. Schools tend to provide different sports experiences for males and females (135–137). Many schools, especially at the middle and high school level, continue to have separate physical education classes for boys and girls. The schedule for female teams' practice is often determined by when males are not using the facilities, and coaches of male teams are paid more than those coaching female teams. Girls are almost routinely excluded from contact sports such as football, rugby, and soccer, and boys are discouraged from participating in girls' activities such as dancing, skipping rope, and using the balance beam. When students persist in pursuing activities reserved for the opposite sex they are often labeled tomboys or sissies.

## Gender Segregation/Separation

Studies done in the late 1970s and middle 1980s revealed that some teachers discouraged male-female interaction. Instead of encouraging mixed-gender groups, some teachers assigned different chores to boys and girls. For example, girls put things in order while boys moved furniture. Teachers separated boys and girls when assigning seats or areas to hang up clothes and when forming study and work groups and committees (134, 138, 139). Lockheed and Harris reported a particularly pernicious management approach:

*In classrooms, assignment to mixed-sex seating adjacencies or groups often is used as a punishment designed to reduce student interaction instead of as a learning technique designed to foster cooperative interaction. (139, p. 276)*

It is unclear how many teachers engaged in these practices in the past and whether teachers continue to do so now. Research is needed to determine if these practices continue and if they are widespread.

## Encouragement of Behavior Differences

Although all teachers want their students to be well-behaved, according to research that was conducted in the 1970s to middle 1980s they appear to have different standards for males and females. Beginning in preschool, teachers tend to encourage gender-stereotypic behavior (94, 140–144). Teachers praise boys more than girls for creative behavior and girls more than boys for conforming behavior. Boys are rewarded for functioning independently, whereas girls are rewarded for being obedient and compliant. Boudreau believes this form of discrimination harms females: "The pattern of reinforcement that young girls receive may lead them to stake their sense of self-worth more on conforming than personal competency" (94, p. 73).

To the extent that these results are still current, teachers who encourage these gender differences can certainly cause problems for girls in situations that require creativity, assertiveness, or independence.

There is also evidence that teachers accept different kinds of inappropriate behavior from males and females without disciplining them for misbehaving. Huffine, Silvern, and Brooks found that kindergarten teachers discipline males and females for different kinds of misbehavior. They report that

*Aggression in boys is acceptable while in girls it is not. The reverse seems to be true of disruptive talking. Teachers expect and/or accept talking from girls, at least much more so than from boys. Thus, the stereotypic behaviors, aggressiveness and loquacity, may be acquired and/or maintained by the differential teacher responses to these behaviors. (142, p. 34)*

## Intolerance of Male Behavior Patterns and Biased Classroom Management Techniques

As was noted previously, educators, especially female educators, tend to be less tolerant of "male-typical" behaviors. African American males are especially likely to suffer the consequences of teachers' intolerance. Many African American males, and females as well, express their emotions much more intensely than most European Americans. When European American teachers observe African American males behaving aggressively and assertively, they tend to assume that the students are much angrier or upset than they actually are. Attributing a level of anger to African American students that would be correct for European American students who behaved in a similar way, teachers become uncomfortable, even anxious, and concerned about what they incorrectly anticipate will happen next. As a result, they intervene when no intervention is necessary. If teachers appreciated the cultural context of African American males' seemingly aggressive behavior toward others and understood that such behavior is unlikely to cause the physical fight or whatever else they expect to occur, they would be less likely to have to intervene to make themselves feel more at ease in the situation. This, in turn, would lessen the likelihood that African American males would get into trouble needlessly.

Teachers tend to reprimand males more often than females and differently as well (29–31, 94, 142). They tend to speak briefly, softly, and privately to girls but publicly and harshly to boys. With younger children they tend to use physical methods like poking, slapping, grabbing, pushing, squeezing, and so on, with boys, and negative comments or disapproving gestures and other forms of nonverbal communication with girls (142). Teachers are more likely to use even harsher disciplinary techniques, such as corporal punishment and suspension, with poor, African American, and Hispanic American males than with middle-class European American males (26, 29, 142, 145–148).

This is unfortunate, because public and harsh reprimands and physical forms of discipline and severe punishments can cause students to react rebelliously to punishments that they feel are too harsh for their "crimes." This may help to explain why males get into trouble in school and why males from poor backgrounds and some non–European American backgrounds tend to get into even more trouble than European American middle-class students (22–26).

## Conclusions

The data just presented clearly indicate that schools play an important role in the formation and maintenance of students' stereotypic views of gender roles. As Meece puts it,

> *Schools have been slow in adapting to recent changes in the social roles of men and women. As a result, schools may be exposing children to masculine and fem-*

*inine images that are even more rigid and more polarized than those currently held in the wider society. Furthermore, the school setting does not seem to provide children with many opportunities to perform behaviors not associated with their gender. Therefore, schools seem to play an important role in reinforcing rigid gender distinctions. (113, p. 67)*

---

**SELF-QUIZ: Critical Incidents**

It is not always easy to apply a set of principles to a real-life situation when some of the principles that apply to a specific situation appear to lead to apparently contradictory solutions to the problem. Describe how you think teachers should handle each of the following critical incidents.

1. After raising her hand repeatedly to volunteer answers to her teacher's questions without being called on, a fifth-grade student complains that her teacher is unfair because the teacher always calls on the boys to answer the difficult questions. The teacher does not believe she is correct.
2. An African American tenth-grade male in a predominantly poor neighborhood school tells his teacher in no uncertain terms to get off his case and stop telling him about the value of a high school diploma. He insists that a high school diploma does not help African Americans. The teacher tells the student he is wrong. The next day the student brings in some articles which confirm that African American males who graduate high school do not earn significantly more than those who do not.
3. A teacher overhears two seniors say they plan to protest the prejudice they experienced in school by wearing some outlandish clothes to the graduation ceremony rather than the conservative clothes and cap and gown prescribed by the school administration.

---

## *Summary*

Many factors contribute to the gender differences observed in school. Males and females are biologically predisposed to function differently. Males and females are reinforced for behaving differently, and they learn different roles by observing adults behaving in gender-stereotypical ways. Further, they are exposed to gender-biased information. Society is structured in ways that promote gender differences. For the present, we are unable to determine which combination of factors contribute to a particular gender difference, how these factors interact to produce the differences, and the relative amount of influence each factor exercises in the case of any particular difference. We also do not know why some individuals conform to these gender stereotypes and others do not. Much more research is needed before scientific answers can be provided to these important questions.

Schools play a significant role in creating and maintaining gender differences. Gender bias exists in the textbooks students use, the unequal amounts of attention and different kinds of feedback and encouragement they receive from their teachers, the gender segregation they experience, and so on. Although these factors tend to reproduce gender differences, substantial numbers of students resist their influences to varying degrees.

Students belong to ethnic groups, socioeconomic classes, and gender groups. Bias against students in school occurs as a result of the interplay between the ways in which teachers relate to students in terms of these three characteristics. Bias against any group of students for any reason is undesirable and should be eliminated.

## Activities

1. Compare how your professors relate to different groups of students. You can study almost any aspect of their teaching. For example, count the number of times they call on students who volunteer, the number of times they praise students' contributions, and so on. Then compare the results for different groups of students such as males and females and European Americans and non–European Americans.

2. Interview males and females from different ethnic and socioeconomic backgrounds in the courses you are taking about some of the issues discussed in this chapter. What are their opinions about the origins of gender differences? Do students opinions vary with their gender, ethnic, or socioeconomic backgrounds?

3. Review the textbooks and other materials your professors assign in the courses you are taking. Are they free from gender bias? Do they deal with the gender issues inherent in the topics they cover? Do they focus exclusively or primarily on European Americans to the exclusion of other ethnic groups?

4. Compare the amount of time your professors devote to the gender issues inherent in the courses they teach. Do you find that some professors are more sensitive to and interested in gender issues than others?

## References

The following references present evidence that some gender differences in students' behavior in school and academic achievement may have a physiological base.

1. Frankenhaeuser, M., von Wright, M. R., Collins, A., von Wright, J., Sedvall, G., & Swahn, C. G. (1978). Sex differences in psychoneuroendocrine reactions to examination stress. *Psychosomatic Medicine, 40*(4), 334–343.
2. Grossman, H., & Grossman, S. (1994). *Gender Issues in Education*. Needham, MA: Allyn and Bacon.
3. Halpern, D. F. (1986). *Sex Differences in Cognitive Abilities*. Hillsdale, NJ: Erlbaum.
4. Jacklin, C. N., Maccoby, E. E., & Doering, C. H. (1983). Neonatal sex-steroid hormones and timidity in 6–18-month-old boys and girls. *Developmental Psychobiology, 16*, 163–168.
5. Jacklin, C. N., Maccoby, E. E., Doering, C. H., & King, D. R. (1984). Neonatal sex-steroid hormones and muscular strength in boys and girls in the first three years. *Developmental Psychobiology, 17*, 301–310.
6. Jacklin, C. N., Wilcox, K. T., & Maccoby, E. E. (1988). Neonatal sex-steroid hormones and intellect abilities of six-year-old boys and girls. *Developmental Psychobiology, 21*, 567–574.

7. Kimura, D. (1980). Sex differences in intrahemispheric organization of speech. *Behavior and Brain Sciences, 3*, 240–241.
8. Kimura, D. (1983). Sex differences in cerebral organization for speech and praxic functions. *Canadian Journal of Psychology, 37*, 19–35.
9. Kimura, D. (1985). Male brain, female brain: The hidden difference. *Psychology Today, 19*, 50–58.
10. Levy, J., & Gur, R. C. (1980). Individual differences in psychoneurological organization. In J. Herron (Ed.), *Neuropsychology of Left-Handedness*. New York: Academic Press.
11. Maccoby, E. E., & Jacklin, C. N. (1974). *The Psychology of Sex Differences*. Stanford, CA: Stanford University Press.
12. Maccoby, E. E., & Jacklin, C. N. (1980). Sex differences in aggression: A rejoinder and reprise. *Child Development, 51*, 964–980.
13. Marcus, J., Maccoby, E. E., Jacklin, C. N., & Doering, C. H. (1985). Individual differences in mood: Their relation to gender and neonatal sex steroids. *Developmental Psychobiology, 18*, 327–340.
14. McGlone, J. (1980). Sex differences in human brain asymmetry: A critical survey. *Behavioral and Brain Sciences, 3*, 215–263.
15. McKeever, W. F. (1987). Cerebral organization and sex: Interesting but complex. In S. U. Philips, S. Steele, & C. Tanz (Eds.), *Language, Gender, and Sex in Comparative Perspective*. Cambridge, England: Cambridge University Press.
16. Parsons, J. E. (Ed.). (1980). *The Psychobiology of Sex Differences and Sex Roles*. Washington, DC: Hemisphere Publishing.
17. Ray, W. J., Newcombe, N., Semon, J., & Cole, P. M. (1981). Spatial abilities, sex differences and EEG functioning. *Neuropsychologia, 19*, 719–722.
18. Seward, J. P., & Seward, G. H. (1980). *Sex Differences: Mental and Temperamental*. Lexington, MA: Lexington Books.
19. Shucard, D. W., Shucard, J. L., & Thomas, D. G. (1987). Sex differences in the pattern of scalp-recorded electrophysiological activity in infancy: Possible implications for language development. In S. U. Philips, S. Steele, & C. Tanz (Eds.), *Language, Gender, and Sex in Comparative Perspective*. Cambridge, England: Cambridge University Press.
20. Springer, S. P., & Deutsch, G. (1981). *Left Brain, Right Brain*. New York: W. H. Freeman.
21. Susman, E. J., Inoff-Germain, G., Nottelmann, E. D., Loriaux, D. L., Cutler, G. B., & Chrousos, G. P. (1987). Hormones, emotional dispositions, and aggressive attributes in young adolescents. *Child Development, 58*, 1114–1134.

References that indicate that males exhibit more behavior problems and get into more trouble in school than females are included next.

22. Center, D. B., & Wascom, A. M. (1987). Teacher perceptions of social behavior in behaviorally disordered and socially normal children and youth. *Behavior Disorders, 12*(3), 200–206.
23. Duke, D. L. (1978). Why don't girls misbehave more than boys in school? *Journal of Youth and Adolescence, 7*(2), 141–157.
24. Epstein, M. H., Cullinan, D., & Bursuck, W. D. (1985). Prevalence of behavior problems among learning disabled and nonhandicapped students. *Mental Retardation and Learning Disability Bulletin, 13*, 30–39.
25. Ludwig, G., & Cullinan, D. (1984). Behavior problems of gifted and nongifted elementary school girls and boys. *Gifted Child Quarterly, 28*(1), 37–39.
26. National Black Child Development Institute. (1990). *The Status of African American Children: Twentieth Anniversary Report*. Washington, DC.

The following references detail differences in teachers' tolerance for male and female behavior patterns.

27. Fagot B. I. (1985). Beyond the reinforcement principle: Another step toward understanding sex roles. *Developmental Psychology, 21*, 1097–1104.
28. Marshall, J. (1983). Developing antisexist initiatives in education. *International Journal of Political Education, 6*, 113–137.
29. Woolridge, P., & Richman, C. L. (1985). Teachers' choice of punishment as a function of a student's gender, age, race, and IQ level. *Journal of School Psychology, 23*, 19–29.

Teachers' use of different management techniques with the sexes is discussed in the following references.

30. Eccles, J. S., & Blumenfeld, P. (1985). Classroom experiences and student gender: Are there differences and do they matter? In L. C. Wilkinson & C. B. Marrett (Eds.), *Gender Influences in Classroom Interaction*. New York: Academic Press.

31. Fagot, B. I., & Hagan, R. (1985). Aggression in toddlers: Responses to the assertive acts of boys and girls. *Sex Roles, 12*(3), 341–351.

These references document that parents reinforce children for behaving in gender-stereotypical ways.

32. Block, J. H. (1984). *Sex Role Identity and Ego Development*. San Francisco: Jossey-Bass.
33. Fagot, B. I. (1978). The influence of sex of child on parental reactions to toddler children. *Child Development, 49*, 459–465.
34. Lewis, M., & Weintraub, M. (1979). Origins of early sex-role development. *Sex Roles, 5*(2), 135–153.
35. O'Brien, M., & Huston, A. C. (1985). Development of sex-typed play behavior in toddlers. *Developmental Psychology, 21*(5), 866–871.

The following references deal with the reinforcement of gender-appropriate behavior by toddlers and preschoolers.

36. Fagot, B. I. (1977). Consequences of moderate cross-gender behavior in preschool children. *Child Development, 48*, 902–907.
37. Fagot, B. I. (1985). Beyond the reinforcement principle: Another step toward understanding sex roles. *Developmental Psychology, 21*, 1097–1104.
38. Lamb, M. E., Easterbrook, A. M., & Holden, G. W. (1980). Reinforcement and punishment among preschoolers: Characteristics, effects, and correlates. *Child Development, 51*, 1230–1236.
39. Lamb, M. E., & Roopnarine, J. L. (1979). Peer influences on sex-role development in preschoolers. *Child Development, 50*, 1219–1222.

The following references discuss the role of cognitive awareness and modeling in children's sex-role acquisition.

40. Andersen, E. S. (1978). *Learning to Speak with Style: A Study of the Socio-Linguistic Skills of Children*. Unpublished doctoral dissertation. Stanford University.
41. Bem, S. L. (1983). Gender schema theory and its implication for child development: Raising gender aschematic children in a gender schematic society. *Signs, 8*, 598–616.
42. Bem, S. L. (1985). Androgyny and gender schema theory: A conceptual and empirical integration. In T. B. Sonderegger (Ed.), *Nebraska Symposium on Motivation: Psychology of Gender*. Lincoln: University of Nebraska.
43. Busey, K., & Bandura, A. (1984). Influence of gender constancy and social power on sex-linked modeling. *Journal of Personality and Social Psychology, 47*(6), 1292–1302.
44. Eagly, A. H. (1987). *Sex Differences in Social Behavior: A Social-Role Interpretation*. Hillsdale, NJ: Lawrence Erlbaum.
45. Fagot, B. I. (1985). Changes in thinking about early sex-role development. *Developmental Review, 5*, 83–98.
46. Hargreaves, D. J., & Colley, A. M. (1987). *The Psychology of Sex Roles*. New York: Hemisphere Publishing.
47. Weintraub, M., Clemens, L. P., Sockloff, A., Ethridge, T., Gracely, E., & Myers, B. (1984). The development of sex role stereotypes in the third year: Relationships to gender labeling, gender identity, sex-typed toy preference, and family characteristics. *Child Development, 55*, 1493–1503.

The role of parents' behavior, expectations, and beliefs in fostering gender differences in students' confidence about their academic abilities and in their choice of academic courses is discussed in the references listed next.

48. Baker, D. P., & Entwisle, D. R. (1987). The influence of mothers on the academic expectations of young children: A longitudinal study of how gender differences arise. *Social Forces, 65*, 670–694.
49. Bempechat, J. (1990). *The Role of Parent Involvement in Children's Academic Achievement: A Review of the Literature Trends and Issues*. No. 14. New York: ERIC Clearinghouse on Urban Education, Institute for Urban and Minority Education.
50. Eccles, J., Adler, T. F., & Kaczala, C. M. (1982). Socialization of achievement attitudes and beliefs: Parental influences. *Child Development, 53*, 310–321.
51. Eccles, J., & Jacobs, J. E. (1986). Social forces shape math attitudes and performance. *Signs, 11*, 367–389.
52. Eccles, J., Kaczala, C. M., & Meese, J. L. (1982). Socialization of achievement attitudes and beliefs: Classroom influences. *Child Development, 53*, 322–339.
53. Entwisle, D. R., & Baker, D. P. (1983). Gender and young children's expectations for performance in arithmetic. *Developmental Psychology, 19*(2), 200–209.
54. Entwisle, D. R., & Hayduk, L. A. (1982). *Early Schooling*. Baltimore: The Johns Hopkins University Press.

55. Jacobs, J., & Eccles, J. (1985). Gender differences in math ability: The impact of media reports on parents. *Educational Researcher, 14*(3), 20–25.
56. Parsons, J. E., Adler, T. F., & Kaczala, C. M. (1982). Socialization of achievement attitudes and beliefs: Parental influences. *Child Development, 53,* 310–321.
57. Parsons, J. E., Kaczala, C. M., & Meese, J. L. (1982). Socialization of achievement attitudes and beliefs: Classroom influences. *Child Development, 53,* 322–339.
58. Yee, D. K., & Eccles, J. S. (1988). Parent perceptions and attributions for children's math achievement. *Sex Roles, 19*(5/6), 317–333.

References that discuss the role of schools in the reproduction of inequities in society are listed next.

59. Connell, R. W. (1989). Curriculum politics, hegemony, and strategies of social change. In H. A. Giroux & R. I. Simon (Eds.), *Popular Culture, Schooling and Everyday Life.* Granby, MA: Bergin & Garvey.
60. Grant, C. A., & Sleeter, C. E. (1988). Race, class, and gender and abandoned dreams. *Teachers College Record, 90*(1), 19–40.
61. Kelly, G., & Nihlen, A. (1982). Schooling and the reproduction of patriarchy: Unequal workloads, unequal rewards. In M. Apple (Ed.), *Culture and Economic Reproduction in Education.* Boston: Routledge Kegan Paul.
62. Valli, L. (1986). *Becoming Clerical Workers.* Boston: Routledge Kegan Paul.
63. Weiler, K. (1988). *Women Teaching for Change: Gender, Class & Power.* Granby, MA: Bergin & Garvey.
64. Witt, S. H. (1979). Native women in the world of work. In T. Constantino (Ed.), *Women of Color Forum: A Collection of Readings.* ERIC ED 191–975.
65. Wolpe, A. (1981). The official ideology of education for girls. In M. McDonald, R. Dale, G. Esland, & R. Fergusson (Eds.), *Politics, Patriarchy and Practice.* New York: Falmer Press.

These references deal with student resistance to school.

66. Anyon, J. (1984). Intersections of gender and class: Accommodation and resistance by working class and affluent females to contradictory sex-role ideologies. *Journal of Education, 166*(1), 25–48.
67. Arnot, M. (1982). Male hegemony, social class and women's education. *Journal of Education, 164*(1), 64–89.
68. Connell, R. W., Dowsett, G. W., Kessler, S., & Aschenden, D. J. (1982). *Making the Difference.* Boston: Allen and Unwin.
69. Fuller, M. (1980). Black girls in a London comprehensive school. In R. Deem (Ed.), *Schooling for Women's Work.* Boston: Routledge and Kegan Paul.
70. Gaskell, J. (1985). Course enrollment in high school: The perspective of working class females. *Sociology of Education, 58*(1), 48–59.
71. Kessler, S., Ashenden, R., Connell, R., & Dowsett, G. (1985). Gender relations in secondary schooling. *Sociology of Education, 58*(1), 34–48.
72. Ogbu, J. U. (1987). Variability in minority school performance: A problem in search of an explanation. *Anthropology & Education Quarterly, 18*(4), 312–334.
73. Simon, R. (1983). But who will let you do it? Counter-hegemonic possibilities for work education. *Journal of Education, 165*(3), 235–256.
74. Thomas, C. (1980). *Girls and Counter-School Culture.* Melbourne Working Papers. Melbourne, Australia.
75. Willis, P. (1981). Cultural production is different from cultural reproduction is different from social reproduction is different from production. *Interchange, 12*(2/3), 48–68.

Administrative imbalance is the focus of the following references.

76. Fennema, E., & Ayer, M. J. (Eds.). (1984). *Women and Education: Equity or Equality?* Berkeley, CA: McCutchan.
77. Frazier, N., & Sadker, M. (1973). *Sexism in School and Society.* New York: Harper & Row.
78. Lockheed, M. E. (1984). Sex segregation and male preeminence in elementary classrooms. In E. Fennema & M. J. Ayer (Eds.), *Women and Education: Equity or Equality?* Berkeley, CA: McCutchan.
79. SUNY study finds school management still white male dominated. (1990). *Black Issues in Higher Education, 7*(5), 23.

The following references provide evidence that gender bias in curriculum materials has been reduced but not eliminated.

80. Cooper, P. (1989). Children's literature: The extent of sexism. In C. Lont & S. Friedly

(Eds.), *Beyond Boundaries: Sex and Gender Diversity in Education*. Fairfax, VA: George Mason University Press.
81. Cooper, P. (1987). Sex role stereotypes of stepparents in children's literature. In L. Stewart & S. Ting-Toomey (Eds.), *Communication, Gender and Sex Roles in Diverse Interaction Contexts*. Norwood, NJ: Ablex.
82. Dougherty, W., & Engel, R. (1987). An 80s look for sex equality in Caldecott winners and honors books. *Reading Teacher, 40*, 394–398.
83. Heinz, K. (1987). An examination of sex occupational role presentations of female characters in children's picture books. *Women's Studies in Communication, 11*, 67–78.
84. Hitchcock, M. E., & Tompkins, G. E. (1987). Basis readers: Are they still sexist? *Reading Teacher, 41*(3), 288–292.
85. Nilsen, A. P. (1987). Three decades of sexism in school science materials. *School Library Journal, 34*(1), 117–122.
86. Purcell, P., & Stewart, L. (1990). Dick and Jane 1989. *Sex Roles, 22*(3/4), 177–185.
87. Tetreault, M. K. T. (1985). Phases of thinking about women in history: A report card on the textbook. *Women's Studies Quarterly, 13*(3/4), 35–47.
88. Timm, J. (1988). *Cultural Bias in Children's Storybooks: Implications for Education*. Paper presented at the annual meeting of the American Educational Research Association, New Orleans.
89. Vaughn-Roberson, C., Thompkins, M., Hitchcock, M. E., & Oldham, M. (1989). Sexism in basal readers: An analysis of male main characters. *Journal of Research in Childhood Education, 4*, 62–68.
90. White, H. (1986). Damsels in distress: Dependency themes in fiction for children and adolescents. *Adolescence, 21*, 251–256.
91. Woodill, G. (1987). Critical issues in the use of microcomputers by young children. *International Journal of Early Childhood, 19*(1), 50–57.

The references listed next deal with gender differences in teacher attention.

92. Becker, J. (1981). Differential treatment of males and females in mathematics classes. *Journal of Research in Mathematics Education, 12*, 40–53.
93. Benz, C. R., Pfeiffer, I., & Newman, I. (1981). Sex role expectations of classroom teachers, grades 1–12. *American Educational Research Journal, 18*(3), 289–302.
94. Boudreau, F. A. (1986). Education. In F. A. Boudreau, R. S. Sennott, & M. Wilson (Eds.), *Sex Roles and Social Patterns*. New York: Praeger.
95. Brophy, J. E. (1985). Interaction of male and female students with male and female teachers. In L. C. Wilkinson & C. B. Marrett (Eds.), *Gender Influences in Classroom Interaction*. New York: Academic Press.
96. Brophy, J. E. (1986). Teaching and learning mathematics: Where research should be going. *Journal for Research in Mathematics, 17*, 323–346.
97. Eccles, J. S., & Blumenfeld, P. (1985). Classroom experiences and student gender: Are there differences and do they matter? In L. C. Wilkinson & C. B. Marrett (Eds.), *Gender Influences in Classroom Interaction*. New York: Academic Press.
98. Fennema, E., & Peterson, P. L. (1985). Autonomous learning behavior: A possible explanation of gender-related differences in mathematics. In L. C. Wilkinson & C. B. Marret (Eds.), *Gender Influences in Classroom Interaction*. New York: Academic Press.
99. Fennema, E., & Peterson, P. L. (1986). Teacher student interactions and sex-related differences in learning mathematics. *Teaching and Teacher Education, 2*(1), 19–42.
100. Fennema, E., Reyes, L., Perl, T., Konsin, M., & Drakenberg, M. (1980). *Cognitive and Affective Influences on the Development of Sex-Related Difference in Mathematics*. Symposium presented at the annual meeting of the American Educational Research Association, Boston.
101. Gore, D. A., & Roumagoux, D. V. (1983). Wait-time as a variable in sex-related differences during fourth-grade mathematics instruction. *Journal of Educational Research, 76*(5), 273–275.
102. Leinhardt, G., Seewald, A. L., & Engel, M. (1979). Learning what's taught: Sex differences in instruction. *Journal of Educational Psychology, 71*(3), 432–439.
103. Lockheed, M. (1982). *Sex Equity in Classroom Interaction Research: An Analysis of Behavior Chains*. Paper presented at the annual meeting of the American Educational Research Association, New York City.
104. Minuchin, P. P., & Shapiro, E. K. (1983). The school as a context for social development. In P. Mussen, & E. M. Hetherington (Eds.),

*Handbook of Child Psychology,* Vol. 4, (4th ed.). New York: Wiley.
105. Morrison, T. L. (1979). Classroom structure, work involvement and social climate in elementary school classrooms. *Journal of Educational Psychology, 71,* 471–477.
106. Morse, L. W., & Handley, H. M. (1985). Listening to adolescents: Gender differences in science classroom interaction. In L. C. Wilkinson & C. B. Marrett (Eds.), *Gender Influences in Classroom Interaction.* New York: Academic Press.
107. Pflaum, S., Pascarella, E., Boswick, M., & Auer, C. (1980). The influence of pupil behaviors and pupil status factors on teacher behaviors during oral reading lessons. *Journal of Educational Research, 74,* 99–105.
108. Putnam, S., & Self, P. A. (1988). *Social Play in Toddlers: Teacher Intrusions.* ERIC ED 319–529.
109. Stake, J., & Katz, J. (1982). Teacher-pupil relationships in the elementary school classroom: Teacher gender and student gender difference. *American Educational Research Journal, 19,* 465–471.

The following references deal with gender differences in teacher feedback.

110. Dweck, C. S., Davidson, W., Nelson, S., & Enna, B. (1978). Sex differences in learned helplessness: The contingencies of evaluation feedback in the classroom, an experimental analysis. *Developmental Psychology, 14*(3), 208–276.
111. Frey, K. S. (1979). *Differential Teaching Methods Used with Girls and Boys of Moderate and High Achievement Levels.* Paper presented at the annual meeting of the American Educational Research Association, Minneapolis.
112. Hodes, C. L. (1985). Relative effectiveness of corrective and noncorrective feedback in computer assisted instruction on learning and achievement. *Journal of Educational Technology Systems, 13*(4), 249–254.
113. Meece, J. L. (1987). The influence of school experiences on the development of gender schemata. *New Directions for Child Development, 38,* 57–73.
114. Parsons, J. E., Kaczala, C. M., & Meese, J. L. (1982). Socialization of achievement attitudes and beliefs: Classroom influences. *Child Development, 53,* 322–339.
115. Simpson, A. W., & Erickson, M. T. (1983). Teachers' verbal and nonverbal communication patterns as a function of teacher race, student gender, and student race. *American Educational Research Journal, 20,* 183–198.

Gender differences in academic expectations are discussed in the following references.

116. Bem, S. (1977). On the utility of alternative procedures for assessing psychological androgyny. *Journal of Consulting and Clinical Psychology, 45,* 196–205.
117. Bernard, M. (1979). Does sex role behavior influence the way teachers evaluate students? *Journal of Educational Psychology, 71,* 553–562.
118. Casserly, P. L. (1975). *An Assessment of Factors Affecting Female Participation in Advanced Placement Programs in Mathematics, Chemistry, and Physics.* Washington, DC: National Science Foundation.
119. Dusek, J. B., & Joseph, G. (1983). The bases of teacher expectancies: A meta-analysis. *Journal of Educational Psychology, 75,* 327–346.
120. Hallinan, M. T., & Sorensen, A. B. (1987). Ability grouping and sex differences in mathematics achievement. *Sociology of Education, 60*(2), 63–72.
121. Luchins, E. (1976). *Women Mathematicians: A Contemporary Appraisal.* Paper presented at the annual meeting of the American Association for the Advancement of Science, Boston.
122. Phillips, R. (1980). Teachers' reported expectations of children's sex roles and evaluation of sexist teaching. *Dissertation Abstracts International, 41,* 995–996-A.

Ethnic differences in the ways teachers perceive and relate to students is the focus of the following references.

123. Grant, L. (1984). Black females' "place" in desegregated classrooms. *Sociology of Education. 57,* 98–110.
124. Grant, L. (1985). *Uneasy Alliances: Black Males, Teachers, and Peers in Desegregated Classrooms.* Paper presented at the annual meeting of the American Educational Research Association, Chicago.
125. Pollard, D. (1979). Patterns of coping in Black school children. In A. W. Boykin, A. Franklin, & F. Yates (Eds.), *Research Directions of Black Psychologists.* New York: Russel Sage.
126. Washington, V. (1982). Racial differences in teacher perception of first and fourth grade pupils on selected characteristics. *Journal of Negro Education, 51,* 60–72.

The following references deal with the adverse results of gender differences in teacher attention, feedback, and expectations.

127. Brush, L. R. (1980). *Encouraging Girls in Mathematics: The Problems and the Solutions.* Boston: Abt Associates.
128. Eccles, J., Adler, T. F., Futterman, R., Goff, S. B., Kaczala, C. M., Meece, J., & Midgley, C. (1983). Expectations, values, and academic behavior. In J. T. Spence (Ed.), *Perspectives on Achievement and Achievement Motivation.* San Francisco: W. H. Freeman.
129. Fox, L., Brody, L. A., & Tobin, D. (Eds.). (1980). *Women and the Mathematical Mystique.* Baltimore: The Johns Hopkins University Press.
130. Fennema, E., & Sherman, J. (1977). Sex-related differences in mathematics achievement, spatial visualization, and affective factors. *American Educational Research Journal, 14,* 51–71.

The following references describe how teachers and other school personnel foster sex differences in the courses and activities students choose.

131. Farris, C. (1982). *Sex Fair Knowledge, Attitudes, and Behaviors of Vocational Educators: A Research Report.* Utica, NY: SUNY College of Technology.
132. Hopkins-Best, M. (1987). The effects of students' sex and disability on counselors' agreement with postsecondary career goals. *School Counselor, 35*(1), 28–33.
133. Parmley, J. D., Welton, R. F., & Bender, M. (1980). *Opinions of Agricultural Teachers, School Administrators, Students and Parents Concerning Females as Agriculture Students, Teachers and Workers in Agriculture.* ERIC ED 209–488.
134. Roberts, E. J. (Ed.). (1980). *Childhood Sexual Learning: The Unwritten Curriculum.* Cambridge, MA: Ballinger.
135. Schaffer, K. F. (1981). *Sex Roles and Human Behavior.* Cambridge, MA: Winthrop.
136. Stockard, J., Schmuck, P. A., Kemper, K., Williams, P., Edson, S. K., & Smith, M. A. (1980). *Sex Equity in Education.* New York: Academic Press.
137. Tavris, C., & Wade, C. (1984). *The Longest War: Sex Differences in Perspective,* (2nd ed.). New York: Harcourt Brace Jovanovich.

Gender segregation and separation is the focus of the following articles.

138. Guttenberg, M., & Gray, H. (1977). Teachers as mediators of sex-role standards. In A. Sargent (Ed.), *Beyond Sex Roles.* St. Paul, MN: West.
139. Lockheed, M. E., & Harris A. M. (1984). Cross-sex collaborative learning in elementary classrooms. *American Educational Research Journal, 21*(2), 275–294.

The next references deal with the fact that teachers encourage different behaviors in male and female students.

140. Caplan, P. J. (1977). Sex, age, behavior, and school subject as determinants of report of learning problems. *Journal of Learning Disabilities, 10,* 60–62.
141. Fagot, B. I. (1977). Consequences of moderate cross-gender behavior in preschool children. *Child Development, 48,* 902–907.
142. Huffine, S., Silvern, S. B., & Brooks, D. M. (1979). Teacher responses to contextually specific sex type behaviors in kindergarten children. *Educational Research Quarterly, 4*(2), 29–35.
143. Lamb, M. E., Easterbrook, A. M., & Holden, G. W. (1980). Reinforcement and punishment among preschoolers: Characteristics, effects, and correlates. *Child Development, 51,* 1230–1236.
144. Schlosser, L., & Algozzine, B. (1980). Sex behavior and teacher expectancies. *Journal of Experimental Education, 48,* 231–236.

The following references describe how teachers use different classroom management techniques with various ethnic and socioeconomic groups.

145. Glackman, T., Martin, R., Hyman, I., McDowell, E., Berv, V., & Spino, P. (1980). *Corporal Punishment in the Schools as It Relates to Race, Sex, Grade Level and Suspensions.* Philadelphia: Temple University, National Center for the Study of Corporal Punishment in the Schools.
146. Richardson, R. C., & Evans, E. T. (1991). *Empowering Teachers to Eliminate Corporal Punishment in the Schools.* Paper presented at the annual conference of the National Black Child Developmental Institute. Washington, DC.
147. Stevens, L. B. (1983). *Suspension and Corporal Punishment of Students in the Cleveland Public Schools, 1981–1982.* Cleveland, OH: Office of School Monitoring and Community Relations.
148. Woolridge, P., & Richman, C. (1985). Teachers' choice of punishment as a function of a student's gender, age, race and I. Q. level. *Journal of School Psychology, 23,* 19–29.

# Chapter 6

# Gender Appropriate Education

Chapters 1 and 3 explored a number of gender inequities such as gender disparities in educational outcomes, gender bias in the treatment of students, and gender differences in the roles for which schools prepare students. This chapter examines the advantages and disadvantages of four alternative ways of dealing with these inequities. Chapters 9 through 11 describe techniques educators can use to implement these four approaches when they select assessment, instructional, and classroom management techniques. The chapter does not take a position about which of these four alternatives is the most appropriate in relation to any specific gender difference. Rather, it presents the arguments for and against each approach and includes exercises that enhance the readers' insight into their own views on gender issues. The chapter also describes the problems gay and lesbian students experience in and out of school and examines what educators can do to assist students with these problems.

## Gender Equity in Education: A Controversial Issue

What is gender equity and how can gender equity be achieved in school? Educators' opinions vary. Some educators equate equity with sameness. Their point of view is that gender equity is achieved when males and females participate in academic and nonacademic courses and extracurricular activities to the same degree, their achievement is the same, they are treated the same by their teachers, and they are prepared for the same societal roles.

Other educators define equity in terms of fairness. Assuming that there are biologically or culturally based educationally relevant differences between male and female students, they believe equity requires each gender to be treated in accordance with its biological make-up and cultural preference. To them, educational equity is achieved when males and females are treated in accordance with their different needs, when the genders have an opportunity to participate in whichever courses and activities they prefer and to achieve up to their different potentials, and when they are prepared for different societal roles.

How teachers define gender equity in school is extremely important because it influences how they perceive their students' behavior, the goals they set for them, and how they relate to them.

## *Controversial and Noncontroversial Practices*

Educators may disagree about the broad issues involved in defining gender equity, but most would probably agree that certain current educational practices are unfair and should be corrected. For example, even though educators disagree about the cause or causes of gender differences and have different comfort levels with the status quo, most would probably agree that teachers should:

- Select textbooks, readers, and biographies that include the contributions of both males and females
- Pay equal attention to all students who volunteer answers or ask questions regardless of their gender
- Call on male and female students equally often
- Provide the same kind and amount of help to all students
- Praise female and male students equally for high achievement, creativity, and effort
- Attribute the cause of students' academic problems accurately
- Be equally attentive to the misbehavior of males and females
- Avoid excessively harsh punishments with all students
- Discourage dependent, helpless, and excessively conforming behavior in all students

However, they probably disagree about whether they should:

- Select textbooks and other reading materials that portray males and females fulfilling nontraditional roles
- Permit males and females to choose to work and play in single-sex groups
- Separate boys and girls for activities such as physical education and sex education
- Assign students to single-sex groups during class to protect females from being dominated by males
- Select male teachers for male students and female teachers for female students
- Encourage students to conform to the same standards of behavior regardless of their ethnic and socioeconomic backgrounds
- Use similar classroom management procedures with males and females
- Utilize the same instructional approaches and assessment procedures with all students regardless of their ethnic and socioeconomic backgrounds.

## Positions on Gender Differences

Excluding practices that most educators would probably agree are unfair, the following are the four most common positions that have appeared in the literature regarding controversial gender issues like the ones just listed.

**1.** *Educators should not treat males and females the same* (8, 9). Educators should prepare the genders to fulfill different societal roles because there are natural, physiological differences between the sexes, and they should accommodate their instructional practices to existing gender differences. This quotation exemplifies the position that teachers should not treat males and females the same:

> *Boys who rise to the top in school often resemble girls in many important ways.... Scholastic honor and masculinity, in other words, too often seem incompatible.... The feminized school simply bores many boys, but it pulls some in one of two opposite directions. If the boy absorbs school values, he may become feminized himself. If he resists, he is pushed toward school failure and rebellion.* (8, pp. 13, 33)

Do you agree that being a "real boy" is incompatible with being a good student? Do you agree that being a "real boy" in the sense that the term is usually used is a desirable personality characteristic? What is your opinion about the author's concern that schools feminize males?

**2.** *Educators should cease fostering gender-role differences that are unnatural, outdated, and harmful* (1–4, 6). They should prepare students for the androgynous roles that are increasingly available to them in society. They should also encourage and prepare students to do what is necessary to transform our sexist society into a less sexist one. The following quote is an example of this position.

> *In American society, men are supposed to be masculine, women are supposed to be feminine, and neither sex is supposed to be much like the other. If men are independent, tough, and assertive, women should be dependent, sweet, and retiring. A womanly woman may be tender and nurturant, but no manly man may be so.... I have come to believe that we need a new standard of psychological health for the sexes, one that removes the burden of stereotype and allows people to feel free to express the best traits of men and women....*
>
> *Traditional sex typing necessarily restricts behavior. Because people learn, during their formative years, to suppress any behavior that might be considered undesirable or inappropriate for their sex, men are afraid to do "women's work" and women are afraid to enter a "man's world." Men are reluctant to be gentle and women to be assertive. In contrast, androgynous people are not limited by labels. They are able to do whatever they want, both in their behavior and their feelings.* (2, p. 32)

Do you agree that students should be encouraged to become androgynous? If you do, you probably favor discouraging students from accepting and acting out any gender-stereotypic roles, whatever they may be.

*At the core of any radical pedagogy must be the aim of empowering people to recognize and work for a change in the social, political, and economic structure that constitutes the ultimate source of class-based power and domination. (4, p. 427)*

Do you agree that teachers should prepare students to change society in the ways suggested by the author of this statement?

**3.** *Educators should decide for themselves whether they want to prepare students to fulfill different gender roles or encourage students to fulfill similar roles* (5). The desirability or lack of desirability of gender roles is something for the individual professional or the group to decide.

*If we value the higher levels of aggressiveness in males, then schools should encourage aggression, competition, and assertion more in females. This might mean more emphasis on competitive athletics for girls, perhaps beginning in early elementary school, or perhaps even in the preschool years. In the academic classroom, it might mean encouraging reticent girls to speak up more forcefully in debates or to become more competitive about their success in mathematics courses. If, on the other hand, we value the low level of aggressiveness of females, we might seek to reduce the level of aggressiveness in boys, while simultaneously encouraging peaceful cooperation for them. . . . We might want to de-emphasize competitive sports in favor of cooperative sports or noncompetitive ones such as jogging. In the classroom, we would avoid competitively structured learning and work toward cooperatively structured learning. . . . Which of these alternatives is chosen, of course, is a matter of values. (5, pp. 64–65)*

Do you agree that gender roles are inherently neither desirable nor undesirable, but depend on the values of different individuals and societies? If so, does that mean that societies have the right to establish different expectations for their male and female members? Does it also follow that different ethnic and socioeconomic groups have the right to expect the schools to respect their freedom to bring up their children to fulfill the gender roles they believe most appropriate? Or should the greater society determine the gender roles for all the subgroups living within its boundaries?

**4.** *Educators should empower students to decide for themselves whether to conform to any particular gender role or to be androgynous* (7).

*To force everyone into the new mold may violate the individual as much as to force them into the older stereotypes. . . . Freedom to choose according to individual need would seem to be the preferred way of dealing with the complex problem of man/woman roles. (7, p. 202)*

Should teachers not involve themselves in shaping their students attitudes about gender roles?

## *Legal Requirements*

Title IX of the Education Amendments Act was designed to correct the biased treatment males and females received in school. Some of the provisions of Title IX that protect students from gender bias also restrict the rights of educators to decide for themselves about how to respond to certain gender issues.

Title IX requires schools to provide equal educational opportunities to all students regardless of gender. As it did in the 1970s and 1980s, Title IX serves as the main legal basis for efforts to eliminate gender-discriminatory educational practices. Its requirements include:

- Students may not be denied admission to schools or subjected to discriminatory admissions practices on the basis of their gender.
- Once admitted, students may not be excluded from participation in, be denied the benefits of, or be subjected to discrimination while participating in any academic, extracurricular, research, occupational training, or other educational program or activity.
- All courses and activities, except human sexuality courses, must be open to all students regardless of their gender. If offered, human sexuality courses must be available to all students, but they can be taught separately to males and females.
- Standards for student participation in physical education activities and ability groupings within these activities must be objective and applied equally to all students regardless of gender. Separate athletic teams may be provided for males and females for contact sports or for other sports when the separation is justified by differences in skills. However, if a school has a contact sport for males only, a noncontact alternative team sport for females must be provided.
- Dress codes must be applied equally to males and females.
- Graduation requirements must be the same for both genders.
- Textbooks and other instructional materials are exempted from Title IX regulations due to potential conflicts with freedom of speech rights guaranteed by the First Amendment and other legislation.

---

**SELF-QUIZ: Critical Incidents**

This self-quiz is designed to provide you with some insight into the approaches you may use to resolve gender issues. First, describe how you think the teacher involved should handle each of the following critical incidents, then put yourself in the teacher's place. Disregard the description of the teacher's point of view. Instead, imagine what your viewpoint would

*Continued*

## SELF-QUIZ: Critical Incidents  *Continued*

be and how you would deal with the problem. If you prefer a number of different approaches to the incidents, try to determine the factors that led you to select the particular approaches you would use in each critical incident.

1. The father of a Hispanic American preschool student comes to school irate because his son told him that the teacher encouraged him to play in the housekeeping/doll house area. He tells the teacher he does not want his son to play "girls' games" or with "girl things." The teacher believes that doll and housekeeping play are important for all children because they foster caring and nurturing qualities in children and androgynous gender roles.

2. A group of second-grade boys does not want some of the girls to join in their game in the schoolyard. The teacher believes students should learn to get along with both genders. The teacher also wants to encourage female students to participate in traditionally male activities and vice versa.

3. A fourth-grade student suggests that the teacher should have a spelling bee with the boys against the girls, as some other fifth-grade teachers do in their classes. The teacher, who feels that the students are already too competitive, wants them to learn to be more cooperative. In addition, the teacher believes in bringing the genders together rather than identifying them as competing groups.

4. One of an educator's best students, an eighth-grade Hispanic American female, informs the teacher that she is not going to continue in the program in high school because she is not planning to go to college. When the teacher asks why, she replies that in her family and culture college is for boys. She says her plans are to finish high school, find a job for a while, get married, have four or five children, and stay home. The teacher believes that females should be encouraged to go on to college so they can have the career and other opportunities a college degree provides.

## SELF-QUIZ: Gender Differences

The following incident was reported by a school principal.

> *Allen attended a parochial school where the playgrounds were segregated by gender. In one playground the girls skipped and jumped rope, in the other, the boys played football. Allen often stood on the sidelines and chatted with several other non-athletic boys. Allen's teacher was concerned and arranged privately with several of the male athletes to include Allen and his friends in the daily football game. The teacher warned that if they failed to do so, all of the boys in the class would be punished. (32, p. 208)*

How do you feel about the gender separation that existed on the playgrounds? What is your opinion about the way the teacher responded to Allen and his friends' behavior? What might have been the teacher's reason for responding in that manner? How would you have responded?

## Sexual Orientation

Although adolescents have many problems centered around their emerging sexual drives and sexual orientation, people disagree about whether these topics are fit for discussion in school. Many educators feel they are. However, in general, sexuality and especially sexual orientation is a forbidden subject in many schools, and many individuals and community groups demand that it remain so. For example, only 1 out of 28 school districts boards in the New York City public school system voted to include the approved elementary school curriculum that deals with homosexual orientation in their schools (10).

### Problems

Many heterosexual adolescents are concerned about their sexual orientation because of one or two homosexual experiences or fantasies. Although research indicates that there are no innate reasons why lesbian, gay, and bisexual students should have more problems than other students, because of society's homophobic attitudes many of them have a very difficult adolescence (11, 12, 14, 17, 18, 20, 23, 24, 27–29, 31). They experience a great deal of discrimination and prejudice both in and out of school, and they also have a great deal of difficulty adjusting to their sexual orientation.

Because gay and lesbian students are brought up in a homophobic society and have little access to information that portrays lesbians and gays in a positive way, many of them suffer from homophobia and believe they are sick, evil, inferior, and disgusting. These ideas can lead to emotional problems such as depression, shame, and guilt, low self-esteem, and self-hatred or at least ambivalence toward their sexual orientation. In turn, their emotional problems can cause them to drop out of school, abuse substances, and commit suicide. Some homosexual students attempt, usually unsuccessfully, to change their sexual orientation. Most students hide their homosexuality, thereby living in fear that they will be discovered. Kissen describes their plight in the following manner.

> *If, like most gay adolescents, they try to hide their identity, they live in constant fear that someone will discover they are gay. Even if they are successful at concealment, they must live every day as a lie, pretending to be someone they are not, and surrounded by homophobic jokes. . . . Anyone who spends time in a high school is surely aware that homophobia—fear and hatred of gay people—is the last "acceptable" form of bigotry among adolescents. Young people who would not dream of uttering (or would not dare to utter) a racial or religious epithet still unthinkingly toss around "queer" and "faggot," probably the most often heard insults in any high school. ( 20, p. 2)*

Sometimes the desire to be true to themselves, to feel good about themselves, and to stop hiding significant aspects of themselves from others in order to build a relationship based on honesty and trust leads gay, lesbian, and bisexual students to declare their sexual orientation to others (to come out). When they do, family conflicts and parental rejection can lead them to run away from home and to engage in prostitution. Loss of the friendship of and abuse by their heterosexual peers often follow. Ross-Reynolds offers this description of the problems of a gay and a lesbian student:

> *Andy is a middle-class, White sixteen-year-old who ran away from his family home in Oregon after suffering years of abuse from his father after the man read his son's love letters from another boy. . . . Andy worked in a fast food restaurant in the evenings and attended high school during the day, resolving to complete high school and get his diploma, despite the obstacles caused by the relocation. Instead of a supportive environment at his new school, Andy found his peers hostile and harassing. Openly gay to his classmates and teachers, Andy was mocked during class time by other students, and received no support from teachers. After he was physically assaulted at the bus stop after school Andy felt pushed to the point of either quitting school or demanding action.*
>
> *Nina is a Black fifteen-year-old from Harlem. She had difficulty coping with the rejection she faced in her inner-city high school because she was up front about being a lesbian. . . . Name-calling, harassing notes, and verbal threats of violence, including rape, began to turn an upbeat, cheerful girl into a jumble of dysfunction and misery. As Nina faced the unpleasant task of steeling herself for two more years of such assaults, she found herself moving toward leaving school (29, pp. 444–445).*

Children of gay and lesbian parents can also experience many problems both in and out of school. Students who are brought up by openly gay or lesbian parents are exposed to the same homophobic attitudes as gay and lesbian students. Even though they may be straight, their parents' sexual orientation can expose them to prejudiced treatment in school. Students whose parents come out to them and others after many years of living or pretending to live straight lives have difficult adjustments to make. Like gay and lesbian students, children of gay and lesbian parents need all the help and support they can get in school.

## *Causes*

As was just noted, students who are worried about their sexual orientation and gay, bisexual, and lesbian students need help and understanding, as do all students with serious problems. However, many educators believe that school is not the place to deal with or even discuss differences in sexual orientation. Dunham describes the situation in the schools as follows:

> *While mental health professionals have worked to create positive and meaningful programs for the gay and lesbian population, educational systems have been considerably less eager to recognize and respond to the needs of this minority group.*

*Public schools have continued to treat homosexuality as a forbidden subject. (15, p. 3)*

Various causes of the current invisibility of gay and lesbian students in the schools have been identified. Some educators think it reflects society's justifiable desire to keep sexual orientation out of the school curriculum. Others who are more critical of the schools attribute the "problem" to homophobic attitudes among educators, their lack of the courage needed to advocate for the rights of gay and lesbian students, and the failure of school personnel to correct many educators' misinformation about the causes and "cures "of homosexuality.

A few school districts have developed projects such as Project 10 in Los Angeles and the Harvey Milk School in New York City that offer special services to homosexual and bisexual students (16, 29). Project 10 provides help to students who remain in their local schools. The Harvey Milk School offers an alternative school setting for those who wish to escape the difficulties inherent in being openly homosexual in a regular high school setting. Both types of programs have their share of critics who believe that homosexual students should be helped to convert to heterosexuality, but the Harvey Milk School has been criticized by supporters of gay and lesbian rights for capitulating to discrimination and homophobia—"ghettoizing" nonheterosexual students, removing them from the mainstream, and providing them with inferior educational opportunities. However, because these programs are rare, for the most part, lesbian, gay, and bisexual students have to rely on the assistance and understanding of individual teachers and counselors.

## *Solutions*

Concerned educators offer the following suggestions for helping students who are concerned about their sexual orientation (13, 14, 21, 26, 29).

- Resist community pressure to avoid relating to the needs of students who are concerned about their sexual orientation.
- Refer students to community agencies and resources where they can obtain assistance.
- Protect students from harassment, criticize such incidents when they occur, and express disapproval of jokes about gays.
- Modify homophobic attitudes. Because values are caught, not taught, teach students to accept each other regardless of sexual orientation by modeling acceptance. Include issues and topics that affect gay and lesbian students in the curriculum (e.g., gay rights and contributions in social studies classes, gay lifestyles in health and psychology courses, and gay and lesbian authors in English courses). Oppose censorship of texts and library material that demonstrate respect for lesbian and gay rights and lifestyles. Dispel myths about people with nonheterosexual orientations. Have students experience the

effects of discrimination and homophobic attitudes on students by role playing. Advocate for students rights. Include homosexual role models.

*A healthy socialization process involves positive role models. Ideally, the socialization experiences for gay and lesbian adolescents will include learning from competent gay and lesbian adults. Observing how successful adults develop productive and ethical lifestyles, resolve problems of identity disclosure, obtain support, manage a career, and build relationships can be extremely valuable for teenagers. (17, p. 121)*

It will not be easy for educators to carry out these suggestions. As Rofes points out,

*Because many educators believe that homosexuality is sick, sinful, or criminal, it is tremendously difficult for them to truly adopt an "objective" stance when addressing gay and lesbian issues in the classroom.... By allowing positive treatment of homosexuality in the classroom, teachers are vulnerable to witch-hunts by parents and school committees attempting to root out homosexual teachers. In certain parts of the nation, laws have been proposed and successfully passed that forbid positive discussion of homosexuality in public school classrooms. (30, p. 451)*

In addition, because "Gay and lesbian adolescents continue to be socialized to conceal their identities—educated to be invisible within the school community and the community at large," (15, p. 5) they are often reluctant to come out—to disclose their sexual orientation to others.

## *Summary*

Some ways that some teachers treat the genders differently are clearly discriminatory or illegal, and some of the current differences in the schools outcomes for males and females are clearly undesirable. Except for these differences, educators disagree about their role vis-à-vis the current gender differences observed among many students. Educators' positions on gender issues include the following: teachers should stop fostering gender differences; they should treat each gender in accordance with their unique, natural, and desirable needs; each educator should decide how she or he wants to deal with gender differences; teachers should empower students to make such decisions for themselves.

Although adolescents have many problems concerning their sexual orientation, sexual orientation is a forbidden subject in many schools. Some educators believe that this is as it should be. Many others fault the schools for failing to help students with their problems. They suggest that educators should modify their own homophobic attitudes and those of their students, protect students from harassment, advocate for homosexual students' rights, include homosexual role

> **Myths About Gay and Lesbian Students**
>
> 1. *Effeminate boys and masculine females and those who like to cross-dress or play with toys that are thought of as in the domain of opposite gender grow up to become gay and lesbian.* Research indicates that although some gay and lesbian students are more likely to exhibit cross-gender behaviors when they are children and adolescents, many do not, and many children who exhibit these behaviors do not grow up to be gay or lesbian.
> 2. *One homosexual experience means that a person is and will be homosexual.* In reality, neither homosexual nor heterosexual experimentation is unusual. Human sexuality exists along a continuum from completely heterosexual to completely homosexual, with many people somewhere in between the extremes but close to the heterosexual end.
> 3. *Discussing gay and lesbian issues encourages students to become homosexuals.* There is no evidence to support this notion.
> 4. *Lesbian and gay teachers provide role models that encourage students to become lesbians and gays.* Homosexuality is not caught by observing lesbian and gay models.
> 5. *Gay and lesbian adults sexually abuse children and recruit them to their life-styles.* Children and adolescents are much more likely to be abused by heterosexual adults.
> 6. *Homosexuality is a sickness or a disorder.* The American Psychological Association and the American Psychiatric Association both state that it is not a disorder.
> 7. *Homosexual behavior is rare in most animal species.* Research indicates that the opposite is true.
> 8. *Because gays are incapable of establishing long-term relationships they lead lonely isolated lives.* Many gay and lesbian couples enjoy long-term relationships.
> 9. *Homosexuality is a choice that one makes.* Research indicates that in our society most homosexuals at first reject their homosexuality and resist thinking of themselves as homosexuals (19, 25, 30).

models and issues and topics that affect gay and lesbian students in the curriculum, oppose censorship of texts and library material that demonstrate respect for lesbian and gay rights and life-styles, and dispel myths about people with non-heterosexual orientations. In today's environment, this will not be easy for educators to accomplish.

> **SELF-QUIZ: Gay and Lesbian Sexual Orientations**
>
> 1. What is your opinion about the following statement?
>
>    *In a democratic country no citizen should be forced to live under the fear of homophobia. Fear is unhealthy for the individual and our democracy.... We need not endorse particular private sexual acts to protect the civil rights of all citizens.* (22, p. 285)
> 2. Should sexual orientation issues be included in the curriculum? Should educators discuss their students sexual orientation problems with students?
> 3. What should educators do when community organizations and parents prefer or demand policies that conflict with their views of whether and how to deal with sexual orientation issues and problems?

## Activities

1. Ask some of your fellow students to respond to the critical incidents presented earlier. Do you notice any gender or ethnic differences in their responses?

2. How knowledgeable are your fellow students about Title IX? Make up and administer a short quiz to them. Do you notice any gender differences in the extent of their knowledge?

3. Ask some gay or lesbian students whether they have experienced any of the problems described in this chapter. Ask them if any of their teachers knew about their sexual orientation, how the teachers reacted to the information, and how they would have prefered them to have reacted.

4. Administer a questionnaire based on the myths about homosexuality to some of your fellow students. Do they believe the prevalent myths or do they know the facts? Do you notice any gender differences in their beliefs?

## References

The following references discuss various positions on gender differences in school.

1. Becker, J. B. (1986). Influence again: An examination of reviews and studies of gender differences in social influence. In J. S. Hyde, & M. C. Linn (Eds.), *The Psychology of Gender*. Baltimore: The Johns Hopkins University Press.
2. Bem, S. L. (1983). Traditional sex roles are too restrictive. In G. Leone & M. T. O'Neill (Eds.), *Male-Female Roles: Opposing Viewpoints*. St. Paul, MN: Greenhaven Press.
3. Block, J. H. (1984). *Sex Role Identity and Ego Development*. San Francisco: Jossey-Bass.
4. Giroux, H. A. (1981). Hegemony, resistance, and the paradox of educational reform. In H. A. Giroux, A. N. Penna, & W. F. Pinar. *Curriculum & Instruction: Alternatives in Education*. Berkeley, CA: McCutchan.
5. Hyde, J. S. (1984). Gender differences in aggression. In Hyde, J. S. & Linn, M. C. (Eds.), *The Psychology of Gender: Advances Through Meta-Analysis*. Baltimore: The Johns Hopkins University Press.
6. Jacklin, C. N. (1989). Female and male: Issues of gender. *American Psychologist, 44*(2), 127–133.
7. Schlafly, P. Personal communication, May 1989.
8. Seward, J. P., & Seward, G. H. (1980). *Sex Differences: Mental and Temperamental*. Lexington, MA: Lexington Books.
9. Wardle, F. (1991). Are we shortchanging boys? *Child Care Information Exchange, 79,* 48–51.

Opposition to teaching about sexual orientations is documented in the next reference.

10. Columbia Broadcasting System. (1993, April 4). *Sixty Minutes, The Rainbow Curriculum*. Author.

These references describe the plight of gay, lesbian, and bisexual students and their possible solutions.

11. Benvenuti, A. (1986). *Assessing and Addressing the Special Challenge of Gay and Lesbian Students for High School Counseling Programs*. ERIC ED 279–958.
12. Cates, J. A. (1987). Adolescent sexuality: Gay and lesbian issues. *Child Welfare, 66,* 353–364.
13. Chang, C. L. (1980). Adolescent homosexual behavior and the health educator. *Journal of School Health, 50*(9), 517–521.
14. Coleman, E., & Remafedi, G. (1989). Gay, lesbian, and bisexual adolescents: A critical challenge to counselors. *Journal of Counseling and Development, 68,* 36–40.
15. Dunham, K. L. (1989). *Educated to Be Invisible: The Gay and Lesbian Adolescent*. ERIC ED 336–676.
16. Friends of Project Inc. (1991). *Project 10 Handbook: Addressing Lesbian and Gay Issues in Our Schools. A Resource Directory for Teachers, Guidance Counselors, Parents and School-Based*

*Adolescent Care Providers*, (3rd ed.) ERIC ED 337–567.
17. Gonsiorek, J. C. (1988). Mental health issues of gay and lesbian adolescents. *Journal of Adolescent Health Care, 9,* 114–122.
18. Hetrick, E. S., & Martin, A. D. (1987). Developmental issues and their resolution for gay and lesbian adolescents. *Journal of Homosexuality, 14*(1/2), 25–42.
19. Hubbard, B. M. (1989). *Entering Adulthood: Living in Relationships.* Santa Cruz, CA: ETR Associates.
20. Kissen, R. M. (1991). *Listening to Gay and Lesbian Teenagers.* ERIC ED 344–220.
21. Krysiak, G. J. (1987). A very silent and gay minority. *School Counselor, 34*(4), 304–307.
22. Lenton, S. M. (1980). A student development response to the gay issue. In F. B. Newton & K. L. Ender (Eds.), *Student Development Practices.* Springfield, IL: Charles C Thomas.
23. Martin, A. D. (1982). Learning to hide: The socialization of the gay adolescent. *Adolescent Psychiatry, 10,* 52–65.
24. Martin, A. D., & Hetrick, E. S. (1988). The stigmatization of the gay and lesbian adolescent. *Journal of Homosexuality, 15*(3), 163–183.
25. Public Broadcasting System. (1993). *Gay By Nature or Nurture.* Author.
26. Powell, R. E. (1987). Homosexual behavior and the school counselor. *School Counselor, 34*(3), 202–208.
27. Remafedi, G. (1987). Adolescent homosexuality: Medical and psychological implications. *Pediatrics, 79*(3), 331–337.
28. Remafedi, G. (1987). Male homosexuality: The adolescent's perspective. *Pediatrics, 79*(3), 326–330.
29. Ross-Reynolds, G. (1982). Issues in counseling the "homosexual" adolescent. In J. Grimes (Ed.), *Psychological Approaches to Problems of Children and Adolescents.* Des Moines: Iowa State Department of Public Instruction, Division of Special Education.
30. Rofes, E. (1989). Opening up the classroom closet: Responding to the educational needs of gay and lesbian youth. *Harvard Educational Review, 59*(4), 444–453.
31. Schneider, M. S., & Tremble, G. (1985). Gay or straight: Working with the confused adolescent. *Journal of Social Work and Human Sexuality, 4,* 631–660.

The incident in the section "Questions for Further Thought and Discussion" was included in the following reference.

32. Hebert, T. P. (1991). Meeting the affective needs of bright boys through bibliography. *Roeper Review, 13*(4), 207–212.

# Chapter 7

# Assessment in a Diverse Society

Assessment is an integral part of the educational process. Assessment provides the information educators need to determine whether their students have acquired the knowledge, skills, abilities, and other objectives of the curriculum. If they have not, it helps educators understand why not. Do the students have the potential and motivation to accomplish the objectives? Did the educators use inappropriate instructional or motivational techniques? What additional assistance do the students require? What are their strengths and weaknesses? These are just a few of the many questions assessment helps answer.

Because our society is so diverse, until recently, assessment procedures, particularly standardized tests, were not very accurate when used with many students. The situation has improved somewhat in recent years. Nowadays educators are much more knowledgeable about the bias typically found in the assessment strategies and materials and the harmful effects of biased assessment on students. New, less-biased procedures and materials have been developed. However, the sad fact is that many school districts do not use these approaches.

This chapter describes how inattention to students' ethnic, socioeconomic, linguistic, contextual, and gender characteristics can bias the results of assessments. It examines various alternative solutions educators and others can employ when they assess students. It describes how educators can avoid biased and discriminatory assessment by adapting their assessment procedures to their students' characteristics and selecting appropriate nonbiased/nonsexist assessment materials and procedures.

## *Student Characteristics*

This section describes some of the many differences among students that require adaptations in the assessment process to avoid bias and describes and evaluates suggestions for adapting the assessment process to these differences. As was noted in Chapter 1, it is important to avoid overgeneralizations and stereotypical statements about students. The ethnic, socioeconomic, and gender differences discussed in this chapter are meant to sensitize assessors to differences that may possibly characterize students, not to encourage them to judge students by their ethnic background, name, skin color, or gender.

## *Familiarity with the Assessment Process*

Not all students are accustomed to being assessed, especially in a one-to-one situation. Students who are unfamiliar with assessment procedures often become anxious when they are assessed (1–6). Research indicates that a small amount of anxiety can motivate students to do their best when they are assessed; but too much anxiety can interfere with their performance (4).

> *The way many standardized tests are composed and given do, in fact, elicit or at least allow strong debilitating motivational dynamics such as test anxiety to operate. Such motivational test bias will cause many children to perform well below their optimal level of functioning in the test situation, thereby invalidating their results if one is interested in what the children have learned, as opposed to whether they can demonstrate that learning under heavy testing pressure. (4, p. 4)*

Immigrant and refugee students who have never been assessed, especially on a one-to-one basis, are likely to be anxious during the assessment process (2, 3, 5). There is also considerable evidence that African American and poor students are more anxious in assessment procedures than European American and middle-class students (1, 4, 6)

> *Some Hispanics come from countries where students are seldom assessed individually as they are in the United States. The strangeness and unfamiliarity of this situation may make Hispanic students anxious to the point that their anxiety interferes with their ability to demonstrate their achievement and potential. (3, p. 175)*

Students come to the assessment process with different test-taking skills. Their test-wiseness, their capacity to utilize the characteristics and format of an assessment procedure or the assessment situation to solve the problems included in an assessment procedure, affects their ability to perform up to their actual level. Students who have not acquired test-taking skills (such as when to ask the assessor for clarification or assistance, when to work fast, when to guess and to skip difficult items, how to rule out items in multiple choice items that are obviously meant to mislead or entrap students, how to mark an answer sheet, and so on) may be unable to demonstrate what they actually know and can do.

> *Many Native American Indian students fail to exhibit successful test-taking behaviors due to a multiplicity of underlying causes. Cultural beliefs in some*

*tribes may bar competitive behaviors in an academic setting. The student may underestimate the seriousness of the test or fail to adopt a successful response strategy which may involve selective scanning for known items, techniques of using partial information to guess correct answers, or efficient time use. (9, p. 3)*

Research has consistently indicated that improving students' test-taking skills, including those of African American, Hispanic American, Native American, and poor students also improves their scores on assessment procedures (7, 8, 10–16). Five to fourteen hours of instruction time spread out over five to seven weeks appears to be the effective range of instructional time needed to improve students' test-wiseness. Ten hours has been recommended by a number of researchers.

Some educators disagree with this approach. They feel it is unethical and misleading to teach test-taking skills to students. Others argue that because students who lack test-taking skills are unable to demonstrate what they can do and what they know, improving their skills through training makes results of assessment more accurate and less biased. Haladyna and colleagues suggest that there are ethical and unethical ways to prepare students for standardized tests (11). Some of the approaches they consider unethical include modifying the curriculum to match the test, teaching students the actual items in the test, and practicing alternate forms of the test. Examples of approaches they believe to be ethical include teaching test-taking skills and motivating students to want to perform their best.

---

**SELF-QUIZ: Test-Wiseness**

Were you a test-wise student when you were younger? Which if any techniques did your teachers employ to improve your test-taking skills? Which techniques would you employ to improve your students' test-taking skills? Which techniques do you think are unethical?

---

## *Motivation*

All students are not equally motivated to do their best when they are assessed. Some students may not realize that the assessment being conducted is designed to evaluate them. This is especially true of Hispanic American, Native American, and Southeast Asian American students, who come from cultures where they are not evaluated in the same way (3, 20). In fact, some Native American students who have not been exposed to a great deal of testing in reservation schools tend to view a test as a game. As a result, they do not try to do as well as they might if they understood the significance of the situation (20).

Many European American females, particularly those from less affluent and working-class backgrounds, have mixed feelings about and are uncomfortable with success in courses or occupations traditionally thought of as being in the male domain. This applies to a lesser degree to African American females (see

Chapter 10). There is also evidence that some African American students, especially males, are motivated to avoid success in school or at least are not motivated to try to succeed (see Chapters 3 and 11). Students who are not motivated to succeed in school may be equally unmotivated to perform their best on school-related assessments. Therefore, it may be necessary for assessors to motivate such students to try their best. If this fails, they should at least take students' lack of motivation into consideration when they interpret and report the results they obtain.

Students' motivational styles also affect their motivation to succeed. Assessors who are aware of students' motivational styles can utilize their knowledge to increase students' motivation to maximize their performance. For example, students who are brought up to view their family as their main reference point when evaluating themselves are more likely to respond positively to statements such as if they do their best during the assessment their family will be proud of them and it will reflect positively on their families and communities. This may be an especially effective approach with Hmong Americans, who have extremely strong loyalty to their kinship group, as the following description indicates. The Hmong believe that

> *A person exists as a member of a specific kin group. . . . The fate of the group determines its individual members' status and identities. People think of themselves as a collective group with an identity and responsibility. Individuals' actions determine the status of the kin group by reflecting on its honor and on the public respect the group can command. Thus a person's achievements are important insofar as they reflect on her or his extended family, and, in turn, affect the well-being of its members. (21, pp. 6–7)*

In comparison to European American students, Hispanic Americans are also brought up to have a greater loyalty to their families and communities.

> *Hispanics have a strong identification with and loyalty to their family and community. As a result, Hispanic students may be highly motivated to do things that have significance for their families, friends, and community. (3, p. 38)*

When attempting to motivate students to do their best when they are assessed, it is also helpful to know whether individual recognition or anonymity is stressed in their culture. Some students try to do their best if they anticipate that their achievement will be recognized publicly, others when they are assured that their anonymity will be preserved. Many non-European students and some European Americans, especially females, have difficulty with public recognition. An Hispanic American educator reported: "When I was a student, I was tremendously embarrassed any time I was singled out. I would have preferred my recognition in private" (3, p. 87).

Are students brought up to behave cooperatively or to compete with others? Would students respond better to competitive or cooperative motivating techniques during the assessment process? Chamberlain and Medinos-Landurand point out that

*In American society, students who do not value or are not skilled in competition are at a serious disadvantage in the testing process. These students do not understand or accept the concept of doing their "best" and working to do better than others during a test. (18, p. 118)*

As the following quotations indicate, Hispanic Americans, Hawaiian Americans, and Native Americans, among others, tend to prefer cooperative environments.

*Cooperative learning is very essential for Central Americans. Cooperation and collectivity are always regarded as very essential values, while in this country what is valued is individualism and competition. (Carlos Cordova, San Francisco University, San Francisco, California) (24, p. 19)*

*Because of their belief that it is bad manners to try to excel over others, some Hispanic students may not volunteer answers or they may even pretend not to know the correct answer when called on. (22, p. 358)*

*There is evidence that Hawaiians are seldom concerned with the pursuit of success for the purely personal satisfaction involved.... Hawaiians apparently derive little personal pleasure from competing successfully against others and, in fact, avoid individual competition.... As an illustration, many children in our school refused to accept material rewards (e.g., cokes or candy) for high grades or successful competition unless the rewards could be shared with their friends. (25, pp. 55–56)*

*Native American parents desire their children to be successful, just as any other parents, but in a manner that is consistent with the cooperative and non-competitive tribal, community, and family values and aspirations. (17, p. 46)*

Would comparing students to their peers be an effective or ineffective motivational device? In some cases, particularly with students who have been brought up in individualistic cultures, such comparisons can be highly motivating. However, students who have learned that such comparisons are bad may do whatever necessary to avoid appearing to be competitive with other individuals. After a friend has given the wrong answer, how will students who have been brought up to function cooperatively rather than competitively respond when they are called on to give the correct answer? Although it is difficult for many European American teachers to believe, many non–European American students, especially Hispanic Americans and Native Americans, pretend that they do not know the answer to a question or a problem if one of their peers has not given the right answer.

*Calling upon a boy or girl to correct an answer or to supply information in response to a question missed by someone else, creates a problem situation for, in the Latino code of ethics, it is not considered proper for any individual to secure attention at the expense of another person (showing up his ignorance, for instance). (19, p 78)*

*If a question is asked and one child cannot answer it, no one else will because that means they would have placed themselves in a superior position over their peer. [American Indian student] (23, p. 135)*

## Perception of Assessors

What is the history of the relationship between the students' ethnic or socioeconomic groups and the group the assessors represent? Have the students personally experienced prejudice, oppression, rejection, or abuse by members of the assessors' ethnic or socioeconomic group? Have they been brought up to anticipate such treatment? How will students perceive and relate to assessors who are not members of their ethnic, socioeconomic, or regional group and whom they do not know? Will students perform poorly during assessment sessions because they are suspicious of their assessors and not because of a lack of potential or achievement? Will they feel more relaxed and perform better if they are familiar with the assessor?

Research (which needs to be updated) suggests that Hispanic American students perform better with Hispanic American examiners (27, 30). As the following quotation reveals, many African American students are brought up to be suspicious of the motives and intentions of European Americans.

*Black children are taught early to be suspicious of whites.... Thus Blacks grow up believing that whites cannot be trusted. Whether this is true or not is hardly the question, for we are dealing here with* perceptual *realities of Blacks.... The effect of such an attitude on any testing situation in which the instrument is administered by a white is obvious.... From an intercultural point of view the testing situation is even more complicated. The situation itself, in all probability, is defined as being* cold *in the negative sense of that Black term. Black Americans looking at Euro-American interactional style often brand whites as cold and aloof. This feeling about whites will then be intensified if the situation is kept under the control of the tester. Not only does this environment ignore the means by which significant information is generally passed on among blacks ... but it eliminates the possibility of establishing the kind of relationship that makes anything but hostile responses seem appropriate to the testee. In this sense it is not the questions per se which cause Black children difficulty, it is the testing environment in general and especially the techniques that are used to ask the questions. (28, pp. 338–339)*

Research about whether these attitudes actually affect how African American students react to the ethnic background of assessors has yielded inconsistent results. Studies of African American students that do not consider student characteristics such as age, mistrust of European Americans, socioeconomic background, or other situational factors (such as the level of difficulty of the assessment procedure and the role of the assessor) tend to find that assessors' ethnic background does not affect the results of assessment procedures. However, results that consider these factors have indicated the opposite. For example, preschool African American students perform better with African American assessors (31). African American students who mistrust European Americans also perform better with African American assessors, but ethnic background has no effect on those who do not mistrust European Americans (32). Although assessors' ethnic background does not affect the results of assessments of middle-class African American students, research that was done in the 1970s and early 1980s indicates that African Americans students from low income backgrounds perform better with African American assessors. They score higher on standardized tests when given social reinforcement by African American assessors and give them longer and elaborate responses (26, 33).

The reasons for these age and socioeconomic effects have not been explored. Some researchers have suggested that because young children are likely to be unfamiliar with European Americans and have less interaction with them as individuals, they are less likely to trust them. They also propose that students from low-income backgrounds are better able to overcome their discomfort with an unfamiliar and/or threatening assessment procedure when their assessors are familiar. Although most assessors are unfamiliar to students, the administrative procedures for most standardized tests discourage assessor familiarity or friendliness. They also provide little or no opportunity for assessors to engage students in activities that will help them to gain their trust.

There is also evidence that some students from some cultures may perform better with same-gender rather than different-gender assessors. In some cultures students try harder with male assessors because in their culture males are more highly regarded and respected than females (29).

## Communication Style

Students' communication styles can also influence the results of their assessments. As was noted in Chapter 6, assessors who prefer direct expression may mistakenly think that African American and Hispanic American students who use a more poetic and analogous speech pattern are "beating around the bush," cannot think straight, or have communication problems (3, 22).

Also as noted previously, some students (e.g, Hispanic Americans and Japanese Americans) expect others to be sensitive enough to their feelings and problems that it is unnecessary for them to be open and direct about their needs. If they have to do so, they may experience a loss of self-respect and think that others have also lost respect for them as well (3, 34, 36).

> *Because Hispanics tend to feel that it reflects negatively on their self-worth to admit that they do not know something or cannot do something, Hispanic students who are less accustomed to asking questions and expressing doubts and confusions may not admit that they do not understand directions or items included in assessment procedures. (3, p. 176)*

Therefore, assessors should not assume that students who do not ask for help in understanding directions and so on are really ready to perform the required assessment task.

Children are brought up to be more or less loquacious with adults. For example, many Native American, Asian and Pacific American, and Hispanic American students are expected to talk less and listen more when they converse with adults in comparison to European American students (3, 18, 35). Thus, they may respond in as few words as possible during assessment procedures and be penalized for not saying enough or providing enough details.

## *Learning Style*

### *Dependent Versus Independent Learners*

No children are brought up to be completely dependent on or independent of adults. However, some youngsters are trained to accomplish things on their own, others are brought up to be more dependent on the aid, support, opinions, and feedback of their parents and other significant adults. It is important to know whether students are prepared to be relatively self-reliant and independent during the assessment process or require a great deal of guidance and feedback to perform at their optimum level. Most standardized assessment procedures do not permit assessors to provide dependent learners with the supportive environment they require to demonstrate their accomplishments.

### *Reflective/Analytical Versus Spontaneous/Intuitive*

No one is completely reflective/analytical or spontaneous/intuitive, but there are cultural differences among people along this continuum. Therefore, it is important to know whether children's cultures stress analyzing and reflecting on questions and problems and being sure to know the answer or solution before saying anything, or emphasize responding intuitively and spontaneously in terms of what occurs to them immediately. Shade describes the difference as follows:

> *Some people are rather anxious to insure that they gather all the information possible before being asked to respond and they have a need to be accurate. These individuals are considered to be* reflective *while those individuals who respond immediately to what is presented without regard to the fact they may be erroneous are labeled as* impulsive *learners. (40, p. 17)*

How long does it take for students to prepare their answers when called on in class or asked to respond to a question during the assessment process? Native American students tend to look at all sides of an issue, examine their possible implications, and make sure they know the answer before they are ready to express their opinion. Assessors who do not allow students sufficient time to prepare their answers before calling on someone else or moving on to the next item may mistakenly believe that the students do not know something, are slow learners, and so on (41).

### Risk Taking

How sure do students have to be that they know the answer, can complete a task, or have a correct opinion before they will risk a response during assessment? How likely are they to choose an answer they are not completely sure of on a multiple choice item that deducts for incorrect answers?

> *A Japanese youth . . . should remain silent rather than exhibiting a faulty understanding or command of a skill. To put forth a mistaken answer or an unperfected skill is a personal disgrace and an insult to the teacher and the discipline. (34, p. 19)*

> *A reluctance to try too soon and the accompanying fear of being "shamed" if one does not succeed may account for the seemingly passive uninterested and unresponsive attitude of Indian students. (39, p. 28)*

> *The Hispanic culture discourages guessing (hablando sin saber). Thus, Hispanic students may be penalized on assessment procedures which require students to respond when they are uncertain of the correct answer. (3, p. 177)*

### Global Perception Versus Analysis of Details

Some students, such as African Americans and Hispanic Americans, tend to be global learners; others, including many middle-class European Americans, typically are more analytical. Global learners perceive things in a holistic manner. They perceive the whole of an event, idea, or image and the relationships between its parts simultaneously. They see everything as a part of the whole and use few discrete categories to notice differences among the parts. Analytic learners can easily divide the whole into subcategories based on differences. Therefore, students' performance on achievement and other types of assessment procedures may depend, in part, on whether the tasks they are required to perform fit their particular global or analytic learning style.

### Stimulation and Variety

Students differ in terms of their tolerance for and willingness to continue to perform assessment tasks that are boring, monotonous, tedious and repetitious. Research indicates that the performance of African American students who come from homes that are highly stimulating increases when the format of an assessment procedure includes more task variation, but the performance of African American and European American students from homes that are not highly stimulating does not improve with increased variability (38; also see "High Versus Low Stimulation" in Chapter 10.) Boykin explains this on the basis of the home environment to which many African Americans are accustomed.

> *The home and immediate ecological environments of a preponderance of Black children afford levels of physical stimulation that are high in both intensity and variability. . . . One consequence of growing up in such environments may be a heightened responsiveness to stimulus change. . . . It would seem reasonable,*

*moreover, that in a problem solving context, Black children would find tasks presented in a relatively monotonous fashion even more intolerable than their counterparts from more placid settings. Thus, it would seem that increased variation should have a greater positive effect on the task performance of Black children. (38, pp. 470–471)*

### Activity Level

Students' willingness to sit still for long periods of time is greatly influenced by their ethnic and socioeconomic backgrounds (37). Because some students may have difficulty sitting quietly and completing sedentary assessment activities for long periods of time, their performance may indicate their difficulty in adjusting to the requirements of the assessment situation, not what they have achieved or learned or what they could accomplish if they were assessed in a more culturally appropriate manner.

### Pace

People from different cultures work and play at different paces. Some students attempt to accomplish as much as possible within a given period of time; others prefer a relaxed, steady pace. Slower-working students who correctly answer all the items that they have time to complete on standardized tests may receive a lower score than students who rush through the test and miss items that those working at a slower pace answer correctly. It is important, therefore, to determine whether students can demonstrate what they know and have achieved in school on timed evaluations or merely appear to have accomplished less than they have because they are unable to complete the evaluation procedure.

Some students who are accustomed to working at a slower pace—African Americans, Brazilian Americans, Filipino Americans, Hawaiian Americans, and Samoan Americans, among others—may make more errors when required to work as fast as they can. Students accustomed to a faster pace—for example, Japanese Americans and Chinese Americans—continue to perform as well when they are told to work as fast as they can (42–44). For all of these reasons, it is essential to use untimed procedures when assessing students who are not accustomed to rushing through things.

### Response Style

Cultures differ in the degree to which they encourage intense or subdued responses to life. For example, in comparison to European American students, African American students are more likely to respond intensely to things in general and to select extreme responses on scales that ask if they strongly agree or just agree, or if they strongly disagree or just disagree (45, 46). Therefore, assessors should consider students' response style when they interpret their responses to items on assessment procedures.

## Assessment Materials and Procedures

The materials and procedures that assessors use are another significant source of bias. The primary sources of such bias are technical bias, content bias, format bias, and linguistic bias.

### Technical Bias

Assessment procedures must be reliable and valid. If they are not, then decisions based on the data they provide will be discriminatory. For an assessment procedure to be useful the score/results that are obtained should be correct. For example, students who have behavior problems should appear that way to different observers, and they should appear to have problems regardless of the particular time they are observed or evaluated or the particular situation in which they are evaluated. If this is not true, then judgments about students might depend on the persons who observe them, the time at which they are observed, or the situation in which they are observed. Procedures are reliable when they produce consistent results regardless of the observer, the time, or the situation.

Procedures that are reliable for some students may be unreliable when used with other students. Because the reliability of most procedures is determined by studying their use with predominantly European American students, many procedures may be unreliable when used with non-European students. For example, observers who are biased against certain groups such as African American students or who do not know about the cultural determinants of their behavior may perceive that behavior differently than observers who are not prejudiced against these students or knowledgeable about their culture.

Procedures that are valid measure what they claim to measure and accomplish what they are designed to achieve. For example, intelligence tests or tests of learning potential are supposed to measure students' ability to learn and to predict how much students will learn in certain situations when they are given certain kinds and amounts of assistance. If they do not measure a student's capacity to learn and predict accurately how students will function in specific learning situations, they are invalid, useless, and even harmful.

For example, students' current knowledge about a particular item (such as how far is it from one place to another or the height of the average American adult male) or their ability to perform a particular task (such as forming a design from blocks) can indicate their learning potential or help assessors to predict how they will learn in the future, but only under certain conditions. The students must have been exposed to the information or task and have had sufficient practice to learn it; they must be motivated to demonstrate their knowledge or ability to assessors; and they have to be permitted to do so in a way that fits their performance style. Non–European American, poor, and limited English proficient students are not always exposed to the same materials, tasks, environments and so on as European American, middle-class, and English proficient students. They may not be as motivated to demonstrate their ability and knowledge during the assessment procedure, and they have different learning and communication styles. Therefore, procedures that are valid with European American middle-class students may be invalid when used with non–European American and poor students.

## *Content Bias*

Content bias may occur because different teachers, schools, and school districts include different content in the courses they offer at each grade level and because students bring different experiences to the assessment situation for contextual and cultural reasons.

Because of differences in the contents of the curriculum to which students are exposed, students' scores on standardized achievement tests may depend on the match between what the procedure measures and what they have been taught (47, 50, 52). After determining that third- and fourth-grade students obtained different scores on each of four standardized reading achievement tests, Good and Salvia concluded that one cannot always determine whether "a student's reading score reflects deficient reading skills or the selection of a test with poor content validity for the pupil's curriculum" (52, p. 56).

Inner city schools, rural schools, and suburban schools include very different skills in their curriculum. Migrant students who move from school to school may miss a considerable amount of course content. For these reasons, assessment procedures may evaluate students on what they should have been taught, not on what they were actually taught (47).

Some educators believe curriculum-based assessment is an effective way to avoid such content bias. Curriculum-based assessment is an approach that aims to assess students in terms of the curriculum that they have actually been exposed to in class. This avoids the bias that results in assessing students on knowledge and skills that they have not studied or practiced and including items that depend on family and community values. The advantages and disadvantages of this approach are discussed later in this chapter.

Some educators claim that the contents of many assessment materials are biased against non–European American and poor students because the context of their lives and their cultural backgrounds expose them to very different experiences than those of middle-class American students. "A body of knowledge based on the experiences of a white middle class community cannot help but create a disadvantage for members of communities which differ from the mainstream" (50, p. 178).

These educators suggest that questions such as how far is it from one place to another are only relevant if students are familiar with the places, asking why it is better to pay bills by check rather than cash is not relevant to children whose parents cannot afford a checking account, and whether it is better to build houses from bricks rather than wood depends on the geographic region in which students grow up.

Measuring independence or motor control by determining if children can drink out of a cup or ride a tricycle or throw a ball overhand can lead to incorrect conclusions if they still drink from a bottle, play soccer rather than baseball, are too poor to own a tricycle, or live in an area where the traffic makes it is too dangerous for children to ride a tricycle. Evaluating students' short-term memory by having them repeat a series of digits backward or forward can provide accurate information for students who have had an opportunity to practice remembering numbers in a series. However, some students come from places where they and their friends have telephone numbers and street addresses, others come from rural areas in the United States or elsewhere where there is little reason to remember numbers.

Some items are biased because they involve family and community values. The answers to such items as what you should do if a smaller child hits you, why it is better to give money to a charitable organization than to a street beggar, and what you should do if you lose something that belongs to your friend depend on the values and experiences to which students have been exposed.

Other educators and psychologists question whether such items are really biased (49, 55). They claim that one cannot determine if an item or content is biased merely by examining it, because that is too subjective; they maintain that one has to actually determine statistically whether an item is more difficult for one group than another; and they point out that some items that were judged to be biased have turned out to be no more difficult for the group that they are supposed to be biased against than for any other group. Presently, there is very little research to support this point of view.

Educators who believe that there is a great deal of content bias in assessment procedures have suggested that one way to reduce such bias is to eliminate any items that are more difficult for some groups than for others (51, 55, 59). They complain that although test publishers eliminate items that are more difficult for one gender or the other in order to eliminate gender bias, they do not do the same thing for items that are more difficult for certain ethnic, socioeconomic, or regional groups.

Other educators and psychologists feel that the differences in the scores that various groups receive on these items represent real differences in ability or achievement between groups (54). They advise test publishers to continue to include such items in their assessment materials.

In the 1970s and early 1980s educators and psychologists developed a number of culture-specific assessment instruments, primarily for African Americans, that included content that was more relevant to the students' experiences, pictures of African Americans in more culturally relevant situations, and so on. The majority of these instruments were designed to evaluate African Americans' personality characteristics, their priorities in life, the extent to which they are aware of and identify with their African heritage, their knowledge of the oppressive nature and effects of racism, their willingness to resist anti–African American pressures and threats, their attitudes toward African American issues, their mistrust of European Americans, and their identification with African American values, customs, and institutions (48, 53, 56–58, 60).

Research indicates that persons assessed with these instruments provide more data and data that is more valid. The instruments can be used to obtain information about certain aspects of students' personalities and their attitudes about European American teachers and European American values. However, they provide only a limited amount of the information needed to evaluate African American students functioning in school.

A number of culture-specific instruments have also been developed for use with Hispanic American students. Most of these instruments are designed to be administered in Spanish to limited English proficient students who have not assimilated to the mainstream European American culture (see the section on linguistic bias). Few of them are designed for use with English proficient Hispanic American students.

There are very few culture-specific assessment instruments available for other groups. This may indicate that it is not profitable to develop and market culture-specific procedures for small numbers of students. Thus, for the present, culture-specific instruments are not a viable option for assessors who wish to avoid content bias.

## *Format Bias*

The format of an assessment procedure refers to how tasks, questions, and so on, are posed to students and how students are required to respond to them. Format characteristics such as whether students are asked to recognize the correct answer or solution to a problem or to produce it themselves; whether they respond orally, in writing, or by performing a task; whether there are time limits; whether items get progressively more difficult; and what materials the students work with—all can affect students' performance. When there is a poor match between how students function and the format of an assessment procedure, students may not be able to show what they know and can do. Space permits a discussion of only a few examples of format problems.

Students who are immigrants or who have attended atypical schools on reservations may have difficulty adjusting to the unfamiliar format of many standardized tests. For example, some assessment procedures require students to fail five, six, or even seven similar items before they can go on to the next group of items. This can be devastating to students who respond poorly to such experiences and to students who are not accustomed to taking tests in which they fail many items and still do well. Assessment materials that can be used with students who function at many different levels often contain both very easy and very difficult problems on the same page. This can be very frightening and demoralizing to students who see many problems or items that are too difficult for them and do not understand that the difficult ones are for students who are older or in a higher grade.

As was noted earlier, some students, particularly African Americans, Hispanic Americans, and Native Americans, cannot always show what they can do on timed procedures. Stringent time limits galvanize some students to work efficiently and perform at their optimal level, but those who are anxious or who work at a slower pace perform less adequately under time pressures (4).

> *Achievement tests with stringent time limits do not just measure what skills children have acquired or what they know but in addition whether or not they can demonstrate this knowledge quickly and under time pressure and testing stress. (4, p. 16)*

Providing these students with the time they need to complete an assessment at the pace at which they are accustomed to work yields more accurate information about what they know and can do (61).

Cultural factors may make it difficult for some students to engage in certain required activities during the assessment process. For example, on assessment of fine motor coordination, Hmong American children would not demonstrate that they could use pincers to pick up an object because the raisins they were required to pick up resembled Hmong medicines that they were warned to avoid (62).

Finally, whether students are required to respond orally or in writing, in a multiple choice or short essay format, verbally or kinesthetically, and so on, during the assessment process can determine if they are able to demonstrate their true capability and achievement. To deal with this problem, Gardner suggests that

> *Achievement tests should be designed so that students have some room for flexibility. For example a cluster of three or four items that examine a particular skill from different viewpoints and tests it in different ways could be set. . . . [so that] a pupil who can answer any one of them correctly will have demonstrated his/her mastery of that skill and should receive full credit for it—even if he/she had erred on some of the other items in that cluster. (43, p. 234)*

## *Linguistic Bias*

Assessments conducted in a language or dialect in which students are not proficient or in only one language when students require two languages to function adequately and explain themselves fully do not provide a true picture of what students know or can do.

### *Limited English Proficiency*

At first glance, one might think that LEP students should be assessed in their native languages. However, the choice of which language or languages should be used to assess students is a much more complicated issue.

Students who have no proficiency in English clearly need to be assessed in their native language. Those who are truly proficient in English can be assessed completely in English. However, many other students need to be assessed in two languages to demonstrate what they know and can do.

Many limited English proficient students have two vocabularies—a home vocabulary and a school vocabulary. Students in bilingual programs learn a great deal of the content of the curriculum in their native language. Students in English as a second language programs or in regular English language classes learn much of the material in English. Thus, until students are completely proficient in English, those in bilingual programs may have to use their native language to demonstrate their mastery of school-related material, and those in English as a second language or English submergence programs will be unable to demonstrate their school-related achievement unless it is assessed in English. Regardless of the program students are in, their English vocabulary is likely to be limited to what they are learning in school for quite some time. As a result, students are likely to have to use their native languages to express most of what they have learned at home and in their community. These differences must be taken into account when decisions are made regarding the language or languages in which students should be as to assessed in general. Because students need to be assessed in the language in which they will function best on each particular task, skill, or knowledge area, individual differences in native language and English language proficiency must be considered when decisions are made about the language or languages in which each aspect of the assessment should be conducted. A general principle to follow is to make sure students are assessed in both English and their native languages, because research indicates that limited English proficient students usually score higher when assessed in both languages rather than in either their native language or English alone (61, 63).

The goal of providing students with linguistically appropriate assessment services in the more than one hundred languages spoken by limited English proficient students in the United States has proved difficult to achieve for two reasons. Very few of the educators and psychologists who are responsible for assessing students are bilingual. This is particularly true for languages other than Spanish, and, except for Spanish language materials, there is very little assessment material in the many languages spoken by the millions of limited English proficient students in the public schools. The two approaches that have been used to overcome these difficulties are to translate assessment materials into other languages and to use interpreters during the assessment process. Both of these approaches are problematic.

Translating materials into students' native languages can improve the performance of limited English proficient students (61, 64). However, a number of problems must be avoided before these benefits can be achieved.

Using material translated into students' native languages when their preferred language for the task or problem is English because they have learned it in English will not benefit students.

Poorly translated materials will not improve the validity of an assessment. Back translations can eliminate this problem. In a back translation the material that has been translated from English is translated back into English in order to detect any distortion in meaning that resulted from original translation. If the meanings of the back translation and the original are the same, then the translation is probably correct. If they are different, there is good chance that the meaning was changed when the material was translated from English. It is also important to be sure that students speak the dialect of the translation to avoid linguistic bias.

Translating material will not necessarily eliminate its content bias. Therefore, it is often necessary to adapt the content as well the language of the material to the cultural, contextual, and linguistic characteristics of the students with whom they are to be used. Actual examples of content change in translations include changing the question "How are a peach and a plum alike?" to "How are an orange and a banana alike?"; replacing a marble game with a card game; and modifying "How far is it from New York to Chicago" to "How far is it from New York to Puerto Rico."

Sometimes it is also necessary to accept alternative correct answers to some items. For example, to middle-class European American children, what is absurd about a picture of man carrying an umbrella upside down is that the umbrella is in a position in which it will not protect him from rain. However, to Puerto Rican American children the absurdity is that a *man* is carrying an umbrella in any position because males do not carry umbrellas. On a vocabulary test a translated word may have more than one meaning. For example, translating "courage" into "*valor*" becomes problematic because "*valor*" means "value" as well as "bravery" in Spanish.

Translating material often changes the level of difficulty of items. "Dog," a very easy word to read or spell in English translates to "*perro*" in Spanish, a more difficult word because of the double r. Translating "building" to "*edificio*" makes the item easier.

Translating materials does not make the norms of a standardized assessment procedure any more appropriate for students who are not well-represented in the norm sample, nor does it eliminate the format bias of procedures that provide students with only limited amounts of time, require them to make many errors before they are allowed to go on to the next group of problems, and so on.

> *It was discovered that some Vietnamese children, when asked to pick up the blue block, would instead pick up the green block. The Vietnamese language classifies colors into four families: green, red, yellow, and purple. Blue is in the green family, so that words for green and blue are similar (Xahn). To distinguish it is necessary to say "Xahn lo" (blue like the sky) or "Xahn la cay" (green like the leaves) to ensure that the child correctly differentiates between green and blue. (62, p. 482)*

Assessors who cannot evaluate limited English proficient students and interview their parents in their native language require the assistance of interpreters. As the following quote indicates, when properly used interpreters can be very helpful.

> *I strongly believe in the use of language and cultural mediators or interpreters, as I have seen dramatic differences in the behaviors of both children and adults. We find a significant difference in how quickly the family develops trust and*

*responds, how much information they volunteer, and how well they establish a relationship. (68, p. 9)*

The use of untrained or poorly prepared interpreters, however, can create many problems (65). Untrained interpreters may identify with the student and want the student to do well. This may lead interpreters to prompt the right answer from the student or modify students' answers so that they are closer to the acceptable response. Interpreters who are not equally fluent in both languages may translate incorrectly to the student or assessor. Interpreters who are fluent in the student's languages but not knowledgeable about their cultural background may translate correctly but conduct the assessment in a culturally inappropriate manner or fail to notice content and format bias. If they are from a different socio-economic, religious, racial, or ethnic background than the students, the interpreters may be prejudiced against them.

To avoid or at least minimize these potential problems, interpreters should be trained in the principles of assessment, human development, and so on. They should be equally competent in both languages, equally familiar with mainstream culture and the students' culture, and, if possible, familiar with the communities in which students live and the subgroups to which they belong. The references at the end of the chapter contain much useful information on the training and use of interpreters in the assessment of culturally and linguistically different students (66–69).

### *Dialect*

Although in the 1970s a few studies found that nonstandard dialect speakers are not penalized when they are assessed in standard English (70–73), the vast majority of research at the time and virtually all that has been carried out since then indicates that nonstandard dialect–speaking students who are poor, African American, Native American, Hispanic American, or from Appalachian areas perform poorly when they are assessed in standard English (74–77, 79, 80, 82–85, 87–91, 94–97). There is also considerable evidence that these biased results can lead educators to underestimate students' academic achievement and language ability. (78, 80, 83, 84).

The following are some of the causes of dialect bias during the assessment process.

- Educators and others discriminate against nonstandard English dialects (see Chapter 6).
- Questions on assessment procedures are often asked using vocabulary that is not familiar to students—i.e., "behind the sofa" rather than "in back of the couch," "beginning to climb" instead of "starting to climb" (97). As a result, students appear to lack information and skills that they actually possess and would be able to demonstrate if they understood the question or directions.
- Some dialect speakers may read material written in their own dialect better than material in standard English (93).

- Students tend to remember better material that is in their dialect (74, 83).
- Students are better able to discriminate between sounds that are present in their own dialect (77, 81, 91).
- Students may misunderstand items and directions because they are given in a different dialect. As an example, European American students who are asked to find which of four pictures shows "delight" may have little difficulty identifying the picture of a girl happily eating an ice cream cone. However, African American students who do not speak standard English may hear "de" (the) "light" and select the picture of a boy reading who needs a light (86).
- What may appear to be articulation problems and other types of speech disorders can be omissions and substitutions that conform to speech patterns present in a student's dialect (82, 95).

Suggestions for avoiding bias during the assessment of nonstandard English speakers include the following (80, 84, 87, 88, 92, 94, 95):

- Become knowledgeable about the characteristics of the dialects spoken by the nonstandard English–speakers. There are many descriptions of the major differences between standard English and the various nonstandard English dialects that can help you to avoid mistaking dialect differences for possible speech disorders (76, 98, 99).
- Examine your attitudes about nonstandard dialects for possible bias.
- Avoid stereotyping all members of a group as nonstandard speakers. Determine whether each individual student is a standard or nonstandard dialect speaker. Keep in mind that working-class and younger students are more likely to use nonstandard dialects.
- Use assessment procedures only with students who use the dialect for whom the test has been standardized.
- Do not consider differences in oral reading due to dialect differences such as mispronunciations or adding or omitting endings that indicate plurals, tense, and the like, as reading errors.
- Accept answers that conform to a student's dialect as correct even though they may not be acceptable according to the manual.
- Make sure students understand the directions and the items included in any assessment procedure. Be prepared to use alternate instructions in both dialects and to express the contents in both dialects.

## Gender Bias

The contents and language of an assessment procedure can also be biased against one gender or the other. Although the effect is not very large, each gender is more likely to answer correctly test items that deal with objects and topics that interest them and those that use same-gender pronouns (male students do somewhat better when pronouns are he, him, and his, and females score higher when pronouns refer to she, her, and hers). Studies conducted in the 1970s and early 1980s indicate that test items tend to include more male pronouns and more material that fits stereotypical male interests. If this situation has not been corrected in recent years, female students may still be placed at a disadvantage when they are assessed with these materials (100–106).

## *Formal, Standardized, Norm-Referenced Assessment Versus Informal, Nonstandardized, Criterion-Referenced Assessment*

Assessment procedures can be divided into two categories: formal, standardized, norm-referenced procedures, and informal, nonstandardized, criterion-referenced procedures. Assessors use the terms somewhat differently and do not always agree about which are which. In general, formal assessment procedures are those that deviate from regular classroom practices. They are usually designed to determine how students are doing in relation to criteria that are more universal and less applicable or geared to the particular students' situations. In order to make such comparisons, formal procedures are administered and scored in a standardized way. The interpretation of the scores is typically accomplished by comparing an individual's score to norms obtained from a sample of students that are believed to represent the population of students with whom the procedure will be used. Standardized achievement tests are good examples of these procedures.

Informal procedures are those that can easily be incorporated into the classroom without interfering with daily activities. Informal procedures typically involve evaluating what students do, how they function, and what they have learned in relation to the curriculum they are exposed to or the goals and standards of their particular teacher or school. This can be done in an unstructured manner by observing how students function and evaluating their work or in a structured way by using observation checklists and scales and lists of specific evaluative criteria.

Unlike norm-referenced assessment approaches, in which individual students are compared to a norm sample of students, criterion-referenced assessment is designed to compare an individual student to a set of criteria or performance standards such as the number of words spelled correctly or the skills needed to perform a specific task. Criterion-referenced assessment procedures describe students' achievement, knowledge, behavior, and so on, rather than compare students to each other (107, 108).

*In norm-referenced testing, learning a particular skill is important only to the extent that differential learning allows the examiner to rank individuals in order, from those who have learned many skills to those who have learned few. The emphasis is on the relative standing of children rather than on absolute mastery of content. On the other hand, criterion-referenced testing interprets achieve-*

## References

Test anxiety is the focus of the following references.

1. Clawson, T. W., Firment, C. K., & Trower, T. L. (1981). Test anxiety: Another origin for racial bias in standardized testing. *Measurement and Evaluation in Guidance, 13*(4), 210–215.
2. Dao, M. (1991). Designing assessment procedures for educationally at-risk Southeast Asian–American students. *Journal of Learning Disabilities, 24*(10), 594–601.
3. Grossman, H. (1984). *Educating Hispanic Students: Cultural Implications for Instruction, Classroom Management, Counseling, and Assessment.* Springfield, IL: Charles C Thomas.
4. Hill, K. T. (1980). *Eliminating Motivational Causes of Test Bias. Final Report, October 1, 1976, through March 31, 1980.* ERIC ED 196–936.
5. Nguyen, K. T. (1984). *Assessing and Counseling Vietnamese Exceptional Students: Some Cultural Factors to Be Considered.* Santa Clara, CA: Santa Clara County Office of Education.
6. Payne, B. D. (1984). The relationship of test anxiety and answer-changing behavior: An analysis by race and sex. *Measurement and Evaluation in Guidance, 16*(4), 205–211.

The following references discuss students' familiarity with assessment procedures and the effects of training in test-wiseness on students' subsequent performance.

7. Bangert-Drowns, R. L., Kulik, R. L., & Kulik, C. C. (1983). Effects of coaching programs on achievement test scores. *Review of Educational Research, 53,* 571–585.
8. Benson, J., Urman, H., & Hocevar, D. (1986). Effects of test-wiseness training and ethnicity on achievement of third- and fifth-grade students. *Measurement and Evaluation in Counseling and Development, 18*(4), 154–162.
9. Brescia, W., & Fortune, J. C. (1988). *Standardized Testing of American Indian Students.* Las Cruces, NM: New Mexico State University. ERIC/CRESS.
10. Bridgeman, B., & Buttram, J. (1975). Race differences on nonverbal analogy test performance as a function of verbal strategy training. *Journal of Educational Psychology, 67*(4), 586–590.
11. Haladyna, T. M., Nolen, S. B., & Hass, N. S. (1991). Raising standard achievement scores and the origins of test score pollution. *Educational Researcher, 20*(5), 2–7.
12. Kalechstein, P., Kalechstein, M., & Doctre, R. (1981). The effects of instruction on test-taking skills in second-grade black children. *Measurement and Evaluation in Guidance, 13*(4), 198–202.
13. McPhail, I. P. (1985). Instructional strategies for teaching test-wiseness. In C. Brooks (Ed.), *Tapping Potential: English Language Arts for the Black Learner.* Urbana IL: National Council of Teachers of English.
14. Samson, G. E. (1985). Effects of training in test-taking skills on achievement test performance: A quantitative synthesis. *Journal of Educational Research, 78*(5), 266.
15. Sarnacki, R. E. (1979). An examination of test-wiseness in the cognitive test domain. *Review of Educational Research, 49,* 252–279.
16. Schubert, J., & Cropley, A. (1972). Verbal regulation of behavior and IQ in Canadian Indian and white children. *Developmental Psychology, 7,* 295–301.

The relationship between students' motivation and their functioning during assessment procedures is discussed in these references.

17. Burgess, B. J. (1978). Native American learning styles. In L. Morris, G. Sather, & S. Scull (Eds.), *Extracting Learning Styles from Social/Cultural Diversity: A Study of Five American*

*Minorities*. Norman, OK: Southwest Teacher Corps Network.
18. Chamberlain, K. P., & Medinos-Landurand, P. (1991). Practical considerations for the assessment of LEP students with special needs. In E. V. Hamayan & J. S. Damico (Eds.), *Limiting Bias in the Assessment of Bilingual Students*. Austin, TX: PRO-ED.
19. Condon, E. C., Peters, J. Y., & Sueiro-Ross, C. (1979). *Special Education and the Hispanic Child: Cultural Perspectives*. Philadelphia: Temple University, Teacher Corps Mid-Atlantic Network.
20. Deyhle D. (1987). Learning failure: Tests as gatekeepers and the culturally different child. In H. E. Trueba (Ed.), *Success or Failure?* Rawley, MA: Newbury House.
21. Goldstein, B.L. (1988). In search of survival: The education and integration of Hmong refugee girls. *Journal of Ethnic Studies, 16*(2), 1–27.
22. Grossman, H. (1990). *Trouble Free Teaching: Solutions to Behavior Problems in the Classroom*. Mountain View, CA: Mayfield.
23. Lyons, G. (1979). A high school on an Indian reservation: A question of survival, developing goals, and giving leadership. *British Educational Administration Society, 7*, 130–138.
24. National Coalition of Advocates for Students. (1988). *New Voices: Immigrant Students in U.S. Public Schools*. Boston: Author.
25. Slogett, B. B. (1971). Use of group activities and team rewards to increase individual classroom productivity. *Teaching Exceptional Children, 3*(2), 54–66.

The effects of assessor characteristics on the outcome of assessment procedures is discussed in the following references.

26. Gantt, W. N., Wilson, R. M., & Dayton, C. M. (1974–1975). An initial investigation of the relationship between syntactical divergency and the listening comprehension of black children. *Reading Research Quarterly, 10*(2), 193–211.
27. Garcia, A. B., & Zimmerman, B. J. (1972). The effect of examiner ethnicity and language on the performance of bilingual Mexican-American first graders. *Journal of Social Psychology, 87*, 3–11.
28. Gay, G., & Abrahams, R. D. (1973). Does the pot melt, boil, or brew? Black children and white assessment procedures. *Journal of School Psychology, 11*(4), 330–340.
29. Gollnick, D., & Chinn, P. (1988). *Multicultural Education in a Pluralistic Society*. St. Louis: Mosby.
30. Mishra, S. P. (1980). The influence of examiners' ethnic attributes on intelligence test scores. *Psychology in the Schools, 17*(1), 117–121.
31. Ratusnik, D. L., & Koenigsknecht, R. A. (1977). Biracial testing: The question of clinicians' influence on children's test performance. *Language, Speech, and Hearing Services in Schools, 8*(3/4), 5–14.
32. Terrell, F., & Terrell, S. L. (1983). The relationship between race of examiner, cultural mistrust, and the intelligence test performance of black children. *Psychology in the Schools, 20*, 367–369.
33. Terrell, F., Terrell, J. L., & Taylor, J. (1981). Effects of type of reinforcement on the intelligence test performance of retarded black children. *Psychology in the Schools, 18*, 225–227.

These references deal with the relationship between communication style and assessment results.

34. California State Department of Education. (1987). *Handbook for Teaching Japanese-Speaking Students*. Sacramento, CA: Author.
35. Crago, M. (1988). *Cultural Context in Communicative Interaction of Inuit Children*. Unpublished doctoral dissertation. Montreal: McGill University.
36. National Council of La Raza. (1986). *Beyond Ellis Island: Hispanics—Immigrants and Americans*. Washington, DC. Author.

The influence of students' learning style on their functioning during the assessment process is the focus of the following references.

37. Almanza, H. P., & Mosley, W. J. (1980). Cultural adaptations and modifications for culturally diverse handicapped children. *Exceptional Children, 46*(8), 608–614.
38. Boykin, A. W. (1982). Task variability and the performance of black and white school children. *Journal of Black Studies, 12*(4), 469–485.
39. Longstreet, E. (1978). *Aspects of Ethnicity*. New York: Teachers College Press.
40. Shade, B. J. (1979). *Racial Preference in Psychological Differentiation: An Alternative Explanation for Group Differences*. ERIC ED 179–672.
41. Tharp, G. (1989). Psychocultural variables and constants: Effects on teaching and learn-

ing in schools. *American Psychologist, 44*(2), 349–359.

How the pace at which students work and play can affect the results of assessments is the focus of the following references.

42. Ayabe, H. I. (1978). Ethnic-culture, reflection impulsivity and locus of control. *Educational Perspectives, 17*(4), 10–12.
43. Gardner, W. E. (1977). A model for creating a more hospitable achievement test environment for black elementary students. *Negro Educational Review, 28*(3/4), 229–236.
44. Levine, R. V., West, L. J., & Reis, H. T. (1980). Perceptions of time and punctuality in the United States and Brazil. *Journal of Personality and Social Psychology, 38*(4), 541–550.

African American students' tendency to select extreme responses on Likert Scales is documented in these references.

45. Bachman, J. G., & O'Malley, P. M. (1984). Yea-saying, nay-saying and going to extremes: Are black-white differences in survey results due to response styles? *Public Opinion Quarterly, 48,* 409–427.
46. Bachman, J. G., & O'Malley, P. M. (1984). Black-white differences in self-esteem: Are they affected by response styles? *American Journal of Sociology, 90*(3), 624–639.

Content bias in assessment procedures is the focus of the next articles.

47. Bagby, S. A. (1981). *Educational Testing for Migrant Students.* Las Cruces, NM: ERIC Clearinghouse on Rural Education and Small Schools.
48. Baldwin, J. A., & Bell, Y. R. (1985). The African Self-Consciousness Scale: An Africentric personality questionnaire. *Western Journal of Black Studies, 9*(2), 61–68.
49. Clarizio, H. F. (1982). Intellectual assessment of Hispanic children. *Psychology in the Schools, 19*(6), 61–71.
50. Conroy, A. A. (1992). The testing of minority language students. *Journal of Educational Issues of Language Minority Students, 2,* 175–186.
51. Fagen, J. (1987). Golden Rule revisited: Introduction. *Educational Measurement: Issues and Practice, 6*(2), 5–8.
52. Good, R. H., III, & Salvia, J. (1988). Curriculum bias in published norm-referenced reading tests: Demonstrable effects. *School Psychology Review, 17*(1), 51–60.
53. Hawley, L., & Williams, R. L. (1981). Feeling-tone and card preference of black college students for the TCB and TAT. *Journal of Non-White Concerns, 10*(1), 45–48.
54. Jaeger, M. M. (1987). NCME opposition to proposed Golden Rule legislation. *Educational Measurement: Issues and Practice, 6*(2), 21–22.
55. Rooney, J. P. (1987). Golden Rule on "Golden Rule." *Educational Measurement: Issues and Practice, 6*(2), 9–12.
56. Terrell, F., & Taylor, J. (1978). The development of an inventory to measure certain aspects of black nationalist ideology. *Psychology, A Quarterly Journal of Human Behavior, 15,* 31–33.
57. Terrell, F., & Terrell, S. (1981). An inventory to measure cultural mistrust among blacks. *Western Journal of Black Studies, 5*(3), 180–185.
58. Weaver, V. (1981). Racial attribution, story length, and feeling-tone of young black males to TCB and TAT. *Journal of Non-White Concerns, 10*(1), 31–43.
59. Weiss, J. (1987). The Golden Rule bias reduction principle: A practical reform. *Educational Measurement: Issues and Practice, 6*(2), 23–25.
60. Williams, R. L., & Johnson, R. C. (1981). Progress in developing Afrocentric measuring instruments. *Journal of Non-White Concerns, 10*(1), 3–18.

Format bias is the focus of these references.

61. Llabre, M. M. (1988). *Test-Related Factors Affecting Test Performance of Hispanics.* Paper presented at the annual conference of the American Education Research Association, New Orleans.
62. Miller, V., Onotera, R. T., & Deinard, A. S. (1984). Denver Developmental Screening Test: Cultural variations in Southeast Asian children. *Journal of Pediatrics, 104*(3), 481–482.

The effects of linguistic bias is the focus of these references.

63. Bergan, J. R., & Marra, E. B. (1979). Variations in IQ testing and instruction and the letter learning and achievement of Anglo and bilingual Mexican-American children. *Journal of Educational Psychology, 71*(6), 819–826.
64. Levandowski, B. (1975). The difference in intelligence test scores of bilingual students on an English version of the intelligence test

as compared to a Spanish version of the test. *Illinois School Research, 11*(3), 47–51.

The following references deal with effective use of interpreters during the assessment process.

65. Del Green Associates. (1983). *A Review of Research Affecting Educational Programming for Bilingual Handicapped Students*. Final Report. ERIC ED 267–555.
66. Figueroa, R. A. (1989). Using interpreters in assessments. *Communique, 17*(7), 19.
67. Langdon, H. W. (1988). *Interpreters/Translators in the School Setting Module*. Sacramento: California State Department of Education.
68. Metz, I. B. (1991). Comments. In M. Anderson & P. F. Goldberg (Eds.), *Cultural Competence in Screening and Assessment: Implications for Services to Young Children with Special Needs Ages Birth Through Five*. Minneapolis: PACER Center.
69. National Clearinghouse for Bilingual Education. *Meet the Needs of Handicapped Language Minority Students and Their Families*. Washington, DC: National Clearinghouse for Bilingual Education.

The following researchers have not found bias when nonstandard dialect speakers are assessed in standard English.

70. Desberg, P., Marsh, G., Schneider, L. A., & Duncan-Rose, C. (1979). The effects of social dialect on auditory sound blending and word recognition. *Contemporary Educational Psychology, 4*, 14–144.
71. Frentz, T. S. (1971). Children's comprehension of standard and Negro nonstandard English sentences. *Speech Monographs, 38*, 10–16.
72. Hockman, C. H. (1973). Black dialect reading tests in the urban schools. *Reading Teacher, 26*, 581–583.
73. Nolen, P. (1972). Reading of non-standard dialect materials, a study at grades two and four. *Child Development, 43*, 1092–1097.

The references listed here describe bias resulting from assessing nonstandard dialect speakers with standard English procedures and how to avoid it.

74. Baratz, J. (1969). *Language and Cognitive Assessment of Negro Children: Assumptions and Research Needs*. Paper presented at the annual meeting of the American Speech and Hearing Association, Washington, DC.
75. Benmaman, V., & Schenck, S. J. (1986). *Language Variability: An Analysis of Language Variability and Its Influence upon Special Education Assessment*. ERIC ED 296–532.
76. Bliss, L. S., & Allen, D. V. (1981). Black English responses on selected language tests. *Journal of Communication Disorders, 14*, 225–233.
77. Bryen, D. N. (1976). Speech-sound discrimination ability on linguistically unbiased tests. *Exceptional Children, 42*(4), 195–201.
78. Burke, S. M., Pflaum, S. W., & Knafle, J. D. (1982). The influence of Black English on diagnosis of reading in learning disabled and normal readers. *Journal of Learning Disabilities, 15*(1), 19–22.
79. Byrd, M. L., & Williams, H. S. (1981). *Language Attitudes and Black Dialect: An Assessment. (1) Language Attitudes in the Classroom. (2) A Reliable Measure of Language Attitude*. ERIC ED 213–062.
80. Cartledge, G., Stupay, D., & Kaczala, C. (1984). *Formal Language Assessment of Handicapped and Nonhandicapped Black Children*. ERIC ED 250–348.
81. Evans, J. S. (1972). Word-pair discrimination and imitation abilities of preschool Spanish-speaking children. *Journal of Learning Disabilities, 7*(9), 49–56.
82. Fisher, D., & Jablon, A. (1984). An observation of the phonology of black English speaking children. In Queens College Department of Communication Arts and Sciences. *Working Papers in Speech-Language Pathology and Audiology*. Flushing, Queens: City University of New York.
83. Harber, J. R. (1980). Issues in the assessment of language and reading disorders in learning disabled children. *Learning Disability Quarterly, 3*(4), 20–28.
84. Hemingway, B. L., Montague J. C., Jr., & Bradley, R. H. (1981). Preliminary data on revision of a sentence repetition test for language screening with black first grade children. *Language, Speech, and Hearing Services in Schools, 12*, 145–152.
85. Jensen, L. J. (1976). Dialect. In P. A. Allen (Ed.), *Findings of Research in Miscue Analyses: Classroom Implications*. Urbana, IL: National Council of Teachers of English.
86. Mackler, B., & Holman, D. (1976). Assessing, packaging, and delivery: Tests, testing, and race. *Young Children, 31*(5), 351–364.

87. Musselwhite, C. R. (1983). Pluralistic assessment in speech-language pathology: Use of dual norms in the placement process. *Language, Speech, and Hearing Services in Schools, 14,* 29–37.
88. Norris, M. K., Juarez, M. J., & Perkins, M. N. (1989). Adaptation of a screening test for bilingual and bidialectal populations. *Language, Speech, and Hearing Services in Schools, 20*(4), 381–390.
89. Ramstad, V. V., & Potter, R. E. (1974). Differences in vocabulary and syntax usage between Nez Perce Indian and white kindergarten children. *Journal of Learning Disabilities, 7*(8), 35–41.
90. Rivers, L. W. (1978). The influence of auditory-, visual-, and language-discrimination skills on the standardized test performance of Black children. *Journal of NonWhite Concerns, 6*(3), 134–140.
91. Ross, H. W. (1979). Wepman Test of Auditory Discrimination: What does it discriminate? *Journal of School Psychology, 17*(1), 47–54.
92. Seymour, H. N., & Seymour, C. M. (1977). A therapeutic model for communicative disorders among children who speak Black English vernacular. *Journal of Speech and Hearing Disorders, 42,* 238–246.
93. Thurmond, V. B. (1977). The effect of Black English on the reading test performance of high school students. *Journal of Educational Research, 70*(3), 160–163.
94. Vaughn-Cooke, F. B. (1980). Evaluation the language of black English speakers: Implications of the Ann Arbor decision. In M. F. Whileman (Ed.), *Reactions to Ann Arbor: Vernacular Black English and Education.* Arlington VA: Center for Applied Linguistics.
95. Wartella, A. B., & Williams, D. (1982). *Speech and Language Assessment of Black and Bilingual Children.* ERIC ED 218–914.
96. Weiner, F. D., Lewnay, L., & Erway, E. (1983). Measuring language competence of Black American English. *Journal of Speech and Hearing Disorders, 48,* 76–84.
97. Williams R. L., & Rivers, L. W. (1972). *The Use of Standard Versus Non-Standard English in the Administration of Group Tests to Black Children.* Paper presented at the annual meeting of the American Psychological Association, Honolulu.

The following references provide descriptions of expected differences that may occur in responses on some standardized tests given to speakers of nonstandard dialects.

98. Deyhle, D. (1985). Testing among Navajo and Anglo students: Another consideration of cultural bias. *Journal of Educational Equity and Leadership, 5,* 119–131.
99. Hunt, B. C. (1974–1975). Black dialect and third and fourth graders' performance on the Gray Oral Reading Test. *Reading Research Quarterly, 10,* 103–123.

The following references discuss gender bias in test items.

100. Brown, F. G. (1980). Sex bias in achievement test items: Do they have any effect on performance? *Teaching of Psychology, 7*(1), 24–26.
101. Doolittle, A. E. (1986). *Gender-Based Differential Item Performance in Mathematics Achievement Items.* ERIC ED 270–464.
102. Dwyer, C. A. (1979). The role of tests in producing sex-related differences. In M. A. Witting & A. C. Peterson (Eds.), *Sex-Related Differences in Cognitive Functioning: Developmental Issues.* New York: Academic Press.
103. Ekstrom, R. B., Lockheed, M. E., & Donlon, T. F. (1979). Sex differences and sex bias in test content. *Educational Horizons, 58*(1), 47–52.
104. Faggen-Steckler, J., McCarthy, K. A., & Tittle, C. K. (1974). A quantitative method for measuring sex "bias" in standardized tests. *Journal of Educational Measurement, 11,* 151–161.
105. Plake, B. S., Hoover, H. D., & Loyd, B. H. (1980). An investigation of the Iowa Test of Basic Skills for sex bias: A developmental look. *Psychology in the Schools, 17*(1), 47–52.
106. Tittle, C. K. (1974). Sex bias in educational measurement: Fact of fiction? *Measurement and Evaluation in Guidance, 6,* 219–226.

# Chapter 8

# Instruction in a Diverse Society

The goal of this chapter is to improve educators' ability to adapt their instructional methods to the ethnic, socioeconomic, and gender diversities among students. The chapter describes how students' relationship, cognitive, and motivational styles; time orientations; interests; degree of self-confidence; and comfort levels with certain educational activities differ. It also suggests how educators can accommodate their instructional techniques to these differences.

## Relationship Style

How students have learned to relate to adults and their peers affects how they learn in school.

### Participatory Versus Passive Learning

Some children are brought up to be active participants in the learning process. They are expected to ask questions of adults, discuss ideas, and so on. These students perceive educators as guides who lead and stimulate students' active learning. Other children are expected to be less active and more passive recipients of instruction and information. They tend to perceive teachers as fountains of information and students as passive learners. Active participatory learning has proven to be more effective than passive learning with most students, but all students are not equally prepared to function in such an environment. African American students prefer and learn more effectively in an interactive, participatory learning environment (1, 3). However, many Hispanic American, Asian American, and Pacific American students are expected to be passive learners. The following quotations describe the passive learning styles of Hispanic Americans and Southeast Asian Americans.

> *The Hispanic culture requires good students to be passive learners—to sit quietly at their desks, pay attention, learn what they are taught and speak only when they are called upon. Anglo educational methods often require students to be active students—to show initiative and leadership, to volunteer questions and answers, and to question the opinion of others. (2, p. 188)*

> *Since they have been taught to learn by listening, watching (observing), and imitating, these students may have a difficult time adjusting to learning by active doing and discovering.... There is a lesser emphasis, as compared to the American school system, on critical thinking and judgmental questions. If a teacher were to ask a question on the relationship between two concepts, one might see Indochinese students searching through their notes or books for the answers, or they may display reluctance or discomfort. (4, p. 42)*

In recent years, educators have begun stressing the value of active participatory learning. However, students who are not comfortable with this approach may require a great deal of direct instruction and supervision during self-directed activities until they become comfortable with a more active role. Meanwhile, some students may not fulfill their academic potential and their behavior may be incorrectly attributed to insecurity, shyness, or excessive passivity. The following quote describes how this applies to some Asian and Pacific American students.

> *The child does not volunteer to answer. He just sits and waits for his teacher to call upon him. So in the eyes of the American teacher, Asian children, as compared to American students, are dull, passive, unresponsive, and lack initiative. Most of the time, Asian children are ignored because of their absolute silence in class. (5, p. 11)*

### *Aloof, Distant Versus Involved Personal Relations*

Cultures differ in terms of the degree of personal involvement teachers are supposed to have with their students. In some cultures, educators' interest in and involvement with students are expected to be restricted to their functioning in school. In other cultures, educators are expected to be interested and involved with them as persons who are also students. In comparison to males, females prefer closer personal relationships with their teachers. As the following quotes indicate, Hispanic American and Native American students, among others, may learn more when their teachers show more interest in their out of school life.

> *While I was in school in Mexico I felt as if my teachers, the nuns, were my friends as well as my teachers. They asked about my family and my personal life. When I came here the teachers seemed very cold and aloof. It was very hard for me to adjust to the differences. (2, p. 46)*

> *Village students tend to expect highly personalized, emotionally intense relationships.... with their teachers.... Village students consider it legitimate to expect a teacher to "care about" them as total persons, not as learners of a particular subject matter. (6, p. 312)*

## Dependent Versus Independent Learning

There are significant ethnic and gender differences in the extent to which students are trained to accomplish things on their own and to arrive at their own independent opinions and decisions, or are brought up to be dependent on the aid, support, opinions, and feedback of their parents and other adults. Compared to European American students, many, but not all, non–European American students, especially Hispanic Americans, Native Americans, Filipino Americans, and Southeast Asian Americans tend to be more interested in obtaining their teachers' direction and feedback (2, 9, 12, 16).

> *Filipino children may be passive and may not show initiative, creativity, or independence. They may be reluctant, afraid, or slow to make decisions in the classroom. . . . To Filipino children, family approval is very important, and they usually rely on their parents to make decisions for them. (9, p. 34)*

In most cultures, females, especially young ones, are more adult-oriented than males. Females achieve more when adults are present than when they are absent (10). There is suggestive evidence that when they are young, their self-esteem is more dependent on feedback from others; males' self-esteem, however, may be more dependent on their ability to master their environment (8). European American females are also more likely to use learned helplessness when they are older as a way of influencing others (14). This is not true of African American females.

The genders are not equally susceptible to the influence of other people (7, 11, 13, 15, 17). Although some research indicates the contrary (15), girls are more likely than boys to modify their opinions and attitudes to conform to others and to copy what others model; boys tend to maintain their ideas and opinions despite what others may think or feel.

The reason why many females seek their teacher's feedback, learn more in their presence, and are more willing to modify their opinions to conform to those of others whereas males function independently is unclear. Some educators argue that females learn better in interpersonal situations whereas males learn better in impersonal ones; they believe females' learning is enhanced when they and their teachers are equally involved in the process of examining their experiences together; and they tend to evaluate the female style more favorably than the male style. Other educators attribute the difference to what they believe is female students' inability to function independently and feel that females need to develop independent learning skills.

Both learning styles have advantages and disadvantages. Some situations call for the ability to work independently and to maintain one's own opinions and attitudes in the face of opposition. Other situations require students to be able to work well with others and to modify their ideas and opinions when others have more experience, knowledge, and training. Students who cannot distinguish between these two situations and those who are too inflexible to adjust to others' opinions as the situation demands are at a distinct disadvantage. Thus, the most helpful approach educators can use may be to help all students learn to function in a bicultural manner.

## Peer- Versus Adult-Oriented

In some cultures children look primarily to adults for guidance, support, and direction; children in other cultures, for example Hawaiian Americans, tend to learn from and are guided by other children and youth. Thus, research suggests that Hawaiian American students prefer to work with their peers in study groups rather than have teachers lecture to them and they learn more effectively in peer groups (18, 19).

Females are more adult-oriented; they seek the help, support and feedback of their teachers. Males are more responsive to feedback from their peers (20–23, 25). However, males who lack self-confidence in their abilities also require teacher feedback to perform well (24).

Educators would do well to consider these differences when they select students for such instructional activities as peer tutoring and decide how much teacher supervision to provide them.

## Individualistic Versus Group-Oriented

Although no culture expects children to be completely individualistic or group-oriented, there are important cultural differences in the degree to which these relationship styles are emphasized. In some cultures, children are brought up to be relatively individualistic. Such children prefer to work alone. When they are assigned to groups, in comparison to more group-oriented students, they are likely to continue to work independently, neither soliciting nor offering assistance. Native American children are an example (18, 26). Although they may not be competitive with their peers, students who prefer to work alone may require considerable assistance before they can function well in cooperative learning environments.

# Cognitive Style

All students do not perceive things the same way or use the same problem-solving techniques. The following are some of the most important cognitive style differences among students.

## Reflective/Analytical Versus Impulsive/Spontaneous/Intuitive

Students differ in terms of how long they think about things before arriving at conclusions. Some children are brought up to analyze and reflect on questions and problems and to be sure they know the answer or solution before saying anything. Others respond more intuitively and spontaneously to the problems presented to them in terms of what occurs to them immediately.

> Some people are rather anxious to insure that they gather all the information possible before being asked to respond and they have a need to be accurate. These

*individuals are considered to be* reflective *while those individuals who respond immediately to what is presented without regard to the fact they may be erroneous are labeled as* impulsive *learners. (30, p. 17)*

Temperamental, ethnic, and gender factors help to determine which of these cognitive styles students use (29). Native Americans are an example of students who tend to look at all sides of an issue, examine their possible implications, and make sure they know the answer before they are ready to express their opinion (18).

Research conducted in the 1970s indicated that in comparison to males, females are better able to delay judgment until they have the information they need to begin a task. They are also able to wait for a more desirable reward or outcome rather than settle immediately for something less desirable (27, 28). More research is needed to determine whether this is still the case.

Students who are more reflective usually have an advantage over their more spontaneous peers. As a result, some educators who believe that all students should be reflective/analytical learners use techniques that have been recommended to modify the learning style of students with culturally determined impulsive, spontaneous, intuitive learning characteristics. This remains controversial.

In addition, some educators do not allow reflective students sufficient time to prepare their answer (wait time) before calling on someone else. This impedes students' learning and may lead teachers to conclude that they are unprepared or slow learners.

### *Global Perception Versus Analysis of Details*

As noted in the previous chapter, global learners perceive things in a holistic manner. They perceive the whole of an event, idea, or image and the relationships between its parts simultaneously. They see everything as a part of the whole and use few discrete categories to notice differences among the parts. Analytic learners can easily divide the whole into subcategories based on differences. Global learners tend to do better in whole language approaches and sight vocabulary. Because analytic learners process individual parts sequentially and gradually build up to an understanding of the whole, a phonetic approach in which the parts of words are analyzed to obtain the meaning of the whole word is more to their liking. In comparison to European American students, African American, Asian and Pacific American, Hispanic American, and Native American students have a more global perceptual style (31–35).

*The Native American sees little or no differentiation between religion and daily life, has little trouble with the anthropomorphism of inanimate objects, practices holistic medicine. . . . The Anglo, on the other hand, sees medicine as separate from nutrition and reading as separate from science or social studies or math. . . . The Anglo compartmentalizes by subject rather than seeing them all as a part of the relation to the person. (35, p. 24)*

> *Afro-American people tend to prefer to respond to and with "gestalts" rather than to or with atomistic things. Enough particulars are tolerated to get a general sense of things. There is an impatience with unnecessary specifics. Sometimes it seems that the predominant pattern for mainstream America is the preoccupation with particulars along with a concomitant loss of a sense of the whole. (32, p. 38)*

Unfortunately for global learners, the teaching style of many European American educators does not match their learning style.

> *Many a new topic in school is approached in an analytic, sequential manner. The topic is introduced a little bit at a time, in a carefully sequenced manner. Often the overall picture (global view) of a topic is not presented until the end of a teaching sequence. For many Native Indian children (and others) this approach would be much more effective if the overall purpose and the overall structure were described before the analytic sequence was begun. The term "advance organizers" has been used by some educators to describe this approach." (33, p. 26)*

> *There is the belief that anything can be divided and subdivided into minute pieces and that these pieces add up to a whole. Therefore dancing and music can be taught by the numbers. Even art is sometimes taught this way. This is why some people never learn to dance. They are too busy counting and analyzing. (32, p. 38)*

## *Aural, Visual, and Verbal Learners*

Although all children without visual or auditory impairments learn both visually and aurally, there are significant culturally influenced differences among students. It is important to know whether students' cultures prepare people to be primarily aural or visual learners, or both, because this would influence whether particular students would learn more efficiently if material were presented orally or visually.

Do people learn visually by observing what transpires in their worlds or by reading about things? Are students better at remembering what they have seen or what they have read? Because of their life-styles, Native American students tend to be visual learners (33, 37, 39).

> *They scrutinize the face of adults; they recognize at great distances their family's livestock. They are alert to danger signs of changing weather or the approach of predatory animals. (37, p. 333)*

> *Native Indian students frequently and effectively use coding with imagery to remember and understand words and concepts. That is, they use mental images to remember or understand, rather than using word association. This suggests that use of metaphors, images or symbols is more effective than dictionary-style definitions or synonyms in helping many Native Indian students learn difficult concepts. (33, p. 26)*

On the other hand, many students, including African Americans, Hispanic Americans, Haitian Americans and Hmong Americans, tend to be aural learners (2, 29, 36, 38).

*Haitians usually have a highly developed auditory ability as evidenced by the oral traditions and rote learning methods. When presented with flow charts and diagrams they may require additional assistance in attaching meaning to the visual presentation. (36, p. 33)*

The Hmong do not have a written language; therefore they have highly developed aural skills. "The Hmong are used to hearing long songs one or two times and then repeating them. Use of repetitive patterns and rhymes assists memorization" (38, p. 33).

Thus, it is extremely important to adapt instructional techniques to students' preferences for aural, visual, or verbal cognitive styles. At the very least, educators should employ a multisensory approach when they instruct a group of diverse learners.

## Kinesthetic/Active/Energetic Learning Versus Calm, Inactive Verbal Learning

Students' ability to sit still for long periods of time is greatly influenced by their cultural background. Knowing whether youngsters are expected to sit in a quiet and controlled manner in most situations or are allowed to be active and noisy enables educators to use instructional techniques that both permit students a level of activity that approximates what they are accustomed to and provide them with ways to discharge their energy.

In general, in comparison to European Americans, African American students are more active and less able to adjust to the sedentary learning environments of American schools.

*In many American schools and especially in inner city schools, children are expected to talk or to move about only when directed to do so by teachers.... Those children who talk and move about with or without teacher directions do not meet normative standards and expectations.... Euro-American children possess the movement repertoire that will satisfy the normative standards and expectations governing child behavior in elementary classrooms while the richer movement repertoire of Black children does not satisfy those normative standards. (40, p. 610)*

In comparison to females, males prefer learning that involves active manipulation to more sedentary learning environments (42). Because of these ethnic and gender differences, educators should know which of their students learn best by doing, manipulating, touching, and experiencing, and which prefer more sedentary approaches such as lectures, reading, written and oral explanations, and discussions of ideas.

Students also differ in terms of whether they function better in highly stimulating or more calm learning environments. African American and Hispanic American students are used to more stimulation than students typically experience in school. That may be why African American and Hispanic American students perform better and achieve more when the curriculum includes many different materials, makes frequent use of nonverbal instructional forms such as visual media or manipulative games, and allows more student autonomy than in classrooms that are teacher controlled, use a great deal of verbal learning, and involve limited use of different materials (44).

Numerous authors have suggested adapting the instruction techniques to African American and Hispanic American students' interest in music, singing, movement, and variety (41, 43). The following quote is an example of such suggestions.

*Many African American children are exposed to high-energy, fast-paced home environments, where there is simultaneous variable stimulation (e.g., televisions and music playing simultaneously and people talking and moving in and about the home freely). Hence, low-energy, monolithic environments (as seen in many traditional school environments) are less stimulating. . . . Variety in instruction provides the spirit and enthusiasm for learning. When instructional strategies facilitate stimulus variety, using combinations of oral, print, and visual media, African-American students perform better. Instructional activities should include music, singing, and movement. (43, pp. 118–119)*

### Nonverbal Cues

Students' sensitivity to nonverbal cues is influenced by their ethnic background and gender. As noted previously, African Americans, Asian and Pacific Americans, and Hispanic Americans tend to be more aware of and tuned into subtle nonverbal cues than European Americans. Females are also more sensitive than males to nonverbal cues (45, 46). Since people sometimes say things they do not mean and mean things they do not say, students who are sensitive to educators' nonverbal communication as well as their verbal communication may learn and understand more because they perceive more.

### Trial and Error Versus "Watch Then Do"

In some cultures people tend to learn by trial and error. They observe, read about, or are told how something is done. Then they practice it under the supervision of a more knowledgeable and skilled individual. Learners are expected to make mistakes, because "practice makes perfect." In other cultures, individuals are expected to continue to watch how something is done as many times and for as long as necessary until they feel they can do it. Only when they are sure they can succeed do they demonstrate their ability to others.

Students who grow up in trial and error cultures can usually take in stride the mistakes they make in public when they volunteer answers or are called on.

Those who are accustomed to a "watch then do" approach have greater difficulty exposing themselves in public while they are learning from their mistakes. This is particularly true of Native American students (35, 47, 48).

*Native Americans spend much more time watching and listening and less time talking than do Anglos. If they are interested in something they watch how it is done, they inspect the product, they watch the process, they may ask a quiet question or two. Then they may try it for themselves, often out of the public eye. They are their own evaluator to determine whether their effort was successful or needs improvement. When they feel comfortable, they will show what they have done to someone else, usually someone they trust. (35, p. 26)*

*A reluctance to try too soon and the accompanying fear of being "shamed" if one does not succeed may account for the seemingly passive uninterested and unresponsive attitude of Indian students. (47, p. 28)*

Students who are uncomfortable with trial and error learning and exposing their errors to others may need educators to supervise them less and not pressure them to try things before they are ready to do so.

### *Argumentative/Forensic Instruction Versus Direct Instruction*

Although all cultures use many different teaching techniques with children, only in some cultures do adults teach children by raising leading questions about their beliefs in order to guide them to a more correct or accurate understanding of things. In other cultures, children are accustomed to being told what is correct and unaccustomed to having their beliefs questioned critically.

*Anglo education emphasizes verbal inquisitiveness, an argumentative discourse that is termed "forensics." In the Anglo-dominated school system, the child is encouraged, even pressured, both to ask and analyze questions . . . . There is consequently a built-in clash between the ethnic (Raza) home tradition and the Anglo school tradition of constant and formal questioning. The WASP "inquisition" would be highly hostile to the Mexican-American attitude of tolerance. (49, p. 64)*

As a result, educators may have to consider students' cognitive styles when deciding whether and how often to use instructional approaches that involve class discussions, debates, analysis of controversial topics, and the examination of students' opinions and beliefs.

### *Learning from Examples, Stories, and Morals Versus Direct Instruction*

In some cultures (for example, Native American cultures), in addition to being told things directly, children are led to an understanding of life through the legends they learn, the morals of the stories they are told, and the examples they are shown. For them, direct instruction can be effectively supplemented by these more seemingly time-consuming instructional strategies.

## *Motivational Style*

In some respects all students are similarly motivated. They would rather succeed than fail and learn to read than remain illiterate. However, because their cultural backgrounds help shape their perceptions about the value and role of education, they also have different motives.

### *Motivation to Succeed in School*

Although students' desire to succeed in school is often influenced by a number of interrelated motivations, typically one or two reasons are paramount. Some students may desire to succeed academically, to go to college, to earn a lot of money, and to be successful materialistically; some strive to succeed in order to receive honor and prestige; and others may believe it is important to learn for its own sake.

Students' motivation to succeed in school is affected by ethnic, socioeconomic, and gender factors. As was noted in Chapter 3, some older African American and Hispanic American students, especially poor males, are motivated to avoid success in school or have lost their motivation to try to succeed (50–55). Many non-European and poor students are alienated, distrustful, angry, and disillusioned about the schools they attend and the teachers that instruct them because of the prejudice and discrimination they encounter. They believe that even if they do well in school, they will not obtain the same benefits that European American upper-class males receive from succeeding in school, particularly in the vocational area, and some of them are pressured by their peers not to conform or to do well in school because to do so is to act white.

For these reasons numerous African American and Hispanic American students, especially males, purposefully avoid academic success by cutting school and not studying. Many students who do achieve up to their potential hide their true motives by becoming disciplinary problems, acting the class clown, or keeping their efforts and accomplishments from their peers.

Although the evidence is somewhat inconsistent, it appears that many European American and Hispanic American females, particularly those from less affluent and poor backgrounds, have mixed feelings about and are uncomfortable with success in courses or occupations traditionally thought of as being in the male domain (57–61, 63). This applies to a lesser degree to African American females.

Research indicates that there are at least three reasons for this (56, 57, 61, 63). Some females are concerned that they may seem less feminine and be less popular with males if they outperform them in these areas. A second reason why some females are uncomfortable with success is that success provokes a conflict between their desires to achieve and their more traditional perception of the ideal female as less oriented to achievement and individualism than to collaboration and egalitarianism. In this vein, Tannen explains that

> *Appearing better than others is a violation of the girls' egalitarian ethic: People are supposed to stress their connection and similarity. . . . It is no wonder that girls fear rejection by their peers if they appear too successful and boys don't. Boys from the earliest age learn that they can get what they want—higher status—by displaying superiority. Girls learn that displaying superiority will not get them what they want—affiliation with their peers. For this they have to appear the same as, not better than their friends. (63, pp. 217–218)*

A third reason is the belief held by many non-European Americans including Hispanic Americans and Asian and Pacific Americans that a female's place is in the home (2, 38). For example, Lewis and colleagues explain that "There is also a suspicion among the Hmong regarding girls who are educated beyond the three or four years required for basic literacy and math skills. . . . The fear is that they will become like western women" (38, p. 32). There is also suggestive evidence that some males may be uncomfortable with success if they perceive success in school as a feminine characteristic (62).

Because of these gender, socioeconomic, and ethnic differences, educators should not assume that all of their students are equally motivated to succeed in school. They should be knowledgeable about each student's motivation and then decide how to handle each individual case. Although this may be a difficult task for secondary-level teachers who have many classes, this goal is more feasible for elementary-level teachers.

## *Learning on Demand Versus Learning What Is Relevant or Interesting*

Are students prepared to spend equal time and energy learning whatever material is presented to them by teachers regardless of what they think and feel about the material? Or will their reactions to material depend on whether or not it interests them? All cultures require all children to learn many things whether they want to or not. However, some students, have been brought up in cultures in which they have considerable leeway to learn what is useful and interesting to them rather than what some others have decided they should learn. Other students are better prepared to study whatever teachers present to them. For example, Cortes believes that Hispanic American students whose parents are not well-educated are less willing to learn things that do not interest them.

> *Relevance is particularly important for students who do not come from families with high educational attainment. For students from families with examples of significant school achievement, education has built in relevance. They have role models . . . they are raised with the concept of a career. . . . Such a student is more likely to accept and play the educational game. (64, pp. 34–35)*

Other authors agree that Hispanic American students are less able to learn on demand.

*Anecdotal evidence suggests that efficiency, automation and technology tend to be highly prized among Anglos, whereas humanistic concerns and open acceptance of affective temperament take precedence among Chicanos. Given such variations in cultural concerns, it is not surprising that the tendency to learn liked materials more readily than disliked materials is more intensified among Chicanos than Anglos. (65, pp. 114–115)*

*To the extent that response to demand could be called a learning style, the Hispanic population tends to demonstrate that tendency much less frequently than a middle-class, white group that is socialized almost from early childhood to produce on demand as is expected in school. (67, p. 19)*

Native American students have been described in the following way:

*They prefer to learn information that is personally interesting to them; therefore, interest is a key factor in their learning. When these students are not interested in a subject, they do not control their attention and orient themselves to learning an uninteresting task. Rather, they allocate their attention to other ideas that are more personally interesting, thus appearing detached from the learning situation. (68, p. 69)*

Some educators believe that students should attend to whatever their teachers present to them because their teachers know best. Other educators think that students should not be so compliant if what they are expected to learn is busy work that has no apparent relationship to their interests and goals or is not at their level. These educators tend to believe that teachers should not be quick to capitalize on students' willingness to learn whatever they are given. Instead they should use the feedback from their students to improve their instructional practices.

Some students who are not ready to learn on demand may be willing to attend to material that does not interest them if teachers personally appeal to them to do so. For example, Kleinfeld reports that Native American students may be motivated to learn in order to please others and to avoid offending or hurting them. "Appealing to interpersonal values rather than purely academic values in a learning situation often motivates village students" (66, pp. 18–19).

Kleinfeld also points out that whereas Native American educators are comfortable appealing to such motives, European American teachers who believe that students should be motivated to learn for intrinsic reasons may be reluctant to make the kinds of personal appeals that are necessary to motivate students. A Native American teacher responded to a Native American student as follows: "He just wouldn't attend speech class. Then I told him he was hurting the teacher's feelings because she thought he didn't like her. At that point he said he would go" (66, pp. 18–19). On the other hand a European American teacher reported, "He said he would study if I wanted him to. But I felt I should tell him that he should study it for himself not me" (66, pp. 18–19). Asian and Pacific American students may also respond to personal appeals: "Asian children are often found to be motivated extrinsically by their parents and relatives. They study hard because they want to please their parents and impress their relatives" (69, p. 84).

It is important to enhance the intrinsic motivation of students, especially if they have become discouraged because of the frustrations they experience in school. However, with some students it may be effective to temporarily use personal appeals to encourage students to engage in school work that will provide them with the successful experiences necessary to increase their intrinsic motivation.

### *Object- Versus People-Oriented Learners*

All children in all cultures must learn many abstract concepts. However, some cultures deemphasize abstract learning and are more people-oriented. As a result, some students are interested in solving math problems about people rather than those that involve only numerical computations and studying human geography (how people live) rather than physical geography (rivers, topography, and so on), whereas other students may prefer more abstract, object-oriented curricular contents. In comparison to European Americans, Hispanic Americans, African Americans, and Native Americans are more people-oriented (2, 70, 71).

> *In comparison to the Anglo culture, the Hispanic culture emphasizes people over ideas. . . . As a result some Hispanic students may relate better to a person-centered rather than thing- or idea-centered curriculum. (2, pp. 42–43)*

> *Research has suggested that white children are very object-oriented. That is, they have numerous opportunities to manipulate objects and discover properties and relationships. Consequently, this society's educational system is very object-oriented. Classrooms are filled with educational hardware and technology. . . . Research with black children, in contrast, has found them to be very people-oriented. Most black children grow up in large families where they have a great deal of human interaction. . . . When this cultural trait is acknowledged, the result will be more human interaction in the learning process. (71, pp. 19–20)*

### *Cooperative, Competitive, and Individualistic Learners*

Cultures differ in the degree to which they stress cooperation, competition, and individualism. Therefore, it is important to know whether particular students respond better to competitive, individualistic, or cooperative motivating techniques and learning environments. Nowadays educators are encouraged to use cooperative learning and peer tutoring with students, but some students are less receptive than others to these approaches.

There are many significant ethnic, socioeconomic, and gender differences in students' preferences for competitive or cooperative learning environments. As was noted in the previous chapter, some students, including African Americans, Asian and Pacific Americans, Filipino Americans, Hawaiian Americans, and Hispanic Americans, tend to be brought up to be cooperative, whereas other cultures typically encourage students to be more competitive and/or individualistic.

European American gifted, average, and low-ability females, particularly those from poor backgrounds, usually prefer cooperative learning environments and may learn better in certain kinds of cooperative situations. In group settings they are more oriented toward group rather than individualistic goals. European American males tend to respond better to competitive and individualistic situations whether they are high or low achievers. (21, 72–77, 79, 81, 82, 84, 85, 88, 89). These gender stereotypes do not apply to the same degree to Native American and Hispanic American males, who grow up in much less competitive environments (80, 83, 86, 87).

Ethnic groups also have different approaches to cooperation. In the European American culture, for example, when people are working cooperatively everyone is supposed to do her or his share. To carry one's load is a guiding principle. Because this is not true of all cultures, the difference can create problems for teachers. Jaramillo points out that a European American teacher

> *is likely to be personally irked if he finds that some child isn't doing his share when engaged in a group task. Latin cultures typically do not put such requirements on individuals when they are working as part of a group. A group member who does not happen to be working will not be offensive. Those members of the group who best qualify or are most interested in performing the task will probably take it upon themselves to do the bulk of the labor. It is generally understood that each individual has special talents, and he will contribute when these talents are called for. (78, p. 9)*

Some students are taught to be self reliant—to be individualistic and to rely only on themselves to accomplish their goals and deal with the challenges, difficulties, and problems they face. Other students are brought up to expect and count on the help and the cooperation of others and to reciprocate in kind. Individualistic students who prefer to work on their own may have difficulty adjusting to working in groups or committees, even though they are noncompetitive.

These ethnic and gender differences have important educational implications. Since some students learn more efficiently in cooperative learning environments whereas others learn more in competitive or individualistic settings, their achievement depends in part on whether their teacher's instructional style matches their own cooperative, competitive, or individualistic learning style. Educators should consider these ethnic differences when they select learning environments and reward systems for students.

Students who learn better in competitive or individualistic situations tend to have an advantage because these environments predominate (90). However, the positive results of cooperative learning on many students' achievement, attitudes, and interpersonal relationships has been demonstrated repeatedly (91–101). Typically, interethnic relationships improve and students learn more, get along better with their peers, and feel better about themselves, their peers, and school when they learn in cooperative environments.

However, research also indicates, that these results characterize only some, not all students. In general, females, African Americans, Hispanic Americans, and students who have a cooperative learning style tend to experience the greatest academic gains from cooperative learning (21, 102, 103). Students who prefer competitive learning environments do better under competitive situations. (104).

Research suggests that female students tend to achieve more in single-sex cooperative learning situations than in mixed-sex cooperative groups (105, 106). There are many possible reasons for this. Moody and Gifford believe one of the reasons for this is that females participate and lead less in mixed-gender groups. They suggest that

> *Females are forced to take leadership and responsibility in laboratory groups when working with only other females.... If increased female leadership and participation is desired, then grouping by gender can accomplish this objective.* (106, p. 16, 17)

Another reason why females are often the losers in mixed-sex groups is because although they tend to be the providers of assistance they are rejected by males when they ask for assistance. In addition, as was noted earlier, in mixed-sex cooperative groups females often revert to a pattern of not interacting with male students, allowing males to dominate them and viewing themselves as less helpful, less important, and less visible (107, 109, 112, 113, 114, 116, 118), and there is some evidence that they may behave more competitively than they otherwise do (115). Males may actually learn more and perform better than females in cooperative mixed-sex groups because they often ignore females, contribute most of the ideas, do most of the talking, and typically function as the group leaders (108, 109, 110, 117).

Peterson and Fennema point out other problems that can result in mixed-sex cooperative groups (111). They suggest that although girls' achievement may improve in cooperative learning groups, such groups may make girls even less independent, and that could further impair their already inadequate high-level thinking skills in courses such as mathematics. They are also concerned that cooperative activities may impede the higher-level mathematics achievement of independent, competitive boys.

In mixed groups, girls tend to be equally responsive to requests from and reinforcement by either sex. However, boys are responsive primarily to other males (119–122). Females are also less likely than males to participate in group discussions and to assume leadership positions (123–126).

Females can benefit from mixed-gender cooperative groups. They are more likely to do so when they have been given advanced training, so they can function as experts/leaders of the group, and they have had prior experience with the group task, so they are familiar with what is to be learned, and when educators prepare students to function in a more egalitarian manner.

The experiences of some African American students in mixed-ethnic cooperative groups may be similar to the negative experiences of many females (112, 127). Piel and Conwell claim that

> *White children and black children may not be getting the same experience from a cooperative learning experience. . . . If white children assume leadership roles and black children assume more subservient roles then the purpose for cooperative groups seems to be somewhat diminished. (112, p. 14)*

There is also some evidence that some African American students perform best when they cooperate with other African Americans and compete with European Americans (128).

Finally, there is suggestive evidence that whether or not students benefit from cooperative learning depends in part on their self-concepts (129). When students with high and low self-concepts work together, those with high self-concepts are less likely to function cooperatively, thereby thwarting the goals of the cooperative learning experiences.

Thus, educators should not assume that cooperative learning experiences will automatically benefit all students. Students, especially those who are likely to dominate others and those who tend to allow others to assume dominant positions, must be prepared for cooperative learning in order for all of the members of the group to reap the benefits associated with this approach.

Experts suggest that the following components are required for an effective cooperative learning experience. These steps should be considered as a list of characteristics of effective cooperative learning approaches rather than as steps to follow exactly as listed.

- Familiarize yourself with the variety of cooperative learning techniques available to teachers. The references in the bibliography are a good source of information.
- Inform students of the cooperative procedures they should follow and teach them how to follow them.
- Prepare all students, especially those that are accustomed to accepting subservient positions, to assume the expert/leadership role.
- Sensitize all students, especially male students and others who are prone to use group situations to dominate others, to the importance of allowing all students to take on all the roles available to group members.
- Determine your students' learning styles. Those who have a cooperative learning style may be ready to profit from such experiences. However, you may need to prepare those who tend to do better in competitive or independent learning situations to function better in more cooperative settings before they can profit from them.
- Monitor the groups closely to discourage the kinds of problems discussed earlier and intervene as quickly as possible when problems arise.

> **SELF-QUIZ: Selecting Students for Cooperative Learning Experiences**
>
> With which students do you think cooperative learning should be used? Do you think that cooperative learning should be used primarily with those who appear to favor this type of learning or with all students? Would you assign students to cooperative learning groups? If so, what criteria would you use to determine which students to assign to such groups? Would you allow students to choose their own learning environments?

## *Risk Taking*

Will students choose tasks that are challenging and novel if these also involve risk of failure or rejection, or will they stick to those that are familiar? Will they be adventurous or play it safe? How sure do students have to be that they know the answer or that their opinion is correct before they will risk responding to their teacher's question?

With many exceptions, girls tend to react less positively than boys to difficult and challenging situations. They often are less persistent when faced with difficult tasks in school and are less likely to take risks (130–132), and they tend to expect to do less well and perform less adequately than boys following failure or the threat of failure (133, 134). European American students appear more willing to take risks than Asian and Pacific American students (135, 136).

These cultural inhibitions may make it difficult for some Asian and Pacific American students, other groups of non–European American students with similar inhibitions, and females to take risks or bounce back from failure. These cultural inhibitions may also make it difficult for some gifted and talented students from these backgrounds to capitalize on their gifts and talents in creative ways.

## *Time Orientation*

Because time is a primary concern in the United States, it is easy to assume that all cultures have similar attitudes about time. However, this is not the case.

### *Present Versus Future Orientation*

There are significant differences in the extent to which people sacrifice present satisfactions for future goals. Although all ethnic groups are concerned about and prepare for the future, some are more present- than future-oriented.

> *The time many Mexican Americans value most is the present. Finishing a conversation with an old friend may be more important than keeping an appointment with a doctor. Making plans for the future may be less important than living to the fullest at the moment in hand. Many Mexican Americans perceive the time-serving ways of the Anglo as a misappropriation of the present.... The entire system of American education revolves about a ritualistic adherence to the*

> *ticking of the clock. What is the Mexican American child's reaction to the rigid schedules and the incessant pressures to plan for the future? How does he view a reward system that is programmed to respond to him at six week intervals? (142, p. 641)*

> *Pacific peoples have learned to focus on meeting present needs and expecting little change. Americans value change, are future oriented, and expect that objectives will be achieved as a result of hard work. (139, p. 264)*

Other ethnic groups, such as European Americans and some Asian Americans, are more future-oriented. Because individuals differ in these respects, it is important to know whether students can work toward the accomplishment of long-term goals and rewards or are more responsive to short-term goals, immediate satisfaction, and immediate reinforcement. It is also important to ask whether students who have a tedious, boring, or irksome job to do will start it immediately, postpone it to a more convenient time, or wait until it's almost too late to complete it.

## *Punctuality*

Do people keep to rigid schedules, or are beginning and ending times flexible? Is time measured exactly or approximately? When students arrive late to class or a meeting are they unmotivated or merely operating in a different time frame? How do people perceive lateness? In some cultures, when a person is late it reflects primarily on the late person, who is seen as irresponsible. In others, lateness is perceived as a statement about the late person's disrespectful attitude toward those who have been kept waiting.

Are students accustomed to starting tasks when they are supposed to, and completing them within a specified time period? If they are not, they will have problems functioning in American schools. African Americans, Hispanic Americans, and Native Americans, among others, have a much more flexible attitude about time and punctuality (141, 144).

> *On the whole, Anglo Americans perceive time as a precious commodity to be conserved and budgeted carefully.... Hispanic societies, on the other hand, tend to treat time in a casual manner, accommodating its passage to their needs, rather than letting themselves be controlled by it.... In school, all activities are segmented into a strict time schedule which orchestrates the entire class to perform the same tasks in exact unison. For the Hispanic student, this imposition of a rigid chronological regimentation brings unfamiliar confusion and confinement for, at home, he has always been master of his "time" and been allowed to exercise his individuality within the casual rhythm of family life. (140, p. 67)*

> *Three Eskimo high school seniors given scholarships to a Washington university flunked out after their first semester. High school counselors who came to investigate the failure of such promising students found them cowering in their dormitory rooms and discovered they had been terrified by the ringing of bells and*

*classes ending in such a flurry of activity and of the rush of students to other classes to be on time. No one in their village had owned a watch or clock; thus they were unprepared for the university situation. (137, p. 5)*

## Pace

As was noted in the previous chapter, students who are accustomed to working at a slower pace make more errors when instructed to work as fast as they can. Students accustomed to a faster pace continue to perform as well when they are told to work as fast as they can (138, 143).

Condon and colleagues point out that Hispanic American students have difficulty keeping to the fast pace set by many European American teachers.

*The entire curriculum of the school is crowded into a tight schedule which features endless sequences of fast-moving and closely-timed activities, such as quizzes, tests and spelling bees. The emphasis placed on a "clock-watch" performance of assigned tasks becomes a haunting nightmare for any learner functioning at a slower tempo, as is the case for Hispanic children who have been brought up in a relaxed home atmosphere where minutes (sometimes hours or days) are not seen as critical factors. (140, p. 68)*

Educators who reward students for the amount of work they accomplish—how many problems or pages they have done—rather than the quality of their work may unwittingly cause some of them to make mistakes. They may also give students the message that it is more important to complete something fast than to do it correctly.

# Self-Confidence

Students' self-confidence about school success depend on their beliefs in their ability to learn and their ability to control their own lives (their locus of control). Males and females tend to differ in both of these respects. Ethnic and socioeconomic differences appear to be primarily in the area of students' beliefs about their abilities to control their lives.

## Ability to Learn

Gender differences in students' self-confidence about school has been the subject of considerable research. Although it is not true of African Americans, in most ethnic groups females tend to be less self-confident than males about school, especially in situations that are in the "male domain" such as mathematics and science courses, in competitive situations, and when they lack objective information about how well they have done or can do in situations that involve mastery of tasks in the male domain (145–152). Females are not less self-confident than males in courses such as reading that are not perceived to be in the male domain and in situations that involve their perceived ability to develop friendly relationships with others, to be popular, to resolve conflicts with others, to break bad habits, to gain self-insight, and so on. There is little evidence that there also are gender differences in students' overall self-concepts and self-esteem (21).

As was noted in Chapter 3, students from different ethnic and socioeconomic backgrounds start school equally confident about their ability to learn. Unfortunately, after spending a number of years in school, many, but far from all, poor, African American, Hispanic American, and Native American students lose much of their self-confidence about school.

### Locus of Control

Students differ in the extent to which they believe they are in control of and responsible for what happens to them in their lives in general and in school in particular. There is no consistent evidence that males and females differ in the extent to which they believe that they are in control of and responsible for what happens to them outside of school. The results of studies that have examined how students explain their school-related experiences as contrasted to experiences in their lives in general paint a different picture. Although a few researchers have found no gender differences, most studies indicate that males and females attribute their academic successes and failures to different factors. Researchers who have compared males' and females' beliefs about whether they or external factors have greater influence over their general school performance have found that in comparison to males, females, especially those with from poor backgrounds, are more likely to attribute their general academic performance to internal factors (153, 157, 165). In courses such as math and science that are thought to be in the male domain, females tend to attribute their poor performance to internal factors such as lack of ability and their success to external factors such as luck rather than effort or ability (154–156, 158, 160, 162, 163, 166). Males' attributions are different. They are more likely to attribute their failures to external factors and their success to internal factors across courses and subjects (159, 161–164).

There are significant ethnic differences in students' locus of control (140, 167–170). European American students are most likely to believe that they rather than external factors control what happens to them. Japanese and Chinese Americans follow close behind. Hispanic American students tend to have a more external locus of control (168). The following quotation compares the optimistic European American view embodied in the expression "If at first you don't succeed, try, try again." to the fatalism of Hispanic Americans, who do not have the same confidence in their ability to shape their lives.

> *This optimistic outlook on life is not shared by most Spanish speakers who have learned that one should not expect too much of life, and that it is best to dismiss the future with a fatalistic shrug of the shoulders*—que sera, sera *(what will be will be)*. (140, p. 63)

As was noted in Chapter 3, African Americans and Native Americans do not assume that they can control many aspects of their lives because they are aware of their lack of power in an environment characterized by pervasive prejudice against them. Because of this, they are less optimistic that they can assure themselves a good life by their own efforts (167, 169).

*White folks think that because they have a good day today every day has to be good. They can't take bad times. Black folks know better. They're happy for any good days that come their way because they know they can't have them all the time. (167)*

In general, research conducted primarily in the 1960s indicated that students with an internal locus of control tended to achieve more in school than those whose locus of control was external, because they tried harder to succeed and to improve when they did poorly (171–174). However, whether this principle applies to poor, African American, Native American, and Hispanic American students has been a matter of controversy. Some educators argue that because many of these students grow up in a racist and prejudiced environment, it may be self-destructive for them to believe that they are completely in control of their lives in spite of the racism and prejudice that surrounds them. Students who correctly understand when external factors beyond their control are to blame for their failures may strive to change them, but students who incorrectly blame themselves or hold themselves responsible for failure caused by unfairness, prejudice, and economic injustice may give up.

Sometimes students who are often the victims of prejudice and discrimination incorrectly blame these factors for problems they themselves cause. This can shield them from the self-criticism that is necessary for self-improvement. Thus, although it is important for students not to blame themselves for the problems others cause them, it is also important for them not to blame others for problems they cause themselves.

To date, there is insufficient research to determine the relationship between locus of control and school achievement for students who belong to groups that experience prejudice and discrimination.

Students who can attempt to accomplish things that involve the possibility of failure and can bounce back from the unavoidable failures that all students experience from time to time will do better over time than those who avoid possible failure and who are too discouraged by failure to try again. Students who avoid difficult and challenging situations deny themselves growth opportunities, and students who incorrectly attribute their poor performance to their imagined lack of ability are less likely to attempt to succeed the next time they face a similar challenge.

### *Self-Confidence Enhancement*

Research indicates that dedicated teachers can improve their students' self-concepts and self-esteem when they make the effort to do so (175–181). The first step is to identify students who lack self-confidence. This can be done informally by observing students at work, at play, and during their interactions with others. You can also talk with them about what they think of themselves. Several validated formal assessment instruments are available for this purpose. The Piers-Harris Children's Self-Concept Scale (186) and the Self-Observation Scales (184) provide information about students' overall perceptions of themselves. Other instruments—such as the Perceived Competency Scale for Children (183), the Nowicki Strickland Locus of Control Scale for Children (185), and the Coopersmith Self-Esteem Inventory (182)—have a more narrow focus. Some of these instruments may be dated because they were developed in the late 1960s and early 1970s. In addition, as was noted in the previous chapter, they may not be culturally appropriate for some students. You may find a culture-specific instrument to be more valid for your purposes, especially if you are working with African American students.

Many suggestions have been offered to enhance students' self-confidence in their ability to learn and control their lives. The following techniques can be used to improve students' confidence in their ability to learn (21, 175–181).

- Good instructional techniques individualized to students, strengths and weaknesses are probably the most effective way to enhance students' self-confidence. Selecting work at their ability levels, organizing their assignments to ensure success, and providing support and information when they need it can help many students with poor self-concepts succeed despite their beliefs that they can't.
- You may be able to counteract students' pessimistic self-perceptions by helping them see the strengths and skills they bring to each task, by expressing your personal belief that they can succeed, and by explaining how their past experiences can be poor predictors of the present if they practice, study, and concentrate more and learn from their mistakes. Students can learn vicariously by reading books and seeing films about others who have had experiences like theirs. Exposing students who don't believe that they can succeed to stories of real-life people who have actually done so can be inspirational.
- If students see their accomplishments as inadequate because they judge themselves by culturally inappropriate standards, help them to be more accepting of themselves and their cultural styles
- Provide students with opportunities to succeed in areas where they feel adequate so that their positive feelings in one area will generalize to other areas.
- Encourage students to make positive rather than negative statements about themselves and reinforce them when they do so.

These approaches can help students believe that they have the power to achieve what they set out to accomplish.

- Demonstrate your trust and faith that they can be self-managing and self-motivating enough to attain the goals they determine for themselves with a minimum of external guidance.

- In keeping with their maturity level, allow students to choose among alternative learning activities, centers, manipulatives, and instructional materials and permit them to generate or develop some of the alternatives themselves within limits you set. This will enhance their perceptions that they, and not others, are responsible for what they do in class. This also gives them another opportunity to experience your faith in them.
- Provide dependent students with assistance only when they request it, and gradually wean them from needing your assistance.
- Ask students what they think about their own work rather than expressing your opinion. This demonstrates your faith that they can evaluate themselves
- Teach students who seek extrinsic rewards to reward themselves.

As has been noted throughout this text, students from certain ethnic groups are more likely to suffer experiences that attack their self-confidence. Thus, many, but certainly not all, of the students in these ethnic groups can profit from instructional techniques that are designed to counteract these harmful experiences. The following self-confidence–enhancing suggestions are representative of the techniques educators can use (187–193).

Pepper lists the following aspects that should be included in a self-concept enhancement program for Native American students.

*Teach the true history of the American Indian and the value of Indian culture to all children. . . . Value and accept the Indian child as he is. . . . Use words that build the Indian child's self-esteem and feelings of adequacy. . . . Show faith in the Indian child so he can believe in himself. . . . Plan for experiences that are guaranteed to give success. (192, pp. 143–144)*

The following seven-step process has been shown to be effective with African American students (188).

- Students discuss people's dreams and aspirations and what might become of them.
- Students analyze their ability to make decisions and their power at home in their community and at school.
- Students identify their personal desires and dreams and the kind of person they would like to become.
- Students set a short-term goal.
- Students prepare a plan of action to meet the goal and identify the individuals and material resources available to them.
- Students' progress toward the achievement of the goal is monitored periodically.
- At the end of the period, students analyze their actions to understand why their goals were or were not met.

The many multicultural activities described in Chapter 4 can improve students' faith in their ability to learn and control their lives. As Wood points out, studying the history and contributions of non–European Americans increases students' self-confidence.

> *When students become aware of the worth of their own histories, they can come to value their own perceptions and insights. They will not have to rely upon the history of the dominant culture to validate their experiences and truths. Rather they can look to themselves as useful members of a cultural tradition that empowers them to speak with their own voices. This has indeed been the experience of minorities in this country as they have strived to recover a sense of their own worth within an understanding of their value to the culture at large. Teachers need to incorporate such a historical perspective within the curriculum for all children, so that this sense of self-worth will permeate their social actions. (193, p. 235)*

## Interests

As was noted previously, some educators believe that schools cater to the interests of European Americans and offer non–European American students an irrelevant curriculum that contributes to their school-related problems. African American educators are particularly critical of the "Eurocentric" curriculum of American schools. To correct this, they suggest that teachers should include in the daily curriculum ethnocentric materials and content that deal with topics and themes that are relevant to other ethnic groups.

> *Most African-American children sit in classrooms, yet are outside the information being discussed. The white child sits in the middle of the information, whether it is literature, history, politics or art. The task of the Afrocentric curriculum is finding patterns in African-American history and culture that help the teacher place the child in the middle of the intellectual experience. This is not an idea to replace all things European, but to expand the dialogue to include African-American information. (194, p. 46)*

Other educators disagree. For example, former Secretary of Education William Bennet stated, "I think it will further alienate the poor who are already tenuously connected to American culture. . . . It's a mistake to think that these kids are going to get any more interested in schools by studying more about Africa" (195, p. 45).

Research is not very supportive of the latter position. Although children and youth share many interests in common, ethnic and gender groups do have somewhat different interests. For example, a study of the reading interests of African American and European American sixth-grade students found that the two books most preferred by African American students were the books least preferred by European American students. (200).

Chapter 4 and the references at the end of this chapter include many suggestions for making the curriculum more relevant to all students, not just European American males (194–201).

## Acceptable and Unacceptable Learning Activities

Students differ not only in how they prefer to learn, but also in what they prefer to learn. For example, because of their religious or moral upbringing some students are unable to participate in various school activities. Jehovah's Witnesses do not allow their children to participate in holiday celebrations. Some Christian groups do not want their children to participate in discussions of morality. Hispanic females may be uncomfortable about participating in physical education activities that require them to wear shorts, and "Indian students may not feel comfortable participating in some activities required in biology and other science classes. Destruction of life for the sole purpose of examining an organism may not be tolerable" (202, p. 44).

## Field-Sensitive and Field-Independent Learning and Behavior Characteristics

There is considerable evidence that some of the learning characteristics described earlier are interrelated. Researchers have identified two groups of learning characteristics, which have been labelled field-sensitive and field-independent. Research conducted in the 1970s indicates that some ethnic groups tend to be primarily field-sensitive (e.g., African Americans and Hispanic Americans) whereas others are predominantly field-independent (e.g., European Americans). Within most ethnic groups, females tend to be more field-sensitive than males.

No group or individual is completely field-independent or field-sensitive. An individual or an ethnic group may function in a predominantly field-sensitive or field-independent way, but aspects of the opposite styles also exist in their personalities. Some examples of characteristics that tend to belong to either the field-sensitive or field-independent personality type are (29)

- *Whether people rely more on internal clues such as their own feelings, ideas, values, and experiences to understand the world around them (field-independent) or on information from their surroundings (field-sensitive)*
- *Whether they prefer solitary activities, personal time, and more distant, aloof relationships (field-independent) or are sociable, gregarious, and interested in helping people (field-sensitive)*
- *Whether they work better individually (field-independent) or in groups (field-sensitive)*
- *Whether they are relatively indifferent to the feelings, ideas, opinions, attitudes, and so on, of others when they decide what to do or how to do it (field-independent) or are sensitive to and responsive to what others feel and think and consider how their actions may affect others (field-sensitive)*
- *Whether they prefer to maintain considerable physical distance when they talk with others (field-independent) or to be in close proximity to them (field-sensitive)*
- *Whether they are indifferent to praise and criticism from others (field-independent) or react intensely to being praised and criticized (field-sensitive)*

- *Whether they function better in competitive situations (field-independent) or under cooperative conditions (field-sensitive)*
- *Whether they prefer to work independently (field-independent) or seek feedback, guidance, and approval from others (field-sensitive)*
- *Whether they prefer abstract, theoretical tasks such as math computational problems (field-independent) or tasks that involve human issues and concerns such as math word problems (field-sensitive)*
- *Whether they respond better to impersonal rewards such as money, toys, candy, time off, and so on (field-independent) or personal rewards such as praise, smiles, pats on the back, and the like (field-sensitive)*

## *Avoiding Misleading Stereotypes*

As noted in the preface and throughout this text, the learning characteristics discussed in this chapter do not apply to all members of a given ethnic or gender group. Whether people conform to a particular ethnic or gender stereotype depends on many different factors. Two of these factors, their socioeconomic background and their acculturation, are discussed next.

### *Socioeconomic Effects*

In the United States, middle-class students are less likely to conform to traditional gender stereotypes. As a result of research that was conducted primarily in the 1970s, we now realize that ethnic stereotypes also do not apply equally to all socioeconomic classes (203–211). In the United States, ethnic differences between African Americans or Hispanic Americans and European Americans are greatest among poor individuals and smallest among middle- and upper-class individuals. This may be because members of these groups may have to reject their ethnic background and assimilate to the European American middle-class culture in order to succeed in a European American middle-class–dominated society. There is also suggestive evidence that socioeconomic class does not play as important a role among some other ethnic groups—for instance, Jewish Americans, Chinese Americans, and Japanese Americans. The cause of this may possibly be that it is less necessary for them to deny their cultural heritages in order to enter the middle class.

It is often difficult to determine whether ethnicity or socioeconomic class is more influential in a particular situation. Thus, Havighurst asks,

> *A given person is a middle-class black, or a working-class black. Is he more accurately described by his social class or by his ethnicity? Another person is an upper-working-class Pole or an upper-middle-class Pole. Which takes precedence for him, his ethnicity or his social class? (206, pp. 56–57)*

Because ethnic and socioeconomic factors interact to influence ethnic and gender traits, numerous educators attribute some of the learning characteristics of many non–European American students described in this text to socioeconomic, not ethnic, factors. They claim that in the United States there is a vast difference between the child-rearing practices, learning styles, behavior styles, standard of living, experiences, access to the many advantages offered to most citizens, and so on, of the poor and of the middle and upper classes. They believe that because African American, Native American, and Hispanic American students are more likely than European American students to come from poor backgrounds, many of the differences some people attribute to ethnicity are actually the result of contextual factors associated with socioeconomic class.

Unfortunately, few researchers have studied socioeconomic differences within the many ethnic groups in the United States. Given the lack of research in this area, it is presently impossible to state with any degree of accuracy which, if any, of the learning characteristics attributed in this chapter to an ethnic group in general or to a particular gender within that ethnic group are actually restricted to a particular socioeconomic class within that group. Perhaps the most reasonable conclusion at this time is that educators should not assume that any particular learning trait is equally characteristic of all socioeconomic classes within a particular ethnic group.

## *Acculturation Effects*

Poor and non–European American students have at least four options for resolving the cultural conflicts they experience when their learning and behavior characteristics do not meet the expectations of the middle-class European American–oriented schools (212, 213). They can maintain the values, beliefs, and practices of their cultural heritage and reject the mainstream culture (traditional/cultural resistance). They can reject their heritage culture and adopt the mainstream culture (assimilation/cultural shift). They can identify with and accept both cultural systems and select which one is more appropriate for a given situation (bicultural/cultural incorporation). They can combine and alter both their original cultural norms and the alternate ones to create a new unique set of norms (cultural transmutation).

Many non–European American students have maintained most aspects of their culture including their learning and behavior characteristics, which are different then those expected by school personnel. The learning and behavior characteristics of others who have lost or given up a great deal of their traditional culture parallel those of European American middle-class students. Some are bicultural, and some are functioning in a way that represents, at least to some degree, cultural transmutation.

The pace at which individuals assimilate to a different culture, the type of acculturation they choose, and the areas in which they manifest these different types of acculturation depend on many factors. Some of these factors are their age at immigration, their gender, their level of education, whether they are immigrants or refugees, the number of generations their family has been living in the other culture, their previous intercultural experience, the length of time they have been exposed to the other culture, the degree to which they interact with members of the other culture, their ability to speak the language of the other culture, the amount of compatibility between the two cultures, their attitudes about the other culture, the relationship between members of the original and the other cultures, the amount of support they have within their original cultural group, the ethnic make up of their neighborhood, and the types and degree of pressure and encouragement they experience to maintain their original culture or to assimilate (213, 215, 217–220, 224, 227, 229, 231).

## *Assessing Learning Characteristics and Acculturation*

For the many reasons just cited, one cannot understand students' learning characteristics on the basis of their names, ethnic backgrounds, or skin shade. It is necessary to understand each student as a unique individual, rather than stereotypically. To do so, educators can assess the learning styles of all students, regardless of their gender and ethnic background, and the degree and type of acculturation of non-European and poor students.

### *Learning Characteristics*

Students' learning characteristics can be evaluated informally. The various characteristics discussed in this chapter can serve as checklists or guides for observing how they learn. Educators can also choose from a wide selection of formal assessment procedures for evaluating students' learning characteristics (233–237). Some are designed for students in general (e.g., the Learning Style Inventory [234, 237]); others are aimed at non–European American students in particular (e.g., the Ramirez and Castaneda Behavior Rating Scales [212]).

The regular and primary versions of the Learning Style Inventory involve students in the assessment process by having them state whether or not various statements apply to them. Following are some sample items from the instrument.

> The things I remember best are the things I hear.
> Noise usually keeps me from concentrating.
> I like to be given choices of how I can do things.
> I like to be told exactly what to do.

The Ramirez and Castenada Behavior Rating Scale is designed to evaluate whether students are field-sensitive or field-independent learners. Although the instrument was designed for use with Hispanic American students, it can be useful to evaluate students from other ethnic groups. It is also a useful tool to examine some gender stereotypes, because many, but certainly not all, females prefer a field-sensitive learning style, whereas males tend to be more field-independent.

The scale also has items to evaluate whether teachers employ field-sensitive or field-independent instructional styles. By using both the teaching style and learning characteristics sections of this instrument, teachers can determine

**The Ramirez and Castenada Behavior Rating Scale**

| Field-Sensitive | Field-Independent |
|---|---|
| *Student* | |
| Likes to work with others to achieve a common goal | Prefers to work independently |
| Seeks guidance and demonstration from teacher | Likes to try new tasks without teacher's help |
| Is sensitive to feelings and opinions of others | Is task oriented; is inattentive to social environments when working |
| *Teacher* | |
| Encourages cooperation and development of group feeling; encourages class to think and work as a unit | Encourages competition between individual students |
| Humanizes curriculum; attributes human characteristics to concepts and principles | Relies on graphs, charts, and formulas |
| Is sensitive to children who are having difficulty and need help | Encourages independent student achievement; emphasizes individual effort |

whether their teaching style matches a particular student's learning characteristics and so accommodate their teaching to her or his needs. The table shows examples of items in the students' and teachers' versions.

## *Acculturation*

As was noted in the previous chapter, it takes immigrant students who have spent the first four, five, or more years of their lives somewhere else a number of years to assimilate to a significant degree to the way things are done in the United States, even if they and their parents want to learn the new ways as quickly as possible. Thus, if immigrant students have not been here at least for a few years, you can assume that their classroom functioning will be affected by many of the cultural factors the students or their parents brought with them. The same principle would apply to many other students who have to adjust to unfamiliar school environments, including Native American students, rural students, and students who attend schools that serve children and youth from a different socioeconomic class.

Students' cumulative folders should include the information you need to determine how long they have been in this country, whether they attended school prior to coming here, and if so, the kind of school experiences they had. You can also obtain some information about Native American or rural students from their cumulative folder. However, you may have to rely on the students themselves, their parents, and sometimes agencies that are working with the students for most of the information you need.

Additional information can be obtained in the following ways.

**1.** *Observe the students' behavior.* Answer the following questions about students' behavior.

1. Do students socialize only with students from their same ethnic or social backgrounds, only with European American students, or with all types of students?
2. What language do bilingual students prefer to use when they are not in class (at lunch, recess, after school): English only, their native language, or a mixture of both?
3. Do students dress like typical European American students or in ways that identify them as members of a different group?
4. What do the statements students make about the European American culture and the culture of their homes reflect about their cultural identity? Do they express pride in their ethnic or racial background or reject it? Do they comment positively or negatively about the European American culture?
5. Do students' reactions to national and ethnic holidays indicate a bicultural identity or a preference for one type of holiday over the other?

**2.** *Consult with colleagues.* Ask colleagues (other teachers, paraprofessionals, and so on) who are knowledgeable about students' cultures to observe them and tell you whether they think their actions indicate they are traditional, assimilated, or bicultural.

**3.** *Interview the student.* Ask students if any of the classroom procedures, routines, rules, or social patterns are difficult for them to follow or conflict with how they are used to doing things at home. Inquire about whether they ever feel pressured in school to behave in ways that make them uncomfortable because they behave differently at home or in their neighborhoods. Determine whether students listen to and watch music, radio, movies, and television programs in their native language, English, or both languages. Listen to how students describe themselves. Do they say that they are Mexican, Vietnamese, Russian and so on; Mexican American, Vietnamese American, Russian American, and so on; or just American?

There are numerous formal assessment instruments for evaluating students' acculturation (214, 216, 217, 222–226, 228, 230). These instruments study the extent to which students are involved in their original and the European American cultures by requiring them to respond to a series of questions about their friendships both in and out of school, the activities they engage in, their recreational habits, the language or languages they speak, their attitudes and values, how they identify themselves, and so on. Typical items include: "What is the ethnic origin of your friends—exclusively Hispanic, Vietnamese, Chinese Americans; mostly Hispanic, Vietnamese, Chinese Americans; both Hispanic, Vietnamese, Chinese Americans and European Americans; mostly European Americans; exclusively European American? How do you call yourself—Hispanic, Vietnamese, Chinese;

## SELF-QUIZ: Informal Assessment

1. Compare the following three Korean American teenagers in terms of their level of acculturation to the United States along the traditional, bicultural, assimilated continuum.
2. Would you use different instructional strategies with each student because of their different types of acculturation? If so, how would you teach them differently?

Jae came to the United States when he was going on 10 years old. He has been here for five years. He speaks both Korean and English with friends and also at home. He reads English and Korean newspapers and magazines, watches Korean and English TV, eats European American and Korean food, and admires both Americans and Koreans. He belongs to some American groups but goes to a Korean church. His friends speak many languages, but most of them are English speaking. His closest friend is a Vietnamese American immigrant.

Jae does not want to lose his ability to speak Korean. He deplores the fact that there are no Korean books for his age group to read. Responding to a question about how he identifies himself, he stated,

> I'm Korean... because I'm from Korea.... My brains, you know are washed up by Korean culture. Then I speak Korean. Even though I work with American Kids, I still don't forget I'm Korean and I look forward to getting along more with Korean people. And when I get a job, I'll look Korean even though I'll have citizenship because I don't have white skin. They'll still be prejudiced a little bit that I'm Oriental. They're not going to look at me as American.... So I'm Korean. (232, p. 13)

Mi Cha has been in the United States for seven years, since she was 9. She considers herself Korean American. Her friends speak English and Korean, but she spends most of her time with a group of Korean teenagers who belong to a Korean church. She describes herself in the following way.

> I can't really speak good English. I can speak fluently in Korean but I don't know about deep words, you know. So I'm in the middle. Half English and half Korean. I know I'm Korean. I'm more into Korea than America. That's why I hang around a lot with Korean people who are older than me. They teach me a lot in Korean and I really learn a lot of Korean there. I will probably live my whole life here, probably learn American as I grow. But if you don't join Korean people you don't learn.
>
> I would marry a Korean guy.... I think we could get along better.... American people think differently than Korean people.... I'm not going to be over men. It's better if they're over me. But they'll not rule me where I have to do every little thing like that... I want an equal chance but I could serve him. It will be easier for me. (232, p. 13)

Danny has been in the United States for 11 or 12 years, since he was 5 or 6 years old. Danny does not remember anything about Korea. He does not know much about Korea and would like to learn more. However, he does not appear to be too interested in visiting his native land. He speaks both languages fluently, but he prefers to speak English because he is embarrassed by the mistakes he makes in Korean. He cannot read Korean. He would like to learn, but does not have the time. Although he identifies himself as Korean American, he feels more American than Korean.

He dates both Korean and European American girls. His best friend is European American. He only knows a few Korean friends, and they all speak English. He says that the new Korean kids in school have their own friends. He would like to help them, but he is too busy with football practice and other things.

His mother cooks Korean food at home. Although he claims to like Korean foods, he does not eat much spicy Korean food any more.

(Adapted from (232), with permission.)

Hispanic, Vietnamese, Chinese American; American? What kind of music do you prefer to listen to—Hispanic, Vietnamese, Chinese, American?"

Some instruments also include questions about students' parents such as their citizenship, the languages they speak, the kind of jobs they work at, the amount of education they have completed, and the number of children they have had, because assimilated and nonassimilated families tend to differ along these lines. One instrument is based on a series of questions designed to determine whether the persons being assessed consider themselves to be "insiders" or "outsiders" in relation to the dominant culture (222).

The students' answers are then compared to a sample group of students from similar backgrounds, enabling educators to determine the extent to which students have remained traditional, assimilated, or become bicultural, whether they identify with one or both cultures, and whether they are growing up in an assimilated or a traditional home.

Until recently, most experts viewed acculturation as a process of change along a continuum from unassimilated to highly assimilated (215–217, 221, 223, 225, 227, 228, 230). Therefore, most instruments indicate students' overall level or type of acculturation along this continuum—the extent to which they are traditional, assimilated, or bicultural. Because these instruments yield a score that indicates students' general level of acculturation, they can easily be misinterpreted. We now realize that students and others do not assimilate at the same pace in all areas of their lives. Thus, an overall score can underestimate the extent of their assimilation in one area and overestimate their adaptation in another. As Mendoza and Martinez state,

> *Some cultural traits tend to be assimilated more rapidly than others. Language usage, dress customs, and technological necessities, for instance, are generally incorporated much faster than abstract or less tangible qualities that involve values, sentiments, esthetic preferences, or attitudes on various socialization practices. (224, p. 73)*

Despite the limitation of the instruments currently available, the information they provide can serve as a starting point for continued examination of how students deal with cultural incompatibilities. Most of these instruments currently available assess Hispanic Americans. However, they can be adapted, and translated if necessary, for use with other ethnic and language groups.

These formal and informal procedures will provide you with a place to begin; they will give you a general understanding of the degree to which students are acculturated; and they will help alert you to the possible existence of cultural differences. However, they do not provide the information needed to determine whether students are characterized by a particular cultural trait—information that is necessary to enable you to consider individual students' cultural characteristics when you choose educational approaches to use with them. To do this requires more detailed information about the way individual students function in school.

## Summary

There are significant gender and ethnic differences in students' relationship, cognitive, and motivational styles; time orientations; interests; degree of self-confidence; and comfort level with certain educational activities. When educators adapt their instructional approaches to these learning characteristics, students learn more efficiently.

These learning characteristics do not apply to all members of a given ethnic or gender group. Students' socioeconomic background and level of acculturation help to determine whether particular students will conform to a particular ethnic or gender stereotype. In order to understand each student as a unique individual, educators can assess their learning characteristics and the degree and type of their acculturation to European American middle-class–oriented schools.

## Activities

**1.** Ask some students from different cultural backgrounds in the courses you are taking or some friends to describe their learning style preferences. You can interview them informally or prepare an informal questionnaire. Do you notice any of the cultural differences reported in this chapter?

**2.** Using the list of learning characteristics included in this chapter as a guide, prepare descriptions of the traits that you believe are characteristic of male and female students. Then ask a few of your friends or fellow students to review your list and tell you which traits they do and do not accept as being characteristic of their group.

**3.** Interview some individuals from an ethnic group that interests you and prepare a description of the educationally relevant cultural characteristics of the group as they perceive them.

**4.** Use the Ramirez and Castaneda Behavior Rating Scale to compare the learning characteristics of some of your male and female professors. Do you observe any of the gender differences reported in the literature?

## References

The following references discuss participatory and passive learning.

1. Gersten, R., & Keating, T. (1987). Long-term benefits from direct instruction. *Educational Leadership, 44,* 28–31.
2. Grossman, H. (1984). *Educating Hispanic Students: Cultural Implications for Instruction, Classroom Management, Counseling, and Assessment.* Springfield, IL: Charles C Thomas.
3. Grossman, H. (1994). *Special Education in a Diverse Society.* Needham, MA: Allyn and Bacon.
4. Kang-Ning, C. (1981). Education for Chinese and Indochinese. *Theory into Practice, 20*(1), 35–44.
5. Wong, M. K. (1978). Traditional Chinese culture and behavior patterns of Chinese students in American classrooms. In *Second*

*Annual Forum on Transcultural Adaptation (Proceedings): Asian Students in American Classrooms.* Chicago: Illinois Office of Education.

Ethnic differences in whether students prefer aloof and distant or involved and personal relations with teachers are included in this reference.

6. Kleinfeld, J. (1975). Effective Teachers of Indian and Eskimo High School Students. *School Review, 83*(2), 301–344.

Ethnic and gender variability in students' preferences for dependent or independent learning is the focus of these references.

7. Becker, B. J. (1986). Influence again: An examination of reviews and studies of gender differences in social influence. In J. S. Hyde & M. C. Linn (Eds.), *The Psychology of Gender.* Baltimore: The Johns Hopkins University Press.
8. Brutsaert, H. (1990). Changing sources of self-esteem among girls and boys in secondary school. *Urban Education, 24*(40), 432–439.
9. California State Department of Education. (1986). *Handbook for Teaching Pilipino-Speaking Students.* Sacramento: Author.
10. Caplan, P. (1979). Beyond the box score: A boundary condition for sex differences in aggression and achievement striving. In B. Maher (Ed.), *Progress in Experimental Personality Research,* Vol. 9. New York: Academic Press.
11. Cooper, H. M. (1979). Statistically combining independent studies: A meta-analysis of sex differences in conformity research. *Journal of Personality and Social Psychology, 37,* 131–146.
12. Dao, M. (1987). *From Vietnamese to Vietnamese American.* San Jose: San Jose State University.
13. Eagly, A. H., & Carli, L. L. (1981). Sex of researchers and sex-typed communications as determinants of sex differences in influenceability: A meta-analysis of social influence studies. *Psychological Bulletin, 90,* 1–20.
14. Parsons, J. E. (1982). Sex differences in attributions and learned helplessness. *Sex Roles, 8*(4), 421–432.
15. Van Hecke, M., Tracy, R. J., Cotter, S., & Ribordy, S. C. (1984). Approval versus achievement motives in seventh-grade girls. *Sex Roles, 11*(1), 33–41.
16. Wauters, J. L., Bruce, K. M., Black, D. R., & Hocker, P. N. (1989). Learning styles: A study of Alaskan Native and non-Native students. *Journal of American Indian Education,* Special Issue, August, 53–62.
17. Wulatin, M. L., & Tracy, R. J. (1977). *Sex Differences in Children's Responses to Achievement and Approval.* Paper presented at the meeting of the Midwestern Psychological Association, Chicago.

Factors that influence whether students are peer oriented or adult oriented are discussed in the following references.

18. Tharp, R. G. (1989). Psychocultural variables and constants: Effects on teaching and learning in schools. *American Psychologist, 44*(2), 349–359.
19. Tharp, R. G., & Gallimore, R. (1988). *Rousing Minds to Life: Teaching, Learning and Schooling in Social Context.* Cambridge, England: Cambridge University Press.

Gender differences in seeking teacher help, support, and feedback are the focus of the following reference.

20. Eiszler, C. F. (1982). *Perceptual Preference as an Aspect of Adolescent Learning Styles.* ERIC ED 224–769.
21. Grossman, H., & Grossman, S. (1994). *Gender Issues in Education.* Needham, MA: Allyn and Bacon.
22. Henry, S. E., Medway, F. J., & Scarbro, H. A. (1979). Sex and locus of control as determinants of children's responses to peer versus adult praise. *Journal of Educational Psychology, 71*(5), 604–612.
23. Nelson-LeGall, S., & Glor-Scheib, S. (1983). *Help-Seeking in Elementary Classrooms: An Observational Study.* ERIC ED 230–286.
24. Stewart, M. J., & Corbin, C. B. (1988). Feedback dependence among low confidence preadolescent boys and girls. *Research Quarterly for Exercise and Sport, 59*(2), 160–164.
25. Sullivan, H. J. (1986). Factors that influence continuing motivation. *Journal of Educational Research, 80*(2), 86–92.

This reference explores student differences in individualistic or group orientation.

26. Barnhardt, C. (1982). Tuning-in: Athabaskan teachers and Athabaskan students. In R. Barnhardt (Ed.), *Cross-Cultural Issues in Alaskan Education,* Vol. 2. ERIC ED 232–814.

Factors that contribute to differences among students in terms of reflective/analytical versus impulsive/spontaneous/intuitive cognitive styles are discussed in these references.

27. Farkas, G., Grobe, R. P., Sheenan, D., & Shuan, Y. (1990). Cultural resources and school success: Gender, ethnicity, and poverty groups within an urban school district. *American Sociological Review, 55*, 127–142.
28. Forslund, M. A., & Hull, R. E. (1974). Teacher sex and achievement among elementary school pupils. *Education, 95*, 87–89.
29. Grossman, H. (1990). *Trouble Free Teaching: Solutions to Behavior Problems in the Classroom*. Mountain View, CA: Mayfield.
30. Shade, B. J. (1979). *Racial Preference in Psychological Differentiation: An Alternative Explanation for Group Differences*. ERIC ED 179–672.

Ethnic contributions to students' preferences for global perception or analysis of details is the subject of the following references.

31. Chan, D. M. (1986). Curriculum development for limited English proficient exceptional Chinese children. *Rural Special Education Quarterly, 8*(1), 26–31.
32. Hilliard, A. (1976). *Alternatives to I. Q. Testing: An Approach to the Identification of Gifted Minority Children*. Sacramento: Final Report to the California State Department of Education.
33. More, A. J. (1987). Native Indian learning styles: A review for researchers and teachers. *Journal of American Indian Education, 27*(1), 17–29.
34. More, A. J. (1989). Native Indian learning styles: A review for researchers and teachers. *Journal of American Indian Education,* Special Issue, August, 15–28.
35. Rhodes, R. W. (1988). Holistic/teaching learning for Native American students. *Journal of American Indian Education, 27*(2), 21–29.

The effects of ethnic background on students' preferences for aural, visual, or verbal learning situations are discussed in these references.

36. Hallman, C. L., Etienne, M. R., & Fradd, S. (1982). *Haitian Value Orientations*. Monograph Number 2. ERIC ED 269–532.
37. John, B. (1972). Styles of learning—styles of teaching: Reflections of the education of Navajo children. In D. Cazden, V. John, & D. Hymes (Eds.), *Functions of Language in the Classroom*. New York: Teachers College Press.
38. Lewis, J., Vang, L., & Cheng, L. L. (1989). Identifying the language-learning difficulties of Hmong students: Implications of context and culture. *Topics in Language Disorders, 9*(3), 21–37.
39. Swisher, K., & Deyhle, D. (1989). The styles of learning are different, but the teaching is just the same: Suggestions for teachers of American Indian youth. *Journal of American Indian Education,* Special Issue, August, 1–14.

Kinesthetic/active, energetic, stimulating learning environments and calm, inactive verbal learning environments are contrasted in the references below.

40. Almanza, H. P., & Mosley, W. J. (1980). Cultural adaptations and modifications for culturally diverse handicapped children. *Exceptional Children, 46*(8), 608–614.
41. Boykin, A. W. (1984). Reading achievement and the social-cultural frame of reference of Afro-American children. *Journal of Negro Education, 53*(4), 464–473.
42. Eiszler, C. F. (1982). *Perceptual Preference as an Aspect of Adolescent Learning Styles*. ERIC ED 224–769.
43. Franklin, M. E. (1992). Culturally sensitive instructional practices for African-American learners with disabilities. *Exceptional Children, 59*(2), 115–122.
44. Simpson, C. (1981). Classroom organization and the gap between minority and nonminority student performance levels. *Educational Research Quarterly, 6*(3), 43–53.

The following studies indicate that females are more sensitive to nonverbal cues.

45. Hall, J. C. (1978). Gender effects in decoding nonverbal cues. *Psychological Bulletin, 85*, 845–857.
46. Rosenthal, R., Hall, J. A., DiMatteo, M. R., Rogers, P. L., & Archer, D. C. (1979). *Sensitivity to Non-Verbal Communication*. Baltimore: The Johns Hopkins University Press.

These references are concerned with trial and error learning.

47. Longstreet, E. (1978). *Aspects of Ethnicity*. New York: Teachers College Press.
48. Rhodes, R. W. (1990). Measurement of Navajo and Hopi brain dominance and learning styles. *Journal of American Indian Education, 29*(2), 29–40.

Argumentative/forensic instruction versus direct instruction is the focus of the following reference.

49. Burger, H. G. (1972). Ethno-lematics: Evoking "shy" Spanish-American pupils by cross-cultural mediation. *Adolescence, 6*(25), 61–76.

Ethnic and gender variations in students' motivation to succeed in school is the focus of these references.

50. Comer, J. P. (1990). What makes the new generation tick? *Ebony, 45*(10), 34, 37, 38.
51. Ford, D. Y. (1991). *Self-Perceptions of Social, Psychological, and Cultural Determinants of Achievement Among Gifted Black Students: A Paradox of Underachievement.* Unpublished doctoral dissertation, Cleveland State University, Ohio.
52. Ford, D. Y. (1992). The American achievement ideology and achievement differentials among preadolescent gifted and nongifted African American males and females. *Journal of Negro Education, 61*(1), 45–64.
53. Fordham, S. (1988). Racelessness as a strategy in Black students' school success: Coping with the burden of "acting White." *Urban Review, 18,* 176–207.
54. MacLeod, J. (1987). *Ain't No Makin' It: Leveled Aspirations in a Low-Income Neighborhood.* Boulder, CO: Westview.
55. Ogbu, J. U. (1990). Minority education in comparative perspective. *Journal of Negro Education, 59,* 45–57.

References that deal with gender differences in motivation to avoid success are listed next.

56. Crovitz, E. (1980). A decade later: Black-white attitudes toward women's familial roles. *Psychology of Women Quarterly, 5*(2), 170–176.
57. Fleming, J. (1978). Fear of success, achievement related motives and behavior in Black college women. *Journal of Personality, 46,* 694–716.
58. George, V. D. (1981). *Occupational Aspirations of Talented Black Adolescent Females.* ERIC ED 206–976.
59. George, V. D. (1986). Talented adolescent women and the motivation to avoid success. *Journal of Multicultural Counseling and Development, 14*(3), 132–139.
60. McCorquodale, P. (1983). *Social Influences on the Participation of Mexican American Women in Science* (N.I.E. Final Report 6–79-011). Tucson: University of Arizona.
61. Roberts, L. R. (1986). *Gender Differences in Patterns of Achievement and Adjustment During Early Adolescence.* ERIC ED 288–134.
62. Stockard, J., Schmuck, P. A., Kemper, K., Williams, P., Edson, S. K., & Smith, M. A. (1980). *Sex Equity in Education.* New York: Academic Press.
63. Tannen, D. (1990). *You Just Don't Understand.* New York: William Morrow.

These references describe ethnic group differences in students' willingness to learn on demand.

64. Cortes, C. E. (1978). Chicano culture, experience and learning. In L. Morris, G. Sather, & S. Scull (Eds.), *Extracting Learning Styles from Social/Cultural Diversity: A Study of Five American Minorities.* Norman, OK: Southwest Teacher Corps Network.
65. Garza, R. T. (1978). Affective and associative qualities in the learning styles of Chicanos and Anglos. *Psychology in the Schools, 15*(1), 111–115.
66. Kleinfeld, J. (1975). *Effective Teachers of Indian and Eskimo Students.* Fairbanks: Institute of Social, Economic, and Government Research, University of Alaska.
67. Rabiannski-Carriuolo, N. (1989). Learning styles: An interview with Edmund W. Gordon. *Journal of Developmental Education, 13*(1), 18–20, 22.
68. Walker, B. J., Dodd, J., & Bigelow, R. (1989). Learning preferences of capable American Indians of two tribes. *Journal of American Indian Education,* Special Issue, August, 63–71.
69. Yao, E. L. (1987). Asian-immigrants students—Unique problems that hamper learning. *NASSP Bulletin, 71*(503), 82–88.

These references argue that Native American and African American students are less object-oriented and more people-oriented learners.

70. Burgess, B. J. (1978). Native American learning styles. In L. Morris, G. Sather, & S. Scull (Eds.), *Extracting Learning Styles from Social/Cultural Diversity: A Study of Five American Minorities.* Norman, OK: Southwest Teacher Corps Network.
71. Hale, J. (1978). Cultural influences on learning styles of Afro-American children. In L. Morris, G. Sather, & S. Scull (Eds.), *Extracting Learning Styles from Social/Cultural Diversity: A Study of Five American Minorities.* Norman, OK: Southwest Teacher Corps Network.

The references listed here focus on ethnic and gender differences in preferences for competitive, cooperative, and individualistic learning environments.

72. Allen, J. L., O'Mara, J., & Long, K. M. (1987). *The Effects of Communication Avoidance, Learning Styles and Gender upon Classroom Achievement.* ERIC ED 291–111.
73. Alvino, J. (1991). An investigation into the needs of gifted boys. *Roeper Review, 13*(4), 174–180.
74. Dalton, D. W., Hannafin, M. J., & Hooper, S. (1989). Effects of individual and cooperative computer assisted instruction on student performance and attitudes. *Educational Technology Research and Development, 37*(2), 15–34.
75. Englehard, G., Jr., & Monsas, J. A. (1989). Performance, gender and the cooperative attitudes of third, fifth, and seventh graders. *Journal of Research and Development in Education, 22*(2), 13–17.
76. Fennema, E. H., & Peterson, P. L. (1985). Autonomous learning behavior: A possible explanation of gender-related differences in mathematics. In L. C. Wilkinson & C. B. Marrett (Eds.), *Gender Influences in Classroom Interaction.* New York: Academic Press.
77. Harpole, S. H. (1987). *The Relationship of Gender and Learning Styles to Achievement and Laboratory Skills in Secondary School Chemistry Students.* ERIC ED 288–728.
78. Jaramillo, M. L. (1973). *Cautions When Working with the Culturally Different Child.* ERIC ED 115–622.
79. Kagan, S., & Madsen, M. C. (1972). Rivalry in Anglo-American and Mexican children of two ages. *Journal of Personality and Social Psychology, 24,* 214–220.
80. Kagan, S., Zahn, G. L., & Gealy, J. (1977). Competition and school achievement among Anglo-American and Mexican-American children. *Journal of Educational Psychology, 69*(4), 432–441.
81. Lewis, M. A., & Cooney, J. B. (1986). *Attributional and Performance Effects of Competitive and Individualistic Feedback in Computer Assisted Mathematics Instruction.* ERIC ED 271–287.
82. Lockheed, M. E., Harris, A. M., & Nemceff, W. P. (1983). Sex and social influence: Does sex function as a status characteristic in mixed-sex groups of children? *Journal of Educational Psychology, 75,* 877–888.
83. McClintock, C. (1974). Development of social motives in Anglo-American and Mexican children. *Journal of Personality and Social Psychology, 29,* 348–354.
84. Moely, B. E., Skarin, K., & Weil, S. (1979). Sex differences in competition-cooperation behavior of children at two age levels. *Sex Roles, 5*(31), 329–342.
85. Peterson, P., & Fennema, E. (1985). Effective teaching, student engagement in classroom activities, and sex-related differences in learning mathematics. *American Educational Research Journal, 22*(3), 309–334.
86. Strube, M. J. (1981). Meta-analysis and crosscultural comparison: Sex differences in child competitiveness. *Journal of Cross-Cultural Psychology, 12*(1), 3–20.
87. Swisher, K. (1990). Cooperative learning and the education of American Indian/Alaskan Native students: A review of the literature and suggestions for implementation. *Journal of American Indian Education, 29*(2), 36–43.
88. Webb, N. M., & Kenderski, C. M. (1985). Gender differences in small-group interaction and achievement in high- and low-achieving classes. In L. C. Wilkinson & C. B. Marrett (Eds.), *Gender Influences in Classroom Interaction.* New York: Academic Press.
89. Wilkinson, L. C., Lindow, J., & Chiang, C. P. (1985). Sex differences and sex segregation in students' small-group communication. In L. C. Wilkinson & C. B. Marrett (Eds.), *Gender Influences in Classroom Interaction.* New York: Academic Press.

The following reference documents the fact that competitive learning environments predominate in American schools.

90. Johnson, D. W., & Johnson, R. T. (1987). *Learning Together and Alone: Cooperation, Competition and Individualization,* (2nd ed.). Englewood Cliffs, NJ: Prentice Hall.

These references document the positive effects of cooperative learning.

91. Aronson, E., Blaney, N., Sikes, J., & Snapp, M. (1978). *The Jigsaw Classroom.* Beverly Hills: Sage.
92. Asher, C. (1986). Cooperative learning in the urban classroom. *ERIC Digest, 30.*
93. DeVries, D. K., Edwards, K. J., & Slavin, R. (1978). Biracial learning teams and race relations in the classroom: Four field experiences using Teams-Games-Tournaments. *Journal of Educational Psychology, 70,* 356–362.

94. DeVries, D. K., & Slavin, R. E. (1978). Teams-Games-Tournaments: A research review. *Journal of Research and Development in Education, 12,* 28–38.
95. Humphreys, B., Johnson, R. T., & Johnson, D. W. (1982). Effects of cooperative, competitive and individualistic learning on students' achievement in science class. *Journal of Research in Science Teaching, 19*(5), 351–356.
96. Johnson, R. T., & Johnson, D. W. (1981). Effects of cooperative and individualistic learning experiences on interethnic interaction. *Journal of Educational Psychology, 73,* 444–449.
97. Johnson, D. W., Johnson, R. T., Holubec, E. J., & Roy, P. (1984). *Circles of Learning.* Alexandria, VA: Association for Supervision and Curriculum Development.
98. Johnson, R. T., Johnson, D. W., Scott, L. E., & Ramolae, B. A. (1985). Effects of single-sex and mixed-sex cooperative interaction on science achievement and attitudes and cross-handicap and cross-sex relationships. *Journal of Research in Science Teaching, 22*(3), 207–220.
99. Johnson, D. W., Maruyama, G., Johnson, R., Nelson, D., & Skon, L. (1981). Effects of cooperative, competitive, and individualistic goal structures on achievement: A meta analysis. *Psychological Bulletin, 89,* 47–62.
100. Schofield, J. W. (1982). *Black and White in School: Trust, Tension, and Tolerance.* New York: Praeger.
101. Slavin, R. E., & Oickle, E. (1981). Effects of cooperative learning teams on student achievement and race relations: Treatment by race interactions. *Sociology of Education, 54,* 174–180.

The selective benefits of cooperative learning are described in these references.

102. Calderon, M. E., Tinajero, J. V., & Hertz-Lazarowitz, R. (1992). Adapting cooperative integrated reading and composition to meet the needs of bilingual students. *Journal of Educational Issues of Language Minority Students.* Special Issue, *10,* 79–106.
103. Glassman, P. (1988). *A Study of Cooperative Learning in Mathematics, Writing and Reading as Implemented in Third, Fourth and Fifth Grade Classes: A Focus upon Achievement, Attitudes and Self-Esteem for Males, Females, Blacks, Hispanics and Anglos.* ERIC ED 292–926.
104. Knight, G. P., Nelson, W., Kagan, S., & Gumbiner, J. (1982). Cooperative-competitive social orientation and school achievement among Anglo-American and Mexican-American children. *Contemporary Educational Psychology, 7,* 97–106.

The positive effects of single-sex cooperative groups on females is discussed in these references.

105. Kahle, J. B., & Lakes, M. K. (1983). The myth of equality in science classrooms. *Journal of Research in Science Teaching, 20,* 131–140.
106. Moody, J. D., & Gifford, V. D. (1990). *The Effect of Grouping by Formal Reasoning Ability, Formal Reasoning Ability Levels, Group Size, and Gender on Achievement in Laboratory Chemistry.* ERIC ED 326–443.

Documentation of the effects of mixed-sex groups on students is found in the following references.

107. Chalesworth, W. R., & LaFrenier, P. (1983). Dominance, friendship utilization and resource utilization in preschool children's groups. *Ethology and Sociobiology, 4,* 175–186.
108. DeVries, D. K., & Edwards, K. J. (1974). Student teams and learning games: Their effects on cross-race and cross-sex interaction. *Journal of Educational Psychology, 66*(5), 741–749.
109. Lockheed, M. E., & Harris, A. M. (1984). Cross-sex collaborative learning in elementary classrooms. *American Educational Research Journal, 21*(2), 275–294.
110. Lockheed, M. E., Harris, A. M., & Nemceff, W. P. (1983). Sex and social influence: Does sex function as a status characteristic in mixed-sex groups of children? *Journal of Educational Psychology, 75,* 877–888.
111. Peterson, P., & Fennema, E. (1985). Effective teaching, student engagement in classroom activities, and sex-related differences in learning mathematics. *American Educational Research Journal, 22*(3), 309–334.
112. Piel, J. A., & Conwell, C. R. (1989). *Differences in Perceptions Between Afro-American and Anglo-American Males and Females in Cooperative Learning Groups.* ERIC ED 307–348.
113. Powlishta, K. (1987). *The Social Context of Cross-Sex Interactions.* Paper presented at the biennial meetings of the Society for Research in Child Development, Baltimore.
114. Siann, G., & Macleod, H. (1986). Computers and children of primary school age: Issues and questions. *British Journal of Educationol Technology, 17,* 133–144.

115. Skarin, K., & Moely, B. E. (1974). *Sex Differences in Competition-Cooperation Behavior of Eight-Year-Old Children*. ERIC ED 096–015.
116. Underwood, G., McCaffrey, M., & Underwood, J. (1990). Gender differences in a cooperative computer-based language task. *Educational Research, 32*(1), 44–49.
117. Webb, N. (1984). Microcomputer learning in small groups: Cognitive requirements and group processes. *Journal of Educational Psychology, 76*(6). 1076–1088.
118. Wilkinson, L. C., Lindow, J., & Chiang, C P. (1985). Sex differences and sex segregation in students' small-group communication. In L. C. Wilkinson & C. B. Marrett (Eds.), *Gender Influences in Classroom Interaction*. New York: Academic Press.

Gender differences in responsiveness to peers' requests and reinforcement is discussed in the following references.

119. Fagot, B. I. (1985). Beyond the reinforcement principle: Another step toward understanding sex roles. *Developmental Psychology, 21*, 1097–1104.
120. Lamb, M. E., Easterbrook, A. M., & Holden, G. W. (1980). Reinforcement and punishment among preschoolers: Characteristics, effects, and correlates. *Child Development, 51*, 1230–1236.
121. Serbin, L. A., Sprafkin, C., Elman, M., & Doyle, A. B. (1984). The early development of sex differentiated patterns of social influence. *Canadian Journal of Social Science, 14*(4), 350–363.
122. Wilkinson, L. C., & Marrett, C. B. (Eds.). (1985). *Gender Influence in Classroom Interaction*. New York: Academic Press.

Gender differences in leadership assumption and participation in mixed-sex groups are treated in the following references.

123. Lockheed, M. E. (1977). Cognitive style effects on sex status in student work groups. *Journal of Educational Psychology, 69*, 158–165.
124. Lockheed, M. E. (1985). Sex and social influence: A meta-analysis guided by theory. In J. Berger & M. Zeldich (Eds.), *Status, Attributions, and Rewards*. San Francisco: Jossey-Bass.
125. Lockheed, M. E., & Hall, K. P. (1976). Conceptualizing sex as a status characteristic: Application to leadership training strategies. *Journal of Social Issues, 32*(3), 111–124.
126. Webb, N. M., & Kinderski, C. M. (1985). Gender differences in small group interaction and achievement in high-and low-achieving classes. In C. Wilkinson & C. B. Marrett (Eds.), *Gender Influence in Classroom Interaction*. New York: Academic Press.

The experiences of different ethnic groups in cooperative learning groups is discussed in these references.

127. Conwell, C. R., Piel, J. A., & Cobb, K. B. (1988). *Students' Perceptions When Working in Cooperative Problem Solving Groups*. ERIC ED 313–455.
128. Fry, P. S., & Coe, K. J. (1980). Achievement performance of internally and externally oriented black and white high school students under conditions of competition and cooperation expectancies. *British Journal of Educational Psychology, 50*, 162–167.

This reference discusses the relationship between students' self-concepts and the outcome of cooperative learning activities.

129. DeVoe, M. W. (1977). Cooperation as a function of self-concept, sex and race. *Educational Research Quarterly, 2*(2), 3–8.

The focus of the references listed here is gender differences in risk taking and reactions to challenges and failure.

130. Ginsburg, H. J., & Miller, S. M. (1982). Sex differences in children's risk-taking behavior. *Child Development, 53*(2), 426–428.
131. Licht, B. G., Kistner, J. A., Ozkaragoz, T., Shapiro, S., & Clausen, L. (1985). Causal attributions of learning disabled children: Individual differences and their implications for persistence. *Journal of Educational Psychology, 77*(2), 208–216.
132. Licht, B. G., Linden, T. A., Brown, D. A., & Sexton, M. (1984). *Sex Differences in Achievement Orientation: An "A" Student Phenomenon*. ERIC ED 252–783.
133. Miller, A. (1986). Performance impairment after failure: Mechanisms and sex differences. *Journal of Educational Psychology, 78*(6), 486–491.
134. Reyes, L. H. (1984). Affective variables and mathematics education. *Elementary School Journal, 84*(5), 558–581.

These references discuss ethnic difference in risk taking.

135. Kishi, G., & Hanohano, M. (1992). *Hawaiian-American vs Caucasian-American Values*. Paper presented at the Council for Exceptional Children Topical Conference on Culturally and Linguistically Different Exceptional Children, Minnesota.
136. Kitano, M. K. (1986). Gifted and talented Asian children. *Rural Special Education Quarterly, 8*(1), 9–13.

These references deal with different ethnic concepts of time.

137. Allameh, J. (1986). *Learning Among Culturally Different Populations*. ERIC ED 273–137.
138. Ayabe, H. I. (1978). Ethnic culture, reflection impulsivity and locus of control. *Educational Perspectives, 17*(4), 10–12.
139. Brady, M. P., & Anderson, D. D. (1983). Some issues in the implementation of P.L. 94–142 in the Pacific Basin Territories. *Education, 103*(3), 259–269.
140. Condon, E. C., Peters, J. Y., & Sueiro-Ross, C. (1979). *Special Education and the Hispanic Child: Cultural Perspectives*. Philadelphia: Temple University, Teacher Corps Mid-Atlantic Network.
141. Dodd, J. M. (1992). *Preventing American Indian Children from Overidentification with Learning Disabilities: Cultural Considerations during the Prereferral Process*. Paper presented at the Council for Exceptional Children Topic Conference on Culturally and Linguistically Diverse Exceptional Children, Minneapolis.
142. Felder, D. (1970). The education of Mexican Americans: Fallacies of the monocultural approach. *Social Education, 34*(6), 639–642.
143. Levine, R. V., West, L. J., & Reis, H. T. (1980). Perceptions of time and punctuality in the United States and Brazil. *Journal of Personality and Social Psychology, 38*(4), 541–550.
144. Morgan, C. O., Guy, E., & Celini, H. (1986). The rehabilitation of disabled Native Americans. *Journal of Rehabilitation, 52*, 25–311.

Gender differences in students' confidence in their ability to succeed in school are the focus of the following references.

145. Eccles, J., Adler, T. F., & Meece, J. L. (1984). Sex differences in achievement: A test of alternate theories. *Journal of Personality and Social Psychology, 68*, 119–128.
146. Hyde, J., & Fennema, E. (1990). *Gender Differences in Mathematics Performance and Affect: Results of Two Meta-Analyses*. Paper presented at the annual meeting of the American Educational Research Association, Boston.
147. Levine, G. (1990). *Arithmetic Development: Where are the Gender Differences?* Paper presented at the annual meeting of the American Educational Research Association, Boston.
148. Matyas, M. L. (1984). *Science Career Interests, Attitudes, Abilities, and Anxiety Among Secondary School Students: The Effects of Gender, Race/Ethnicity, and School Type/Location*. ERIC ED 251–309.
149. Meece, J. L., Parsons, J. E., Kaczala, C. M., Goff, B., & Futterman, R. (1982). Sex differences in math achievement: Toward a model of academic choice. *Psychological Bulletin, 91*, 324–348.
150. Richman, C. L., Clark, M. L., & Brown, K. P. (1984). General and specific self-esteem in late adolescent students: Race x gender x SES effects. *Adolescence, 20*(79), 555–566.
151. Stevenson, H. W., & Newman, R. S. (1986). Long-term prediction of achievement and attitudes in mathematics and reading. *Child Development, 57*, 646–659.
152. Travis, C. B., McKenzie, B. J., & Wiley, D. L. (1984). *Sex and Achievement Domain: Cognitive Patterns of Success and Failure*. ERIC ED 250–601.

The reference that follows deals with gender differences in students' perceptions of their ability to exert control over their lives and their attribution of the cause of their successes and failures in school.

153. Dyal, J. A. (1984). Cross-cultural research with the locus of control construct. In H. M. Lefcourt (Ed.), *Research with the Locus of Control Construct. Vol. 3: Extensions and Limitations*. New York: Academic Press.
154. Evans, E. D., & Engleberg, R. A. (1988). Student perceptions of school grading. *Journal of Research and Development in Education, 21*(2), 45–54.
155. Frey, K. S., & Ruble, D. N. (1987). What children say about classroom performance: Sex and grade differences in perceived competence. *Child Development, 58*, 1066–1078.
156. Lewis, M. A. (1989). *Consistency of Children's Causal Attributions Across Content Domains*. ERIC ED 306–488.
157. Lopez, C. L., & Harper, M. (1989). The relationship between learner control of CAI and locus of control among Hispanic students.

*Educational Technology Research and Development, 37*(4), 19–28.
158. McMahan, I. D. (1982). Expectancy of success on sex-linked tasks. *Sex Roles, 8,* 949–958.
159. Powers, S., & Wagner, M. J. (1983). *Achievement Locus of Control of Hispanic and Anglo High School Students.* ERIC ED 230–355.
160. Reyes, L. H., & Padilla, M. J. (1985). Science math and gender. *Science Teacher, 52*(6), 46–48.
161. Ryckman, D. B., & Peckman, P. D. (1986). Gender differences in attribution patterns in academic areas for learning disabled students. *Learning Disabilities Research, 1*(2), 83–89.
162. Ryckman, D. B., & Peckman, P. D. (1987a). Gender differences in attribution for success and failure. *Journal of Early Adolescence, 7,* 47–63.
163. Ryckman, D. B., & Peckman, P. D. (1987b). Gender differences in attribution for success and failure across subject areas. *Journal of Educational Research, 81,* 120–125.
164. Stipek, D. J. (1984). Sex differences in children's attributions for success and failure on math and spelling tasks. *Sex Roles, 11*(11/12), 969–981.
165. Turner, R. R. (1978). Locus of control, academic achievement, and follow through in Appalachia. *Contemporary Educational Psychology, 3,* 367–375.
166. Willig, A. C., Harnisch, D. L., Hill, K. T., & Maehr, M. L. (1983). Sociocultural and educational correlates of success-failure attributions and evaluation anxiety in the school setting for Black, Hispanic and Anglo children. *American Educational Research Journal, 20*(3), 385–410.

Ethnic differences in students' perceptions of their ability to exert control over their lives is the focus of these references.

167. Ashe, R. Personal communication.
168. Ayabe, H. I. (1977). *Measuring Locus of Control at the College Level.* Paper presented at the annual conference of the Hawaiian Psychological Association, Honolulu.
169. Shade, B. J. (1979). *Racial Preference in Psychological Differentiation: An Alternative Explanation for Group Differences.* ERIC ED 179–672.
170. Tashakkori, A., & Thompson, V. D. (1990). *Race Differences in Self-Perception and Locus of Control During Adolescence and Early Adulthood.* ERIC ED 327–806.

The relationship between locus of control and school achievement is discussed in these references.

171. Coleman, J. S., Campbell, E. Q., Hobson, C. J., McPartland, J., Mood, A. M., Weinfeld, F. D., & York, R. L. (1966). *Equality of Educational Opportunity.* Washington, DC: U.S. Government Printing Office.
172. Crandall, V., Katkovsky, W., & Crandall, V. (1965). Children's beliefs in their own control of reinforcement in intellectual and academic achievement situations. *Child Development, 36,* 91–109.
173. Epps, E. G. (1969). Negro academic motivation and performance: An overview. *Journal of Social Issues, 25*(3), 5–11.
174. Wilson, K. R., & Allen, W. R. (1987). Explaining the educational attainment of young black adults: Critical familial and extra-familial influences. *Journal of Negro Education, 56*(1), 64–76.

These references discuss the efficacy efforts to improve students' self-confidence.

175. Canfield, J., & Wells, H. C. (1976). *100 Ways to Enhance Self-Concept in the Classroom.* Englewood Cliffs, NJ: Prentice Hall.
176. De Charms, R. (1976). *Enhancing Motivation.* New York: Irvington.
177. Hauserman, N., Mitler, J. S., & Bond, F. T. (1976). A behavioral approach to changing self-concept in elementary school children. *Psychological Record, 26,* 111–116.
178. Lane, J., & Muller, D. (1977). The effect of altering self-descriptive behavior on self-concept and classroom behavior. *Journal of Psychology, 97,* 115–125.
179. Olszewski, P., Kulieke, M. J., & Willis, G. B. (1987). Changes in the self-perceptions of gifted students who participate in rigorous academic programs. *Journal for the Education of the Gifted, 10*(4), 287–303.
180. Scheier, M. A., & Kraut R. E. (1979). Increasing educational achievement via self-concept change. *Review of Educational Research, 49,* 131–149.
181. Schulman, J. L., Ford, R. C., & Busk, P. (1973). A classroom program to improve self-concept. *Psychology in the Schools, 10,* 481–487.

Instruments for assessing students' self-confidence are described in the following references.

182. Coopersmith, S., & Feldman, R. (1974). Fostering a positive self-concept and high self-

esteem in the classroom. In R. H. Coop & K. White (Eds.), *Psychological Concepts in the Classroom*. New York: Harper & Row.
183. Harter, S. (1982). The perceived competency scale for children. *Child Development, 53,* 87–97.
184. Katzenmer, W. G., & Stenner, A. J. (1970). *Self-Observation Scale*. Durham, NC: NTS Research Corporation.
185. Norwicki, S., & Strickland, B. (1973). A locus of control scale for children. *Journal of Consulting Psychology, 40,* 148–154.
186. Piers, E. V., & Harris, D. B. (1969). *Children's Self-Concept Scale (The Way I Feel About Myself)*. Nashville: Counselor Recordings and Tests.

Suggestions for enhancing the self-confidence of poor and non–European American students are included in the following references.

187. Draper, I. L, Kimbrough, A. H., Jones, J. W., & Pierce, B. (1992). *Using "Self-Esteem Through Culture Leads to Academic Excellence (SETCLAE)" Transmission of Culture*. Paper presented at the Council for Exceptional Children Topical Conference on Diverse Exceptional Children, Minneapolis.
188. Frasier, M. M. (1979). Rethinking the issues regarding the culturally disadvantaged gifted. *Exceptional Children, 45*(7), 538–542.
189. Hale-Benson, J. E. (1986). *Black Children: Their Roots, Culture, and Learning Styles*, (rev. ed.). Baltimore: The Johns Hopkins University Press.
190. Hankerson, H. E. (1980). Understanding the young black exceptional child: An overview. In E. Jackson (Ed.), *The Young Black Exceptional Child: Providing Programs and Services*. ERIC ED 204–919.
191. Mack, F. R-P. (1987). Understanding and enhancing self-concept in black children. *Momentum, 18*(1), 22–25.
192. Pepper, F. C. (1976). Teaching the American Indian child in mainstream settings. In R. L. Jones (Ed.), *Mainstreaming and the Minority Child*. Reston, VA: Council for Exceptional Children.
193. Wood, G. H. (1984). Schooling in a democracy: Transformation or reproduction: *Educational Theory, 34*(3), 219–239.

The following references offer guidelines and suggestions on how to make course contents more relevant and interesting to non–European American students.

194. Asante, M. K. (1991). Putting Africa at the center. *Newsweek, 118*(13), 46.
195. Kantrowitz, B. (1991). A is for ashanti, b is for black. *Newsweek, 118*(13), 45–48.
196. Cheng, L. L. (1989). Intervention strategies: A multicultural approach. *Topics in Language Disorders, 9*(3), 84–91.
197. Flores, J. M. (1989). Barrio folklore as a basis for English composition. *Equity & Excellence, 24*(2), 72.
198. Gay, G. (1988). Designing relevant curricula for diverse learners. *Education and Urban Society, 20*(4), 327–340.
199. Martinez, D. I., & Ortiz de Montellano, B. R. (1988). *Improving the Science and Mathematic Achievement of Mexican American Students Through Culturally Relevant Science*. Las Cruces: ERIC/CRESS, New Mexico State University.
200. Palmer, P. A., & Palmer, B. C. (1983). Reading interests of middle school black and white students. *Reading Improvement, 20*(2), 151–155.
201. Pugh, S. L. (1989). Literature, culture, and ESL: A natural convergence. *Journal of Reading, 34*(4), 320–329.

This reference provides examples of acceptable and unacceptable learning experiences.

202. Nazzaro, J. N. (1981). Special problems of exceptional minority children. In J. N. Nazzaro (Ed.), *Culturally Diverse Exceptional Children in School*. ERIC ED 199–993.

The following references discuss the interrelationship between socioeconomic class and ethnicity.

203. Chan, K., & Rueda, R. (1979). Poverty and culture in education: Separate but equal. *Exceptional Children, 45,* 422–427.
204. Cooper, J. G. (1977). *The Effects of Ethnicity upon School Achievement*. ERIC ED 157–675.
205. Dillard, J. M., & Perrin, D. W. (1980). Puerto Rican, Black, and Anglo adolescents' career aspirations, expectations, and maturity. *Vocational Guidance Quarterly, 28,* 313–332.
206. Havighurst, R. J. (1976). The relative importance of social class and ethnicity in human development. *Human Development, 19,* 56–64.
207. Johnson, N. J., & Sanaday, P. R. (1971). Subcultural variations in one urban poor population. *American Anthropologist, 73,* 128–143.

208. Kagan, S., & Ender, P. B. (1975). Maternal responses to success and failure of Anglo-American, Mexican American, and Mexican children. *Child Development, 46,* 452–458.
209. Laosa, L. M. (1977). Socialization, education and continuity: The importance of the sociocultural context. *Young Children, 32*(5), 21–27.
210. Sarason, S. B. (1973). Jewishness, blackness, and the nature-nurture controversy. *American Psychologist, 28,* 962–971.
211. Wilson, W. J. (1978). *The Declining Significance of Race.* Chicago: University of Chicago Press.

These references discuss students' acculturation and how to evaluate it.

212. Ramirez, M., & Castaneda, A. (1974). *Bicultural Democracy, Bicognitive Development and Education.* New York: Academic Press.
213. Berry, J. W., Kim, U., Minde, T., & Mok, R. (1987). Comparative studies of acculturative stress. *International Migration Review, 21*(30), 491–511.
214. Cloud, N. (1990). *Measuring Level of Acculturation in Bilingual, Bicultural Children.* Paper presented at the annual meeting of the American Educational Research Association, Boston.
215. Cloud, N. (1991). Acculturation of ethnic minorities. In A. M. Ambert (Ed.), *Bilingual Education and English as a Second Language: A Research Handbook 1988–1990.* New York: Garland.
216. Cuellar, I., Harris, L. C., & Jasso, R. (1980). An acculturation scale for Mexican American normal and clinical populations. *Hispanic Journal of Behavioral Sciences, 2*(3), 199–217.
217. Franco, J. N. (1983). An acculturation scale for Mexican-American children. *Journal of General Psychology, 108,* 175–181.
218. Koh, T., & Koh, S. D. (1982). A note on the psychological evaluation of Korean school children. *P/AAMHRC Research Review, 1*(3), 1–2.
219. Lee, E. (1988). Cultural factors in working with Southeast Asian refugee adolescents. *Journal of Adolescence, 11,* 167–179.
220. Leung, E. K. (1988). Cultural and acculturational commonalities and diversities among Asian Americans: Identification and programming considerations. In A. A. Ortiz & B. A. Ramirez (Eds.), *Schools and Culturally Diverse Exceptional Students: Promising Practices and Future Directions.* Reston, VA: ERIC Clearinghouse on Handicapped and Gifted Children, Council for Exceptional Children.
221. Lin, K., & Masuda M. (1983). Impact of refugee experience: Mental health issues of Southeast Asian refugees. In R. F. Morales (Ed.), *Bridging Cultures.* Los Angeles: Asian American Health Center.
222. Mainous, A. G., III. (1989). Self concept as an indicator of acculturation in Mexican Americans. *Hispanic Journal of Behavioral Sciences, 11*(2), 178–189.
223. Martinez, R., Norman, R. D., & Delaney, H. D. (1984). A Children's Hispanic Background Scale. *Hispanic Journal of Behavioral Sciences, 6*(2), 103–112.
224. Mendoza, R. H., & Martinez, J. L. (1981). The measurement of acculturation. In A. Baron, Jr. (Ed.), *Explorations in Chicano Psychology.* New York: Holt.
225. Olmedo, E. L. (1980). Quantitative models of acculturation: An overview. In A. M. Padilla (Ed.), *Acculturation: Theory, Models, and Some New Findings.* Boulder, CO: Westview Press.
226. Olmedo, E. L., & Padilla, A. M. (1978). Empirical and construct validity of a measure of acculturation for Mexican Americans. *Journal of Social Psychology, 105,* 179–187.
227. Padilla, A. M. (1980). The role of cultural awareness and ethnic loyalty in acculturation. In A. M. Padilla (Ed.), *Acculturation: Theory, Models, and Some New Findings.* Boulder, CO: Westview Press.
228. Suinn, R. M., Rickard-Figueroa, K., Lew, S., & Vigil, P. (1987). Asian Self-Identity Acculturation Scale: An initial report. *Educational and Psychological Measurement, 47,* 401–407.
229. Szapocznik, J., & Kurtines, W. (1980). Acculturation, biculturalism and adjustment among Cuban Americans. In A. M. Padilla (Ed.), *Acculturation: Theory, Models, and Some New Findings.* Boulder, CO: Westview Press.
230. Szapocznik, J., Kurtines, W. M., & Fernandez, T. (1979). *Bicultural Involvement and Adjustment in Hispanic American Youth.* ERIC ED 193–374.
231. Wong-Rieger, D., & Quintana, D. (1987). Comparative acculturation of Southeast Asian and Hispanic immigrants and sojourners. *Journal of Cross-Cultural Psychology, 18*(3), 345–362.
232. Golden, J. G. (1990). The acculturation of three Korean American students. *Teaching and Learning, 5*(1), 9–20.

Instruments for evaluating students' learning styles are listed and discussed in the following references.

233. Dunn, R., & Dunn, K. (1978). *Teaching Students Through Their Individual Learning Styles: A Practical Approach.* Reston, VA: Reston Publishing Company.
234. Keefe, J. (1979). Learning style: An overview. In *Student Learning Styles: Diagnosing and Prescribing Programs.* Reston, VA: National Association of Secondary School Principals.
235. McCarthy, B. (1980). *The 4 Mat System: Teaching to Learning Styles with Right/Left Mode Techniques.* Oak Brook, IL: Excel.
236. Perrin, J. (1982). *Learning Style Inventory: Primary Version.* Jamaica, NY: St. John's University.
237. Renzulli, J., & Smith, L. (1978). *The Learning Style Inventory: A Measure of Student Preference for Instructional Techniques.* Mansfield Center, CT: Creative Learning Press.

# PART II: Teaching Exceptional, Diverse, and At-Risk Students in the General Education Classroom

Sharon Vaughn, Candace S. Bos, Jeanne Shay Schumm

CHAPTER 9

# Planning and Grouping Strategies for Special Learners

# Interview

## Lisa Geller

Lisa Geller is a third-grade teacher at South Pointe Elementary School in Miami, Florida. Of the 35 students in Lisa's class, 5 have learning disabilities. Lisa's faculty has chosen an inclusion model of service delivery for students with disabilities. Ellen Fascano is the special education teacher who works with Lisa. Her role is to provide instruction for students with learning disabilities in the general education classroom during the reading and language arts block, and then to pull individual students, as necessary, to work on specific objectives identified on the IEP. Because Lisa and Ellen work daily in the same classroom, collaborative planning is a must.

> Each week, Ellen and I sit down to talk about what the students with disabilities are doing. This is really important because we have parent conferences with the parents of all of our students four times a year, and Ellen and I both meet with the parents of the special education students. Although Ellen actually is responsible for the grades of the students with disabilities, we confer about their progress and decide on their grades jointly.
>
> At the beginning of the year Ellen and I review the IEP for all of the children and develop plans for individual students. But really our planning is ongoing. We also conduct an informal reading test at the beginning, middle, and end of the year for the students so that we can keep track of their progress in reading and make revisions and additions to our plans. We also do a great deal of informal observation and keep checklists about student progress, and we input our observations into the computer every week. The philosophy of our school is to record one observation per subject area per week. As you can imagine, this takes a great deal of work, and we need to meet every week to accomplish it all. But it is really important as we think how to meet individual student needs.
>
> When I do my unit and lesson planning, I talk with Ellen about what areas might be difficult for the students with disabilities. She lets me know the most sensitive areas and gives me suggestions for how I can make adaptations to help students learn the material.
>
> Part of our planning is related to how we group students for reading instruction. The philosophy at our school is for each student to feel that he or she is important and one person is not better than the other, so we use a variety of grouping patterns—and most of the grouping is mixed, in terms of student achievement levels. If you came into our reading class, this is what you'd see. First we do whole-class activities, such as reading a literature book together, and then some follow-up activities. Once again, Ellen is really helpful here because she lets me know where the students with disabilities might have some trouble and suggests some adaptations that I might make. I'm getting better at being sensitive to what they can and can't do while I'm teaching and making on-the-spot changes to help them learn.
>
> During the follow-up activities, my kids always have a "study buddy." Usually we try to choose the buddy that they work with so that a high achiever is working with a student who is having difficulty reading. It's great because the high achievers feel that they are being teachers, and they are learning something too. The low achievers are only working with one student, so they don't feel embarrassed or feel that they can't do it. It works well.
>
> During part of the reading time we divide up into smaller groups for skill lessons. Ellen pulls all the students with disabilities into one group. The other students are placed in mixed achievement-level groups of six to ten students. I teach one group, and three other teachers come to our class to teach the other groups. This is unusual, but it really works. The other three teachers rotate from class to class to provide individual attention to students. I really like this small-group time because we can zero in on what each student in the class needs to work on.
>
> You can see that the students with disabilities don't really feel that they are in a lower group. In our class we just say Ms. So-and-so's group is this table, and so on. The special education group is just another group. They look forward to that time because Ellen is a wonderful teacher, she's very caring, she loves the kids.
>
> So we have whole-class instruction, student pairing for activities, and small-group instruction for skills. We also have cooperative learning groups for special projects, and also Ellen or I pull students who might need to work on a specific skill in phonics or comprehension. As you can see, we use many different grouping formats, which involves a great deal of planning and coordination. I've been very happy with the way we grouped our students this year. Next year I probably would take even more time, pull the students who are having difficulty, and really try to focus more on the ones who can achieve more and try to challenge them. That's just my own personal goal.

## Introduction

Planning for the success of all students in your class involves careful consideration of the needs of individuals as well as of those of the class as a whole. As our interview with Lisa indicates, she recognizes that in order for this to happen she needs to "plan time for planning" every week. Part of this planning time is hers alone and part is for collaborative planning with other professionals in the school. Although Lisa is meticulous with her beginning-of-the-year planning, she also recognizes that it is important to keep setting new goals for meeting the individual needs of her students.

Part of Lisa's instructional planning is the way she organizes students for instruction through grouping. She knows that sometimes whole-class instruction is appropriate and necessary, but also realizes that at times she must incorporate small groups and student pairing into her plans in order to meet individual student needs.

In this chapter you'll learn strategies for planning for individual student needs within the framework of planning for the class as a whole. You'll also learn about how to incorporate a variety of grouping strategies to promote student success in your instructional planning. The focus of this chapter is not on your role in planning the IEP for students with special needs. Rather, the chapter focuses on how to make plans for your own classroom—plans that will attend to the learning needs of all students.

## Model of the Planning Process

If you ask experienced teachers how they plan, you are likely to get a collection of very different answers. Like any kind of planning (planning a budget, planning a personal schedule, planning a trip) individuals have different styles—and it is important for you to learn from other professionals and then develop your own.

In developing your own planning routines, it is helpful to think about how and when planning occurs and the factors that influence planning. The **Flow of the Planning Process Model** (Figure 2.1) can help structure your thinking (Schumm et al., 1995). This model indicates the sequence and relation among three types of planning and the factors that influence planning.

### Types of Planning

For most teachers, planning is not just what is written in plan books, which often include only a general outline of what is going to happen in class. The "real" plan is in the head of the teacher and is developed and

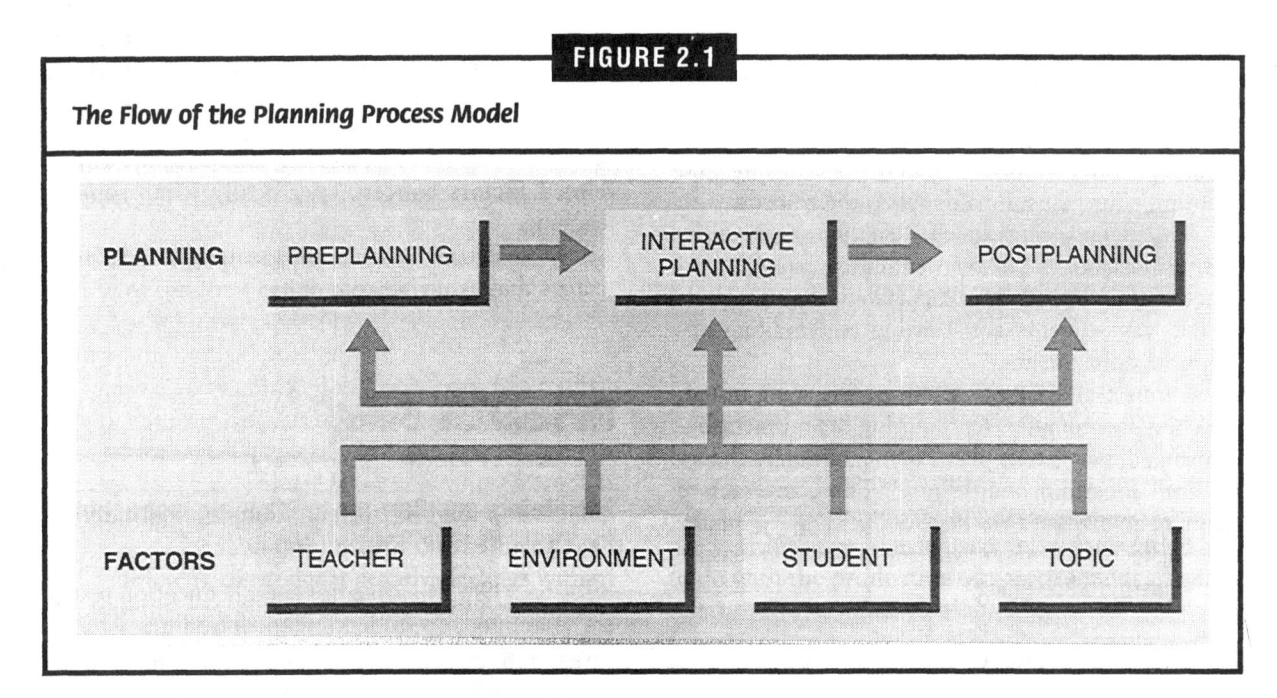

**FIGURE 2.1**

**The Flow of the Planning Process Model**

PLANNING: PREPLANNING → INTERACTIVE PLANNING → POSTPLANNING

FACTORS: TEACHER | ENVIRONMENT | STUDENT | TOPIC

Used by permission of *EEC* and the University of Calgary Press.

revised on an ongoing basis. Whether planning is for an entire school year, for a unit, or for an individual lesson, planning occurs at three stages—preplanning, interactive planning, and postplanning—as the Flow of the Planning Process Model indicates.

***Preplanning*** Preplanning involves decisions about what to teach and how to teach it. This advance preparation, which occurs at many levels, includes activities such as developing unit or lesson plans, gathering materials, identifying resources, and deciding on instructional methods. Preplanning also involves gathering information about the students' prior knowledge of the topic being taught, and their level of skill development, so that instructional plans are appropriate for meeting individual needs.

> In a survey of 775 classroom teachers, 98 percent reported that their knowledge and skills for planning for general education students was excellent or good, but only 39 percent said that their knowledge and skills for planning for special education students was excellent or good (Schumm & Vaughn, 1992).

***Interactive Planning*** Your goals for the year, plans for a unit, or outline for a lesson may be carefully drawn on paper and imagined in your head, but as you begin to implement your plans, you may need to make changes to promote learning for all students. For example, you may observe that one or more students are having difficulty learning a skill or concept. That's when interactive planning comes in. **Interactive planning** involves monitoring students' learning, and adapting your plans in response to their needs.

You might say to yourself, "Isn't interactive planning just teaching?" The two certainly overlap, but interactive planning differs somewhat, in that it focuses on the way students are learning and making appropriate adjustments.

Lampert and Clark (1990, p. 21) have noted, "teaching is a complex act requiring the moment-by-moment adjustments of plans to fit continually changing and uncertain conditions." Thus, interactive planning involves the on-the-spot decisions you make as a teacher to respond to student needs and to ensure that learning takes place.

***Postplanning*** Postplanning is follow-up planning, and frequently occurs at the end of a lesson. After a lesson you may reflect on the way students performed, then use that information to guide your planning for subsequent instruction. For example, you might realize that you covered less material than you anticipated, and might need to adjust your plans for the next day.

Or perhaps many students did not grasp what you were teaching, and you may need to develop plans for reteaching the lesson—in a different way.

When evaluating a lesson, you may also reflect on how you would teach it in the future, or simply think, "When I teach that lesson next year, I'll be certain to make some changes." In other words, you evaluate what occurred and decide what to keep and what to leave out in the future.

Overall, postplanning involves thinking about and evaluating a lesson, and determining how student needs can best be met in future lessons, units, or in school years to come.

### Factors That Influence Planning

The Flow of the Planning Process Model includes four interrelated factors that influence planning: teacher, environment, student, and topic. These factors can have a strong impact on what you plan, how you plan, and even how much you plan.

**Teacher-related factors** are those that pertain to you as a planner not only for your class as a whole, but also for students with special needs. **Environment-related factors** pertain to the context in which you teach and include state, local, and class-level factors. **Student-related factors** pertain to who your students are, how they learn, and how they respond to instruction—both academically and socially. **Topic-related factors** concern specifically what you are teaching.

Table 2.1 presents examples of each of the four factors that influence planning.

## Research Brief

### Facilitators and Barriers to Planning Instruction for Students with Special Needs

Prior to 1990, the topic of general education teachers' planning for students with disabilities was restricted to research on the classroom teachers' role in the IEP process. Because larger numbers of students with disabilities were being placed in general education settings for all or part of the school day, research was needed in the ways teachers plan and make adaptations for exceptional students.

To explore this topic, Schumm and Vaughn (1992) conducted a survey with 775 general education teachers (elementary, middle school, and high school) to determine what they do to plan and make adaptations for students with disabilities. The survey included a section in which to identify factors that can impact planning for mainstreamed students: both facilitators and barriers to planning.

Responses to survey items among teachers in various grade groupings were similar. In general, classroom teachers viewed fellow professionals (special education teachers, school-based curriculum specialists such as reading resource teachers, fellow teachers, department chairs, and guidance counselors) as those who help in the planning process.

Budgetary factors (particularly the need for larger classes) were identified as the greatest barriers. Need to cover curriculum objectives, access to equipment and materials, and lack of planning time were also identified as factors that inhibit planning.

Meeting the instructional needs of all your students takes careful advance planning (preplanning), adjustments during lessons to be certain that learning is taking place (interactive planning), and reflection and evaluation to improve instruction in the future (postplanning). The need for conscientious planning of all three types is particularly important when you teach diverse learners, including students with disabilities. The task might seem daunting, but it can be done. First, it can be accomplished by considering the

### TABLE 2.1

**Four Factors That Influence Planning**

*Teacher-Related Factors*
- attitudes and beliefs about planning in general, and motivation to do so
- attitudes and beliefs specific to planning for students with special needs, and motivation to do so
- knowledge and skills in planning and making accommodations for students with special needs
- knowledge of and experience and interest in the subject matter you are teaching
- amount of planning time
- confidence in planning and making adaptations

*Environment-Related Factors*
- state and school-district guidelines and policies regarding planning and curriculum
- school-level guidelines and policies regarding planning and curriculum
- grade-level, department, or subject-area guidelines and policies regarding planning and curriculum
- state-adopted textbooks and available materials
- access to specialists (i.e., reading resource specialists, special education teachers, school counselors)
- scheduling of special classes: physical education, special education, ESL classes, music, and art
- scheduling of special holidays, assemblies, and special activities
- physical arrangement and condition of school and classroom

*Student-Related Factors*
- class size
- engagement and interest in the topic and tasks
- motivation
- learning strategy preferences
- level of background knowledge
- behavior patterns
- acceptance of adaptations
- language and cultural differences
- difficulty with basic skills

*Topic-Related Factors*
- new or review material
- prior knowledge of topic
- interest level of topic
- number and complexity of new concepts or skills introduced
- clarity of topic presentation in curricular materials
- importance of topic in relation to overall curriculum

reality of your situation: the teacher, student, environmental, and topic-related factors. It can also be accomplished by using planning procedures specifically designed to focus on individual needs within the framework of planning for the class as a whole. In the next sections, you'll read about procedures for long-term, unit, and lesson planning.

## Long-Term Planning

It is interesting to observe three or four teachers in the same school who teach the same grade (at the elementary level) or the same grade and subject (at the secondary level). Even in schools in which teachers use the same state-adopted textbooks and follow the same state or district curriculum objectives, you are likely to see differences, particularly in the ways teachers accommodate individual student needs. Many of these differences stem from the type of **long-term planning** (planning for the whole school year) teachers do to meet individual student needs. This section presents suggestions for ways to include individual student needs in your long-term preplanning, interactive planning, and postplanning for your class as a whole.

Few travelers would start out on a cross-country trip without a map. Long-term planning is your map for the school year. Long-term preplanning is essential to helping you get the big picture in respect to curriculum and classroom management. It can help you set a plan for moving from unit to unit and developing a sense of continuity. Most important, it can help you set a framework for meeting the individual needs of your students throughout the year.

### Procedure for the Course Planning Routine

If you are an elementary teacher, you'll probably teach a number of subjects: language arts, reading, mathematics, science, social studies, and so on. If you are a secondary teacher, you'll need to prepare for one or more courses. In either case, it's important to develop a master plan for what you'll teach and how to teach it. Of course, you'll need to work within your "planning parameters," but even so you'll have many decisions to make for your own class.

The six-stage **Course Planning Routine**, developed by researchers at the University of Kansas (Lenz et al., 1993), is a guide for long-range planning for classrooms with diverse learners. This guide includes procedures for setting goals for the course, getting the course off on the right foot, monitoring and managing the course during the year, and closing the course. As an elementary teacher you can use this routine in your planning for each subject. As a secondary teacher you can use this routine for planning each course. In either case, the Course Planning Routine can help you get the big picture:

**Stage 1—ReflActive Planning Process**—consists of seven steps designed to help teachers think through an overview of the course. The steps are easy to remember because they're organized by the acronym **SMARTER** (Lenz et al., 1993, p. 14–15):

What process did this teacher undertake in planning this geography lesson? What factors influenced this process?

- Select the critical content outcomes and turn them into a set of 10 questions that everyone in the class will be able to answer at the end of the course.
- Map the organization of the critical content of the entire course and create a visual device that will help students see their progress in mastering course content.
- Analyze why the critical course content might be difficult to learn, based on:

  | | |
  |---|---|
  | quantity | complexity |
  | interest | student background |
  | relevance | organization |
  | abstractness | external conditions (e.g., calendar) |

- Reach decisions about the types of routines, devices, or learning strategies that should be used throughout the course to address learning difficulties.
- Teach using these routines regularly throughout the year to inform students about the devices and strategies being used and to involve students in constructing the devices and strategies in explicit ways.
- Evaluate mastery of the critical course content and related processes for high achievers, average achievers, low achievers, and others.
- Reevaluate course decisions and revise plans for the next unit or for next year.

Stage 2—Community of Learners—guides teachers through a series of questions related to creating a community of learners in the classroom, one in which every student feels accepted as a full participant:

- How can I nurture the community of learners enrolled in this course so that connections among them are strengthened and students help each other learn?
- How can I include everyone enrolled in the course in the learning process, such that each person becomes an involved learner?
- How can I determine the strengths and resources of course participants to ensure they can be contributed to the community?
- How can I circumvent and compensate for the limitations of course participants?

Stage 3—Target Students—helps teachers focus on individual needs by identifying four types of student: high-, average-, and low-achieving students, as well as those with disabilities. (In some classes, identifying a student who speaks English as a second language may also be helpful.) The teacher keeps these target students in mind during all aspects of planning. In planning for diversity in the classroom, it's difficult—if not impossible—to plan for the needs of every single student for every single lesson. This is particularly true in high schools where teachers may instruct over 100 students in a day! Identifying target students is a practical, realistic technique that helps make teaching more sensitive to diversity.

Stage 4—Course Launching—involves developing a plan for getting the course under way. Launching involves a plan for:

- developing rapport with students
- communicating course goals and expectations to students
- describing classroom routines and procedures
- generating enthusiasm and interest in the course

Stage 5—Course Maintenance—revisits the course map developed during Stage 1 periodically to make certain that everything is on track and to make any necessary revisions. At the beginning of the school year, it will be helpful to mark specific dates on your calendar for conducting a review of the course map.

Stage 6—Course Closure—serves as a course evaluation. The 10 questions outlined in the course map are once again revisited to determine how well all students have fared in learning the content. During this stage the teacher and students also discuss issues related to the learning community and how well goals were achieved.

The Course Planning Routine can serve as your road map for a grading period, a semester, or an entire school year. Its strengths include a system for considering individual student needs through target students, planning for academic goals through 10 questions, and planning for social goals through questions about the community of learners. As with any planning, the Course Planning Routine takes time. But the payoff is having a clear idea of where you're going and how you're going to get there! Tips for Teachers 2.1 provides time-management suggestions.

## An Example of the Course Planning Routine

Jeanette Robinson teaches a self-contained fifth-grade class in a suburban elementary school. Of the 24 students in Jeanette's class, 3 are students with learning disabilities who are mainstreamed into the class for science and social studies.

Jeanette used the Course Planning Routine to plan her overall goals for teaching a semester-long course on earth science. Her questions were based on overall objectives presented in her textbook and in her district science curriculum guide. Figures 2.2 and 2.3 illustrate Jeanette's Course Organizer and Course Map for science instruction during the school year.

## Unit Planning

After you establish "the big picture" for what you want to accomplish during the school year, the next step is to plan for units of study. An **instructional unit** is actually a series of lessons related to the same topic. For example, your school district's mathemat-

---

# TIPS FOR TEACHERS

### 2.1 Time Management for Teachers

As you begin to plan for a new school year, you may start wondering, "How am I going to get all of this done?" Time management for teachers is complex—so much to do and so little time. With careful planning and prioritizing, however, you can accomplish a great deal. Here are some tips:

1. Keep your radar out for time-management tips from other teachers. They know the job and can give you hints for getting things done.
2. Write "to do" lists, and keep them short. Use the 80–20 rule suggested by Alan Lakein (1973). Twenty percent of the items on your list should yield 80 percent of the value. In a list of 10 items, identify 2 and have a plan for getting them done.
3. As you look at your "to do" list, identify 5-minute tasks, 15-minute tasks, and 1-hour tasks (and try to figure out when they can be done). You'd be surprised at what you can accomplish during in-between times, with a little planning.
4. Set realistic goals. For example, you may not be able to contact every parent every week, but you can make a commitment to contacting five parents a week. Before you know it, you'll have contacted all the parents of students in your class.
5. Schedule time for contacting fellow professionals, for planning and coordinating. Say to yourself, "I'll contact two fellow professionals per week. This week I'll talk to the teacher of the gifted and talented students in my class and to the teacher of the special education students."
6. Learn how to delegate. Can someone help you with all or part of a project? Perhaps a parent, paraprofessional, volunteer, or student can assist you with tasks.
7. Think about how technology can help. Keep your eye out for computer programs to help with your grading, planning, and so on.
8. Avoid the temptation to overplan. As a teacher, you will be interrupted by parents, administrators, and, naturally, by students. It is important to keep these interruptions in mind and to realize that they are part of the job.
9. Plan for long-term, monthly, weekly, and daily goals, but be prepared to change your plans. Be flexible with your plan when legitimate situations arise.
10. Schedule a time every day for conferences. Meet with certain students on Monday, others on Tuesday, still others on Wednesday, and so on.
11. Plan for 60-second lessons while students are engaged in seatwork.
12. Take note of students who arrive early or leave late, and meet with them during those times.
13. Once or twice a week, make an appointment for lunch with a student.
14. Schedule conference times, and have students sign up for a conference with you.
15. This is the tough part: schedule time for planning. The payoff for a short time spent planning is tremendous.

ics curriculum guide may require you to teach a series of lessons on measurement, which includes lessons on liquid measurement, distance, and so on. The length of the unit will depend on the topic. Some may last only a few days, others may last a month or more. In this section, you'll read about a unit-planning framework for planning for diverse student needs, the **Planning Pyramid** (Schumm et al., 1994).

## Procedure for the Unit Planning Pyramid

The Unit Planning Pyramid is a framework or a way of thinking about planning instruction to enhance learning for all students. The Pyramid is designed as a flexible tool that teachers can adjust to their personal style of planning and teaching. It involves careful identification of what needs to be taught, and careful attention to individual student's needs to determine how the information will be taught.

**Degrees of Learning** The primary component of the Planning Pyramid (see Figure 2.4), the **Degrees of Learning**, make up the body of the Pyramid and will help you examine the content to be taught and prioritize concepts in an instructional unit. The Degrees of Learning are based on the premise that although all students are capable of learning, not all students will learn all the content covered. The three Degrees of Learning are the base of the Pyramid, the middle level of the Pyramid, and the top of the Pyramid.

The base of the Pyramid, considered the foundation of the lesson, consists of information that is essential for all students to learn. This section of the Pyramid is directed by the question, "What do I want *all* students to learn?"

The middle part of the Pyramid represents information that is next in importance. This is information that *most* (but not all) students are expected to learn or grasp. This level of the Pyramid includes supplementary facts and information about ideas

### FIGURE 2.2

**Course Organizer**

Name of Course: _____ *Earth Science* _____

is about

*Our planet, its place in space, how it changes naturally and due to pollution, and what we need to do to preserve it.*

**Course Questions:**

1. What is the atmosphere?
2. How do storms form?
3. How do scientists predict weather changes?
4. What is the Earth's crust?
5. What is the Earth's surface made of?
6. What are sources of energy and how are these energy resources used?
7. What are the sources of air, water, and land pollution?
8. How does pollution affect natural resources?
9. What is the solar system and what objects can be found in space?
10. How has space been studied and what instruments are used to study it?

Adapted from Vaughn, S., Schumm, J. S., Lenz, K., Schumaker, J., Deshler, D., Morocco, C., Gordon, S., Riley, M., Fuchs, L., & Fuchs, D. (1995). *Planning for academic diversity in America's classrooms: Windows on reality, research, change, and practice.* Lawrence, KS: University of Kansas Center for Research on Learning.

and concepts presented at the base of the Pyramid. The guiding question is "What do I want *most* students to learn?"

The top of the Pyramid represents information that the teacher believes will enhance basic concepts and facts about the topic or subject. This type of information will be acquired only by a few students who have an added interest in and desire to learn more about the subject. It is information that the classroom teacher may not emphasize or elaborate on during a class, but that students might read in a text or retain from a brief mention in class. The guiding question at this level is, "What information will a *few* students learn?"

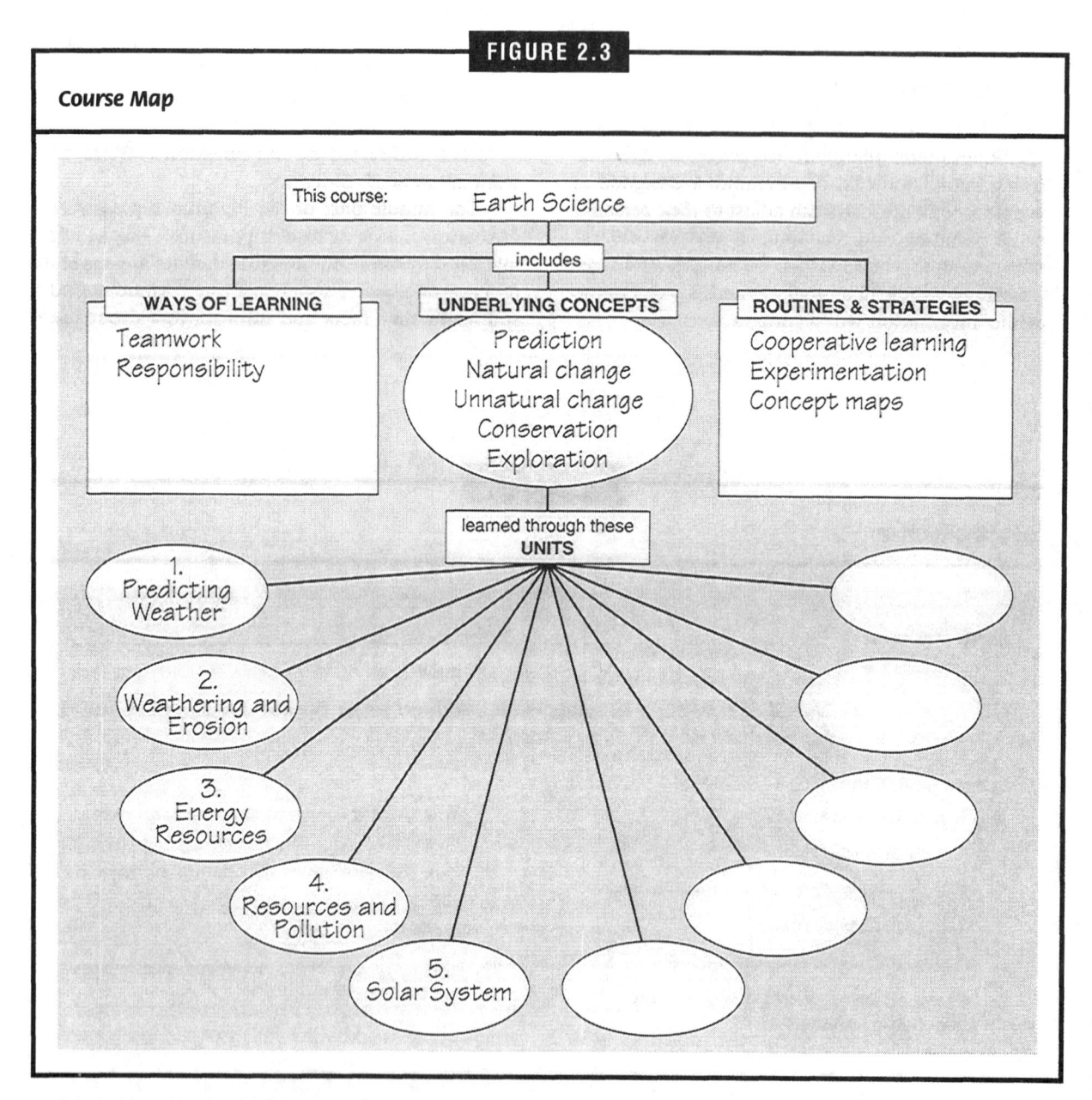

**FIGURE 2.3**

**Course Map**

```
                    This course:  Earth Science
                              |
                           includes
           ┌──────────────────┼──────────────────┐
    WAYS OF LEARNING    UNDERLYING CONCEPTS    ROUTINES & STRATEGIES
    Teamwork                Prediction          Cooperative learning
    Responsibility          Natural change      Experimentation
                            Unnatural change    Concept maps
                            Conservation
                            Exploration
                              |
                    learned through these
                            UNITS
```

1. Predicting Weather
2. Weathering and Erosion
3. Energy Resources
4. Resources and Pollution
5. Solar System

Adapted from Vaughn, S., Schumm, J. S., Lenz, K., Schumaker, J., Deshler, D., Morocco, C., Gordon, S., Riley, M., Fuchs, L., & Fuchs, D. (1995). *Planning for academic diversity in America's classrooms: Windows on reality, research, change, and practice.* Lawrence, KS: University of Kansas Center for Research on Learning.

## FIGURE 2.4

**Planning Pyramid**

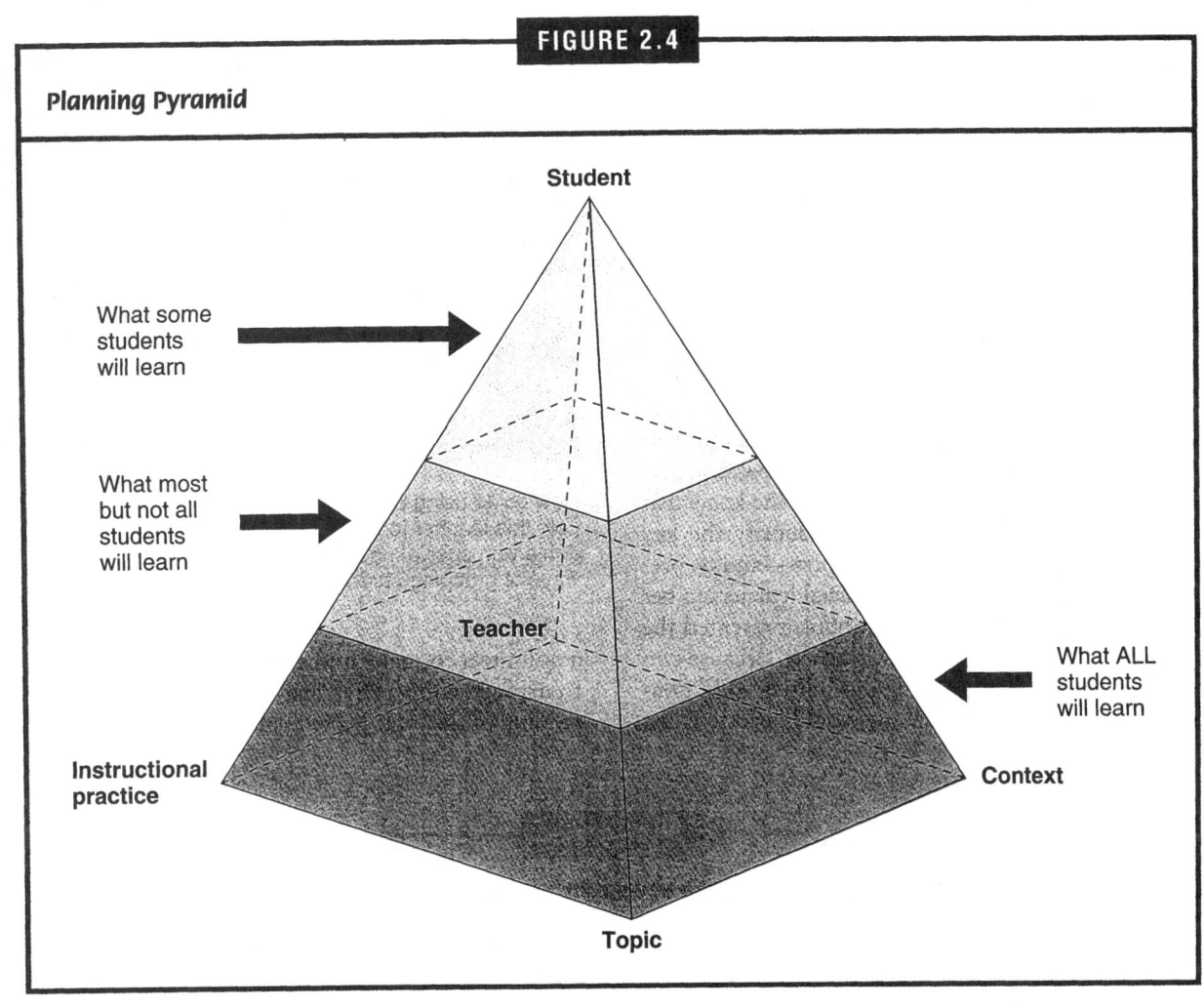

*Pyramid diagram with labels: Student (apex), Topic, Instructional practice, Context (base corners), Teacher (center). Arrows indicate: "What some students will learn" (top section), "What most but not all students will learn" (middle section), "What ALL students will learn" (bottom section).*

Schumm, J. S., Vaughn, S., & Leavell, A. G. (1994, May). Planning Pyramid: A framework for planning for diverse students' needs during content area instruction. *The Reading Teacher, 47* (8), 608–615. Nancy Padak and Timothy Rasinski (Eds.). Copyright by the International Reading Association.

**Cautions and Comments** A few cautions and comments about the Planning Pyramid:

- All students must have the opportunity to be presented with or exposed to the same information, although presentation of the information may vary somewhat according to a student's needs.
- All students must have equal access to information representing all levels of the Pyramid.
- Students should not be assigned to a particular level of the Pyramid based on their ability—students who learn at the middle and top levels do so based on their interests, prior knowledge, or personal experience.
- Activities at the base of the Pyramid should not be less stimulating (e.g., handouts, worksheets) than those at the other levels, nor should the upper levels be viewed as the place for creative, fun activities.

**Deciding What Concepts to Teach** After teachers have used the Planning Pyramid for a while, it is easier to determine what concepts belong at each degree of learning. Initially, teachers find it helpful to use a self-questioning process to determine what concepts to teach. Table 2.2 provides a list of questions you might ask to guide your thinking.

After you decide on the concepts to be taught, you can record them on the Unit Planning Form (see Figure 2.5). This form also provides areas in which to record the unit title, materials and resources needed, instructional strategies and adaptations to be used, and evaluation or products that will serve as unit outcome measures.

## An Example of the Unit Planning Pyramid

Jeanette used the Planning Pyramid to structure a unit on weathering and erosion. She predicted that this would be a difficult unit for her students because they had little prior knowledge of this topic. She knew that it would be important for her to identify the key concepts she wanted students to learn—and to predict adaptations necessary for special learners in her class. She liked the way the textbook presented the material, and wanted to follow it closely. Because two of the students with learning disabilities were nonreaders, however, she knew she would need to enlist a volunteer to make audiotapes of the chapters and to arrange cooperative learning groups for in-class reading of the text. Jeanette also planned to have in-

How could using unit and lesson planning pyramids help this teacher to adapt instructional activities for students with special needs? How should this teacher plan ways of grouping students for instruction?

### TABLE 2.2

**Questions to Guide Thinking about Concepts to Be Taught**

*Questions Pertaining to the Topic*

Is the material new or review?

What prior knowledge do students have of this topic?

How interesting is the topic to individual students?

How many new concepts are introduced?

How clearly are the concepts presented in the textbook?

How important is this topic in the overall curriculum?

*Questions Pertaining to the Teacher*

What prior knowledge do I have of this topic?

How interesting is the topic to me?

How much time do I have to plan for the lesson?

What resources do I have available to me for this unit?

*Questions Pertaining to the Students*

Will a language difference make comprehension of a particular concept difficult for a student?

Is there some way to relate this concept to the cultural and linguistic backgrounds of my students?

Will students with reading difficulties be able to function independently in learning the concepts from textbooks?

Will there be students with high interest or prior knowledge of these concepts?

Will my students have the vocabulary they need to understand the concepts to be taught?

What experiences have my students had that will relate to this concept?

Schumm, J. S., Vaughn, S., & Leavell, A. G. (1994, May). Planning Pyramid: A framework for planning for diverse students' needs during content area instruction. *The Reading Teacher, 47* (8), 608–615. Nancy Padak & Timothy Rasinski (Eds.). Copyright by the International Reading Association.

**FIGURE 2.5**

**Unit Planning Form**

UNIT PLANNING FORM

- What some students will learn.
- What most students will learn.
- What ALL students should learn.

Date: _____ Class Period: _____

Unit Title: _____

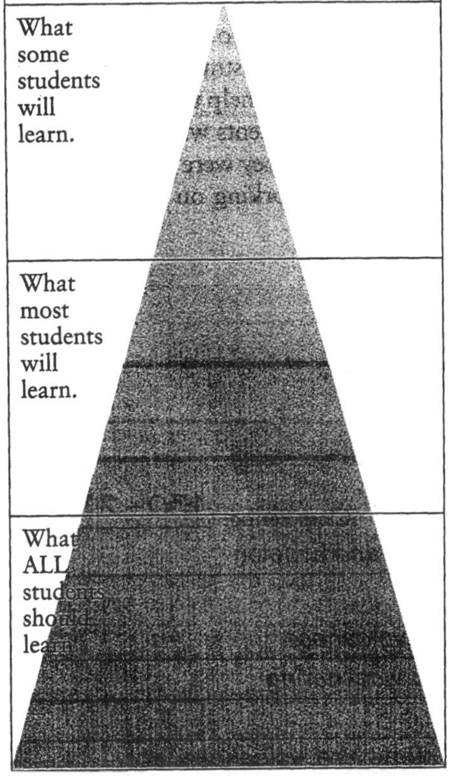

Materials/Resources:
_____
_____
_____
_____
_____
_____

Instructional Strategies/Adaptations:
_____
_____
_____
_____
_____
_____

Evaluation/Products:
_____
_____
_____
_____
_____
_____

Schumm, J. S., Vaughn, S., & Harris, J. (1995). *Collaborative planning for content area instruction.* Published by TEC.

class study time (with study buddies) before tests. To plan the weathering and erosion unit, Jeanette used the Unit Planning Form shown in Figure 2.6.

# Lesson Planning

Your overall plan for the school year is in place. Your plan for a unit of study is detailed. Now it's time to focus on a particular instruction session—the lesson. The earlier recommendation that you develop your own planning style is particularly important for lesson planning. As you consider your lesson-planning style, you'll want to think about how to plan to promote learning for all students. The Lesson Planning Pyramid can help.

## Procedure for the Lesson Planning Pyramid

The Lesson Planning Pyramid can be used for an individual lesson or to add depth and detail to the Unit Planning Pyramid described earlier. The Lesson Planning Pyramid does not necessitate a great deal of paperwork, and contains most of the elements teachers think are necessary to plot out a lesson.

With the Lesson Planning Pyramid, as with the Unit version, you focus on identifying concepts to be taught by asking, "What do I want all, most, and some of the students to learn as a result of the lesson?" As you can see from Figure 2.7, the Lesson Planning Form also provides areas in which to record materials, evaluations, in-class assignments, and homework assignments. In addition, there is an agenda area on which to list activities that will occur during the lesson.

In lesson planning it is important to think not only about the teacher, student, and topic, but also about the environment and the instructional strategies you will use. The questions in Table 2.3 (page 54) can guide your thinking about the environment and instructional strategies.

## An Example of the Lesson Planning Pyramid

Jeanette used her Lesson Planning Form as a guide for her lesson plan for the science lesson on the earth's surface. This lesson included many new terms that she knew would be unfamiliar to her students. The vocabulary was important for students to learn because it would be used throughout the unit. Her lesson plan included specific strategies for teaching the vocabulary, and visuals to help the vocabulary come alive. Also, by having students write in learning logs, she could monitor what they were learning. She knew that while they were working on the learning logs,

---

**FIGURE 2.6**

**Jeanette's Sample Unit Plan**

### UNIT PLANNING FORM

Date: Sept. 1–30    Class Period: 1:30 – 2:30
Unit Title: Weathering and Erosion

| | |
|---|---|
| What some students will learn. | • How Earth looked during Ice Age<br>• Disasters caused by sudden changes<br>• Geographic examples of slow and fast changes |
| What most students will learn. | • Compare and contrast weathering and erosion<br>• How humans cause physical and chemical weathering<br>• Basic types of rocks |
| What ALL students should learn. | • Basic components of Earth's surface<br>• Forces that change crust are weathering and erosion |

Materials/Resources:
- Guest speaker on volcanoes
- Video: erosion and weathering
- Rock samples
- Library books – disasters, volcanoes, etc.
- Colored transparencies for lectures

Instructional Strategies/Adaptations:   Experiments!
- Concept maps
- Cooperative learning groups to learn material in textbook
- Audiotape of chapter
- Study buddies to prepare for quizzes and tests

Evaluation/Products:
- Weekly quiz
- Unit test
- Learning logs (daily record of "What I learned")
- Vocabulary flash

## FIGURE 2.7

**Lesson Planning Form**

Date: _____  Class Period: _____  Unit: _____

Lesson Objective(s): _____

_____

_____

| Materials | Evaluation |
|---|---|
| | |

| In-Class Assignments | Homework Assignments |
|---|---|
| | |

### LESSON PLANNING FORM

| Pyramid | Agenda |
|---|---|
| What some students will learn. | |
| What most students will learn. | |
| What ALL students should learn. | |

Schumm, J. S., Vaughn, S., & Harris, J. (1995). *Collaborative planning for content area instruction.* Published by TEC.

---

**TABLE 2.3**

**Questions to Guide Thinking about Environment and Instructional Strategies**

---

*Questions Pertaining to Environment:*

Are there any holidays or special events that are likely to distract students or alter instructional time?

How will the class size affect my teaching of this concept?

How well do my students work in small groups or pairs?

*Questions Pertaining to Instructional Strategies:*

What methods will I use to motivate students and to set a purpose for learning?

What grouping pattern is most appropriate?

What instructional strategies can I implement?

What learning strategies do my students know (or need to learn) that will help them master these concepts?

What in-class and homework assignments are appropriate for this lesson?

Do some assignments need to be adapted for students with disabilities?

How will I monitor student learning on an ongoing, informal basis?

---

Schumm, J. S., Vaughn, S., & Leavell, A. G. (1994, May). Planning Pyramid: A framework for planning for diverse students' needs during content area instruction. *The Reading Teacher, 47* (8), 608–615. (Nancy Padak & Timothy Rasinski, Eds.). Copyright by the International Reading Association.

she'd need to check in with students with writing difficulties to monitor their learning orally. Figure 2.8 shows Jeanette's plan.

## Monitoring Student Learning during the Lesson

As you read earlier in this chapter, interactive planning is planning that occurs during a lesson. When you recognize that students are not "getting it," you adjust or alter your plans to respond to student needs. Monitoring what students understand is critical for interactive planning. Monitoring helps you keep in touch with what students are learning and remain sensitive to the troubleshooting you must do when students experience difficulty. The most typical kinds of monitoring are to ask questions during class and to circulate around the room, checking in with students during individual or group seatwork. Some quick strategies for monitoring follow.

**Informal member checks** are frequent, quick checks to see whether students understand. For example, after Susan Moore taught her third graders a lesson about the four food groups, she asked for a "thumbs up" hand signal if they understood, "thumbs down" if they did not.

At frequent intervals during a lesson you can ask students to summarize key points. This helps keep students on their toes while helping you keep tabs on what they are learning.

McTighe and Lyman (1988) described the **Think–Pair–Share** method, which can be used during peer monitoring activities. This strategy yields high student involvement and verbal interaction. Students are first encouraged to think individually about a topic for 2 minutes. Then students pair up to discuss the topic. The teacher then signals the pairs of students to share their responses with the entire class. The Think–Pair–Share method involves all students in active idea processing throughout the school day.

Class notes are the most tangible record of what students have learned during a lesson. Often students with learning disabilities have a difficult time taking notes during class, and thus have difficulty preparing for tests. One way to provide support is to have **collaborative open-note quizzes** (Schumm & Lopate, 1989). After completing a lecture, divide the students into small cooperative learning groups. Allow students some time to discuss the lecture and summarize key points. Students should also revise their notes, adding information from their fellow students. Then, give students questions about the lecture to answer as a group. Through sharing, students with learning problems are provided the opportunity to "fill in the gaps" of what they missed during a lesson and also to see examples of the way other students take notes.

## An Overview of Instructional Grouping

As you make your long-range, unit, and lesson plans, you'll want to plan for a variety of grouping patterns. At the beginning of the chapter you read that Lisa uses a variety of grouping patterns: sometimes whole

## FIGURE 2.8

*Jeannette's Sample Lesson Plan*

Date: Sept. 1    Class Period: 1:30 – 2:30    Unit: Weathering and Erosion
Lesson Objective(s): The students will describe components of the earth

**Materials**
Colored transparencies
Rock samples

**Evaluation**
Learning logs
Oral summaries

**In-Class Assignments**
Write in learning log

**Homework Assignments**
Draw diagram of Earth's layers
Make vocabulary flash cards

### LESSON PLANNING FORM

| Pyramid | Agenda |
|---|---|
| What some students will learn. • Examples of 3 types of rocks | Introduce key vocab. using transparencies |
| | Work in coop. groups to read chapter |
| | Discuss chapter |
| What most students will learn. • Crust made of 3 types of rock • How rocks are formed | Show rock samples |
| | Have students write in learning logs |
| What ALL students should learn. • Earth has 3 layers • Outer layer is where we live • Crust is constantly changing | Have several students read log entries aloud |
| | Assign homework — Recommend extra reading for students who want to learn more about rocks |

---

class, sometimes small groups, and sometimes pairs of students. Sometimes Lisa combines students with similar achievement levels; sometimes she mixes high and low students. Part of Lisa's planning is to think about which grouping pattern seems most appropriate for each learning objective.

There is no easy answer to the question of how best to group students for instruction. Consequently, the issue of grouping has triggered vigorous debate among educators, parents, and students. Our experience is that almost everyone has an opinion based on personal experience as a teacher, parent, or student. Your personal experience has already helped you shape ideas about how grouping should occur in the

# TECH TALK

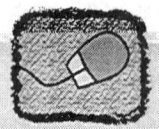

## Computers and People with Special Needs

Teaching students with special needs and disabilities has undergone a revolution since the late 1970s through the introduction of adaptive computer technologies. Adaptive technology refers to the use of computers—both hardware and software—to help challenged individuals overcome a limiting condition in their lives. This can happen in many different ways. A vision-impaired student can have text read out loud to her using special software and a sound card and speakers, a paralyzed individual can use a puff switch to activate a communications board or keyboard, or a mute individual can have words spoken to them.

Adaptive computer technologies involve the special modification and use of interface devices such as keyboards, mice, and touch screens. Likewise, output devices must also be adapted as well. In the case of a blind or visually limited individual, a printer can be redesigned to output raised Braille letters, rather than print, or text output on a monitor can be magnified.

A good online source on adaptive input and output devices can be found at Vanderbilt University's Assistive Technology Viewer:

http://peabody.vanderbilt.edu/projects/proposed/asttech/home.htm.

An excellent introduction on adaptive technology that not only deals with technical issues, but also addresses questions about the appropriate use of computers for people with special needs is Arlene Brett and Eugene F. Provenzo, Jr.'s *Adaptive technology for special human needs* (Albany, New York: State University of New York Press, 1995). Also see Chapter 6, "Technology for Inclusion" in Eugene F. Provenzo, Jr., Arlene Brett, and Gary N. McCloskey's *Computers, Curriculum, and Cultural Change: An Introduction for Teachers* (Mahwah, N.J.: Lawrence Erlbaum Associates, Publishers, 1999).

---

school and in the individual classroom. In this section you'll learn more about grouping from an historical standpoint, as well as current trends and issues associated with grouping students. The section also includes a description of various grouping configurations you might use in the classroom, as well as suggestions for implementing flexible grouping patterns to promote successful learning for all students.

> John Philbreck of the Quincy, Massachusetts, school system initiated the graded system in 1847. It is likely that Philbreck was influenced by Horace Mann's and Colonel Francis W. Parker's reports of the ordered curriculum they had observed in Prussia (Button & Provenzo, 1983).

## Traditional Instructional Grouping

In the mid-1800s, preoccupation with improving the productivity of public education in the United States gave rise to "graded" schools. A teacher assigned to a specific grade could teach the entire class. The graded system spread widely across the United States, thus establishing the most durable form of grouping in our educational system, age-level grouping, or grades.

Teachers quickly realized, however, that a single grade included a wide range of academic levels. As Berliner and Casanova note (1993, p. 6), teachers often resort to grouping by ability because of an "inescapable fact of life: students differ dramatically from one another."

**Homogeneous** or **same-ability grouping** is the practice of putting students at approximately the same achievement level together for instruction. School-level ability grouping is called **tracking**. At the school level, students might be assigned to a particular class. In an elementary school, for example, one teacher might be assigned all the high-achieving students, another teacher all the average-achieving students, and a third teacher all the low-achieving students. At the middle- or high-school level, high-achieving students might be assigned to accelerated courses, average-achieving students to regular courses, and low-achieving students to remedial courses. Students are assigned to tracks based on their grades, achievement test scores, and (in some cases) behavior. The idea of homogeneous grouping is that the content and pacing of instruction can be better controlled to meet individual needs.

> The first ability-grouped classes originated in 1862 in the St. Louis, Missouri, public schools, under the direction of superintendent William T. Harris (Otto, Wolf, & Eldrige, 1932).

Although research on the effectiveness of homogeneous grouping was inconsistent, early reviewers of such literature generally recognized the positive impact of homogeneous grouping, particularly for children with learning difficulties (Miller & Otto, 1930; Whipple, 1936). In 1957, the launching of the Soviet satellite, *Sputnik*, caused many people in the United States to think our country trailed in the space race, and prompted a definite increase in the practice of grouping students in classes, tracks, or streams according to their level of achievement. The reasoning was that the brightest students should be grouped together to get the training in science and mathematics they would need to compete internationally. Thus, tracking became an integral part of education in the United States.

During the 1950s, the practice of **within-class same-ability grouping** for reading and mathematics began to take hold in elementary classes (Harris & Sipay, 1980). Within-class same-ability grouping occurs when students in a single classroom are placed with other students of similar abilities for an entire school year. The goal of same-ability small groups is to reduce the range of abilities between group members so that the teacher can instruct students who are functioning on approximately the same level. For example, the reading and math groups in an elementary school classroom might be based on similar student achievement (high, medium, or low) in each area. The teacher would pull one group at a time for instruction while the other groups focused on completing workbook assignments or silent readings. Within-class same-ability grouping for reading and mathematics was a dominant practice in elementary schools until recent years.

> The Joplin Plan, started in Joplin, Missouri (Floyd, 1954), involves regrouping students across grade levels. For example, all first-, second-, and third-grade students reading on the first grade level would be moved to the same group during reading time.

# MAKING A DIFFERENCE
## The 60-Second Lesson

### Using Lesson Reaction Sheets

Student monitoring provides an excellent opportunity for 60-second lessons. Lesson Reaction Sheets are one quick way to monitor students' understanding. After a lesson is completed, have your students write a brief reaction to it. Provide your students with the following questions:

- What did you learn from this lesson?
- What was confusing about the lesson?
- What else would you like to know about the topic?

It should take students only a few minutes to write answers to these questions. You may need to find another time to ask these questions of students who have difficulty writing, so that they can answer orally.

The early 1960s witnessed the ultimate attempts at homogeneity: the resource room for students with disabilities (Cruickshank et al., 1961) and special programs for the gifted. More recently, with the new influx of non-English-speaking immigrants to the United States, separate classes for students with limited English proficiency (LEP) have been established in many areas of the United States.

## Current Trends in Instructional Grouping

Ability grouping, tracking, and placing students in resource rooms have been the norm in the United States for years. Schooling in the United States is now in a phase in which educators are exploring new alternatives to traditional ways of organizing students for instruction (Barr, 1995). The trends described here summarize current thinking about grouping.

### Trend #1: A critical examination of homogeneous grouping

Although many alternatives to homogeneous grouping had been proposed, the trend toward homogeneous grouping—including the expansion of pull-out programs—continued (Barr & Dreeben, 1991) into the early 1990s. Recently a number of criticisms of homogeneous grouping have been raised, including the following (Oakes, 1992):

- There is little evidence that homogeneous grouping results in substantial academic advantages (Slavin, 1987).
- Homogeneous grouping "widens the gap" between high and low achievers (Slavin, 1987).
- Homogeneous grouping restricts friendship choices (Hallinan & Sorensen, 1985).
- Although homogeneous grouping may enhance the motivation and self-esteem of high-achieving students, it lowers the motivation and self-esteem of low-achieving students (Oakes et al., 1991).
- Homogeneous grouping frequently results in social stratification, in which students representing minority groups are overrepresented in low-ability tracks (Oakes, 1990).
- The quality of instruction in low-ability classes is frequently inferior. Emphasis in typical low-ability classes is more on lower-level skills and discipline, and less on higher-level thinking (Goodlad, 1984; Hiebert, 1983).

The trend in general education is toward **heterogeneous** or **mixed-ability grouping**, in which students with a range of achievement levels are put together for instruction. Heterogeneous grouping (rather than lock-step same-ability grouping) is being advocated to avoid the inevitable stratification resulting from traditional ability groups and tracking policies (Marshall & Weinstein, 1984; Webb & Cullian, 1983).

## Research Brief

### Students' Perceptions of Grouping

What do students think about grouping practices for reading instruction? Elbaum, Schumm, and Vaughn (1995) surveyed 549 elementary students (grades 3, 4, and 5), including 23 students with learning disabilities, to find out what students think. Results revealed that students at all levels of reading ability liked mixed-ability groups and mixed-ability pairs most, followed by whole-class instruction. Same-ability groups and working alone were the least popular formats. Students in mixed-ability groups were perceived as getting more help from classmates, working more cooperatively, and making more progress in reading than those in same-ability groups. Same-ability groups were perceived to be desirable for nonreaders only.

### Trend #2: Movement of inclusion of students with disabilities in general education settings

Students with disabilities are spending more and more of their school day in general education settings. This movement toward inclusion broadens the range of student diversity in the classroom. Inclusion, coupled with the movement toward heterogeneity discussed earlier, means that classroom teachers must learn new strategies and organizational procedures for meeting the needs of individual students.

### Trend #3: A critical examination of "what's best" for all students

Those who oppose—or at least question—mixed-ability grouping do so out of concern for what will happen to students at the extremes of the ability spectrum. Two typical questions follow:

- Will mixed-ability grouping slow down the academic progress of gifted and high-achieving students?
- Can mixed-ability grouping enable teachers to provide the intensive, direct instruction needed by low-achieving students?

The answer to the first question is that there is no conclusive evidence about the effect of mixed- versus same-ability grouping for the academic success of gifted and high-achieving students. Indeed, an examination of the literature on grouping can be interpreted in very different ways. Allan (1991) concluded from such an examination that students who are gifted and high-achieving benefit from some form of same-ability grouping, and that opportunities should be maintained for accelerated instruction of such students with their high-achieving peers. Allan concluded, "The strongest positive academic effects of grouping for gifted students result from either acceleration or classes that are specially designed for the gifted and use specially trained teachers and differentiated curriculum and methods" (p. 65). Slavin (1991) examined the same literature and determined that the evidence to support same-ability grouping for high achievers was sparse, and that the modest academic benefits cannot compensate for maintaining an unequitable system. Slavin's conclusion is that students who are high achieving "will do well wherever they are" (p. 70).

Similarly, there is no clear-cut answer to the second question. There is little definitive evidence that ability grouping (including pull-out programs) positively impacts the academic achievement of low-achieving students. "Nor—given the widespread practice of undifferentiated whole-class instruction in general education classrooms—is there much encouragement that low-achieving students in that setting will receive the intensive, direct instruction they need (Baker & Zigmond, 1990; McIntosh et al., 1993). It is abundantly clear that the type of instruction needed to improve the basic skills of students who are low-achieving needs to be improved, regardless of the setting.

What are the six key elements of effective cooperative learning? What are some special considerations for students with disabilities when working in cooperative learning groups?

### Trend #4: Exploration of alternatives to same-ability grouping

For many years, educators continued with tracking and other forms of same-ability grouping simply because other alternatives were not available. Recently, however, researchers and teachers have begun to explore alternatives to traditional practices. These alternatives are not necessarily "new," but they are "improved" in respect to meeting the needs of a wide range of students. For example, whole-class instruction—teaching the whole class at the same time—is hardly "new." What is "improved" is that ways to meet diverse individual needs during whole-class instruction have been developed and tested in classrooms.

### Trend #5: Emphasis on flexible grouping

Research has not identified one "best" grouping pattern, in terms of academic and social benefits to students. Many teachers are beginning to realize that using a variety of grouping patterns is most appropriate for classrooms with a wide range of student diversity. These teachers are beginning to recognize that different grouping patterns are appropriate for different purposes.

The use of a variety of grouping patterns is called **flexible grouping**. As Table 2.4 demonstrates, when grouping students you can think about different group sizes, composition, materials, purposes, and leadership.

## TABLE 2.4

**Grouping Decisions**

*Size*
    Individuals
    Pairs
    Small groups
    Half class
    Whole class

*Composition (placement in group determined by)*
    ability
    interests
    skill levels
    prior knowledge (content)
    prior knowledge (strategies)
    random
    friendship
    sex
    English proficiency
    cultural background
    behavior
    teacher selection
    student selection
    standardized test scores
    administrator preference
    parent preference
    previous success with group

*Materials*
    teacher-chosen
    student-chosen
    same materials for all groups
    different levels of different topics
    different levels of similar topics
    different materials and different activities—
        same level

*Purposes*
    skill development
    skill practice
    projects
    written assignments
    reading assignments
    problem solving
    discussions

*Leadership*
    teacher-led
    student-led

Adapted from: Flood, J., Lapp, D., Flood, S., & Nagal, G. (1992). Am I allowed to group? Using flexible patterns for effective instruction. *The Reading Teacher, 45*(8), 608–616. Copyright by the International Reading Association, James Baumann, Editor.

Unsworth (1984, p. 300) listed five principles of flexible groups:

- There are no permanent groups.
- Groups are periodically created, modified, or disbanded, to meet new needs as they arise.
- At times there is only one group consisting of all pupils.
- Groups vary in size from 2 or 3 to 9 or 10 students, depending on the group's purpose.
- Group membership is not fixed; it varies according to needs and purposes.

### Trend #6: Emphasis on helping students learn the process of working in various grouping patterns

Teachers can group students for the purpose of working together to complete an assignment or project, to solve a problem, or to practice basic skills. It is unwise, however, to assume that students will automatically know how to work with each other. The current trend is not only to group students so that they can accomplish tasks together, but also to show students *how* to work together. Working collaboratively, students can learn such lessons as how to give and receive help, how to listen and respond to the ideas of others, and how to complete a task as a team. The teacher needs to structure group work, however, so that these valuable lessons are not lost.

In the upcoming sections you'll read about different grouping patterns and how to implement them in your classroom. Particular emphasis is placed on how to meet the needs of students with disabilities in each grouping pattern. You will also learn to teach students how to work effectively in groups. Finally, you'll learn how to incorporate different grouping patterns as part of a flexible grouping plan.

## Planning for Flexible Grouping

For flexible grouping to be successful, careful planning is essential. Without thoughtful preplanning, flexible grouping sometimes doesn't occur. The temptation becomes not to group at all, but to fall into the pattern of whole-class teaching followed by individual practice, a less than ideal pattern for meeting individual needs (Radencich & McKay, 1995). As you think about a lesson, keep grouping in mind by asking yourself the following questions:

- What is the best group size for teaching this lesson?

- What is the best group size for seatwork and follow-up activities?
- What is the best composition of learners for each group, with respect to student academic ability and work habits?
- What materials are needed for each group?
- Will the groups be teacher-led, student-led, or cooperative?
- What room arrangement is necessary for the grouping plan?
- When students move from one group to another, how can I ensure quick and smooth transitions?

## Grouping Patterns

There are many ways to group students of varying abilities for instruction. This section describes different grouping patterns and includes guidelines for classroom implementation of these grouping arrangements. The discussions focus on ways to create student groups of different sizes (whole class, small group, pairs, and single student).

### Whole Class

**Whole-class grouping** is the pattern most students in the United States have experienced most often. Indeed, whole class is the most frequently used grouping pattern. Whole classes can comprise students of same or mixed ability. Quite often the decision of whether to track students or group them by ability is a districtwide or schoolwide decision. You may or may not be part of that decision-making process. Even in a "same-ability" class, however, you'll quickly note that students in your class have a range of differences to which you, the teacher, need to attend.

Keeping the whole class together is appropriate for a variety of reasons:

- building classroom community
- establishing classroom routines
- introducing new units of study
- introducing new skills and concepts
- conducting whole-class discussions
- developing common experiences
- listening to guest speakers
- viewing educational videos

Many teachers like whole-class grouping because it makes planning fairly simple, with one instructional plan (including one set of instructional activities) for the whole group. Whole-class grouping also makes classroom management easier, in that teachers do not have to divide their time among different groups. Being in a mixed-ability whole class can improve the self-esteem of low-achieving students by helping them feel less isolated from their higher-achieving peers.

There are some drawbacks to whole-class grouping, however. The primary problem is that it is more difficult to attend to individual needs during whole-class grouping. Students with learning difficulties are likely to try to fade into the woodwork and not participate fully in class activities (Brozo, 1990). The pace of instruction might be too fast for some students and too slow for others. Moreover, the content might be too difficult for some students and too easy for others.

The Planning Pyramid discussed earlier in this chapter is particularly important to use when planning whole-group instruction. With whole-class grouping, it is important not only that you monitor what students are learning, but also that you think about necessary adaptations to ensure success for all students. For example, if whole-class instruction involves a reading assignment followed by a discussion, you'll need to plan adaptations, such as listening to an audiotape of the reading assignment, for students who are nonreaders.

### Small Groups

Small groups consist of three or more students. In this section you'll read about same-ability small groups, mixed-ability small groups, and cooperative learning groups.

***Same-Ability Small Groups*** Students in same-ability groups are at approximately the same level (as determined by achievement tests, informal tests, or teacher judgment). Although the current trend is away from permanent same-ability groups, some teachers still prefer to have same-ability groups as part of their overall grouping plan. In Yvette Myers' fourth-grade class, for example, six students are reading below the second-grade level. Yvette finds it necessary to provide this group of students with direct instruction in word recognition, three times a week, but she also includes many other types of grouping patterns during the school day so that the students don't feel isolated from the class as a whole.

# TIPS FOR TEACHERS

## 2.2 Effective Grouping Strategies for Small, Same-Ability Groups

1. Instead of having an arbitrary number of groups (for example, three groups), make sure that you have enough groups to handle individual differences.
2. Plan for appropriate pacing of instruction.
3. For students who have difficulty learning, plan to reteach concepts and skills, using different methods and explanations.
4. Keep student assignment to groups fluid, so that students can be moved to more appropriate groups, as necessary.
5. Disband groups that have served their purpose.
6. Be flexible about the time spent with each group. A rigid schedule will not permit you to work with groups that need extra or reduced time.
7. Avoid using student membership in a same-ability group to determine involvement in other activities. For example, if students are in the "yellow" group for extra help in reading, don't put the "yellow" students together for science or social studies projects.
8. A good rule of thumb is to keep groups of students who need extra help small, and to provide students with the intensity of instruction they need.

Adapted from: Good, T. L., & Brophy, J. E. (1994). *Looking in classrooms* (6th ed.). New York: HarperCollins Pubs., Inc.

---

The pros and cons of same-ability groups were discussed earlier in this chapter. If you elect to use same-ability groups as part of your total grouping plan, Tips for Teachers 2.2 includes some suggestions for their most effective use.

**Mixed-Ability Small Groups** Students in mixed-ability groups represent a wide range of levels. Group placement may be determined by many different criteria, from student interest to needed skill lessons. Mixed-ability groups are created for special purposes and are fluid, in that they tend to change throughout the school year and even throughout the school day. In fact, students can belong to more than one group at one time. Once the goals of the project are achieved, the groups are reorganized.

Mixed-ability groups can be organized for a variety of purposes, including the following:

- conducting minilessons on an as-needed basis
- completing a project
- preparing a presentation for the class
- completing a follow-up assignment
- practicing new skills
- discussing a reading assignment

The composition of students can be grouped in a number of ways, some of which follow:

- Interest. Students with similar interests can be placed together in small groups. Teachers can determine student interests through surveys and group discussions, and place students together for an assignment such as creating a volcano during science time. Interest groups tend to yield impressive products because students in the group are highly motivated.
- Skills to be learned. Several students who are experiencing difficulty with a particular skill, such as antonyms, may be placed in a small group. This may give them the extra time and support they need. If necessary, the teacher can intervene with this group for the purpose of reinforcing the needed skill. Once the skill is mastered by individual group members, they no longer need to be in this particular group.
- English proficiency. For students who need help understanding English, you can provide very necessary support by including in the group a bilingual classmate with greater proficiency.

- Level of basic skills. Depending on the purpose of the group and the task to be completed, it may be helpful to group students who are better readers, writers, or mathematicians with students who may need assistance.
- Prior knowledge. Students can be grouped according to how much they already know about a topic. If you are teaching a lesson on dinosaurs, for example, you may want to develop mixed-ability groups of students who know a great deal about dinosaurs and students who are new to the topic.

Finally, two types of groups do not depend on students' knowledge or needs:

- Student-selected. The teacher may give students time to create their own small groups at specific times during the week. One instance of this type of grouping occurs when the teacher asks students to discuss with their classmates the books they read independently over the weekend.
- Random assignment. Random assignment to groups for special projects can be done to expose students to different classmates throughout the year.

The advantages of small, mixed-ability groups are both social and academic. Socially, students learn how to work collaboratively, communicate effectively in groups, and give and receive help. Academically, students become more engaged in their learning and spend more time on-task.

The disadvantages mainly concern classroom management. Teachers can be in only one place at a time. When the class is divided into groups, the possibility for misbehavior increases. Therefore, guidelines for student responsibilities during small-group activities need to be communicated clearly and reinforced consistently. The research conducted in cooperative learning groups has yielded classroom procedures for maximizing productivity in small, mixed-ability groups. Those procedures are discussed in the next section.

## Cooperative Learning Groups

The purpose of this section is to provide an overview of cooperative learning. In **cooperative learning groups**, students work together toward a common goal, usually to help one another learn academic material (Slavin, 1991). Students not only help explain material to each other and provide mutual support, but also give group members multiple perspectives (Morrow & Smith, 1990). In cooperative learning groups, students perceive that the main goal of the group is that all students learn and that each member of the group is critical for group success. As the Research Brief indicates, research in cooperative learning has yielded positive outcomes.

Goor and Schwenn (1993, p. 8) identified six key elements of cooperative learning:

- Teams are formed to maximize heterogeneity.
- Positive interdependence is structured through shared goals and rewards.
- Management systems are established to maximize group learning.
- The room is arranged to facilitate small-group activity.
- Students are taught skills necessary to cooperate and teach one another.
- The structure of each cooperative learning activity is chosen to match the goals of the lesson.

# Research Brief

### Benefits of Cooperative Learning

The benefits of cooperative learning are well documented in the research literature. Slavin (1991) synthesized the research in this area with the following highlights:

1. Cooperative learning is most successful when there are group goals coupled with individual accountability.
2. Achievement effects of cooperative learning have been positive for high-, average-, and low-achieving students across grade levels—elementary through high school.
3. Social effects of cooperative learning have been demonstrated in terms of improving self-esteem, intergroup relations, acceptance of students with disabilities, and attitudes toward school.

Cooperative groups consist of three to six students, with typically about four per group (Wilcox et al., 1987) and should include high, average, and low achievers (Slavin, 1987). Some teachers create permanent cooperative learning groups that are seated together for an entire school year. Other teachers keep the groups together for a grading period; still others for a single project.

To ensure full student participation, each member of a cooperative learning group is assigned a role. It is the teacher's responsibility to explain the roles thoroughly, including why each role is important. For example, one student can serve as timekeeper, another as quiet control, another as secretary or scribe, and still another as an encourager or "cheerleader."

> Of all recent education innovations, cooperative learning has undergone the most extensive research, including research on both academic and social outcomes for students of different grade levels, achievement levels, and cultural backgrounds (Slavin, 1961).

While the cooperative learning groups are in session it is the teacher's job to listen and observe how students work as a group. When necessary the teacher models collaborative behaviors, such as how to give and receive help, and how to ask what others think. It is also important to praise groups that are following guidelines and to redirect groups that are not. The teacher also needs to clarify directions or clear up any misconceptions students may have about the topic. As you can see, cooperative learning time is an active time for the teacher as well as for the students.

Many teachers are concerned about how to grade students for cooperative learning work. What happens if one student does all the work for the group? Should everyone get the same grade? What happens if one group member does nothing? In determining a grade for the group product, it's probably best to have both an individual score and a group score. When making the cooperative learning assignment, announce a group goal and an individual goal. For example, you might be teaching a lesson on the layers of the Earth. The group project might be to complete a drawing of the Earth and its layers, and to ensure that each group member can name the layers. The group goal is to complete the drawing and teach the names of the layers to group members. The individual goal (followed by a quiz) is to demonstrate knowledge of the layers.

It is important for students to evaluate the group process, as well as to earn a "grade" for a project. Evaluating the process makes students aware of the importance of working together and of the steps necessary for enhancing group dynamics.

Goor and Schwenn (1993) offer some special considerations for students with disabilities working in cooperative learning groups. Students with learning and behavior disorders may have difficulty monitoring their own learning, following directions, and in social skills. Some students may have difficulty participating fully in groups when their basic skills in reading, writing, and mathematics are not on a par with those of their peers. Goor and Schwenn make the following recommendations:

1. Make certain that students with disabilities are clear about the procedures for working in cooperative groups.
2. Be sure that students are assigned to a group that provides the necessary support.
3. Make certain that the role you assign a student with disabilities is appropriate for that student. For example, the job of recorder may be inappropriate for a student who cannot write, unless that student is allowed to tape record the session and then make an oral summary.
4. For students who have difficulty staying on-task, develop signals for keeping excess movement and noise to a minimum.
5. Monitor student learning consistently to make certain that students are picking up on key concepts and not becoming more focused on group process than on learning the designated material.

## Learning Partners in Pairs

Pairing occurs when students work together in groups of two, sometimes called **dyads**. Depending on the task, pairs can be either same- or mixed-ability. When two students of the same ability level are placed together for an assignment, they can offer each other support, corrective feedback, and praise. For example, two students who are about the same level in mathematics might work together to solve word problems.

Pairing also can be effective when students of differing ability levels work together. When one student in such pairs acts as teacher to the other student, **peer tutoring** occurs (Cohen, Conway, & Gow, 1988). When peer tutoring involves a student with learning disabilities, that student can serve as either the tutor or the tutee of a general education student (Eiserman, 1988). Academic and social benefits for both tutor and tutee have been documented in research (King, 1982). An example of mixed-ability pairs might be a more able reader serving as partner to a less able reader to complete the reading of a science chapter.

Another way to place two students together for reading instruction is known as **cross-age pairing**. In this scenario, an older and younger student are "buddies" in a mutually beneficial reading activity (Morrice & Simmons, 1991). Benefits of this method include motivation to read (for the younger student), and application and reinforcement of previously learned language arts concepts (for the older student). Cross-age pairing has been shown "to boost the self-esteem of each of the buddies" (Morrice & Simmons, 1991, p. 573). Some suggested activities to use during cross-age pairing are creating Big books, making cards and writing letters for the holidays, and participating in science projects (Morrice & Simmons, 1991). In a study on the effectiveness of cross-age pairing, it was concluded that both students in the pairs improved in their ability to work cooperatively with another student (Morrice & Simmons, 1991).

Pairs can also be based on friendships, interests, or can be random. The important things to think about when planning for student pairing are the task to be completed and the kind of support your students need to complete that task.

Student pairing can be used for the following activities:

- revising written assignments
- practicing new skills
- developing fluency in reading or computation
- preparing for tests
- completing reading assignments
- solving problems
- conducting library research
- conducting science experiments
- reflecting about stories or books read

Many teachers like to use student pairs because pairing provides students with additional support and helps them learn how to work as a team. Pairing involves minimal planning and is easily implemented in the classroom. Many students like pairing because it makes learning more fun and helps them feel less isolated. Students like to give and receive help. As one third-grade student put it, "Two heads are better than one."

One potential pitfall of student pairing is that students can get off-task and spend more time socializing than working. Another problem is that a student who is asked to "tutor" another student may simply not know what to do, and both students get frustrated. In some classrooms, higher-achieving students are asked too often to help their lower-achieving peers, and resentment occurs. Finally, some students may simply prefer to work alone. These problems can be minimized. Tips for Teachers 2.3 suggests ways to make the most of student pairs.

When students work together, they can learn to encourage each other. Tips for Teachers 2.4 provides a list of encouraging words and phrases you can post in your class to serve as a reminder. You can also model the use of encouraging words during whole-group, small-group, and one-on-one instruction.

### One-on-One Instruction

Research indicates that general education teachers rarely make extensive individualized plans for students (Schumm & Vaughn, 1991). However, teachers do have one-to-one instructional encounters with students throughout the day. For example, while you are monitoring students as they complete seatwork, you may observe that one student doesn't understand. So you do some quick reteaching. During writing instruction you may have one-to-one conferences with students about their writing.

In yet another scenario, a student assigned to a special education resource room might be in your class for only 15 minutes of a language arts period. In such cases, you may want to consult with the special education teacher to plan activities for the best use of that 15 minutes each day. The advantage of one-to-one instruction is that you can zero in on a student's individual needs. The obvious disadvantage is finding the time to do it.

# TIPS FOR TEACHERS

## 2.3 Making the Most of Working with Pairs

*Set procedures for peer tutoring, such as:*
1. Give everyone a chance to be a tutor—every student has something to share with a peer.
2. Give the tutor very specific suggestions about what to teach and how to teach it.
3. Keep tutoring sessions short for students with short attention spans.

*Set procedures for collaborative pairs, such as:*
1. Give specific guidelines about the responsibilities of each partner.
2. Hold each partner accountable for fulfilling responsibilities.
3. Give students the opportunity to work with a variety of partners.

*Set rules, such as:*
1. Talk only to your partner.
2. Talk only about your assignment (project).
3. Use a low voice.
4. Cooperate with your partner.
5. Try to do your best.

Used by permission of Douglas and Lynn Fuchs, Vanderbilt University.

# TIPS FOR TEACHERS

## 2.4 Encouraging Words

*Words of Acceptance*
You really seem proud of yourself for figuring that out.
What do you think you could do to feel better about it?
You seem frustrated. Try it this way.
You seem to really feel good about that.
I really like working with you.

*Words of Appreciation*
I really appreciate your . . .
That was nice of you to . . .
That was great, the way you . . .

*Words That Show Confidence*
Keep going. I know you can do it.
I have confidence in you.
I know this is hard, but you'll figure it out.

*Words That Recognize Effort and Improvement*
In just one week you learned . . .
Look how much you have improved.
You really worked hard on that!
Yes, you got some wrong, but look how many you got right!

"Good ways to encourage your tutees" (1991). *Valued Youth Program: Tutor Workbook.* The Coca-Cola Company, pg. 9. By permission of International Development Research Association, San Antonio, TX.

# SUMMARY

- The Flow of the Planning Process Model indicates the sequence and relation between three types of planning (preplanning, interactive planning, and postplanning) and factors that influence planning (teacher, environment, topic, and student).
- In long-range planning, planning parameters such as state, district, and school guidelines for curriculum and instruction must be considered.
- The Course Planning Routine, a guide for long-range planning, includes procedures for setting goals for the course, getting the course off on the right foot, monitoring and managing the course during the year, and closing the course.
- The Planning Pyramid, a framework for unit and lesson planning, helps you examine the content to be taught and prioritize concepts to ensure learning for all students.
- Current trends in instructional grouping include a critical examination of homogeneous grouping, a movement toward inclusion of students with disabilities in general education settings, critical examination of "what's best" for all students, exploration of alternatives to ability grouping, and an emphasis on flexible grouping as well as on helping students learn how to work in various grouping patterns.
- A variety of group sizes—whole class, small group, pairs, and individual student—can be used for instruction. The decision about which size is most appropriate depends on student needs and the learning activity being planned.
- Students can be grouped in a number of ways, including interests, skills to be learned, English proficiency, and prior knowledge.
- In cooperative learning groups, students work together toward a common goal, usually to help each other learn academic material. Students in cooperative learning groups perceive that the group's main goal is that all students learn and that each member of the group is critical for group success.

# Key Terms and Concepts

collaborative open-note quizzes
cooperative learning groups
Course Planning Routine
cross-age pairing
Degrees of Learning
dyads
environment-related factors
flexible grouping
Flow of the Planning Process Model
heterogeneous grouping
homogeneous grouping
informal member checks
instructional unit
interactive planning
long-term planning

mixed-ability grouping
peer tutoring
Planning Pyramid
postplanning
preplanning
same-ability grouping
SMARTER
student-related factors
teacher-related factors
think–pair–share
topic-related factors
tracking
whole-class grouping
within-class same-ability grouping

## Think and Apply

1. Now that you have read Chapter 2, reread the interview with Lisa. How does Lisa plan with Ellen, the special education teacher? How does she use flexible grouping?
2. Use the Course Planning Routine to develop initial plans for a course you might teach. Compare your plans with those of a classmate who is teaching the same (or a similar) course.
3. Interview 3 classroom teachers to elicit their tips for time management. Probe for specific suggestions for finding time to meet the special needs of students either individually or in small groups. Share their tips with your classmates.
4. Teach a lesson based on the Planning Pyramid. Write a reflective statement about the lesson. What went well? What would you change? How did the lesson impact a student with special needs? An average-achieving student? A high-achieving student?
5. Use the Planning Pyramid to develop a unit plan and for an individual lesson within that unit. Compare your plans with those of a classmate.
6. Imagine that you have been assigned to a task force to make a proposal about whether or not to keep tracking at your school. In preparation for the first meeting you have been asked to draft a position statement explaining your stance on the issue. Develop a brief statement explaining your thoughts.
7. Describe an appropriate instructional activity that would be appropriate for each of the following group sizes: whole class, small group, pairing, individual.

## Read More about It

1. Cohen, E. (1994). *Designing groupwork: Strategies for the heterogeneous classroom* (2nd ed.). New York: Teachers College Press.

   Comprehensive handbook to help make your students' small groupwork productive. Includes chapters on planning groupwork, preparing students for cooperation, setting expectations, and applications for groupwork in classrooms in which some students speak English as a second language.

2. Johnson, D. W., & Johnson, R. T. (1991). *Learning together and alone: Cooperative, competitive, and individualistic learning* (3rd ed.). Boston: Allyn & Bacon.

   Comprehensive overview of cooperative learning, with specific instructions for ways to implement different cooperative learning methods, such as Cooperative Integrated Reading and Composition (CIRC), Student Teams–Achievement Divisions (STAD), and Teams–Games–Tournaments (TGT).

3. Moran, C., Stobbe, J., Baron, W., Miller, J., & Moir, E. (1992). *Keys to the classroom: A teacher's guide to the first month of school.* Newbury Park, CA: Corwin.

   How do you get the school year off on the right foot? This teacher-friendly guide for elementary teachers provides specific suggestions for preparing the classroom, structuring routines, planning the first day, and activities for the first month. It also includes sample letters to parents, in both English and Spanish.

4. Radencich, M. C., & McKay, L. J. (Eds.). (1995). *Flexible grouping for literacy in the elementary grades.* Boston: Allyn & Bacon.

   Provides guidelines for planning and implementing flexible grouping for reading and writing instruction in elementary classrooms. Provides detailed descriptions of ways to implement a variety of grouping options.

5. Slavin, R. E. (1990). *Cooperative learning: Theory, research, and practice.* Englewood Cliffs, NJ: Prentice-Hall.

   A detailed manual for structuring cooperative and individualized learning. Includes a chapter on teachers' concerns about cooperative and individualized learning that is particularly helpful in considering students who are low and high achieving as well as students who are socially isolated and disruptive.

6. Vaughn, S., Schumm, J. S., Lenz, K., Schumaker, J., Deshler, D., Morocco, C., Gordon, S., Riley, M., Fuchs, L., & Fuchs, D. (1995). *Planning for academic*

*diversity in America's classrooms: Windows on reality, research, change, and practice.* Lawrence, KS: University of Kansas Center for Research on Learning.

This monograph reports findings from a series of investigations conducted by four research groups. Each group investigated general education teachers' planning for students with disabilities. The monograph includes practical suggestions for planning and implementing instruction for students with disabilities.

7. Schumm, J. S., Vaughn, S., & Sobol, M. C. (1997). Are they getting it? How to monitor student understanding in inclusive classrooms. *Intervention in School and Clinic, 32* (3), 168–171.

This article provides a summary of 12 monitoring strategies gleaned from the professional literature. Particular emphasis is placed on specific things teachers can do to gather data about what and how students are learning.

# CHAPTER 10

# Teaching Students with Learning Disabilities or Attention Deficit Disorders

# Interview

## Tammy Gregory

Tammy Gregory is one of four second-grade teachers at Canyon Verde Elementary School in Tucson, Arizona. This is Tammy's third year teaching. In her class of 31 students, Tammy has one student with learning disabilities, Adrian, and one student with attention deficit disorder, Lenny.

When you talk with Tammy and watch her teach, it is clear that she believes all students can be successful learners, and that her job is to modify the content and the curriculum for the various learners in her classroom. This is certainly the case with Adrian, whose learning disabilities relate most to the speed at which he processes information. It takes him longer to understand what is being said during classroom discussions and presentations. He reads slowly whether he is reading aloud or to himself. His responses to questions are often slow and labored, and the ideas are not clearly stated. He also writes slowly. He is almost always the last or next-to-last student to finish a written assignment, and often does not complete work in the time allowed.

Tammy regularly makes accommodations for Adrian so that he is a successful learner in her classroom. Because his writing is slow, she sometimes reduces the length of the assignment so that he can complete it in the time allowed. Tammy says, "The key is that Adrian understands and has mastered the skill. If he can demonstrate mastery answering 5 problems instead of 10 problems in math, then he has learned and reached his goal."

Tammy has also set up an informal buddy system in her room. Students regularly help each other with assignments. Tammy has Adrian sitting next to one student who is an able helper and high achiever and another student who is an average achiever and who likes to problem solve and work with Adrian on assignments. This arrangement gives Adrian the opportunity to work with two very different students who like to work with others and provide support for him. Although speed of processing can make Adrian appear slow and not very adept at many skills, his teacher has taken the time to learn about his interests and his strengths and to share those with the other students. It is not unusual to hear Tammy say to the class, "Check with Adrian on that, he's a real expert."

Tammy has also made accommodations for Lenny, a student with attention deficit disorders including hyperactivity and impulsivity. At the beginning of the year, Tammy thought that Lenny would be "the child that led her into early retirement." He moved constantly (even when sitting), and was out of his seat, sharpening his pencil, talking to and bothering the other students. During class discussion he would answer before Tammy had a chance even to ask the students to raise their hands. He rarely completed assignments. Tammy felt that Lenny could do much of the work, but that his attention problems got in the way of his being a successful learner. To help Lenny, Tammy thought about and modified the structure of her classroom and schedule. Tammy comments,

> Lenny attends best when he knows what is "on tap" for the day. Each day I review the schedule for the day and put a copy of it on the board, on the corner of Lenny's desk, and on my desk. As each activity is completed, Lenny checks it off and rates himself for that activity on three criteria: paying attention, effort, and work completed. At first I also rated Lenny, but now I am comfortable with his self-monitoring. At lunch and during the end of the day wrap-up, I take several minutes to review with Lenny his self-monitoring. Based on his performance, Lenny receives good work day certificates to take home for his parents to sign, and on Friday afternoon he can receive a "Job Well Done" pass to watch a video or participate in other activities with the other good workers in the school. For me, taking this extra time with Lenny is well worth the progress Lenny has made and the sanity that has been restored to my classroom.

Tammy also makes other modifications for Lenny, such as reducing the number of math problems assigned by having him complete only the odd or even numbered problems. She also helps Lenny, Adrian, and other students in her class break multiple-step or complex tasks and projects into smaller tasks. Tammy comments, "Even reading a book and writing a book report can be divided into five or six steps the students can complete one-by-one. This substantially increases the likelihood of students getting these projects done in a timely manner."

Adrian and Lenny have made good progress this year in school, both in terms of their learning and their positive self-concepts as learners. Tammy is concerned, however, about their transition into third grade, where more emphasis will be placed on written work and complex assignments and less time will be spent on teaching basic skills and individualizing for different students' needs. She is wondering what to communicate to Adrian and Lenny's teachers next year, so that they can continue as successful learners.

## Introduction

Think about Tammy's philosophy and practice of teaching students with learning disabilities and attention problems. To what extent do the practices she implements with Adrian and Lenny reflect the type of teacher you are or want to be? The first section of this chapter provides an overview of students with learning disabilities (LD), and the second section focuses on students with attention deficit disorder (ADD). As you read, think about ways the strategies suggested for these students can also be used for other students in elementary and secondary classrooms.

## Learning Disabilities

The disabilities of students who have visual impairments, are deaf or hard of hearing, or have overall cognitive delays usually are apparent. In contrast, you probably will not recognize students with learning disabilities in your classroom until you have the opportunity to see how they learn. Only in the last 25 years have learning disabilities, sometimes referred to as the "invisible disability," been recognized in our schools. This section provides definitions and characteristics of learning disabilities, as well as suggestions for meeting the needs of students with learning disabilities in your classroom.

### Definitions and Types of Learning Disabilities

The issue of how to define learning disabilities has received considerable attention in the field since 1963, when Samuel Kirk suggested the term "specific learning disabilities" at the organizational meeting of the Learning Disabilities Association (LDA) (formerly called the Association for Children with Learning Disabilities, ACLD). At that time, children with learning disabilities were referred to by such terms as perceptually handicapped, brain-injured, and neurologically impaired and were served in classrooms for students with mental retardation or, in most cases, were not receiving any specialized services in the public schools.

The term **specific learning disabilities** represents a heterogeneous group of students who, despite adequate cognitive functioning and the ability to learn some skills and strategies quickly and easily, have great difficulty learning other skills and strategies. For example, students with specific reading disabilities may participate quite well in class discussions but have difficulty reading the text and taking tests. Other students may have great difficulty with math, but have little difficulty with tasks that incorporate reading and writing.

The operational guidelines for the definition of specific learning disabilities are specified in the rules and regulations for IDEA, and indicate that a multidisciplinary team may determine that a child has a specific learning disability if:

> The Learning Disabilities Association is a parent and professional organization that provides many resources related to learning disabilities. Contact information: Learning Disabilities Association, 4156 Library Road, Pittsburgh, PA 15234, telephone: (412) 341-1515.

- the student does not achieve commensurate with his or her age and ability level in one or more of several specific areas when provided with appropriate learning experiences
- the student has a severe discrepancy between achievement and intellectual ability in one or more of these seven areas:
   a. oral expression
   b. listening comprehension
   c. written expression
   d. basic reading skills
   e. reading comprehension
   f. mathematics calculation
   g. mathematics reasoning
- the student needs special education services

A student is not regarded as having a specific learning disability if the discrepancy between ability and achievement is primarily the result of any of the following:

- visual, hearing, or motor disability
- mental retardation
- emotional disturbance
- environmental, cultural, or economic disadvantage

Although many definitions of learning disabilities have been developed (see Figure 5.1), secondary science teacher Joseph Blankenship's ideas about learning disabilities are similar to those of many other general education teachers. He comments that initially these students may not seem different from other students. They participate in classroom discussions and appear to understand the content covered. But as assignments are submitted and tests given, he quickly realizes that students with learning disabilities have difficulties with reading, writing, studying, and organizing their time.

Learning disabilities represent a group of disorders that cause students to have learning and academic difficulties. Currently, although no generally accepted classification systems exist for students with learning disabilities (Keogh, 1993; Speece, 1994), types of learning disabilities have been discussed in the literature and used in medical and psychological reports for many years. Some of the most frequently used terms follow:

- **Dyslexia**—severe difficulty in learning to read, particularly as it relates to decoding
- **Dysgraphia**—severe difficulty learning to write, including handwriting
- **Dyscalculia**—severe disability in learning mathematical concepts and computation (Baroody & Ginsburg, 1991)

As a teacher, when you find these diagnostic terms in medical and psychological reports, you need to ask the following question:

*What behaviors or learning characteristics should I expect when a student has been identified as having learning disabilities?*

For example, when Lynn Ann Chang reviewed the special education files of students who would be in her fourth-grade classroom the following year, she noticed that an evaluation in second grade identified Jessica as having dyslexia. Lynn Ann met with Jessica's current third-grade teacher, special education teacher, and mother to learn more about what this meant for Jessica and to plan for having Jessica in her classroom. Lynn Ann learned that Jessica had experienced significant difficulties in learning to read, particularly learning to understand the relationship between sounds in the oral language and the symbols they represented. In second grade, Jessica was reading at a preprimer level and could not consistently

---

**FIGURE 5.1**

**IDEA Definition of Learning Disabilities, and Major Components of the Definition**

**DEFINITION**

The term "children with specific learning disabilities" means those children who have a disorder in one or more of the basic psychological processes involved in understanding or in using language, spoken or written, which disorder may manifest itself in imperfect ability to listen, think, speak, read, write, spell, or to do mathematical calculations. Such disorders include such conditions as perceptual handicaps, brain injury, minimal brain dysfunction, dyslexia, and developmental aphasia. Such terms do not include children who have learning problems which are primarily the result of visual, hearing, or motor handicap, of mental retardation, of emotional disturbance, or of environmental, cultural, or economic disadvantage.

**MAJOR COMPONENTS**

- ✓ difficulty with academic and learning tasks
- ✓ discrepancy between expected and actual achievement
- ✓ disorder in basic psychological processing
- ✓ exclusion of other causes

identify the beginning or ending sounds of words. Jessica liked books, however, and when they were read to her, could retell and answer questions about stories written for children her age. Since that evaluation, Jessica has been receiving small-group reading instruction from the special education teacher and tutoring in an after-school program. Lynn Ann decided to assign a buddy to assist Jessica in reading her science and social studies texts, and she also incorporated high-interest, low-vocabulary books into her reading instruction. Jessica's teachers have encouraged her to use different strategies to help her decode and remember words. Her sight vocabulary has grown significantly, and she is now reading at a second-grade level.

# Research Brief

## Developmental, Neurological, and Genetic Nature of Reading Disabilities

Currently, the National Institute for Child Health and Human Development is sponsoring a number of research centers and projects that are investigating the nature of reading disabilities, particularly as it relates to learning to read (Lyon, 1994; 1998). This research has been summarized by Lyon (1994; 1998), with the following findings:

- Although schools identify approximately four times as many boys as girls as having reading disabilities, studies show that as many girls are affected as boys.
- Reading disabilities persist. Of the students who have reading disabilities in the third grade, about 75 percent still have significant problems in ninth grade.
- The ability to read and comprehend depends upon rapid and automatic recognition of words. Slow and inaccurate decoding are the best predictors of difficulties in reading comprehension.
- The ability to decode words depends on the ability to segment words into syllables and sounds. Difficulty with this task is central to dyslexia.
- There is strong evidence that reading disabilities are inherited, and affect the processing of information by the brain.

In addition, two major types of dyslexia have been identified (Eden et al., 1995; Lyon et al., 1991). The most prevalent type is language-based and results in students having difficulty processing sounds, which in turn affects the use of phonics rules to decode words and spell (Olson et al., 1990; Stanovich, 1988). The second, less frequent type relates to the visual aspects of reading and results in students having difficulty remembering words and developing sight vocabulary (Stanovich et al., 1991; Van Strien et al., 1995; Vellutino et al., 1994).

## Characteristics of Students with Learning Disabilities

Because learning disabilities are heterogeneous, it is very difficult to list a set of characteristics that adequately describes all students with learning disabilities. You will find that students with learning disabilities seem more different from each other than alike, in relation to how they learn, but certain overriding characteristics will help you in identifying these students:

- *unexpected* difficulty or low performance in one or more academic areas (unexpected in that your general impressions of the student would not lead you to predict that he or she would have difficulty)
- ineffective or inefficient information-processing or learning strategies in the area(s) of difficulty

Furthermore, the reasons for this low performance vary according to the strengths and weaknesses of the learner, and the learning strategies he or she employs. For example, Tamara and Randy, two students in Carla Huerra's third-grade classroom, were identified as having specific learning disabilities and were reading and spelling at an early first-grade (primer) level. Both students have difficulty developing an automatic sight vocabulary to use when reading and writing, but the strategies each of them uses are very different, as are the individualized educational programs Carla and the special education teacher use with each student.

Carla *observes* the students to better understand their learning styles, including their strategies and motivation for learning, and their interests. She listens to each of them as they read aloud and retell what they have read. She notes the miscues each of them makes when reading, and watches for the strategies they use when they come to a word they do not recognize automatically or to something they do not seem to understand. She also observes both students during writers' workshop, as they compose first (and subsequent) drafts of their work.

Carla's observations reveal that Tamara has strong oral language skills. She capitalizes on these skills when she reads, and uses the meaning and the syntax (word order or grammar) of the language as her primary strategies for figuring out unknown words. When she does not know a word, she skips it or substitutes a word that more or less makes sense. She shows little evidence of using phonics to figure out unknown words. Carla notes that even though Tamara sees a word many times, either in context or written by itself, it is not easy for her to recognize it automatically, so that it becomes part of her sight vocabulary. When Carla observes Tamara's writing, she notes that Tamara has wonderful ideas but spends much of her time asking other students how to spell words, or changing what she was originally going to write so that she can use words she knows how to spell. She does this despite the classroom rule that, "Spelling doesn't matter on drafts; spell it the way you think."

Like Tamara, Randy has difficulty memorizing words so that they become part of his sight vocabulary and can be retrieved automatically when he reads or writes. Randy's strategies for reading are very different from Tamara's, however. Randy's reading is very slow because he tries to sound out the words (uses his phonic analysis skills). He is able to get a number of the individual sounds, but has trouble blending them together to make a word. Although the words that result may not make sense, he does not seem to monitor this by going back and rereading. Randy's writing also reflects his use of his somewhat successful phonic analysis, in that even high-frequency, irregular words are spelled phonetically (e.g., *cum* for *come*, *wuz* for *was*).

In talking with David Ross, Tamara and Randy's special education teacher, Carla learned that her observations were the same as his. Both students have visual-memory and auditory-processing difficulties that make it hard for them to learn to automatically recognize words. Each student, however, uses very different strategies and strengths to compensate (i.e., Tamara relies on her strong oral language skills and Randy relies on "somewhat successful" phonic analysis).

Together, Carla and David have *planned and designed* educational programs to support these students. For studying content areas such as science and social studies, Carla relies on partner reading and the use of trade books written at different reading levels. She also allows students to demonstrate their knowledge through oral reports, posters, and pictures, rather than only through traditional written reports and tests. During writers' workshop, Carla has helped each student develop a spelling dictionary. For reading, Carla and David work together to help Tamara and Randy expand the strategies they use to

> Approximately 85 percent of the elementary-age students with learning disabilities have difficulties reading, particularly in decoding words.

What are some learner characteristics that might help you identify a student with possible learning disabilities? How might you work with an inclusion specialist or special education teacher to plan and design an education program to support such a student?

## TABLE 5.1

### Signals for Possible Learning Disabilities

*Signals for learning disabilities* are characteristics of students with learning disabilities. Because these students are a heterogeneous group, only certain signals will apply to any one student.

- has trouble understanding and following directions
- has a short attention span; is easily distracted
- is overactive and impulsive
- has difficulty with handwriting and fine motor activities
- has difficulty with visual or auditory sequential memory
- has difficulty memorizing words or basic math facts
- has difficulty allocating time and organizing work
- is unmotivated toward tasks that are difficult
- has difficulty segmenting words into sounds, and blending sounds
- confuses similar letters and words, such as *b* and *d,* and *was* and *saw*
- listens and speaks well, but decodes poorly when reading
- has difficulty with tasks that require rapid naming of pictures, words, and numbers
- is not efficient or effective in using learning strategies

---

decode unknown words. For Tamara, this includes learning to identify the first sound(s) in the words and to use this information, along with meaning, to help her identify the unknown word. They are also helping Tamara to see similar patterns in words (e.g., word families: -ake, make, take, lake). For Randy, their help includes getting him to ask himself the question, "Does this make sense?" and to take more risks, instead of laboriously sounding out each word.

Table 5.1 presents some characteristics that, although they might not apply to all students with learning disabilities, have helped signal to general education teachers which students might have specific learning disabilities. Several of these characteristics refer to difficulties in attention. Students with learning disabilities often have difficulties with attention and, in some cases, hyperactivity. About 35 percent of students with learning disabilities also have attention deficit disorders (Barkley, 1990) which are discussed later in this chapter.

As students with learning disabilities continue to fail in school, they are likely to develop emotional and behavioral disabilities, depression, and low self-esteem as learners (Huntington & Bender, 1993; Montgomery, 1994). A longitudinal study of the self-concept of students with and without LD indicated, however, that the self-concepts of the other achieving groups decreased from kindergarten through fifth grade, and that students with LD did not have lower self-concepts than other students (Vaughn et al., 1992).

What are the lifelong outcomes for students with learning disabilities? There is no single answer for all students, but we do have evidence that some individuals with learning disabilities are quite successful in adult life and that they learn to adjust and make accommodations for the disabilities. (For example, Albert Einstein, Nelson Rockefeller, and Thomas Edison all had significant learning disabilities.) What are the social and education factors that predict success for individuals with learning disabilities? Research indicates that successful adults with learning disabilities make realistic adaptations for their learning disabilities, take control of their lives, are goal oriented, and persist at these goals. Successful adults with learning disabilities have indicated that one or more significant people have supported their adjustments during school, post-secondary training, and young adult life (e.g., Raskind, Goldberg, Higgins, & Herman, 1999; Speckman et al., 1993). Increased access to vocational training programs and support programs in colleges has also served to increase success (Gerber et al., 1992; Vogel et al., 1993).

It is important for teachers and parents to assist individuals with learning disabilities to successfully retrain their experiences related to learning disabilities (Gerber, Reiff, & Ginsberg, 1996), as those who are able to do so experience higher levels of vocational success (Gerber, Ginsberg, & Reiff, 1992). Teachers can assist with retraining by encouraging individuals to identify their strengths and to be aware of their weaknesses.

# Research Brief

## Learning Disabilities and Juvenile Delinquency

The incidence of learning disabilities is generally much higher in delinquents (18 to 55 percent) than in the general population. Similarly, teens who have learning disabilities report more contact with the law than their non-learning-disabled peers (e.g., Bryan et al., 1989; Keilitz & Dunivant, 1986; Spreen, 1988).

Two theories have been suggested as to why this is the case. The *school failure theory* suggests that school failure, including poor academic achievement, leads to persistent delinquency. The *susceptibility theory* suggests that learning disabilities may be linked to certain underdeveloped personality skills, such as general impulsiveness and poor judgment, which lead to increased susceptibility to delinquent behavior through unwise social choices. Waldie and Spreen (1993) conducted follow-up interviews with 65 individuals with learning disabilities who were diagnosed between ages 8 and 12 and reported police contact during an interview at age 18. During an interview at age 25, 62 percent had persisting problems with the law. Data analysis, which demonstrated that poor judgment and impulsivity were the two factors involved, supports the susceptibility theory.

## Prevalence of Learning Disabilities

Today, more students are identified as having specific learning disabilities than any other type of disability and it is recognized as a worldwide condition (Gersons-Wolfensbergert & Ruijssenaars, 1997). According to the *Sixteenth Annual Report to Congress on the Implementation of the Individuals with Disabilities Education Act* (United States Department of Education, 1995), 10 percent of school-age children were identified as disabled, and over 5 percent were identified as having learning disabilities. During the last 2 decades, the number of students identified as having learning disabilities has increased substantially. For example, during the 1979–1980 school year, 1,281,379 students with learning disabilities were identified and served in the public school system. This number increased to 2,064,892 by 1989–1990, and to 2,444,020 in 1993–1994.

Why does the percentage of students with learning disabilities continue to increase? Several factors are related to the answer, including the following (Hallahan, 1992; Lerner, 1993):

- *Growing public awareness of learning disabilities.* As more parents and general education teachers learn about the characteristics of students with learning disabilities, they become more attuned to watching for signs and seeking assistance within the school system.
- *Greater social acceptance.* Learning disabilities are among the disabilities viewed as more socially accepted and with fewer negative connotations than others.
- *Limited alternatives for other students at-risk.* Due to limited alternative programs, the tendency is to identify students who may be failing for reasons other than specific learning disabilities, so that they may receive services.
- *Social and cultural influences on central nervous system integrity.* Demographics would suggest that more children are being born of parents whose income falls below the poverty level, who may be addicted to drugs and alcohol, and who are teenagers (all factors that increase chances of these children being at risk for learning disabilities).
- *Increasing needs for literacy at work and in daily life.* As we move into an information age that requires better educated individuals, schools are demanding more of students, and higher literacy levels are necessary for jobs and the tasks of daily life.

Also of interest is the number of boys versus girls identified as having learning disabilities—with boys identified from twice to as many as eight times more often than girls (Shaywitz & Shaywitz, 1988). Data from the U.S. Department of Education (1994) indicates a ratio of approximately four boys to every girl. Recent research on the genetic bases of dyslexia would suggest that the ratio of boys to girls should be more equal (Shaywitz et al., 1990). Males may be more vulnerable to referral and identification, however, because boys generally exhibit more disruptive behaviors that are difficult to manage in school.

## Identification and Assessment of Students with Learning Disabilities

Most students with learning disabilities are identified because of difficulties with academic achievement. Teachers—usually the first professionals to notice the students' learning strengths and weaknesses and academic skills—play an important role in identifying students with learning disabilities.

Louise Parra, a first-grade teacher, comments on the importance she places on being alert for students who may have learning disabilities. She comments,

> As a first-grade teacher, it is very important that I understand learning disabilities and keep alert for children who are not learning at the same rate or with the same ease that I would expect of them. If I notice these children in the first grade and begin collaborating with the special education teacher, other specialists, and the children's families, then I can assist in preventing these children from developing the poor self-esteem that frequently develops if they continue to fail and are not supported.

Of all the members of a prereferral or multidisciplinary team, classroom teacher(s) and parent(s) have the most experience with a student. Referral from the classroom teacher is one of the most important predictors as to whether a student will be identified as learning disabled. A recent study of 236 referrals made in an intermediate school district in the midwest, for example, indicated that 128 students (approximately 45 percent) were identified by the multidisciplinary teams as eligible for special education as learning disabled (Fugate et al., 1993).

Jackie Darnell, a classroom teacher, shared observations and information (see Figure 5.2) about a student, Cassandra, at a multidisciplinary conference during which it was decided that, because of math disabilities, Cassandra was eligible for special education services.

The information Jackie provided clearly identified her concerns in the area of math computation. She also provided information about strategies she had already tried with Cassandra. Because Jackie felt that the computer programs were the most helpful, she and the special education teacher decided to work together to identify additional computer programs for Cassandra. The special education teacher would work with Cassandra on how to use a calculator and build skills in computation of multiplication problems. Both teachers would use manipulatives to build Cassandra's understanding of division and fractions. Tips for Teachers 5.1 (page 141) suggests what classroom teachers should consider before referring a student who seems to have learning disabilities.

## Instructional Techniques and Accommodations for Students with Learning Disabilities

Because the group of students with learning disabilities is so diverse, no one approach or technique is relevant for all students with learning disabilities. In fact, many special education teachers describe themselves as having to be necessarily eclectic in their philosophy and approaches to teaching to match the different learning styles these students exhibit. Effective classroom teachers report that they must use their "best teaching practices" to teach students with learning disabilities.

Len Hays, a seventh-grade English teacher elaborates on "best teaching practices":

> When I work with students who have been identified as learning disabled or who are at risk, it requires my best teaching. By this I mean that I must be very organized in the manner in which I present a literature unit or an English lesson. First, I give an overview of the lesson and explain the activities and what is expected of the students. I also make sure that when I lecture, I use an overhead projector to write important information. If I want the students to understand a process, such as how to revise an essay to add "color," then using the overhead projector lets me demonstrate the process and my thinking as I edit. I find that using the overhead allows me to model not only the questions I ask myself as a writer, but to show the changes I make. It is also important that I organize the learning activities and working groups so that students have the opportunity to practice the skills that are the focus of the lesson. Whether we are working on editing skills or doing a critical analysis of a book, I always work to relate the learning to the students' daily lives. Finally, I try to be creative and humorous. That is just part of being a middle school teacher and dealing with adolescence.

---

*Although some students with learning disabilities receive instruction in a special education classroom, more and more of these students receive all their education in the general education classroom, with support from the special education teacher or a paraprofessional.*

## FIGURE 5.2

**Information Shared by Jackie Darnell, the Classroom Teacher, at a Multidisciplinary Conference**

**Name:** Cassandra
**Age:** 10
**Grade:** 5th

**Literacy:**
- 4th to 5th grade level
- Enjoys reading as a leisure-time activity, and uses the library on a regular basis.
- Enjoys writing fantasy and drama, and uses both character and plot development; patterns many of her stories after the popular girl-oriented series.
- Participates in literature discussion groups and can answer a variety of questions about the literature, including underlying theme and application questions.
- Can write a report with introduction and two supporting paragraphs.
- Spells at fourth-grade level, using phonic and structural analysis for unknown words.
- Can use a word processor to write and revise written work.

**Math:**
- Second-grade achievement level.
- Adds and subtracts with regrouping, but makes computation errors in the process and with basic facts.
- Understands basic concept of multiplication but does not know basic facts or how to use for simple word problems.
- Has difficulty understanding simple, one- and two-step word problems.
- Has not yet memorized 50% of the basic addition and subtraction facts.
- Knows multiplication facts 0, 1, 5, and 10.
- Understands concept of multiplication as repeated addition. Does not compute multiplication problems.
- Does not demonstrate concept of division and does not know division facts.
- Demonstrates concept of simple fractions 1/2, 1/3, 1/4.
- Solves word problems. Errors are generally in computation and basic facts rather than problem representation.
- Describes math as least favorite subject.
- Struggles to learn basic math facts, despite incentive program, coordination with parents, and use of computer programs at school.

**Social/Emotional:**
- Well liked by peers, both boys and girls.
- Quiet, does not ask for help when needed.
- Works well in cooperative groups but usually does not take leadership roles.
- Good sense of humor.

# TIPS FOR TEACHERS

## 5.1 What to Consider in Referring Students Suspected of Learning Disabilities

- In which academic areas of learning (e.g., listening comprehension, oral expression, basic reading skills, reading comprehension, basic writing skills, written expression, math computation, math reasoning and problem solving) is the student successful, and in which areas is the student having difficulties?
- What are the academic achievement levels in these areas and what are representative examples of the student's work?
- How does the student compare with other students in the classroom in areas of success and difficulty?
- What factors (other than specific learning disabilities) might be contributing to the learning problems experienced by the student (e.g., frequent moves, absences, recent traumatic life events, vision or hearing impairments, emotional disorders)?
- Are the student's first language and language of instruction the same, or is the student learning academics while also acquiring a second language or dialect?
- What learning or compensatory strategies does the student currently use to aid in learning?
- How does the student perceive him- or herself as a learner, and what is the student's attitude toward school and learning?
- What strategies and accommodations have been tried, and how did they work?

---

This section presents some general teaching strategies that are effective for students with learning disabilities. You will find many more ideas in the chapters about teaching reading, writing, content area subjects, mathematics, and in the Appendix on Learning Strategies. The general strategies in this chapter include the following:

- Provide a framework for learning.
- Model the processes and strategies.
- Present information in multiple ways.
- Allow students to demonstrate learning in multiple ways.
- Teach students to use memory strategies.
- Teach self-regulation and self-monitoring.
- Provide opportunities for extended practice and application.
- Use learning tools and aids (e.g., computers, calculators, spell checkers).
- Adjust work load and time requirements.

These strategies have been shown to be effective when teaching students with learning disabilities.

**Provide a Framework for Learning** Students are more successful when they have a good idea of where they are going. Research on the use of advance organizers would suggest that this is even more important for students with learning disabilities, learning problems, or limited background knowledge for the task being taught (Mayer, 1979). The concept of advance organizers was introduced in the 1960s by David Ausubel. He defined an **advance organizer** as information presented "in advance of and at a higher level of generality, inclusiveness, and abstraction than the learning task itself" (Ausubel & Robinson, 1969, p. 606).

Keith Lenz and his colleagues (Lenz, 1983; Lenz et al., 1987) developed 10 steps for using an advance organizer. Lenz found that when content area teachers in middle and high schools used this framework for learning, adolescents with learning disabilities could experience significant improvements in both the quality and quantity of learning.

Three factors seem important to the success of advance organizers. First, students with learning disabilities are taught how to listen for and use the advance organizer. Students might complete a worksheet (see Figure 5.3) as they listen to the teacher introduce each part of the advance organizer. Second, after using the advance organizer worksheet, the teacher and students discuss the effectiveness of its use and how and when it might be used in various

## FIGURE 5.3

**Headings and Questions to Include on a Student Worksheet for Advance Organizer**

**Advance Organizer Worksheet**

Name:
Date:
What is the topic?

What is the framework or picture for the information?

What do I need to do or what are the assignments?

What do I need to learn?

What is the important vocabulary?

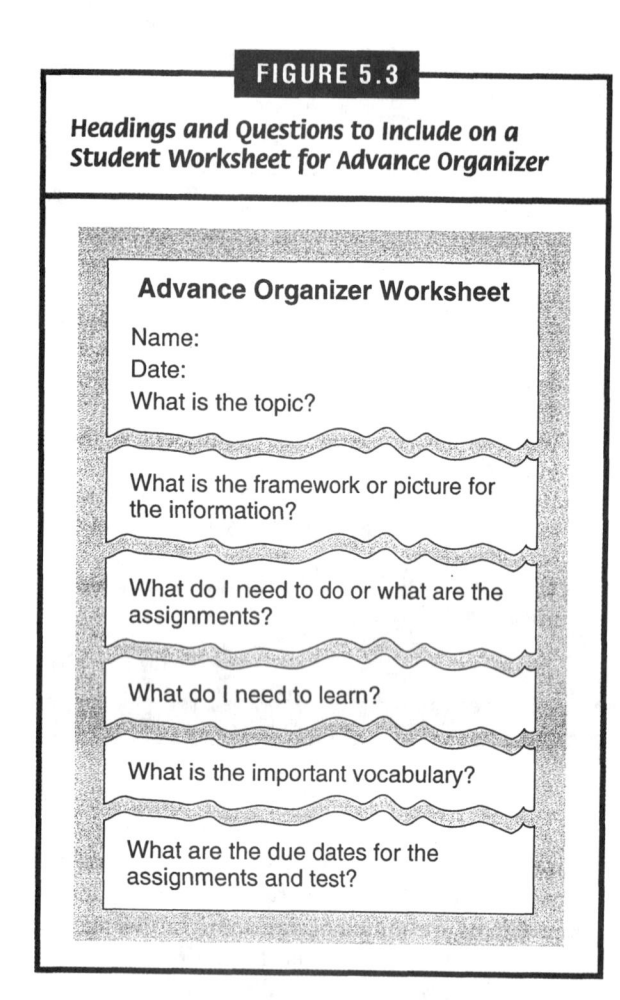

What are the due dates for the assignments and test?

*What are nine general teaching strategies that are helpful for all students but are especially effective for students with learning disabilities?*

content classes. Third, before an advance organizer is presented, the teacher cues the students that it is going to be used.

One critical aspect of the advance organizer is that it provides basic information or activates the students' background knowledge (refer to Step 5 in Tips for Teachers 5.2). Students with learning disabilities often have information about the topics, skills, or strategies being taught but do not automatically think about this information (e.g., Borkowski et al., 1989; Bos & Filip, 1984; Wong, 1991; Wong & Wong, 1986). The chapters on reading and content-area instruction discuss specific techniques for activating students' background knowledge.

**Model Processes and Strategies** One key to success for students with learning disabilities is to make the learning visible. Think back to your experiences as a student. How did you learn to find the main idea when you were reading? Many teachers traditionally used the technique of repeatedly asking students questions such as, "What is the main idea of this story?" until a student provided the right answer (e.g., Durkin, 1978–1979). Students were expected to infer how to find the main idea. In the last 20 years, however, intervention research on teaching reading comprehension and other cognitive processes has emphasized that teachers and students should model and discuss the **cognitive strategies** (i.e., thinking processes) they use for tasks such as finding the main idea of the story (e.g., Echevarnia, 1995; Moll, 1990; Palincsar, 1986; Tharp & Gallimore, 1988). Teachers use discussions (referred to as **instructional conversations**) to make visible the thinking processes needed for understanding. Isabel Beck and colleagues (Beck, McKeown, Hamilton, & Kucan, 1998) use a "Questioning the Author" strategy to get students to really grapple with text.

In the following dialogue, the teacher is helping students to better understand story elements, using an instructional conversation to make learning more visible (Englert et al., 1994). In this example, the teacher is working with two students who have partner-read a narrative story about a bear and are now telling the rest of the students about the story.

**T:** Tell us about the story.
**Ann:** [Begins . . . by retelling random incidents from the story]
**T:** You already said we were going to talk about the characters, setting, and problem. Who are the characters in that story?
**Dee:** There is Brother Bear, Papa Bear, and . . . [Shows pictures from the book]
**T:** Who would you say is the main character?
**Ann:** They were all main characters because they were all together throughout the story.
**T:** When we try to figure out the main character, what is the question we ask ourselves?
**Ann:** What the author wants us to know.
**T:** Remember when we try to figure out the main character, we ask ourselves, "Who is . . ."
**Ann:** [Ann fills in] ". . . the story mostly about?"
**T:** Could you answer that question by saying it's mostly about everybody there? (p. 21)

Rather than providing the answer, the teacher is modeling what question to ask to determine who the main character is.

Whether teaching reading, math, or written expression, research on students with learning disabilities consistently has demonstrated that making the learning strategies visible improves learning significantly (e.g., Bos & Anders, 1990; Englert et al., 1991; Wong, 1991).

# TIPS FOR TEACHERS

## 5.2 Steps in Using an Advance Organizer

1. Inform students of advance organizers.
   - Announce advance organizer.
   - State benefits of advance organizer.
   - Suggest that students take notes on the advance organizer.
2. Identify topics or tasks.
   - Identify major topics or activities.
   - Identify subtopics or component activities.
3. Provide an organizational framework.
   - Present an outline, list, or narrative of the lesson's content.
4. Clarify action to be taken.
   - Explain your actions.
   - State actions expected of students.
5. Provide background information.
   - Relate topic to the course or to a previous lesson.
   - Relate topic to new information.
6. State the concepts to be learned.
   - State specific concepts and ideas from the lesson.
   - State general concepts and ideas broader than the lesson's content.
7. Clarify the concepts to be learned.
   - Clarify by examples or analogies.
   - Clarify by nonexamples.
   - Caution students about possible misunderstandings.
8. Motivate students to learn.
   - Point out relevance to students.
   - Be specific, personalized, and believable.
9. Introduce vocabulary.
   - Identify and define new terms.
   - Repeat and define difficult terms.
10. State the general outcome desired.
    - State objectives of instruction and learning.
    - Relate outcomes to test performance.

Adapted with permission from: Lenz, B. K. (1983). Promoting active learning through effective instruction. *Pointer, 27*(2), 12.

***Present Information in Multiple Ways*** Students with learning disabilities have difficulty processing information when it is presented in only one way. To assist these students, it is important to present the information in multiple ways. Bruce Ford incorporates a number of activities, materials, and ways of presenting information as he plans a unit on cells for his ninth-grade science class.

> Modeling strategies and processes and using instructional conversations as the major means of teaching may be uncomfortable at first for teachers accustomed to more traditional lecture or question/answer formats.

> When I think about planning for biology class, I think about what are the key knowledge and skills that I want the students to understand and use. I know that if I just present the information, using a lecture, and have the students read the textbook, a good number of the students will not be able to access the information. So I find myself being creative and constantly on the lookout for additional resources that I can integrate into the unit. Right now, when we do the unit on cells, I have a great video from "Nova" that I use. I have also developed a study guide that I have students complete as we go through the unit. It incorporates pictures of cells and allows them to label the parts of the cell and their functions. The study guide also provides the outline for my lecture notes. The study guide is critical because many of the students in my class cannot take adequate notes and the study guide serves as a structure for their note taking. One activity that I use is an experiment where students have to view cells during the reproduction cycle with a microscope. This activity allows the students to work in teams and develop a group report of their findings. I ask the students to be sure to include drawings. I have found that some of my students with learning disabilities excel at this activity. The experiment allows them to work in teams and move around the room. Having them incorporate drawings is something that these students often excel in, even though they struggle with writing.

**Allow Students to Demonstrate Learning in Multiple Ways** The majority of students with learning disabilities have writing problems that persist over time (Graham & Harris, 1989; Mather & Roberts, 1995). A high-school teacher of students with learning disabilities explains the situation this way, "The adolescents in my program do not want to write. They do not even want to answer questions in writing. Writing a theme for a class is torture" (Bos & Vaughn, 1994, p. 214). Yet writing and tests are the major vehicles used to demonstrate learning. Modifying the manner in which students demonstrate learning enables students with learning disabilities to be more successful in the classroom.

Tips for Teachers 5.3 gives ideas for presenting information in multiple ways.

**Teach Students to Use Memory Strategies** Research has consistently demonstrated that students with learning disabilities are less effective at employing memory strategies than their peers (Swanson, 1993; Swanson & Cooney, 1991; Torgesen & Goldman, 1977). For the classroom teacher, this means that students with learning disabilities will not automatically use **memory strategies** such as rehearsing information they are learning, categorizing the information to make it easier to learn, using visual imagery to "see" the information mentally, and using acronyms to remember lists. By teaching students with learning disabilities how to organize and associate information, how to use mnemonic devices and key words, and how to use rehearsal strategies, you can help them remember information, whether they are beginning readers developing an automatic sight vocabulary or high-school students studying for a science test. Take, for example, the use of acronyms to remember lists of information. The sentence, "Kings play cards on fine green sofas," can help students remember the biological classification system:

Kingdom
Phylum
Class
Order
Family
Genus
Species

It is important not only to teach students memory strategies, but also to *cue students to use their memory strategies when they work on a task.* (For more information about teaching memory strategies, see the appendix, "Making a Difference through Action Learning: Teaching Study Skills, Learning Strategies, and Self-Advocacy." This chapter's 60-Second Lesson describes a fun way to have students develop acronyms.

***Teach Self-Regulation and Self-Monitoring*** By having students keep track of how well they are understanding or performing, they can gain incentives for learning and change their learning patterns to more effective ones. Research suggests that students with learning disabilities are not as adept as their peers at monitoring their own performance (e.g., Bos & Filip, 1984; Harris et al., 1994; Wong, 1991) and effective teachers promote self-monitoring (Pressley, Rankin, & Yokoi, 1996). One way to help students with learning disabilities is to teach them to ask themselves questions about their learning and performance. General questions that students can ask themselves include the following:

- What is my purpose for learning or doing this?
- What is my plan for doing this task?
- Does what I am learning, reading, or doing make sense?
- What do I already know about this topic?
- How am I doing with my work?
- What are the main points I am learning?
- How can I use this elsewhere?

## TIPS FOR TEACHERS

### 5.3 Ideas for Presenting Information and Demonstrating Learning in Multiple Ways

*Ideas for Presenting Information*

- Demonstrate the process or strategy.
- Lecture, writing key points on an overhead projector as you talk.
- Lecture, stopping at natural breaks so that students, working in pairs, can discuss what they see as the major ideas.
- Use a graphic organizer or map to show the relationship among the ideas you are presenting.
- Use a video or movie that presents the key points.
- Have students listen to books on tape.
- Have students conduct experiments to test hypotheses or discover relationships.
- Use pantomimes and skits to explain concepts.
- Have students role-play.
- Use computer simulations.
- Use manipulatives to demonstrate and then have the students use manipulatives.
- Use analogies, metaphors, and examples to further explain concepts.
- Have students use visualization and imagery to see ideas and their relationships.

*Ideas for Demonstrating Learning for Math*

- For students who have difficulties aligning numbers, use graph paper.
- Have students draw a visual representation of the story problem and then complete the math computation. Give partial credit for correct visual representation, even if math computation is incorrect.
- Allow students who do not know their math facts to use math fact matrixes or calculators.
- Allow for time extensions.

*Ideas for Demonstrating Learning for Content Areas*

- Give tests orally and have students respond orally (students can tape-record their responses). (The special education teacher or paraprofessional can often assist in this activity.)
- Allow time extension on tests and projects.
- For projects, help students divide the project into steps and develop a timeline for completing each step.
- Have students use a picture or sequence of pictures to demonstrate understanding of a concept or process.
- Have students develop a skit or pantomime and present it to the class.
- Use word processing and spell checkers.

## MAKING A DIFFERENCE
### The 60-Second Lesson

**Teaching Students to Develop Acronyms**

One activity that students of all ages seem to enjoy and profit from is learning to develop and memorize acronyms for lists of information that must be learned. When you teach a list to students, have them form cooperative groups, with each group working on developing an acronym to help them remember the list. Then each group can report on its acronym.

---

The use of **self-recording** and graphing has been shown to be effective for students with learning and attentional problems (e.g., Martin & Manno, 1995; Rooney et al., 1984; Trammel et al., 1994). Teaching students to self-monitor assignment completion, using an assignment sheet such as the one in Figure 5.4, has been shown to be effective in increasing assignment completion (Trammel et al., 1994). Following are several important aspects to consider:

- Students should record when assignments are due, then mark not only for assignment completion but also for turning in the assignment.
- General education teachers can initial the assignment sheet, thereby providing an easy means of communicating to the special education teacher and parents. The special education teacher can review and discuss the assignment sheet and the assignments with the student.
- Students should set goals to increase their assignment completion, rewarding themselves when they reach their goals.

**Provide Opportunities for Extended Practice and Application** Students with learning disabilities need extended practice and additional opportunities to apply their learning, to ensure continued mastery (Bos & Vaughn, 1994; Kameenui & Simmons, 1990). To create these opportunities when other students in the class may not benefit from them, teachers must be adept at instructional management.

Margaret Duran, a fifth-grade teacher, comments on the way she organizes her classroom to promote opportunities for extended practice and maintenance of skills and strategies:

> One of the most difficult aspects of teaching is juggling the grouping of students and scheduling of activities to assure that students who need more time to learn have that opportunity available. I find that using readers' and writers' workshops has allowed me the flexibility I need. Within these workshops I embed lessons that focus on different skills and strategies. I select the skills/strategies based on students' needs, and we usually work on those skills/strategies for 1 to 3 weeks. I usually teach nine 10- to 15-minute lessons a week so that I focus on three skills/strategies at the same time. The students who are most academically at risk usually work on two of the three skills/strategies. This allows the students who need the most guidance to receive regular small-group instruction and to work consistently on a specific skill or strategy. In their writing folders, there is a list of these skills/strategies and space to record when we worked on them and for the student and me to judge mastery level. When I do individual conferences with the students, we review the skill/strategy list, update the records, monitor progress, and set goals. I find that for students with learning disabilities or who are academically at risk, I have more individual conferences to monitor progress, and we do more maintenance checks to see that the students are continuing to use the skills/strategy effectively in their writing.

As for materials, the fourth- and fifth-grade teachers have been working on these workshops for several years and regularly add text and materials, particularly materials for extended practice.

**Use Learning Tools and Aids** With the new technology and its increasing availability, more students with reading, writing, and math disabilities are able to overcome their academic problems through the use of technologically based learning tools (Lewis, 1993; Woodward & Rieth, 1997). Also, teachers are better able to organize their classrooms and use technology to facilitate effective cooperative learning activities (Bryant & Bryant, 1998). The best known tool is the computer, with its peripherals and programs. Students with handwriting and spelling disabilities have been helped by word processors and their built-in spell checkers. Through speech synthesizers and such software as *Talking Text Writer,* students with reading

**FIGURE 5.4**

*Assignment Sheet for Monitoring Assignment Completion*

X = Completed and Turned In
I = Incomplete/Not Turned In
O = No Assignment

Name _____

| 1 | 2 | 3 | 4 | 5 | 6 |
|---|---|---|---|---|---|
| Mon. | | | | | |
| | X I O | X I O | X I O | X I O | X I O |
| Tues. | | | | | |
| | X I O | X I O | X I O | X I O | X I O |
| Wed. | | | | | |
| | X I O | X I O | X I O | X I O | X I O |
| Thurs. | | | | | |
| | X I O | X I O | X I O | X I O | X I O |
| Fri. | | | | | |
| | X I O | X I O | X I O | X I O | X I O |

Reprinted with permission from: Trammel, D. L., Schloss, P. J., & Alper, S. (1994). Using self-recording, evaluating, and graphing to increase completion of homework assignments. *Journal of Learning Disabilities, 27* (2), 75–81. Copyright 1994 by PRO-ED, Inc.

and writing difficulties have had the opportunity to hear what they write and then to read along with the computer. More and more children's literature is available on CD-ROM, an increasingly available medium that allows readers to hear as well as read the text, to have words and pictures in the text explained, and to have words provided in another language. Drill and practice programs for math facts, such as *Math Blasters Plus*, have provided many students with the opportunity to review and practice their math facts in an interactive game format. See Tech Talk on page 149 for more information about **computer-assisted instruction (CAI)**.

> Whether learning skills or strategies, students with learning disabilities have difficulty transferring or applying these skills and strategies to other learning situations (Borkowski & Turner, 1990; Wong, 1994).

Although computers and multimedia learning environments can play an important role in assisting students with learning disabilities to reach academic success, limited access to hardware and software, classroom constraints, lack of professional development in technology, and unavailability of special education technology specialists will continue to serve as barriers to making full access a reality (Okolo et al., 1993). Other learning tools recommended for students with learning disabilities include calculators, spell checkers, and tape recorders.

**Adjust Work Load and Time** Adjustments of work load and time allocations can be useful accommodations for students with learning disabilities. Adjustments to the work load can include both the amount of work given and the manner in which it is given. Reducing the amount of work may be a very reasonable accommodation when the goal of an assignment or test is for the student to demonstrate mastery (and it can be demonstrated with less work). For example, if the purpose of a math assignment is to demonstrate mastery in using addition and subtraction with regrouping to solve verbal math problems, then completing the odd-numbered problems rather than all the problems may provide adequate evidence of mastery. This type of accommodation is reasonable for students who are slow in math computation because their knowledge of math facts is not at an automatic level. Another accommodation—providing time extensions for tests or completion of large projects—has been helpful to students with learning disabilities.

Another way to adjust work is to divide it into smaller sections or tasks. Having students work on groups of 5 problems at a time rather than the complete set of 20 can make a task more manageable for the student and give the teacher additional opportunities to provide feedback and encouragement as each five-problem set is completed. Helping students to break a complex task, such as reading a book and writing a report, into smaller tasks and to develop a timeline for completing each task can also improve successful task completion. As a teacher you will find that many of the accommodations and teaching ideas suggested in this section will also assist students with attention deficit disorders.

## Attention Deficit Disorders

Many students with learning disabilities also demonstrate attention problems. Danny Moreira, a tenth-grade student, found out during the ninth grade that he has an attention deficit disorder (ADD):

> It has been an enormous relief to me, because all of my life I have been called names like "spaced out," "lazy," "hyper," and "daydreamer," yet I always knew that I was doing the best I could and that it was difficult for me to behave any other way. Ever since I was very young I was very intense and had extra energy to work on areas of interest, but I also became easily bored and distracted. I've been reading and talking to my counselor about ADD, and what they say is that people with ADD have a hard time making friends. That has sure been true for me. I get bored with what people are saying. I interrupt. I am also somewhat impulsive so that if I am thinking something I just blurt it out and sometimes I say the wrong thing. I've gotten much better and the friends I have now understand me. I must say, though, that finding out I had an attention deficit really took the weight off of me. I feel like I've had a boulder removed from my shoulders.
>
> School was a disaster for me, largely because I was so bored and the work all seemed so repetitive and tedious. I've only had one teacher who I felt understood me, Mrs. Golding, my third-grade teacher. I'll never forget her. For math, she would tell me I only had to do the problems until I got five in a row right, then I could stop. At recess she

# TECH TALK

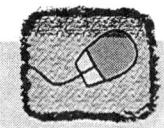

## Computer-Assisted Instruction

**Computer-assisted instruction** (CAI) involves learning through the use of computers and multimedia systems. In contrast, computer-managed assessment and instruction uses computers and multimedia systems to obtain and manage information about the learner and learning resources so as to prescribe and better individualize instruction for the students.

What does the research have to say about the effectiveness of computer-assisted instruction? Word processing, paired with writing instruction, consistently produces a positive though relatively small impact on students' writing and their attitude toward writing (Bangert-Drowns, 1993; Cochran-Smith, 1991). Critical to the success of word processing for students with learning disabilities, however, is that it be coupled with systematic instruction in writing (MacArthur, 1993).

The research in reading is also encouraging, although at this point most of the research conducted has been on drill and practice word-recognition programs rather than on multimedia computer systems and CD-ROM books (Higgins & Boone, 1993). Computer-assisted instruction in math has also shown promise (for reviews see Mastroprieri et al., 1991; Woodward & Carnine, 1993).

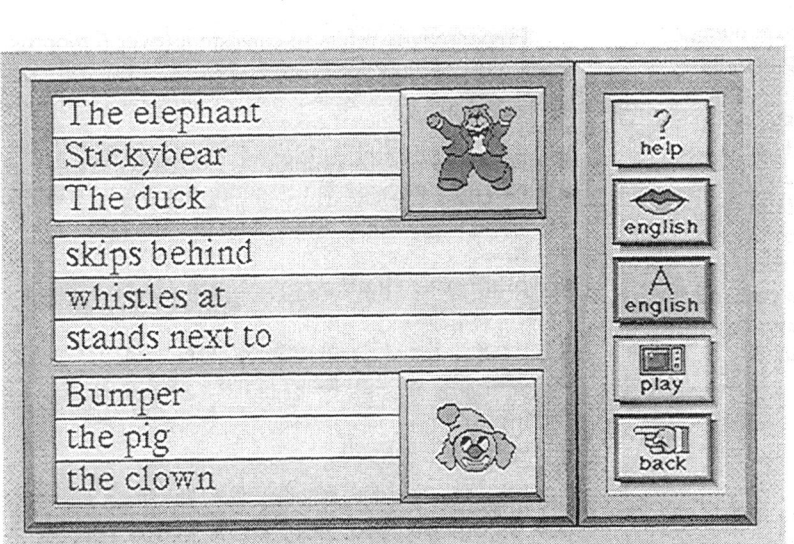

In *Where in the World Is Carmen Sandiego?*® by Broderbund, students explore and learn about dozens of the world's great cities and diverse cultures. School Editions include teacher guides and classroom activities to help teachers provide follow-up activities for the game in which students practice their writing and research skills. Courtesy of Broderbund.

Screen from *Sticky Bear's Reading Room.* Courtesy of Optimum Resource, Inc.

would help me get involved in games with other children and insist that I be included.

Students with attention deficit disorder have been identified for well over a century (e.g., Still, 1902), but only recently have we begun to address the educational implications of their disorder in schools. Parent groups such as Children and Adults with Attention Deficit Disorders (CH.A.D.D.) have applied pressure at the local, state, and national levels so that appropriate educational services would be developed for their children (Children and Adults with Attention Deficit Disorders, 1988, 1992). Additionally, teachers and other school personnel, recognizing that students with ADD come to school with behaviors that interfere with their successful learning, are increasingly requesting information that provides instructional guidelines that will help them meet the needs of students with ADD. Linda Wellens, a veteran kindergarten teacher, explains her experiences with ADD this way:

> IDEA does not recognize Attention Deficit Disorder as a separate category of disability. In 1991, the United States Department of Education clarified that students with ADD may be eligible for special education services under IDEA as "Other Health Impaired" or they may be served if they have another disability (e.g., learning disability, serious emotional disturbance).

I know that every year at least one of the students in my class will have serious attention problems. I don't mean the usual behaviors that a 5-year-old and 6-year-old display. I mean serious problems focusing on what we are doing, controlling themselves, and following directions even after everyone else in the room has caught on to the routines. I can usually tell after the first two weeks of school, but I try everything I can think of to structure the classroom for the child before I mention it to the parents or school counselor. I find that parents are relieved to discover that another adult has confirmed what they know about their child. Most of these parents are totally stressed out having to deal with the problems day and night and are looking for help.

## Definitions and Types of Attention Deficit Disorders

Some teachers wonder whether there is such a thing as ADD, or whether parents and children use it as an excuse for their behavior (Reid et al., 1993). Research studies provide compelling evidence that ADD is a true disorder (Barkley, 1990; McBurnett et al., 1993). According to the *Diagnostic and Statistical Manual of Mental Disorders* (DSM-IV) (American Psychiatric Association, 1994), **attention deficit disorder** has two distinct factors: (1) inattention and (2) hyperactivity–impulsivity (McBurnett et al., 1993). Students who display either or both of these characteristics can be identified as having ADD. There is increasing support for the notion that youngsters with attention deficit disorder without hyperactivity display different achievement patterns than those with both attention deficit disorder and hyperactivity (Marshall, Hynd, Handwerk, & Hall, 1997).

**Inattention** refers to consistent (over 6 months) and highly inappropriate levels of the following behaviors:

- failing to pay close attention to details, and making careless mistakes that are inconsistent with the child's developmental level
- failing to sustain attention to tasks and/or play activities
- failing to listen, even when spoken to directly
- failing to complete tasks
- having difficulty with organization
- resisting to work on tasks that require sustained attention
- losing materials and objects
- becoming easily distracted
- being forgetful

Students need to display six or more of the above symptoms for a sustained period of time.

**Hyperactivity** refers to consistent (over 6 months) and highly inappropriate levels of the following behaviors:

- fidgeting or squirming
- having a difficult time remaining seated during class, even when other students are able to do so
- running or climbing excessively when it is not appropriate
- having difficulty playing quietly
- acting as though he or she is "driven by a motor"
- talking too much

**Impulsivity** refers to consistent (over six months) and highly inappropriate levels of the following behaviors:

- blurting out answers

- difficulty waiting for their turn
- interrupting others or butting into activities

Students must display six or more of the preceding characteristics to be identified with hyperactivity–impulsivity.

## Characteristics of Students with Attention Deficit Disorders

There is general agreement that ADD manifests itself early in a youngster's life. In fact, the precursors to ADD have been identified in infancy (Ross & Ross, 1982). Some early indicators of ADD include poor sleeping and eating habits, difficult temperament, and high levels of activity. By the time youngsters are 3 years old, approximately 50 percent of those who will later be identified as having ADD demonstrate such behaviors as high levels of activity, behavior problems, and short attention span (Barkley, 1990). Therefore, it is not uncommon that many of the behaviors associated with ADD will be demonstrated by children as early as kindergarten and first grade. The core characteristics of ADD include the following:

- poor sustained attention and vigilance
- impulsive or poor delay of gratification
- hyperactivity or poorly regulated activity
- diminished rule-governed behavior
- increased variability of task performance

The common developmental features that distinguish ADD from mild attention or hyperactive problems follow:

- onset in early childhood
- chronic over time
- generally pervasive across situations
- deviant from age-based standards
- increased co-morbidity with other learning and psychiatric disorders

Typically, teachers notice that these students are restless, inattentive, and have a difficult time with routines. These observations are often confirmed by parents. Tips for Teachers 5.4 describes what teachers and parents can do to explain ADD to others.

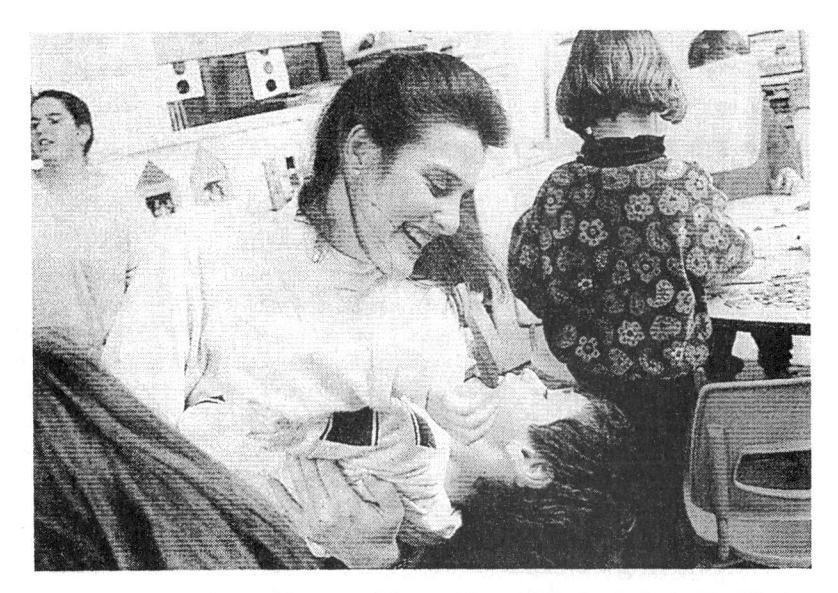

What are some signs of hyperactivity and impulsivity in students identified as having attention deficit disorder? What can you do to help students with ADD in your classroom?

Individuals with ADD do get better as they get older, but more than half of them continue to complain of impulsivity, inattention, low self-esteem, and restlessness as adults (Hechtman et al., 1980). See Table 5.2 for a description of the characteristics of ADD in adolescents.

Perhaps one of the most distinctive characteristics of ADD is the likelihood that it will co-occur with another disability, such as learning disabilities or conduct disorders. Many students with ADD (25 to 68 percent of them) are also identified as learning disabled (McKinney et al., 1993; Shaywitz & Shaywitz, 1988). Approximately 30 percent of students with ADD also display conduct disorders (Fowler, 1992). Thus, students with ADD frequently have other behavior or academic difficulties.

## Prevalence of Attention Deficit Disorders

A conservative estimate of the number of students with ADD is 3 percent (Schiller & Hauser, 1992). Current best estimates of the prevalence rate of ADD are from 3 percent to 5 percent (Barkley, 1990). As with learning disabilities, the exact number of individuals with ADD is difficult to determine because many children with ADD have not been identified (Rapport, 1994). Furthermore, recording the number of students with ADD is difficult because there is no

# TIPS FOR TEACHERS

## 5.4 Ten Tips for Parents and Teachers for Explaining ADD to Children and Others

- *Tell the truth.* This is the central, guiding principle. First, educate yourself about ADD, then put what you have learned into your own words, words the child can understand. Don't just hand the child a book or send the child off to some professional for an explanation. Explain it to yourself, after you have learned about it, then explain it to the child. Be straightforward and honest and clear.
- *Use an accurate vocabulary.* Don't make up words that have no meaning, or use inaccurate words. The child will carry the explanation you give him or her wherever he or she goes.
- The *metaphor of nearsightedness* is useful in explaining ADD to children. It is accurate and emotionally neutral.
- *Answer questions.* Ask for questions. Remember, children often have questions you cannot answer. Don't be afraid to say you don't know. Then go find the answer. Books by professionals who deal with ADD are good sources of information; see for example, Paul Wender's *Hyperactive Children, Adolescents, and Adults,* and Russell Barkley's *Attention Deficit Hyperactivity Disorder.*
- *Be sure to tell the child what ADD is not.* ADD is not stupidity, retardation, defectiveness, badness, and so on.
- *Give examples of positive role models.* Use role models either from history, such as Thomas Edison, or from personal experience, such as a family member (mom or dad).
- *If possible, let others know the child has ADD.* Let others in the classroom know (after discussing this with the child and parents), and let others in the extended family know. Again, the message should be that there is nothing to hide, nothing to be ashamed of.
- *Caution the child not to use ADD as an excuse.* Most kids, once they catch on to what ADD is, go through a phase of trying to use it as an excuse. ADD is an explanation, not an excuse. They still have to take responsibility for what they do.
- *Educate others.* Educate the other parents and children in the classroom, as well as members of the extended family. The single strongest weapon we have to ensure that children get proper treatment is knowledge. Spread the knowledge as far as you can; there is still a great deal of ignorance and misinformation out there about ADD.

---

### TABLE 5.2

**Characteristics of Attention Deficit Disorder in Adolescents**

Adolescents with attention deficit disorder will manifest many of the following characteristics (Shaywitz & Shaywitz, 1988):

- less activity than younger children with ADD
- restlessness
- behavior problems or antisocial conduct
- low self-concept
- inattentiveness
- impulsiveness
- depression
- academic difficulties in school
- problems with relationships
- difficulty maintaining jobs
- difficulty following through on tasks
- problems with drugs/alcohol
- difficulty following directions
- procrastination
- impatience, easily frustrated or bored

separate category for ADD under the Individuals with Disabilities Education Act. Students with ADD may be identified as having a health impairment or a secondary condition, when ADD and another disability (e.g., learning or emotional disabilities) overlap. Other students, who do not qualify under IDEA as students with ADD, do qualify under Section 504 of the Vocational Rehabilitation Act (discussed in Chapter 1). Again, however, as in the case of IDEA, the number of students with ADD is not recorded.

Prevalence estimates of students with ADD consistently report higher rates for males than for females. Some reports indicate that the ratio of males to females is 3 to 1, with other studies reporting ratios as high as 6 to 1 (e.g., Rapport, 1994). It is difficult to determine why the rate is so much higher for boys, but there is some reason to believe that ADD may manifest itself differently in girls than in boys and that the identification instruments are based on the behavioral manifestation of ADD in boys. There is evidence that girls with ADD are more likely to be withdrawn (and thus less likely to be identified) than boys with ADD, who are likely to be hyperactive.

## Instructional Guidelines and Accommodations for Students with ADD

Because students with ADD are likely to spend all or most of their school time in general classroom settings (Fowler, 1992), much of their educational program is likely to be the responsibility of the classroom teacher. What are the characteristics of teachers who are effective with students with ADD? According to Lerner and colleagues (Lerner et al., 1995), "in many respects, they are simply good teachers" (p. 96). Lerner and colleagues indicate that the following characteristics help teachers to work successfully with students who have ADD:

- *Positive attitudes toward mainstreaming and inclusion of students with ADD.* These attitudes are reflected in the way teachers accept students and promote students' acceptance by the classroom community.
- *Ability to collaborate as a member of an interdisciplinary team.* Teachers who have students with ADD in their classrooms have an opportunity to work with other professionals and family members who will be monitoring the students' academic and behavioral progress, response to medication, and self-esteem.
- *Knowledge of behavior-management procedures.* Most students with ADD in your classroom will demonstrate difficulty following directions, remembering routines, attending to task, and organizing themselves and their work. Behavior-management skills are essential to adequately meet the needs of students with ADD.
- *Personal characteristics.* To teach students with ADD, you need understanding, compassion, patience, concern, respect, responsiveness, and a sense of humor.

In addition to the preceding characteristics, educational and medication-related interventions can also be helpful in your work with students with ADD.

**Educational Interventions** As indicated in Chapter 2, teachers should begin any educational intervention with planning. Maria Nahmias has served as a consultant to parents and teachers on how to effectively meet the needs of students with ADD in the classroom. Based on her extensive experience she recommends that teachers consider the following key points when planning **educational interventions** for students with ADD (Nahmias, 1995):

- *Use novelty in instruction and directions.* Highlight important instructions and key points with colored pens, highlight markers, or flair-tip pens. Bold key information or underline it. Use "oral cueing" to identify key words or ideas in the directions.
- *Maintain a schedule.* As indicated earlier, students with ADD have a difficult time learning rules and routines; thus, it is critical that these be changed as infrequently as possible. Change is difficult for students to adjust to and often promotes behavior problems. Post rules and schedules in the room and on index cards on the students' desks.
- *Provide organizational assistance.* Provide guidelines for how the students should maintain their desks, materials, and schedules. Provide opportunities at the beginning of each week for students to organize and then reward them for doing so. Ask students to keep a notebook for each of their classes and to write their assignments and due dates in the notebook.

- *Provide rewards consistently and often.* All students like to receive positive feedback about their performance and behavior; however, the frequency, intensity, and consistency of rewards needs to be increased for students with ADD. Whenever possible, involve the student in selecting the rewards.
- *Be brief and clear.* Think about instructions before stating them, and provide them as briefly and in as well-organized a way as possible. Present the critical information in chunks so that it is more easily understood and remembered. Keep instructional lessons brief to maintain students' attention.
- *Arrange the environment to facilitate attention.* Consider where the student is sitting. Are there other students who might promote good behavior and organizational skills? Are you able to quickly and easily maintain eye contact as well as physical contact with the student? Be sure to consider how to minimize distractions.
- *Provide optimal stimulation.* There is some support for the notion that optimal stimulation facilitates learning for students with attention deficit disorder. For example, students with ADD who were provided background music while doing arithmetic problems performed better than non-ADD students under the same conditions (Abikoff, Courtney, Szeibel, & Koplewicz, 1996).

Planning lessons for students with ADD within the context of planning for the class as a whole is a challenge. The primary focus of planning should be on what accommodations are needed to make the lesson effective for all students, including a student with ADD. Figure 5.5 names the types of problems frequently manifested by students with ADD, and provides potential solutions. Figure 5.6 (on page 156) provides a sample lesson plan with supports identified for a student with ADD.

A problem frequently noted by parents and teachers of students with ADD is homework. These students have a difficult time recording assignments, knowing when they are due, and establishing an organizational sequence that enables them to complete the task on time. For this reason, homework record sheets are often developed and implemented by teachers and then monitored by parents. Figure 5.7 (on page 157) provides an example of a daily assignment log.

The following guidelines will help reduce the trauma often associated with homework for students with ADD.

- *Unfinished classwork remains in class.* This helps students to differentiate between classwork and homework. If unfinished classwork becomes homework (as an "add on" to the already assigned homework), students can easily become overwhelmed.
- *Identify the minimum amount to demonstrate learning.* Understanding and mastering the task is more important than completing an extensive amount of work. Consider shortening the task for these students. It is better that they do a small amount well than a lot of work poorly.
- *Provide timelines for tasks associated with long-term assignments.* Rather than telling students the date a long-term assignment is due, help them problem solve a timeline for completing the key components of the assignment. Pair them with a buddy or work cooperatively with parents to ensure that each component in the timeline is completed.

Although no one educational treatment package has been demonstrated to yield successful outcomes for students with ADD (Fiore et al., 1993), the best treatment procedures to date are those that involve a range of instructional supports and accommodations.

**Effects of Stimulant Medications** Students with ADD are frequently identified by a team that includes a physician. The physician often recommends that these students be provided **stimulant medications** to assist in the treatment of their disorder. This decision can be a tumultuous one for parents who, unsure about the outcomes associated with medical treatment, fear negative side effects. Parents need to be informed as to how to recognize possible side effects so that, should they occur, they can inform the physician. Linda Wellens, a kindergarten teacher comments,

> This year I had a student, Alex, who was identified as hyperactive–impulsive. His mother called me frequently to check on how he was doing in school. He had been kicked out of three preschools before he even started kindergarten, and she was worried about how he would perform. Alex just couldn't sit still. He would try to stay in his seat and then would jump up and start playing with toys or building with blocks. He

### FIGURE 5.5

**Educational Interventions**

| PROBLEM | SOLUTION |
|---|---|
| Listening | Provide visual displays (flowcharts, pictorials, wheels); prereading questions/terms at end of chapter; assigned reading; keyword note-taking system to expand memory jogs during daily review; advance note-taking organizers from subtitles in textbook. |
| Distractibility | Minimize visual distractors in the environment; don't have interesting activities going on in one corner of the room while expecting the student to do his or her seatwork. |
| Attention Span | Have student work in short units of time with controlled activity breaks (i.e., reading break or magazine break); activities need to be interspersed throughout instruction. |
| Short-Term Memory | Offer review systems in a flashcard style so frequent practice can be done independently; material may need to be reviewed frequently. |
| Task Completion | Present work in short units (i.e., five problems on paper cut into quarters rather than on one sheet); timeframes should be short, with clear deadlines and checkpoints to measure progress; have a model available so product can be examined if directions can't be retained. |
| Distractibility | Have as few distractions as possible; provide a "quiet corner" for anyone who wishes a distraction-free place to work. |
| Impulsivity | Show the student how to do the work; have a checklist for what he needs to do, and have a reward system tied to the completion of all the steps. |
| Inattention to Detail | Emphasize detail through color coding or isolation. |
| Test Taking | Have the student review critical details and main ideas in a flashcard system to support attention and practice specific retrieval. |

From: Rooney, K. J. (1995). Teaching students with attention disorders. *Intervention in School and Clinic, 30*(4), 221–225. Copyright 1995 by PRO-ED, Inc. Reprinted by permission.

## FIGURE 5.6

**Lesson Plan for Students with Attention Deficit Disorder**

**Objective:**
Students will understand the difference between an adverb phrase and an adjective phrase.

**Methods for Presentation:**
Demonstrations, examples, overheads, worksheets, student samples for analysis.

**Materials Needed:**
Overhead projector, worksheets, examples.

**Workplan and Timeframes for Presentation:**

|  |  |
|---|---|
| 2:00 PM – 2:05 PM | Review definition of adverb/adjective; have students write definition of each term from memory and then correct them to the book's definition. |
| 2:05 PM – 2:15 PM | Explain and discuss the difference between an adjective phrase and an adverb phrase; demonstrate examples on the overhead. |
| 2:15 PM – 2:25 PM | Have students write an operational rule and share their versions. |
| 2:25 PM – 2:35 PM | Have students produce an example of an adverb phrase and an adjective phrase. |
| 2:35 PM – 2:40 PM | Explain and demonstrate assignment. |

**Supports for Attention:**
Frequent shifts in activities.
Activities interspersed with instruction.
Demonstration as well as oral presentation.

**Review System:**
Record of instruction will be written in a bound notebook. Study card (homework) will be produced for the grammar review system.

**Demonstration of Knowledge (Independent Use):**
Homework. Study card from the grammar book section (pp. 54–56). The card will include the topic, the rule or instruction, and an example of each. Examples corrected in class, and errors highlighted and corrected on the card.

From: Rooney, K. J. (1995). Teaching students with attention disorders. *Intervention in School and Clinic, 30*(4), 221–225. Copyright 1995 by PRO-ED, Inc. Reprinted by permission.

## FIGURE 5.7

**Daily Assignment Log**

Name _____

Date _____

| Materials | Subject | Class Assignment | Done | Homework | Done |
|---|---|---|---|---|---|
| ☐Y ☐N | | | ☐Y ☐N | | ☐Y ☐N |
| ☐Y ☐N | | | ☐Y ☐N | | ☐Y ☐N |
| ☐Y ☐N | | | ☐Y ☐N | | ☐Y ☐N |
| ☐Y ☐N | | | ☐Y ☐N | | ☐Y ☐N |
| ☐Y ☐N | | | ☐Y ☐N | | ☐Y ☐N |
| Totals Y__ N__ | | | Totals Y__ N__ | | Totals Y__ N__ |

From: Kemp, K., Fister, S., & McLaughlin, P. J. (1995). Academic strategies for children with ADD. *Intervention in School and Clinic, 30*(4), 203–210. Copyright 1995 by PRO-ED, Inc. Reprinted by permission.

---

just seemed to need a frequent release. He was a handful, but I managed to set up a behavior modification program that was highly effective. One of the things that helped the most is that his parents, his physician, and the psychologist agreed that he would benefit from medication. Then we worked as a team to monitor his reaction and progress.

Several medications can help alleviate many of the symptoms of ADD. The medication works like a pair of eyeglasses, helping the individual to focus. It can also reduce the sense of inner turmoil and anxiety that is so common with ADD. Stimulant medication works by adjusting a chemical imbalance that affects the neurotransmitters in the parts of the brain that regulate attention, impulse control and mood (Hallowell & Ratey, 1994). Swanson and colleagues (Swanson et al., 1993) have completed a comprehensive review of the effect of stimulant medication on children with ADD. Table 5.3 provides a

### TABLE 5.3

***Treatment of Children with Attention Deficit Disorder with Stimulant Medication***

*What You Should Expect:*

- improved ability to modulate motor behavior and overactivity
- increased concentration or effort on tasks
- improved self-regulation and reduced impulsivity
- increased compliance and effort
- decreased physical and verbal aggression
- decreased negative behaviors during social interactions
- increased amount and accuracy of academic work
- about 70 percent of children respond favorably
- possible side effects such as facial tics, loss of appetite, difficulty sleeping, and psychological effects on cognition and attribution
- no significant improvement of academic skills
- no significant improvement of athletic or game skills
- no significant improvement of positive social skills
- no long-term improvement in academic achievement
- no long-term reduction in antisocial behavior or arrest rate

Adapted from Swanson et al. (1993). Effect of stimulant medication on children with attention deficit disorder: A "review of reviews." *Exceptional Children, 60,* 154–162. Copyright 1993 by the Council for Exceptional Children. Reprinted by permission.

---

summary of the treatment outcomes you should expect when youngsters with ADD are provided stimulant medication. More children receive medication to control ADHD symptoms than for any other childhood disorder (Barkley, 1990).

The one thing all professionals agree on about treatment of ADD with medication is that it should always be considered as one component of an overall treatment plan (Accardo et al., 1991; Barkley, 1990; Goldstein & Goldstein, 1990; Swanson et al., 1993). As Lerner and colleagues state (Lerner et al., 1995), "Medication should not be considered a 'silver bullet' or the single solution to the problems the student is facing. Rather, medical treatment should be recognized as one part of a total interdisciplinary management and intervention program" (p. 175). Schools, parents, the physician, and the counselor or psychologist all need to work as a team to develop a coordinated effort to meet the needs of students with ADD.

## SUMMARY

- The term "learning disabilities" is used to describe a heterogeneous group of students who, despite adequate cognitive functioning, have difficulty learning, particularly academics.
- Dyslexia, dysgraphia, and dyscalculia are three types of learning disabilities that refer to extreme difficulty learning to read, write, and do mathematics, respectively.
- Students with learning disabilities represent a range of characteristics that include low performance in one or more academic areas, unexpected low performance considering their overall ability, and ineffective or inefficient information processing.
- The number of individuals identified as learning disabled is approximately 5 percent of the school-age population, which accounts for over half of all students identified as having disabilities.
- Because the characteristics of students with learning disabilities are heterogeneous, the types of learning accommodations vary. Accommodations that generally assist students with learning disabilities include: providing a framework for learning, modeling the processes and strategies,

presenting information and allowing students to demonstrate learning in multiple ways, teaching students to use memory strategies, teaching self-regulation, providing opportunities for extended practice and application, using learning tools and aids, and adjusting work loads and time requirements.
- Attention deficit disorder (ADD) refers to difficulty in attention and has two factors: inattention and hyperactivity–impulsivity. Students can display one or both of these factors.
- A conservative estimate of the number of students with ADD is 3 percent.
- The core characteristics of ADD are poor sustained attention and vigilance, impulsivity with poor delay of gratification, hyperactivity and poorly regulated activity, diminished rule-governed behavior, and increased variability of task performance.
- Classroom interventions to assist students with ADD include: using novelty in instruction and directions, maintaining a schedule, providing organizational assistance, providing rewards consistently and often, communicating briefly and clearly, and arranging the environment to facilitate attention.

# Key Terms and Concepts

advance organizer
attention deficit disorder (ADD)
cognitive strategies
computer-assisted instruction (CAI)
dyscalculia
dysgraphia
dyslexia
educational interventions
hyperactivity
impulsivity
inattention
instructional conversations
memory strategies
self-recording
specific learning disabilities
stimulant medications

# Think and Apply

1. Now that you have read Chapter 5, review Tammy's experiences in working with Adrian and Lenny. If you could talk to Tammy and the parents of Adrian and Lenny, what other questions would you ask them? What would you suggest Tammy tell Adrian and Lenny's third-grade teachers to help them succeed next year? List any questions or ideas you have now about teaching students with learning disabilities and attention deficit disorder. Discuss your questions and ideas with your fellow students, your instructors, and teachers in the field. Also check the list of questions or concerns you developed from reading Chapter 1, and see whether you can check any of them off your list. Record your answers and file your personal inquiry in your teaching portfolio.

2. Think about several students you know, have taught, or are currently teaching who are not achieving as you would expect. Using the definition of learning disabilities and the exclusionary factors, predict whether their learning difficulties are due to specific learning disabilities or other reasons.

3. Select a lesson in which you are going to teach a new skill or strategy. Think about how you can modify the lesson to provide more opportunities for you and the students to model or demonstrate the skill or strategy, and more opportunities for the students to practice the skill or strategy.

4. Modify a lesson or unit you are going to teach, increasing the number of ways students can learn the information or skills, and the number of ways in which they can demonstrate learning.

Think about the needs of students with learning disabilities or attention deficit disorders.

5. Write or call the following organizations, request copies of their publications and resources, and keep them in a designated file for use in your classroom with parents or other teachers.

- Attention Deficit Disorder
   Advocacy Group
  8091 South Ireland Way
  Aurora, CO 80016
  (800) 487-2282
- Children and Adults with
   Attention Deficit Disorder
  499 N.W. 70th Avenue, Suite 101
  Plantation, FL 33317
  (954) 587-3700
- A.D.D. Warehouse
  300 Northwest 70th Avenue, Suite 102
  Plantation, FL 33317
  (305) 954-8944
  (800) 233-9273
- Learning Disabilities Association of America
  4156 Library Road
  Pittsburgh, PA 15234
  (412) 341-1515

## Read More about It

1. Bos, C. S., & Vaughn, S. (1998). *Strategies for teaching students with learning and behavior problems* (4th ed.). Boston: Allyn & Bacon.

   Provides specific strategies that teachers, school personnel, and parents can use to facilitate the academic and personal growth of students with special needs. Also describes the major theories and approaches to learning.

2. Deshler, D. D., Ellis, E. S., & Lenz, B. K. (1996). *Teaching adolescents with learning disabilities: Strategies and methods.* Denver, CO: Love.

   Provides descriptions of the characteristics of adolescents with learning disabilities and specific strategies for instruction. The roles of the teacher, parent, and family members as well as appropriate programs for providing successful interventions for adolescents with learning disabilities are described.

3. Gillingham, A., & Stillman, B. W. (1973). *Remedial training for children with specific disability in reading, spelling, and penmanship.* Cambridge, MA: Educators Publishing Service.

   Based on the principles for teaching reading to dyslexic students, this phonics-based approach uses a multisensory technique to teach the structure of language and the alphabetic principle. A number of programs have been developed that are based on these same principles.

4. Hallowell, E. M., & Ratey, J. J. (1994). *Driven to distraction: Recognizing and coping with attention deficit disorder from childhood through adulthood.* New York: Touchstone.

   Useful to different audiences, including those who know little about ADD and those who are well informed. Topics addressed include: definition, the child with ADD, the adult with ADD, ADD in couples, ADD and the family, subtypes of ADD, diagnosis, treatment, and biology.

5. Hampshire, S. (1982). *Susan's story: An autobiographical account of my struggle with dyslexia.* New York: St. Martin's Press.

   Provides an interesting account of a young woman's experiences in school and life. Her dyslexia was difficult for her to deal with, and in many cases even more difficult for others.

6. Lerner, J. W., Lowenthal, B., & Lerner, S. R. (1995). *Attention deficit disorders: Assessment and teaching.* Pacific Grove, CA: Brooks/Cole.

   Provides an overview of ADD from an educational perspective. Topics covered include: definition, ADD and the law, assessment, educational interventions, working with families, medical treatment, and the biological bases of ADD.

7. Moss, P. B. (1990). *P. Buckley Moss: The people's artist*. Waynesboro, VA: Shenandoah Heritage.

   Ms. Moss has become a successful artist and advocate for individuals with learning disabilities. This book conveys her feelings concerning the need to look for the creative strengths many students with learning disabilities hide because of fears related to their difficulties learning in school.

8. Smith, S. (1986). *No easy answers*. Cambridge, MA: Winthrop.

   Sally Smith is a successful woman with learning disabilities who owns a private school for students with learning disabilities. She explains the difficulties of growing up with learning disabilities, and describes some of the strategies used in her school to effectively meet students' educational and social needs.

9. Wong, B. Y. L. (1996) *The ABC's of learning disabilities*. San Diego: Academic Press.

   This book discusses the concept of learning disabilities, as well as major research findings regarding learning-disabled children, adolescents, and adults. It also encourages the beginning student to identify the big picture and to think about implications of issues and research findings.

CHAPTER *11*

# Teaching Students with Communication Disorders

# Interview

## Lorri Johnson

Lorri Johnson is one of five third-grade teachers at Drexel Elementary School. This is her first year of teaching. In her class of 31 students, one (Samatha) has a communication disorder. She also has two students with learning disabilities, one of whom receives support from both the speech and language pathologist (SLP) and the special education teacher.

Lorri believes that all children can learn and that her job is to create a learning community that supports this belief. Although she utilizes the districtwide curricula, she is quick to modify, supplement, and augment the curricula to fit her students' needs. For example, she uses the language arts textbook only as a resource for activities to build communication and written language skills. These activities she embeds in thematic units on such typical third-grade topics as fantasy and weather.

Samatha, the student with communication disorders, works with the speech and language pathologist, Nancy Meyers, for 30 minutes twice a week. Nancy and Lorri check with each other informally about once a week regarding Samatha's progress and what is working. This communication often occurs during lunch or when both teachers are in the teachers' work room.

As Lorri describes Samatha, it is clear that she understands Samatha's needs and makes accommodations to help her communicate successfully in the classroom. Lorri notes,

> The way I would describe Samatha is as a late bloomer when it comes to language. Early in the year, Nancy and I sat down with Samatha's file, and we discussed her history and needs. Samatha did not start talking until she was almost 3 years old, despite the fact that she is an only child. Although she babbled and seemed to be talking to herself when she played as a toddler, she did not use words in her play or to communicate with others. Her mom reported that she did appear to understand what others were saying to her. At age 4, Samatha began attending Head Start and was identified as a child with speech and language disorders. She started working with a speech and language pathologist at that time. She has continued to receive services since then. Both Nancy and I agree that talking is difficult for Samatha. Her sentences are short, and she continues to have difficulty producing complex sentence structures, does not use adjectives and adverbs to elaborate, and has significant difficulty with verb tenses and irregular verbs. Samatha also has a limited vocabulary when she speaks, and I am oftentimes unsure if she is getting the concepts that I am teaching.
>
> I feel that I work to make my class successful for Samatha in several ways. First, I usually don't call on Samatha in large class discussions unless she raises her hand. We have a deal that she can't use this rule to escape listening and learning and that I expect her to contribute to large group discussions at least several times a day. But this way she gets to pick the opportunities. Second, I have a habit of frequently "checking for understanding." During lessons, I regularly ask students if they are understanding. To keep the class active, I have them use thumbs up, stand up, clap hands, etc. to indicate if they understand. I think Samatha and the other students feel comfortable telling me they don't understand, for I encourage and praise them for the questions they ask. Third, I have Samatha take leadership roles that require her to talk when we work in small groups, and I encourage her to help other students when doing independent seat work. Finally, through reading and writing, I can focus on the areas that are difficult for her in oral language. For example, we have been working on using adjectives to make our writing more interesting. Samatha has really improved in this area of writing, and now I am asking the students to take their new descriptive written language and use it more when they talk.
>
> I guess overall, I feel that Samatha is a successful learner in my class, but I would like to know more about communication disorders so I can provide more encouragement and assistance.

## Introduction

Lorri and many other teachers (both elementary and secondary) share these feelings. They learn a lot about teaching reading and writing, but much less about the development of oral communication, the characteristics of students with communication disorders, strategies for identifying these students, and techniques for promoting oral communication and language development in general education classrooms. This chapter focuses on those areas and should provide you with a number of techniques and strategies for working with students who have communication disorders or other disabilities that result in delayed communication development.

## Communication Disorders

Communication is the process of exchanging ideas and information (Owens, 1998) and a natural part of life: Society places high value on oral communication. Both in school and society, communication is a powerful resource. For example, we use communication to do the following:

- develop and maintain contact and relationships with others
- gain and give information
- control and persuade
- create and imagine
- communicate feelings
- monitor our own behavior when we talk to ourselves

Even though written communication plays a key role in school, speaking and listening are the most frequently used means of learning. Consequently, students with communication disorders may experience difficulties in many aspects of school, including both learning and social situations.

The term **communication disorders** refers to difficulties with the transfer of knowledge, ideas, opinions, and feelings (Oyer et al., 1987). Communication is thought to be disordered when it deviates from the community standards enough to interfere with the transmission of messages, stands out as being unusually different, or produces negative feelings within the communicator (Payne & Taylor, 1998). Communication disorders range in severity from mild to profound. They may be developmental or acquired through injuries or diseases that affect the brain. A communication disorder may be the primary disability, or it may be secondary to other disabilities (ASHA, 1993). For example, students with learning disabilities and mental retardation often have secondary language disabilities and receive services from a speech and language pathologist.

When students enter school, they are expected to communicate by listening and speaking. Some students may have difficulty transmitting the message or information. For example, when Sarah entered kindergarten her speech was so difficult to understand that both the teacher and students had to listen to her for several days before they began to figure out what she was trying to communicate. Sarah has difficulty with speech, or the vocal production of language. Jeffrey, on the other hand, has difficulty understanding the message of others and communicating his message to others. His speech (vocal production) is adequate, but the message is unclear. Jeffrey's difficulties lie in the area of language. Language, the major vehicle humans use for communicating, is a "code whereby ideas about the world are represented through a conventional system of arbitrary signals for communication" (Bloom & Lahey, 1978, p. 4). The American Speech–Language–Hearing Association (1993) has divided communication disorders into the three broad categories: speech disorders, language disorders, and hearing disorders. This chapter deals with speech and language disorders, whereas Chapter 9 discusses students with hearing disorders.

> Of students with communication disorders, 53 percent have speech disorders. By far the most typical speech disorders are articulation disorders (47 percent), with voice disorders (4 percent) and fluency disorders (2 percent) far less frequent (Leske, 1981).

### Speech Disorders

Individuals have **speech disorders** when their communication is unintelligible, unpleasant, or interferes with communication (Van Riper & Emerick, 1984). The vocal production of language has three components: articulation, fluency, and voice. **Articulation** has to do with the production of speech sounds, **fluency** refers to the flow and rhythm of language, and **voice** focuses on the quality of speech, including resonance, pitch, and intensity.

**Articulation Disorders** By far, the most common speech disorders, **articulation disorders** occur when students are unable to produce the various sounds and sound combinations of language (Hulit & Howard, 1997). It is not unusual for speech and language pathologists to work with elementary-age children who have a delay in the development of articulation, because the ability to produce the speech sounds continues to develop through age 8. Learning to produce the speech sounds, no matter what the language, usually proceeds in a fairly consistent sequence, but there may be as much as a three-year variance between the time early learners start producing a particular sound and the time late learners start producing the sound (Bernthal & Bankson, 1998; Yavas, 1998). Figure 6.1 demonstrates the developmental progression of speech sounds and clarifies why many children enter school still in the process of learning to produce such sounds as *r, l, s, ch, sh, z, j, v,* and voiced and voiceless th and zh.

It is also interesting to note that the production of speech sounds generally develops earlier in girls than in boys. Table 6.1 compares the development of girls and boys, noting the age at which 90 percent of the girls and boys can articulate the sounds. If you teach kindergarten through second grade, you will have the opportunity to hear these sounds developing in some of your students. Even if these sounds are not fully developed, children's speech by the time they enter kindergarten should be at least 90 percent intelligible.

The types of articulation disorders are sound substitutions, omissions, additions, and distortions. Substitutions and omissions are the most common errors. In *substitutions,* one sound is substituted for another. Common substitutions include /w/ for /r/ (*wabbit* for *rabbit*), /t/ for /c/ (*tat* for *cat*), /b/ for /v/ (*balentine* for *valentine*), and /f/ for /th/ (*free* for *three*). *Omissions* occur when a sound is not included in a word. Because blends are later developing, many omission errors have the second sound in the blend omitted (e.g., *boo* for *blue, pity* for *pretty*).

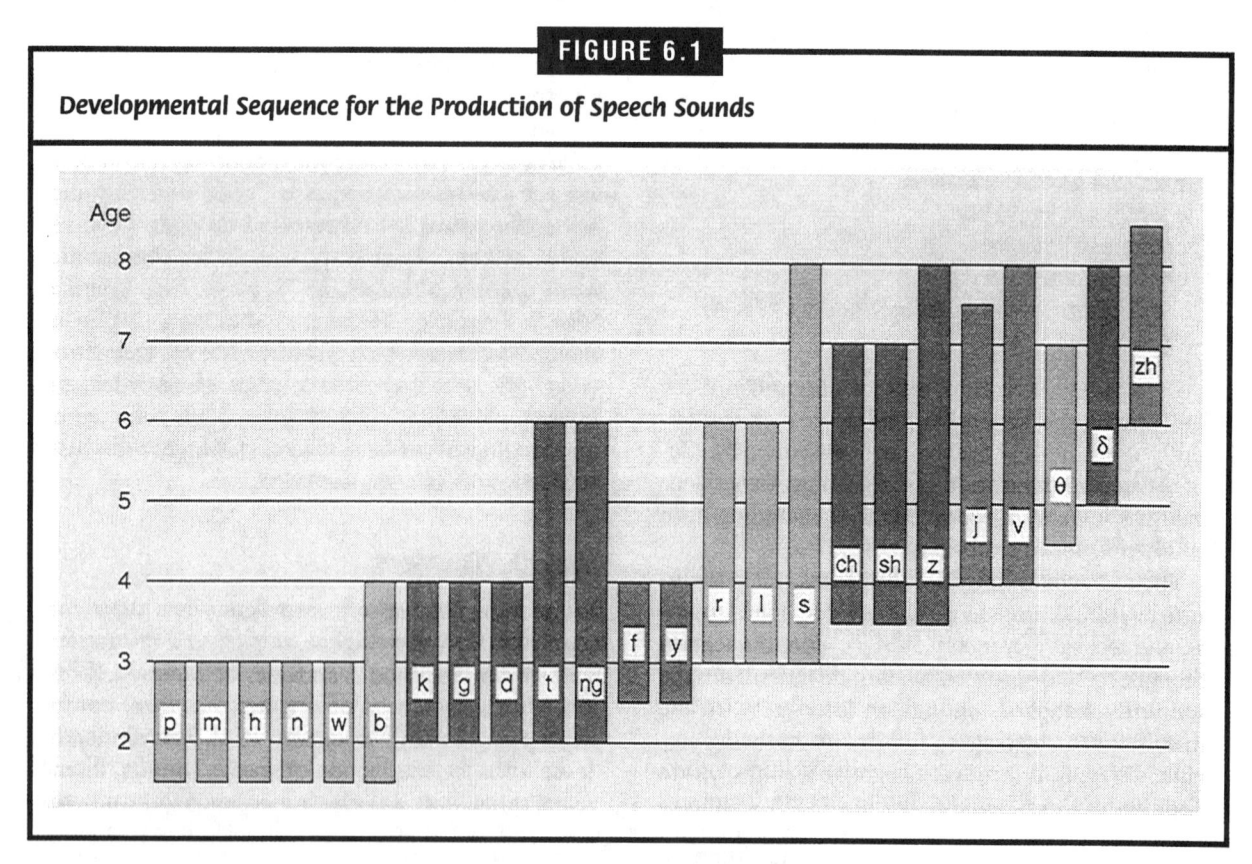

**FIGURE 6.1**

**Developmental Sequence for the Production of Speech Sounds**

Reprinted with permission from Sander, E. K. (1972). When are speech sounds learned? *Journal of Speech and Hearing Disorders, 37,* 62.

Final sounds also are commonly omitted, particularly the later-developing sounds such as /s/, /sh/, /z/, and voiced and voiceless /th/. As a classroom teacher, it will be important for you to listen for children whose articulation is developmentally delayed or whose articulation errors are so frequent that they significantly affect intelligibility. You will want to talk with the speech and language pathologist about these children.

Articulation is affected not only by development but also by regional dialects and cultural uses. Variations or dialects of a language are products of historical, cultural, geographic, social, economic, ethnic, and political factors (Hedge, 1996). For example, Bostonians often use /er/ for /a/ (as in idea/ider and data/dater), and Southerners draw out vowels. **African American Vernacular English** (AAVE) is used by some African Americans and reflects the complex racial and economic history of the African American in the United States. The features of AAVE are characteristic of the dialect as a whole but vary in individual speakers.

> Variations in speech or language that are used by a group of individuals from a geographic region or from a social or cultural group are not communication disorders. Rather, these variations (e.g., Black Vernacular English and Appalachian English) are dialects.

Articulation of English sounds is also affected when students are learning English as a second language (ESL). Sounds made in one language may not be made in another language or may not be made in the same manner. As a classroom teacher, it is important for you to remember that differences in articulation due to regional or cultural dialects or English as a second language should not be considered disorders. (For more information about AAVE and ESL, see Chapter 10, "Teaching Culturally and Linguistically Diverse Students.")

**Fluency Disorders** Whereas articulation disorders involve difficulty with the production of the sounds, **fluency disorders** refer to difficulty with the rate and flow of speech. **Stuttering**, the most common fluency disorder, is an interruption of the forward flow of speech (Palmer & Yantis, 1990). All of us are nonfluent to some degree when we communicate. We hesitate in the middle of sentences, break the flow of language with meaningless sounds and fillers (e.g., ah, um, you know, like), repeat parts of words, and speak very quickly. We are more nonfluent in stressful, novel, or exciting situations. When we have difficulty thinking of a word, we may stutter.

> Boys are four times more likely to stutter than girls.

This normal dysfluency becomes stuttering when the disruptions in speech are accompanied by aware-

### TABLE 6.1

**Comparison of the Development for Speech Sound Production in Boys and Girls***

**BOYS**

| Age | 3 | 4 | 5 | 6 | 7 |
|---|---|---|---|---|---|
| | p | ng | y | zh | f |
| | b | | | wh | l |
| | m | | | j | r |
| | h | | | | ch |
| | w | | | | sh |
| | d | | | | s |
| | n | | | | z |
| | k | | | | th (voiceless) |
| | t | | | | v |
| | g | | | | th (voiced) |

**GIRLS**

| Age | 3 | 4 | 5 | 6 | 7 |
|---|---|---|---|---|---|
| | p | l | j | sh | s |
| | b | t | y | ch | z |
| | m | | | r | th (voiceless) |
| | w | | | zh | v |
| | d | | f | f | th (voiced) |
| | n | | | wh | |
| | k | | | | |
| | g | | | | |
| | h | | | | |
| | ng | | | | |

*The age at which 90 percent of boys and girls can articulate sounds. *Note:* Vowel sounds are produced correctly by 90 percent of all children by age 3. Consonant blends—tr, bl, pr, and so on—develop between ages 7 and 9.

Reprinted with permission from Work, R. S. (1994). Articulation disorders. In S. Adler & D. A. King, (Eds.), *Oral communication problems in children and adolescents* (p. 3). Boston: Allyn & Bacon.

ness, anxiety, or compensatory behavior (Cantwell & Baker, 1987; Curlee & Siegel, 1997). Most young children, at different times during the preschool years, are nonfluent in a manner that resembles stuttering. Four of five children move through these times spontaneously usually by age five (Sheehan & Martyn, 1970), and fewer than 1 percent of school-age children have stuttering problems. Although Sharon Kutok, a speech and language pathologist in Tucson, serves few students at the high-school level, several of these students have problems with stuttering.

**Voice Disorders** Voice disorders relate to the quality of the voice itself. Usually, four dimensions are considered:

- Quality
- Resonance (nasality)
- Pitch (high or low)
- Intensity (loud or soft)

The most typical type of voice disorder found in school-age children is the presence of vocal nodules caused by yelling and other forms of vocal abuse that affect voice quality. Vocal nodules, which develop because the vocal mechanism is used incorrectly or overused, are somewhat like calluses on the vocal folds. If the nodules become too large, students can lose their voices and require surgery. Generally, it takes consistent and prolonged abuse for nodules to develop, but it is important to caution students about "yelling till they are hoarse" or talking a great deal using "pretend or contrived voices," such as the guttural, hoarse voices that monsters or aliens might make.

> Students who have had corrective surgery for a cleft palate may have difficulties with resonance, and often receive speech therapy to learn to control the flow of air.

Few school-age children have the other types of voice disorders—resonance (e.g., difficulty producing the nasal sounds of /m/, /n/, and /ng/), pitch and intensity. Should you notice students with these difficulties, talk with your speech and language pathologist.

### School-Age Language Disorders

**Language disorders** are the other major area of communication disorders discussed in this chapter. Language functions as an integral part of the communication process because it allows us to represent ideas, using a conventional code. A person's ability to understand what is being communicated is referred to as **comprehension** or **receptive language**, whereas a person's ability to convey the intended message is referred to as **production** or **expressive language**.

Students with language disorders may have developmental delays in comprehension or receptive language. These students frequently ask for information to be repeated or clarified. In school these students may have difficulties with the following processes:

- following directions
- understanding the meaning of concepts (particularly technical or abstract concepts)
- seeing relationships among concepts (e.g., temporal, causal, conditional relationships)
- understanding humor and figurative language
- understanding multiple meanings
- understanding less common and irregular verb tenses
- understanding compound and complex sentences
- detecting breakdowns in comprehension

Students with production or expressive language difficulties generally communicate less frequently than their peers. These students may have difficulty doing the following:

- using correct grammar
- using compound and complex sentences
- thinking of the right word to convey the concept (word retrieval or word finding)
- discussing abstract concepts
- changing the communication style to fit different social contexts
- providing enough information to the listener (e.g., starting a conversation with "He took it to the fair," when *He* and *it* have not been previously identified)
- maintaining the topic during a conversation
- repairing communication when the listener doesn't understand

To help us think about language and language disorders, language has been divided into **content** (semantics), **form** (phonology, morphology, and syntax), and **use** (pragmatics) (Bloom & Lahey, 1978). It is the interaction of content, form, and use that creates language.

## Language Content

Semantics (content) refers to the ideas or concepts we are communicating, and the relationships among those concepts. When you teach content (as in social studies or science), you are teaching concepts and the labels for those concepts (vocabulary). For example, students often ask for the label for an idea (e.g., "What is that?" or "What are you doing?"), and they ask about what a word means (e.g., "What is a penguin?" or "What does freedom mean?"). By providing that information, we teach content.

Teaching content focuses on teaching vocabulary, word categories and relationships, multiple meanings, and figurative language. Gloria Huerra, a high-school social studies teacher, comments,

> Grouping words by categories and using relationship words (like *if . . . then* and *because*) are often difficult for students with language impairments or English language learners. It is also the multiple meanings of words and the figurative language that holds up their learning. I consistently highlight these in our discussions of social studies. One way that I highlight them is by writing them on the overhead projector and discussing them prior to reading. Then I cue the students to look for them when they read. We discuss them after reading by finding them in the text and reviewing their use.

In what ways might developmental delays in language be manifested? What aspects of communication are important in identifying students with possible language-learning disabilities?

**Vocabulary** As students develop language, their **vocabulary** and their ability to understand and talk about abstract concepts increase quickly. For example, children's speaking vocabulary when they enter school is estimated to be about 2,500 words (Owens, 1995). In comparison, when technical words are discounted, average adult speakers use about 10,000 words in everyday conversation, and an estimated 60,000 to 80,000 words are known and used by the average high-school graduate (Carroll, 1964). In comparison, students understand or comprehend even more words. Owens (1995) suggests that at age 6, students' comprehension vocabulary is between 20,000 and 24,000 words, increasing (by age 12) to more than 50,000 words. Even in math, vocabulary increases, with second-grade vocabulary focusing on such terms as *addition, estimation, subtraction,* and *regrouping* (in comparison to eighth-grade terms such as *absolute value, circumference, equation,* and *finite set*). School provides an important opportunity for children to expand their vocabularies.

**Word Categories and Word Relationships** During school-age years, students' ability to understand and organize abstract concepts increases significantly (McLaughlin, 1998; Owens, 1995). Students learn to group concepts by abstract features (such as animate and inanimate), spatial features, temporal relationships, or by function. For example, in learning about fossils, students learn to simultaneously classify different types of fossils (e.g., trilobites, crinoids, brachiopods) according to plant/animal, extinct/not extinct, and location (e.g., sea, fresh water, or land). By using **semantic feature analysis**, in which the categories or critical features are placed along one axis of a matrix and the specific vocabulary along the other axis, teachers can guide student discussion about the relationships among concepts and then visually represent those relationships (see Table 6.2). Relationships can be noted as positive, negative, or no relationship, or can be rated as to the degree of relationship along a scale. Instructional research shows a substantial increase

## TABLE 6.2

**Semantic Feature Analysis for a Chapter on Fossils**

### Relationship Chart

Key:
- + = positive relationship
- − = opposite or negative relationship
- o = no relationship
- ? = uncertain

| Important Words | Type of Life — Plant | Type of Life — Animal | Location — Sea | Location — Lakes | Location — Land | Extinct? — Extinct | Extinct? — Not Extinct |
|---|---|---|---|---|---|---|---|
| trilobites | | | | | | | |
| crinoids | | | | | | | |
| giant cats | | | | | | | |
| coral | | | | | | | |
| bryozoans | | | | | | | |
| guide fossils | | | | | | | |
| dinosaurs | | | | | | | |
| fresh water fish | | | | | | | |
| brachiopods | | | | | | | |
| small horses | | | | | | | |
| ferns | | | | | | | |
| enormous winged bugs | | | | | | | |
| trees | | | | | | | |

in the comprehension and learning of students with learning disabilities and language disorders when these kinds of feature analysis are incorporated into the teaching routine (Bos & Anders, 1990, 1992; Reyes & Bos, 1998).

Clearly, the ability to understand the relationships among concepts is important to successful learning. Types of relationships include the following categories:

- Comparative (taller than)
- Spatial (above, under)
- Temporal-Sequential (before, first)
- Causal (because, therefore)
- Conditional (if . . . then)
- Conjunctive (and)
- Disjunctive (either . . . or)
- Contrastive (but, although)
- Enabling (so that, in order that)

Teaching relationship vocabulary is important for students' understanding of content subjects such as science, social studies, and math.

**Multiple Meanings** Students also learn to deal with **multiple meanings** of words during school-age years (Menyuk, 1971; Nippold, 1998). For example, *bank* has several meanings and can function as both a noun and verb:

> Lou sat on the *bank* fishing.
> You can *bank* on him to be there.
> Put your money in the *bank* for now.

Students with communication disorders and other disabilities generally have more limited vocabularies, and their word meanings are generally more concrete and less specific than those of other students (Bishop & Adams, 1992; Gerber, 1993; Nelson, 1998). These students also have greater difficulty understanding multiple meanings and when to apply which meaning.

As Mary Armanti got to know Krista, a student with communication disorders in her third-grade class, she discovered that Krista's vocabulary was very limited. During sharing or small-group discussion, Krista used simple words and did not expand on her ideas (compared to the other students). Concerned about Krista's limited vocabulary, Mary worked with the speech and language pathologist to develop some classroom strategies to increase Krista's vocabulary. These strategies included Mary elaborating on what Krista said, that is, to model for Krista how to use a more complex, rich vocabulary. For example, when Krista volunteered, "The egg hatched," as she watched a bird nest outside the classroom window, Mary elaborated on her statement, "Yes, the bird's egg just hatched. The new bird is so tiny and fuzzy."

**Figurative Language** Another area of language content, **figurative language**, represents abstract concepts and usually requires an inferential rather than literal interpretation. Figurative language allows students to use language in truly creative ways (McLaughlin, 1998; Nippold, 1998; Owens, 1995). The primary types of figurative language include:

- *idioms* (It's raining cats and dogs.)
- *metaphors* (She watched him with an eagle eye.)
- *similes* (He ran like a frightened rabbit.)
- *proverbs* (The early bird catches the worm.)

Table 6.3 presents some common American English idioms.

Students with language disorders and other disabilities, and students from other cultures or for whom English is a second language, tend to have difficulty with figurative language. Yet figurative language, particularly idioms, prevails in the classroom. Classroom research shows that teachers use idioms in approximately 11 percent of what they say, and that approximately 7 percent of the sentences in third- to eighth-grade reading programs contain idioms (Lazar et al., 1989).

## Shoe

© Tribune Media Services. Inc. All rights reserved. Reprinted with permission.

## TABLE 6.3

**Common American English Idioms**

**Animals**
- a bull in a china shop
- as stubborn as a mule
- going to the dogs
- playing possum
- a fly in the ointment
- clinging like a leech
- grinning like a Cheshire cat

**Body Parts**
- on the tip of my tongue
- raised eyebrows
- turn the other cheek
- put your best foot forward
- turn heads

**Clothing**
- dressed to kill
- hot under the collar
- wear the pants in the family
- fit like a glove
- strait-laced

**Colors**
- gray area
- once in a blue moon
- tickled pink
- has a yellow streak
- red-letter day
- true blue

**Games and Sports**
- ace up my sleeve
- cards are stacked against me
- got lost in the shuffle
- keep your head above water
- paddle your own canoe
- ballpark figure
- get to first base
- keep the ball rolling
- on the rebound

**Foods**
- eat crow
- humble pie
- that takes the cake
- a finger in every pie
- in a jam

**Plants**
- heard it through the grapevine
- resting on his laurels
- shrinking violet
- no bed of roses
- shaking like a leaf
- withered on the vine

**Tools and Work**
- bury the hatchet
- has an axe to grind
- hit the nail on the head
- jockey for position
- throw a monkey wrench into it
- doctor the books
- has a screw loose
- hit the roof
- nursing his wounds
- sober as a judge

**Vehicles**
- fix your wagon
- like ships passing in the night
- on the wagon
- don't rock the boat
- missed the boat
- take a back seat

**Weather**
- calm before the storm
- haven't the foggiest
- steal her thunder
- come rain or shine
- right as rain
- throw caution to the wind

Reprinted with permission from Owens, Jr., R. E. (1995). *Language disorders: A functional approach to assessment and intervention* (2nd ed., p. 347). Boston: Allyn & Bacon. Compiled from Boatner, Gates, & Makkai (1975); Clark (1990); Gibbs (1987); Gulland & Hinds-Howell (1986); Kirkpatrick & Schwarz (1982); Palmatier & Ray (1989).

## Language Form

Difficulties with the form of language are usually quite noticeable to classroom teachers. Students not only have difficulty pronouncing certain sounds and using prefixes, suffixes, and endings on words, but they also use sentences that have poor word order and grammar. As mentioned earlier, form refers to the structure of the language and includes phonology, morphology, and syntax.

**Phonology** Phonology focuses on the sounds of language and the rules that determine how those sounds fit together. **Phonemes** are the smallest linguistic units of sound that can signal a meaning difference. In English there are approximately 45 phonemes or speech sounds, classified as either consonants or vowels. (The section on articulation disorders also includes information relevant to the development of phonemes.)

The ability to listen to and produce sounds is important not only for oral language but also for reading and writing (written language). As students learn to decode unknown words while reading and spell words as they write, one strategy they use is to "sound out the word" or "sound spell." Students who have difficulty generating rhyming words, segmenting words into their individual sounds, or producing individual sounds and then blending them together to make words often have difficulty using the "sound out, sound spell" strategy. These skills develop in the preschool and early elementary years as students experiment with sounds and sound patterns while they play with words and learn to read and write. These skills, referred to as **phonological awareness**, pertain to students' ability to understand that words contain sounds and that sounds can be used as linguistic building blocks to construct words (Mann, 1984). This difficulty with phonological awareness has been identified as the most common type of reading disability (Adams, 1990; Goswami & Bryant, 1990; Mann, 1984; Smith, 1998; Tangel & Blachman, 1995; Torgesen, 1997). Consequently, the ability to listen and produce sounds plays an important role in the development not only of oral language but also of written language.

> Different languages have different sounds. When sounds are not made in a student's first language, the student does not listen for or discriminate those sounds. One aspect of learning a second language is "retraining the ear" to listen for the sounds unique to that second language.

**Morphology** Whereas phonology focuses on sounds, morphology focuses on the rule system that governs the structure of words and word forms. And as phonemes are the smallest sound units, **morphemes** are the smallest units of language that convey meaning. There are two different kinds of morphemes: *root words*, or words that can stand alone (e.g., cat, run, pretty, small, inside), and *affixes* (prefixes, suffixes, and inflectional endings) that, added to words, change the meaning of the words (e.g., cat*s*, *re*run, small*est*, *trans*form*ation*).

Learning the different affixes and their meanings can help elementary and secondary students to decode words, spell words, and determine the meaning of words. For example, students who do not recognize or know the meaning of the word *predetermination* can break it into the root word *determine* (to decide), the prefix *pre* (before), and the suffix *tion* (denoting action in a noun). Then the students can decode the word and decide that the meaning of *predetermination* is "a decision made in advance."

Developmentally, inflectional endings are the easiest to learn, followed by suffixes, and then prefixes (Owens, 1995; Rubin, 1988). Although inflectional endings can be taught through conversation, suffixes and prefixes usually require more direct instruction in both oral and written form (Moats & Smith, 1992). The most frequently used prefixes in American English are *un-*, *in-*, *dis-*, and *non-*. You can use the common prefixes, suffixes, and inflectional endings presented in Table 6.4 as a guide for teaching morphology.

**Syntax** Syntax (sometimes referred to as *grammar*) focuses on the rules that govern the order of words in sentences. During the school-age years, students continue to grow in their ability to use more complex sentence structures (Scott, 1988). Even though most students understand and generate basic sentences by age 5 (McNeill, 1970; Nippold, 1998), first graders produce sentences that are neither completely grammatical (*He'll might go to jail*) nor reflect the syntactical complexities of the English language.

Some of the most difficult structures are complex sentences that express causation (*because*), conditionals (*if . . . then*), and enabling relationships (*so that*). Passive sentences (*The boy was chased by the*

## TABLE 6.4

**Common Prefixes, Suffixes, and Inflectional Endings**

| Derivational | | Inflectional |
|---|---|---|
| *Prefixes* | *Suffixes* | |
| a- (in, on, into, in a manner) | -able (ability, tendency, likelihood) | -ed (past) |
| bi- (twice, two) | -al (pertaining to, like, action, process) | -ing (at present) |
| de- (negative, descent, reversal) | -ance (action, state) | -s (plural) |
| ex- (out of, from, thoroughly) | -ation (denoting action in a noun) | -s (third person marker) |
| inter- (reciprocal, between, together) | -en (used to form verbs from adjectives) | -'s (possession) |
| mis- (ill, negative, wrong) | -ence (action, state) | |
| out- (extra, beyond, not) | -er (used as an agentive ending) | |
| over- (over) | -est (superlative) | |
| post- (behind, after) | -ful (full, tending) | |
| pre- (to, before) | -ible (ability, tendency, likelihood) | |
| pro- (in favor of) | -ish (belonging to) | |
| re- (again, backward motion) | -ism (doctrine, state, practice) | |
| semi- (half) | -ist (one who does something) | |
| super- (superior) | -ity (used for abstract nouns) | |
| trans- (across, beyond) | -ive (tendency or connection) | |
| tri- (three) | -ize (action, policy) | |
| un- (not, reversal) | -less (without) | |
| under- (under) | -ly (used to form adverbs) | |
| | -ment (action, product, means, state) | |
| | -ness (quality, state) | |
| | -or (used as an agentive ending) | |
| | -ous (full of, having, like) | |
| | -y (inclined to) | |

Reprinted with permission from Owens, Jr., R. E. (1995). *Language disorders: A functional approach to assessment and intervention* (2nd ed., p. A–62). Boston: Allyn & Bacon.

---

*girl*) also are developed later, often not until age seven. Students with language impairments, and English language learners, are often delayed in the development of syntax. In the case of students who are learning English as a second language, they may understand complex syntax, particularly if similar syntax is found in their first language, but may be uncomfortable producing it.

Regardless of the reason for the delay, one helpful strategy is to listen to the students' language and determine where they are in the developmental sequence. For example, Rebecca Blair, a third-grade teacher, noticed that several of her students with language-learning disabilities were not using the past participle during class discussions, on the playground, or during small-group discussions (*has/ have* + *verb*). She talked with Jean Gleason, the speech and language pathologist, who agreed that this would be a good skill to work on, since all three students were able to use simple past tense. To teach the skill directly, Rebecca worked with the three students as they wrote a language-experience story in which she controlled the use of verb tense by requiring them to use the past participle. The story follows:

> Once upon a time there was a very hungry boy named Jason. Jason decided that he would eat everything he could find in the refrigerator. All day long he has gone to the refrigerator and eaten whatever food he could find. By the end of the day,
>
> Jason has eaten 3 pickles.
> Jason has eaten 5 olives.
> Jason has eaten 8 slices of cheese.
> Jason has eaten 25 grapes.
> . . . . . . . . . . . .
> Now Jason has a stomach ache.

In discussing the story, Rebecca compared the simple past tense with the past participle and had the students think of other instances in which they could use the past participle. Rebecca had the students write other stories with similar formats, and Jean, at the same time, worked on the same skill with the students. Rebecca also gave each student a quick "thumbs up" whenever she heard them use the past participle. Within 3 months, the past participle became part of their everyday language.

As sentence complexity increases, so does the average length of the sentences. Table 6.5 shows the growth in the number of words per communication unit. From early elementary school to high school, students grow from an average of 7 words per communication unit to almost 12 words. During the early elementary grades, students also continue to increase in their ability to use irregular noun plurals (e.g., *mice, sheep, men*) and irregular verbs (see Table 6.6). In students with communication disorders and other disabilities, development of these irregular forms is often delayed by several years (Koziol, 1973; Nelson, 1998).

## Language Use

The area of most important linguistic growth during the school-age years is language use, or pragmatics (Owens, 1995; Reed, 1994). **Pragmatics** refers to the purposes or functions of communication, or how we use language to communicate (Roberts & Crais, 1989). During the school years, students become quite adept in using communication for a variety of functions. During later school years students use language proficiently including figurative language, sarcasm, jokes, and multiple meanings (Schultz, 1974). Students also learn to vary their communication style, or **register**, according to the listener's characteristics and knowledge of the topic. By the age of 13 students can switch from peer register to adult register (depending on the person with whom they are talking) and from formal register to an informal register, depending on the setting and circumstances (McKinley & Larson, 1991; Owens, 1996).

### TABLE 6.5

**Average Number of Words per Communication Unit**

| | Average Number of Words per Communication Unit (mean) | | |
|---|---|---|---|
| Grade | High Group | Random Group | Low Group |
| 1 | 7.91 | 6.88 | 5.91 |
| 2 | 8.10 | 7.56 | 6.65 |
| 3 | 8.38 | 7.62 | 7.08 |
| 4 | 9.28 | 9.00 | 7.55 |
| 5 | 9.59 | 8.82 | 7.90 |
| 6 | 10.32 | 9.82 | 8.57 |
| 7 | 11.14 | 9.75 | 9.01 |
| 8 | 11.59 | 10.71 | 9.52 |
| 9 | 11.73 | 10.96 | 9.26 |
| 10 | 12.34 | 10.68 | 9.41 |
| 11 | 13.00 | 11.17 | 10.18 |
| 12 | 12.84 | 11.70 | 10.65 |

Reprinted by permission of Loban, W. (1976). *Language development: Kindergarten through grade twelve* (p. 27), Res. Report #18. Urbana, IL: National Council of Teachers of English.

Young children use language for such functions as gaining and holding attention, obtaining and giving information, directing and following others, expressing feelings, and role playing (White, 1975). By

### TABLE 6.6

**Development of Irregular Verbs**

| Age in Years | Irregular Verbs |
|---|---|
| 3-0 to 3-5 | Hit, hurt |
| 3-6 to 3-11 | Went |
| 4-0 to 4-5 | Saw |
| 4-6 to 4-11 | Ate, gave |
| 5-0 to 5-5 | Broke, fell, found, took |
| 5-6 to 5-11 | Came, made, sat, threw |
| 6-0 to 6-5 | Bit, cut, drove, fed, flew, ran, wore, wrote |
| 6-6 to 6-11 | Blew, read, rode, shot |
| 7-0 to 7-5 | Drank |
| 7-6 to 7-11 | Drew, dug, hid, rang, slept, swam |
| 8-0 to 8-5 | Caught, hung, left, slid |
| 8-6 to 8-11 | Built, sent, shook |

Adapted from Shipley, K., Maddox, M., & Driver, J. (1991). Children's development of irregular past tense verb forms. *Language, Speech, and Hearing Services in Schools, 22,* 115–122.

adolescence, students demonstrate communication competence (Mobbs et al., 1993; Nippold, 1998; Owens, 1995; Wiig & Semel, 1984) in that they are able to do the following:

- express positive and negative feelings and reactions to others
- present, understand, and respond to information in spoken messages about persons, objects, events, or processes that are not immediately visible
- take the conversational partner's perspective
- comprehend the speaker's mood
- comprehend nonverbal communication
- understand and present complex messages
- adapt messages to the needs of others
- use clarification and repair in conversation
- based on prior experience, approach verbal interaction with expectations of what to say and how to say it
- relate a narrative cohesively and sequentially
- communicate a point of view logically
- select different forms of messages according to the age, status, and reactions of listeners
- use sarcasm, humor, and multiple meanings
- make deliberate use of figurative language

Language is used for many different communication activities. One activity that occurs frequently in school and in other settings is conversation.

To determine whether students are having difficulty with the use of language, you can assess their conversational skills. Take a few minutes to think about several students you know or with whom you are currently working. Think about how they use language to communicate in social contexts. Do they vary their communication style depending on the listener? Do they present enough information for the listener to understand the message? If the listener is not understanding, do they take action to clarify what they said? For students who do have difficulty with these areas, working on language use may be an appropriate goal.

## Metalinguistics

Students who use **metalinguistics** can think about, analyze, and reflect on language as an object in much the same way one can describe tables or friends (Hulit & Howard, 1997; Wallach & Miller, 1988). Metalinguistics also involves understanding that language is a code for representing sounds, words, and ideas. The Research Brief presents the results of developmental research on metalinguistics.

## Research Brief

### Development of Metalinguistic Abilities

Young children learn to use language without really understanding how it operates and functions. They use the linguistic rules that govern language, but if you asked them to tell you about or explain the rules, they would have great difficulty. As children mature, however, they become more sophisticated language learners. They develop *metalinguistics* skills, or the ability to talk about and reflect on language as if it were an object. Reed (1994) notes that metalinguistics involves talking about language, seeing it as an entity separate from its function. It is the ability to judge the correctness of language and to correct it. Wallach and Miller (1988) have arranged information on the development of metalinguistic skills to correspond in rough approximation to Piaget's stages of cognitive development (see Table 6.7).

It is evident from this table that during stage two (ages 2 to 6), children develop the metalinguistic skills critical for decoding words (when reading) and for learning to spell (when writing) (Kamhi, 1987; Nelson, 1998; Smith, 1998; Tangel & Blachman, 1995; van Kleeck, 1990). These skills include ascertaining word boundaries in spoken and printed sentences, rhyming, making sound substitutions, segmenting words into syllables and sounds, and blending syllables and sounds into words. Research consistently demonstrates the reciprocal relationship between early reading and writing and the development of these metalinguistic skills (e.g., Blachman, 1989; Bradley & Bryant, 1985; Kamhi & Catts, 1989).

What competencies in the pragmatics of language do these students probably possess? How does the way children typically use language change as they mature into adolescence?

## FoxTrot by Bill Amend

FOXTROT © 1995 Bill Amend. Reprinted with permission of Universal Press Syndicate. All rights reserved.

## TABLE 6.7

### Stages of Children's Metalinguistic Development

*Stage One (Ages 1½ to 2):*
- Distinguishes print from nonprint
- Knows how to interact with books: right side up, page turning from left to right
- Recognizes some printed symbols, e.g., TV character's name, brand names, signs

*Stage Two (Ages 2 to 5½ or 6):*
- Ascertains word boundaries in spoken sentences
- Ascertains word boundaries in printed sequences
- Engages in word substitution play
- Plays with the sounds of language
- Begins to talk about language parts and about talking (speech acts)
- Corrects own speech/language to help the listener understand the message (spontaneously or in response to listener request)
- Self-monitors own speech and makes changes to more closely approximate the adult model; phonological first; lexical and semantic speech style last
- Believes that a word is an integral part of the object to which it refers (word realism)
- Able to separate words into syllables
- Inability to consider that one word could have two different meanings

*Stage Three (Ages 6 to 10):*
- Begins to take listener perspective and use language form to match
- Understands verbal humor involving linguistic ambiguity, e.g., riddles
- Able to resolve ambiguity: lexical first, as in homophones; deep structures next, as in ambiguous phrases ("Will you join me in a bowl of soup?"); phonological or morphemic next (Q: "What do you have if you put three ducks in a box?" A: "A box of quackers.")
- Able to understand that words can have two meanings, one literal and the other nonconventional or idiomatic, e.g., adjectives used to describe personality characteristics such as *hard, sweet, bitter*
- Able to resequence language elements, as in pig Latin
- Able to segment syllables into phonemes
- Finds it difficult to appreciate figurative forms other than idioms

*Stage Four (Ages 10+):*
- Able to extend language meaning into hypothetical realms, e.g., to understand figurative language such as metaphors, similes, parodies, analogies, etc.
- Able to manipulate various speech styles to fit a variety of contexts and listeners

Reprinted with permission from Wallach, G. P., & Miller, L. (1988). *Language intervention and academic success* (p. 33). San Diego: College Hill.

As a teacher, you will want to talk about language, how it works, and the rules that govern language. Playing word games such as the ones suggested in the 60-Second Lesson is one way to build this type of language learning into those free moments during the day.

## Prevalence of Communication Disorders

Approximately 7 to 10 percent of school-age children receive services for communicative disorders, but only 2 to 3 percent of these children have a primary

# MAKING A DIFFERENCE
## The 60-Second Lesson

*Promoting Language through Word Games*

Often teachers find themselves before or just after a transition with several minutes that need to be filled. Playing word games is a great way to fill the time and to promote language and metalinguistic skills. Listed here are several word games you and your students can play. You may want to make lists based on the words you generate from these games and post them for student reference.

### For Younger Students

*Rhyming Words:* Select a word. Use a word from a word family (e.g., -at, -ight, -an, -end) to provide lots of opportunities for rhyming. Or have a student select a word. Then have the other students give rhyming words. You may want to write the words so that students can see the similarities between words. If you want students to select the words, put each word on a slip of paper and place them in a container such as a hat or jar, then have students draw words from the container.

*Sound Substitutions:* Select a word (e.g., hat). (Again—use of word-family words helps.) Say the word and write it on the board. Then ask students what word will be made if the first sound (e.g., /h/) is changed to another sound (e.g., /b/).

*Syllables:* Have a student select a word and say it. Then repeat the word slowly and have the students clap once for each syllable in the word.

*Opposites:* Select pairs of simple word opposites (e.g., hot/cold, easy/hard, big/little, happy/sad). Say one word from each pair and have students say the opposite.

### For Older Students

*Antonyms:* Select pairs of word opposites (e.g., cool/warm, hard/soft, cruel/gentle, empty/full, tame/wild). Write one word from the pair on a card and put it in a container. Have a student draw a card, say the word, and have other students say or write the opposite word.

*Synonyms:* Select a word with several synonyms (e.g., eat, pretty, pants, laugh). Say one word and have students name as many synonyms as they can.

*Homonyms:* Select a word with at least one homonym (e.g., fare, sale, male). Say and spell one word and have students give the homonyms.

*Multiple Meanings:* Select a word that has several meanings, write it on the board, and have students give examples of sentences that use the different meanings of the word (e.g., I have a **run** in my stocking. Let's go for a **run**. In the long **run,** it isn't very important. I have to **run** and pick up a sandwich.)

*Suffixes:* Select a suffix (e.g., -tion). Discuss its meaning, and then have students provide examples of words that use this suffix (e.g., determination, nomination, participation). Have students also tell what the root word is. (You can play the same game with prefixes.)

---

disability of communication disorders (United States Bureau of the Census, 1993). Why is this the case? Many school-age children who receive services from a speech or language pathologist have another disability that is considered the primary disability (e.g., learning disabilities, mental retardation, hearing impairment, severe or multiple disabilities). For example, nearly 50 percent of children with mild retardation have some type of communication disorder (National Institute of Neurological Disorders and Stroke, 1988). Of school-age children with communication disorders, most have difficulties in the areas of language and articulation. In comparison, only 4 percent of students with communication disorders have voice disorders, and only 2 percent have fluency disorders (stuttering) (Leske, 1981). Over

85 percent of the students with communication disorders are mainstreamed into general education classes (United States Department of Education, 1994).

> Over 85 percent of students with communication disorders spend most of the school day in general education classes.

Within this population, communication disorders occur 3 to 4 times more often in boys than girls (National Advisory Neurological Disorders and Stroke Council, 1990). Recall that speech sounds develop later in boys than girls (refer to Table 6.1). This trend is evident in most aspects of communication, including the development of language, and may be responsible for the higher identification of boys than girls.

A greater percentage of preschool-age children than school-age children are identified with communication disorders as their primary disability (approximately 10 to 15 percent of the population, or 70 percent of preschoolers with disabilities) (ASHA's Committee on Prevention of Speech, Language, and Hearing Problems, 1984; National Institute of Neurological Disorders and Stroke, 1988). Children identified as having communication disorders at the preschool age are often classified as having learning disabilities as they move into elementary school and experience academic difficulties (Kelly, 1998; Mallory & Kerns, 1988).

> Evaluation of students for possible language delays or disorders often includes collecting a language sample. Sampling involves tape recording students as they interact, then analyzing the students' utterances for characteristics such as mean length of utterance, types of utterances, vocabulary, topic maintenance, and turn taking.

## Identification and Assessment of Students with Communication Disorders

Most students with communication disorders are identified in preschool or during the early elementary grades. If a communication disorder is suspected, it will be important for the student to have a hearing screening and to determine if there is a history of chronic ear infections. One role that general education teachers play is that of observer and listener for students who may have significant difficulty communicating. Particularly in the elementary grades, the classroom teacher spends more time with the students than any other individual in school.

When Sharon Kutok, a speech and language pathologist, spoke about what teachers should watch, she commented, "Classroom teachers are good at identifying students with language disabilities. When identifying students with receptive language problems, typical teacher comments are, 'When these students are listening to a presentation they look away and don't focus. When I ask a question, they don't seem to know what is going on. I don't know if the students don't understand me or if they can't answer my question.'"

For expressive language difficulties, Sharon noted that, "Classroom teachers indicate that these students give answers that have no relationship to the question. They use short sentences or just words, and sometimes the words are out of order. Those are the kinds of symptoms that teachers notice when identifying students with language difficulties."

As a classroom teacher, you have the opportunity to observe students using language in the classroom (during both academic and social activities), as well as on the playground, and during other activities such as art, music, and physical education. What should you look for in the area of language? Tips for Teachers 6.1 presents questions you can ask about your students to determine the possibility of difficulties with language. The questions are grouped according to the three areas of language: form, content, and use. If a language delay is evident, then you should consider making a referral to the speech and language pathologist.

If students are English language learners, or if their first dialects are other than Standard English, consult with a speech and language pathologist and a bilingual education or ESL teacher when observing students for language differences associated with second language/dialect acquisition or possible language difficulties. (See Chapter 10 for additional information.)

## Instructional Guidelines and Accommodations for Students with Communication Disorders

Most students with communication disorders are educated in general education classrooms. Although these students may work (individually or in small groups) with a speech and language pathologist several times a week for 30 minutes or so, they spend the rest of their school days with the classroom teacher and students. Consequently, students with communication disorders have many more opportunities to develop effective communication in the classroom than in the limited time spent with the speech and language pathologist. You, the classroom teacher, play a major role in facilitating the development of effective communication for these students.

Speech and language pathologists are one of your best resources for ideas facilitating speech and language development. As more schools adopt inclusion policies, speech and language pathologists are more frequently teaming with classroom teachers. Two major benefits of these teams are that you and the SLP have more opportunities to learn from each other, and students other than those identified as having communication disorders profit from the communication activities (Haynes et al., 1990).

## Facilitating Speech Development

Generally, specific remediation of articulation errors, voice disorders, and stuttering is provided by the speech and language pathologist. The major goal of the general education teacher is to provide opportunities for the student to communicate in the classroom using the most natural, nonthreatening situations possible (LaBlance et al., 1994). If students are to generalize what they are learning in therapy, you will also need to work with the SLP to get specific information on the skills students are targeting and to discuss strategies you can use to help them generalize those skills. One such strategy is to develop a personal cueing system for students who have difficulty responding in a large group. Robert Encino, a seventh-grade science teacher, explains how he developed such a system with Kim.

# TIPS FOR TEACHERS

### 6.1 Identifying a Student with Possible Language Disorders

Language Form
- Does the student mispronounce sounds or words and omit endings?
- Does the student comprehend and produce types of sentences similar to those of other students in the classroom?
- Is the student's language as elaborate and descriptive as that of other students in the classroom?
- Are the student's comprehension and production of grammatical rules similar to those of other students in the classroom?

Language Content
- Does the student comprehend and produce vocabulary as rich and varied as that of other students in the classroom?
- Does the student comprehend others' ideas and express his or her ideas as effectively as other students in the classroom?
- When talking, does the student have significant difficulty finding the word he or she wants to use (i.e., word-finding difficulties)?
- Does the student comprehend and use figurative language and multiple meanings of words similar to that of other students in the classroom?

Language Use
- Does the student use language for different purposes, including: to gain attention, ask for and tell about information, express and respond to feelings, use imagination to understand and tell stories and jokes, express opinions and persuade, and for greetings, introductions, and farewells?
- Does the student take turns appropriately in conversations?
- Does the student initiate conversations?
- Does the student maintain topic during a conversation?
- Does the student have more than one style of interacting, depending upon the listener, situation, and topic?
- Does the student recognize when the listener is not understanding, and act to clarify communication for the listener?

Kim was a student in my fifth period who stutters. I was aware that she often knew an answer and wanted to share her knowledge, but I was unsure of when she felt confident enough to do so. I met with Kim one day during planning period, and we agreed on a system where she would open her hand, palm-side up on her desk if she wanted to respond. What I found was that this reduced her anxiety, and during the semester her hand was open more and more frequently. Eventually, we discontinued the system because she felt that she didn't need it any longer.

It is also important for students with speech disorders that the classroom be a safe environment in which to practice oral communication. Tips for Teachers 6.2 provides some strategies for helping promote a classroom community that accepts and encourages meaningful student communication.

Some students with physical disabilities and other severe disabilities cannot communicate effectively through speech, gestures, or writing. **Augmentative communication** systems attempt to compensate for, temporarily or permanently, the impairment and disability patterns of individuals with severe expressive and receptive language disorders (ASHA, 1993). Augmentative communication is a means for students with limited or no speech to join the classroom community. Tech Talk describes different types of augmentative communication.

## Facilitating Language Development

Opportunities for teaching oral language abound during general education classroom activities—whether they occur in the classroom itself or on the playground, during field trips, or in the lunch room. It is also in these settings that language becomes more natural and purposeful than is the case in the therapy setting.

As a classroom teacher, you are constantly teaching oral language. When you teach students new concepts and vocabulary in content area subjects, you are teaching oral language. When students learn how to give oral reports or retell a story, how to introduce themselves, or how to use irregular verbs, they are developing language skills. What are some general guidelines you can use to facilitate language devel-

## TIPS FOR TEACHERS

### 6.2 Creating an Accepting Classroom Community for Students with Speech Disorders

- Create an atmosphere of ease and comfortable pacing. Avoid an atmosphere that creates time pressures and tensions.
- Listen in a calm and thoughtful manner to what students have to say. Allow time for students to finish their thoughts. Don't disregard ideas just because students have difficulty expressing them.
- Do not criticize or point out speech errors. You may, however, demonstrate correct speech by correctly repeating what the students said.
- Classroom rules should not allow for ridicule of students or their speech errors.
- Take care not to place students with speech problems in situations in which their communication difficulties might interfere or are highlighted.
- Use flexible grouping so that students have opportunities to talk in small groups and with a partner.
- Allow time for students to respond. Students often need time to get their ideas organized and to plan their communication. Speech may be labored and slow.
- Develop cueing systems in which students can let you know when they are comfortable responding.
- Reading aloud in a slow, easy manner can be a good opportunity for students to practice fluency strategies or new sounds they are learning. Students become more fluent with multiple readings, so the use of repeated reading may be beneficial.
- Avoid competition among students, particularly when it highlights oral communication.

# TECH TALK

## Augmentative Communication

*Augmentative communication* is used to supplement the communication skills of persons for whom speech is not possible or is unintelligible (Lewis, 1993). There is a long history of the use of alternative means of communicating. Suddath and Susnik (1991) suggest such traditional methods as "multiple choice questions, eye blinks, gestures, sign language, communication boards, communication books, alphabet boards, and even primitive Morse Code Systems" (p. i).

What has changed the type of augmentative communication in the recent past is the availability of the computer and voice synthesizers. One approach focuses on the method the individual uses to make choices—by scanning or by direct selection. Other approaches focus on unaided or low technology devices, such as communication boards, alphabet boards, and communication books. In contrast to low technology devices, high-technology devices require external devices, such as voice output or a speech synthesizer with a large vocabulary, multiple input modes, and a built-in printer. For example, the Liberator by the Prentke Romich Company (800-262-1990) allows for input through direct selection and one of several scanning modes. Output is through a printer, the eight-line LCD display, or a speech synthesizer. Another system, the DeltaTalker, has both prerecorded speech and a speech synthesizer. This communication device also has a menu-type computer touch screen. Pegasus LITE by Words+ (800-869-8521) is a talking screen for Windows and features all the latest developments in high-tech augmentative communication systems.

Lewis (1993) suggests considering the following questions when making decisions about high technology communication devices:

- What type of speech output does the device offer? Is the speech intelligible? Is it appropriate for the student in terms of age and gender?
- Are other types of output provided?
- What input modes are available to the student? Direct selection? Scanning? What physical abilities does the student need to operate the device?
- How are message choices presented to the user? Does the student see letters, words, graphics, or a combination of these?

A child using a low-tech communication board

A student is shown using the Pegasus LITE by Words+. The talking screen for Windows features the latest technology in augmentative communication.

- How much vocabulary can be stored in the device? Are there strategies for increasing the quantity of vocabulary? For increasing the user's speech in selecting vocabulary?
- How easy is the device for the student to use in communication situations? Can the student (or a teacher or parent) change or add messages easily?
- Is the device portable and durable enough to withstand daily use?
- Is the communication device compatible with other technologies that the student uses, such as computers and environmental control units?
- What is the cost of the device? (page 393).

opment in your classroom? Bos and Vaughn (1998) suggest the following guidelines to help shape your instruction:

- Teach language in purposeful contexts.
- Teach comprehension (receptive language) and production (expressive language).
- Use effective teaching strategies when presenting a new concept.
- Help students see the connections or relationships among concepts.
- Use conversation as the major milieu for teaching rather than questions or drill and practice.
- Give students enough time to respond.
- Adjust the pace, chunk information, and check for understanding.
- Use self-talk to explain what you are doing or thinking.
- Use parallel talk to describe what others are doing.
- Use modeling to help students get practice and feedback on a specific language skill.
- Use expansion and elaboration to demonstrate how an idea can be expressed in a more complex or mature manner, and provide more information.
- Use language as an intrinsic motivator.

Specific ideas for using these guidelines are presented in the following section.

**Teaching Language in Purposive Contexts** Whether you are teaching students causal relationships such as the effect of heat on water, or how to request information by telephone, it is important to teach language in the context of meaningful activities. It is difficult to imagine teaching someone how to use a screwdriver or a needle and thread without having the tools at hand, demonstrating how to use them, and then letting students practice. The same is true for language. Hence, when you cannot create a "real" situation, use such techniques as simulations and role-play to create authentic learning experiences. Tips for Teachers 6.3 explains how to use barrier games to teach language.

# TIPS FOR TEACHERS

### 6.3 Using Barrier Games to Promote Language

It is not always possible to create authentic learning environments when you teach language, but we know that the best, quickest way to learn language is when it is purposeful and taught in context. One way to promote purposeful language and to help students build their comprehension and production of descriptive language, particularly locative prepositions, is to use barrier games. These games (frequently used by speech and language pathologists to teach prepositions) can be a great activity for the entire class or used as a filler activity after students complete their work.

*The Game:* Students work in pairs, with a barrier placed between them so that they cannot see each other's work. The materials usually consist of blocks for building or paper and colors for making a picture. The lead student builds a simple structure or colors a simple design or picture. Then the lead student describes to the second student how to make what he or she has built or drawn. The second student is encouraged to ask questions when the directions are unclear. After the second student has finished his or her project, the barrier is removed, the two projects are compared, and differences discussed. Then the roles are reversed. Students can keep track of the number of projects they make accurately.

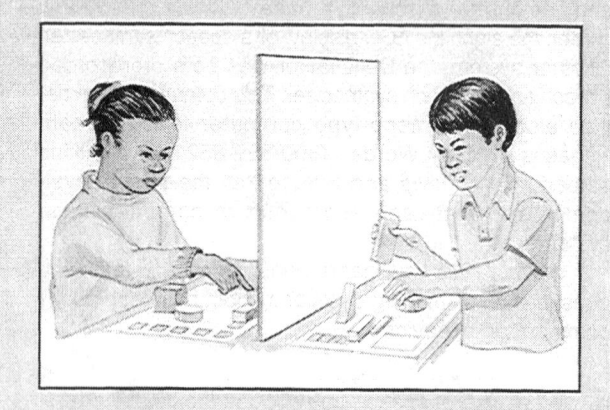

If you use competition, do not have the students in one pair compete against each other. Instead, have one team compete against another team. Also, this should not be a timed task, because the goal is to promote the use of descriptive language.

***Teaching Comprehension and Production*** Give students opportunities to develop both their understanding (comprehension) and their ability to express (production) the new structures (form), vocabulary (content), and ways of using language (use) that they are learning. When teaching the vocabulary associated with a new unit, for example, provide students with opportunities not only to listen to explanations but also to discuss their knowledge of the vocabulary and to use the new terms in their discussion and writing. The pause procedure provides these opportunities (Di Vesta & Smith, 1979; Ruhl et al., 1990). Using this procedure, the teacher pauses at logical breaks in the lecture or discussion, and the students discuss what they are learning (with a partner or in a small group) and review their notes.

***Presenting New Concepts*** Critical to learning new content or concepts is the use of effective teaching strategies. As you may recall from the earlier discussion of vocabulary development, students' knowledge of concepts grows exponentially during the school-age years. By using effective teaching strategies (see Tips for Teachers 6.4), you help students with language impairments and English language learners to gain the concepts and content necessary for success in content-area classes.

***Demonstrating Connections among Concepts*** One important way we learn about concepts is by understanding the relationships or connections between concepts. If you listen to a conversation in which a new idea is being explained, you'll undoubtedly hear statements such as, "It's like . . . ," or "You can compare it to . . ." or "It's like . . . except that . . ." or "It's almost the opposite of . . . ." These phrases all help students understand and see the connections among concepts. Because students with language problems have difficulty making those connections, it is important that you highlight them as you and the students discuss new concepts. For example, when Peggy, a first-grade teacher, was introducing the concept of *squirm* because it was important for understanding the book her students were to discuss and read, she asked the students, "What does squirm mean?" "Show me with your body how you can squirm."

## TIPS FOR TEACHERS

### 6.4 Presenting New Language Concepts or Content

When teaching new language concepts or patterns, keep the following strategies in mind:

- Gear the activities to the students' interests and cognitive level.
- Get the students' attention before engaging in communication activities.
- Bombard the student with the concept or skill frequently throughout the day in a functional manner.
- When speaking, place stress on the target concept or language pattern.
- Pause between phrases or sentences so that the student has time to process the new concept or language pattern.
- Decrease the rate of presentation when first introducing the concept or language pattern.
- When introducing a new concept or language pattern, use familiar, concrete vocabulary and simple sentence patterns (Bloom, Miller, and Hood, 1975; Reed, 1994).
- If possible, present the new concept or language pattern by using more than one input mode (e.g., auditory, visual, kinesthetic). Gestures and facial expressions that are paired with a specific language pattern often assist students in understanding the form. For example, giving a look of puzzlement or wonder when asking a question can serve as a cue to the students.
- Pair written symbols with oral language. For instance, demonstrating morphological endings such as *s* (plurals) and *ed* (past tense) can be done in writing. The students can then be cued to listen for what they see.

Reprinted with permission from Bos, C. S., & Vaughn, S. (1998). *Strategies for teaching students with learning and behavior problems* (4th ed., p.89). Boston: Allyn & Bacon.

"What other things can squirm?" "Now that we know what squirm is, what other words mean something similar to squirm?" "Is squirm similar to wiggle?" "What would be the opposite of squirm? If you weren't squirming, you would be ____."

At more advanced levels, when students make comparisons among books written by the same author, when they compare the relationships between addition and multiplication versus subtraction and division, and when they compare the similarities between the Korean and Vietnam Wars, the emphasis is on making connections. These kinds of discussions help students see the relationships among concepts and better understand semantic relationships (such as contrastives, comparatives, causals, conditionals). The use of feature analysis (refer to Table 6.2) and other graphic organizers (see Chapter 16) can help students see the relationships.

**Using Conversation** As students with language impairments work, think, and play in your classroom, you need to create opportunities for them to engage in conversations with you and with other students. One way to do this is to use discussion groups rather than a question–answer format for reviews of books and current events. Nancy Meyers, the speech and language pathologist who works with Lorri Johnson, chose to work in Lorri's classroom while the literature groups meet. Once a week she joins Samatha's literature group. As she listens and joins in the conversation about the book being discussed, Nancy has the opportunity to model language patterns on which Samatha is working.

At least several times a week, engage students in conversations. (This may take some forethought and effort on your part, for observational research has shown that classroom teachers, in general, are not as responsive to students with language impairments as they are to average and high-achieving students [Pecyna-Rhyner et al., 1990]). Let the students direct the topics of these conversations, which need not be long and, in secondary settings, can be accomplished as students enter the room. Tips for Teachers 6.5 provides more ideas for promoting language through conversations. Use these ideas and share them with parents.

## TIPS FOR TEACHERS

### 6.5 Promoting Language through Conversations

- Talk about things in which the child is interested.
- Follow the child's lead. Reply to the child's initiations and comments. Share his/her excitement.
- Don't ask too many questions. If you must, use questions such as how *did/do . . ., why did/do . . ., and what happened . . .* that result in longer explanatory answers.
- Encourage the child to ask questions. Respond openly and honestly. If you don't want to answer a question, say so and explain why. *(I don't think I want to answer that question; it's very personal.)*
- Use a pleasant tone of voice. You need not be a comedian, but you can be light and humorous. Children love it when adults are a little silly.
- Don't be judgmental or make fun of a child's language. If you are overly critical of the child's language or try to catch and correct all errors, he/she will stop talking to you.
- Allow enough time for the child to respond.
- Treat the child with courtesy by not interrupting when he/she is talking.
- Include the child in family and classroom discussions. Encourage participation and listen to his/her ideas.
- Be accepting of the child and of the child's language. Hugs and acceptance can go a long way.
- Provide opportunities for the child to use language and to have that language work for him/her to accomplish his/her goals.

Reprinted with permission from Owens, Jr., R. E. (1995). *Language disorders: A functional approach to assessment and intervention* (2nd ed., p. 416). Boston: Allyn & Bacon.

**Using Wait Time** When speech and language pathologist, Sharon Kutok, talks about the most important principles in teaching students with language impairments, the first one she mentions is **wait time**. "For some students, waiting is important. Wait time gives students the opportunity to understand what has been said and to construct a response. These students may have particular difficulty with form (e.g., syntax), and need the extra time to think about the form they should use in constructing their response."

> Students with word-retrieval problems may use circumlocutions (talking around the word) when they are having difficulty retrieving a word, as in "It's the thing, you know, the thing you write on" (Owens, 1995).

Students who have difficulty with content may have difficulty also with **word retrieval** or word finding (German, 1992). A word retrieval problem is like having the word on the tip of your tongue but not being able to think of it. Two examples demonstrate how difficulty with word retrieval can affect the flow of communication. The first conversation (about making an Easter basket) is a dialogue between two third graders—one with typical language and the other with word-retrieval problems (Bos & Vaughn, 1998).

> Susan: Are you going to make, uh, make, us . . . one of these things (pointing to the Easter basket on the bookshelf)?
> Cori: Oh, you mean an Easter basket?
> Susan: Yeh, an Easter basket.
> Cori: Sure, I'd like to, but I'm not sure how to do it. Can you help me?
> Susan: Yeah, first you need some, uh, some, uh . . . the things you cut with, you know. . .
> Cori: Scissors.
> Susan: Yeah, and some paper and . . . uh, the thing you use to stick things together with.
> Cori: Tape?
> Susan: No, uh, uh, . . . sticky stuff.
> Cori: Oh, well let's get the stuff we need.
> Susan: Let's go, to, uh, uh, the shelf, uh, where you get, you know, the stuff to cut with.
> Cori: Yeh, the paper, and let's also get the glue (p. 82).

In the second example, an adolescent explains how to fix a tire:

> "Well . . . to fix a tire . . . or your wheel . . . you gotta take the tire off . . . you gotta lift up . . . you jack up the car and use this thing . . . it's square metal wrench . . . to loosen the bolts . . . you know the nuts . . . then you take the wheel off the axes. First you ask the guy at the garage if he will fix the tire. You lock up the car so it won't . . . you put the car in gear so it stays put" (Chappell, 1985, p. 226).

It is clear from these two examples that wait time is important for students with word-retrieval problems. In addition to increasing wait time, strategies that teachers can use during classroom discussions include:

- using multiple-choice formats so that students need only recognize one word in a group, rather than generate the word
- providing a cue, such as the initial sound or syllable, the category name or function, a synonym or description, or a gesture demonstrating the word
- restating a question so that it requires a yes or no response rather than an open-ended answer (German, 1993)

By teaching students with word-finding problems to categorize words, make visual images of words, learn synonyms, and make word associations (e.g., bread/butter; plane/fly), you can help them recall words, thereby increasing the accuracy and fluency of their expressive language (Gerber, 1993; German, 1993; McGregor & Leanard, 1995).

**Adjusting the Pace** Students with language delays and other disabilities, and English language learners, often have difficulty comprehending what is being said during class, particularly in content-area classes. Teachers need to adjust the pace so that these students have time to process language input. The flow of instruction does not have to suffer, but when you discuss new or difficult concepts or ideas, slow the pace and highlight key ideas by writing them on the board or overhead projector and repeating them.

Reducing the amount of information in each segment is helpful also. For example, Bob Stern, a high-school science teacher, used to introduce the terms for a new science chapter by writing them on the board and discussing them as a group when he introduced the chapter. After Bob noticed that his students with language problems listened to the first five words and recorded three of them in their science notebooks, he decided to chunk the words into groups of three to five, introducing them when they were needed.

Checking for understanding is also important for facilitating language development in classroom settings. Teachers generally identify a group of several students by whom to gauge the pace of instruction and the decision as to when to move on. Make sure that your group includes the students with language problems.

**Using Self-Talk and Parallel Talk** Students, particularly young students with language delays, need to hear language that is connected to activities. In **self-talk**, teachers describe what they are doing or thinking; in **parallel talk**, teachers describe what students are doing or thinking. As you and the students work or play, describe what everyone is doing. Maria Ferraro, a first-grade teacher who works in an inner-city school, regularly uses parallel and self-talk when she joins students at the different centers in her classroom.

> When I join a center, I try to sit down and join in the activities rather than asking students questions. My goal is to become part of the group. As I join in the activity, I describe what I am doing and what other students in the group are doing. For example, I might say, "José is making a clay animal. It's blue and right now he is putting a ferocious snarl on the animal's face. I wonder what kind of animal it is? I think I'll ask José." In this way, the students get to hear how words can describe what someone is doing, and it focuses the attention on José and the ongoing activities.

**Using Modeling** Modeling plays an important role in the process of learning language. Whether students are learning a new sentence structure, new vocabulary, or a new function or use for language, modeling is a powerful tool. For example, Sharon Kutok and Armando Rivera, the speech and language pathologist and the eighth-grade English teacher at Vail Middle School, decided to improve their students' conversational skills during literature groups. Both Armando and Sharon were concerned about the number of students who did not clarify what they were saying when other students clearly did not understand (but did not request clarification).

To teach clarification skills, Armando and Sharon began discussing clarifying conversations. During their discussion they role-played, first as students who could not effectively clarify what they were saying, then as students who clarified effectively. They exaggerated the examples, and the students seemed to really enjoy their modeling. Next, Armando and Sharon joined the literature groups and continued to model as they participated in discussions. At the end of the period, they asked students to summarize what they had learned, and whether they thought they could become more effective at clarifying what they said and asking others to clarify if they did not understand. During the next 2 weeks, Armando had the students in each literature group rate the group's effectiveness in clarification. When Sharon returned in 2 weeks, both teachers observed a difference in the students' discussions, particularly in their ability to clarify ideas and ask for clarification. The students also thought that their skills had improved. In discussing the change, both teachers and students agreed that the modeling Armando and Sharon had done on the first day was an important key to their learning. Peer modeling, discussed in Chapter 2, can also be a powerful tool.

**Promoting Language through Expansion and Elaboration** Language **expansion** is a technique used to facilitate the development of complex language form and content. By repeating what students say, but in a slightly more complex manner, the teacher demonstrates how their thoughts can be more fully expressed. For example, Susie Lee, a first-grade teacher, is working to get Rob to use adverbs to describe his actions. As he finished several math problems, Rob reported, "I got the first one easy. The second one was hard." Susie replied, "Oh, you got the first one *easily*. The second one was hard." Note that you do not want to imply that you are correcting the student, but simply showing him or her a more complex way of expressing the thought. Note also that you should expand only one of two elements at a time. Otherwise, the expansion will be too complex for the student to profit from it.

You can use language **elaboration** to build upon the content of the student's language and provide additional information on the topic. For example, Chris, a fourth-grade student with language disabilities, was explaining that snakes have rough skin. Teacher Peggy Anderson elaborated on Chris's idea by commenting, "Yes, and snakes have smooth skin on their bellies and so do lizards. Are there other animals in the desert that have smooth skin on their bellies?"

**Using Language as an Intrinsic Motivator** Language is a powerful enabling tool and carries a great deal of intrinsic motivation for students. Rather than using praise (e.g., "I like the way you said that" or "Good talking"), you can capitalize on the naturally reinforcing nature of language. During a cooking activity, for example, teacher Jon Warner asked students, "How can we figure out how much two-thirds of a cup plus three-fourths of a cup of flour is?" After Lydia explained, Jon said, "Now we know how to figure that out. Shall we give it a try?" Later, Jon asked how to sift flour. After Randa explained, Jon said, "I've got it, how about the rest of you? Do you think you can sift the flour just the way Randa explained to us?" Instead of commenting on how "good" their language was and disrupting the flow of communication, Jon complimented Lydia and Randa by letting them know how useful the information was.

These students are working in a cooperative learning group. Which instructional accommodations described in this chapter might the teacher use for her students who have communication difficulties?

When students' purposes and intents are fulfilled because of their language, their language is naturally reinforcing, and students learn that language is a powerful tool for controlling the environment (Bos & Vaughn, 1998; Nelson, 1998; Owens, 1995).

## SUMMARY

- Communication is a powerful tool in school and society. For example, we communicate to develop and maintain relationships, to gain and give information, to express feelings, and to control others and the environment.
- Communication disorders include speech, language, and hearing disorders. Speech disorders involve difficulties with articulation, fluency, and voice. Language disorders involve difficulties with content (semantics), form (phonology, morphology, and syntax), and use (pragmatics). Hearing disorders are discussed in Chapter 9.
- Language can be divided into comprehension (receptive language) and production (expressive language).
- Although most basic language skills develop before children enter school, language continues to evolve through the school-age years, a process that includes a large growth in vocabulary, more complex sentence structures, use of prefixes, suffixes, multiple meanings, figurative language, complex semantic relationships (e.g., causal, conditions, enabling), and more sophisticated uses of language (e.g., adjustments to the register of communication, use of sarcasm and humor).
- Approximately 7 to 10 percent of school-age children are identified as having communication disorders, but only 2 to 3 percent have communication disorders as their primary disability. Approximately 10 to 15 percent of the preschool population is identified as having communication disorders.
- An important role classroom teachers play is to identify students who may have speech and language impairments.

- For students with speech disorders, the classroom teacher's role is to create a nonthreatening environment in which students can communicate.
- Classroom teachers play an important role in facilitating the development of language. The classroom is an ideal setting to use such language techniques as self and parallel talk, expansion and elaboration, modeling, and conversations. It is also important to adjust the pace and wait time.

## Key Terms and Concepts

articulation disorders
augmentative communication
African American Vernacular English
communication disorders
comprehension
content
elaboration
expansion
expressive language
figurative language
fluency disorders
form

language disorders
language use
metalinguistics
modeling
morphemes
morphology
multiple meanings
parallel talk
phonemes
phonological awareness
phonology
pragmatics
production

receptive language
register
self-talk
semantic feature analysis
semantics
speech disorders
stuttering
syntax
use
vocabulary
voice disorders
wait time
word retrieval

## Think and Apply

1. Now that you have read Chapter 6, review Lorri's experiences in working with Samatha. If you could talk to Lorri, what other questions would you ask her? List any questions or concerns you have now about teaching students with communication disorders. Discuss your questions with your fellow students, your instructor, and a speech and language pathologist. Also, check the list of questions or concerns you developed from reading Chapter 1 to see whether you can check any of them off your list. Record your answers and file your personal inquiry in your teaching portfolio.
2. What are the major components of oral language? Listen to a conversation between two students and think about how the components function and interact.
3. Listen to students as they move from one school setting to another (e.g., classroom, playground, lunchroom). Determine how their use of language and its formality varies.
4. Interview a speech and language pathologist. Get information about the number and type of students served, typical ages, type of speech or language problems, and ideas for classroom teachers.
5. Teach a lesson involving new content or vocabulary. Pay particular attention to wait time, pacing, and opportunities for the students to discuss what they are learning with partners or in small groups. Notice how this affects students who usually don't respond in class.
6. When teaching, consciously use the techniques of parallel talk, expansion, and elaboration. How does this affect the expressive language of the students whose language is typically less elaborated and complex?

# Read More about It

1. Diamond, S. (1993). *Language lessons in the classroom*. Phoenix, AZ: ECL Publications.

   Provides activities and lessons for general education classrooms to develop language skills for grades K–5.

2. Langdon, H. with Cheng, L. L. (1992). *Hispanic children and adults with communication disorders: Assessment and intervention*. Gaithersburg, MD: Aspen.

   Provides important information about speech and language assessment and intervention with Hispanic children whose first language is Spanish. Also provides information about the acquisition and development of English as a second language in Spanish speakers.

3. Nippold, M.A. (1998). *Later language development: The school-age and adolescent years* (2nd ed.). Austin, TX: Pro-Ed.

   Reviews language development during the school-age years including the development of figurative language, conversation, vocabulary, and word finding.

4. Owens, Jr., R. E. (1995). *Language disorders: A functional approach to assessment and intervention* (2nd ed.). Boston: Allyn & Bacon.

   Provides a comprehensive look at language disorders and presents a model for assessment and teaching that stresses the use of functional environments, conversations as the instructional milieu, and meaningful contexts. Also provides information about second-language and second-dialect learners.

5. Reed, V. A. (1994). *An introduction to children with language disorders* (2nd ed.). New York: Macmillan.

   Reviews normal language development and includes a chapter about the language of students with different types of disabilities (e.g., mental retardation, autism, learning disabilities, deaf/hard of hearing). Also includes information on language assessment and intervention.

6. Shames, G. H., Wiig, E. H., & Secord, W. A. (Eds.) (1998). *Human communication disorders* (5th ed.). New York: Merrill/Macmillan.

   Provides a comprehensive introduction to the field of communication disorders, discusses language differences and disorders, and the communication disorders of special populations.

7. Simon, C. S. (1993). *300+ developmental language strategies for clinic and classroom*. Tempe, AZ: CommiCog.

   This sourcebook offers strategies for building general oral language and pragmatic skills and includes ideas for teaching English language learners.

8. Strong, C. J., & North, K. H. (1995). *The magic of stories: Literature-based language intervention*. Eau Claire, WI: Thinking Publications.

   This program utilizes children's literature and 22 strategies to help students understand and retell stories.

9. Wiig, E. H., & Semel, E. (1984). *Language assessment and intervention for the learning disabled*. Columbus, OH: Merrill.

   Provides many ideas for facilitating the development of semantics, morphology, syntax, and pragmatics, as well as an overview of several language curriculums.

# CHAPTER 12

# Teaching Students with Emotional and Behavioral Disorders

# Interview

## Juline Truesdell

Juline Truesdell has been a primary teacher for 5 years, during which time she has worked with many students who were identified as emotionally and behaviorally disordered. We interviewed her about one of her students who was identified as "seriously emotionally disturbed" as a preschooler.

> My greatest challenge as a teacher was a student named Lenox, who was identified as seriously emotionally disturbed and placed in my classroom for part of the school day. Lenox was in my class during his first-grade year. The first day of school he ran into my classroom swinging his lunch box, bumping into other students on his approach to me. When no more than four inches from me he looked up and shouted, "Are you my teacher?"
>
> The first 2 months of school were difficult for both of us. Lenox was very rebellious and aggressive and he had a very hard time controlling himself. He wanted the other children to like him but he threw tantrums when they did not give him his way, and so many of the children were afraid of him. I worked very hard with him so that he could sit with one of the groups of children during the day, but I found I often had to separate him from other students. He often sat at a desk by himself, away from the other children. I know he didn't like that because he continued to say to me, "Why can't I sit with my group?" I always told him why he was separated but he seemed to forget seconds later. He just didn't seem to be able to control himself and when he sat with the other students he would call them bad names and hit them and interfere with their work. The other students would complain and say that they didn't want him to be in their group.
>
> Once in a while he would have a good day and he would get a smiley face on his report to take home and I could tell that made a difference. But then the next day he would come in and have a terrible day. It was very difficult to predict his behavior. Then I decided to try something new. Lenox really liked me, and so I set up a program with him where he would get a point for each of the five periods in the day. If he got all five points, I would spend 5 minutes with him at the end of the day. Sometimes we would talk, color together, play games or read a book, but it would be time just for the two of us. If he got five points for 4 days in a row, I would bring lunch for him and the two of us would eat together alone in the room. The program made a big difference in how Lenox behaved. He started to work better with other students and he reduced considerably the amount of hitting and fighting. He was able to work with his group most of the day. I can truly say I hated to see him leave at the end of the year. I loved this child. I always have. He gave me so many problems and such a hard time, but there was something about him I'll never forget.

## Introduction

The relationships established between classroom teachers and their students with emotional and behavioral disorders, like that of Juline and her student Lenox, are often among the more meaningful relationships experienced by both. Sharon Andreaci, a sixth-grade teacher, describes a student with emotional problems who was mainstreamed into her classroom part-time and spent the rest of the day in the special education resource room.

> Diana was her name, and you could just tell by looking into her eyes that something was wrong. She had been raped by a member of her family, and she never seemed to recover. She would see spirits and think evil things were coming to get her. She would say very strange things to me and to other students in the class. I felt that the support she got that year from me and the [other] students . . . really helped her feel better accepted. I have followed her in school, and checked to see how she is doing. Now she is in a regular ninth-grade class and is participating in counseling.

General education teachers indicate that the students they feel are the most difficult to mainstream into their classrooms are students who demonstrate serious emotional and behavioral disorders (Schumm & Vaughn, 1992). Even special education teachers find students with serious emotional and behavioral problems to be a challenge. As Mark Stitz, a sixth-grade teacher, indicates, "Teaching the content that I am interested in is the fun part. Meeting the needs of students with behavior problems is the work." Teaching students with emotional and behavioral disorders is indeed a challenge, but for teachers who understand and implement the types of instructional adaptations necessary to meet these students' educational needs, the results can be very satisfying. And as experienced teachers have reported, the positive impact their efforts have on their students' lives can greatly reward teachers, and stay with them forever.

Although some students with emotional or behavioral disorders receive at least part of their educational program in self-contained special education classrooms or in specialized settings (e.g., alternative schools for students with specific problems, hospital settings), approximately 50 percent of students identified as having emotional or behavioral disorders spend part or all of their school day in general education classrooms (Knitzer et al., 1990). Therefore, general education teachers must be knowledgeable in the techniques and skills necessary to work with these students.

## Definitions of Emotional and Behavioral Disorders

What does it mean to be emotionally disturbed? What types of behaviors would you expect to see? As with many other disabilities, there is no clear line between those who have disabilities and those who do not. Often the question is decided by how severe the problem is, and how persistent. As a teacher, you will come in contact with students who display a range of emotional and behavioral problems.

The National Mental Health Association's National Mental Health and Special Education Coalition Workgroup on Definition (Forness & Knitzer, 1992) uses the descriptor **emotional or behavioral disorders** for students whose behavior falls considerably outside the norm. The federal government uses the term *emotional disturbance* in its criteria for placement of students in special education. The federal definition of emotional disturbance is provided in Figure 7.1.

It is not the responsibility of general education teachers to determine whether a student qualifies as emotionally disturbed, but teachers do have the responsibility of referring students for possible special education placement (by requesting evaluation of students who present significant emotional or behavioral problems in their classrooms). The federal definition of emotional disturbance can help you determine whether the behaviors of a student warrant referral for special education.

> Although the terms *behaviorally disordered* and *emotional disturbance* are often used to mean the same thing, a movement exists to emphasize the term "behaviorally disordered," which professionals believe is the less stigmatizing label. Nevertheless, the Individuals with Disabilities Education Act still uses the term "serious emotional disturbance."

> **FIGURE 7.1**
>
> **The Federal Definition of Serious Emotional Disturbance**
>
> The federal government defines emotionally disturbed as follows:
>
> (i) The term means a condition exhibiting one or more of the following characteristics over a long period of time and to a marked degree, which adversely affects educational performance including:
>
>   (A) An inability to learn which cannot be explained by intellectual, sensory, or health factors;
>
>   (B) An inability to build or maintain satisfactory interpersonal relationships with peers and teachers;
>
>   (C) Inappropriate types of behavior or feelings under normal circumstances;
>
>   (D) A general pervasive mood of unhappiness or depression; or
>
>   (E) A tendency to develop physical symptoms or fears associated with personal or school problems.
>
> (ii) The term includes children who are schizophrenic. The term does not include children who are socially maladjusted, unless it is determined that they are seriously emotionally disturbed.
>
> The Individuals with Disabilities Education Act: 25C.F.R.

## Prevalence of Students with Emotional or Behavioral Disorders

Higher prevalence rates are reported for mild emotional or behavioral disorders, and lower prevalence rates for more severe disorders. Prevalence varies, depending on the criteria used. Estimates for emotional and behavioral disorders range from 0.5 percent to 20 percent or more of the school-age population (Kauffman, 1993). Reports indicate a general prevalence rate of 3 percent to 6 percent of the student population (Achenbach & Edelbrock, 1981; Brandenburg et al., 1990). Approximately 0.8 percent of students receive special education services because of emotional disturbance (U.S. Department of Education, 1990; 1994). Thus, students with emotional or behavioral disorders are regarded as underserved.

The National Mental Health Association (1986) summarized the following issues as reasons for the *underidentification* of students with emotional and behavioral disorders:

- Social stigma is associated with the label "seriously emotionally disturbed."
- Eligibility for categorization as emotionally disordered is not clearly explained.
- There is a lack of uniformity in the identification process.
- A lack of funding may limit school districts' willingness to identify these students.
- There is often a lack of appropriate services when students are identified.

Although few professionals disagree that students with emotional and behavioral disorders are underidentified, there is less certainty as to why so many of the students identified are males. Males consistently outnumber females in all prevalence reports for serious emotional disturbance (Quay & Werry, 1986; Rosenberg et al., 1992). Particularly in specialized programs for students with emotional and behavioral disorders, males outnumber females by as much as 8 to 1.

> In the first few years following the implementation of IDEA, McLaughlin and Owings (1992) found that rural school districts identified fewer students with learning disabilities and emotional disturbance than did more populated areas. The authors suggest that this lower identification rate is the result of social, cultural, and economic factors.

# Types and Characteristics of Emotional or Behavioral Disorders

Think about classrooms you have observed or taught in. Which students got your attention first—those who were quiet and withdrawn, or those who were acting out and disturbing others? Not surprisingly, students who demonstrate such **externalizing behaviors** as aggression, hitting, and shouting are much more likely to come to the teacher's attention and therefore to be identified as behavior-disordered than are students who exhibit more **internalizing behaviors**, such as shyness, withdrawal, or depression.

Emotional and behavioral disorders can be classified broadly as externalizing or internalizing. Students who exhibit externalizing behaviors (e.g., conduct disorders, acting out, aggression, tantrums, and bizarre behaviors) tend to interfere with others. Students who exhibit internalizing behaviors (e.g., fear, immaturity, tenseness, withdrawal, worry) tend to be less disturbing to others but still very distressing to themselves and their families.

Considering the behaviors of students as either externalizing or internalizing can be useful for classroom teachers. First, it helps you become aware that students with internalizing problems also need help, even though they do not call attention to themselves in the same way as those with externalizing problems. Second, being able to identify the type of behavior problem gives you a basic idea of what to do.

Quay and colleagues (Quay & Peterson, 1987; Quay & Werry, 1986) have identified the major subtypes of externalizing and internalizing emotional and behavioral disorders that teachers are likely to encounter. These subtypes include: conduct disorder, motor excess and attention problems, socialized-aggression, pervasive developmental disorder, immaturity, and anxiety–withdrawal. During your career as a teacher, you will have students who display a range of these behaviors, some mild and some severe. Understanding these categories will help you not only to more accurately describe your students' behavior to professionals, but also to respond appropriately to your students. One classification system frequently used by counselors, psychologists, and physicians is described next.

*What internalizing behaviors might signal the possible presence of emotional or behavioral disorders? How are externalizing behaviors different?*

The *Diagnostic and Statistical Manual of Mental Disorders* (DSM) classification system is based on the reference book of the same name, published by the American Psychiatric Association. Currently in its fourth edition, the book is commonly referred to as the *DSM-IV*. Its purpose is to provide a uniform nomenclature from which clinicians and researchers may discuss, research, diagnose, and treat mental disorders.

The book describes specific criteria necessary for the diagnosis of each disorder, as well as symptoms, indicators of severity, and any variations of the disorder.

Symptoms affected by culture, age, sex, or other variables are discussed, along with the prevalence and progression of the disorder. Each disorder is given a code (usually four or five numbers).

Counselors, psychologists, psychiatrists, and medical doctors who have had extensive training in diagnostic procedures generally use the DSM-IV. Although teachers need not be fluent in its content, familiarity with its use can facilitate communication with school counselors, psychologists, and doctors who may use DSM-IV disorder classification titles, symptoms, and codes.

A copy of the DSM-IV should be available from the school counselor or psychologist, or a local library or bookstore.

It is important to remember that the DSM-IV is an independent classification system. The disorders delineated and their characteristics may be different from those in other classification systems, although some overlap can be expected. Also, many students with emotional/behavioral disorders display learning difficulties, and may have learning disabilities (Rock, Fessler, & Church, 1997) and/or attention deficit disorders (Bussing, Zima, Belin, & Forness, 1998).

## Conduct Disorders

Behaviors associated with **conduct disorder** include hitting, fighting, throwing, temper tantrums, teasing, acting defiant or disobedient, being irritable or overactive, difficult to get along with, uncooperative, inconsiderate, resistive, jealous, quarrelsome, distractable, irresponsible, and inattentive. Some students with conduct disorders provoke peers into hitting them or others. Students with conduct disorders who are defiant often resist direction from adults. When teachers call home to describe a student's lack of compliance, they often find frustrated parents who feel their child is not as responsive to them as they would like.

Not surprisingly, teachers have no difficulty recognizing students who display conduct disorders. Their aggressive, interfering behaviors are probably the greatest source of frustration for classroom teachers. Identifying students with extreme conduct disorders may be easy, but developing successful strategies for managing them can be difficult.

Students with mild-to-moderate conduct disorders can be handled in the general education classroom by effective behavior-management strategies and cooperation with the school counselor, psychologist, and parents. Students with more extreme conduct disorders are challenging to all adults and may be removed from the classroom for all or part of the school day for special education. More than 50 percent of students with conduct disorders continue to demonstrate difficulties as adults and often have adjustment problems throughout their lifetimes (Kazdin, 1993). Although their intelligence is often well within the normal range (Sattler, 1988), students with conduct disorders often display low academic achievement (Gold & Mann, 1972; Vaughn et al., 1992).

Furthermore, the most common secondary special education service provided to students with behavior disorders is speech and language intervention (Griffith, Rogers-Adkinson, & Cusick, 1997).

## Research Brief

### Developmental Pathways to Conduct Disorders

Loeber and colleagues (1993) conducted a long-term study of the **developmental pathways** associated with conduct disorder. Some students follow one pathway, others follow more than one. Those who follow multiple pathways are most at risk. The pathways (covert, overt, and disobedience) and related behaviors follow:

Covert behavior: stealing, lying, burglary, use of drugs and alcohol

Overt behavior: aggression, coercion, bullying, manipulation of others, escalated interactions with teachers, parents, and peers

Disobedience: noncompliance, oppositional–defiant behavior, resistance to adult influence

## Motor Excess

Although most parents of 2-year-olds perceive **motor excess** as a perfect descriptor of their child, the term refers to the restless, overactive behavior (also referred to as *hyperactivity*) displayed by some students. These students cannot sit still for long periods of time, even when they are doing something they enjoy. Described as acting as though they were driven by a motor, they tend to be tense, unable to relax, and overly talkative. Note that motor excess does *not* refer to students who have difficulty remaining quiet all day or who seem restless in their seats. As a teacher you will find that many students dislike sitting still and remaining quiet. Wise teachers build into the day brief, structured transition times during which students can move around and visit with their classmates.

## Socialized-Aggression

Few people have not engaged in some type of antisocial behavior at some point in their lives (Bullis & Walker, 1994). The term **socialized-aggression** is used to refer to students who routinely engage in antisocial behavior. Adults describe them as hanging around with the wrong kinds of kids, displaying behaviors that are not typical of others in their age group, harassing others, and stealing and damaging property. School behaviors that get these students into trouble include truancy and cutting classes. Socialized-aggression is also associated with **group behavior**; that is, behaviors are displayed in the presence of other group members. Parents and teachers often worry that they have little influence over the behavior of students loyal to delinquent friends. Students with socialized-aggression often belong to gangs. Students' attraction to gang life is apparent in many inner cities as well as in suburban and rural areas (Jankowski, 1991; Morales, 1992). Law enforcement agencies categorize **gangs** into the following four groups:

- *delinquent* youth gangs that are loosely structured and recognize each other by the way they dress and look
- *turf-based* gangs—also loosely structured, but committed to defending a reputation or neighborhood
- *crime-oriented,* or drug gangs—engage in robbery, burglary, or sale of controlled substances for monetary gain
- *violent* hate gangs whose members commit assaults or hate crimes against specific types of people

Students may be attracted to gangs through a desire for companionship, acceptance, and success.

> The categories of emotional and behavioral disorders described in this chapter are cultural constructs and may be regarded differently in different cultural settings. Teachers need to consider the cultural and ethnic background of students and how their behavior would be interpreted in light of that background. Students from diverse cultural backgrounds need to be assessed carefully, with consideration of their community and environment (Rogoff & Morelli, 1989), as well as their knowledge of the English language (August & Hakuta, 1997).

Many such students feel that they have not been accepted by traditional society (Goldstein & Huff, 1993).

A high rate of overlap exists among conduct disorders, attention problems, and socialized-aggression. For example, many students who have attention problems might also display behaviors associated with conduct disorders, such as aggression and acting out.

## Research Brief

### Five Types of Aggression

Lancelotta and Vaughn (1989) examined five subtypes of aggression. In *provoked physical aggression,* one student hits or taunts another, who retaliates. In *unprovoked physical aggression,* a student acts aggressively with no apparent prompting. In *verbal aggression,* one student screams, yells, or uses other verbal expression to attack another. In *outburst aggression,* a student "blows up." In the last type of aggression, *indirect aggression,* a student does something sneaky or tricky to get back at another student. Neither boys nor girls like students who use indirect aggression. Both sexes are the most tolerant about provoked aggression, but girls are less tolerant of all types of aggression than are boys. All subtypes of aggression were related to low social acceptance by classmates except provoked physical aggression. Teachers' ratings were closer to boys' ratings of peer acceptance than to similar ratings by girls.

## Pervasive Developmental Disorder

Pervasive developmental disorder can be classified as either externalizing or internalizing, depending on the type(s) of behavior manifested. Students who exhibit behaviors characterized as **pervasive developmental disorder** express farfetched, unusual, or unbelievable ideas. These students may say strange things to the teacher (e.g., "The blue dog is in the hallway and it is going to get me when I leave.") and may also exhibit repetitive speech, and unusual behaviors such as excessive rocking, nail biting, or head knocking. Students with this disorder may relate to others (including family members) as if they were inanimate objects rather than people. Students may also ignore or resist signs of affection and love and fail to interact with or adapt to others. You are unlikely to have students identified with pervasive developmental disorders in your classroom.

## Immaturity

Behaviors associated with **immaturity** include lack of perseverance, failure to finish tasks, short attention span, poor concentration, and frequent day dreaming or preoccupation. Students might stare into space excessively; appear absentminded, inattentive, or drowsy; and seem clumsy or poorly coordinated.

Immature students often come to the attention of teachers because they show little interest in schoolwork and need prodding to participate. Teachers might feel frustrated at the amount of effort necessary to keep these students interested and involved.

These students often seem overly dependent on parents or caretakers and have difficulty being responsible members of a group (whether the classroom or the family). Students with severe immaturity often have difficulty interacting with other people, using social skills, and playing with children their own age. These students may frequently retreat into fantasy and develop fears that are out of proportion to the circumstances.

## Depression

Many students with emotional and behavioral disorders are also prone to depression (Klein & Last, 1989; Kovacs et al., 1988). Mental health workers and educators have realized only recently that depression is a widespread, serious problem among children and adolescents (Forness, 1988). Whereas depression is more prevalent in adult women than men, school-age boys are as likely as girls to exhibit depression (e.g., Lefkowitz & Tesiny, 1985; Lobovits & Handal, 1985).

Teachers often have difficulty identifying students who are depressed (Sarcco & Graves, 1985). The following behaviors may indicate depression:

- acting sad, lonely, and apathetic
- exhibiting low self-esteem
- displaying avoidance behaviors (particularly, avoiding social experiences)
- having chronic complaints about eating, sleeping, and elimination
- refusing or fearing going to school or other public places
- talking of suicide

## Anxiety–Withdrawal

The term **anxiety–withdrawal** includes two highly related major behaviors. *Anxiety* refers to extreme worry, fearfulness, and concern (even when little reason for those feelings exists). Simple reassurance is rarely effective. *Withdrawal* describes the typical behavior of students who are anxious or depressed; they frequently withdraw from others and appear seclusive, preferring solitary activities. Withdrawn students are often timid or bashful around others, even people they know, thinking of themselves (and described by others) as loners with few friends, if any. Often preferring to work alone, in class these students may avoid group work, volunteering, or answering questions. Teachers and parents often attribute such behavior to low self-confidence and poor self-concepts.

As you can see from the preceding descriptions, students with behavior disorders display a wide range of characteristics. Perhaps the most consistent characteristic of these students is their inability to maintain satisfying relationships with others (e.g., Kauffman, 1993; Walker et al., 1995).

# Causes of Emotional and Behavioral Disorders

Although the rate of sexual abuse among individuals with disabilities is unknown, 62 percent of the 13- to 18-year-old females with emotional disorders in one study were sexually abused before the age of 16 (Brooks, 1985). Also, poverty is related to mental health problems in children (Tarnowski & Rohrbeck, 1993).

Despite a general understanding that the emotional and behavioral disorders of students do not reflect directly on parents, dysfunctional parenting contributes to behavior disorders in children (Kaiser & Hester, 1997). On the basis of the research we currently have, our best understanding is that emotional and behavioral disorders result from both environmental and genetic factors, and that in some cases one set of factors plays a greater role than the other. For example, a student exposed to family violence may be more likely to display violent behaviors (Jacobs, 1994; Sanson et al., 1993), but some students who are mentally ill may have heritable explanations for their symptoms (e.g., Lombroso et al., 1994; McGuffin et al., 1994). Regardless of the cause, early intervention is needed (Kaiser & Hester, 1997).

Whether emotional or behavioral disorders have social or organic causes, they are treated with three groups of medications: stimulants, antidepressants, and antipsychotics.

*Stimulants* target the central nervous system and are believed to help the brain release certain chemicals that make it possible to focus on particular stimuli rather than be overwhelmed by all present at a given moment. Thus, stimulants increase attention and reduce impulsive and intrusive behavior. Examples of stimulants include Cylert, Ritalin, Dexedrine, and Benzedrine. Some of the possible side effects caused by stimulants include a loss of appetite, insomnia, growth retardation, muscle tics, depression, and nervousness.

*Antidepressants* are often used in the treatment of depression, anxiety disorders, bed wetting, compulsive and obsessive behavior, stomachaches, anxiety attacks, and muscle tics. Antidepressants have a sedative effect; they reduce mood swings and levels of stress, making tasks seem less overwhelming. Examples of antidepressants include Elavil, Tofranil, and Prozac. Some of the possible side effects of antidepressants include nausea, dry mouth, loss of appetite, insomnia, and seizures.

*Antipsychotics* are tranquilizers used in the treatment of severe cases of behavioral disorders. These drugs reduce delusions and hallucinations, severe anxiety, depression, and hyperactivity. Examples of antipsychotics include Haldol, Thorazine, Mellaril, Navane, and Stelazine. Possible side effects of antipsychotics include listlessness, passiveness, impaired cognitive performance, dry mouth, increase in appetite, weight gain, enuresis, and motor difficulties.

Although not included in the preceding classifications, lithium is another commonly used medication in the treatment of emotional and behavioral disorders. Lithium is used in the treatment of severe mood disorders, such as manic-depression. Some of the possible side effects include nausea, excessive need to urinate, thirst, tremors, dizziness, diarrhea, vomiting, abdominal pain, shaking, exhaustion, and distorted or slurred speech.

# Identification and Assessment of Students with Emotional and Behavioral Disorders

How are students with emotional and behavioral disorders identified? Some students with severe disorders are recognized by parents and other adults before they start attending school. These students may receive early treatment through a combination of educational interventions, medications, play therapy, and family counseling. Other students have emotional and behavioral disorders that remain latent until students are older or that become apparent in structured settings such as the school. Older students may not have received specialized services outside the school setting.

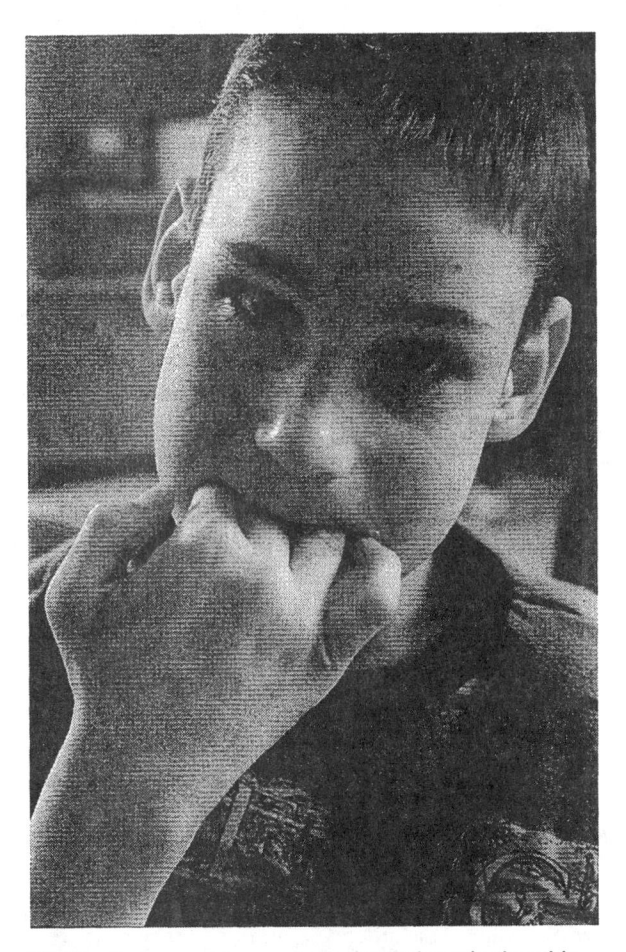

What criteria would you use to determine whether this student's behavior warrants referral for evaluation for the presence of an emotional or behavioral disorder?

How should classroom teachers decide whether a student's behavior is problematic enough to warrant referral to special education or other specialized services? The following criteria provide indications of disturbance and the likelihood for referral (e.g., Clarizio & McCoy, 1983; Morgan & Reinhart, 1991):

- *Behavior–Age discrepancy:* The social and behavioral problems exhibited must be unusual or deviant for the student's age. For example, clinging to adults is common in very young children but is deemed inappropriate for school-age children.
- *Frequency of occurrence of the behavior:* Under stress, all people exhibit characteristics of emotional or behavioral disorders, such as whining, withdrawal, mood swings, or depression. These behaviors and feeling states are not considered problems if they occur only occasionally.
- *Number of symptoms:* Display of one or more behavior problems at some time does not indicate that a person has an emotional or behavioral disorder, but students who frequently display several related symptoms should be considered for referral. The greater the number of symptoms, the greater the likelihood of a serious emotional disturbance.
- *Inner suffering:* Signs of inner suffering include low self-esteem, less interaction with others, appearance of sadness or loneliness, and general malaise. Inner suffering interferes with learning, social relationships, and achievement.
- *Persistence of the behavior:* Persistence refers to the continuation of the emotional or behavioral problems over time, despite substantive efforts on the part of adults and the student to change the behaviors. A behavior problem is persistent when several types of interventions have not resulted in long-term change.
- *Self-Satisfaction:* Students who appear to be generally happy with themselves reflect a measure of self-satisfaction. They show positive affect, and the willingness to give and receive affection and pleasure. A lack of self-satisfaction contributes to problems that interfere with personal growth and development as well as academic and social success but that may not signal the presence of an emotional or behavioral disorder.
- *Severity and duration of the behavior:* All dimensions of a student's behavior can be classified in terms of two important criteria: severity and duration. *Severity* refers to how extreme the problem is and the extent to which it varies from expected behavior. *Duration* (or persistence) refers to the length of time the problem has occurred. A problem that persists over a long period of time is said to be *chronic*. Most students who are identified as having emotional or behavioral disorders must deal with their problems throughout their lifetimes.

When identifying a student with possible emotional or behavioral disorders, ask the following questions:

- How often does the behavior occur? How long has the problem persisted?
- Under what conditions does the behavior occur? To what extent does this behavior occur in different settings, such as the classroom, playground, or home?
- What are the *antecedents* of the behavior; that is, what events occur before the behavior is exhibited, triggering the behavior? What are the *consequences,* that is, what occurs as an outcome of the behavior after the student exhibits the behavior?
- Does the problem not arise in certain situations?
- To what extent does the student develop and maintain positive relationships with other people? Does the student seem happy or display satisfaction at any time?
- How severe is the problem? To what extent is the behavior deviant from that of other students of the same age?
- To what extent is this a problem in the relationship between you and the student, or a problem in the student?

Tips for Teachers 7.1 offers suggestions for gathering information before referring a student with possible emotional or behavioral disorders.

> Self-stimulation—repetitive sensory stimulation, such as twirling, patting, flapping, staring at lights, and swishing saliva—is common behavior in students with severe emotional disturbance.

## TIPS FOR TEACHERS

### 7.1 Making Referrals for Students with Emotional or Behavioral Disorders

- Keep a journal that includes the dates, times, and contexts of student behaviors that you regard as deviant or bizarre.
- Be specific, using behavioral terms to describe what occurs. As much as possible, avoid including value judgments. For example, a journal entry might read, "Mark got up from his seat, pushed John out of his chair, and then ran around the room flapping his arms."
- Record any relevant information from parents, such as their descriptions of the student's behavior at home or telephone calls concerning the student. Keep parents informed of the problem, both in writing and by telephone.
- Also record relevant information from other teachers or school personnel who know the student.
- Keep samples of the student's work in different subjects, and a record of skills the student can and cannot perform. If student's academic performance is inconsistent, note this as well.

## Teaching Guidelines and Accommodations for Students with Emotional or Behavioral Disorders

Many teachers realize that understanding and recognizing the behaviors of students with emotional and behavioral disorders is the first step in providing appropriate interventions. The most important role of the teacher is to establish an academic community and climate that promotes the learning and acceptance of all students, including students with emotional and behavioral problems (Walker, Colvin, & Ramsey, 1995). How can you do this? This section provides an overview of teaching accommodations to facilitate the academic and social growth of students with emotional and behavioral disorders.

Teachers usually realize that providing appropriate intervention is not sufficient, but that the student's day-to-day environment must be structured to promote mental health. Students who return to abusive families or inappropriate environments that maintain their emotional or behavioral problems are unlikely to achieve much success without changes in these environments. In working with students with serious emotional or behavioral problems, some teachers feel hopeless and give up. Remember, however, that the small things you do often make a big difference in the life of a student, even if the student does not say so or demonstrate significant changes.

No single approach to intervention works for all students with severe emotional and behavioral problems. A systematic, well-organized plan, and documentation of changes in behavior will help you determine whether an intervention is working, however.

### Maintaining an Organized Physical Environment

Look around your classroom or that of another teacher, and evaluate whether the physical environment supports or detracts from the student's ability to behave appropriately (Fimian et al., 1983). The physical arrangement may have a significant effect on the classroom climate as well as on student behavior, particularly that of students with emotional and behavioral problems. Consider the following:

- Is the classroom uncluttered, clean, attractive, and uncrowded?
- Are necessary materials accessible, organized, and stored appropriately?
- Is there sufficient natural light in the classroom?

What physical characteristics of the classroom environment support the learning of students with emotional or behavioral disorders? What characteristics of the classroom climate contribute to a positive emotional environment in which academic and social learning can take place?

- Is the classroom well ventilated?
- Is the noise level appropriate? What objects might be removed or changed to make the room less noisy?
- Is there evidence that housekeeping chores have been taken care of? Is the room clean and orderly?
- Does each student have his or her own physical space, desk, and materials?

Students with emotional and behavioral disorders work best in organized, structured environments in which materials, equipment, and personal items are well maintained, neatly arranged, and presented in a predictable way. You can establish a classroom committee composed of elected students or students you appoint on a rotating basis that allows all students to participate over the school year. This committee might meet weekly to assess the classroom environment and address issues raised by students (perhaps in a student suggestion box).

### Establishing Positive Relationships

Think about the teachers that you remember most from your elementary and secondary school days. What made these teachers special to you? Chances are that you felt they really cared about you, what you learned, and how you felt. The importance of your establishing good relationships with all students is important, but especially so for students with emotional and behavioral disorders. These students probably have had few positive relationships with adults and may act as if they dare you to care about them.

Trust is the foundation for success with students with emotional and behavioral disorders (Henley et al., 1993). Students learn to trust you when you act in predictable ways and do what you say you are going to do. They also learn to trust you when they believe you will do what is best for them, rather than what is best for you.

Remember that disliking the student's behavior is not the same as disliking the student, who needs your respect and caring. "Respect the student—dislike the behavior" is an important motto when you work with students with emotional and behavioral disorders. Think about the language you use when you reprimand students or enforce consequences for inappropriate behavior. Be sure you convince them that their behavior is unacceptable, not they. Jason Landis, a high-school English teacher, says it this way:

> When I correct students I always talk about the behavior and I always let the student know that anyone who behaves like this will be treated the same way. For example, the other day in class I needed to remind a student that no one swears in the class and those who swear will get a detention and therefore, here is your detention. Later on in the period, I encouraged the same student to respond to a question and provided positive feedback for the part of the answer he got correct.

Caring for students with emotional and behavioral disorders should not come with strings attached or expectations that students will reciprocate (Webber et al., 1991). Many of these students have little experience with giving or receiving kindness and warmth. Some are hurting and cannot cope with giving to others. All children need our concern, and students who do not reciprocate need it the most.

Be empathic. Empathy requires genuine concern and interest in understanding the student, no matter how deviant or difficult his or her behavior. Students know when teachers are empathic and concerned about them.

Tips for Teachers 7.2 offers further suggestions for creating an appropriate emotional environment.

# TIPS FOR TEACHERS

## 7.2 Creating an Appropriate Emotional Environment

- *Respond to students' feelings and intentions* rather than to overt behavior. When students with emotional and behavioral disorders act out or become aggressive, the teacher's first reaction might be to respond with anger or hostility—but the student is really saying, "I'm hurting. Pay attention to me."
- *Listen.* Before responding, no matter how certain you are that the student is in the wrong, give the student an opportunity to explain and give his or her version of what occurred. You may not always agree with the interpretation, but by taking the time to listen you demonstrate caring and concern to the student. Listening is a sign of acceptance, an important first step in helping students.
- *Develop a positive relationship* with the student about one topic. All students are interested in and can succeed at something that you can recognize. Discover what this area is and what the student knows about it, then make him or her the class expert.
- *Establish rules and consequences* to help provide the structure that students with emotional and behavioral disorders need.
- *Consider changes you can make.* Evaluate the classroom routines, instructional procedures, and discipline practices you use that may be contributing to the student's behavioral problems.
- *Catch the student being good.* You have many opportunities to recognize the student's inappropriate behavior. A greater challenge is to catch the student being good and recognize that appropriate behavior several times a day.
- *Use humor* to build relationships and to decrease tension. Look for the fun in the way students relate to each other and to you.
- *Create an emotionally safe classroom* environment in which students accept each other's strengths and weaknesses and treat each other with respect and consideration.

## Changing Behavior

The student behaviors teachers most want to change are those they regard as undesirable, such as those that interfere with instruction, other students, or the student's learning. Desirable behaviors—those that enhance instruction, relations with others, and the student's success—are the behaviors teachers most want to see increased. In addition to the behavior-management procedures discussed in detail in Chapter 3, the following guiding principles will help you use consequences for desirable and undesirable behaviors (Morgan & Reinhart, 1991):

- Carefully select the rules you apply, and then follow through consistently. If you try to clamp down on every rule, you may find yourself continually at war with the student.
- Consider consequences carefully, because you must follow through on stated consequences. Do not use threats. When you make remarks such as, "You're going to do this math paper if you have to sit here all day," students soon learn that consequences are not real and that your words cannot be trusted.
- Establish consequences that are not punishing to you. If you are stressed or inconvenienced by the consequence, you might resent the student (a circumstance that would surely interfere with the quality of the relationship you need to establish). For example, staying in at lunch, giving up your planning period, or driving the student home may punish you as much as the student.
- Listen and talk to the student but avoid the trap of arguing. Listen to what the student has to say, and say what you have to say. If you are tempted to argue, recognize that you need a break and set another time to finish the discussion.
- Use logic, principles, and effective guidelines to make decisions. Avoid flaunting your authority as a teacher to make students do something, without giving them a clear sense that it is the right or best thing to do.

- Focus on the problems that interfere most; that is, ignore minor misbehaviors and focus on the important things.
- Inform students that the work they complete is necessary and meaningful for their education. Avoid asking them to complete work "for you."
- As you know, each student is an individual with his or her own attributes and problems. Avoid comparing a student with emotional or behavioral problems to other students. Comparisons do not help students understand and accept themselves, or be understood and accepted by others.
- Students' problems belong to them. They may interfere with your work, but they are not your problems. Resist the temptation to solve students' problems for them. Students need to learn how to resolve conflicts for themselves.
- Recognize your feelings and do not let them control your behavior. When you are upset by a student's behavior in class, it is important not to respond by further upsetting the student. Never "strike back" by humiliating, embarrassing, or berating a student.
- Let the student know how many chances he or she has before a consequence will be applied (and do not add chances later). When you tell a student, "This is the last chance," and he or she continues to behave inappropriately, you need to follow through on whatever consequence was designated.
- Give yourself positive feedback for what you do to enhance student learning and social functioning. Do not be too hard on yourself, especially when you make mistakes. Although there are limitations to what any effective teacher can do, there are always opportunities to be successful in teaching students with emotional and behavioral disorders.

The following procedures should remind you how to target key behaviors you want students to change:

- Whenever possible, involve students and parents in identifying the target behavior. In this way, you work at changing the behavior both at school and at home.
- As when making referrals, describe the behavior in as much detail as possible, including when and with whom it typically occurs.
- Get the student's input on the behavior, as well as his or her suggestions for what might help reduce it.
- Describe the target behavior in writing, using the terms expressed by the student, the parent, and yourself so that everyone involved understands the problem.
- Establish a procedure for eliminating the behavior and providing positive consequences when the behavior does not occur. Involve parents in distributing positive consequences as well.

Many techniques exist for helping students change their behavior. Figure 7.2 provides an example of a behavior contract between a student and a teacher. The 60-Second Lesson (page 208) shows how even simple devices can work.

Most special education teachers who instruct youngsters with behavioral and emotional problems implement a level system as a means of controlling behavior (Farrell, Smith, & Brownell, 1998). A level system attempts to provide a guide for managing student behavior through an organized framework based on token economies and the application of behavioral principles whereby students are provided with privileges based on their behavior. Expectations for student behavior and associated privileges are increased as the student moves up the level system. Students who reach a high enough ladder on the level system may be placed for part or all of the school day in the regular classroom.

## Resolving Conflicts and Promoting Self-Control

Dealing with conflict between students and between a student and a teacher is an ongoing issue for teachers at all grade levels. Conflicts are inevitable in a classroom community; they occur with students who have emotional and behavioral disorders as well as among other students.

Morgan and Reinhart (1991) suggest the use of conflict reports as a strategy for **conflict resolution**. Conflict reports not only enable students to debrief after a conflict, but also give them an opportunity to practice writing skills. A conflict report might include the following items:

- Describe the conflict you were involved in (fighting, taking an object that belongs to another, pushing).

### FIGURE 7.2

**Sample Student–Teacher Contract**

Date: _____

Ms. Gonzalez will draw a star next to Paul's name on the bulletin board and give Paul one point when he does any of the following in her classroom:

1) When the teacher asks a question, he raises his hand and waits for the teacher to call on him before talking.
2) He stays seated in his chair while working on class assignments.
3) When other kids in the class are bothering him, he tells the teacher about their behavior instead of yelling at and/or hitting the other kids.

After Paul has earned 12 points from his teacher, Ms. Gonzalez, he may select one of the following rewards:

1) He may have extra time to work on the computer.
2) He may serve as the teacher's helper for a day.
3) He may be in charge of caring for the class pet for the day.
4) He may serve as a peer tutor for a day (for a subject decided upon by the teacher).

After Paul has received 12 points, he begins earning the points again. Another reward will be given when 12 points have been earned.

I, Paul B. O'Brien, agree to the conditions stated above, and understand that I will not be allowed any of the rewards until I have earned 12 points by doing the activities stated above.

_____
(student's signature)

I, Ms. Gonzalez, agree to the conditions stated above. I will give Paul one of the aforementioned reinforcers only after he has received 12 points.

_____
(teacher's signature)

---

- Briefly list who was involved in this conflict.
- Briefly list who else witnessed (but was not involved in) the conflict.
- Describe where the conflict took place (in the back of the classroom, in line going to lunch, at recess).
- Briefly describe how the conflict started. What did you do? What did they do? Describe what you said. Describe what they said.
- What else would you like to say or do to the other people involved in the conflict?
- What did you do to try to stop the conflict?
- What did they do to try to stop the conflict?
- Whom do you think might be able to help stop or resolve the conflict?
- Write a brief set of procedures for resolving the conflict. Be specific. Be sure to tell who will do what, and when.

One of the advantages of a conflict report is that both participants have an opportunity to write all they know about it and to give their side of the story. Furthermore, the process of reporting provides time to debrief and let anger or resentment subside. Some teachers train students in conflict resolution as part of the regular curriculum. Students serve on an

*What steps should this teacher take to help the students resolve their conflict? What specific skills can students be taught to use in preventing future interpersonal conflicts?*

informal hearing board to resolve conflicts without teacher intervention. This training lets students practice the important skill of conflict negotiation.

By teaching students to set personal goals you also help them to develop self-control. Setting and monitoring positive personal goals contributes to students' positive self-concept and higher self-esteem. The 60-Second Lesson (page 209) describes a simple activity for helping students establish personal goals.

## Research Brief

### School-Based Wraparound

Students with behavior disorders and emotional disturbances are among the most highly segregated students with disabilities. A recent attempt to provide appropriate services to students with behavior disorders and their families has resulted in wraparound approaches that extend services to families and students (Eber, Nelson, & Miles, 1997). Wraparound planning involves considering the actual needs of the students within their home–school community rather than shopping for the program that will accept the student. Wraparound services can be used to provide supports that are coordinated through school, home, and community settings. To initiate wraparound planning, the following steps should be considered (Eber, Nelson, & Miles, 1997): issue identification, agenda setting, strengths, goal setting and needs, prioritization of needs, strategy development, securing commitments, follow-up communication, and process evaluation.

## MAKING A DIFFERENCE
### The 60-Second Lesson

#### Using a Timer to Change Behavior

**Purpose:** To increase appropriate behavior, such as "on-task" behavior, and to reduce inappropriate behavior, such as being "out-of-seat"

**Materials:** Kitchen timer

**Procedure:**
1. Show students the kitchen timer and indicate that you will be using it to cue students to look for on-task behavior in the class. Discuss with students what behaviors will be included (e.g., working, performing an assignment, asking a question, reading a text).
2. Indicate that the timer will ring at different intervals and that all groups or individuals who are on task when the timer rings will be awarded a point.
3. Set the timer initially for a range of times (from 5 to 10 minutes), then for longer periods of time.

Adapted from: Wolf, M. M., Hanley, E. L., King, L. A., Lachowicz, J., & Giles, D. K. (1970). The timer-game: A variable interval contingency for the management of out-of-seat behavior. *Exceptional Children, 37,* 113–117.

# MAKING A DIFFERENCE
## The 60-Second Lesson

### Helping Students Establish Personal Goals

**Purpose:** To establish personal goals

**Materials:** Index card or small piece of paper; pencil or pen

**Procedure:**
1. Ask students to think about people they most admire. For younger students, discuss the meaning of *admire*.
2. Ask students to identify the qualities of people they admire and examples of their behavior that demonstrate these qualities.
3. Now ask each student to write on the index card one quality for which they would like to be admired.
4. Ask students to keep the card in a prominent place (taped on their assignment folder or inside their desk, for example).
5. Throughout the year, ask students to look at the card and assess the extent to which they express the quality or trait for which they most want to be admired.

---

## Using the Life-Space Intervention

The Life-Space Intervention (LSI) (Wood & Long, 1994), originally discussed by Redl (1959), can be used to help students with emotional and behavioral problems cope with a crisis situation. According to Redl, the LSI has two primary goals:

- to provide emotional "first aid" so that the student can regain composure and return to as normal an activity level as possible
- to take advantage of the conflict situation to assist students in confronting and resolving their own personal conflicts

Although many professionals feel that the Life-Space Intervention is best applied by trained professionals familiar with counseling procedures, teachers can apply the key principles of the Life-Space Intervention. When the emotional problem or conflict is serious and warrants the help of a trained counselor, however, the teacher needs the good judgment to make an immediate referral.

Long, Morse, and Newman (1980) provided the following suggestions for the application of the LSI by teachers:

- Shake off or drain off the frustration and upset through the use of humor, physically shaking the problem away, or diffusing tension by allowing the student to talk about the problem. Drain off enough frustration so that the student can talk about the issue.
- Be as courteous as you would be if you were dealing with a friend or another adult. Give the student time to adequately explain his or her side of the story, and listen attentively. If you ask questions, be sure to give the student time to think and respond to them.
- Conduct the LSI in as private a place as possible. No one wants to exhibit problems, throw tantrums, or be extremely upset in front of others. Find a private, quiet place to conduct the session.
- Eliminate barriers between you and the student. Position yourself at eye level, for example. With a young child, pull up small chairs and sit down so that you are at the same level.
- Ask the student to provide his or her interpretation of the event. Listen carefully and be sure that you clarify any misunderstandings, but do not give in to his or her misperceptions of the situation. Confront the student, if necessary, to point out that there is another way to view the situation.
- Discuss what needs to be done to resolve the situation. If an apology is needed, role-play and rehearse how that can be done. If the conflict

needs to be further discussed and resolved with another person, plan procedures for doing so.
- Discuss what to do the next time a similar situation develops. How can you prevent a conflict? Discuss procedures for eliminating problems in the future.
- Do not assume that you understand how the student feels. Many times teachers assume that the student is angry, hurt, or disappointed. Ask how the student is feeling (to check whether you are correct).
- Avoid invalidating students' feelings by claiming that they could not possibly feel the way they say they do. Students with emotional and behavioral disorders often say outrageous things that they mean at the time. Listen carefully without judging or denying their feelings. Allow time for students to ask you questions and to prepare a follow-up.
- Teach problem solving skills (such as those presented in Chapter 4).

### Adapting Instruction

Students with emotional and behavioral problems often have academic difficulties (Vaughn et al., 1992), are underachievers in school (Kauffman, 1989), and are often missing basic academic skills (Browder & Shear, 1996). An important factor that positively affects students with emotional and behavioral disorders is the extent to which they are busy in purposeful, authentic activities. Activities need to be viewed by students as personally relevant and related to learning skills they need. Effective teachers explain to students *why* they are studying a topic, *why* they do an assignment, and *how* their learning will contribute to their success as students and in the future. Teachers can also adapt instruction in the ways described in the following sections.

**Provide Instruction That Allows All Students to Succeed** Academic failure or frustration can exacerbate a student's emotional or behavioral disorder. Without creating a parallel program or watering down the curriculum, teachers can adapt and modify assignments and expectations so that students can succeed. One simple strategy is to look for opportunities to reinforce and reward students for what they know or have done correctly. Another is to enhance motivation and performance by changing activities when students are failing. Students with emotional and behavioral disorders may have difficulty accomplishing particular types of tasks. In many cases, you can change the task so that students can demonstrate

## TIPS FOR TEACHERS

### 7.3 Providing Opportunities for Student Success

- When you correct papers, point out correct responses rather than mistakes.
- Before students submit papers, ask them to look carefully to see whether they can find an error. Call on students to describe mistakes they find, and praise them for finding and correcting the mistakes. Point out that everyone makes mistakes and that with practice we can reduce the number and types of mistakes we make.
- When a student with emotional or behavioral disorders asks for help, start by asking him or her to find something correct on his or her paper.
- Find opportunities for a student to "shine" in front of classmates. Even small recognitions are valuable.
- Notice improvement. If the student usually gets three right on the weekly spelling test and this week gets five right, let the student know that you notice the change. Recognition of progress toward a goal motivates students more than recognition that comes only after the goal has been attained.

knowledge without performing tasks that upset them. Tips for Teachers 7.3 offers additional suggestions for giving students opportunities for success.

**Provide Opportunities for Students to Learn Academically and Socially** Use different groupings—individual, small group, paired, and large group—to give students opportunities to acquire academic and social skills. Students with emotional and behavioral disorders may have difficulty learning in whole-class instruction but do well in small-group or paired learning situations. Also provide opportunities for students to be tutored and to serve as tutors themselves. Learning to work with others is an important skill for students with emotional and behavioral disorders. Recall from Chapter 2 the specific suggestions for grouping practices that enhance learning for all students.

Social learning also contributes to the success of students with emotional and behavioral disorders. Social learning involves observing and modeling or imitating the behavior of others (e.g., Bandura, 1971, 1973). To what extent can you expect students to imitate the appropriate behaviors of classmates, and what can you do to accelerate this process? Research suggests that students with emotional and behavioral disorders are unlikely to imitate "better" behaviors in the classroom unless teachers provide directed experiences to promote this behavior (Hallenbeck & Kauffman, 1995). Tips for Teachers 7.4 offers a strategy for guiding students to learn appropriate behaviors from classmates.

**Use a Variety of Commercial and Individually Created Materials** Assignments built to maximize success and capture students' interest reduce inappropriate behaviors. By providing high interest materials, you can keep students involved in the task. High interest is a characteristic of educational technologies, for example. Having students compose essays, complete tests, and practice skills on the microcomputer may provide better motivation than more traditional activities.

Also provide alternative ways for students to complete tasks and demonstrate learning. For example, students might give oral recitations, describe what they know to other students who have already mastered the material, or perform learning outcomes. Allow students to express their individual learning-style preferences. For instance, some students work better standing up, others while sitting on the floor, still others while sitting in bean bag chairs. As long as students are working, learning, and not interfering with the progress of others, appropriate alternatives for completing tasks make sense.

## TIPS FOR TEACHERS

### 7.4 Guiding Students to Learn Appropriate Behaviors from Classmates

1. Identify student "models" and their behaviors that you want other students to emulate. For example, "Joaquin has his math book open to page 38 and is looking at me to indicate that he is ready. Show me that you are ready by doing the same thing."
2. Monitor whether the student with emotional or behavioral disorders follows the model. Look for approximations and provide positive reinforcement. For example, "Sheilah (student with emotional or behavioral problems) is getting her math book out. What are the next two things you need to do, Sheilah, to indicate that you are ready?"
3. Provide frequent feedback when the student performs the desired behaviors. Look for as many chances as possible to recognize desirable behaviors.
4. Students who view themselves as "like" a model are more likely than not to imitate desirable behaviors. You can facilitate this process by identifying ways in which students' behaviors are similar. For example, "Sheilah (student with emotional or behavioral disorder) and Joaquin are not talking while they are getting ready for the homework assignment. Good for them!"

# TECH TALK

## Interactive Multimedia

In this era of advancing technology, interactive multimedia are playing an important role in education. Computer-assisted learning can act as a supplement to existing resources. The Vocational Rehabilitation Learning Resource Package (VRLR), a self-paced learning package, is discussed at the following website: http:www.clt.uts.edu.au/Cameron.html/

Interactive Multimedia, Inc. provides educational games for all ages. Its fully interactive CD-ROM allows the user to choose the direction, action, and outcome of the overall experience. The user can explore entire areas of information through different media thoroughly at his or her convenience. The information is presented on a CD-ROM using high-impact audio, video, and animations. The CD-ROM is capable of being viewed on all Windows 95/98/NT and 3.x systems.

ESL/ELT Multimedia Software produces *Euro*Plus+ *Flying Colours,* which is a software application for serious learners of English who favor an academic approach. The learner can do a variety of things, including listening to dialogues and taking part in them, watching video clips, and reading passages. The student can practice pronunciation by recording his or her voice and comparing it with that of a native speaker. Students can also check their understanding by doing a multitude of different exercises with immediate feedback. *Euro*Plus+ is available at four levels, each providing about 150 hours of intensive study. *Euro*Plus+ provides a number of supporting tools such as Audio Dictionary, Tape Recorder, Browser, and Spelling Teacher. A demonstration can be downloaded at http://users.bigpond.net.au/ESL_Multimedia. Details regarding this software can be obtained at this site.

SLIM SHOW is an interactive multimedia authoring software for MS-Windows. It has a compact runtime engine that allows the teacher to create professional-looking multimedia projects containing graphics, text, sound, music, video clips, buttons, animation objects, and text-to-speech objects. Projects can be made for distribution on diskettes, CD-ROMs, the Internet, or other media. It can be used to create tutorials and educational programs. It requires Windows 3.1/95/98/NT and SVGA 640x480 by 256 or better. A sound card is needed to hear the audio.

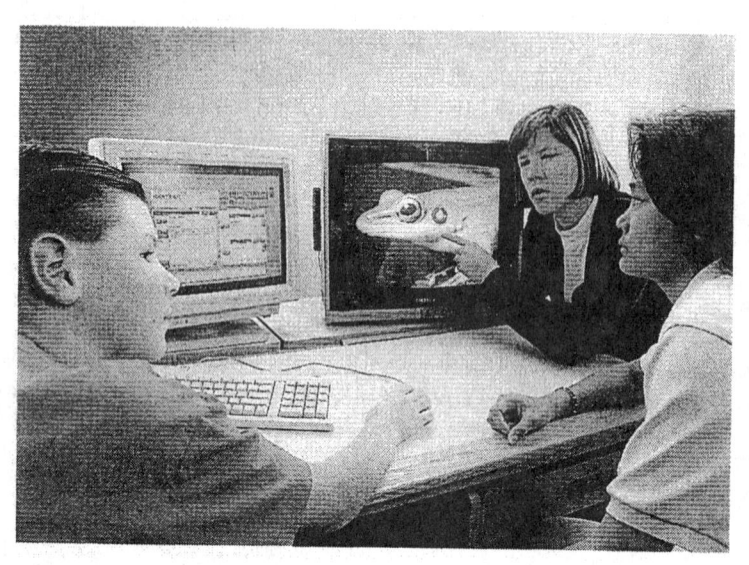

Courtesy of Video Discovery.

The program has several features, including an authoring program for making multimedia projects to run on Windows 3.1x, 95/98, and NT. It supports button objects for interactivity, includes a print option, contains an easy-to-use visual authoring environment with no programming, no scripting, and no pages—just click, drag, and drop. They have several projects, including Multimedia Playroom, that focus on educational activities for kids, such as learning to tell time, a music encyclopedia, 100 questions and answers, and more. A SlimShow tutorial made with *Slim Show* can be downloaded for free, and third-party tools for creating multimedia project material can be accessed at http://www.pcww.com/web_mat/presentations.html. Software can be ordered at 1-800-242-4775 or 1-713-524-6394. Fax: 1-713-524-6398. Mail: PSL, P.O.Box 35705, Houston, TX 77235-5705, USA.

Educational Software Institute (ESI) provides interactive software for all ages. They produce *A+LS–Advanced Learning System* Complete Series, which is a system of fully managed educational software. The A+LS Multimedia Curriculum Authoring System provides teachers full multimedia authoring capabilities. Importantly, all of these features are integral to each and every A+LS subject title, providing schools with a true building-block approach to a fully integrated curriculum solution. Macintosh users require a 68040-based machine or better, System 7.5.3 Update 2 or higher, and 8 MB RAM. Windows users require a 486 processor or higher, Windows 3.11 or higher, Win95 Service Pack 1 or higher, 8MB RAM for Win3.11, 16 MB RAM for Win95, Windows-compatible mouse, and Windows-compatible sound card and speakers or headphones (recommended). Contact ESI for Network/Site License policy, pricing, and availability. Floppy diskettes are available upon request at a slightly increased price. This complete series, which contains 43 titles, provides administrators, teachers, and students with a unique, fully authorable, and open instruction management and learning system. It gives teachers the flexibility to provide their students with a wide range of instructional software, along with the ability to create, for each student, an individualized lesson sequence. A+LS also provides a complete range of fully correlated instructional software in the areas of reading, writing, mathematics, social studies, and science. This entire curriculum is managed, graded, and reported through a comprehensive, easy-to-use management system with the ability to print study material assignments, and tests. Details about this software can be obtained online at http://www.edsoft.com, or at Educational Software Institute, 4213 South 94th Street, Omaha, NE 68127. Phone 1-800-955-5570. Fax: 1-402-592-2017.

Parrot Software provides programs that focus on speaking English. These programs can be set up to provide the directions in either spoken or written form. The number of different directions can be set between 1 and 3 to increase the difficulty of the task. The program runs on any Windows-compatible word processor. The font includes 150 characters that can be scaled between 3 and 127 points. The specific characters include those from the International Phonetic Alphabet, along with others found in scientific articles using phonetic characters. It requires Windows 3.x or Windows 95.

Parrot Software also produces an interactive version of the *Brubaker Workbook Series* on the computer. This software allows the teacher to create in seconds exactly the kind of workbook that is needed. This program provides an extensive source of language and cognitive exercises that allow the teacher to create a workbook that specifically targets a child's unique deficits. The teacher indicates the types of deficits demonstrated by a particular child by clicking on an extensive list of language and cognitive concepts. The teacher also indicates target area, cognitive and language concepts, difficulty level, response type, print size, spacing, and typeface. The program uses these options to create the most appropriate exercises from a huge database. The exercises selected can be viewed on-screen before a personalized workbook is printed. With over 1,500 new exercises on disk, the combinations are all-encompassing and comprehensive, allowing individuals to progress through the same exercise with several levels of difficulty or different exercises with one concept. The workbook can be saved and printed all or in part at any time. It requires Windows 3.x or 95, 8 MB of RAM, a printer, and a mouse. Details can be found online at http://www.parrotsoftware.com.

For further information, there are books that demonstrate how to create vibrant multimedia environments to enhance a child's educational and play experience, and a multimedia guide that includes a history of children's software and profiles of the latest technologies. Details regarding these and other similar books can be obtained at http://www.amazon.com.

## SUMMARY

- Students with emotional and behavioral disorders exhibit behaviors that are significantly different from the norm, and that persist over a long period of time.
- Emotional and behavioral disorders are grouped into two broad categories: externalizing and internalizing.
- Externalizing behaviors are characterized by acting out, aggression, and interfering, attention, and conduct problems.
- Internalizing behaviors are viewed as more self-directed, such as being anxious, worried, and depressed.

- There are six major classifications of emotional and behavioral disorders: conduct disorder, attention problems, socialized-aggression, pervasive developmental disorder, immaturity, and anxiety–withdrawal. Some of these classifications fit the externalizing category, some the internalizing category, and some fit both, depending on the specific manifestation of the problem behavior.
- The criteria considered when interpreting emotional or behavioral problems include: behavior–age discrepancy, frequency of occurrence of behavior(s), number of symptoms, inner suffering, persistence of behavior, self-satisfaction, and severity and duration of behavior(s).
- Points to consider when teaching students with emotional and behavioral disorders include: altering the environment, targeting and changing behavior, promoting academic and social factors that enhance learning, providing successful experiences, providing ample opportunities for students to learn, monitoring and changing activities, and using alternative behavior-management strategies.

## Key Terms and Concepts

anxiety–withdrawal
conduct disorder
conflict resolution
developmental pathways
Diagnostic and Statistical Manual of Mental Disorders (DSM)
emotional or behavioral disorders
externalizing behaviors
gangs
group behavior
immaturity
internalizing behaviors
motor excess
pervasive developmental disorder
social learning
socialized-aggression

## Think and Apply

1. Now that you have read Chapter 7, consider the behaviors of Lenox, the student in Juline's first-grade class described at the beginning of the chapter. Make a list of the types of behaviors you would expect Lenox to exhibit. Consider the suggestions provided in the chapter and list instructional and behavior-management practices you could implement to enhance this student's success. File your responses in your teaching portfolio and add ideas as you read this book.
2. Identify a practicing teacher you can interview, and ask him or her the following questions:
    a. To what extent have students in your class exhibited symptoms of emotional and behavioral disorders? What kinds of problems do you see?
    b. Do you think that more students have emotional and behavioral problems today than in the past? Why or why not?
    c. To what do you attribute students' emotional and behavioral problems?
    d. What advice would you give to teachers about working effectively with students with emotional and behavioral disorders?

    Compare the teacher's answers with your own ideas and those of your classmates.
3. Most school districts have special classrooms or programs for students with severe emotional and behavioral disorders. Make arrangements to visit one of these classrooms or programs. How do these educational settings differ from the general education classroom? What types of resources are available to meet the special learning needs of these students?

# Read More about It

1. Coleman, M. C. (1996). *Emotional and behavioral disorders: Theory and practice.* Boston: Allyn & Bacon.

   Provides a complete overview of children and adolescents with behavioral and emotional problems, including internalizing and externalizing problems, assessment, and educational issues.

2. Knitzer, J., Steinberg, Z., & Fleisch, B. (1990). *At the school house door: An examination of programs and policies for children with behavioral and emotional problems.* New York: Bank Street College of Education.

   A comprehensive examination of the types of programs available for school-age children with emotional and behavioral disorders, this book also describes the educational, political, and social policies that influence intervention programs for these students.

3. MacCracken, M. (1973). *Circle of children.* Philadelphia: J. B. Lippincott.

   This personal account of one teacher's experiences instructing students with emotional disorders poignantly describes the frustrations and successes teachers are likely to encounter when working with this student population.

4. Quay, H. C., & Werry, J. S. (1986). *Psychopathological disorders of childhood.* New York: Wiley.

   A comprehensive overview of the classification, research, and intervention effects of treating students with emotional and behavioral disorders. This book identifies the types of problems frequently found in students and expands on the subtypes presented in this chapter.

5. Walker, H. M., Colvin, G., & Ramsey, E. (1995). *Antisocial behavior in school: Strategies and best practices.* Pacific Grove, CA: Brooks/Cole.

   Provides background on identification, classification, and intervention strategies for addressing antisocial behavior of students in school settings.

CHAPTER *13*

# Teaching Students with Mental Retardation and Severe Disabilities

# Interview

### Susie Speelman, Mary Robinson, and Steve Canty

Susie Speelman is an **inclusion support teacher** at Sunrise Elementary School, Tucson, Arizona. Susie's job involves supporting students with mental retardation, severe disabilities, physical disabilities (e.g., cerebral palsy), and visual impairments in general education classrooms. To do this Susie works closely with the general education teachers at Sunrise to learn what the different classes will be doing and to make the necessary accommodations or adaptations so that students with disabilities can be successful and learn at their level.

Susie has been in this position for 3 years and, therefore, knows well the children whom she supports. Susie does not work alone—besides herself there are six educational assistants (EAs) or paraprofessionals who support the 10 children with whom she works in 10 different kindergarten-through-fifth-grade classrooms. When talking about making accommodations, Susie comments:

> The key to making inclusion work is to have good working relationships with the classroom teachers and to assist them in feeling that they are capable of teaching students with significant disabilities. In working in the different classrooms, one generalization that I can make is that it is the attitude and knowledge of the classroom teacher that is oftentimes the key to a student's success. If the teacher has a "can do" attitude and considers the student a viable member of the class, then the stage is set for the student's success. My job becomes one of providing the supports for the student's learning. This may be an EA who works in the classroom part- or full-time, using assistive technology such as a communication board, or my directly working with the student. While it may appear more challenging to support these children at the upper elementary level where the work includes more pencil and paper tasks, I have found that many of my students have become fascinated with the various hands-on projects and activities that are emphasized at the upper elementary level in content subjects such as math, science, social studies, and art.

Melody's work in Mary Robinson's fifth-grade class is a good example of how a student with mild to moderate mental retardation is integrated into the classroom community. One of Melody's strengths is math. With the help of the EA and peer tutors, she is developing many functional math skills, such as reading prices and knowing how much money is necessary to make a purchase. Melody is also memorizing basic addition and subtraction facts. While the other students are working on timed tests or on the computer, Melody also works on a timed test or on computer programs for math facts. In this way she participates like the other students, but the content of her work is different.

Many of Melody's goals focus on communication and social development and are worked on throughout the school day. Mary, Susie, and the EA know that Melody is working on asking for help instead of waiting for someone to notice her, and also on looking up and speaking clearly. The team finds opportunities throughout the day to work on these goals. Mary comments on how she integrates Melody's goals into the class routines:

> Now that I know Melody, it is easy to integrate her goals with the other students' goals. For example, students are expected to be independent in this classroom, and we use lots of semistructured activities such as writer's workshop and literature study groups. Each requires that the students take responsibility for getting materials, working on projects, and evaluating their own learning. Melody is responsible for getting and putting away her writing folder, her literature log, and her reading folder just like the other students. As a reminder, I have a picture of each taped on her desk. When she has difficulty remembering to get or put away her materials, I can point to the picture of what she needs to get or put away. This serves as a cue, without calling undue attention to her.

José, another student Susie supports, is in Steve Canty's third-grade class. José has severe disabilities, is nonverbal, and uses a wheelchair. One of the most difficult challenges with José is to get him actively involved in the classroom activities. Steve comments:

> José tends to let others make decisions for him and he sits back and watches instead of participating. Therefore, making choices is one of José's major goals. Susie and I have worked hard at providing José lots of opportunities and helped his peers also give José choices throughout the day.
>
> For example, when the students were designing their own money, one of José's classmates gave him three choices of designs for their joint project.

Susie, Mary, and Steve all agree that an important key to the successful integration of Melody and José is co-planning and ongoing communication not just among themselves, but with the EAs, with parents, and with other specialists who work with these students, including the speech and language pathologist and the occupational therapist.

## Introduction

Like Mary and Steve, you will probably have students like Melody and José in your class. This chapter provides information about these students. It also presents a process for curriculum modification and describes strategies you can use to support students with mental retardation and severe disabilities in your own classroom.

## Definitions and Types of Mental Retardation and Severe Disabilities

The populations of individuals considered to have mental retardation or severe disabilities are quite heterogeneous, as is evident in our interview with teachers at Sunrise Elementary. This section discusses the definitions and types of mental retardation and severe disabilities.

### Mental Retardation

Students with mental retardation have limited intellectual functioning, which affects their learning. These students have slower rates of learning and are particularly challenged by complex and abstract tasks. Students with mental retardation are just like other students in your class in that they are members of families, have friends and neighbors, have personalities shaped by both their innate characteristics and life experiences, and have aspirations to become adults, get jobs, and fall in love (Orelore & Sobsey, 1996; Smith, 1998). Yet, to be successful in general education classrooms, they also need additional support and accommodations. In planning for this support, it is helpful to have some knowledge about mental retardation and how it affects learning.

The underlying concept associated with mental retardation is that students have limited abilities to learn. Historically, definitions of mental retardation focused on limitations in intellectual functioning (as measured by intelligence tests). More recent definitions are broader, focusing on four major concepts:

- **Intellectual functioning:** Individuals who have mental retardation have substantial limitations in **intellectual functioning** and have been characterized as having "significantly subaverage intellectual functioning." On measures of intellectual functioning, "significantly subaverage" has been defined as an IQ of 70 to 75 or less, and includes about 3 percent of the population.
- **Adaptive behavior:** Students who have mental retardation also have significant limitations in adaptive skills or behavior. **Adaptive behavior** refers to "the effectiveness or degree with which individuals meet the standards of personal independence and social responsibility expected for age and cultural group" (Grossman, 1983, p.1).
- **Developmental period:** Students who have mental retardation demonstrate limitations in intellectual functioning and adaptive behavior during the **developmental period**, before the age of 18. Persons who acquire limited intellectual functioning after that age are not referred to as having mental retardation but instead as having traumatic brain injury, or whatever the cause of the disability (Smith, 1998).
- **Systems of support:** This term refers to the coordinated set of services and accommodations matched to a student's needs, and can include teachers and specialists, specialized programs and methodologies, and assistive technology. When appropriate supports are provided over a sustained period, the life functioning of students with mental retardation will generally improve (AAMR, 1992).

Using these four themes, in 1992 the American Association on Mental Retardation (AAMR) defined **mental retardation** as follows:

> *Mental retardation* refers to substantial limitations in present functioning. It is characterized by significantly subaverage intellectual functioning, existing concurrently with related limitations in two or more of the following applicable adaptive skill areas: communication, self-care, home living, social skills, community use, self-direction, health and safety, functional academics, leisure and work. Mental retardation manifests before age 18 (p. 1).

The following four assumptions are essential to the application of this definition:

- Valid assessment considers cultural and linguistic diversity, as well as differences in communication and behavioral factors.

- The existence of limitations in adaptive skills occurs within the context of community environments typical of the individual's age peers and is indexed to the person's individual needs for supports.
- Specific adaptive limitations often coexist with strengths in other adaptive skills or other personal capabilities.
- With appropriate supports over a sustained period, the life functioning of the person with mental retardation will generally improve (AAMR, 1992, p. 5).

In comparison to previous definitions, the current definition stresses the interaction among: (1) the environment in which the person functions, (2) the person's capabilities, and (3) the need for varying levels of support (Beirne-Smith, Ittenbach, & Patton, 1998).

In addition, the new definition reflects a change in the classification system. The traditional system emphasized the individual's degree of retardation (i.e., mild retardation [IQ scores of 50–55 to 70–75], moderate retardation [35–40 to 50–55], severe retardation [20–25 to 35–40], profound retardation [below 20–25]). The new classification system emphasizes the level of supports needed to facilitate the individual's integration into the community (Meyen & Skrtic, 1995). Figure 8.1 presents this new classification system, along with examples of support at each level. The classification system incorporates a multidimensional approach that includes emotional, psychological, and related health factors.

The cause of the mental retardation, although known only about 50 percent of the time (Beirne-Smith et al., 1998), is one way people think about different types of mental retardation. Chromosomal disorders are probably the best known cause of mental retardation. **Down syndrome**, one of the most common chromosomal disorders, is often what people think of when mental retardation is mentioned. Yet Down syndrome occurs in only about 1 in 700 live births and accounts for less than 10 percent of all individuals with mental retardation (Kozma & Stock, 1993). **Fetal Alcohol Syndrome** (FAS), one of the top three known causes of birth defects (Griego, 1994), refers to a spectrum of birth defects caused by the mother's drinking during pregnancy, and is fast becoming the leading cause of mental retardation (March of Dimes, 1993). Children with FAS may experience some degree of mental retardation, poor coordination, learning disabilities, psychosocial behavior problems, physical abnormalities, and speech and language problems (Umansky & Hooper, 1998).

### Severe Disabilities

**Severe disabilities** are often described as a condition in which typical life activities are significantly affected. The Association for Persons with Severe Handicaps (TASH), defines persons with severe disabilities as:

> individuals of all ages who require extensive ongoing support in more than one major life activity in order to participate in integrated community settings and to enjoy a quality of life that is available to citizens with fewer or no disabilities. Support may be required for life activities such as mobility, communication, self-care, and learning as necessary for independent living, employment and self-sufficiency (Meyer et al., 1991, p. 19).

Among those considered to have severe disabilities are students whose mental retardation is severe or profound, who are autistic, who have dual sensory impairments (i.e., deaf–blind), or who have multiple disabilities (e.g., significant mental retardation and physical disabilities, or mental retardation and a sensory disability).

**Autism** Autism is a physical disorder of the brain that causes a developmental disability. Although persons diagnosed as autistic are considered to have a severe disability, the range in ability levels within this group is varied (Powers, 1989). Some individuals with autism may function independently or almost independently. Kim Peek, the character played by Dustin Hoffman in the movie *Rainman*, is an example of an individual who has autism but generally functions independently (and even has some specific cognitive abilities in the genius range).

The physical features of people with autism may not suggest a disability. Rather, the disability generally is manifested in their language and their personal and social behavior. According to the Individuals with Disabilities Education Act (1997) *autism* means:

> A developmental disability significantly affecting verbal and nonverbal communication and social interaction, generally evident before age 3,

## FIGURE 8.1

**1992 Classification System for Mental Retardation**

| LEVEL OF SUPPORT | DESCRIPTION OF SUPPORT | EXAMPLE |
|---|---|---|
| Intermittent | Support on an "as needed basis." Characterized by episodic nature, person not always needing the support(s), or short-term supports needed during life-span transitions (e.g., job loss or an acute medical crisis). Intermittent supports may be high or low intensity when provided. | Counseling support needed as student adjusts to school at the beginning of each year and as the student begins job training programs in high school. |
| Limited | An intensity of supports characterized by consistency over time, time-limited but not of an intermittent nature, may require fewer staff members and less cost than more intense levels of supports (e.g., time-limited employment training or transitional supports during the school to adult period). | Support provided to a high-school student with mild mental retardation as they take specially designed courses in learning strategies/study skills, functional English, and applied math. Support provided by a job developer as student works in the afternoons. |
| Extensive | Supports characterized by regular involvement in at least some environments (such as work or home) and not time limited ( e.g., long-term support and long-term home living support). | Support provided to an elementary-age student with a moderate or severe disability who works in the general education classroom. An educational assistant provides the major support during reading, language arts, math, and science, with peers and the classroom teacher providing the major support at other times of the day. |
| Pervasive | Supports characterized by their constancy, high intensity; provided across environments; potentially life-sustaining nature. Pervasive supports typically involve more staff members and intrusiveness than do extensive or time-limited supports (Luckasson et al., 1992, p. 26). | Ongoing support provided to a student who is medically fragile and in need of constant support by a staff member. |

Adapted from Luckasson, R., Coulter, D. L., Polloway, E. A., Reiss, S., Schalock, R. L. Snell, M. E., Spitalnik, D. M., & Stark, J. A. (1992). *Mental retardation: Definition, classification, and systems of supports.* Washington, DC: American Association on Mental Retardation, p. 26.

that adversely affects a child's performance. Other characteristics often associated with autism are engagement in repetitive activities and stereotyped movements, resistance to environmental change or change in daily routines, and unusual responses to sensory experiences. The term does not apply if a child's educational performance is adversely affected primarily because the child has a serious emotional disturbance (34 C.F.R., Part 300, Sec. 300.7[b][1]).

> When autism was first identified in the 1940s, it was thought to be a psychosocial problem caused by parents' aloof or hostile behavior. Later, autism was classified under physical impairments. Not until the IDEA amendments of 1990 was autism treated as a separate disability category.

After having Jason, a student with autism, in his seventh-grade language block for several months, Robert Hernandez expressed these thoughts, "I was worried about how it would work with the other students; if it would take away from them. I was concerned that Jason would be a distraction to the students. But now that Jason has been part of our class for several months, I feel that the more he is in the classroom, the less the children even notice the noise or occasional outbursts. The students had to learn that Jason will do things that are not okay for them to do."

Tips for Teachers 8.1 presents Robert's advice for working with students like Jason in the classroom.

**Multiple Disabilities** Individuals with **multiple disabilities** have mental retardation that is severe or profound, as well as one or more significant motor or sensory impairments or special health needs. For example, a person with severe mental retardation might also have cerebral palsy or epilepsy (Orelore & Sobsey, 1996; Westling & Fox, 1995). Types of multiple disabilities include: mental retardation with physical disabilities (e.g., cerebral palsy, spina bifida, seizure disorders), or mental retardation with severe behavior disorders, or mental retardation with a visual or hearing impairment. It is reasonable to expect that two of every five students with severe and multiple disabilities will have a sensory impairment (Sobsey & Wolf-Schein, 1991).

> Fifty to sixty percent of persons with cerebral palsy also experience a mental disability.

Like all students, students with multiple disabilities have learning needs that require a *holistic* approach to education (an approach in which the student is viewed as a whole person). In determining educational goals and teaching strategies, professionals consider factors such as the student's emotions, cognitive processes, and other factors that interact

## TIPS FOR TEACHERS

### 8.1 A Teacher's Advice for Working with Students with Autism

- *Don't let the behavior overwhelm you.* Develop a behavior-management plan and implement small steps. Decide what you will put up with and what behaviors must stop, and target those.
- *Talk to the student's parents and other teachers*, and find out what works and what does not work with this student.
- *Systematically expect more and more of the student.* At first the student might only be required to sit with the class with whatever it takes (a favorite object), then the student may be required to hold the reading book.
- *Develop a picture and word schedule for daily activities.* Use this to prepare the student for transitions to new activities. Introduce changes in routine slowly, and let the student know in advance that these changes are going to occur.
- *Use peers to help redirect the student's behavior* and to interest him or her in the task.
- *Take "ownership" of the student* so that he or she feels like a real member of the class.

*What factors must be taken into account when planning instruction for students with severe or multiple disabilities?*

with the environment to produce behavior (Siegel-Causey et al., 1995).

**Dual Sensory Impairments** Students with **dual sensory impairments** (also referred to as **deaf–blind**) present unique challenges in that the two main channels (auditory and visual) of receptive communication and learning are impaired. Although difficult to determine, the cognitive abilities of students with dual sensory impairments can vary from severe retardation to giftedness. Downing and Eichinger (1990) noted that individuals who are deaf–blind may have diverse combinations of vision and hearing impairments with normal or gifted intelligence, or they may have additional mental, physical, and behavioral disabilities. Because these individuals do not receive clear and consistent information from either sensory modality, a tendency exists to turn inward. These individuals may appear passive, not responding to or initiating interactions with others. Tips for Teachers 8.2 provides a list of teaching strategies and guidelines for interacting with individuals with dual sensory impairments.

# Prevention of Mental Retardation

The President's Committee on Mental Retardation reported that more than 50 percent of all cases of mental retardation could have been prevented. Maternal use of alcohol and drugs during pregnancy, as well as maternal infections (such as HIV) are among the fastest-growing causes of mental retardation that can be prevented. For example, women who smoke heavily during the last 6 months of pregnancy are 60 percent more likely to have children with mental retardation (Bergstein, 1996). McLaren and Bryson (1987) estimated that as many as 15 percent of the cases of mild retardation are a result of child abuse or neglect, and that 1 in 30 newborns will experience a serious head trauma before the age of 18. Poverty can cause mental retardation through increased chances of lead poisoning, inadequate diet, inadequate health care (including immunizations), unsafe neighborhoods, and environmental pollutants (Smith, 1998). In fact, Menolascino and Stark (1988) stated that poverty is a determinant in 75 to 80 percent of people with mental retardation at higher IQ levels. Following are some simple prevention strategies:

**Prenatal**
- Avoid using alcohol, drugs, and smoking.
- Avoid sexually transmitted diseases.
- Obtain appropriate medical care.
- Maintain good health and nutrition.
- Immediately treat infections.
- Obtain genetic testing and prenatal tests, if indicated.

**Postnatal**
- Provide proper nutrition and medical care.
- Obtain proper immunizations.
- Use infant and child car seats and seat belts in automobiles.
- Prevent lead or other chemical intake.
- Eliminate child abuse and neglect.
- Eliminate poverty and associated conditions.

# Prevalence of Mental Retardation and Severe Disabilities

Prevalence of persons with mental retardation is difficult to determine because different definitions and methodologies are used to determine retardation. Generally, however, prevalence is estimated to be about 1 to 2 percent of the population. According to the federal government, slightly more than 1 percent of the school-age population is identified as having mental retardation and requiring special education services (U.S. Department of Education, 1997), with approximately 90 percent of those

# TIPS FOR TEACHERS

### 8.2 Environmental Accommodations for Students with Dual Sensory Impairments

- Develop a tactile schedule for your student. Each activity of the day has an object that represents it. For example: math—calculator; lunch—spoon; reading—a small book.
- Along with the schedule, objects can be used to make choices, get information from the environment or convey a message (e.g., handing the teacher a small pillow might mean the student wants his or her position changed, choosing a small ball would communicate what the student wants to do during recess).
- Tactually or visually identify your student's belongings with a consistent, meaningful symbol. This will help facilitate independence (e.g., a pencil taped on the desk, a safety pin on the tag of his or her coat).
- Have clear pathways marked with objects that serve as cues. Consistent furniture, or tactile or visual runners on the wall help promote orientation and the student's independent mobility. Important places should be distinguished by special cues.
- To encourage your student to use his or her remaining hearing or vision, add light, color, sound, vibration, interesting textures, and colors to objects.
- Firmly touch the student's shoulder to signal that an interaction is going to occur.
- Introduce yourself by using a consistent symbol for your name. This could be a ring, watch, or other piece of jewelry you always wear that the student could easily touch. Or it could be a distinguishing feature, such as your hair or glasses. Name signs or the finger spelling of the first letter of your name could also be signed in the palm of the student's hand as a consistent symbol for your name.

Adapted from Rikhye, C. H. Gotheif, C. R., & Appell, M. W. (1989). A classroom environment checklist for students with dual sensory impairments. *Teaching Exceptional Children*, 22(1), 44–46; California Deaf–Blind Services (1992). *How to interact with individuals with dual sensory impairments* (Fact Sheet). California: Author.

---

students having mild retardation. Prevalence of multiple disabilities is difficult to determine, as different states use different classification systems (e.g., some states include students with multiple disabilities under the category of physical disabilities). The United States Department of Education (1994) reports that about 0.13 percent of the general population has multiple disabilities or dual sensory impairments.

It is interesting to note that the prevalence of children born with severe disabilities is on the rise. Some screening and early intervention has led to a reduction in causes (e.g., most hospitals now screen to determine whether babies have phenylketonuria [PKU], so that it can be treated before mental retardation occurs), but the number of children being born exposed to drugs and alcohol is increasing. In addition, because medical advances have also resulted in more high-risk and low birth weight babies living and living longer, more children with disabilities are reaching school age.

## Characteristics of Students with Mental Retardation and Severe Disabilities

When you consider the characteristics of students with mental retardation and severe disabilities, not every student will have all the characteristics discussed. As a group, however, students with mental retardation and severe disabilities display these characteristics more often than the general population (Mihail, 1995). The characteristics are grouped into four areas: intellectual functioning, social skills, motor skills, and communication.

### Intellectual Functioning

Students with mental retardation and severe disabilities, although they have many diverse learning characteristics, generally learn slowly and often fail to notice relevant features of what is being taught, do not demonstrate learned skills spontaneously, and have difficulty generalizing learned skills to new situations (Noonan Siegel-Causey, 1990). These students also have difficulty learning complex skills and abstract concepts, and learn less overall than other students learn. Many students with mental retardation and severe disabilities experience memory deficits, either remembering incorrectly or not remembering automatically. These students frequently need additional cues to help them focus their attention.

Students with mild retardation learn academic tasks such as reading, writing, and math—sometimes achieving up to a sixth-grade level in some areas by the end of high school. These students, however, usually have more success with basic academic skills (such as decoding and math computation) than with more abstract and applied skills, such as reading comprehension and math problem-solving (Thomas & Patton, 1990). Students also have significant difficulty making connections among ideas and generalizing newly learned knowledge and skills to new situations (Drew et al., 1996). The following strategies promote skill and strategy acquisition and generalization:

- Engage students actively in learning.
- Teach the strategy or skill in small steps or segments.
- Check frequently for understanding.
- Use actual materials and real life experiences or simulations.
- Teach students to use self-talk to "talk themselves through" activities.
- Have students perform the skill or strategy repeatedly.
- Provide many examples to promote generalization.
- Use the skill or strategy in several different learning situations to promote generalization.

Given that students with mental retardation have slow learning rates and significant difficulty learning higher-level thinking skills and abstract concepts, what they learn should be necessary to their daily functioning and serve them in their adult lives. The *Brigance Diagnostic Inventory of Essential Skills* (Brigance, 1981) provides one means of assessing higher-level functional skills (see Table 8.1).

Because students with mental retardation have many opportunities to experience failure, they can develop poor motivation for learning, and set low goals (Balla & Zigler, 1979). They also learn not to trust their own solutions, and look to others for cues (Zigler & Burack, 1989). Many students with mental retardation display **biased responding**—saying "yes" because they want to please the teacher or hide their confusion (Sigelman et al., 1981).

For Lilly, an eleventh grader with Down syndrome and mild mental retardation, it is important that her teachers accommodate her slower rate, more concrete style of learning, and low level of confidence in her ability to learn. Lilly, who attends Madison High School, is mainstreamed for physical education, art (her favorite class), and home economics.

Grace Fong, her home economics teacher, makes several accommodations for Lilly. Although Lilly can decode the words in many recipes, directions, and other readings in the class, Grace found that Lilly often does not understand what she is reading. To help Lilly and several other students in her class, Grace uses paired reading and has the students check often for understanding. The students read with partners, stopping at the end of each paragraph or section to discuss that paragraph (or section), consistently using the cue, "What was this mainly about?" Lilly can check for understanding as she reads, instead of reading the entire assignment and then realizing that she has not understood. When reading recipes and directions for sewing, the pairs stop after each ingredient or direction and discuss what to do. Grace finds that this approach helps increase not only Lilly's success in comprehending what she reads, but also her confidence in her reading skills. Grace also finds that, in the long run, with paired reading all her students do better (and enjoy the interactions that naturally occur).

## Social Skills

Students with mental retardation and severe disabilities have friends and participate in social activities, but often have difficulties developing friendships. Such difficulties may be due to behaviors that deter interactions or to the lack of opportunity (Westling & Fox, 1995). With the move toward inclusive learning communities, students have more opportunities to make friends.

The "Circles of Friends" (Forest & Lusthaus, 1989) is one example of an activity that can promote social support for students with disabilities as they are integrated into general education classrooms. In this

## TABLE 8.1

**Functional Skills Assessed by the Brigance Diagnostic Inventory of Essential Skills**

| Area | Subtests | Area | Subtests |
|---|---|---|---|
| *Functional Word Recognition* | Basic sight vocabulary<br>Direction words<br>Abbreviations<br>Warning/safety signs<br>Reads number words | *Health and Safety* | Medical vocabulary<br>Medical labels<br>Health evaluation form<br>Health practices and attitude rating scale<br>Self-concept rating scale<br>Warning labels |
| *Schedules and Graphs* | Reads class schedule<br>Reads television schedule<br>Identifies and interprets graphs | *Money and Finance* | Price signs<br>Computes totals for amounts of money<br>Making change<br>Comprehends and computes purchase savings<br>Computes expenses using charts and tables<br>Balancing a checking account<br>Manages a checking account<br>Computes interest on loans<br>Reads and comprehends a credit agreement<br>Application for a credit card<br>Reads and comprehends monthly credit statement |
| *Forms* | School information form<br>Computer base form | | |
| *Measurement* | Equivalent values of coins and the dollar bill<br>Total values of collections of coins and bills<br>Conversion of coins<br>Time<br>Equivalent units of time<br>Conversion of units of time<br>Equivalent calendar units<br>Conversion of calendar units<br>Calendar<br>Dates<br>Ruler<br>Equivalent units of measurement<br>Conversion of units of measurement<br>Meters and gauges<br>Concepts of Fahrenheit temperature | | |
| | | *Travel and Transportation* | Traffic signs<br>Traffic symbols<br>Car parts vocabulary<br>Identifies car parts<br>Application for driver's instruction permit<br>Auto safety rating scale<br>Gas mileage and cost<br>Mileage table<br>Bus schedule and map of route<br>Road map |
| *Vocational* | Attitude rating scale<br>Personality rating scale<br>Responsibility and self-discipline rating scale<br>Job interests and aptitudes<br>Health and physical problems/handicaps<br>Application for a social security number<br>Choosing a career<br>Employment signs<br>Employment vocabulary<br>Employment abbreviations<br>"Help wanted" advertisements<br>Simple application for employment<br>Complex application for employment<br>Job interview questions<br>Job interview preparation rating scale<br>Job interview rating scale<br>W-4 form<br>Future time on clock<br>Past time on clock<br>Time duration on clock<br>Payroll deductions<br>Federal income tax return—Form 1040A<br>Unemployment compensation form | *Food and Clothing* | Food vocabulary<br>Food preparation vocabulary<br>Basic recipe directions<br>Food labels<br>Conversion of recipes to different servings<br>Foods for a daily balanced diet<br>Computes cost of purchasing different quantities<br>Food quantity at best price<br>Personal sizes of clothing<br>Clothing labels |
| | | *Oral Communication and Telephone Skills* | Speaking skills<br>Speaking skills rating scale<br>Listening skills<br>Listening skills rating scale<br>Telephone<br>Telephone book<br>Telephone Yellow Pages |

Reprinted with permission from Brigance, A. H. (1981). *Brigance Diagnostic Inventory of Essential Skills*. North Billerica, MA: Curriculum Associates.

activity, each student in the classroom completes a picture of his or her circles of friends, following the steps in Tips for Teachers 8.3.

Some students, particularly those with autism, may seem uninterested in the people around them, seldom making eye contact, initiating, or responding to interactions. Students with severe disabilities often engage in isolated inappropriate behaviors such as stereotypic or self-injurious behaviors. **Stereotypic behaviors** include rocking, flapping fingers, twirling or spinning objects, and grinding teeth. **Self-injurious behavior**, which occurs in only 5 to 15 percent of individuals with severe retardation, may consist of head banging, scratching, or biting oneself, and is difficult to understand. One of several theories about why students exhibit these behaviors is that they are a means of communicating or regulating their own level of awareness (Helmstetter & Durand, 1991; Johnson, Baumgart, Helmstetter, & Curry, 1996). Because students are unable to express their desires or dislikes verbally, they express them through their behavior.

## Motor Skills

Some students with mental retardation, and most students with severe disabilities, have physical disabilities (Beirne-Smith et al., 1994) and also experience delays in sensory and motor development. The

---

# TIPS FOR TEACHERS

### 8.3 Providing School Support through Circles of Friends

Circles of Friends (Forest & Lusthaus, 1989) is an activity that can be used when students with disabilities are going to be integrated into general education classrooms. In this activity, each student in the classroom completes a picture of his or her circles of friends, using the following steps:
1. Students draw four circles.
2. In the first circle, students list the people closest to them, the people that they love.
3. In the second circle, students list the people they really like (but not enough to put in the first circle).
4. In the third circle, students list groups of people they like or people they do things with (e.g., scouts, soccer team).
5. In the fourth circle, students list people paid to be in their lives (e.g., doctor, dentist).

After students have completed their own circles of friends, the teacher describes the circles for a "fantasy person" who is similar to the student who will be joining the class. For example, a student might have only Mom listed in the first circle, with the second and third circles empty. In the fourth circle are a number of doctors and therapists. Through discussion, the teacher and students talk about how the student must feel and how this fantasy person is similar to the student with disabilities who is going to join the class. Finally, the teacher and students plan on how they can become part of the circles of friends for the student with disabilities through such activities as classroom ambassadors, telephone buddies, lunch buddies, and reading buddies.

How might the Circles of Friends activity contribute to providing social support for students with disabilities in your classroom?

Adapted from Forest, M., & Lusthaus, E. (1989). Promoting educational equality for all students: Circles and maps. In S. Stainback, W. Stainback, and M. Forest (Eds.), *Educating all students in the mainstream of regular education.* (pp. 45–57). Baltimore: Brookes.

physical disabilities commonly found among individuals with severe disabilities include cerebral palsy, spina bifida, seizure disorders, hydrocephalus, and cardiovascular disorders. (Chapter 9 discusses physical disabilities in more detail.) Many students with severe disabilities cannot move independently, and need assistance through wheelchairs, walkers, and braces. Other students may have limited voluntary movement of any type, and may experience difficulty grasping items, holding their heads up, and rolling over.

## Communication Skills

Students with mental retardation and severe disabilities often have difficulties communicating. Delayed speech and other speech problems are more common in students with severe disabilities than in other students. Additionally, language development may be inhibited or significantly delayed in students who have more limited cognitive abilities on which to build language skills, fewer experiences, and less exposure to activities than their nondisabled peers.

For many students with mild mental retardation, speech problems also are mild and can be corrected with help from a speech and language pathologist. Mental retardation affects not only how students communicate, however, but also the content and quality of their communication. These students use shorter, less complex sentences with fewer relative clauses and words with more concrete meanings. They also exhibit poorer recall of sentences (Bernstein & Tiegerman, 1993).

Students with severe disabilities may not acquire speech, or their speech may be difficult to understand for those who do not interact with them often (Parette & Angelo, 1996). It is important to realize that a lack of speech does not preclude communication. Communication can occur through gestures, facial expressions, eye blinks, behavior, and through alternative and augmentative communication (such as the high- and low-technology communication devices introduced in Chapter 6). Low-technology devices can involve pictures or drawings at which the student points to convey a message. High-technology devices can provide voice output (speech synthesizers) and can be programmed with many messages.

A **communication board** is one example of augmentative communication. The essential elements are the board itself and the symbols or pictures. The board can be made of sturdy paper or a board, or it can be a regular or simplified computer keyboard, or a computer screen. The symbols or symbol systems selected depend on the learner and the environment in which he or she lives. Symbols should be selected according to what students need and want to communicate. In constructing communication boards, Lewis (1993) suggests that the following questions need to be addressed:

- What choices will the student be able to make?
- How will the choices be represented on the board?
- How will the student make his or her selections?
- How many choices will be available and how will they be arranged on the board?
- How will the communication board be constructed?

Figure 8.2 presents examples of common symbol systems, which include: *Core Picture Vocabulary* (Johnston, 1985), *Talking Pictures* (Leff & Leff, 1978), *Pic Syms* (Carlson, 1984), *Oakland Schools Picture Dictionary* (Kirstein & Bernstein, 1981), *Picture Communication Symbols* (Johnson, 1985), and *Blissymbols* (Bliss, 1965).

This chapter's Tech Talk (page 230) describes a computer program (The Communication Board-Maker) teachers can use to create communication boards.

Communication is an important area for students with mental retardation and severe disabilities because it gives them some control over their environment and a way to fulfill their wants and needs. It is also an important key to being socially accepted.

The students in Robert Hernandez's seventh-grade class imitated the noises that Jason, a student with autism, made. Robert and the special education teacher discussed with the class how Jason is learning to communicate. "Right now he does not use words, but he makes noises and uses his communication board. The noises he makes are [the way] he communicates, so . . . you need to respect this communication and not make fun of it. Your job is to listen closely and watch the communication board to learn what Jason is saying." Ideas to help students with mental retardation and severe disabilities develop communication skills are discussed in Tips for Teachers 8.4 (page 231).

Approximately 40 percent of children with autism do not speak, and many others use **echolalia**, a repeating of what was said without necessarily understanding the meaning (Powers, 1989). For students with mild retardation, speech difficulties most often occur in articulation and include omissions, substitutions, or distortions of sounds (Beirne-Smith et al., 1994). Speech and language problems are the most frequently diagnosed secondary disability for students with mild retardation (Beirne-Smith et al., 1994).

## Identification and Assessment of Students with Mental Retardation and Severe Disabilities

Before the passage of IDEA in 1975, many students with severe disabilities and mental retardation were not allowed to attend public schools. This federal legislation required that educational services be provided for all students, including students with severe and profound retardation and severe disabilities, with the resulting need for better methods of identification and assessment for educational purposes. With the passage of IDEA amendments in 1986 (P.L. 99-457), these children became eligible to receive special education services as infants, toddlers, and in preschool (see Chapter 1).

Initial identification for students with all but mild mental retardation is usually a medical diagnosis at birth or shortly thereafter. For students with mild mental retardation, initial identification often occurs during preschool when the child's rate of development in cognitive, language, and motor skills is not typical. For these students the emphasis is on developmental and educational assessment, which usually includes measures of general intelligence and measures of adaptive behavior.

Although intelligence tests are still used to determine whether students have mental retardation and severe disabilities, a number of concerns have been raised. First, it can be difficult to know whether the tests accurately reflect the abilities of the students,

### FIGURE 8.2
**Picture Symbol Systems for Communication Boards**

Reprinted by permission from Glennen, S. (1992). Augmentative and alternative communication. In G. Church and S. Glennen (Eds.), *The handbook of assistive technology,* (p. 100). San Diego, CA: Singular Publishing Group.

# TECH TALK

### Communication Board-Maker

The Communication Board-Maker™ (Mayer-Johnson Co. [619-550-0084]) is a software program that allows teachers to create and print communication boards, using the Picture Communication Symbols (Johnson, 1985). This software is available for both Macintosh and IBM compatible systems. The boards are easy to design by using either a menu at the top of the screen or an index of the words for the pictures, or by clicking on the find button at the bottom of the screen and typing in the desired word.

More than 3,000 picture communication symbols are available. The arrangement of the pictures can be modified. Each picture has the written word. The written word for each picture can be deleted or it can be displayed in English, Spanish, or another language. This program provides a simple and efficient way for teachers to construct and modify communication boards.

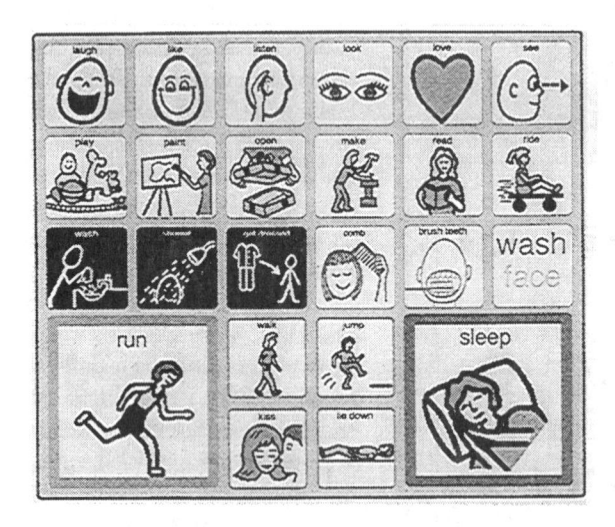

Courtesy of Mayer-Johnson Co.

Adapted from Lewis, R. B. (1993). *Special education technology: Classroom applications* (pp. 388–389). Pacific Grove, CA: Brooks/Cole.

---

particularly given their difficulty with communication and their delayed responses. Second, there is continuing concern regarding cultural influences and biases in tests of intellectual functioning (Baca & Cervantes, 1998). In 1984 the California courts ruled that standardized IQ tests (e.g., Weschler, Stanford-Binet, and Leiter) could not be used to determine eligibility for special education for African American students (*Larry P. v. Riles*, 1984). Factors influencing student performance on intelligence tests include: family history and home life, duration of study in the United States, language proficiency, socioeconomic status, prior educational experiences, and cultural background (Cuccaro, 1996). Currently, emphasis continues to move toward a more functional definition, with intellectual functioning seen as only one aspect to consider in determining mental retardation and severe disabilities.

Another area used to determine evidence of mental retardation is the student's adaptive behavior. One frequently used adaptive behavior scale is the *AAMR Adaptive Behavior Scale—School* (2nd ed.) (Lambert et al., 1993), which includes domains for both adaptive and social behaviors (see Table 8.2 on page 232).

Educational assessments are also used to determine instructional goals and objectives for individual students. According to Westling and Fox (1995), the

## TIPS FOR TEACHERS

### 8.4 Helping Students Develop Communication Skills

Following are areas to consider when assisting students with mental retardation and severe disabilities to develop their communication skills:

**Reason to Communicate**
By anticipating the needs of students with mental retardation and severe disabilities, we often deprive them of reasons to communicate. We need to create situations that motivate students to communicate. An example might be to "accidentally" forget to give them their lunch tickets when the rest of the class receives their tickets, or having every student tell you about the drawing they just did before they can go out to recess. Working on communication skills during everyday activities is known to significantly increase the students' desire to communicate.

**Mode of Communication**
We need to make sure that students have a way, as well as a reason, to communicate. If your students do not use speech, they should have an augmentative communication device. If your students do not have a mode of communication, talk with the school's speech and language pathologist or inclusion specialist about developing or purchasing one.

**Way to Make Choices**
Self-stick notes provide a quick and easy way to provide students with disabilities on-the-spot choices (choosing a word to fill in the blank, choosing a color) to facilitate their participation in class. Just write the choices on the notes and stick them on the students' desks so that they can make the choices.

To help students choose a partner, take pictures of all the students in the class (or use individual class photos) and paste them in a little book or on a board, so that the student with a disability can choose the person with whom he or she wants to work on a class assignment.

---

process of determining instructional needs includes:

- collecting information from existing records
- interviewing parents to determine educational goals
- using adaptive behavior scales, activities, and skill lists to help decide students' needs
- conducting ecological inventories of the students' learning environments

**Functional assessments** determine the skills needed to complete a particular activity or task. **Ecological inventories** assess the different skills a student needs in his or her specific environments. Related service providers also assess the student's speech and physical needs (including vision and hearing, if necessary). The needs and strengths determined by these assessments are then incorporated into the student's IEP goals and objectives or benchmarks.

For all students, but particularly for students with mental retardation and severe disabilities, parents play an important role in assessment. This is evident in IDEA from the emphasis placed on the role of parents in identifying and assessing students with disabilities and in planning for the students' individual education programs. Classroom teachers can also benefit from parent input when these students are included in their classrooms.

When Anne Kiernan, a third-grade teacher, learned that she was going to have a child with autism in her class, she insisted on sitting down with the parents before school started to learn more about the student's strengths and weaknesses. She said, "I wanted to know from John's parents what John was like, ... some of [his] habits ..., what works for them, what doesn't work, and what ... he like[s]. Not to find out negative things—just to talk with them. It was very helpful."

No one knows the student better than his or her family. The family's cultural background influences their perception and attitudes about disabilities. The Research Brief provides a brief summary of three cultural views of disabilities. An understanding of people's diverse views may be helpful to you before you meet with parents.

## TABLE 8.2

**Domains and Subdomains of the AAMR Adaptive Behavior Scale—School**

*Part One*

I. Independent Functioning
   A. Eating
   B. Toilet Use
   C. Cleanliness
   D. Appearance
   E. Care of Clothing
   F. Dressing and Undressing
   G. Travel
   H. Other Independent Functioning

II. Physical Development
   A. Sensory Development
   B. Motor Development

III. Economic Activity
   A. Money Handling and Budgeting
   B. Shopping Skills

IV. Language Development
   A. Expression
   B. Verbal Comprehension
   C. Social Language Development

V. Numbers and Time

VI. Prevocational/Vocational Activity

VII. Self-Direction
   A. Initiative
   B. Perseverance
   C. Leisure Time

VIII. Responsibility

IX. Socialization

*Part Two*

X. Social Behavior

XI. Conformity

XII. Trustworthiness

XIII. Stereotypical and Hyperactive Behavior

XIV. Self-Abusive Behavior

XV. Social Engagement

XVI. Disturbing Interpersonal

Lambert, N., Nihira, K., & Leland, H. (1993). *AAMR Adaptive Behavior Scale—School: Examiner's manual* (2nd ed.). Austin, TX: PRO-ED. Reprinted by permission.

## Research Brief

### Cultural Views of Disabilities

Cultural beliefs can affect the manner in which a family accepts and adapts to a child with a disability. These beliefs can also determine the family's ability to request help and the level of trust they give professionals (Seligman, 1991). Before professionals attempt to provide help to families of diverse backgrounds, they should be aware of how that culture views disabilities, while also taking into account that every family is unique.

**Latin American.** When a child with a disability is born, the disability may be attributed to an external, nonmedical reason (Cheng, 1990). For example, several Latino mothers attributed their children's cleft palates to an eclipse during pregnancy. The disability may also be regarded as a punishment for the adults and as God's will, and be accepted as such. Although some families use extended support to help raise the child, other families may hide the child because of family pride. Individual family values related to the sex and status of the child may influence acceptance of the disability. The disability of a firstborn male might be harder to accept than that of a daughter (Lynch & Hanson, 1992).

**African American.** Some African Americans react with less distress than people of other cultures to having a child with a disability, because of family support and religious beliefs. Disability is often interpreted in either of two ways: as bad luck or misfortune, or less often as the result of "sins of the fathers." The perceived cause of the disability has no apparent effect on interactions with families who have a member with a disability or on how the family itself deals with the disability (Lynch & Hanson, 1992).

**Native American.** Native American families are likely to downplay the birth of a child with a disability. The birth of a child with a disability may be viewed as a "prenatal choice" by the infant, and consequently not be considered a negative event. Some tribes believe that a disability is the consequence of a transgression. The consequence is not seen as a punishment, but just the result (Ponchillia, 1993). Children with disabilities are for the most part accepted and taught to assume useful roles in the community.

See Chapter 10 for more information on accommodating students from diverse cultures.

# Instructional Guidelines and Accommodations for Teaching Students with Mental Retardation and Severe Disabilities

Teachers who have students with mental retardation and severe disabilities in their classrooms are asked to participate in the development of the students' educational plans, work with the students, and communicate and work with the paraprofessionals and specialists who provide support. Douglas Akers, a fifth-grade teacher, has been working for several months with Amy, a student with Down syndrome and moderate retardation who is being included in general education classes for the first time. Reflecting about Amy entering his class, Doug comments,

> I wanted to establish a good rapport with Amy. I wanted her to take directions from me, ... not just to rely on her aide or the special education teacher. I wanted Amy to develop a relationship with me and feel comfortable coming to me or the other students for assistance. I knew this would take time because she has always been in a self-contained special education class. But now she does come to me with her work and with questions.

The instructional guidelines and accommodations discussed here will help you to include students with mental retardation and severe disabilities in your class and to develop a social support network that will facilitate these students' success.

## Role of the General Education Teacher

With the move toward inclusive schools, the roles of special education and general education teachers are less clearly defined. The role of the general education teacher is to be involved in and problem-solve adaptations and curriculum modifications for all students. In an observational study of 15 elementary students with severe disabilities and 15 general education students (Logan & Malone, 1998), results suggest that more individualized instructional supports were provided for the students with severe disabilities including more one-to-one and small group instruction that was done in coordination with the special education staff.

Chris Johnson is a good example of a teacher whose role changed as he worked with a student with disabilities. Upon hearing that he would have Darrell, a student with mild mental retardation, in his eighth-grade applied math class, Chris shared these concerns, "One of my main concerns was what am I going to do for Darrell? How am I possibly going to teach him anything? I don't have a special education degree. I feel as if I need one in order to teach him. How is Darrell going to fit in as a member of the class?"

To alleviate these feelings, Chris met with Darrell's special education teacher, Martha Anderson. They reviewed the applied math curriculum in relation to Darrell's IEP goals and objectives. What they quickly realized was that many of Darrell's goals (including skills in measurement, making change, and using fractions and percentages) could be met within the general curriculum.

Each week Chris discussed the activities and assignments with Martha and she gave him ideas for modifications. Once a week, Martha worked in the room with Chris so that she could keep up with the curriculum and Darrell's progress. At the end of the first month, Chris commented, "Darrell is a member of our class, just like any of the [other] students. He works on math assignments, although I usually modify them by giving him less to complete, by allowing him to use manipulatives and a calculator, and in some

> Despite the movement toward inclusion, less than 10 percent of students with mental retardation and severe disabilities are educated primarily in general education classrooms. Thirty-five states use separate classrooms for educating more than half the students with mental retardation (the ARC, 1992).

cases giving him different assignments from the other students. What I have come to appreciate is that Martha is there to assist me."

One of the teacher's most important roles is to take "ownership" of students with disabilities by demonstrating that these students are members of the class. When this happens, students with disabilities develop a sense of belonging and being accepted. The need for this sense of belonging is part of the reason that spending only part of the day in class may not work for some students with mental retardation and severe disabilities. Schnorr (1990) found that part-time integration negatively affected the acceptance of a student with a severe disability as a class member. For Chris and his class, Darrell was just another member of the applied math class.

## Planning Systems

Planning—critical for all students—is particularly important for students with mental retardation and severe disabilities, whose learning goals may differ substantially from those of other students in the class. One planning system is the Planning Pyramid, introduced in Chapter 2 (Schumm et al., 1994). In the example in Chapter 2, Jeannette Robinson planned a unit on Weathering and Erosion (refer to Figure 2.6).

As she planned, Jeannette wrote in the base of the pyramid what she wanted *all* students to learn. This goal was appropriate for all the students in her class that year, but when Jeannette taught this unit the next year, Steven, a student with autism and limited language and cognitive skills, and Sandra, a student with mild mental retardation, were in her class. During weekly planning time, Jeannette talked about the unit with the inclusion specialist and assistant who supported Steven and Sandra. They decided that Steven's content goals would be to identify three types of weather (i.e., sunny, rainy, and snowy) and the type of clothing worn in each type, and Jeannette noted these specific goals on the unit planning sheet (see Figure 8.3).

> Adults with mental retardation and severe disabilities, most of whom lived in institutions before the 1970s, now live in group homes and supported apartments. In a supported apartment arrangement, the person chooses his or her roommates, and the apartments are located in different areas of the community.

Although Steven would participate in a number of the activities planned for the unit and continue to work on his general language and social goals (e.g., working with others and sharing, communicating wants and feelings), the assistant would work with him on these content goals. In discussion, Jeannette and the team decided that for Sandra a more limited depth of learning and modified quizzes would be appropriate accommodations. You should find the Planning Pyramid helpful for planning lessons and units and making instructional decisions about how

---

**FIGURE 8.3**

**Planning Pyramid with Modifications for a Student with Significant Disabilities**

| What some students will learn. | • How earth looked during Ice Age<br>• Disasters caused by sudden changes<br>• Geographic examples of slow and fast changes |
|---|---|
| What most students will learn. | • Compare and contrast weathering and erosion<br>• How humans cause physical and chemical weathering<br>• Basic types of rocks |
| What ALL * students should learn. | • Basic components of earth's surface<br>• Forces that change crust are weathering and erosion |

* Steven—identify 3 types of weather and the appropriate clothing.

you can accommodate the various learners in your classroom.

When working with a student with severe disabilities you may also participate in planning for the student's long-range goals, which are incorporated into the IEP. **The McGill Action Planning System (MAPS)** (Lusthaus & Forest, 1987) is one example of such a planning system. The purpose of this planning activity is to foster relationships to improve the quality of life for persons with severe disabilities and to facilitate participation in inclusive settings such as a general education classroom.

In the MAPS process, the student, his or her family and friends, and special and general educators establish a team. Because peers are important to the process, students from the classroom generally participate in the team (Vandercook, York, & Forest, 1989). This team answers seven questions, using them to brainstorm methods to plan the student's future in an inclusive environment. Answers to the seven questions help determine the goals and objectives. Figure 8.4 provides an example of the MAPS questions and ideas for Tyrone, a high-school student with severe mental retardation.

*Choosing Outcomes and Accommodations for Children: A Guide to Educational Planning for Students with Disabilities (COACH)* is another planning system for developing an appropriate educational program for students with severe disabilities in the general education setting (Giangreco, Cloninger, & Iverson, 1998). COACH focuses on individualization, family participation, and the active involvement of related service providers.

For students with mental retardation and severe disabilities, it is important to plan beyond the students' school experiences, particularly as these students reach middle and high school. Planning for their transition into adult life in terms of vocation and adult living are critical to their success (Hutchins & Renzaglia, 1998; Wehmeyer, 1995). Person-centered planning (Miner & Bates, 1997) builds from such techniques as MAPS and Circle of Friends to provide long-range planning and transition. As part of the process, the student's circle of support map is developed by the student, family, educators, and other key support persons. Figure 8.5 presents the map for Robert, a 17-year-old student with moderate mental retardation. This process actively involves the student in planning, as is mandated by the Individuals with Disabilities Education Act.

## Functional Assessment, Discrepancy Analysis, and Task Analysis

Functional assessment, discrepancy analysis, and task analysis help determine the skills the student needs to reach established goals. In a functional assessment each goal or activity is broken into steps or subskills, and the student's present performance level is determined for each subskill or step in the activity. For example, the first column of Figure 8.6 shows the steps involved in the activity of getting to school, with the student's performance noted in the second column.

A **discrepancy analysis** reviews each specific step or skill and determines how the student does the step or skill, compared to nondisabled peers (the third column in Figure 8.6 on page 238). If the student is unable to perform a step or skill (i.e., a discrepancy exists), then the teacher determines whether the student should be taught that particular step or skill or whether an adaptation should be made to help the student perform the skill. The fourth column in Figure 8.6 shows the adaptations and instruction that will occur as a result of the functional assessment and discrepancy analysis.

How might functional assessments have aided in placing this student in a work setting? How would you identify the skills the student needs to succeed? What opportunities does this learning situation provide for the functional practice of these skills?

### FIGURE 8.4

**MAPS Questions and Ideas Generated for Tyrone**

**1. What is the individual's history?**

Tyrone developed meningitis shortly after birth, which resulted in brain damage. He learned to walk and talk much later than normal.

**2. What is your dream for the individual?**

Tyrone will find a job in the community, where he can interact with many people, and a place to live with friends.

**3. What is your nightmare?**

Tyrone will be alone after we (parents) pass away.

**4. Who is the individual?**

Tyrone is a young man who loves music and talking to people. He is an only child. He is a sophomore in high school. He loves sports. He gets lonely and bored when alone for long periods of time.

**5. What are the individual's strengths, gifts, and abilities?**

He loves to laugh and smiles a lot. He works hard. He has a great sense of humor. He's energetic. He is sensitive to others' moods.

**6. What are the individual's needs?**

He needs friends his own age with whom to do things. He needs to be more assertive and ask for help, when necessary. He needs to be more independent in food preparation and in getting around the community.

**7. What would the individual's ideal day at school look like and what must be done to make it happen?**

A Circle of Friends should be done with Tyrone so that he has friends to meet when he gets off the bus and to hang out with during lunch and breaks. Tyrone should participate in some community-based instruction. Tyrone should take a Foods class.

Next, a **task analysis** (a further breakdown of each individual step or skill, with the necessary adaptations) is used as a guide to teach the step or skill to the student. For example, the 60-Second Lesson (page 239) describes how to develop a picture task analysis.

The same goals can be assessed across the different environments in which the activities occur. Mary Hinson, Marta's high-school job developer, assessed "arriving and getting started" as part of placing Marta in her first job in an office—putting on labels and doing simple packaging. For a number of steps, the adaptations made at school could easily be made at work.

**FIGURE 8.5**

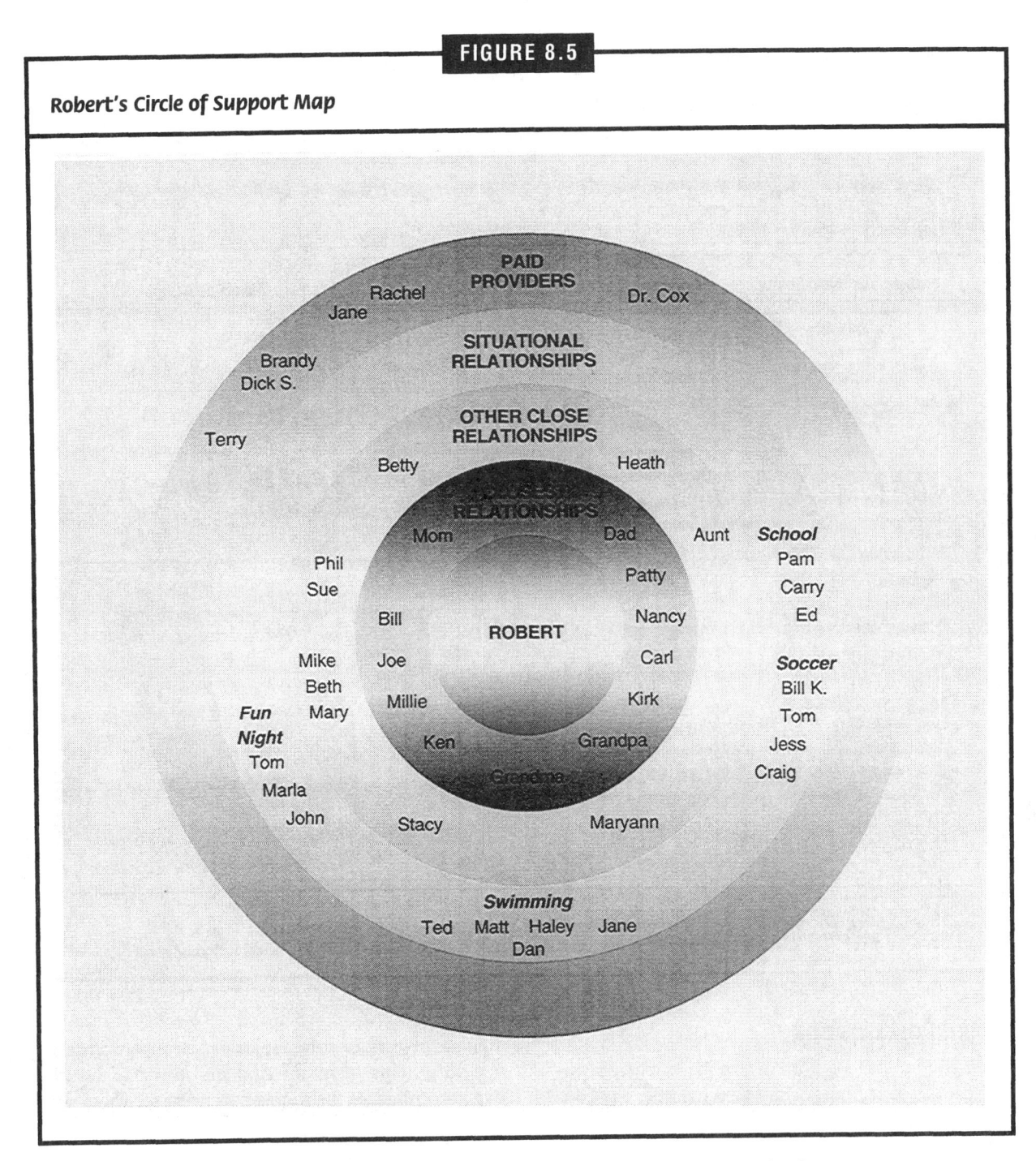

**Robert's Circle of Support Map**

```
                        PAID PROVIDERS
              Rachel                         Dr. Cox
         Jane
                    SITUATIONAL RELATIONSHIPS
       Brandy
       Dick S.
                       OTHER CLOSE RELATIONSHIPS
   Terry
               Betty                    Heath
                      CLOSEST RELATIONSHIPS
                 Mom              Dad       Aunt    School
       Phil                                          Pam
       Sue                       Patty               Carry
              Bill                                   Ed
                              Nancy
       Mike      Joe        ROBERT   Carl          Soccer
       Beth                                         Bill K.
  Fun        Mary    Millie         Kirk            Tom
  Night                                             Jess
       Tom        Ken          Grandpa              Craig
       Marla              Grandma
       John     Stacy              Maryann

                         Swimming
                    Ted  Matt  Haley  Jane
                           Dan
```

Reprinted with permission from Miner, C. A., & Bates, P. E. (1998). Person-centered transition planning. *Teaching Exceptional Children, 30*(1), 66-69.

## FIGURE 8.6

**Functional Assessment/Discrepancy Analysis**

**Student:** Marta is an eighth-grade student with moderate mental retardation and cerebral palsy.
**Activity:** Arriving at school

| Steps of the Activity | Student Performance | Discrepancy Analysis | Teach or Adapt |
|---|---|---|---|
| 1. Arrives at school by bus | + | | |
| 2. Goes to locker | − | Cannot propel herself | Peers will wait by bus |
| 3. Opens locker | − | Doesn't remember combination | Use key lock |
| 4. Gets notebooks, etc. out | − | Can't reach items | Put items in backpack on hook |
| 5. Hangs out/does hair until class | − | Doesn't initiate conversations | Develop "Circles of Friends" |
| 6. Goes to class when bell rings | − | Can't self-propel that far | Ask classmates to help |
| 7. Listens to announcements in homeroom | + | | |
| 8. Raises hand to indicate will eat lunch | + | | |
| 9. Goes to first hour when bell rings | − | Doesn't know which class is at this time | Teach to review a picture schedule and ask for help |

Code: + = can do step    − = cannot do step

## Partial Participation

When you look at a skill to determine whether a student can do it, it is important to remember the concept of **partial participation**, which assumes that an individual has the right to participate in all activities to the extent possible (Downing, 1996; Falvey, 1995). An opportunity to participate should not be denied because a person cannot independently perform the needed skills; instead individualized adaptations should be developed to allow participation and learning, even of only part of the skill. Ferguson and Baumgart (1991) stress the importance of active partial participation by having students make choices, manipulate objects, or communicate. Active participation not only helps maintain students' physical health, but also enhances their image, as peers see them partaking in a meaningful activity. Say, for example, that a class is working on writing sentences, using correct punctuation. A classmate randomly selects three small pictures and places them on Heather's desk. Heather, a student with a severe disability, has to reach out and point to one of the pictures. Her goals are to reach and point, look at her peer, and make decisions in a timely fashion. The peer then holds up the picture for the class to see. The class writes a sentence about it, and Heather must answer a question about it.

# MAKING A DIFFERENCE
## The 60-Second Lesson

*Developing a Picture Task Analysis*

Picture task analyses, by providing visual cues of the steps of a task, enable students with mental disabilities to gain meaningful skills and independence. A picture is taken of each step in a task. Then the pictures are glued (in sequential order) in a manila folder, with a number under each picture. Laminating the whole folder helps preserve the photographs. An erasable pen enables students to cross off pictures as the steps are completed. How might you develop a picture schedule for Marta (see Figure 8.5)?

For more information, see "Using a Picture Task Analysis to Teach Students with Multiple Disabilities," by W. Roberson, J. Gravel, G. Valcante, and R. Maurer in *Teaching Exceptional Children, 1992, 24*(4), 12–16.

---

## Curriculum Adaptations

An important component of adapting materials or instruction is joint planning by the special education and classroom teachers. When Jeannette Robinson heard she was going to have two students with mental retardation and severe disabilities in her classroom (i.e., Steven and Sandra, discussed earlier in this chapter), she was concerned that she would be responsible for writing lesson plans and making all the adaptations. She felt overwhelmed until she realized it was a team process and that the special education teacher and assistant would help her plan. She commented, "I'm so relieved. I feel much more positive now. I didn't know how I was going to do it." Realizing that it is a team process, and that everyone has knowledge to contribute, is important.

The following hierarchy of curriculum-modification questions can be used to help guide teams in making decisions about a student's participation:

1. Can the student participate in the unmodified activity?
2. Can the student participate in the activity with adapted materials, support, or modified expectations?
   - Can the student participate with peer support or with extra adult support?
   - Do materials need to be modified or substituted?
   - Do expectations of the activity (e.g., learning goals, amount of work, method of evaluation) have to be modified?
3. Can the student participate in this activity by working on embedded communication, motor, or social skills?

If the answer to these questions is "no," the team might consider a parallel activity related to the student's educational priorities (as Jeannette and her team did for Steven, when planning the unit on Erosion and Weathering).

## Peer Support and Peer Tutoring

Another important component of teaching accommodations is the development of peer support and peer tutoring. Peers may be the most underrated and underused human resource available in general education classrooms. Nondisabled peers are often creative problem solvers and staunch supporters of students with mental retardation and severe disabilities (Hendrickson, Shookoohi-Tekta, Hamre-Nietupski, & Gable, 1996; Salisbury, Galluci, Palombaro, & Peck, 1995; York & Vandercook, 1991).

Longewill and Kleinert (1998) provide some guidelines for setting up a peer tutoring program in a middle or high school as well as ideas on how to modify assignments for students with more significant disabilities (see Tips for Teachers 8.5). It is important, however, that students not always take the role of "helping" a student with disabilities, which can get in the way of their developing a friendship. Initially, peer support and tutoring requires adult facilitation as needs and strategies are identified, but adult participation should be reduced as friendships and tutoring routines develop. Teachers using Circle of Friends for a student with disabilities often find that classmates want to add the student to their circles and try to finish their work early so they can work with the student. Some teachers find that so many students volunteer, they must use a sign-up sheet, limiting the number of times per month peers can work with a student.

## Strategies to Support Students in General Education Classes

A number of general strategies can be used to support students with mental retardation and severe disabilities in general education classrooms.

**Increasing a Student's Sense of Belonging** One key to success is to create a community to which the student with disabilities has a sense of belonging. Frisbee and Libby (1992) suggest the following strategies to increase this sense of belonging:

- Give the student the same "things" as the other students (e.g., desk, typical seating, locker, name on classroom charts).
- Demonstrate respect for the student by using age-appropriate language, and being a good role model.
- Involve the student in the typical classroom routine.
- Work with your educational team and students to find ways for the student to participate actively in classroom activities.
- Consult with specialists for ideas, and express your concerns.
- Encourage students to find ways to increase learning opportunities for classmates who are challenged.
- Promote equality and interactions with other classmates (e.g., remember to use the word "friend" instead of "peer tutor," and say "go together" rather than "take _____ with you."

# TIPS FOR TEACHERS

### 8.5 Using a Peer Tutoring Program for Students with Significant Disabilities in a Middle or High School

1. Collaborate with your school administration and special education staff to create a peer tutoring course for which the students can receive credit.
2. Inform counselors, faculty, and students of the course and make sure it uses the typical process for enrollment.
3. Do not enroll more peer tutors than there are students to be tutored.
4. Before the students begin tutoring, teach them strategies that they can use to support their tutees.
5. Some students may want to participate in some disability awarenesss training before they begin tutoring.
6. Have tutors develop lists of ideas on how to adapt classes and assignments for their tutees:
   - In art, instead of drawing pictures, have tutees paste pictures from magazines.
   - For a written report, use picture symbols arranged in order and integrate them with written text, depending on the tutee's abilities (symbols could be from the tutee's communication system).
   - For an oral report, have tutee and tutor develop a poster or collage that they can explain.
   - For community-based living projects, assist the tutee in learning about budgeting, nutrition, and shopping.
7. Have students report every 1 to 2 weeks on their tutee's progress and reflect on their own learning.
8. Provide opportunities for cooperative learning as well as tutor/tutee learning situations.

Adapted from Longwill, A. W., & Kleinert, H. L. (1998). The unexpected benefits of high school peer tutoring. *Teaching Exceptional Children, 30* (4), 60–65.

***Accepting Varied Learning Goals*** The most frequently asked question about inclusion is, "How are students going to benefit from my class—what will they get out of it?" Students with mental retardation and severe disabilities may be working on their own goals during class activities. It is important that these goals, however different, be regarded as meeting valued educational needs. Sean Miller, a high-school biology teacher, says his biggest concern was how to grade the student with mild retardation in his class. He comments, "I didn't know what to do. The student was trying and doing her work, but it wasn't high-school level. I wondered if I gave her a passing grade, was it fair to the other students? We (the special education staff and I) ended up sitting down and reviewing her goals and determining a grade based on that. I was comfortable with that idea."

A sheet that demonstrates the relationship between the IEP goals and the activities in the general education classroom helps everyone understand that individual goals can be met through classroom activities. One example, the IEP Goal–Activity Matrix shown in Figure 8.7 is for Manny, a second-grade student with a moderate mental disability. Across the top of the matrix are the subjects and activities, with Manny's IEP goal areas down the side. Each indicates the logical time for Manny to work on his IEP goals during his school day.

**FIGURE 8.7**

**IEP Goal–Activity Matrix**

Student: Manny
Grade: 2nd grade
Semester: Fall 1997
Teachers: Ms. Nichols, Mr. O'Brian

**IEP Goal Areas** / **Subjects/Activities**

| IEP Goal Areas | Opening | Reading/Language Arts | Recess | Math Their Way | Lunch | Science/Social Studies |
|---|---|---|---|---|---|---|
| Writes name and functional words | | X | | X | | X |
| One-to-one correspondence | | | | X | | X |
| Decision making | X | X | X | X | X | X |
| Initiating communication | X | X | X | X | X | X |
| Functional reading | X | X | | | | X |

**Making Environmental Accommodations** *Environmental accommodations* are changes made to the physical learning environment so that each student can participate successfully. These changes are often as simple as having a bean bag chair so that a student with cerebral palsy can be on the floor with peers during story time, or lifting the legs of a desk a few inches so that a wheelchair fits comfortably.

**Team Teaching** As you may recall from Chapter 4, team teaching involves two or more teachers (special and general education) cooperatively teaching a class or particular curriculum or thematic unit. The teachers often have different areas of expertise that build upon each other to make a successful lesson for all students. Team teaching reduces the teacher–student ratio, thereby making small group instruction more feasible (Vaughn, Schumm, & Arquelles, 1997).

**Cooperative Learning** Cooperative learning, also discussed in Chapter 4, is an effective instructional method for including students with mental retardation and severe disabilities (Putnam, 1998; Wilcox et al., 1987). In cooperative learning situations, the class is divided into groups for learning activities that have cooperative goals. Each student has a role, and it is important that each role is valued. Cooperative learning fosters interdependence and helps all involved to develop interpersonal skills (Slavin, 1995). General education teachers need to be comfortable with the idea of having heterogeneous groups for cooperative learning. Hunt, Staub, Alwell, and Goetz (1994) found that having a student with a severe disability in a cooperative group did not in any way hinder the progress of other members.

> Students with mental retardation and severe disabilities need to learn general work habits such as following directions, working with others, accepting feedback and supervision, asking for help, working steadily at a satisfactory rate, doing quality work, and completing the work (Kokaska & Brolin, 1985).

**Accommodating Personal Learning Styles** Accommodating learning styles involves letting students learn and demonstrate what they learn in ways that reflect their individual strengths. Students may share their knowledge through an oral report instead of a written one, or by creating a collage about the topic being studied. High-school teacher Lynn Blankenship, who teaches Independent Living Skills, says that because she encourages students to use various methods of demonstrating their knowledge, having Jessica, a student with moderate retardation, worked out well.

**Providing Hands-On Instruction** Hands-on, or experientially based instruction, relates learning to what students already know and uses real-life activities as teaching tools. This type of instruction provides greater opportunity for students with mental retardation and severe disabilities to be actively involved. The use of learning centers, math manipulatives, science projects, art projects, and computers are examples of hands-on activities that give students with mental retardation and severe disabilities the opportunity to participate.

## Providing Opportunities for Functional Practice

In addition to hands-on activities, opportunities for **functional practice** are also important. When practice is relevant, students can easily see the connection between what they are practicing and its use in real life. For example, you can incorporate into reading instruction activities that stress reading for fun or to obtain information needed for daily life. Suggestions include:

- directions (e.g., for cooking, building a model, repairing an appliance)
- directional orientation and map reading
- menus
- labels on foods, medicines, clothing
- telephone book
- catalogs and advertisements (for selecting something to order)
- schedules (e.g., bus, train, television)
- signs
- newspapers and magazines

Writing activities also can be centered around daily activities, as follows:

- writing a message for a friend
- writing a letter to request something or complain
- writing a postcard or letter to a friend
- making a shopping list
- completing a job application or an application for a library card
- ordering something by filling out a form
- writing down a telephone message

Functional math activities include:

- making change

- counting money
- making a purchase
- using a checking account
- using a credit card
- budgeting money
- telling and estimating time
- reading a calendar
- reading a thermometer
- measuring
- determining weight and height

Students' success in functional activities can often predict the degree to which they will function successfully as adults.

## Encouraging Parental Involvement

Every teacher realizes the importance of parental involvement in a student's education. This involvement is especially important for a student with mental retardation and severe disabilities. Their parents play a key role in determining the student's educational program and the preparation for adult life. Knowing the parents' goals for their child can help everyone work together as a team. The Research Brief presents parents' perspectives on inclusion and curriculum goals for children with severe disabilities.

# Research Brief

### Parents' Perceptions of Goals for Students with Disabilities

A frequently asked question is what types of goals students with mental retardation work on in the general education classroom. Parents are key members of the multidisciplinary team that determines what goals are important for the student. Knowing what parents think and feel is important information for school staff.

Hamre-Nietupski, Nietupski, & Strathe (1992) surveyed 68 parents of students (6–21 years old) with moderate or severe/profound disabilities to determine the relative value these parents placed on the following curricular areas: functional life skills (e.g., making simple meals), academic skills (e.g. addition), and development of friendships and social relationships (e.g., sharing games with peers). Parents of students with moderate disabilities ranked the areas' relative value in the following order: (1) functional life skills, (2) academic skills, and (3) friendship/social relationship development. Parents of students with severe/profound disabilities ranked the areas differently: (1) friendship/social development, (2) functional life skills, and (3) academic skills.

In a survey conducted in the Los Angeles and Orange County areas, of almost 500 parents of students aged 3 to 22 with significant cognitive disabilities reported that they were more positive regarding the impact of inclusion on the mutual social benefits for both their child and other children in the classroom and the acceptance and treatment of their child (Palmer, Borthwick-Duffy, & Widaman, 1998). At the same time the parents were more apprehensive about the quality of the educational services their child received. In the general education classrooms, parents were concerned about how meaningful the content was for their child, the difficulty in modifying lessons and materials, and the opportunity their child would have to get extra help.

What do parents of nondisabled children think about having a child with a severe disability in their child's class? Giangreco, Edelman, Cloninger, and Dennis (1993) surveyed 81 parents of nondisabled children (grades K–8) about their perceptions of their children having a classmate with a severe disability. The results showed that parents not only think that their children are comfortable interacting with a classmate with a severe disability and that this interaction has a positive effect on their children's social and emotional growth, but also that having a classmate with a severe disability has not interfered with their children's receiving a good education. Overall, the parents felt that having a classmate with a severe disability was a positive experience for their children.

As integration of students with mental retardation and severe disabilities into general education classrooms increases, it is important that you learn strategies for accommodating these students in your class. You may need to adapt the curriculum or have the students work on goals not specified in the curriculum. A key to successful integration is collaboration with and support from the specialists who work with these students. Make time for co-planning and ongoing communication, and you can help ensure that students are successful and that you feel positive about the learning experiences of all the students in your class.

# SUMMARY

- Students with mental retardation and severe disabilities represent a diverse group of individuals with varied learning needs and abilities.
- Although ability levels vary, difficulties often occur in four areas: intellectual functioning, and social, motor, and communication skills.
- The causes of mental retardation are unknown in 50 percent of the students with mental retardation, but it is known that many of the causes are preventable.
- An important part of students' success is participation in planning systems, such as the Planning Pyramid and MAPS.
- Functional assessment and discrepancy analysis are means of determining how students perform a skill and whether the skill should be taught or adapted.
- A change in teaching style to incorporate more hands-on and cooperative learning activities can help you include all students in classroom activities.
- Environmental accommodations, team teaching, cooperative learning, hands-on learning, providing practice in functional activities, and getting parents involved are all strategies to promote students' involvement and learning.

## Key Terms and Concepts

adaptive behavior
autism
biased responding
communication board
deaf–blind
developmental period
discrepancy analysis
Down syndrome
dual sensory impairments
echolalia
ecological inventories
Fetal Alcohol Syndrome
functional assessment
functional practice
inclusion support teacher or specialist
intellectual functioning
McGill Action Planning System (MAPS)
mental retardation
multiple disabilities
partial participation
self-injurious behavior
severe disabilities
stereotypic behavior
systems of support
task analysis

## Think and Apply

1. Think about Susie's role as an inclusion specialist in relation to your role as a classroom teacher. If one of Susie's students were to join your class, how would you plan, communicate, and work with Susie so that she could support both you and the student? List the questions you would want to ask Susie before the student joined your class.
2. Review AAMR's definition for mental retardation, and think about two students with mental retardation. Decide which level of support they would need. Discuss with a classmate the pros and cons of this type of classification system.
3. Think about a classroom activity, then use the hierarchy of curriculum-modification questions to determine how a student with mental retardation and severe disabilities could participate in the activity.
4. ABLEDATA is a service with information about more than 20,000 assistive technology products and related services. Call 1-800-227-0216 or

fax 301-587-1967 and ask one of the information specialists to research your area of interest. Report on what you learned.

5. Watch a student with a severe disability participate in a general education activity. Make a list of all the embedded skills you observe the student using (e.g., communicating, reaching).

## Read More about It

1. Drew, C., Hardman, M., & Logan, D. (1996). *Mental retardation: A life cycle approach*. Columbus, OH: Merrill.
   An overview of the field of mental retardation from an educational perspective.

2. Giangreco, M. F. (1997). *Quick guides to inclusion: Ideas for educating students with disabilities*. Baltimore: Brookes.
   This book contains five "Quick-Guides," written for general educators, on topics related to inclusive education. Each Quick-Guide gives a list of 10 guidelines-at-a-glance, as well as a page of text discussing each one, and selected references on the topic. The topics covered are:
   (1) Including Students with Disabilities in the Classroom
   (2) Building Partnerships with Parents
   (3) Creating Partnerships with Paraprofessionals
   (4) Getting the Most out of Support Services
   (5) Creating Positive Behavioral Supports

3. Tashie, C., Shapiro-Barnard, S., Dillon, A. D., Schuh, M., Jorgensen, C., & Nisbet, J. (1993). *Changes in attitudes, changes in latitudes*. Durham, NH: University of New Hampshire, Institute on Disability.
   First in a series of three books, this colorful publication reviews the emerging role of inclusion facilitators and provides, with wit and wisdom, many stories about their experiences.

   Dillon, A. D., Tashie, C., Schuh, M., Jorgensen, C., Shapiro-Barnard, S., Dixon, B., & Nisbet, J. (1993). *Treasures: A celebration of inclusion*. Durham, NH: University of New Hampshire, Institute on Disability.
   Second in the series, this thought-provoking, emotional photo essay on inclusive schooling is a celebration for all the families, students, and school personnel who have worked hard for inclusive schooling in New Hampshire.

   Tashie, C., Shapiro-Barnard, S., Schuh, M., Jorgensen, C., Dillon, A. D., Dixon, B., & Nisbet, J. (1993). *From special to regular, from ordinary to extraordinary*. Durham, NH: University of New Hampshire, Institute on Disability.
   This third book, written to inspire and support families and professionals working toward inclusive schooling, includes strategies for beginning the inclusion process, meeting challenges along the way, and planning for success.

4. The following articles provide general education teachers' perspectives about inclusion of students with mental retardation and severe disabilities:

   Giangreco, M. F., Dennis, R., Cloninger, C., Edelman, S., & Schattman, R. (1993). I've counted Jon: Transformational experiences of teachers educating students with disabilities. *Exceptional Children, 59,* 359–372.

   Janney, R. E. & Snell, M. (1997). How teachers include students with moderate and severe disabilities in elementary classes: The means and meaning of inclusion. *The Journal of the Association for Persons with Severe Handicaps, 22,* 159–169.

   Olson, M. R., Chalmers, L., & Hoover, J. H. (1997). Attitudes and attributes of general education teachers identified as effective inclusionists. *Remedial and Special Education, 18,* 28–35.

   Smith, R. M. (1997). Varied meaning and practice: Teacher's perspectives regarding high school inclusion. *The Journal of the Association for Persons with Severe Handicaps, 22,* 235–244.

   Wood, M. (1998) Whose job is it anyway? Educational roles in inclusion. *Exceptional Children, 64,* 181–195.

   York, J., & Tundidor, M. (1995). Issues raised in the name of inclusion: Perspectives of educators, parents, and students. *Journal for the Association for Persons with Severe Handicaps, 20,* 31–44.

# CHAPTER 14

# Teaching Students with Visual Impairments, Hearing Loss, Physical Disabilities, or Health Impairments

# Interview

## Pat Childers and Diane Batson

Pat Childers, a middle school English teacher, teaches a combination seventh–eighth grade class of thirty students. One of Pat's students is Brandy Walters, an eighth grader who is totally blind and uses braille. Brandy is supported by Diane Batson, an itinerant teacher for students with visual impairments. Diane's diverse caseload includes students with visual impairments, students with multiple disabilities including visual impairments, and students who are both visually impaired and gifted. The vision of most of her students enables them to read print.

When Pat initially learned that Brandy would be a member of her classroom she had several concerns. First, she felt that students would be disrupted by having a second adult, Diane, in the room. Another concern was all the activities Pat believed Brandy would have difficulty doing. Pat's concern increased when Diane started bringing in Brandy's equipment, including a computer with a braille printer that (to Pat) sounded like a popcorn machine.

Because of all the equipment, Diane and Brandy took over a corner of the classroom, where Brandy had a table to herself. Pat found this arrangement unsatisfactory, in that Brandy was isolated from the rest of the class. Pat, who recognized that Brandy had social needs as well as academic needs, commented on her concerns, "Brandy could hide behind that computer and was off in the corner by herself. I moved her right in with the other kids so she'd be part of the classroom community. Then she started making friends with the other kids." At the end of the year Pat described Brandy's role in the class as,

> . . . a part of the gang. The kids never excluded her. She followed the rules just like the rest of them.

One time, when Brandy did not follow a classroom rule, she had to pay the consequences just like the other students. In my room, students who break rules know they have to go out and run a lap around the track. When Brandy had to "do a lap," she took her long cane and used it to independently locate and travel around the track.

Pat and Diane both recognize the importance of working as a team. They learned to work together, noting that being flexible is what made it work. Diane says, "Sometimes Pat would change a lesson at the last minute. There was no way I could get the books, notes, and other written information brailled in time, so Pat would get a peer to read it to Brandy. Somehow, it would always work because Pat was flexible in her teaching."

Flexibility and organization, Pat learned, are equally important for the class to run smoothly. When she selected reading materials for the class or wrote a test, she shared the information with Diane, giving Diane time to prepare the materials in braille so that Brandy could participate in the activity. In fact, after working together for a year, both Pat and Diane commented that they continue to need to improve their co-planning and organization. For students with visual impairments (and the other types of impairments discussed in this chapter), the teachers' preparation prior to teaching is what often determines the degree to which the students can be included in the learning activities of the classroom.

# Introduction

Although there are not many students with visual, hearing, physical, or health impairments, it is not unusual for these students to be educated in general education classrooms. This chapter provides strategies for teaching and accommodating these students in your classroom. Because these students have different needs (based on their disabilities) and usually work with different specialists, this chapter is divided into three sections: *visual impairments* (VI), *hearing loss* or *deaf/hard of hearing* (D/HH), and *physical disabilities and health impairments* (PD/HI). When you work with these students, you will be part of a team that includes not only you, the parents, and the special education teacher who specializes in teaching students who are visually impaired, have a hearing loss, or have physical or health impairments, but also such specialists as orientation and mobility specialists (VI), interpreters (D/HH), physical and occupational therapists, and adaptive physical education teachers.

# Students with Visual Impairments

Both Pat and Diane have learned to modify materials and the environment to meet the needs of students who have visual impairments. This section's discussion of students with visual impairments focuses on instructional strategies you can use to assist these students in your classroom. So that you can better understand these students, the section begins with definitions and types of visual impairments, along with information about the characteristics, prevalence, and identification of students with visual impairments.

## Definitions and Types of Visual Impairments

When glasses or contacts do not correct vision to within normal or near normal limits, students may be considered to have a visual impairment that may require special education services. Several definitions are used to describe visual impairments:

- **Partially sighted** individuals have (with best possible correction in the better eye) a measured visual acuity between 20/70 and 20/200.
- **Blind** individuals are unable to see, and therefore use tactual (touch) and auditory (hearing) abilities to access the environment.
- **Legal blindness** is a condition in which individuals (with the best possible correction in the better eye) have a measured visual acuity of 20/200 or worse, or a visual field restricted to 20 degrees or less.
- **Functional vision** is the amount of usable vision a person has with which to complete a task or interact with the environment.
- **Low vision** describes the visual impairment of an individual who is either partially sighted or legally blind, and refers to the amount of functional vision a person has.

How clearly an individual can see a designated object at a distance of 20 feet is called **visual acuity**. How well an individual can see, using *peripheral* or side vision, is called **visual field**. Students with visual impairments may have limited visual acuity, visual field, or both.

The many causes of visual impairments are usually grouped in the following three areas:

- **diseases** (e.g., cataracts, glaucoma, retinopathy of prematurity)
- **trauma or injury** (e.g., car accidents, a blow to the head)
- **refractive errors** (e.g., myopia, hyperopia)

Although it is helpful to know the cause of a student's visual impairment, it is more important to know how the student uses vision functionally. When Eliosa Mendez was told that Amber, a student with cataracts, would be in her sixth-grade classroom she was very nervous. Mrs. Mendez, whose grandmother had cataracts and was able to read only large print at a very slow pace, was surprised that Amber could see the blackboard (provided that she sat in the front row and Eliosa used white chalk). Amber could read regular print books, although she held them closer than the other students and sometimes used a hand magnifier to see details on maps and drawings. Eliosa quickly learned that although her grandmother and Amber both had the same eye disease, their functional vision varied considerably.

> In the first 5 years of life, vision is responsible for between 80 to 90 percent of what we learn. Only 5 to 10 percent of people who are visually impaired can see nothing at all.

## Characteristics of Students with Visual Impairments

Even though a student with a visual impairment is more like sighted peers than different from them, a visual impairment has an impact on all aspects of development. Its impact on each student varies considerably (Warren, 1994). Students may have difficulty learning concepts, especially those related to space (e.g., up–down, left–right) (Hall, 1982; Hill & Ponder, 1976; Ross & Tobin, 1997). For young children, learning their way around the classroom may be challenging; it is important to help them learn landmarks and cues in their environment so that they can travel independently (Hill & Ponder, 1976). Some students may have difficulty with language skills; for example, they may engage in **echolalia** (inappropriately repeating words or phrases they hear) or they may ask many questions (Andersen et al., 1984; Kitzinger, 1984; Warren, 1994). Motor development, especially eye–hand coordination, is another area of difficulty. For example, these students may have trouble with scissors, write illegibly, or spill liquids when pouring. Students with visual impairments often have significant problems in social development (Kekelis, 1988; MacCuspie, 1996; Read, 1989; Rosenblum, 1997; Sacks & Gaylord-Ross, 1992; Wolffe & Sacks, 1997; Workman, 1986). The Research Brief gives examples and suggests strategies you can use to help students with visual impairments achieve social success in your classroom.

# Research Brief

### The Social Network Pilot Project: A Close Look at the Lives of Adolescents with Visual Impairment

If you give some thought to how typical adolescents spend their time, you will most likely think of a group of teens, friends, "hanging out" at the mall or at a friend's house. Is it the same for students with visual impairment? Karen Wolffe and Sharon Zell Sacks, (1997) conducted the Social Network Pilot Project to look in depth at the experiences of adolescents with visual impairment ages 15 to 21. These researchers followed 16 adolescents with low vision, 16 who were blind, and 16 who were sighted over a 1-year period. Four areas were examined: academic involvement and experience, daily living and personal care activities, recreation and leisure activities, and work and vocational experiences. Both adolescents and parents were asked to complete a series of questionnaires about the adolescents' experiences in each of the four areas. In addition, the researchers called each adolescent three times over a 1-year period and asked the adolescent to think back over the last 24 hours and describe what he/she was doing in 1-hour time blocks. What Wolffe and Sacks found will make you think about your own expectations for students in your classroom who have visual impairments.

When they looked at academic involvement and performance they were surprised to learn that adolescents with visual impairment (both blind and low vision) had less homework than sighted adolescents and they perceived this homework to be easier than did the sighted adolescents. When it came to getting homework done, both the blind and low-vision students reported getting help from their parents, teachers, and teacher assistants while sighted students reported their main source of help was friends followed by parents. Students with visual impairment reported completing homework with guidance from teachers, while sighted students did not report any guidance from the teacher. The students with low vision tended to earn Bs and Cs in school while the sighted and blind students tended to earn As and Bs.

When Wolffe and Sacks looked at work experiences, they found that almost all of the students had some volunteer or paid work experiences. Almost all of the sighted students had found these jobs on their own, but for the students with visual impairment the jobs were found through parents, teachers, and guidance counselors. Job experiences for those who were blind or had low vision were primarily office/clerical in nature, while the sighted students had jobs in a broader range of industries (fast food, retail, outdoor work).

Within their examination of recreation and leisure experiences, Wolffe and Sacks took a close look at the social experiences of adolescents. There were large differences between the sighted students and the two groups of visually impaired students. The sighted students were more likely to be out with friends and doing things in the community when they were not at home. They spent little time recreating with parents or siblings. The low-vision students were most likely to be by themselves doing activities around the house (e.g, listening to music, talking on the phone) and when they did get involved in recreational activities it was generally with a family member. The blind students fell somewhere in between the other two groups, but spent significantly more time alone than the sighted students. The students in the sighted group were four times more likely to be with friends than were the low-vision group, and two times more likely to be with friends than the blind group. One of the most intriguing findings of this study is that low-vision students slept on average 3 hours more a day than sighted students and an average of 2 hours more a day than blind students—an indication that students with low vision and blindness are not as active or involved as their sighted counterparts.

What do the findings of the Social Network Pilot Project mean for you as a general education teacher? First, it is important to help students develop friendships within the classroom. The use of cooperative learning or group activities where students must come together to get a long-term project done is one avenue. Helping students with visual impairment to recognize their own strengths so that they can serve as a "helper" or "tutor" for a peer may serve as the catalyst to a friendship. A second consideration is your role in helping students with visual impairment recognize the variety of jobs and careers available in our society. A disproportionate number of adults with visual impairment are in the "service" professions (e.g., teaching, counseling) and this stems from their lack of awareness that their are other career options available to them. Spending time in your subject area examining careers that would be of interest to all of your students will be valuable for the adolescent with visual impairment.

Wolffe and Sacks have provided researchers and educators with much food for thought when it comes to the experiences of adolescents with visual impairment. As general education teachers it is important for us to consider not only the academic needs of our students but all their needs in helping them to maximize their independence and quality of life.

## Prevalence of Visual Impairments

Visual impairments are considered a low-incidence disability, which means that comparatively fewer students have visual impairments than high-incidence disabilities such as learning disabilities. According to the American Printing House for the Blind (1997), approximately 55,000 students with visual impairments (less than 1 percent of the school population) were counted in the United States in January, 1996. Of students with visual impairments, approximately half have some other disability (often mental retardation). Students with such multiple disabilities, including students who are deaf–blind, are discussed in Chapter 8.

It is estimated that about 25 percent of students with visual impairments are *visual* readers (use large print or some means of enlarging the print), 10 percent are *braille* readers (use braille for reading), and 8 percent are *auditory* readers (listen to tapes or others reading). The remaining students are either *prereaders* (young children) or *nonreaders* who, in addition to their visual impairment, have other disabilities (usually mental retardation) that interfere with their ability to read.

## Identification and Assessment of Students with Visual Impairments

Certain signs may prevent or lessen the damage from a visual impairment or help you identify students to refer for evaluation. Following are common symptoms of visual impairments:

- red-rimmed, swollen, or encrusted eyes
- excessive blinking
- itchy eyes
- eyes that are tearing
- one or both eyes turn inward, outward, upward, or downward
- extreme sensitivity to light
- tilting or turning head to one side to see an object
- squinting or closing one eye to see an object
- covering one eye to view an object
- thrusting head forward to view an object
- headaches, fatigue, or dizziness after doing close work
- tripping, bumping into objects, or appearing disoriented
- recurring styes (i.e., inflamed swelling of gland at margin of the eyelid)

If you suspect that a student has a visual impairment, you should refer the student to the school nurse. To receive educational services from a special education teacher specializing in visual impairments, students must have a documented visual impairment. Written documentation in the form of an eye report is obtained from an ophthalmologist or optometrist.

After a student's visual impairment is identified, the special education teacher who specializes in visual impairments assesses the student's functional vision and compensatory skills (such as listening and orientation skills). Then the multidisciplinary team develops an IEP that addresses any necessary accommodations. **Compensatory skills** are skills needed for independence and include the use of braille, a slate and stylus, and an abacus. During assessment, the special education teacher observes the student in different activities and environments, including your classroom. The special education teacher examines lighting, colors, contrasts, optimal print size, seating preference, and visual features of the environment and suggests modifications and accommodations you can make for the student.

Heather Blair quickly realized that Winnie, a fourth-grade student with low vision, relied on three **sensory channels** (modalities): visual, auditory, and tactile. Heather planned lessons and incorporated experiences that enabled Winnie to gain information through these three channels. All students learn through multiple channels. Students with visual impairments need to recognize their primary and secondary channels for learning. Koenig and Holbrook (1993) have designed a Learning Media Assessment procedure that teachers can use to determine a student's primary and secondary learning channels. The Learning Media Assessment involves observing the student in different situations to determine the manner in which the student attends to and accesses information. Figure 9.1 shows a portion of the Learning Media Assessment for Darren, a second-grade student with low vision. Can you determine Darren's primary and secondary sensory channels for learning?

## Instructional Guidelines and Accommodations for Students with Visual Impairments

Some general education teachers feel overwhelmed when they see the materials and equipment that a student with visual impairments needs in the classroom. Ron Cross, a seventh-grade science teacher, was awestruck the day before school started when Susan Brady, the itinerant special education teacher, carried into his classroom a tape recorder, the science textbook on audiotape and in braille (twelve volumes), and a brailler and braille paper (i.e., the machine and special paper used to write braille). During the year, Susan also provided tactual diagrams of cells and insects (i.e., diagrams that are raised and textured so that the features can be felt). Susan explained that the specialized equipment and materials would enable Josh, who for educational purposes is blind, to succeed in science class. She and Ron reviewed a list of accommodations and teaching suggestions she had prepared. Susan indicated that many of these accommodations, presented in Tips for Teachers 9.1, are also helpful for students who have some usable vision.

**Using Braille and Braille Devices** Some students, such as Josh, may have some usable vision but rely on tactual and auditory information gained by using these learning channels. These students use **braille**, a system of embossed or raised dots that can be read with the tips of the fingers. The basic unit of braille is a cell that contains six dots in two vertical rows of three dots each.

> The Braille code was developed in France in 1829 by Louis Braille, who was blind.

Letters of the alphabet, numbers, punctuation marks, and contractions are formed by combining the dots. Contractions are used to save space. (For example, the entire word *understand* is written as ⠠⠥⠝⠙⠑⠗⠎⠞⠁⠝⠙, whereas the contraction for *understand* takes up only four cells: ⠠⠥⠝⠙). When students learn braille, they learn to spell both the full and contracted forms. Figure 9.2 gives examples of braille forms. Young children exposed to braille before they start school are as ready to learn to read and write as their sighted peers (Rex et al., 1994).

There are several ways to write braille—by using a brailler (also called a *braillewriter*), by using a noiseless portable notetaker such as Braille 'n Speak, and by using a slate and stylus. The Tech Talk (page 256) describes these and other high-tech solutions for students with visual impairments.

**Using Orientation and Mobility Skills** Students with visual impairments learn, from an orientation and mobility specialist, to travel independently in their environments. The goal is to enable the student to enter any environment, familiar or unfamiliar, and to function safely, efficiently, gracefully, and independently (Hill & Ponder, 1976). Consequently, it is not unusual for the student and specialist to work not only in school but also in the community.

The student needs to develop both **orientation skills** (which include understanding one's own body, one's position in space, and abstract concepts such as the layout of a city block) and **mobility skills** (which include going up and down stairs, crossing streets, and

## FIGURE 9.1

**Learning Media Assessment Observation Form**

### USE OF SENSORY CHANNELS

Student: Darren
Setting/Activity: Math Class
Date: 3-22     Observer: S. Jones

| Observed Behavior | Sensory Channel |   |   |
|---|---|---|---|
| teacher writing on board | [V] | T | A |
| Darren picks up pencil | V | (T) | A |
| Darren writes problem on paper | [V] | T | A |
| teacher calls on student who walks to board and solves problem | [V] | T | A |
| Darren reaches in desk and pulls out eraser | V | (T) | A |
| Darren listens to teacher's directions | V | T | (A) |
| Darren turns page of book | [V] | (T) | A |
| Darren picks up pencil | V | (T) | A |
| Darren looks at book | [V] | T | A |
| Darren writes problem on paper | [V] | T | A |
| Darren raises hand | V | (T) | A |
| teacher calls on Darren | V | T | (A) |
| Darren states answer to problem | V | T | (A) |
| teacher tells class to do all problems on the page | V | T | (A) |
| Darren looks at book | [V] | T | A |
| Darren writes problem on page in notebook | [V] | T | A |
|  | V | T | A |
|  | V | T | A |
|  | V | T | A |
|  | V | T | A |

☐ Probable Primary Channel: Visual
○ Probable Secondary Channel(s): Auditory

Form reprinted with permission from Koenig, A., & Holbrook, M. G. (1993). *Learning media assessment of students with visual impairment: A resource guide for teachers.* Austin, TX: Texas School for the Blind and Visually Impaired.

using public transportation). The orientation and mobility specialist or the special education teacher who specializes in visual impairments can help you arrange your classroom to facilitate the student's mobility there.

> Dog guides were first introduced in the United States in 1928. Today approximately 2 percent of individuals who are visually impaired travel with dog guides.

**Using Optical, Nonoptical, and Instructional Aids**
Students who have difficulty seeing street signs, building numbers, and bus signs might use a *monocular*, an optical aid that magnifies a distant object. Other optical aids include many types of magnifiers—hand held, lighted, or with a stand—as well as prescription lenses (glasses or contacts).

Large print is another option for students with visual impairments. Large print books are costly and difficult to store, however, and sometimes embarrass the students. Reading large print may also be tiring, in that it requires exaggerated head movements and adaptive seating positions. Optical aids, on the other hand, are more compact, less costly, and let students have access to all materials (Barraga & Erin, 1992; Corn & Koenig, 1997). The key is to ask students what works for them.

Some aspects to consider when selecting and preparing text is that it is clearly written, has adequate

---

## TIPS FOR TEACHERS

### 9.1 Modifications of the Environment for Students with Visual Impairments

**Physical Environment**
- Announce your presence and identify yourself (e.g., "Hi girls, it's Mr. Johnson, May I join your science group to see how you are working together?"). Also announce your departure (e.g., "Thank you girls for letting me join you. I'm going to check in with Ryan's group now.").
- Leave doors fully opened or closed, and drawers closed, so that the student does not run into them.
- Describe the location of things, especially after rearranging the classroom. Start with the door and travel around the room systematically noting locations.
- Provide an extra desk or shelf space for the student to store materials.
- Provide access to an outlet for a tape recorder, lamp, or other electrical equipment.
- Allow early dismissal from class so that the student has time to travel to other classes.

**Learning Environment**
- Familiarize students with classroom materials (e.g., give them time to visually or tactually explore a globe before asking them to locate the longitude and latitude of a city).
- Have concrete examples students can touch (e.g., in science, have fossils, not just pictures of fossils).
- Provide lessons with tactual and auditory components, and adapt assignments so that students can participate by using alternative sensory channels.
- Consider lighting conditions. Some students do best with natural lighting, others do better with lamps. Backlighting reduces visibility, so avoid standing in front of a window when you present material to the class. Low contrast in materials and between backgrounds and foregrounds reduces visibility.
- Provide written copies of any materials you use on an overhead projector or chalkboard. When you use an overhead projector or chalkboard, say what you are writing as you do it.
- Allow a peer to take notes for the student, but check that the student is still paying attention and participating.
- Provide opportunities for students to work in groups, especially when the assignment has a visual component (e.g., conducting experiments in science class).
- Modify writing activities as necessary by allowing students to dictate into a tape recorder.

### FIGURE 9.2

**The Braille Alphabet, Numbers, and Punctuation**

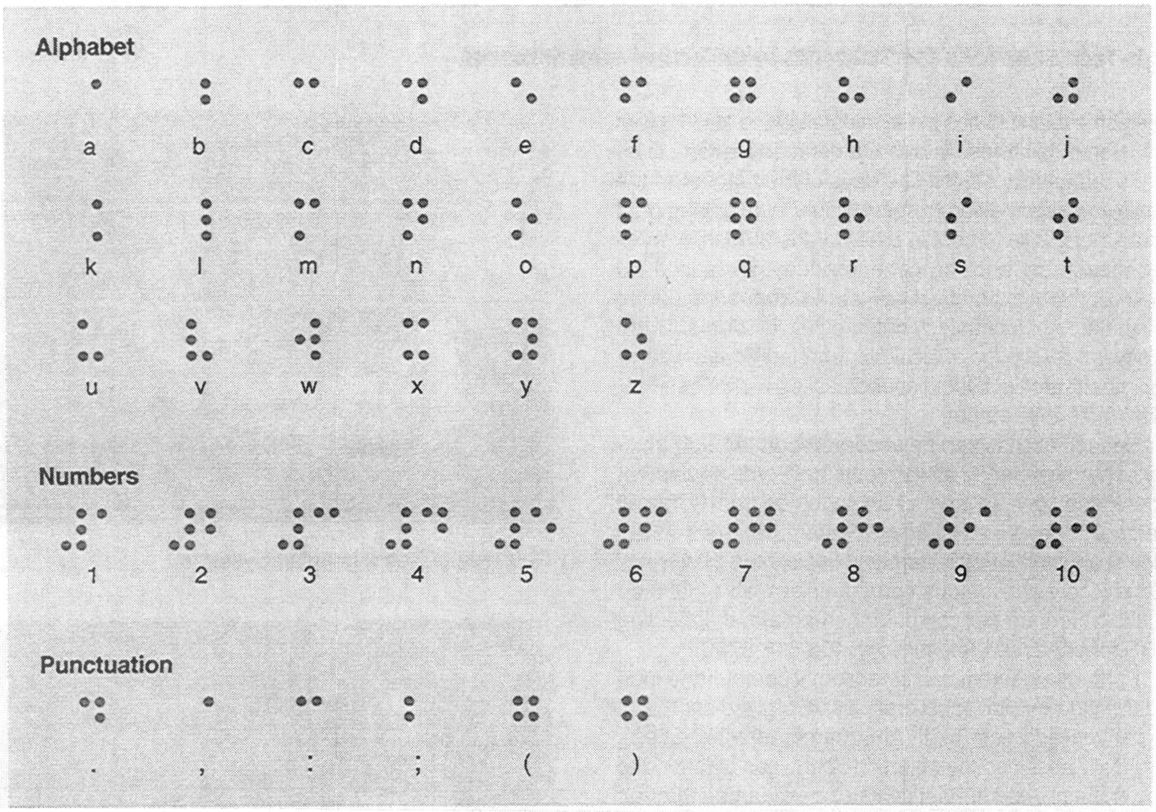

*Alphabet:* a b c d e f g h i j k l m n o p q r s t u v w x y z

*Numbers:* 1 2 3 4 5 6 7 8 9 10

*Punctuation:* . , : ; ( )

---

spacing between letters and words, and is on good quality paper. Reducing the amount of background patterns on the page or providing good contrast between the color of the print and the color of the page is important (Barraga & Erin, 1992).

Nonoptical aids also can help students to maximize visual potential. *Nonoptical aids* are devices that, although not prescribed by a doctor, promote efficient use of vision. Following are some examples of nonoptical aids:

- *lamp* (provides additional light). Lamps with adjustable necks help to minimize glare.
- *reading stand* (used to bring printed material closer to the eyes). Also reduces poor posture and fatigue.
- *bold line paper* (makes writing easier for students with visual impairments). The American Printing House for the Blind manufactures writing paper, graph paper, and large print paper with music staffs.
- *hats and visors* (can help reduce amount of light). Helpful for students who are sensitive to light (photophobic).
- *color acetate* (a plastic overlay that darkens print or increases contrast). Yellow is the color favored by many students with visual impairments.

Several nonoptical aids, available mainly from the American Printing House for the Blind, include the following:

- *Cranmer abacus,* an adapted device for the rapid computation of basic math functions, decimals, and fractions
- *raised line paper,* writing and graph paper with raised lines that can be followed tactually

# TECH TALK

## High-Tech Solutions for Students with Visual Impairments

High-tech equipment has made integrating the student with low vision or blindness into the general education classroom substantially easier. The days of the teacher of the visually impaired having to spend hours transcribing print to braille or braille to print in order for the student with visual impairment and the general education teacher to quickly communicate effectively are disappearing due to the multitude of technology options now available. There are several categories of technology for individuals with visual impairment, including speech access, print enlargement, and braille output.

Speech access can be accomplished through a variety of hardware and software options. Some equipment is designed to read text aloud, such as the Kurzweil Reading Edge (Xerox Imaging System, 800-421-7323) which scans print directly from text or disk and then reads it aloud. There are computer programs available that read the characters on the computer screen aloud, including JAWS for Windows (Telesensory, 408-616-8700).

Print enlargement can be accomplished for the individual with low vision in several ways. Software such as a program called Zoom Text, (Ai Squared, 802-362-3612), specifically designed to enlarge the print, can be added to the computer system. Print can also be enlarged through the use of a Closed Circuit Television (CCTV), a device with an internal camera that is able to project onto a screen the image of a book, worksheet, or any other object placed on its tray (see picture top right).

Special portable computers also facilitate the learning of students with visual impairments who use braille. For example, the Braille 'n Speak is a rechargeable computer, weighing less than a pound, that can serve as a word processor, stopwatch, calendar, and timer (Espinola, 1992). Other products are designed for people who read and write braille, for example, Power Braille and Braille Mate from TeleSensory (415-960-0920). The keys correspond to those on a brailler. An individual who is blind can braille on the Braille 'n Speak and, with the speech synthesizer, can hear the material that has been brailled—a letter, word, sentence, paragraph, or entire file at a time. Information can be transferred by connecting the device to an external braille printer, standard printer, modem, or another computer.

Courtesy of Xerox Imaging Systems

---

- *writing guides,* rectangular templates designed to enable one to accurately place a signature, address an envelope, or write a check
- *measurement tools,* such as braille clocks, rulers, and measuring kits with raised marks

**Testing Accommodations** Classroom tests should be modified to make them accessible for students with visual impairments. Modifications may include assigning alternate items, orally reading sections of the test to the student, using large print or braille answer sheets, providing real objects for items shown in pictures, or coloring pictures to make them easier to see. The special education teacher who works with the student with visual impairments is an excellent resource for suggestions and help with the accommodations. Tips for Teachers 9.2 suggests several simple testing accommodations.

## Students with Hearing Loss

You may have the opportunity to teach a student who is deaf or hard of hearing. Nancy Shipka, a fifth-grade math and science teacher who had that opportunity, worked with a special education teacher specializing in hearing loss and an interpreter. Nancy had no idea what to expect when two students who were deaf joined her math and science class. She was concerned not only that the students' academic performance would not measure up to that of the hearing students in her class, but also about working with a special education team in her classroom.

With the help of the special education team, Nancy worked with the students to determine where they could clearly see the interpreter, Nancy, the chalkboard, and the television monitor. She also learned to face the students directly when speaking and to vary her teaching methods, emphasizing hands-on activities and demonstrations. Nancy also learned that the role of the interpreter is one of facilitating communication. Nancy told the interpreter about difficult concepts ahead of time, and also provided written summaries and class notes so that the interpreter would be prepared to sign difficult or technical concepts.

During the year Nancy asked many questions and learned about students who are deaf or hard of hearing and how to accommodate them in her class. You also may have questions about working with these students. This section explains deafness, hearing loss, and accommodating students with hearing loss.

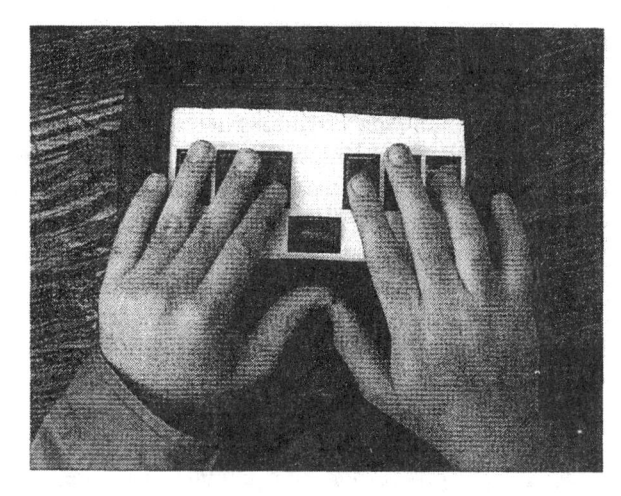

*What low-tech and high-tech solutions available for students with vision impairments can students use in your classroom?*

---

# TIPS FOR TEACHERS

### 9.2 Accommodations for Tests in the General Education Classroom

- Provide test materials in the student's primary learning medium (e.g., braille, large print, audiotape).
- Allow extra time to complete test items.
- Give students who read braille twice as much time as other students to complete a test.
- Give students who read regular or large print time and a half to complete a test (e.g., if the time limit is 30 minutes, give them 45 minutes).
- Read written instructions to students with visual impairment to minimize the amount of reading they need to do (so as to reduce eye fatigue).
- Present test items orally.
- Allow students to write answers on the test material instead of a bubble sheet, or provide a large print bubble sheet.

## Definitions and Types of Hearing Loss

Hearing loss, although often associated with aging, can occur at any time, including from birth. Hearing loss can occur as the result of several factors, including heredity, illness or disease, and excessive prolonged exposure to loud noises. Many of the causes of hearing loss in infants are unknown. Young children identified as having hearing losses before they learn language (2 to 3 years old) are identified as *prelingually deaf*. This early loss of hearing significantly affects language development.

The degree of hearing loss is assessed by observing a person's responses to sounds. The *intensity* of a sound (loud versus quiet) is measured in decibels (dB); the *frequency* of the sound (high versus low) is measured in hertz (Hz). An audiologist tests and plots an individual's responses to sounds on a graph called an **audiogram**, a visual representation of an individual's ability to hear sound. Figure 9.3 shows a comparison of the frequency and intensity of various environmental and speech sounds, plotted on an audiogram.

> American Sign Language, the fourth most common language in the United States, is used also in parts of Canada. Other sign languages (that an ASL signer would not automatically understand) exist in other countries.

## Characteristics of Students with Hearing Loss

A person with normal hearing may have a loss of 0 to 15 decibels in one or both ears. As the loss increases, the amount of usable, or **residual hearing** decreases. Losses can be described as mild, moderate, severe, and profound:

- 15–40 dB = mild hearing loss
- 40–65 dB = moderate hearing loss
- 65–90 dB = severe hearing loss
- greater than 90 dB = profound hearing loss

A person with a mild to moderate loss is usually considered **hard of hearing**. Someone with a severe or profound loss is usually described as **deaf**.

Even a mild hearing loss can have significant educational effects if not recognized early in the student's life. Lauren Resnick, a first-grade teacher, commented that she was surprised at the difference hearing aids made for Rider, a hard-of-hearing student in her class. When Rider was not wearing his hearing aids, he was often off task or seemed uninterested in class activities. With his hearing aids, however, he functioned like the other students in the class.

Hearing loss affects normal speech and language development, which in turn affects English-language reading development. Students who are deaf or hard of hearing and who do not learn English as their primary language may be significantly delayed in English vocabulary development and reading skills.

Students who are deaf use vision as their primary mode of communication and learning. Hard-of-hearing students, on the other hand, generally develop communication and learning skills based on speech rather than vision. Students with mild or moderate hearing losses do not hear all the sounds or words in their environment, and students with severe or profound losses may not hear any of the sounds in their language system. Thus, even though their vocal apparatuses function normally, they experience difficulty learning to produce the speech sounds because they do not get feedback from hearing the sounds they are producing.

Students who are deaf ordinarily use American Sign Language (ASL) as their primary mode of communication. Some hard-of-hearing students may use ASL, but many also use spoken English as their primary mode of communication. **American Sign Language** is a visual, gestural language. (English is an aural, oral language.) ASL is not a visual representation of English, nor is it a simplified language or communication system. ASL is a full, complete language with its own unique grammar and usage.

**Finger spelling**, on the other hand, is a system for representing the English alphabet manually. Finger spelling is used to "spell" names and proper nouns, as well as English words for which no ASL sign exists. Figure 9.4 shows the American finger-spelling alphabet.

Because many students and adults who are deaf speak a common language, ASL, and share similar backgrounds (in that they are deaf), they regard themselves as members of the Deaf culture. Members of the Deaf culture view hearing loss not as a disability but as a common characteristic among their members (Christensen & Delgado, 1993). They share common stories and experiences and the desire to preserve their culture. This is one reason for the strong move-

**FIGURE 9.3**

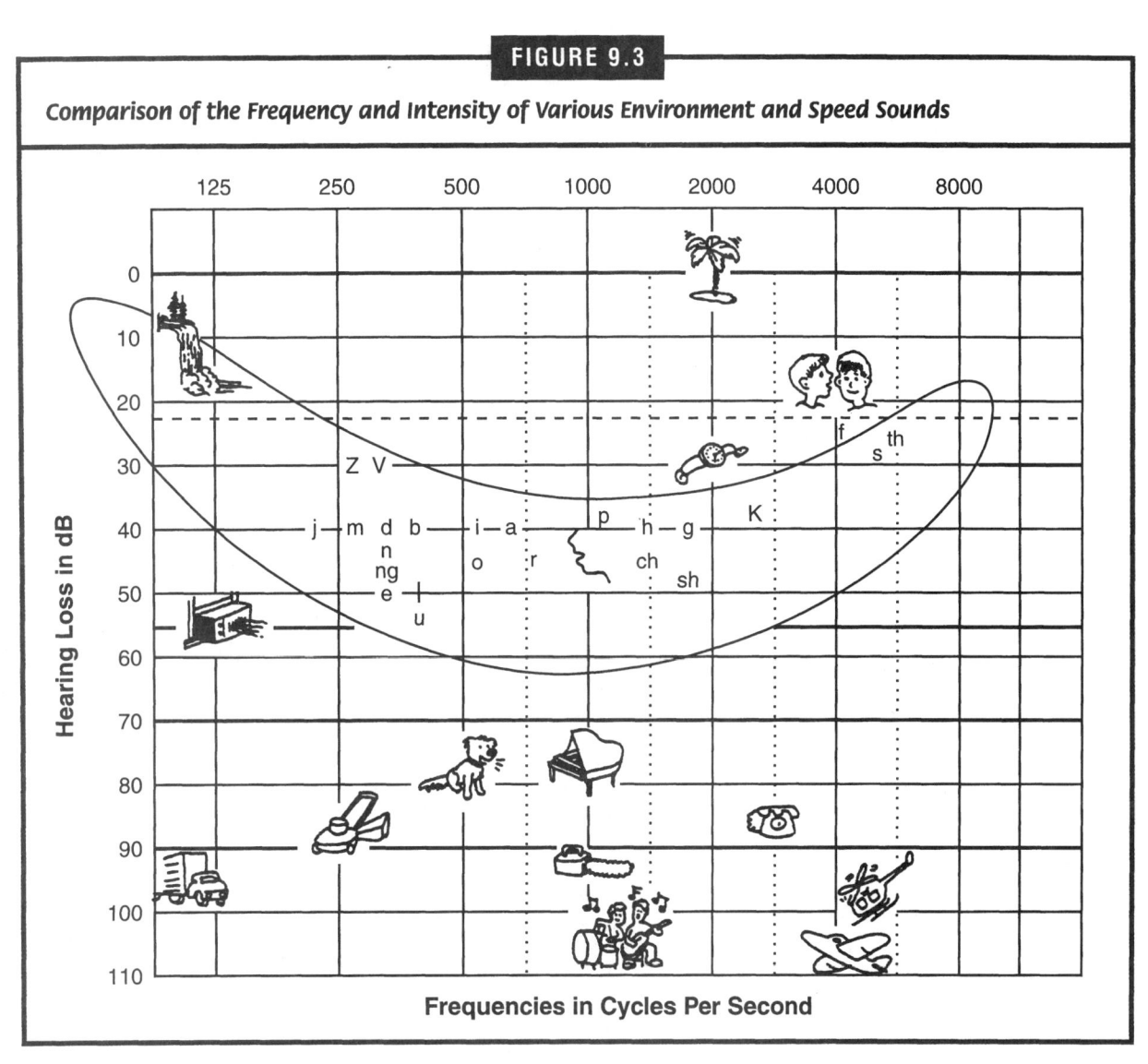

Comparison of the Frequency and Intensity of Various Environment and Speed Sounds

Reprinted with permission from Watkins, S. (Ed.) (1993). *Sky*HI resource manual* (p. G9). Logan, UT: H.O.P.E.

ment to keep special day and residential schools as a placement option for students who are deaf, and for the importance of ASL in the curricula in these schools.

## Prevalence of Hearing Loss

The annual survey from the Office of Demographic Studies at Gallaudet University, which represents 60 percent of all programs, reported that there were approximately 48,000 students who are deaf and hard of hearing in general education classrooms in the United States during the 1996–1997 academic year (Holden-Pitt, 1997). The majority of these students are hard of hearing rather than deaf.

Since the implementation of IDEA, public schools have served more students with hearing loss than have state residential schools. It has been reported that 71 percent of students who are deaf and hard of hearing are attending public academic classes with hearing peers (Holden-Pitt, 1997).

### FIGURE 9.4

**American Finger-Spelling Alphabet**

The manual alphabet as the receiver sees it:

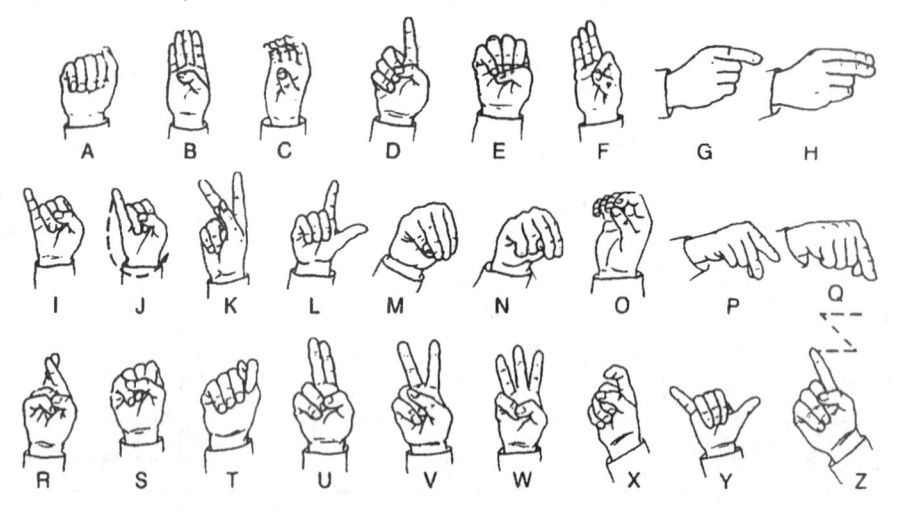

The manual alphabet as the sender sees it:

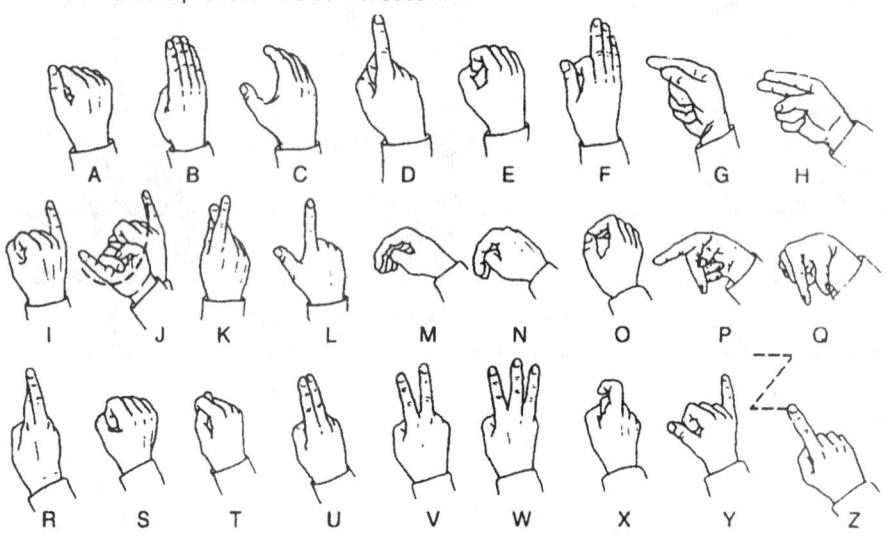

## Identification and Assessment of Students with Hearing Loss

Melanie Brooks, a kindergarten teacher, recalls her first experience identifying a student with a hearing loss. Chelsea had difficulty following directions, often asked that information be repeated, and had difficulty locating the speaker in group discussions. Melanie was also concerned about Chelsea's persistent colds, and she contacted the school nurse.

Together, the school nurse and Melanie began to identify ways to help Chelsea. They discovered that Chelsea had failed her kindergarten hearing screening and had incurred numerous ear infections as an infant and toddler. The district audiologist conducted further testing with Chelsea, discovering a mild-to-moderate hearing loss in both ears. Chelsea was fitted with hearing aids. Melanie and the special education teacher specializing in hearing loss worked with Chelsea to provide resources and adaptations to help her learn better. Melanie recalls her satisfaction at being able to make a difference in Chelsea's life.

Some losses, particularly if they are mild to moderate ones, are first detected during kindergarten screening and by classroom teachers. By the time students are ready to attend school, most moderate, severe, and profound hearing losses have already been detected and identified. You should be aware of the following warning signs:

- daydreaming
- inattention
- behavior problems—frustration
- lethargy
- failure to follow simple verbal commands
- using verbal expressions of misunderstanding (e.g., "Huh?" and "I don't know")
- articulation errors
- limited speech or vocabulary
- inappropriate responses to questions
- difficulties with verbal tasks
- difficulty decoding phonetically
- unusual voice quality (soft, nasal, high pitch, monotonal)
- mouth breathing
- persistent colds

## Instructional Guidelines and Accommodations for Students with Hearing Loss

When a student in your classroom is deaf or hard of hearing, you become an important member of a team that will make educational decisions for the student. In addition to you, the team can include a special education teacher specializing in hearing loss, an interpreter, the student, the parents, a speech and language pathologist, an audiologist, and other resource people.

**Using Amplification** Amplification of sound is one common accommodation made for students with hearing loss. Hearing aids are the most common form of amplification. Thanks to technological advances, hearing aids have improved and continue to do so. In classroom situations, however, even the best hearing aids have limitations. Because hearing aids amplify all sounds in the environment, the student may hear a lot of noise (background and reverberation) in addition to the desired signal (e.g., teacher's voice). In classroom situations, students often use **assistive listening devices** such as FM units. With an FM system, the teacher wears a wireless microphone and the student wears a wireless receiver incorporated with a hearing aid. The microphone amplifies the teacher's voice 12 to 15 decibels above the classroom noise and is not affected by distance.

**Making Classroom Accommodations** Accommodations for students who are deaf may differ from those for students who are hard of hearing. The following

What are some advantages and disadvantages of amplification systems for students with hearing loss? What communication alternatives are available for students who are deaf?

accommodations, however, benefit both types of students:

1. Provide preferential seating.

   - Minimize strain of listening by having the student sit near you and away from loud noises (high traffic areas, doors, air conditioning and heating units).
   - Make sure the student can see you, the interpreter, and visual aids clearly.
   - Eliminate glare from windows or lights.

2. Minimize nonmeaningful environmental noise.

   - Use carpets, rugs, cork, and curtains to help absorb noise.
   - Avoid unnecessary background noise (music, hallway noise).

3. Use visual clues and demonstration.

   - Face the student directly when you talk.
   - Use an overhead projector rather than a chalkboard, so that you can face the student while you write.
   - Use natural gestures.
   - Use modeling to demonstrate how to do different procedures and tasks.
   - Use pictures, diagrams, and graphs.
   - Provide opportunities for experiential learning.

4. Maximize the use of visual media.

   - Provide closed-captioned television (see Tips for Teachers 9.3).
   - Provide access to computers.

5. Monitor the student's understanding.

   - Ask the student to repeat or rephrase important information or directions.
   - Reword statements for clarification.
   - Provide written instructions and summaries.

6. Promote cooperation and collaboration.

   - Use peer and classroom tutors and notetakers.
   - Identify speakers in a group discussion.
   - Inform interpreters of topics before class, and provide study guides or teaching notes.

**Using Interpreters and Notetakers** Interpreters and notetakers are valuable resources in the classroom. Interpreters provide a communication link between students who are deaf and hearing individuals. Transliterators also provide such a link, but use an

---

## TIPS FOR TEACHERS

### 9.3 Using Closed Captioning (CC)

*Closed captioning* is the process of encoding dialogue and sound effects from a program into readable text at the bottom of the television screen (similar to the subtitles in foreign films). *Decoders* are devices that enable you to view the words in a closed-captioning program.

In 1993, the federal Television Circuitry Decoder Act (passed in 1990) took effect. Thanks to this act all televisions marketed in the United States must be capable of decoding closed caption signals. With this development one does not need a special captioning machine to view closed captioned text.

Today, not only many television programs and specials, but also many films, videos, and educational resources are captioned and available for use in the classroom. When you order a film or video, find out whether you can order it captioned. For more information contact:

Captioned Films/Videos for the Deaf
Modern Talking Picture Service, Inc.
5000 Park Street North
St. Petersburg, FL 33709
(800-237-6213)

English-based sign system rather than ASL. It is important that students who use ASL or a sign language system have an interpreter in the educational setting. Although an interpreter facilitates communication between the teacher and the student who is deaf, he or she is not a substitute for you (the classroom teacher). Students who are deaf may at first rely on the interpreter for answers and guidance, but will learn to shift their confidence to you, their teacher.

To understand the information being presented, students who are deaf or hard of hearing need to be visually attentive to the speaker and the interpreter. By permitting these students to photocopy your lecture notes or a classmate's notes, or by providing carbon paper to a peer notetaker, you allow them to focus all their attention on you and the interpreter. Peer or adult notetakers and tutors can also help clarify and explain topics, preteach vocabulary, or review technical terms. Keep in mind that most students who are deaf and some students who are hard of hearing have limited English skills and need teaching techniques that support the development of concepts.

# Students with Physical Disabilities and Health Impairments

Students with physical disabilities or health impairments are a small but diverse group. Disabilities can range from asthma, a comparatively mild condition, to cerebral palsy, which may involve neurological impairment that affects mobility and other functional skills.

One of Lanetta Bridgewater's second-grade students, Emma, has cerebral palsy and is unable to speak, but understands what others are saying and is developing academic skills at a rate similar to her classmates. In planning and working with Emma, Lanetta worked closely with Susie Speelman, the inclusion support teacher you met in Chapter 8. Among the strategies Lanetta and Susie used to facilitate Emma's successful inclusion in Lanetta's classes were time to plan together, making the classroom more accessible for Emma and her wheelchair, use of technology (particularly of assistive devices to enable Emma to make choices and demonstrate her understanding), and reducing the amount of work (so that Emma has enough time to respond).

## Definitions and Types of Physical Disabilities and Health Impairments

Most students with physical disabilities and health impairments may qualify for special education services under three IDEA categories: orthopedic impairment, other health impairment, and traumatic brain injury. IDEA defines **orthopedic impairment** as:

> a severe orthopedic impairment that adversely affects a child's educational performance. The term includes impairments caused by congenital anomaly (e.g., clubfoot, absence of some member, etc.), impairments caused by disease (e.g., poliomyelitis, bone tuberculosis, etc.), and impairments from other causes (e.g., cerebral palsy, amputations, and fractures or burns that cause contractures) (*IDEA,* Section 300.7[7]).

Orthopedic impairments or physical disabilities may not only interfere with the students' coordination and mobility, but also affect their ability to communicate, learn, and adjust. Section 504 of the Vocational Rehabilitation Act of 1973 defines a *physical disability* as an impairment that substantially limits a person's participation in one or more life activities (home, school, or work activities) (Brimer, 1990). By this definition, a person whose impairment is controlled by medication is not considered physically disabled if he or she can participate in home, school, and work activities.

> Asthma is one of the most frequently cited reasons for students missing school. Another is head injury. One in 500 students is hospitalized each year for a head injury.

**Other health impairment** is defined as:

> having limited strength, vitality, or alertness, due to chronic or acute health problems such as heart condition, tuberculosis, rheumatic fever, nephritis, asthma, sickle cell anemia, hemophilia, epilepsy, lead poisoning, leukemia, or diabetes, that adversely affects a child's educational performance (*IDEA,* Section 300.7[8]).

With the 1990 amendments to IDEA, **traumatic brain injury** was identified as a category of disability and defined as:

> an acquired injury to the brain caused by an external physical force, resulting in total or partial functional disability or psychosocial impairment, or both, that adversely affects a child's education performance. The term applies to open or closed

head injuries resulting in impairments in one or more areas, such as cognition; language; memory; attention; reasoning; abstract thinking; judgment; problem-solving; sensory, perceptual, and motor abilities; psychosocial behavior; physical functions; information processing; and speech. The term does not apply to brain injuries that are congenital or degenerative, or brain injuries induced by birth trauma (34.CRF, Sec. 300.7[6][12]).

Common causes of traumatic brain injuries are motorcycle, automobile, and off-road vehicle accidents; sports injuries; and accidents from violence, such as gunshot wounds and child abuse (Russo, 1991).

## Research Brief

### Understanding Causes of Spinal Cord Injury and Traumatic Brain Injury

Spinal cord injuries in young children are most often caused by automobile accidents or child abuse. Automobile accidents, falls, gunshot wounds, and diving accidents cause most spinal cord injuries in adults and older children. Diseases and infections such as measles, polio, meningitis, and HIV can cause permanent damage to the central nervous system, therefore causing physical disabilities and health impairments. A lack of prenatal care and a mother's alcohol and substance abuse during pregnancy can also lead to physical disabilities and health impairments in children.

Over 50 percent of traumatic brain injuries in children and adolescents are caused by motor vehicle accidents, with falls causing another 21 percent. Sports and recreational injuries are the next major cause, followed by violence (Russo, 1991). Child abuse accounts for the majority of infant head injuries, and more than 75 percent of children under the age of three who are physically abused have a traumatic brain injury (Savage, 1993). Infants can also receive traumatic brain injury from being shaken (referred to as *shaken-impact syndrome*). In 10 to 25 percent of the cases, the child dies (Schroeder, 1993).

The following are typical behaviors associated with traumatic brain injuries:

- lowered social inhibition and judgment; lowered impulse control
- faulty reasoning
- numerous cognitive processing difficulties
- lowered initiative and motivation
- overestimation of abilities
- depression
- flat affect with sudden outbursts
- agitation and irritability
- fatigue (Forness & Kavale, 1993; Tucker & Colson 1992; Tyler & Myles, 1990; Witte, 1998).

Physical disabilities and health impairments caused by traumatic brain injury and spinal cord injury are preventable. The case for prevention of traumatic head injuries is clear:

- 63 percent of all children involved in motor vehicle accidents were not wearing restraints.
- 99 percent of those injured in bicycle accidents were not wearing helmets.
- 70 percent of those injured in motorcycle accidents were not wearing helmets.
- 54 percent of those injured while riding on all-terrain and recreational vehicles did not use restraints (Medical Research and Training Center in Rehabilitation and Childhood Trauma, 1993).

The three general categories of physical disabilities and health impairments are: neurological impairments, neuromuscular diseases, and health impairments. A **neurological impairment** is an abnormal performance caused by a dysfunction of the brain, spinal cord, and nerves, thereby creating transmission of improper instructions, uncontrolled bursts of instructions from the brain, or incorrect interpretation of feedback to the brain (Brimer, 1990). Some types of neurological impairment are seizure disorders, cerebral palsy, spina bifida, and traumatic brain injuries. **Neuromuscular diseases** involve both the nerves and muscles. They are neurological problems that affect the muscles. Muscular dystrophy, polio, and multiple sclerosis are examples of this type of physical disability. **Health impairments** include conditions such as asthma, cancer, cystic fibrosis, juvenile diabetes, prenatal substance abuse, fragile health, and communicable diseases like tuberculosis, cytomegalovirus, and HIV infection. As stated in the definition, the chronic or acute health problem must result in limited strength, vitality, or alertness.

## Characteristics of Students with Physical Disabilities and Health Impairments

The following sections describe the characteristics of the most common neurological impairments, neuromuscular diseases, and health impairments. During your teaching career you undoubtedly will have students with these and other illnesses or conditions in your classroom.

**Cerebral Palsy** Students with cerebral palsy are one of the largest groups of children with physical disabilities (Heward, 1996). **Cerebral palsy** is caused by damage to the brain before or during birth. Conditions are classified according to the areas affected and the types of symptoms. The degree of severity varies and is often evidenced by lack of coordination, speech disorders, motor problems, and extreme weakness. Cerebral palsy generally has accompanying problems in such areas as learning, vision, hearing, cognitive functioning, and social–emotional growth (Meyen & Skrtic, 1995). The condition can interfere with head control, arm use, sitting positions, balance, posture, and mobility, and these problems can be exacerbated by fatigue and stress.

As a classroom teacher, you will want to be aware of the student's level of fatigue and stress. Paul Nichols, a high-school math teacher, mentioned that his student, Allison, appeared stressed during tests, particularly if they were long or timed.

> I noticed that whenever we had a timed test with essays, Allison would have difficulty sitting up and holding up her head. At first I thought it was just a way for her to try and get out of the test so I tried to be firm with her. When I spoke to the physical therapist, he mentioned that she may be tired or stressed and then he taught her some relaxation techniques. She is doing better but it is still a difficult time for her. I did explain to her that the timed part was not as important as doing the work so now I give her extended time by allowing her to finish the test with the special education teacher during her resource period.

**Spina Bifida** Spina bifida, a birth defect that occurs when the spinal cord fails to close properly, often causes paralysis of parts of the body but seldom affects intellectual functioning. Most students with spina bifida walk with difficulty and lack complete bladder and bowel control. Some students need to use a catheter, which necessitates training in hygiene and extra time during the day to take care of the catheter. Generally, the school nurse or a special education teacher provides this training if it has not already been provided.

**Epilepsy** The most common neurological impairment in school-age children is convulsive disorders or epilepsy. **Epilepsy** is characterized by a tendency to have recurrent seizures—sudden, excessive, spontaneous, and abnormal discharges of neurons accompanied by alteration in motor function, sensory function, or consciousness (Coulter, 1993).

There are three major types of seizures. *Absence seizures (petit mal)* are characterized by short lapses in consciousness. Students may appear inattentive and often do not realize that they are having seizures. *Tonic–clonic seizures (grand mal)* are characterized by convulsions followed by loss of consciousness. Usually a tonic phase, in which the muscles are rigid, is followed by a clonic phase, in which the arms and legs jerk. Often the student loses consciousness and awakens disoriented and tired. Although these seizures usually last less than 5 minutes, they can be a frightening event for you and your students. Tips for Teachers 9.4 provides some pointers for handling this type of seizure. If a student in your class has this type of seizure disorder, be sure to help the other students in the classroom understand the condition and respond appropriately to the student (Reisner, 1988).

During *complex partial seizures* the electrical discharge is limited to one area of the brain. With a psychomotor seizure, for example, the student seems to be in a dreamlike state and may make random movements such as picking at clothes or repeating phrases, whereas with a focal motor seizure, the student usually has sudden, jerky movements in one part of the body.

**Muscular Dystrophy** Muscular dystrophy is a chronic disorder characterized by the weakening and wasting of the body's muscles. Persons with muscular dystrophy progressively lose their ability to walk and effectively use their arms and hands (Brooke, 1986). There is no cure for muscular dystrophy at this time, and the only prevention is genetic counseling (the condition appears to run in families). Helping the student maintain independence through regular physical therapy, exercise, and necessary physical aids is important. School personnel need to be careful not to lift or

## TIPS FOR TEACHERS

### 9.4 How to Respond to a Student with a Tonic–Clonic (Grand Mal) Seizure in the Classroom

- Ease student to the floor and clear the area around him or her.
- Put something soft under student's head to keep it from banging the floor.
- Do not interfere with the seizure. Turn student gently on his or her side, but do not put anything in the student's mouth and do not try to hold his or her tongue.
- Have someone stay with the student until he or she is fully awake.
- Allow the student to rest afterwards.
- Seek emergency assistance if seizure lasts longer than 5 minutes or if the student requests it.

---

pull a student with muscular dystrophy by his or her arms, because doing so may cause dislocation of limbs. Most students with muscular dystrophy need wheelchairs by the age of 10 to 14, and teachers should be alert for signs of fatigue (Heward, 1996).

**HIV and AIDS** Human immunodeficiency virus (HIV) is a condition that infects and eventually destroys cells in the immune system that protect the body from disease (Colson & Carlson, 1993). A viral infection transmitted through bodily fluids, HIV is responsible for **acquired immunodeficiency syndrome (AIDS)**. Students infected with HIV may eventually experience loss of stamina, developmental delays, motor problems, progressive neurological defects, repeated bacterial infections, psychological stresses, and death (Belman et al., 1988). HIV progresses through stages. In the latency stage, which generally lasts from 2 to 10 years in children, there are no outward symptoms. As the disease progresses through the middle stages, individuals experience a general weakening of the immune system, which results in persistent fevers and infections. In the final stages, opportunistic infections increase in frequency and severity.

Most school districts have established policies regarding the inclusion of students with HIV in general education classrooms. If students in your classroom are identified as having HIV, consult with individuals knowledgeable about these policies, and work with the special education teacher and school nurse in planning for these students. One important question to ask is how the condition currently affects the student's health. Students whose frequent absences are due to recurrent infections may need a homebound teacher. In advanced stages, students may experience a loss of knowledge and skills due to brain degeneration, and a lack of vitality (Kelker et al., 1994).

By knowing and adjusting to the student's capabilities, you enable the student to participate more fully and successfully in classroom activities. For example, Shirley Meeder, an eighth-grade social studies teacher, found that she could adapt assignments for Joey, a student in the middle stages of HIV, by reducing the amount of work required, giving him the option of listening to the textbook on tape, having a notetaker, and letting Joey take tests orally. These modifications helped Joey deal with his limited stamina. The special education teacher helped Shirley provide many of these accommodations.

> At the beginning of 1992, 3,420 students under the age of 13 had been diagnosed as having AIDS. About 80 percent of these children were infected by their mothers.

When Joey suffered from a prolonged infection, he received homebound instruction so that he could keep up with his classmates.

You may need to take some precautions with students with HIV. Casual contact among people in the classroom is not a problem, as this is not how HIV is transmitted (Wishom et al., 1989). But in situations in which you could come in contact with the blood or other bodily fluids of a student with HIV, then protective gloves should be worn (Kelker et al., 1994).

## Prevalence of Physical Disabilities and Health Impairments

Approximately 52,000, or 1.1 percent of all students receiving special education services, are categorized as having orthopedic impairments. Health impairments account for approximately 59,000, or 1.3 percent (U.S. Department of Education, 1993). It is important to remember that some students with physical disabilities and health impairments also have other disabilities and may be classified as having multiple disabilities.

Each year about 5,000,000 children receive head injuries, and of these about 200,000 are hospitalized (Rosman, 1994). About 2 to 5 percent of these children develop severe neurologic complications (Rudolph & Kamei, 1994). The occurrence of traumatic brain injuries increases dramatically during adolescence, with as many as 3 percent sustaining a head injury serious enough to cause school problems (Forness & Kavale, 1993). The following list of physical disabilities, health impairments, and related prevalence information is adapted from Turnbull et al. (1995):

### Cerebral Palsy
- About 500,000 to 700,000 Americans have some degree of cerebral palsy, with about 5,000 to 7,000 infants born with cerebral palsy each year.
- 3 in 1,000 infants are born with cerebral palsy (Bigge, 1991).

### Spina Bifida
- 0.5 to 1 in 1,000 infants are born with spina bifida (Bigge, 1991).
- If one child is born with spina bifida, the chances of the second child being born with spina bifida increase significantly.

### Neuromuscular Diseases
- Considering the more than 40 neuromuscular diseases together, the rate of disabilities is about 1 in 1,000 (Ringel, 1987).

### Seizure Disorders
- Approximately 1 percent of the American population, or about 2,000,000 individuals, have epilepsy. There are 750,000 under the age of 18.

### Asthma
- 5 million children under the age of 18, or about 6.5 percent, have asthma.
- Many do not require special education.

### Cancer
- New cases of childhood cancer are estimated at 8,000 per year.

### Diabetes
- Approximately 120,000 school-age children have juvenile diabetes.

### HIV
- Approximately 310,000 adolescents and 5,000 children had AIDS in 1993.

### Prenatal Substance Exposure
- An estimated 2 in 1,000 infants have fetal alcohol syndrome.
- In the United States, 100,000 infants per year are born drug-exposed.

## Identification and Assessment of Students with Physical Disabilities and Health Impairments

Medical diagnosis usually provides the initial identification of physical disabilities and health impairments. Assessments are carefully designed to take into account that these students may have delayed motor skills or problems staying on task for long periods of time. Sirvis (1988) recommends assessments in the following areas:

- **Activities of daily living** (personal hygiene, eating, dressing, using public transportation)
- **Academic potential** (physical disabilities may or may not affect mental capabilities) Students with neurological damage may have problems with attention, concentration, initiation, or fatigue (Meyen & Skrtic, 1995).
- **Adaptations for learning** (academic and physical adaptations to help students achieve academic success and independence)

- **Communication** (students' ability to express and understand language)
- **Mobility** (students' current and potential range and mode of mobility)
- **Physical abilities and limitations** (positioning and necessary adaptive equipment and techniques that facilitate students' independence)
- **Psychosocial development** (effects of impairment on students' social and emotional functioning)
- **Transition skills** (skills needed for a successful transition into and from school, and between grade levels)

Remember—as a classroom teacher and a member of the education team, you are a valuable resource for information.

## Instructional Guidelines and Accommodations for Students with Physical Disabilities and Health Impairments

Three basic principles can help you accommodate students with physical disabilities and health impairments in your classroom.

- **Use others as resources.** Call on the expertise of the student, parents, other school personnel, and others in health-related professions, as well as the student's classmates.
- **Be flexible in your planning.** Be willing to make last-minute changes in response to day-to-day changes in the student's condition and readiness to learn.
- **Be ingenious and creative.** One of the greatest rewards from working with students is helping them discover their strengths and ways to demonstrate them.

### Transdisciplinary Teaming and Support Providers

Because many students with physical disabilities or health impairments receive services from special education teachers, an occupational or physical therapist, an adaptive physical education teacher, and possibly a speech and language pathologist, effective teaming and communication are crucial. In **transdisciplinary teaming**, all members of the team work together and view the student as a whole, instead of working only on their specialty area (Downing & Bailey, 1990). All team members are aware of the student's goals, and observe each other as they work with the student so that they can share and generalize successful techniques and strategies. Tips for Teachers 9.5 provides further suggestions for working with these and other service providers. You will find these individuals to be an important support team for you and one key to the student's success.

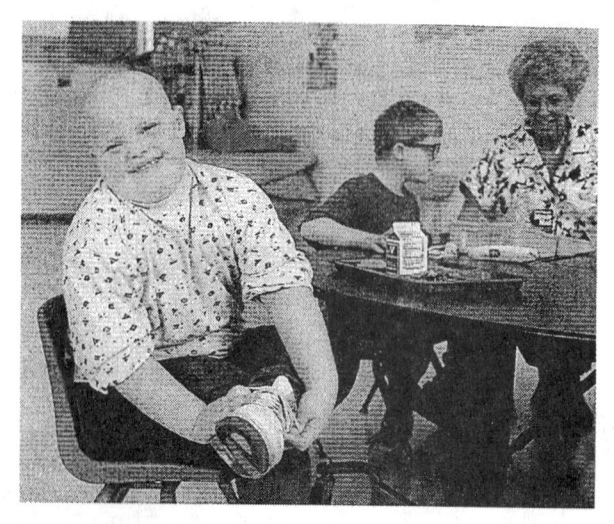

As a classroom teacher, how will you assess and address the needs of a student with a serious health impairment?

**Using Assistive Technology** Recall that IDEA defines *assistive technology* as "any item, piece of equipment, or product system whether acquired commercially off the shelf, modified, or customized, that is used to increase, maintain, or improve functional capabilities of individuals with disabilities." Assistive technology devices are particularly useful for increasing mobility, communicating better, gaining access to computers, performing daily living skills, enhancing learning, and manipulating and controlling the environment (Lewis, 1993). By using such assistive technology as eye-gaze pointing, switch-controlled computing, and writing implements encased in plastic tubing or bicycle handle grips, for example, Lanetta's student, Emma, is able to participate more fully in classroom life. Check whether someone is responsible for assistive technology at the district level in your school district, or work with an educational technology specialist.

**Making Environmental Modifications** In addition to the necessary accessibility modifications (wide aisle for wheelchairs, low drinking fountains, appropriate

# TIPS FOR TEACHERS

## 9.5 Suggestions for Working with Service Providers

Giangreco (1997) provided the following guidelines for working effectively with support service providers:

- Become aware of what support service providers have to offer.
- Approach support service staff as collaborators rather than experts.
- Make sure team members agree on expectations and goals for students.
- Clarify your role as a team member and your relationship with other team members.
- Be clear about the types of supports you need and want.
- Distinguish between needing an "extra pair of hands" and more specialized help.
- Make sure support service providers understand your classroom routines.
- Participate in scheduling support services.
- Have the team evaluate the effectiveness of support services for the student.
- Make sure support services are helping you to do a better job.

Adapted from Giangreco, M. F. (1997). *Quick-guides to inclusion: Ideas for educating students with disabilities.* Baltimore: Brookes.

---

handles), other environmental modifications facilitate independence for students with physical disabilities and health impairments. Wright and Bigge (1991) discuss four types of environmental modifications:

- **changes in location of materials and equipment** (e.g., so that students in wheelchairs can reach items independently)
- **work surface modifications** (e.g., raising a desk so that a wheelchair fits under it)
- **object modifications** (e.g., attaching clips to a student's desk to secure papers)
- **manipulation aids** (e.g., using a page turner to reduce dependency on others)

The 60-Second Lesson provides more quick and easy ideas for helping students become more independent and successful.

**Promoting Literacy Development** Literacy (reading, writing, listening and speaking) development is very important for persons with physical disabilities. It provides students access to language, a means to communicate their ideas, and a way to increase their experiences and knowledge. It also provides a lifelong pleasure activity (Dziwulski, 1994; Light & Kelford-Smith, 1993). Facilitating literacy development (Coleman, Koppenhaver, & Yoder, 1991) includes such suggestions as those that follow.

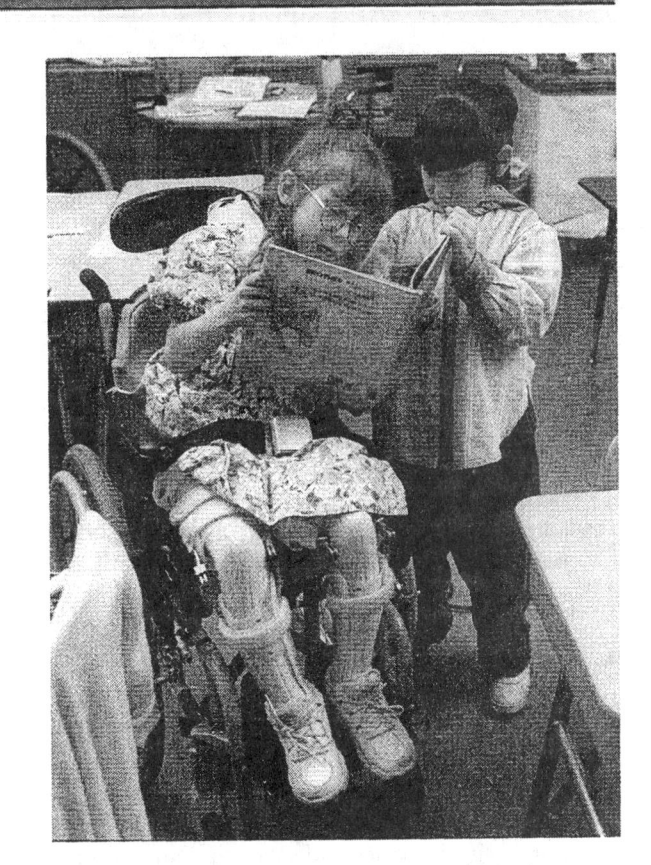

As a classroom teacher, how can you help students with physical disabilities or health impairments in their psychosocial development and peer relations?

# MAKING A DIFFERENCE
## The 60-Second Lesson

### Ways to Promote Independence in Students with Physical Disabilities or Health Impairments

- Retrace or enlarge print with a dark marker to help students see material more clearly.
- Schedule study buddies to help a student with disabilities gather learning materials.
- Assign a classmate or ask for a volunteer to take or copy notes for a student with disabilities.
- Ask students for whom writing is difficult whether they would prefer an oral assignment or test.
- Ask the special education teacher to provide (or advise you on acquiring) materials for securing small objects. Velcro and Dycem mat on a student's desk prevent books, calculators, pencil boxes, and the like, from slipping off.
- Ask parents to provide a bandanna or sweat band, worn on the wrist, to help a student with limited control of facial muscles wipe off excess saliva.
- Arrange with the special education teacher for the assistance of a paraprofessional in moving a student from a wheelchair to a bean bag chair during floor activities, so that the student can be both supported physically and seated on the same level as peers.

---

- **Positioning** Adaptive wheelchairs or other seating devices may act as barriers in the students' ability to see print and pictures. Position students so they can see the print and pictures while listening. This helps them begin to make the connection between print and speech. Ideally, the students should be situated in a way that allows them to help turn the pages so they begin to recognize the left-to-right orientation of text. A person following the text with a finger also helps develop this concept. Page fluffers, (pieces of foam glued to the pages in a book) provide more space between pages, making them easier to turn. Gluing a popsicle stick or paper clip on the edge of the page also makes turning the page easier. A glove with a magnet can be used with the paper clip to help the student be independent. (Dziwulski, 1994).
- **Siblings and peers** Since children with physical disabilities may not have the ability or access for questioning and retelling the story, the inclusion of peers or siblings during storytime could help make the storytime more "lively." Parents have reported that children related text to real life activities and asked and answered a greater variety of questions when peers or siblings were present. The other children also act as models for the child with disabilities.
- **Repeated readings** Research has shown that students benefit from repeated readings as it helps them to recognize printed words and to understand the structure of written language.
- **Print in the environment** Having print everywhere in the students' environment is important. For students with physical disabilities, rememeber that the print needs to be at their eye level based on their adaptive equipment.
- **Accessing literacy** Students with disabilities need a method to independently access storybooks, writing instruments, and other literacy-related items. These could be books on tape or slide projectors with an adaptive switch to independently activate. A designated communication signal should be in place that means they want to use print-related materials.
- **Functional/recreational uses of print** It is important for students to participate in functional and recreational literacy such as developing a grocery list, writing a note to a friend, and reading for enjoyment. Embed literacy into all activities during the day (reading the signs on the restroom door or at the grocery store).
- **Interactive stories** Adaptations need to be made so students with physical disabilities can ask and answer questions about stories to help

develop literacy skills. Communication boards and velcro vests can be constructed to be relevant to a story with new symbols added to represent characters, actions, and feelings dealing with the new stories. One idea is to buy two copies of the book, cut out the pictures from one book, and paste them on an eye-gaze board so the child can predict what is going to happen next in the story.

- **Access to drawing and writing** Drawing and writing can be made easier with adaptive holders for the writing utensil. Taping the paper down also helps the student draw or write. There are various adaptive writing and drawing software programs that can be accessed through Touch Windows or switches to help students with physical impairments.
- **Assistive technology** There is abundant assistive technology available but it needs to be matched up with the students in their homes and schools. Books on disks, drawing and writing software, and other language programs can assist students in developing literacy.

**Educating Classmates** For students with health impairments and physical disabilities, some of the most important modifications relate to informing other students in the class. Classmates, particularly younger students with rare diseases or severe disabilities, will most likely have limited knowledge and many questions. For example, Sexson and Madan-Swain (1993) found that students most often asked the following questions about a classmate with a health problem:

- What's wrong with the student?
- Is the disease contagious?
- Will (the student) die from it?
- Will he or she lose anything (such as limbs, hair)?
- Should we talk about the student's illness or ignore it?
- What will other students think if I'm still friends with this student?

Sexson and Madan-Swain (1993) suggest not only addressing these questions, but also talking about how the student may be different when he or she returns from a prolonged absence.

**Dealing with Death** During your teaching career you may have a student in your class who is dying. In this circumstance, counseling is indicated. Open communication with the student, parents, counselor, and other members of the education team becomes very important so that you can deal with the student's feelings and fears in a consistent and open manner. You may work directly with the school counselor, but you need written permission from parents before you can contact a student's private counselor or psychologist.

Berner (1977) and others suggest that children go through stages as they move toward accepting death. Although not all children go through all stages, and some may be experienced simultaneously, knowledge of these stages can help you understand the behaviors and emotions that may be exhibited by a student who is dying. The stages include:

- shock and disbelief
- crying (sometimes hysterical)
- feelings of isolation and loneliness
- psychosomatic symptoms, which may distract the student from the fatal condition
- panic
- guilt that he or she is to blame
- hostility or resentment toward others
- resistance to usual routines and continuing to live
- reconciliation and beginning acceptance of the inevitability of death
- acceptance

Although the suggestions in Table 9.1 are from parents of children with cancer (Candlelighters Childhood Cancer Foundation, 1993), many apply also to children with other life-threatening illnesses, such as AIDS.

**Providing Instruction of Motor Skills** For students with physical disabilities and health impairments, working on motor skills is an important component of their education program. Many activities that support motor skills can be incorporated easily into daily classroom activities such as increasing control by looking at a classmate during cooperative learning activites or improving fine motor skills by drawing or writing.

As you work with students who have visual, hearing, physical, or health impairments, your repertoire of teaching strategies and knowledge of classroom accommodations and assistive technology will grow. With the help of a number of specialists, who can assist both you and the student, you should feel confident of success in educating your students.

## TABLE 9.1

**Parents' View: What Teachers Should and Should Not Do for a Student with Cancer**

| Helpful Teachers | Less Helpful Teachers |
|---|---|
| ✔ Take time to learn about the treatments and their effects on school performance. | ✔ Fail to learn about the disease and its effects and treatments. |
| ✔ Demonstrate support for parents as well as student. | ✔ Show fear about having the student in class. |
| ✔ Listen to parents' concerns and fears. | ✔ Allow other students to pity the student. |
| ✔ Call or visit during absences. | ✔ Fail to keep ongoing communication with parents and student during absences. |
| ✔ Encourage classmates to call or write during extended absences. | ✔ Ignore problems classmates have in adjusting to friend's disease. |
| ✔ Before re-entry, talk with the student about any fears or concerns. | ✔ Before re-entry, fail to share information about the student and the disease with classmates. |
| ✔ Adjust lessons and assignments based on the student's endurance. | ✔ Do not give the student the benefit of the doubt on assignments and homework. |
| ✔ Follow parental and medical instructions regarding snacks, wearing a hat, bathroom visits. | ✔ Make an issue of the student's differences in front of others. |
| ✔ Treat the student as normally as possible and include the student in as many class activities as possible. | ✔ Do not give the student an opportunity to attempt what others are doing. |

Adapted from The Candlelighters Childhood Cancer Foundation (1993). Advice to educators (adapted from a survey by A Wish with Wings). In *Educating the child with cancer* (pp. 21–22). Bethesda, MD: Author.

# SUMMARY

- Students with visual impairment can be blind or partially sighted, depending on the degree and type of vision loss.
- It is important when planning for a student with visual impairments to consider the student's functional vision.
- Braille is the system of raised dots used for reading and writing by students who cannot read print.
- It is important to make the classroom accessible for students who have visual impairments. These students may need instruction in orientation and mobility skills.
- High and low technology, including computers, have done much to help students who are visually impaired succeed in school.
- Hearing loss is measured by an audiologist, who plots the results of the hearing test on an audiogram.
- Although most children with significant hearing loss are identified prior to beginning school, it is important to watch for signs of mild hearing loss.
- American Sign Language is a visual and gestural language used by many individuals in North America who are deaf.
- Arranging the classroom to reduce background noise and to have the speaker's face visible is important for students with hearing loss.
- Interpreters and notetakers provide a means for students with hearing loss to attend and learn from general education classes.
- The three main types of physical disabilities and health impairments are: neurological impairments, neuromuscular diseases, and health impairments.

- Assistive technology devices can enhance students' independence and learning. Devices range from low-tech items such as handles to high-tech devices such as computers.

- When working with students who have visual, hearing, physical, and health disabilities, you have a number of specialists with whom to collaborate.

## Key Terms and Concepts

acquired immunodeficiency syndrome (AIDS)
American Sign Language
assistive listening devices
audiogram
blind
braille
cerebral palsy
compensatory skills
deaf
echolalia
epilepsy
finger spelling
functional vision
hard of hearing
health impairments
human immunodeficiency virus (HIV)
legal blindness
low vision
mobility skills
muscular dystrophy
neurological impairments
neuromuscular diseases
orientation skills
orthopedic impairment
other health impairment
partially sighted
residual hearing
sensory channels
spina bifida
transdisciplinary teaming
traumatic brain injury
visual acuity
visual field

## Think and Apply

1. In the opening interview, Pat Childers expressed that she lacked the knowledge and experience to work with students like Brandy. Other teachers, such as Nancy Shipka and Lanetta Bridgewater, expressed the same concerns. What systems are in place to help these teachers? Make a list of your questions, the persons you would ask, and the meetings or activities you would plan before a student with disabilities joins your class.

2. Interview and observe two or three of the specialists described in this chapter. Find out about the students with whom they work, their roles and responsibilities, and how they team with general classroom teachers.

3. Develop a file of assistive technology resources in your state and local district. Visit the technology center or specialist and learn more about integrating assistive technology for students with disabilities.

4. Survey a classroom and school to determine accessibility for a student using a wheelchair. List modifications that you think would improve accessibility.

5. Interview several adolescents or young adults with a visual, hearing, physical, or health impairment. Ask the following questions:
   - What impact does (the disability) have on your daily life?
   - How do your routines differ because of (the disability)?
   - How do others react to your disability?
   - What advice would you give classroom teachers about helping other students with (the disability)?

6. Check and see if there is a classroom for students who are deaf/hard of hearing or visually impaired in your school district. Perhaps there is a school for the deaf and blind. Arrange to spend some time in a classroom with these students. Observe the strategies teachers use to communicate with and instruct their students. How do these classrooms function similarly to and differently than general education classrooms?

## Read More about It

**Visual Impairments**

1. Barraga, N. D., & Erin, J. N. (1992). *Visual handicaps and learning* (3rd ed.). Austin, TX: Pro-Ed.

   An introductory textbook with information on designing appropriate instructional settings and programs for students who are visually impaired.

2. Levack, N. (1994). *Low vision: A resource guide with adaptations for students with visual impairments* (2nd ed.). Austin, TX: Texas School for the Blind.

   This is a useful guide for parents and teachers who work with students with low vision. Includes information on teaching adaptations.

3. Torres, I., & Corn, A. L. (1990). *When you have a visually handicapped child in your classroom: Suggestions for teachers* (2nd ed.). New York: American Foundation for the Blind.

   A practical guide with many suggestions for integrating students with visual impairments into mainstream classes.

**Hearing Loss**

1. Lane, H., Hoffmeister, R., & Bahan, B. (1996). *A journey into the Deaf-world*. San Diego, CA: Dawn Sign Press.

   A resource book that details Deaf culture and its role in education.

2. Luetke-Stahlman, B., & Luckner, J. (1991). *Effectively educating students with hearing impairments*. White Plains, NY: Longman.

   An introductory textbook on educating students with hearing loss, includes ideas for teaching these students in general education classrooms.

3. Moores, D. F. (1996). *Educating the deaf: Psychology, principles, and practices* (4th ed.) Boston, MA: Houghton Mifflin.

   A comprehensive textbook that provides an overview of educating deaf students and discusses other aspects of deafness.

**Physical Disabilities and Health Impairments**

1. Batshaw, M. L. (1997). *Children with disabilities: A medical primer* (4th ed.). Baltimore: Brookes.

   An extensive overview of various types of physical disabilities and health impairments.

2. Beverly, C. L., & Thomas, S. B. (1997). Developmental and psycho-social effects of HIV in school-aged population: Educational implications. *Education and Training in Mental Retardation and Developmental Disabilities, 32,* 32–41.

   An informative article describing the developmental and psycho-social characteristics of school-aged persons with HIV and also providing educational implications and strategies to assist educators.

3. Bigge, J. L. (1991). *Teaching individuals with physical and multiple disabilities*. New York: Macmillan.

   A comprehensive textbook on physical and health impairments.

4. Glang, A., Singer, G. & Todis, B. (1997). *Students with acquired brain injury: The school's response*. Baltimore: Brookes.

   A resource for educators that provides practical information on educational issues and approaches to working with students with brain injury.

5. Moffitt, K., Nachahsi, J., & Reiss, J. (Eds.). (1993). *Special children, special care.* Tampa: University of South Florida.

   A practical guide for collaboration among professionals and families caring for children with complex health impairments.

6. Witte, R. (1998). Meet Bob: A student with traumatic brain injury. *Teaching Exceptional Children, 30*(3), 56–60.

   Provides practical information about identifying and educating students with TBI.

7. Nevins, M. E. & Chute, P. (1966). *Children with cochlear implants in educational settings.* (School Age Children Series) Singular Publishing Group.

   Sometimes children who are deaf receive a cochlear implant to improve their hearing. This book is a reader-friendly introduction to working with children with cochlear implants in the classroom.

CHAPTER *15*

# Teaching Culturally and Linguistically Diverse Students

# Interview

## Co-teachers at Mission Way School

Gloria Rodriguez is a fifth-grade bilingual education teacher who co-teaches with Lidia Romo, a fourth-grade bilingual education teacher at Mission Way Elementary School in southwest Arizona. Maria Chavez is the English as a second language (ESL) teacher for this K–5 elementary school. Most students at Mission Way speak Spanish or Spanish and Yaqui, a Native American language, as their first language(s). Although over 85 percent of these students qualify for free lunch, they come from rich cultural communities, such as the Mexican-American barrios or the Yaqui Reservation.

Two years ago, with the support of the principal, Gloria and Lidia decided to co-teach. They made this decision for several important reasons. First, by co-teaching they offer broader cultural and linguistic expertise. Gloria, whose background is Mexican American, grew up in the local barrios, attended a local university, and has been teaching at Mission Way for 5 years. In contrast, Lidia grew up on the Yaqui Reservation, went to a university in northern Arizona, and has been teaching 3 years at Mission Way. She has a rich knowledge of the Yaqui ways.

Second, by co-teaching they believe that they increase their ability to effectively use their approach to multicultural education. This approach, which uses the culture and community as the foundation on which learning and curriculum are built, provides students with the opportunity to learn about and respect their cultural and linguistic heritages. At the same time, the students are learning English and to assimilate into the mainstream of American life.

Third, by co-teaching Gloria and Lidia are able to group students flexibly while many of them make the transition from their first language(s) to English. As in other learning, not all students are ready to make the transition at the same time or at the same rate. The teachers believe that flexibility is important for students to succeed at becoming competent English speakers, readers, and writers. Lidia comments,

> The transition from first language to second language is one of the most complex aspects of bilingual education that we deal with. We often have a good sense for when students are ready to make this transition, but our curriculum and grouping doesn't allow us to meet the students' needs. Team teaching with Gloria helps me better meet the needs of the students and make adjustments tailored to them.

Another reason that Gloria and Lidia decided to team teach is that it seems to give them more time to integrate the family and communities into the school and their classroom. Gloria comments,

> Fourth and fifth grades are often times when students are beginning to be pressured to join gangs. We feel that one reason our students are not as likely to join gangs is because they have a strong sense of respect for their own cultures. We feel that combining our cultural expertise and engaging the students in thematic units built on their cultures serves as a deterrent to joining gangs.

In contrast to Gloria and Lidia, the ESL teacher, Maria, grew up in Puerto Rico and New York City. She attended college in Puerto Rico and then taught for several years in a New York public school serving a Puerto Rican community. She started teaching ESL at Mission Way 2 years ago, when her husband was transferred to the Southwest. Maria has found that although both she and Gloria are considered Latinos or Hispanics, their cultural roots and heritage are different, in much the same way that New Englanders differ from Southerners and Midwesterners.

In her teaching Maria works to broaden the students' knowledge of various cultures to include not only different Latino and Native American cultures, but also European American, African American, and Asian American cultures. In teaching ESL, Maria goes into the classroom or sometimes works with small groups of students in her resource room. On a regular basis, new students are enrolled in Mission Way who speak no English and have limited academic skills in their first language. Maria, whose job is to provide intensive support to these students and their teachers, sees herself also as a resource for the other teachers. She comments,

> I feel like one of my major job roles is that of a school-wide resource. I switch lunch periods during the week so that I have the opportunity to eat with different teachers and find out their needs and offer help. One of my concerns is how to be of assistance to more teachers. I think communication and time are the keys.

## Introduction

Clearly, the cultural and linguistic diversity of Mission Way adds to the richness of the school community and the complexity of teaching. But compared to schools whose students come from many different cultural and linguistic backgrounds, Mission Way is relatively homogeneous.

This chapter focuses on the growing diversity of schools and students in the United States. It also presents the key concepts associated with multicultural education, linguistic diversity, second language learning, and bilingual education. Finally, it discusses instructional strategies for educating students who are culturally and linguistically diverse. As you read this chapter, think about how the ideas presented by Gloria, Lidia, and Maria create schools and classrooms that facilitate the successful education of culturally and linguistically diverse students.

## Diversity in Classrooms and Schools

The United States is one of the most culturally diverse nations in the world. A Mexican immigrant commented, "Before I came to America I had dreams of life here. I thought about tall Anglos, big buildings, and houses with lawns. I was surprised when I arrived to see so many kinds of people—Black people, Asians. I found people from Korea and Cambodia and Mexico. In California I found not just America, I found the world" (Olsen, 1988). This diversity continues to increase as new immigrants relocate in the United States. By the year 2000, non-European Americans are expected to comprise more than one-third of the population, with the two largest minority groups—African Americans (currently over 30 million) and Latino Americans (currently over 22 million)—making up almost a third of the total school enrollment (Grossman, 1995; Orando & Collier, 1998). Asian Pacific Americans are the fastest growing "minority group" in the United States, with over 100 percent growth since 1980 and numbering more than 7 million.

Approximately 30 percent of elementary school students are members of racial and ethnic minority groups (Snyder, 1993). Minorities constitute the majority of public school students in more than 20 of the country's largest school systems, including Miami, Philadelphia, Baltimore, and Los Angeles. Although many of these students do well in school, a substantial number of students come from homes in which families live in poverty and parents are unemployed or underemployed, have little education, few technical skills, and are not fluent in English (Berliner & Biddle, 1995; Garbarino, 1997). Furthermore, education practice oftentimes does not provide a good match with the students' cultures and the curriculum (Jordan, 1985; Orando & Collier, 1998). Tips for Teachers 10.1 has suggestions to help teachers learn about students' home communities.

The average achievement of African Americans, Native Americans, and Latino Americans is consistently lower than that of middle- and upper-class European Americans at every grade level (National Center for Educational Research, 1990). The dropout rates and the grade retention rates are also higher for these groups of students. It is estimated that 48 percent of Native American students, and 40 percent of Latino Americans, do not graduate from high school (Wyman, 1993). African Americans also have high dropout rates, with inner-city youth dropping out at a rate of 80 percent. The dropout rates for Asian Pacific Americans are lower, but when considering those Asian Pacific American students from developing countries only, the rate is high (Grossman, 1995).

> Over 2 million people in the United States are Native Americans, representing over 500 tribal groups and speaking more than 200 languages. The largest tribes are Cherokee and Navajo. The largest populations of Native Americans are in California, Arizona, New Mexico, and Oklahoma.

A disproportionately high percentage of African Americans, Latin Americans, and Native Americans have been identified as having learning disabilities, mild mental retardation, and emotional or behavioral disorders (Drew et al., 1996). In contrast, a disproportionately low percentage of students from these cultural groups have been identified as gifted and talented (VanTassel-Baska et al., 1991).

The reasons for the limited success these students have in school are complex and interrelated, but several factors should be considered (Stephen et al., 1993). First, role models from minority groups are often limited in school, in that many teachers are European Americans and limited mentor programs are available for these students to connect with leaders in

## TIPS FOR TEACHERS

### 10.1 Learning about the Funds of Knowledge in Students' Home Communities

Teachers may begin their teaching careers in schools in which the students' home communities are neither their home community nor similar to their home communities. Some ideas that help teachers learn about the students' home communities are:

- Learn about students' cultural backgrounds. Learn how the culture views the role of teachers and schools, and the role of parents in relation to schools.
- Locate at least one person in the community who can serve as your cultural guide or informant. This can often be a fellow staff member. Develop a relationship in which that person teaches you about the culture and community.
- Be a learner in the classroom. Discuss with students your interest in learning about their cultures, including community activities. Information that can help guide your learning includes: jobs of parents, their special skills and knowledge, special interests of students (at home and in the community), community activities, special occasions and holidays, family structure, family responsibilities and relationships.
- If appropriate and within school policy, visit students' homes and talk with parents and other family members. This is an ideal opportunity to learn more about the students, the households, and culture, including interests of the family, the role of the extended family, the way in which jobs are shared, and the ways in which literacy is used in the home.

---

their communities. Second, discrimination against students from minority groups continues in assessment for and placement in advanced and gifted programs. Third, curriculum and educational practice are often not culturally responsive, with limited integration of information about different cultural groups into the curriculum (Erickson & Mohatt, 1982). Fourth, teaching styles may not match the learning styles of students from diverse cultures (Ladson-Billings, 1995). Fifth, a greater proportion of students from minority groups live in poverty and their poverty levels are lower than that of European Americans (Banks, 1996). Furthermore, the number of children in poverty in the United States continues to rise and is well above most European countries (Banks, 1997a; Berliner & Biddle, 1995).

### Understanding Diverse Cultures

The United States is composed of a shared core culture and many subcultures (Banks, 1997a). Students in our schools are influenced by this core culture, sometimes referred to as the **macroculture**. The United States is such a complex and diverse nation that its core culture is somewhat difficult to describe, but Banks and Banks (1995) suggest the following key components:

- equality of opportunities for individuals in the society
- individualism and the notion that individual success is more important than the family, community, and nation-state
- social mobility through individual effort and hard work
- individualistic attitudes toward values and behaviors
- belief in the nation's superiority
- orientation toward materialism and exploitation of the natural environment

At the same time, students are influenced by their home cultures, or **microcultures**. Microcultures are often based on such factors as national origin, ethnicity, socioeconomic class, religion, gender, age, and disability (Gollnick & Chinn, 1990). Even geographical areas of the country (e.g., New England, Appalachia) can be considered microcultures because of differences in customs and mores.

What is involved in the process of mediating among diverse cultures? What environmental and instructional measures can teachers take to help diverse students mediate between the microcultures of their homes and communities and the macrocultures of their nation and school?

Sometimes the core values of the macroculture and microcultures are relatively similar, but in other cases, the microculture values are quite different from those of the core culture (Banks, 1997a). For example, the emphasis on individuality is generally not as important in African American, Latino American, and Native American ethnic communities as it is in the European American macroculture. Instead, these communities place more importance on group and family values (Hale-Benson, 1986; Ramirez & Castaneda, 1974; Swisher & Deyhle, 1992). Hence, cooperative learning may be a better match than competitive learning for students from these ethnic backgrounds. In fact, cooperative learning activities that support equal status contact between majority and minority groups in pursuit of common goals have been shown to increase cross-ethnic friendships in classrooms (e.g., Kagan et al., 1985; Oishi et al., 1983). Another example of differences between the macroculture and various microcultures in the United States is the value given to personalized knowledge (e.g., knowledge that results from firsthand observation). Although the macroculture values knowledge based on objectivity, and educational institutions emphasize abstract "out-of-context" knowledge, research on women's ways of knowing suggest that women value personalized knowledge (Belenky et al., 1986; Gilligan, 1982; Maher, 1987). Similarly, Ramirez and Castaneda (1974) found that Mexican-American students who were socialized within traditional Latino cultures also responded positively to knowledge presented in a personalized or story format.

When the core values in the macroculture and microculture are relatively different, teachers can help students understand and mediate differences between the cultures. To act as mediators, teachers need to learn about and incorporate the various microcultures and home communities into school life and the curriculum. For example, Luis Moll and his colleagues (e.g., Moll & Greenberg, 1990; Gonzales et al., 1995) have been working as participants and researchers in Tucson's barrio schools for a number of years. Moll's research and ethnographic methods of study provide strategies for teachers to integrate the home and school communities by building on the **funds of knowledge** found in the home community (see Tips for Teachers 10.1).

Learning about the funds of knowledge in the students' home community can help teachers to not overgeneralize characteristics that are often attributed to different cultural groups.

## Cultural Characteristics

In learning about cultural influences there is a tendency to make generalizations based on common beliefs about a culture. As Lynch (1992) notes, however, "Culture is only one of the characteristics that determine individuals' and families' attitudes, values, beliefs, and ways of behaving.... Assuming that culture-specific information ... applies to all individuals from the cultural group is not only inaccurate but also dangerous—it can lead to stereotyping that diminishes rather than enhances cross-cultural competence" (p. 44). Still, having some knowledge of students' **cultural characteristics** serves as a starting point for understanding individual students' behaviors and learning styles.

Knowledge of cultural characteristics can keep teachers from misinterpreting students' actions. One example is the learning style of some Native American groups. Teachers typically encourage students to attempt tasks publicly or to answer questions, even though they are unsure of what to say or do, but the traditional learning styles of some Native American groups encourage learning privately and gaining competence before performing publicly. Learners repeatedly watch an activity and review it in their heads before attempting any kind of public performance (Appleton, 1983; Longstreet, 1978). For example, after watching a medicine man, an apprentice will collect a plant for a specific remedy. If the selection is not correct, the medicine man more than likely will walk to the correct plant and show and explain some characteristics that make it the appropriate plant. The same rich style of watching, modeling, and explaining is used for jewelry making, weaving, and classroom learning.

Werner and Begishe (1968) capture this contrast in learning by comparing the European American philosophy, "If at first you don't succeed, try, try, again" to the Native American philosophy, "If at first you don't think, and think again, don't bother trying." A teacher of Native American students comments, "The Indian students seem to need time to think about things before they take action on their assignment. It is almost like they have to make sure they can do it before they try. . . . If I didn't know better, I could interpret this as they just do not care about doing their assignments" (Swisher & Deyhle, 1992, p. 82).

Díaz-Rico and Weed (1995) suggest that teachers should learn about their students' cultural characteristics to understand the students' actions and help them to integrate the home and school cultures. Following are general areas and questions that teachers can use to guide their inquiry:

- **Time:** How do students perceive time? How is timeliness regarded in their cultures?
- **Space:** What personal distance do students use in interactions with other students and with adults? How does the culture determine the space allotted to boys and girls?
- **Dress and Food:** How does dress differ for age, gender, and social class? What clothing and accessories are considered acceptable? What foods are typical?
- **Rituals and Ceremonies:** What rituals do students use to show respect? What celebrations do students observe, and for what reasons? How and where do parents expect to be greeted when visiting the class?
- **Work:** What types of work are students expected to perform, and at what age, in the home and community? To what extent are students expected to work together?
- **Leisure:** What are the purposes for play? What typical activities are done for enjoyment in the home and community?
- **Gender Roles:** What tasks are performed by boys? By girls? What expectations do parents and students hold for boys' and girls' achievements, and how does this differ by subject areas?
- **Status:** What resources (e.g., study area and materials, study assistance from parents and siblings) are available at home and in the community? What power do parents have to obtain information about the school and to influence educational choices?
- **Goals:** What kinds of work are considered prestigious or desirable? What role does education play in achieving occupational goals? What education level do the family and student desire for the student?
- **Education:** What methods for teaching and learning are used in the home (e.g., modeling and imitation, didactic stories and proverbs, direct verbal instruction)?
- **Communication:** What roles do verbal and nonverbal language play in learning and teaching? What roles do conventions such as silence, questions, rhetorical questions, and discourse style play in communication? What types of literature (e.g., newspapers, books) are used in the home and in what language(s) are they written? How is writing used in the home (e.g., letters, lists, notes) and in what language(s)?
- **Interaction:** What roles do cooperation and competition play in learning? How are children expected to interact with teachers?

Common characteristics in a culture can serve initially to guide teacher inquiry. For example, Kitano (1973) and Cheng (1991) note several characteristics of Asian cultures that may help to explain parents' expectations and students' actions:

- Students are to be quiet and obedient, not calling attention to themselves in a group.
- Didactic methods of learning are common. Teachers are to teach by demonstrating or transmitting knowledge, skills, and strategies. Students are to study and learn.

- Teachers are to be respected and generally not to be challenged.
- In school, students respond when they have something important to share and do not engage easily in free discussion and brainstorming.

Based on these characteristics, a teacher would understand when students from Laos or Vietnam would not consider raising their hands and asking for clarification when a teacher is lecturing (Bliatout et al., 1988) or would not want to be singled out for attention or praise by teachers (Furey, 1986).

In many Native American cultures, the role of time is viewed differently. The time to begin is when people arrive for the gathering. Work is oriented toward the common good of the community rather than personal recognition and fame, and a deep respect for knowledge and wisdom of elders is evident (Pepper, 1976; Swisher & Deyhle, 1992). The role of silence is important, in that it communicates respect and thoughtfulness. Being comfortable with silence helped the counselor in the following scenario establish trust and rapport.

> Norman, a Paiute youth from Reno, Nevada, had an agonizing decision to make. At the age of 18, he had graduated from the Indian Youth Training Program in Tucson, Arizona, and was free to return home to live. Living at home would possibly jeopardize the hard-won habits of diligence and self-control that he had learned away from the home community, in which he had been arrested for juvenile delinquency. As the counselor in Norman's group home, I knew he could possibly benefit by talking over his decision. After school, I entered his room and sat on the chair by his bed, indicating that I was available to help him talk through his dilemma. One-half hour of total silence elapsed. After thirty minutes he began to speak. Silence rather than language had achieved the rapport I sought (Díaz-Rico & Weed, 1995, p. 246).

In African American cultures, interaction is more informal, with greater spontaneity and general participation in the discussion rather than the more focused question and answer format (Ratleff, 1989). In studying a small African American community in the rural Carolinas, Heath (1983) noted that young children in "Trackton" were encouraged to use spontaneous verbal play, rich with metaphors and similes. The use of multiple modes of communication, particularly nonverbal expressions, plays an important role in understanding the meaning of the message.

In many Latin American cultures, the family and community are strongly valued, and time is more flexible. For example, "Adela, a Mexican-American first-grade girl, arrived at school about 20 minutes late every day. Her teacher was at first irritated and gradually exasperated. In a parent conference, Adela's mother explained that braiding her daughter's hair each morning was an important time for the two of them to be together. This family time presented a value conflict with the school's time norm" (Díaz-Rico & Weed, 1995, p. 231). Just as family and community are valued, *interdependence* (rather than independence) is viewed as a strength. Decisions are made as a group, and those who are successful have responsibilities for others. Classrooms that foster learning through cooperation may help students extend their predisposition for interdependence (Banks, 1997c; Díaz-Rico & Weed, 1995; Orando & Collier, 1998).

> Terminology for racial and ethnic groups changes, reflecting both cultural and political decisions and historical development (Nieto, 1996). Using the current preferred terms when referring to groups is important.

Ogbu (1978, 1992) has suggested that some cultural groups seem to cross cultural boundaries more easily than other groups. The case for this idea is built on the information presented in the Research Brief.

# Research Brief

### Crossing Cultural Boundaries

Teachers often ask why some cultural groups seem to cross cultural boundaries and succeed in school more easily than others do. Based on his comparative research, John Ogbu (1978; 1992) has put forth one explanation. In his work, he classified cultural groups as (a) autonomous minorities, (b) immigrant or voluntary minorities, and (c) castelike or involuntary minorities.

- *Autonomous minorities* are considered minorities in a numerical sense, and include Jews, Mormons, and the Amish. In the United States, there are no non-White autonomous minorities.

- *Immigrant or voluntary minorities* are people who have moved to the new society or culture more or less voluntarily—because they desire greater economic opportunities and political freedom. The Chinese and Punjabi Indians are representative United States examples.
- *Castelike or involuntary minorities* are people who were brought to the United States or conquered against their will. Examples in the United States are African Americans, Native Americans, early Mexican Americans in the Southwest, and Native Hawaiians.

Ogbu (1992) suggests that voluntary groups experience initial (but not lingering) problems in school because of language and cultural differences. The involuntary minorities, on the other hand, usually experience greater, more persistent difficulties learning in school. This difficulty for involuntary minorities appears related to several factors:

- **Cultural inversion,** or the tendency to regard certain forms of behavior, events, symbols, and meanings as inappropriate because they are characteristic of European American culture.
- A *collective identity,* in opposition to the social identity of the dominant group, develops as the involuntary minorities are treated as subordinates by European Americans in economic, political, social, psychological, cultural, and language domains.

Hence, in an effort to retain their own identity and roots, students from involuntary minorities may be more oppositional and less motivated to learn in school. Ogbu (1992) explains, "They fear that by learning the White cultural frame of reference, they will cease to act like minorities and lose their identity as minorities and their sense of community and self-worth" (p. 10). In contrast, because voluntary minorities do not feel the need to protect their cultural identity, they do not perceive learning the attitudes and behaviors required for school success as threatening to their own culture, language, and identities. Instead they interpret such learning as *additive,* that is, adding to what they already have (Chung, 1992).

It is important to note that these are generalized types that include groups who may more appropriately "fit" a different type. For example, Cubans who fled Cuba during the 1960s were an involuntary minority, yet many acculturated and became quite successful in the Miami community.

Cummins (1992) suggests that academic success of students from involuntary minority groups is related to the extent that schools reflect the following:

- Minority students' language and culture are incorporated into the school program.
- Minority community participation is encouraged as an integral component of children's education.
- Instruction (pedagogy) is used to motivate students to use language actively in order to generate their own knowledge.
- Professionals involved in student testing (assessment) become advocates for minority students by focusing primarily on ways in which students' academic difficulties are a function of interactions with and within the school context, instead of locating the problem within the students (p. 5).

Do not assume that cultural characteristics are common to all members of a cultural group. Rather, these characteristics serve as a starting point in your education about the cultural diversity of the students you teach. They also provide rich opportunities for students to learn about their cultural backgrounds, the focus of the next section.

## Multicultural Education

**Multicultural education** is "an idea, an educational reform movement, and a process whose major goal is to change the structure of educational institutions so that male and female students, exceptional students, and students who are members of diverse racial, ethnic, and cultural groups will have an equal chance to achieve academically in school" (Banks, 1997a, p. 1). Multicultural education is closely linked to cultural diversity (Yee, 1991) and fosters pride in minority cultures, assists students in developing new insights into their cultures, reduces prejudice and stereotyping, and promotes intercultural understanding (Rubalcava, 1991). In the fullest sense, multicultural education is a total rethinking of the way we conduct schooling in a diverse society within a democratic, civic framework (Lessow-Hurley, 1996).

## Dimensions of Multicultural Education

Multicultural education is much more than a curriculum focused on learning about diverse cultures based on such parameters as gender, ethnicity, and race. It is a thread running through the total curriculum, not a subject to be taught (Tiedt & Tiedt, 1995). Banks (1997c) suggests that multicultural education has four dimensions: content integration, knowledge construction, an equity pedagogy, and an empowering school culture.

**Content Integration** Content integration focuses on using examples and content from a variety of cultures and groups to illustrate concepts, principles, generalizations, and theories. Ethnic and cultural content is infused into the subject areas in a natural, logical way (Banks, 1993a). For example, you can teach students about traditional dress and celebrations in many different cultures by discussing different holidays, the dress worn, and the reasons for the holidays and traditional dress. As a follow-up activity, students can interview their parents and other family members to learn about traditional dress and holidays celebrated by their families.

**Knowledge Construction** Knowledge construction refers to students learning about how implicit cultural assumptions, frames of reference, perspectives, and biases influence the ways that knowledge is constructed. For example, the discovery of America by Europeans has two very different frames of reference when presented from the perspectives of the Native Americans and the Europeans. Similarly, the power of the mind over the body is viewed differently by Asian and European cultures.

**Equity Pedagogy** With an **equity pedagogy**, the teacher attends to different teaching and learning styles and modifies teaching to facilitate the academic achievement of students from diverse cultures. Adjusting the learning process so that Native American students can learn in private or encouraging the use of cooperative learning can accommodate cultural differences and promote academic learning.

**Empowering School Culture** An empowering school culture promotes gender, racial, and social-class equity. Establishing such a culture entails examining the school culture for biases and prejudices, developing strategies to alleviate them, and replacing them with opportunities that promote positive self-esteem for all students. An initial step in creating an empowering school culture is to have the staff share, learn about, and respect their own diversity.

A school's staff can learn about their school community through many of the activities used to help students learn about each other, such as sharing information about heritage, birthplace, family, traditional foods, and hobbies. For example, Stan Williams, the principal at an urban elementary school, takes time each year at the initial full-staff meeting for the staff to interview each other about their families, cultural backgrounds, areas of educational expertise, traditional foods, and hobbies. Then each interviewer uses the information garnered to introduce the interviewee to at least two other staff members. In the past, Stan has also displayed staff photos and profiles in the staff lounge. Stan comments, "When we take time [for] . . . this activity . . . , the staff immediately begins to learn . . . about each other and find common interests that are fostered throughout the school year. It helps to create a sense of equality across all . . . staff jobs (e.g., teachers, paraprofessionals, office staff, building maintenance staff)."

> Multicultural education grew out of the civil rights movement of the 1960s, which called for curriculum reform to reflect the experiences, histories, cultures, and views of African Americans and other groups. Early responses included recognition of ethnic holidays and high-school courses such as "Black Studies."

To implement multicultural education and integrate these four dimensions successfully, multicultural education should be conceptualized as much more than a curriculum or a subject to teach. Several leaders in the field have suggested that viewing the school as a social system and studying and reforming the major variables is necessary to create a learning environment in which students have an equal chance for school success (e.g., Banks, 1997a; Grant & Sleeter, 1993; Ladson-Billings, 1995; Nieto, 1994; Ogbu, 1992). As a social system, Banks (1981, 1997) suggests that the following aspects of the school need to be considered:

- school policy and politics
- school staff: attitudes, perceptions, and actions
- school culture and hidden curriculum

- formalized curriculum and course of study
- assessment and testing procedures
- instructional materials
- learning styles for the school
- teaching styles and strategies
- language and dialects of the school
- counseling program
- community participation and input

As you study the schools in which you teach as social systems and teaching and learning communities, consider these variables and determine the degree to which they foster the overarching goals of multicultural education, that is, to create a learning community in which students not only have equal opportunities for academic success, but also an understanding of and respect for diversity.

## Desired Student Outcomes

Given these dimensions of multicultural education and its overall goals, what are some desired student outcomes that lead to these goals? Tiedt and Tiedt (1995) suggest that students should be able to do the following:

- identify a strong sense of self-esteem, and express the need and right of others to similar feelings of self-esteem
- describe their own cultures, recognizing the influences that have shaped their thinking and behavior
- identify racial, ethnic, and religious groups represented in our pluralistic society
- identify needs and concerns universal to people of all cultures, and compare cultural variations
- recognize, understand, and critique examples of stereotypic thinking and social inequities in real life and literature, and develop solutions for altering their status
- discuss special gender-, ethnic-, age-, and disability-related concerns
- inquire multiculturally as they engage in broad thematic studies related to any field of study

Clearly, these outcomes call for learning curricula that highlight cultural diversity. The next section discusses curricula for multicultural education.

## Multicultural Curricula

Banks (1997b) suggests that since multicultural education was introduced in the 1960s, curricular approaches to multicultural education have evolved, based on the degree to which diversity plays a central role in the curriculum. Banks (1997b) identifies four approaches—contributions, additive, transformation, and social action (see Table 10.1).

How can school culture empower all students to succeed? What student outcomes lead to the goal of creating a learning community in which students understand and respect diversity and have equal opportunity for academic success?

**Contributions Approach** The **contributions approach** is characterized by the insertion of ethnic heroes and discrete cultural artifacts into the curriculum—adding culturally diverse inventors and their inventions to a thematic unit on inventions, for example.

This approach is the easiest to use but has several serious limitations. First, because the heroes are usually presented in isolation, students do not gain an overall understanding of the role of ethnic and cultural groups in the United States. Second, this approach does not address issues such as oppression and discrimination. Instead, it reinforces the Horatio Alger myth in that ethnic heroes are presented with little attention paid to how they became heroes despite the barriers they encountered.

**Additive Approach** The **additive approach** is characterized by the addition of content, concepts, themes, and perspectives without changing the basic structure of the curriculum. Typical examples are adding books about different groups to the literature sets (e.g., Mildred Taylor's *Roll of Thunder, Hear My Cry*), adding a unit on Native Americans to an American history course, or adding a course on ethnic or gender studies to a high school curriculum. This approach offers better integration of multicultural perspectives than the contributions approach, but does not result in a restructured curriculum. For

### TABLE 10.1

**Approaches for the Integration of Multicultural Content**

| Approach | Description | Examples | Strengths | Problems |
|---|---|---|---|---|
| *Contributions* | Heroes, cultural components, holidays, and other discrete elements related to ethnic groups are added to the curriculum on special days, occasions, and celebrations. | Famous Mexican Americans are studied only during the week of Cinco de Mayo (May 5). African Americans are studied during African American History Month in February but rarely during the rest of the year. Ethnic foods are studied in the first grade with little attention devoted to the cultures in which the foods are embedded. | Provides a quick and relatively easy way to put ethnic content into the curriculum. Gives ethnic heroes visibility in the curriculum alongside mainstream heroes. Is a popular approach among teachers and educators. | Results in a superficial understanding of ethnic cultures. Focuses on the lifestyles and artifacts of ethnic groups and reinforces stereotypes and misconceptions. Mainstream criteria are used to select heroes and cultural elements for inclusion in the curriculum. |
| *Additive* | This approach consists of the addition of content, concepts, themes, and perspectives to the curriculum without changing its structure. | Adding the book *The Color Purple* to a literature unit without reconceptualizing the unit or giving the students the background knowledge to understand the book. Adding a unit on the Japanese American internment to a U.S. history course without treating the Japanese in any other unit. Leaving the core curriculum intact but adding an ethnic studies course, as an elective, that focuses on a specific ethnic group. | Makes it possible to add ethnic content to the curriculum without changing its structure, which requires substantial curriculum changes and staff development. Can be implemented within the existing curriculum structure. | Reinforces the idea that ethnic history and culture are not integral parts of U.S. mainstream culture. Students view ethnic groups from Anglocentric and Eurocentric perspectives. Fails to help students understand how the dominant culture and ethnic cultures are interconnected and interrelated. |

### TABLE 10.1
*Approaches for the Integration of Multicultural Content (continued)*

| Approach | Description | Examples | Strengths | Problems |
|---|---|---|---|---|
| *Transformation* | The basic goals, structure, and nature of the curriculum are changed to enable students to view concepts, events, issues, problems, and themes from the perspectives of diverse cultural, ethnic, and racial groups. | A unit on the American Revolution describes the meaning of the revolution to Anglo revolutionaries, Anglo loyalists, African Americans, Indians, and the British. A unit on 20th-century U.S. literature includes works by William Faulkner, Joyce Carol Oates, Langston Hughes, N. Scott Momoday, Saul Bellow, Maxine Hong Kingston, Rudolfo A. Anaya, and Piri Thomas. | Enables students to understand the complex ways in which diverse racial and cultural groups participated in the formation of U.S. society and culture. Helps reduce racial and ethnic encapsulation. Enables diverse ethnic, racial, and religious groups to see their cultures, ethos, and perspectives in the school curriculum. Gives students a balanced view of the nature and development of U.S. culture and society. Helps to empower victimized racial, ethnic, and cultural groups. | The implementation of this approach requires substantial curriculum revision, in-service training, and the identification and development of materials written from the perspectives of various racial and cultural groups. Staff development for the institutionalization of this approach must be continual and ongoing. |
| *Social Action* | In this approach, students identify important social problems and issues, gather pertinent data, clarify their values on the issues, make decisions, and take reflective actions to help resolve the issue or problem. | A class studies prejudice and discrimination in their school and decides to take actions to improve race relations in the school. A class studies the treatment of ethnic groups in a local newspaper and writes a letter to the newspaper publisher suggesting ways that the treatment of ethnic groups in the newspapers should be improved. | Enables students to improve their thinking, value analysis, decision-making, and social-action skills. Enables students to improve their data-gathering skills. Helps students develop a sense of political efficacy. Helps students improve their skills to work in groups. | Requires a considerable amount of curriculum planning and materials identification. May be longer in duration than more traditional teaching units. May focus on problems and issues considered controversial by some members of the school staff and citizens of the community. Students may be able to take few meaningful actions that contribute to the resolution of the social issue or problem. |

Reprinted with permission from Banks, J. A. (1997b). Approaches to multicultural curriculum reform. In J. A. Banks (Ed.), *Multicultural education: Issues and perspectives* (3rd ed., pp. 244–245). Boston: Allyn & Bacon.

example, including a unit on the Plains Indians in a U.S. history class will increase students' understanding of Native Americans, but not as clearly as transforming the curriculum so that the movement to the West is viewed as both an expansion (from a European perspective) and an invasion (from a Native American perspective).

**Transformation Approach** In the **transformation approach**, the basic core of the curriculum is changed and the focus is on viewing events, concepts, and themes from multiple perspectives, based on diversity. Banks (1997b) suggests that, "When studying U.S. history, language, music, arts, science, and mathematics, the emphasis should not be on the ways that various ethnic and cultural groups have contributed to mainstream U.S. society and culture. The emphasis rather, should be on how the common U.S. culture and society emerged from a complex synthesis and interaction of the diverse cultural elements that originated within the various cultural, racial, ethnic, and religious groups that make up the U.S. society" (page 204). In developing multicultural units, it is important to identify the key concept and generalizations associated with that concept. Specific activities can then be planned so that students have the evidence to draw the generalizations and understand the key concept. Table 10.2 provides an example of a unit for high-school students on the key concept of social protest.

**Social Action Approach** The **social action approach** incorporates all the elements of the transformation approach and also includes a cultural critique. Teaching units that use this approach incorporate a problem-solving process in which students make decisions and take actions related to the concept, issue, or problem being studied, following these steps:

1. Identify the problem or question (e.g., discrimination in our school).
2. Collect data related to the problem or question (e.g., what is discrimination; what causes discrimination; what examples are evident in our school).
3. Conduct a value inquiry and analysis (i.e., students examine and reflect on their values, attitudes, and beliefs related to discrimination).
4. Make decisions and establish a plan of social action based on a synthesis of the knowledge obtained in step 2 and the values identified in step 3.

Robinson (1993) describes how a class of African-American middle-school students in Dallas used the social action approach. The important problem they identified was that their school was surrounded by liquor stores. Investigating further, they found that the city's zoning regulations made some areas dry but that their school was in a wet area. Further investigation revealed that schools serving White upper-middle-class students were located in dry areas, whereas schools in poor communities were in wet areas. The students, assisted by their teacher, planned a strategy for exposing this inequity. By using mathematics, literacy, and social and political skills, the students proved their points with reports, editorials, charts, maps, and graphs. In this case the curriculum and the students' learning became a form of cultural critique and social action.

> Concern with gender equity in textbook publishing is an example of transformation and social action approaches in education. In 1972, Scott Foresman was the first to publish curriculum guidelines for recognizing women's achievement, treating girls and boys equally, and avoiding sex-role stereotypes and sexist language.

As a teacher, you will undoubtedly use all four approaches to multicultural education, with the goal of primarily employing the transformational and social action approaches. Tips for Teachers 10.2 presents general strategies for integrating content about cultural groups into the school curriculum, and Tech Talk describes how to create a community video using videography. The curriculum should incorporate opportunities to foster student achievement and cultural competence as well as help students recognize, understand, and critique current social inequities (Ladson-Billings, 1995).

# Linguistic Diversity and Second Language Acquisition

Linguistic diversity is not new in the United States, with its rich history of immigration. Today, as in the past, many students live in homes in which the language spoken is not English. This trend is increasing rather than decreasing. In 1992 a total of 32 million, or one in seven Americans above the age of 5, spoke a language other than English at home—a 34 percent

## TABLE 10.2

### Key Ideas and Activities for a Unit on Social Protest

#### Key Ideas

*Key Concept:* Social Protest

*Key Generalization:* When individuals and groups are victims of oppression and discrimination, they tend to protest against their situation in various ways.

*Intermediate-Level Generalization:* Throughout their experiences in the United States, ethnic minorities have resisted discrimination and oppression in various ways.

*Low-Level Generalization:* Mexican Americans have resisted Anglo discrimination and oppression since Anglo-Americans conquered and occupied the Southwest.

#### Activities

1. To give the students a general overview of Mexican-American history, show them a videotape, such as *Mexican People and Culture,* a videotape in *The Hispanic Culture Series* distributed by Zenqer Video. After showing the videotape, ask the students to discuss the questions:

    a. What major problems have Mexican Americans experienced in the United States?

    b. What actions have been taken by Mexican-American individuals and groups to eliminate the discrimination they have experienced?

2. Ask a group of students to prepare reports that reveal the ways in which the following men led organized resistance to Anglo Americans in the 1800s:

    Juan N. Cortina
    Juan Jose Herrera
    Juan Patron

    The class should discuss these men when the reports are presented. A good reference for this activity is Rodolfo Acuña, *Occupied America: A History of Chicanos,* 3rd ed.

3. Ask a group of students to prepare a report to be presented in class that describes Chicano involvement in strikes and unions between 1900 and 1940. When this report is presented, the students should discuss ways in which strikes and union activities were forms of organized resistance.

4. Ask the students to research the goals, tactics, and strategies used by the following Mexican-American civil rights groups: Order of the Sons of America, League of United Latin-American Citizens, The Community Service Organization, The American G.I. Forum, Federal Alliance of Free Cities, and Crusade for Justice. Ask the students to write several generalizations about the activities of these groups.

5. Ask the students to research the following questions:

    a. How is the "Chicano" movement similar to other Mexican-American protest movements?

    b. How are its goals and strategies different?

    c. When did the movement emerge?

    d. What long-range effects do you think the movement will have? Why?

6. Ask the students to read and dramatize the epic poem of the Chicano movement, *I Am Joaquin,* by Rodolfo Gonzales.

7. Ask the students questions that will enable them to summarize and generalize about how Mexican Americans have resisted Anglo discrimination and oppression in both the past and in contemporary American society.

8. Conclude the unit by viewing and discussing the film *I Am Joaquin,* distributed by El Teatro Campesino, San Juan Bautista, CA.

---

Reprinted with permission from Banks, J. A. (1997a). *Teaching strategies for ethnic studies* (6th ed., pp. 518–519,). Boston: Allyn & Bacon.

# TIPS FOR TEACHERS

## 10.2 Guidelines for Teaching Multicultural Content

- Take time to learn about your culture(s) and how it influences your beliefs and actions. Be sensitive to your attitudes and behaviors.
- To teach cultural content you need knowledge of cultural groups. Read books that survey the histories of cultural groups in the United States. (See Read More about It for suggested books.)
- Make sure that your room conveys positive images of various cultural groups (through bulletin boards, posters, literature, software, and so on).
- Plan time in which you and your students can learn about each other's cultural backgrounds. (See Read More about It for reference books.)
- Be culturally conscious in selecting teaching materials. If the materials you use include stereotypes or present only one perspective, point out the limitation to the students.
- Use trade books, films, videotapes, and recordings to supplement the textbook and to present more varied perspectives.
- Use literature to enrich students' understanding of cultural pluralism.
- Be sensitive to the development levels of your students when you select concepts, content, and activities. Use concrete, specific concepts and activities for students in early elementary grades. As students develop, focus on more abstract concepts and problem solving.
- Use cooperative learning and group work to promote integration.
- Make sure that not only classroom but also school-wide activities (such as plays, sports, and clubs) are culturally integrated.

---

increase between 1980 and 1990. The number of Chinese speakers doubled during this period, and approximately 17 million Americans spoke Spanish in their homes in 1993 (Tiedt & Tiedt, 1995).

José is a good example of such a student. At the age of 4, he immigrated with his parents and three siblings from a rural community in Mexico to an urban Spanish-speaking community in Texas. His parents spoke only Spanish when they arrived. Although José has some exposure to English and his father is taking a night course to learn English, he entered school at age 5 with Spanish as his first language and only a limited knowledge of his second language, English. This same scenario is true of children who immigrate from Central and South American countries, Asian and Pacific Island countries, and Eastern European countries. The U.S. Department of Education estimates that of the 40 million students in public and private schools, over 2 million are English language learners (Díaz-Rico & Weed, 1995; Orando & Collier, 1998).

The implications of this demography are that a growing number of students who enter school in the United States learn English as a second language in school. As a teacher, your knowledge of second language acquisition and general instructional guidelines can help make school a success for students like José.

## Framework for Second Language Acquisition

Ellis (1985; 1994) provides a framework for second language acquisition that can guide you in making accommodations for students whose first language is not English. Ellis suggests that five interrelated factors govern the acquisition of a second language. Figure 10.1 (page 294) depicts the relationship among these factors.

**Situational Factors** Situational factors are related to the context or the situation (i.e., the learning environments) in which the second language learning occurs. Students learn the second language in multiple learning environments—from relatives, friends, and neighbors who speak English, through ESL or bilingual education programs at school, and from peers in the classroom and on the playground.

# TECH TALK

### Using Multimedia and Videography to Create Community Connections

Creating multimedia and videography presentations can integrate multicultural education and the resources of students' home communities into the curriculum. Such activities provide students with opportunities to learn new technology skills and celebrate their home communities and cultures.

Even as simple a process as having students video typical scenes in their neighborhood and interview respected members of the community presents opportunities for planning, developing story boards, writing, and scheduling and conducting interviews. If editing equipment is available, students can learn simple editing skills by piecing together the segments of videotape as they construct the community video.

Multimedia production, or hypermedia, as it is sometimes called, allows students to use a variety of resources from their community to create a presentation that shares what they have learned in an interactive way. Sources can include not only video, but audio for music and interviews, photographs and drawings that can be scanned in, and text such as newspaper headlines and maps. All these information sources can be included in a multimedia format. Software programs such as Hypercard, HyperStudio, or Linkway enable young people to create hypermedia programs with buttons and links that allow the user to experience the material in his or her own unique way.

Constructing a community media product provides many opportunities to learn about the community's "funds of knowledge" and the people the community considers to be experts. These funds of knowledge can extend across many contexts including home life, traditions and celebrations, work, art, and politics. For example, an upper elementary class might decide to focus on home life, traditions, and celebrations. A high-school American government class might select a political subject such as "illegal immigrants" and make connections to the many elements of this issue such as home countries, labor opportunities, or health, education and welfare issues.

Media activities can provide ideal opportunities for students to learn basic videography and computer skills,

---

Environments such as these can provide both formal teaching and more natural opportunities to acquire language. When José's uncle explains the concept "scientist" in Spanish and then pairs it with English, he is providing formal instruction. On the other hand, the instruction is much more natural when José and his uncle converse about what happened in school and his uncle provides José with words in English when José is searching for the English word. One goal of both bilingual education and English as a Second Language (ESL) instruction, is to create environments that are nonthreatening and in which students are willing to take risks and play with the language (Orando & Collier, 1998; Vaughn & Gersten, 1998). Maria, the ESL teacher interviewed

> Students whose first language is not English and who are not fluent in English are sometimes referred to as English language learners (ELL).

such as using a camera, and external microphones for interviews. By using a story board to draw and describe the different parts of the media presentation, students can plan and visualize the end product before they begin to construct it. Community media production also provides natural opportunities for meaningful language arts, art, and social studies activities. For example, students learn about their communities and cultural traditions, as well as who the good sources of this information are in the community. Students write the interviews and practice their interviewing skills with each other. In many communities the arts including dance, visual arts, theater and drama, and traditional dress play an important role. As students construct their presentation, they can learn to integrate scenes from the arts with their interviews for greater interest and to provide pictures of what is being described.

The completed media presentation can be shared in many ways. Copies can be placed in school and local libraries and in the classroom, and a special showing for parents and the community can be held at the school. It is also possible to utilize the World Wide Web for more resources and for further dissemination of their work. Students can create their own web site with internal or external links to related information using any one of several software packages that allow WYSIWYG graphic hypermedia production such as Claris Homepage, Front Page, PageMill, or just by learning to write html code. Access to an Internet Service Provider (ISP) is required to work online.

Resources to help you plan a community media presentation include the following:

1. Gross. L. S., & Ward, L. W. (1991). *Electronic movie-making.* Belmont, CA: Wadsworth. Describes how to make a movie, including preproduction activities (such as developing scripts and story boards), production activities, and postproduction activities (such as editing).
2. Jonassen, D., Peck, K., and Wilson, B. (1999) *Learning with technology: A constructivist perspective.* Upper Saddle River, NJ: Merrill. Provides a constructionist perspective for technology-mediated learning environments as well as practical information about affordable and accessible "mind tools."
3. Male, M. (1997). *Technology for inclusion: Meeting the special needs of all students.* Boston: Allyn & Bacon. This book includes a vision for teachers, advice on increasing student/teacher productivity, and information about access to tools and materials available.
4. Valmont, W. J. (1995). *Creating videos for school use.* Boston: Allyn & Bacon. Written for teachers; explains use of videos in schools; provides many examples of how to use video in class and how to teach basic videography skills.
5. Wigginton, E. (Ed.) *The Foxfire series.* New York: Doubleday. An English teacher in an Appalachian community helped students publish their oral histories, starting with The Foxfire Book in 1972. Information about the Foxfire Teacher Networks is available from Foxfire Teacher Outreach, P.O. Box 541, Mountain City, GA 30562.
6. Zimmerman, W. (1988). *Instant oral biographies: How to tape record, video or film your life stories.* New York: Guarionex Press. Written for students in upper elementary and middle schools; describes how to make oral histories and includes sample forms.

---

at the beginning of this chapter, encourages students to play with the language by experimenting with sounds, words, and syntactic construction. She makes these opportunities for discovery by encouraging experimentation.

Another situational factor that promotes second language acquisition is an environment in which the students' first language and culture are respected and valued. The research consistently demonstrates that valuing students' first language is an important factor for student success (Carter & Chatfield, 1986; Lucas et al., 1990; Thomas & Collier, 1997). One important aspect of valuing the students' language is to learn about their community's funds of knowledge and language (refer to Tips for Teachers 10.1).

**Linguistic Input** Linguistic input refers to input received when reading or listening to a second language. Comprehensible input is a key factor for success (Krashen, 1985). Input is made more

## FIGURE 10.1

**Framework for Second Language Acquisition**

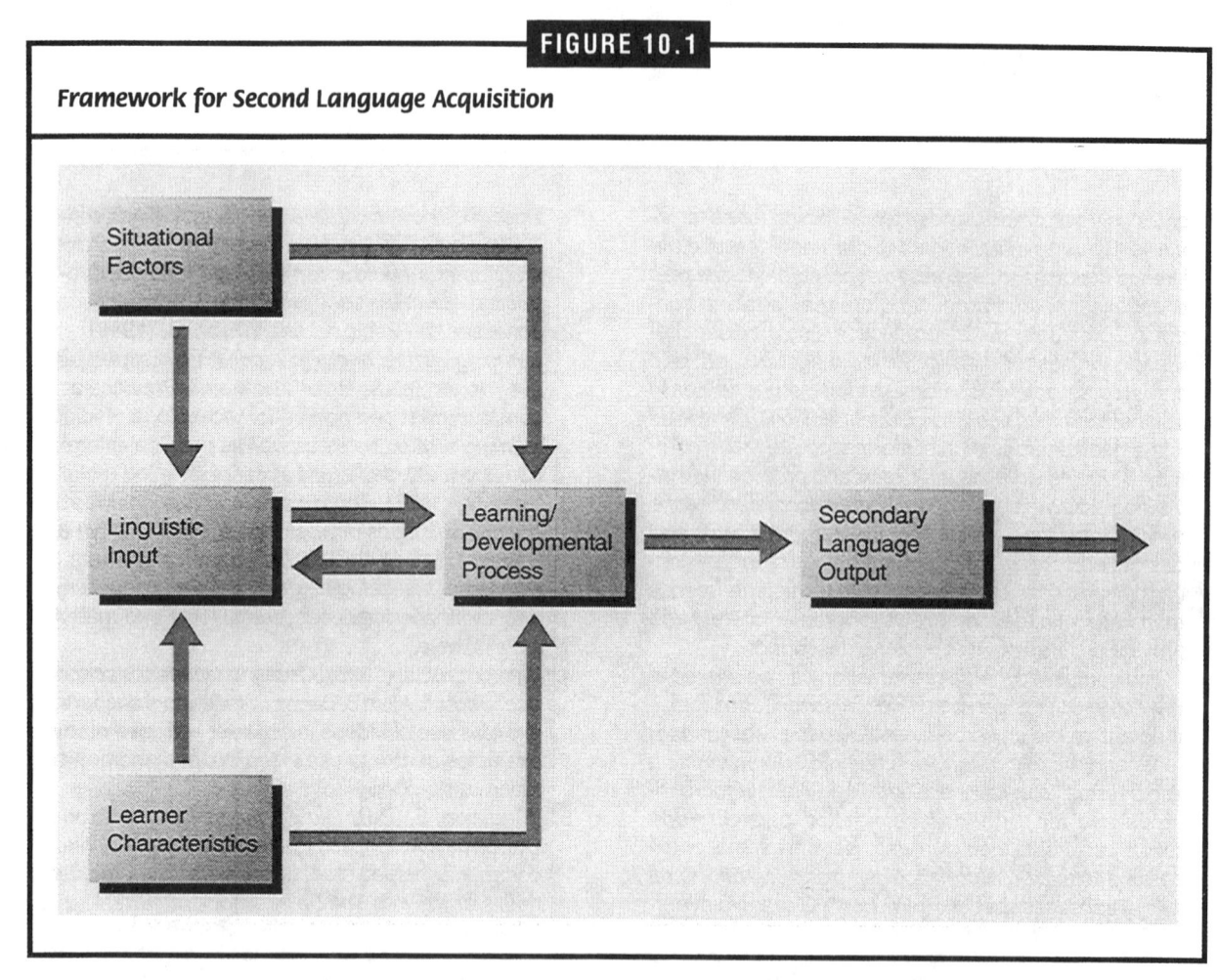

[Diagram: Situational Factors → Linguistic Input ↔ Learning/Developmental Process → Secondary Language Output; Learner Characteristics feeds into Linguistic Input and Learning/Developmental Process; Situational Factors also feeds into Learning/Developmental Process]

Adapted from Ellis, R. (1985). *Understanding second language acquisition*. Oxford: Oxford University Press.

comprehensible by a number of strategies, including the following:

- selecting a topic of conversation familiar to students
- creating a context for what is being discussed
- using simpler sentence construction
- repeating important phrases
- incorporating the students' first language into the instruction
- emphasizing key words to promote comprehensible input

When teaching linguistically diverse students, it is important to consider the linguistic input. Tips for Teachers 10.3 presents guidelines and ideas for making input more comprehensible.

**Learner Characteristics** The third factor affecting second-language acquisition or output is **learner characteristics**. Relevant learner characteristics include the age at which students learn a second language, their aptitude for learning language, their purposes and degree of motivation for learning the second language, their self-confidence in language learning, and their learning strategies.

> Assessment used in screening for proficiency in English includes the Bilingual Syntax Measure (Burt et al., 1980), the IDEA Oral Language Proficiency Test (Ballard & Tighe, 1987), and the Language Assessment Scales (De Avila & Duncan, 1986).

# TIPS FOR TEACHERS

### 10.3 Guidelines for Making Input More Comprehensible for Second Language Learners

- Begin teaching new concepts by working from the students' current knowledge and incorporating the funds of knowledge from the students' community.
- Use demonstrations and gestures to augment oral communication.
- To the degree possible, create the context in which the concepts occur. For example, when teaching about shellfish, visit an aquarium, watch a film, display shells in the classroom.
- Discuss connections between the concepts being taught and the students' home cultures.
- Encourage students to share the new vocabulary in their first language and incorporate the first language into instruction.
- If students share a common first language, pair more proficient second language learners with less proficient peers, and encourage students to discuss what they are learning.
- Highlight key words and phrases by repeating them and writing them.
- Use simple sentence constructions, particularly to present a new or difficult concept.

---

Another important variable is the degree of acquisition or proficiency in the first language. Cummins (1991), in a review of research, concluded that the better developed the students' proficiency and conceptual foundation in the first language, the more likely they were to develop similarly high levels of proficiency and conceptual ability in the second language. He has referred to this as the **common underlying proficiency**, using the analogy of an iceberg to explain this hypothesis and relationship between first and second language acquisition (see Figure 10.2) and why proficiency in the first language complements proficiency in the second language (Cummins, 1981).

As shown in Figure 10.2, both languages have separate surface features, represented by separate icebergs. Below the surface and less visible, however, is the underlying proficiency common to both languages.

No matter which language the person is using, the thoughts that accompany the talking, reading, writing, and listening come from the same language core. One implication of this analogy is that individuals who are **balanced bilinguals** have an advantage over monolingual individuals in that they have greater cognitive flexibility and a greater understanding of language (see the Research Brief that follows).

## Research Brief

### Relationship of Bilingualism to Cognitive Development and Learning

From the early nineteenth century to approximately the 1960s, dominant belief was that bilingualism was detrimental to cognitive development and academic learning. Diaz (1983) summarized the research performed prior to 1962, which built the case for bilingualism as a "language handicap." Researchers found that bilingual children had more limited vocabularies, deficient articulation, and more grammatical errors than monolingual students. One interpretation was that bilingualism caused "linguistic confusion," which affected students' cognitive ability and academic performance. This research overall had many flaws. Bilingual and monolingual groups were not matched for other important variables such as socioeconomic status, for example, and tests for intellectual functioning and learning of bilingual students generally were conducted in English, not in the first or more dominant language.

In 1962, Peal and Lambert published the study now considered the major turning point in the history of the relationship between bilingualism and cognition. This research broke new territory in two respects: it overcame many methodological deficiencies and, in addition, found that bilingualism leads to cognitive advantages over monolingualism. Peal and Lambert concluded that bilingualism provides greater cognitive flexibility, greater ability to think more abstractly, and greater ability in concept formation.

Subsequent research has shown that higher degrees of bilingualism are correlated with increased cognitive abilities in such areas as creativity, knowledge of how language works (*metalinguistics*), concept formation, and cognitive flexibility (Galambos & Goldin-Meadow, 1990; Nieto, 1992; Orando & Collier, 1998; Skutnabb-Kangas, 1981).

**The Learning and Developmental Process** The fourth factor addresses the **learning and developmental process** of second language acquisition and learning. Cummins (1984) suggested that students generally acquire competency in the **basic interpersonal communication skills (BICS)** before becoming competent with **cognitive academic language proficiency (CALP)**. The BICS, or social language, are the conversational competencies we develop with a second language—the greetings and "small talk" between peers, which generally do not require much cognitive effort or social problem solving. The CALP, or academic language, on the other hand, refers to the more cognitively demanding language skills required for the new learning that occurs in school. In general, BICS develop in a second language prior to CALP. Cummins (1981) suggested that it takes from 1 to 2 years to develop BICS, but from 5 to 7 years to develop competence in CALP.

Although these guidelines have been shown to vary widely, depending on situational factors, linguistic input, and learner characteristics, they do have implications for teachers in general education classrooms. You might assume that because students can converse easily with you in their second language, they are ready to learn new concepts, strategies, and skills in the second language. This is not

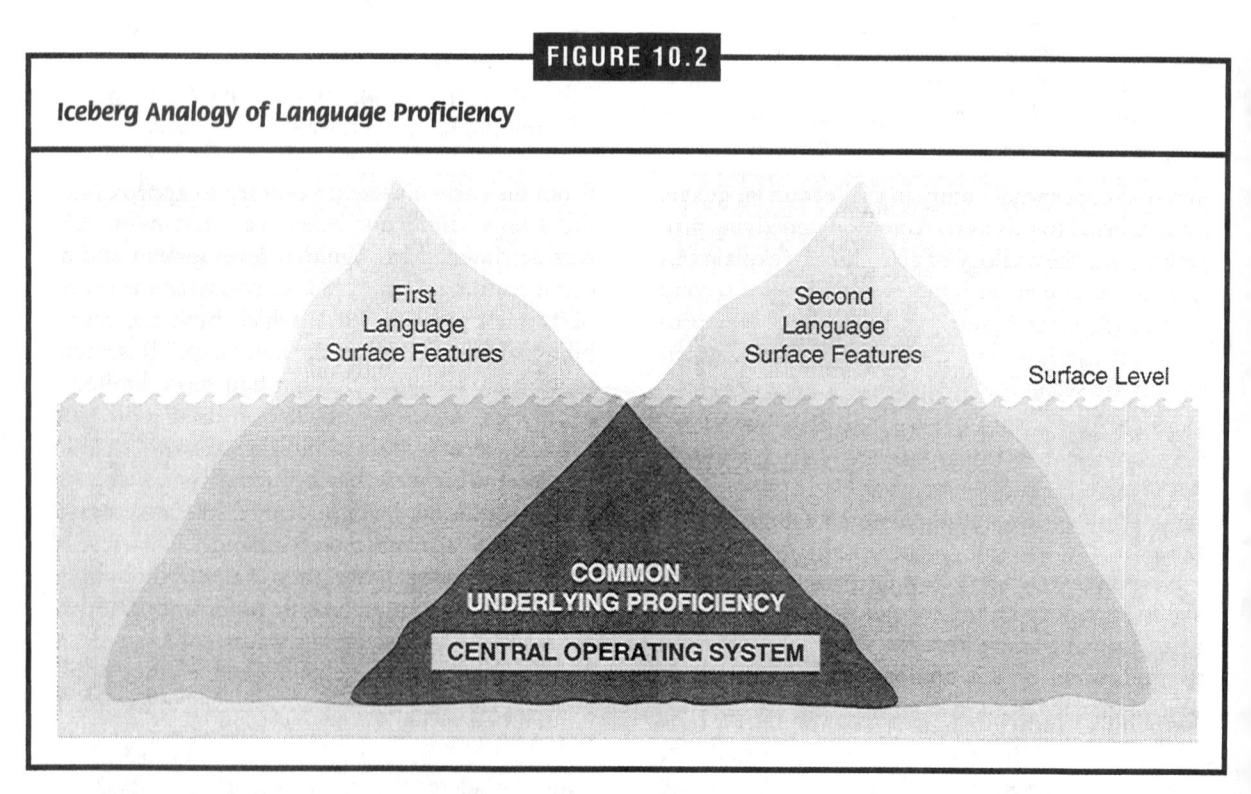

**FIGURE 10.2**

**Iceberg Analogy of Language Proficiency**

First Language Surface Features

Second Language Surface Features

Surface Level

**COMMON UNDERLYING PROFICIENCY**

**CENTRAL OPERATING SYSTEM**

Adapted from Cummins, J. (1981). *Bilingualism and minority language children.* Ontario: Ontario Institute for Studies in Education.

necessarily the case. For example, when Hoang Hy Vinh entered Sarah Miles's third-grade class, Sarah immediately noticed that he conversed easily with other students and with her. Vinh immigrated from Vietnam 2 years ago and began learning English through the school's ESL program. His parents, who take English in a night course, feel that learning English is important for their economic and personal success in America. Still, Vietnamese is the primary language spoken in the home.

As Sarah got to know Vinh, she realized that although his conversational skills were strong enough for him to be comfortable in the classroom community, he was not yet proficient in academic tasks such as reading and writing in English. She also found that to teach new concepts in social studies and science, she needed to provide lots of context. Sarah incorporated an extended segment on farming communities into a thematic unit on California, for example, because Vinh and several other students came from other Asian and Mexican farming communities. From the school and public libraries, she checked out books and magazines about farming and rural life in Vietnam, Mexico, and other Asian countries. The students also visited a California market, as well as Asian and Mexican food markets. They compared the foods from the two markets, and learned how those foods were grown in the three communities. For Vinh and other students from other cultures who were in the process of acquiring English as a second language, providing the link to their cultures helped give them a context in which to build both their language and cognitive skills. This is an example of the **context-embedded communication and instruction** that Cummins (1981) and others (Chamot & O'Malley, 1994; Gersten & Jiménez, 1998; Reyes & Bos, 1998; Ruiz, Garcia, & Figueroa, 1996) recommend as facilitating second language learning. A good teacher incorporates both social (BICS) and academic (CALP) language into every lesson (Orando & Collier, 1998).

**Secondary Language Output** The fifth factor in the framework (Figure 10.1) is **secondary language output**. Students may understand a language (listening and reading), but not be proficient in producing the language (speaking and writing). An important part of developing speaking proficiency is the opportunity to engage in meaningful oral exchanges (in the classroom and the community) and to experiment with oral and written language in nonthreatening environments. Swain (1986) emphasized that not only **comprehensible input,** but also opportunities for students to develop **comprehensible output** by oral practice with the language are important for acquisition of a second language. Feedback from listeners and from self-monitoring enables second-language speakers to develop and fine-tune their oral language.

Also important in a consideration of secondary language output is that receptive language skills typically develop before expressive language skills. It

According to Ellis's framework for second language acquisition, what five factors will influence this student's acquisition of English? What kinds of instructional activities for second language acquisition might you recommend for this student, based on effectiveness research?

> Giving students the opportunity to discuss a new concept in their first language helps to promote content learning for second language learners.

has been well documented that second language learners experience a **silent or nonverbal period** (Ervin-Tripp, 1974; Hakuta, 1974), during which they are absorbing information and language that they cannot demonstrate or do not yet feel comfortable demonstrating (Coelho, 1994). For example, Hakuta (1974) observed a 5-year-old Japanese girl, noting that it took from her arrival in October until the following April for her to begin speaking English. During that intervening period, she attended kindergarten and played with neighborhood English-speaking friends, but did not speak English.

## Language Variation and Dialect

**Language variation**, which refers to the fact that language varies from place to place and from group to group (Wolfram, Adger, & Christian, in press), usually relates to the characteristics of groups of people (such as geographical region, social class, ethnic and cultural backgrounds, age, and gender). **Dialect** generally refers to language variations associated with a regional or social group of people (Wolfram et al., in prep.). All English speakers use a dialect or variation of the English language. Think for a moment. Do you use the term *pop, soda, soda pop, tonic* (or some other term) to label this popular type of drink? The answer depends on your dialect, which most likely relates to where you live and your cultural background. Dialect is also affected by age—use of the term *icebox,* rather than *refrigerator,* is more evident in older people who grew up in times when iceboxes were used.

Language variation or dialects vary in several ways. Regional dialects tend to be distinguished by pronunciation and vocabulary features, whereas social and cultural dialects show variation not only in these areas, but also in grammatical usage (Wolfram et al., in prep.). Dialects also reflect conversation patterns. In a good, satisfying conversation in some speech communities, for example, speakers overlap one another's talk. In other communities, the listener waits for a break to enter a conversation, and the speaker is likely to stop talking when someone else starts speaking.

**African American Vernacular English (AAVE)** is a dialect used by some African Americans. It is the most prevalent native English vernacular dialect in the United States. (The word *vernacular* is included in the term to avoid the stereotype that all African Americans speak AAVE.) Estimates based on socioeconomic demographics show about three-fourths of African Americans speak AAVE. As with any other language or dialect, there is great language variation among speakers of AAVE.

Because of African Americans' historical status as an oppressed and involuntary minority, there has been a tendency to consider AAVE not as a valid language system, but rather as random errors (Labov et al., 1968). Like any other language, however, AAVE has an internally consistent linguistic infrastructure and set of grammar rules. Table 10.3 on pages 299 and 300 presents some common grammatical contrasts between African American Vernacular English and Standard American English. In teaching about diversity, it is important that students study dialects and learn that AAVE is a linguistic system. When teaching Standard American English to students who speak AAVE, it is important to help them understand the systematic differences between the standard and vernacular forms. You can do so by using many of the strategies recommended for second language acquisition.

## Historical Perspective on ESL Instruction and Bilingual Education

Bilingual education and English as a second language instruction (ESL) or English to speakers of other languages (ESOL) for culturally and linguistically diverse students have evolved through the years. Figure 10.3 shows the chronology of this evolution in the United States.

What is interesting about this chronology is the way bilingualism has been tied to assimilation into American culture, and therefore linked to political policy. Bilingualism in our schools and communities dates back to the early colonies. It was common among both the working and educated classes that many official documents were published in German and French as well as English. By the late 1800s, however, language restrictions were being placed on schools. Under strong political pressures to assimilate immigrants, bilingual education was virtually eradicated by the 1930s. After World War II, students from minority cultures were described as "culturally deprived" and "linguistically disabled."

In the early 1960s, however, bilingual education was reborn in Dade County, Florida, as Cuban immigrants requested bilingual schooling for their children. Programs were developed throughout the United States, under the authority of the Bilingual Education Act passed (as Title VII of the Elementary and

## TABLE 10.3

**Grammatical Contrasts between African American Vernacular English and Standard American English**

| AAVE Grammatical Structure | SAE Grammatical Structure |
|---|---|
| **Possessive -'s** <br> Nonobligatory word where word position expresses possession. <br>   Get *mother* coat. <br>   It be mother's. | Obligatory regardless of position. <br><br>   Get *mother's* coat. <br>   It's mother's. |
| **Plural -s** <br> Nonobligatory with numerical quantifier. <br>   He got ten *dollar*. <br>   Look at the cats. | Obligatory regardless of numerical quantifier. <br>   He has ten *dollars*. <br>   Look at the cats. |
| **Regular past -ed** <br> Nonobligatory; reduced as consonant cluster. <br>   Yesterday, I *walk* to school. | Obligatory. <br>   Yesterday, I *walked* to school. |
| **Irregular past** <br> Case by case, some verbs inflected, others not. <br>   I *see* him last week. | All irregular verbs inflected. <br>   I *saw* him last week. |
| **Regular present tense third person singular -s** <br> Nonobligatory. <br>   She *eat* too much. | Obligatory. <br>   She *eats* too much. |
| **Irregular present tense third person singular -s** <br> Nonobligatory. <br>   He *do* my job. | Obligatory. <br>   He *does* my job. |
| **Indefinite an** <br> Use of indefinite *a*. <br>   He ride in *a* airplane. | Use of indefinite *an*. <br>   He rode in *an* airplane. |
| **Pronouns** <br> Pronominal apposition: pronoun immediately follows noun. <br>   Momma *she* mad. She ... | Pronoun used elsewhere in sentence or in other sentence; not in apposition. <br>   Momma is mad. She ... |
| **Future tense** <br> More frequent use of *be going to* (gonna). <br>   I *be going to* dance tonight. <br>   I *gonna* dance tonight. <br> Omit *will* preceding *be*. <br>   I *be* home later. | More frequent use of *will*. <br>   I *will* dance tonight. <br>   I *am going to* dance tonight. <br> Obligatory use of *will*. <br>   I *will* (I'll) *be* home later. |
| **Negation** <br> Triple negative. <br>   *Nobody don't never* like me. | Absence of triple negative. <br>   *No* one ever likes me. |

*Continued*

### TABLE 10.3

*Grammatical Contrasts between African American Vernacular English and Standard American English (continued)*

| AAVE Grammatical Structure | SAE Grammatical Structure |
|---|---|
| **Modals** <br> Double modals for such forms as *might, could,* and *should*. <br>    I *might could* go. | Single modal use. <br>    I *might be able to* go. |
| **Questions** <br> Same form for direct and indirect. <br>    What *it is*? <br>    Do you know what *it is*? | Different forms for direct and indirect. <br>    What *is it*? <br>    Do you know what *it is*? |
| **Relative pronouns** <br> Nonobligatory in most cases. <br>    He the one stole it. <br>    It the one you like. | Nonobligatory with *that* only. <br>    He's the one *who* stole it. <br>    It's the one (that) you like. |
| **Conditional *if*** <br> Use of *do* for conditional *if*. <br>    I ask *did* she go. | Use of *if*. <br>    I asked *if* she went. |
| **Perfect construction** <br> *Been* used for action in the distant past. <br>    He *been* gone. | *Been* not used. <br>    He left a long time ago. |
| **Copula** <br> Nonobligatory when contractible. <br>    He sick. | Obligatory in contractible and noncontractible forms. <br>    He's sick. |
| **Habitual or general state** <br> Marked with uninflected *be*. <br>    She *be* workin'. | Nonuse of *be*; verb inflected. <br>    She's working now. |

Reprinted with permission from Owens, Jr., R. E. (1995). *Language disorders: A functional approach to assessment and intervention* (2nd ed. pp. A-8–A-9). Boston: Allyn & Bacon.

Secondary Education Act) in 1968. Based on the law, suits were brought to ensure better services for students with cultural and linguistic diversities. The most noted case is *Lau v. Nichols,* in which the U.S. Supreme Court ruled that equal treatment is not merely providing students with the same facilities, textbooks, teachers, and curriculum, when students do not understand English.

Bilingual education may be justified as: (1) the best way to attain the maximum cognitive development of ELL students, (2) a means of achieving equal educational opportunity, (3) a means of easing the transition into the dominant language and culture, (4) an approach to educational reform, (5) a means of promoting positive interethnic relations, and (6) a wise economic investment to help ELL students to become maximally productive in adult life for the benefit of themselves and society (Baca & Cervantes, 1998).

Although the Bilingual Education Act and the Civil Rights Act and their rules and regulations have promoted equal access and bilingual education,

## FIGURE 10.3

### Recent Developments in Second Language and Bilingual Education in the United States

**Prior to 1914** Many community schools existed to teach a specific language, such as German. Saturday classes were common.

**1918** World War I brought about reactions against Germany and a resurgence of patriotic feeling; use of "English only" in schools legislated in many states.

**1945** World War II led to realization of need for knowledge of foreign languages: teaching of foreign languages in schools encouraged.

**1958** Soviet launching of *Sputnik* shocked United States' leaders, who then funded schools' efforts to promote key subject areas, including foreign languages.

**1963** Dade County, Florida, initiated bilingual programs for Spanish-speaking Cuban children coming to Miami.

**1964** Civil Rights Act forbade language-based discrimination.

**1968** Bilingual Education Act: Title VII of Elementary and Secondary Education Act promoted bilingual programs in the schools.

**1971** Massachusetts Bilingual Education Act: Law mandating bilingual education for non-English-speaking children; Massachusetts first state, other states followed.

**1974** Bilingual Education Reform Act: Updated 1968 law; mandated language instruction; added study of history and culture in bilingual programs.

**1974** U.S. Supreme Court Decision *Lau v. Nichols* gave non-English-speaking students the legal right to instruction that enables them to participate in education process, and to bilingual instruction, as part of "equal educational opportunity."

**1975** United States Department of Education developed guidelines that specified approaches, methods, and procedures for educating students with limited proficiency in English. These Lau Remedies were not enacted.

**1981** Senator S. I. Hayakawa first introduced a constitutional amendment to declare English the official language of the United States. (Defeated)

**1981** *Castenada v. Pickard* established a framework for determining whether school districts are in compliance with *Lau v. Nichols* decision. The framework for compliance included:
Theory—Is the program based on sound theory?
Implementation—Does the district have an implementation plan?
Results—What kinds of results does the district have for implementing the program?

**1984** California voters passed bill to publish ballots and other election material in English only.

**1985** Secretary of Education William Bennett spoke out against federal bilingual education programs.

**1994** Reauthorization of Bilingual Education Act (Title VII of the Improving American Schools Act, formerly Elementary and Secondary Education Act). In this reauthorization, bilingualism was reconceptualized as a valuable national resource. Bilingual programs are no longer defined by types: maintenance, transitional, and immersion.

**1994** Reauthorization of Improving American Schools Act resulting in language minority students being eligible to receive Title I services, even if the source of disadvantage is determined to be language.

**1998** California state legislature passed the English for the Children Initiative that restricts the programs in which ELL students can participate, including the number of years to several years only and the types of programs to ESL programs.

Adapted from Tiedt, P. L., & Tiedt, I. M. (1995). *Multicultural teaching: A handbook of activities, information, and resources* (p. 4). Boston: Allyn & Bacon.

political developments have moved the country back toward an assimilation philosophy. For example, in 1981, Senator S. I. Hayakawa introduced a constitutional amendment to declare English the official language of the United States. This amendment was defeated, but a growing number of states have passed what has been referred to as "English-only" legislation. More recent legislation has moved to restrict the type and length of programs for ELL students, such as the English for the Children Initiative passed in 1998 by the California state legislature. This legislation limits the number of years ELL students can participate in programs and does not support programs that promote maintenance of the first language along with development of English.

## Instructional Guidelines and Accommodations for Culturally and Linguistically Diverse Students

As a teacher, you will have students from many cultures and students who are in the process of acquiring English as a second language or second dialect. You may or may not be familiar with the culture and language of these students, but it will be important for these students to feel comfortable in your class and to learn. To promote learning, you should incorporate their language and culture into the curriculum, demonstrate that you value their culture and language, have high expectations for these students, and make accommodations so that they can learn successfully. Research into the characteristics of effective teachers of students with cultural and linguistic diversities (Chamot, 1998; Garcia, 1991; Gersten, Marks, Keating, & Baker, 1998; Johnson, Fletcher, & Bos, in press; Ladson-Billings, 1995; Tikunoff, 1983) indicates that such teachers:

- have high expectations of their students and believe that all students are capable of academic success
- see themselves as members of the community and see teaching as a way to give back to the community
- display confidence in their ability to be successful with students who are culturally and linguistically diverse
- communicate clearly, pace lessons appropriately, involve students in decisions, monitor students' progress, and provide immediate feedback
- through culturally relevant teaching, integrate the students' native language and dialect, culture, and community into classroom activities to make input more relevant and comprehensible, to build trust and self-esteem, and to promote cultural diversity and cultural pluralism
- use curriculum and teaching strategies that promote coherence, relevance, progression, and continuity
- structure opportunities for students to use English
- challenge their students and teach higher-order thinking

As you will learn from the next section, schools have developed specific programs to promote second language acquisition.

### Programs for Promoting Second Language Acquisition

Two broad categories of programs have been used in schools in the United States to promote second language acquisition: English as a second language (ESL) instruction and bilingual education. English as a second language generally has as its goal the acquisition of English, whereas the goal of bilingual education is to promote bilingualism or proficiency in both the first and second languages.

**Instruction in English as a Second Language** **English as a Second Language (ESL) instruction** uses English to teach students English as a second language, with limited emphasis on maintaining or developing proficiency in the student's first language. Instruction may be given during a specified instructional time (with students receiving the rest of their instruction in general education classrooms) or it may be integrated into content-area instruction (as is the case with Sheltered English). **Sheltered English** is a type of ESL instruction in which the goal is to teach English language skills at the same time that students are learning content-area knowledge (Chamot & O'Malley, 1994; Northcutt & Watson, 1986). Sheltered English techniques that you can use as a classroom teacher include the following:

- Increase wait time.
- Respond to the message, not to the correctness of the pronunciation or grammar.
- Simplify your language.
- Don't force reluctant students to speak.
- Demonstrate the concept; use manipulatives.
- Make use of all senses.
- Pair or group native speakers together.
- Adapt the materials, don't "water down" the content.
- Learn as much as you can about the language and culture of your students.
- Build on students' prior knowledge.
- Bring students' home language and culture into the classroom and curriculum (Chamot, 1998; Gersten et al., 1998; Reyes & Bos, 1998; Sullivan, 1992; Towell & Wink, 1993).

Schools often use the ESL model when the non-English-speaking students are from several language groups or there are too few students from a common language group to support a bilingual education model. Many educators suggest that students should be encouraged to continue to develop proficiency in their first language, even if it is not formally supported through bilingual education (e.g., Baker, 1993; Cummins, 1989; Orando & Collier, 1998). To promote this, teachers can do the following:

- Encourage students to use their first language around school.
- Provide opportunities for students from the same language group to communicate with one another in their first language (e.g., in cooperative learning groups; during informal discussions).
- Recruit people who can tutor students in the first language.
- Provide, in classrooms and the school library, books written in various languages.
- Incorporate greetings and information in various languages in newsletters and other official school communications (Cummins, 1989).

The ESL teacher is usually considered a resource teacher, in that she works daily, or at least several times a week, with groups of students or whole classes of students for a specified instructional time. In addition, the ESL teacher is usually responsible for assessing the students' language proficiency in English and, depending on the language, in their first language.

> Research indicates that academic and linguistic skills developed in a student's first language usually transfer easily to the second language (Lanauze & Snow, 1989).

When Maria, the ESL teacher interviewed at the beginning of this chapter, was asked about her job and what she believed would make her most effective, she commented,

> I feel fairly comfortable teaching the ESL students. I use a model that requires active learning on the part of the students with lots of use of gestures, demonstrations, and playing with language integrated into the instruction. I also build the

---

## MAKING A DIFFERENCE
### The 60-Second Lesson

#### Teaching a Concept to Second Language Learners

When students do not understand a concept, use one or more of the following strategies:

- Draw a picture.
- Have students with the same first language explain it in that language.
- Re-explain, but simplify the language.
- Demonstrate it.
- Provide examples and, if necessary, nonexamples (i.e., use of nonexamples is typical language used in teaching concepts).

students' culture into the instruction and I encourage the students to use an inquiry model to learn more about their cultures and share them with the other class members. My greatest concern is my ability to serve as a resource for the classroom and bilingual teachers in the school. One way that I feel that I am more effective with classroom teachers is that I am doing more co-teaching. This allows me to demonstrate ESL techniques to the teachers, and I work with the teachers to plan ESL lessons that are relevant to the content being taught in class.

**Bilingual Education** Bilingual education students usually spend the entire day in classrooms designated as *bilingual classrooms*. These students are learning English and may be receiving content instruction in their first language, in English, or in both, according to their level of development in English. Frequently, bilingual education approaches are described as *transitional* or *maintenance*, based on the degree to which the first language is developed and maintained.

> When biliteracy is encouraged in second language learners, literacy skills transfer from one language to the other (Lanauze & Snow, 1989; Johnson et al., in press).

The focus of **transitional bilingual education** is to help students shift from the home language to the dominant language. These programs initially provide content-area instruction in students' native language along with ESL instruction. Students transfer from these programs as soon as they are deemed sufficiently proficient in English to receive all academic instruction in English (Baca & Cervantes, 1998). The time taken for this transition from the students' first language to English varies, depending on the program (Ramirez & Merino, 1990). In programs in which literacy is taught in the first language, with other content taught in English, students may make the transition in 2 to 3 years. In other transition programs, at least 40 percent of the instruction is in the first language—including reading, language arts, math, and sometimes social studies or science—and students usually remain in the programs through fifth or sixth grade (Ramirez, 1992).

**Maintenance bilingual education** fosters the students' first language and strengthens their sense of cultural identity while teaching the second language and culture. Maintenace programs typically provide native language content-area instruction throughout the elementary grades with the amount of native language instruction decreasing as students progress through the program. This model values bilingualism and sees the learning of a second language as a positive addition for the students' cognitive development and life success. This model also places a strong emphasis on incorporating the students' culture and heritage into the instruction. A particularly compelling use of the maintenance bilingual model is in the education of Native Americans (Díaz-Rico & Weed, 1995) in which the goal is to increase the number of speakers of Native American languages and preserve the cultural and linguistic heritage (Reyhner, 1992).

Recently, **two-way bilingual programs** have become an option for students learning English as a second language. In two-way programs, half the students are native speakers of English; the other half speak another language, usually Spanish. Instruction is in English half the time, and in Spanish the other half. The goal is for all students to become fully bilingual and biliterate. Although the number of programs in the United States is limited, estimated at under 200 programs (Willis, 1994), the long-term results from early established programs are promising (Collier, 1989; Crawford, 1995; Thomas & Collier, 1997), with most of the native English and Spanish speakers bilingual and attending college, even though students were from poor, working class backgrounds. Results also indicate that the native English speakers have positive attitudes toward multicultural issues and are more sensitive toward students learning a second language.

When Gloria and Lidia, the bilingual education teachers team teaching at Mission Way, were asked about their model of bilingual education, they described it as best fitting the transition model, with a relatively late transition to English (fourth to fifth grade). One of the reasons Gloria and Lidia chose to team teach was to better meet the needs of their students as they made the transition from skill and content instruction in Spanish to English. Gloria comments,

> During grades four and five we transition the language of instruction to almost exclusively English. For us, the exception is reading and writing. In our literature-based reading program and

writer's workshop, we continue to encourage the students to read some literature written in Spanish and to write some compositions in Spanish, although most instruction is in English. We also discuss the literature in Spanish. In this way students do not lose those Spanish literacy skills that they have developed in the bilingual programs. We feel that this is important not only for them to stay connected to their home community, but [also because] being bilingual and biliterate are highly desired job skills.

## Promoting Language Learning during Content Instruction

Students who are acquiring English as a second language are focusing their attention not only on learning content and vocabulary, but also on learning English. Richard-Amato (1996) described the following stages of second language development related to learning in content classes:

- **Low-Beginning:** Students depend on gestures, facial expressions, objects, pictures, a phrase dictionary, and often a translator to understand or be understood. Occasionally, students comprehend words or phrases.
- **Mid-Beginning:** Students begin to comprehend more, but only when the speaker provides gestural clues, speaks slowly, and uses concrete referents and repetitions. Students speak seldomly and haltingly, show some recognition of written segments, and may be able to write short utterances.
- **High-Beginning to Low-Intermediate:** Students comprehend more, but with difficulty. Students speak in an attempt to meet basic needs but remain hesitant, and make frequent errors in grammar, vocabulary, and pronunciation. Students can read very simple text and can write a little (but writing is very restricted in grammatical structure and vocabulary).
- **Mid-Intermediate:** Students may experience a dramatic increase in vocabulary recognition, but idioms and more advanced vocabulary remain difficult. Students often know what they want to say but grope for acceptable words and phrases. Errors in grammar, vocabulary, and pronunciation are frequent. Students can read text that is more difficult but still concrete, and can write with greater ease than before.
- **High-Intermediate to Low-Advanced:** Students begin to comprehend substantial parts of normal conversation but often require repetitions, particularly with academic discourse. Students are gaining confidence in speaking ability; errors are common but less frequent. Students can read and write text that contains more complex vocabulary and structures than before, but experience difficulty with abstract language.
- **Mid-Advanced:** Students comprehend much conversational and academic discourse spoken at normal rates, but sometimes require repetition. Speech is more fluent and meaning is generally clear, but occasional errors occur. Students read and write with less difficulty materials commensurate with their cognitive development, but demonstrate some problems in grasping intended meaning.
- **High-Advanced:** Students comprehend normal conversation and academic discourse with little difficulty. Most idioms are understood. Students speak fluently in most situations with few errors. Students read and write both concrete and abstract materials and are able to manipulate the language with relative ease (Richard-Amato & Snow, 1992).

Based on this progression of second language development, Richard-Amato and Snow (1992) have developed strategies for general classroom teachers to use in teaching content (see Tips for Teachers 10.4). *The CALLA Handbook: Implementing the Cognitive Academic Language Learning Approach* (Chamot & O'Malley, (1994) also focuses on strategies for teaching second language acquisition within content areas. In addition, it simultaneously teaches learning strategies such as those presented in the Appendix: Making a Difference through Action Learning.

Although planning for culturally and linguistically diverse students takes some creative thinking and modifications of the curriculum, these students will broaden both your horizons and those of the class. In your planning, be sure to provide ample time for students to engage in meaningful conversations about topics related to language and culture.

# TIPS FOR TEACHERS

## 10.4 Teaching Strategies for Promoting Content and Second Language Learning in General Education Classes

**Beginning to Mid-Intermediate Proficiency Level**
- Provide a supportive environment in which help is readily available to second language learners.
- Establish consistent patterns and routines in the classroom.
- Use gestures, visuals, and demonstrations to present concepts.
- Connect content to students' home cultures.
- Simplify grammar and vocabulary.
- Slow the pace of presentation, enunciate clearly, and emphasize key concepts through gesture, facial expression, intonation, and repetition.
- Record your lectures or talks on tape and make them available for students.
- Make copies of your notes, or have another student take notes, so that second language learners can concentrate on listening.
- Build in redundancy by restating the concept in a simpler form, providing examples, and giving direct definitions.
- Extend wait time so that second language learners have time to volunteer.
- Avoid forcing second language learners to speak.
- Arrange cooperative learning so that students with the same first language work together.
- Encourage students to use their second language in informal conversations.
- Whenever possible, use tutors who speak the native language of the second language learners.
- Alter criteria for grading.

**High-Intermediate to Advanced Proficiency Level**
- Add contextual support to your lesson (e.g., advance organizer, study guides, glossaries, videos/films).
- Take into account the linguistic demands of the content.
- Provide opportunities for students to write in the content area.
- Provide opportunities for second language learners to practice critical thinking skills.
- Coach second language learners in appropriate learning strategies for mastering content.

# SUMMARY

- The demographics of our nation and schools are changing, with the number of students with cultural and linguistic diversities increasing.
- In U.S. schools, the number of students whose first language is not English is increasing substantially.
- The macroculture represents the dominant culture of the United States, whereas the microcultures represent the students' home cultures. Teachers can help students understand and mediate the macroculture.
- Learning about your students' home cultures and communities and integrating those cultures and communities into the curriculum is important.
- The goal of multicultural education is to change the structure of schools so that students from different cultural groups have an equal chance to achieve in school.
- Dimensions of multicultural education include content integration, knowledge construction, equity pedagogy, and an empowering school culture.
- Four basic approaches to multicultural education include the contributions, additive, transformation, and social action approaches.
- Five elements that affect second language acquisition are situational factors, linguistic input, learner characteristics, the learning and developmental process, and second language output.

- In considering language proficiency it is important to consider both the basic interpersonal communication skills or social language (BICS) and cognitive academic language performance or academic language (CALP).
- Language varies from place to place and group to group and includes dialects such as African American Vernacular English (AAVE).
- English as a second language instruction and bilingual education are two types of programs for educating second language learners.
- A number of strategies facilitate learning for students who are second language and dialect learners.

## Key Terms and Concepts

additive approach
African American Vernacular English (AAVE)
balanced bilinguals
basic interpersonal communication skills (BICS) or social language
bilingual education
cognitive academic language proficiency (CALP) or academic language
common underlying proficiency
comprehensible input
comprehensible output
content integration
context-embedded communication and instruction
contributions approach
cultural characteristics
cultural inversion
dialect
empowering school culture
equity pedagogy
English as a Second Language (ESL) instruction
English language learners (ELL)
funds of knowledge
knowledge construction
language variation
learning and developmental process
learner characteristics
linguistic input
macroculture
maintenance bilingual education
microcultures
multicultural education
secondary language output
Sheltered English
silent or nonverbal period
situational factors
social action approach
transformation approach
transitional bilingual education
two-way bilingual programs

## Think and Apply

1. Now that you have read Chapter 10, think about the interview with bilingual teachers Gloria Rodriguez and Lidia Romo, and with ESL teacher Maria Chavez. What questions do you have for them about strategies for working with students who are culturally and linguistically diverse? Make a list of the questions and then ask them of an ESL or bilingual education teacher.
2. Visit a school known for its positive emphasis on multicultural education. Watch for evidence of cultural integration and an empowering school culture. Observe a lesson to see how the teacher builds upon the students' cultural diversity.
3. To learn more about your own cultural background, answer the questions posed in the "Cultural Characteristics" section or partner with a fellow student and interview each other.
4. Select a unit you have taught or plan to teach. Review it for its focus on multicultural perspectives. Then, using one of the four approaches to multicultural education (contribution, additive, transformation, social action), modify the unit to include a stronger multicultural emphasis.
5. Select a unit you have taught or plan to teach, and review it to determine how you would modify it for second language or dialect learners.

# Read More about It

1. Agar, M. H. (1980). *The professional stranger: An informal introduction to ethnography.* Orlando, FL: Academic Press.

    A very readable book that provides information on strategies for learning about the home environment.

2. Banks, J. A. (1997). *Teaching strategies for ethnic studies* (6th ed.). Boston: Allyn & Bacon.

    An overview of ethnic studies for Native Americans, African Americans, European Americans, Hispanic Americans, and Asian Americans. This is an excellent resource for videotapes, films, children's literature, and trade books highlighting different ethnic groups.

3. Banks, J. A., and Banks, C. A. M. (Eds.) (1995). *Handbook of research on multicultural education.* New York: Macmillan.

    A reference work in which scholars report on multicultural education from a variety of disciplines and fields. A valuable resource for teachers.

4. Block, C. C., & Zinke, J. A. (1995). *Creating a culturally enriched curriculum for grades K–6.* Boston: Allyn & Bacon.

    Provides activities and short units on different aspects of multicultural education. For each activity, children's literature (rated for difficulty) is provided.

5. Chamot, A. U., & O'Malley, J. M. (1994). *The CALLA handbook: Implementing the cognitive academic language learning approach.* Reading, MA: Addison-Wesley.

    Middle- and high-school curriculum for ELL students that integrates teaching ESL, learning strategies, and higher-order thinking.

6. Delpit, L. (1995). *Other people's children: Cultural conflict in the classroom.* New York: The New York Press.

    Collection of essays about effective ways to teach children from diverse racial, ethnic, and cultural groups.

7. Díaz-Rico, L., & Weed, K. Z. (1995). *The crosscultural, language, and academic development handbook: A complete K–12 reference guide.* Boston: Allyn & Bacon.

    A very readable book about second language acquisition, bilingual education, culture and cultural diversity, and language policies, with many ideas for teaching.

8. Gersten, R. M., & Jimenez, R. T. (Eds.) (1998). *Promoting learning for culturally and linguistically diverse students.* Belmont, CA: Wadsworth.

    Readable book that provides strategies for classroom teachers to use in teaching English language learners.

9. Ladson-Billings, G. (1994). *The dreamkeepers: Successful teachers of African American children.* San Franciso: Jossey-Bass.

    Tells the stories of teachers who are successfully educating African American students.

10. Ovando, C. J., & Collier, V. P. (1998). *Bilingual and ESL classrooms: Teaching in multicultural contexts* (2nd ed.). Boston: McGraw-Hill.

    Provides an overview of bilingual education and ESL that includes teaching strategies.

11. Reyhner, J. (Ed.) (1992). *Teaching American Indian students.* Norman, OK: University of Oklahoma.

    Readings on strategies for teaching Native American students.

12. Ruiz, N. T., Garcia, E., & Figueroa, R. A. (1996) *The OLE curriculum guide: Creating optimal learning environments for students from diverse backgrounds in special and general education.* Sacramento, CA: California Department of Education, Specialized Programs Branch.

    Early literacy curriculum for teaching ELL students that incorporates a sociocultural perspective and includes such teaching components as interactive journals, writers' workshops, literature study, and shared reading.

13. Siccone, F. (1995). *Celebrating diversity: Building self-esteem in today's multicultural classrooms.* Boston: Allyn & Bacon.

    Provides many multicultural activities to promote self-worth and confidence in students (grades K–8).

14. Sleeter, C. E., & Grant, C. A. (1993). *Making choices for multicultural education: Five approaches to race, class, and gender* (2nd ed.). New York: Merrill.

    Critically examines five alternative models of multicultural education that are used in American schools and classrooms today.

15. Spangenberg-Urbschat, & Pritchard, R. (Eds.) (1994). *Kids come in all languages: Reading instruction for ESL students.* Newark, DE: International Reading Association.

    Presents practical strategies for teaching ESL students.

16. Soto, L. D. (1997). *Language, culture, and power: Bilingual families and the struggle for quality education*. Albany, NY: State University of New York Press.

    Documents the story of Puerto Rican community as they struggle to get quality education for their children.

17. Tiedt, P. L., & Tiedt, I. M. (1995). *Multicultural teaching: A handbook of activities, information, and resources* (4th ed.). Boston: Allyn & Bacon.

    Presents general strategies for multicultural education in addition to topical activities and units.

# PART III: Journal Articles

# CHAPTER 16

## The Silenced Dialogue: Power and Pedagogy in Educating Other People's Children

LISA D. DELPIT
*Baltimore City Schools*

*Lisa Delpit uses the debate over process-oriented versus skills-oriented writing instruction as the starting-off point to examine the "culture of power" that exists in society in general and in the educational environment in particular. She analyzes five complex rules of power that explicitly and implicitly influence the debate over meeting the educational needs of Black and poor students on all levels. Delpit concludes that teachers must teach all students the explicit and implicit rules of power as a first step toward a more just society. This article is an edited version of a speech presented at the Ninth Annual Ethnography in Education Research Forum, University of Pennsylvania, Philadelphia, Pennsylvania, February 5–6, 1988.*

A Black male graduate student who is also a special education teacher in a predominantly Black community is talking about his experiences in predominantly White university classes:

> There comes a moment in every class where we have to discuss "The Black Issue" and what's appropriate education for Black children. I tell you, I'm tired of arguing with those White people, because they won't listen. Well, I don't know if they really don't listen or if they just don't believe you. It seems like if you can't quote Vygotsky or something, then you don't have any validity to speak about your *own* kids. Anyway, I'm not bothering with it anymore, now I'm just in it for a grade.

A Black woman teacher in a multicultural urban elementary school is talking about her experiences in discussions with her predominantly White fellow teachers about how they should organize reading instruction to best serve students of color:

> When you're talking to White people they still want it to be their way. You can try to talk to them and give them examples, but they're so headstrong, they think they know what's best for *everybody*, for *everybody's* children. They won't listen, White folks are going to do what they want to do *anyway*.
>
> It's really hard. They just don't listen well. No, they listen, but they don't *hear*—you know how your mama used to say you listen to the radio, but you *hear* your mother? Well they don't *hear* me.

> So I just try to shut them out so I can hold my temper. You can only beat your head against a brick wall for so long before you draw blood. If I try to stop arguing with them I can't help myself from getting angry. Then I end up walking around praying all day "Please Lord, remove the bile I feel for these people so I can sleep tonight." It's funny, but it can become a cancer, a sore.
>
> So, I shut them out. I go back to my own little cubby, my classroom, and I try to teach the way I know will work, no matter what those folk say. And when I get Black kids, I just try to undo the damage they did.
>
> I'm not going to let any man, woman, or child drive me crazy—White folks will try to do that to you if you let them. You just have to stop talking to them, that's what I do. I just keep smiling, but I won't talk to them.

A soft-spoken Native Alaskan woman in her forties is a student in the Education Department of the University of Alaska. One day she storms into a Black professor's office and very uncharacteristically slams the door. She plops down in a chair and, still fuming, says, "Please tell those people, just don't help us anymore! I give up. I won't talk to them again!"

And finally, a Black woman principal who is also a doctoral student at a well-known university on the West Coast is talking about her university experiences, particularly about when a professor lectures on issues concerning educating Black children:

> If you try to suggest that that's not quite the way it is, they get defensive, then you get defensive, then they'll start reciting research.
>
> I try to give them my experiences, to explain. They just look and nod. The more I try to explain, they just look and nod, just keep looking and nodding. They don't really hear me.
>
> Then, when it's time for class to be over, the professor tells me to come to his office to talk more. So I go. He asks for more examples of what I'm talking about, and he looks and nods while I give them. Then he says that that's just my experiences. It doesn't really apply to most Black people.
>
> It becomes futile because they think they know everything about everybody. What you have to say about your life, your children, doesn't mean anything. They don't really want to hear what you have to say. They wear blinders and earplugs. They only want to go on research they've read that other White people have written.
>
> It just doesn't make any sense to keep talking to them.

Thus was the first half of the title of this text born—"The Silenced Dialogue." One of the tragedies in the field of education is that scenarios such as these are enacted daily around the country. The saddest element is that the individuals that the Black and Native American educators speak of in these statements are seldom aware that the dialogue *has* been silenced. Most likely the White educators believe that their colleagues of color did, in the end, agree with their logic. After all, they stopped disagreeing, didn't they?

I have collected these statements since completing a recently published article (Delpit, 1986). In this somewhat autobiographical account, entitled "Skills and Other Dilemmas of a Progressive Black Educator," I discussed my perspective as a product of a skills-oriented approach to writing and as a teacher of process-oriented approaches. I described the estrangement that I and many teachers of color feel from the progressive movement when writing-process advocates dismiss us as too "skills oriented." I ended the article suggesting that it was incumbent upon writing-process advocates—or indeed, advocates of any progressive movement—to enter into dialogue with teachers of color, who may not share their enthusiasm about so-called new, liberal, or progressive ideas.

In response to this article, which presented no research data and did not even cite a reference, I received numerous calls and letters from teachers, professors, and even state school personnel from around the country, both Black and White. All of the White respondents, except one, have wished to talk more about the question of skills versus process approaches—to support or reject what they perceive to be my position. On the other hand, *all* of the non-White respondents have spoken passionately on being left out of the dialogue about how best to educate children of color.

How can such complete communication blocks exist when both parties truly believe they have the same aims? How can the bitterness and resentment expressed by the educators of color be drained so that the sores can heal? What can be done?

I believe the answer to these questions lies in ethnographic analysis, that is, in identifying and giving voice to alternative world views. Thus, I will attempt to address the concerns raised by White and Black respondents to my article "Skills and Other Dilemmas" (Delpit, 1986). My charge here is not to determine the best instructional methodology; I believe that the actual practice of good teachers of all colors typically incorporates a range of pedagogical orientations. Rather, I suggest that the differing perspectives on the debate over "skills" versus "process" approaches can lead to an understanding of the alienation and miscommunication, and thereby to an understanding of the "silenced dialogue."

In thinking through these issues, I have found what I believe to be a connecting and complex theme: what I have come to call "the culture of power." There are five aspects of power I would like to propose as given for this presentation:

1. Issues of power are enacted in classrooms.

2. There are codes or rules for participating in power; that is, there is a "culture of power."

3. The rules of the culture of power are a reflection of the rules of the culture of those who have power.

4. If you are not already a participant in the culture of power, being told explicitly the rules of that culture makes acquiring power easier.

5. Those with power are frequently least aware of—or least willing to acknowledge—its existence. Those with less power are often most aware of its existence.

The first three are by now basic tenets in the literature of the sociology of education, but the last two have seldom been addressed. The following discussion will explicate these aspects of power and their relevance to the schism between liberal educational movements and that of non-White, non-middle-class teachers and communities.[1]

---

[1] Such a discussion, limited as it is by space constraints, must treat the intersection of class and race somewhat simplistically. For the sake of clarity, however, let me define a few terms: "Black" is used herein to refer to those who share some or all aspects of "core black culture" (Gwaltney, 1980, p. xxiii), that is, the mainstream of Black America—neither those who have entered the ranks of the bourgeoisie nor those who are participants in the disenfranchised underworld. "Middle-class" is used broadly to refer to the predominantly White American "mainstream." There are, of course, non-White people who also fit into this category; at issue is their cultural identification, not necessarily the color of their skin. (I must add that there are other non-White people, as well as poor White people, who have indicated to me that their perspectives are similar to those attributed herein to Black people.)

1. *Issues of power are enacted in classrooms.*

These issues include: the power of the teacher over the students; the power of the publishers of textbooks and of the developers of the curriculum to determine the view of the world presented; the power of the state in enforcing compulsory schooling; and the power of an individual or group to determine another's intelligence or "normalcy." Finally, if schooling prepares people for jobs, and the kind of job a person has determines her or his economic status and, therefore, power, then schooling is intimately related to that power.

2. *There are codes or rules for participating in power; that is, there is a "culture of power."*

The codes or rules I'm speaking of relate to linguistic forms, communicative strategies, and presentation of self; that is, ways of talking, ways of writing, ways of dressing, and ways of interacting.

3. *The rules of the culture of power are a reflection of the rules of the culture of those who have power.*

This means that success in institutions—schools, workplaces, and so on—is predicated upon acquisition of the culture of those who are in power. Children from middle-class homes tend to do better in school than those from non-middle-class homes because the culture of the school is based on the culture of the upper and middle classes—of those in power. The upper and middle classes send their children to school with all the accoutrements of the culture of power; children from other kinds of families operate within perfectly wonderful and viable cultures but not cultures that carry the codes or rules of power.

4. *If you are not already a participant in the culture of power, being told explicitly the rules of that culture makes acquiring power easier.*

In my work within and between diverse cultures, I have come to conclude that members of any culture transmit information implicitly to co-members. However, when implicit codes are attempted across cultures, communication frequently breaks down. Each cultural group is left saying, "Why don't those people say what they mean?" as well as, "What's wrong with them, why don't they understand?"

Anyone who has had to enter new cultures, especially to accomplish a specific task, will know of what I speak. When I lived in several Papua New Guinea villages for extended periods to collect data, and when I go to Alaskan villages for work with Alaskan Native communities, I have found it unquestionably easier—psychologically and pragmatically—when some kind soul has directly informed me about such matters as appropriate dress, interactional styles, embedded meanings, and taboo words or actions. I contend that it is much the same for anyone seeking to learn the rules of the culture of power. Unless one has the leisure of a lifetime of "immersion" to learn them, explicit presentation makes learning immeasurably easier.

And now, to the fifth and last premise:

5. *Those with power are frequently least aware of—or least willing to acknowledge—its existence. Those with less power are often most aware of its existence.*

For many who consider themselves members of liberal or radical camps, acknowledging personal power and admitting participation in the culture of power is distinctly uncomfortable. On the other hand, those who are less powerful in any situation are most likely to recognize the power variable most acutely. My guess is that the White colleagues and instructors of those previously quoted did not perceive themselves to have power over the non-White speakers. However, either by virtue of their position, their numbers, or their access to that particular code of power of calling upon research to validate one's position, the White educators had the authority to establish what was to be considered "truth" regardless of the opinions of the people of color, and the latter were well aware of that fact.

A related phenomenon is that liberals (and here I am using the term "liberal" to refer to those whose beliefs include striving for a society based upon maximum individual freedom and autonomy) seem to act under the assumption that to make any rules or expectations explicit is to act against liberal principles, to limit the freedom and autonomy of those subjected to the explicitness.

I thank Fred Erickson for a comment that led me to look again at a tape by John Gumperz[2] on cultural dissonance in cross-cultural interactions. One of the episodes showed an East Indian interviewing for a job with an all-White committee. The interview was a complete failure, even though several of the interviewers appeared to really want to help the applicant. As the interview rolled steadily downhill, these "helpers" became more and more indirect in their questioning, which exacerbated the problems the applicant had in performing appropriately. Operating from a different cultural perspective, he got fewer and fewer clear clues as to what was expected of him, which ultimately resulted in his failure to secure the position.

I contend that as the applicant showed less and less aptitude for handling the interview, the power differential became ever more evident to the interviewers. The "helpful" interviewers, unwilling to acknowledge themselves as having power over the applicant, became more and more uncomfortable. Their indirectness was an attempt to lessen the power differential and their discomfort by lessening the power-revealing explicitness of their questions and comments.

When acknowledging and expressing power, one tends towards explicitness (as in yelling to your 10-year-old, "Turn that radio down!"). When de-emphasizing power, there is a move toward indirect communication. Therefore, in the interview setting, those who sought to help, to express their egalitarianism with the East Indian applicant, became more and more indirect—and less and less helpful—in their questions and comments.

In literacy instruction, explicitness might be equated with direct instruction. Perhaps the ultimate expression of explicitness and direct instruction in the primary classroom is Distar. This reading program is based on a behaviorist model in which reading is taught through the direct instruction of phonics generalizations and blending. The teacher's role is to maintain the full attention of the group by continuous questioning, eye contact, finger snaps, hand claps, and other gestures, and by eliciting choral responses and initiating some sort of award system.

When the program was introduced, it arrived with a flurry of research data that "proved" that all children—even those who were "culturally deprived"—could learn to read using this method. Soon there was a strong response, first from academics and later from many classroom teachers, stating that the program was terrible.

[2] *Multicultural Britain: "Crosstalk,"* National Centre of Industrial Language Training, Commission for Racial Equality, London, England, John Twitchin, Producer.

What I find particularly interesting, however, is that the primary issue of the conflict over Distar has not been over its instructional efficacy—usually the students did learn to read—but the expression of explicit power in the classroom. The liberal educators opposed the methods—the direct instruction, the explicit control exhibited by the teacher. As a matter of fact, it was not unusual (even now) to hear of the program spoken of as "fascist."

I am not an advocate of Distar, but I will return to some of the issues that the program—and direct instruction in general—raises in understanding the differences between progressive White educators and educators of color.

To explore those differences, I would like to present several statements typical of those made with the best of intentions by middle-class liberal educators. To the surprise of the speakers, it is not unusual for such content to be met by vocal opposition or stony silence from people of color. My attempt here is to examine the underlying assumptions of both camps.

*"I want the same thing for everyone else's children as I want for mine."*

To provide schooling for everyone's children that reflects liberal, middle-class values and aspirations is to ensure the maintenance of the status quo, to ensure that power, the culture of power, remains in the hands of those who already have it. Some children come to school with more accoutrements of the culture of power already in place—"cultural capital," as some critical theorists refer to it (for example, Apple, 1979)—some with less. Many liberal educators hold that the primary goal for education is for children to become autonomous, to develop fully who they are in the classroom setting without having arbitrary, outside standards forced upon them. This is a very reasonable goal for people whose children are already participants in the culture of power and who have already internalized its codes.

But parents who don't function within that culture often want something else. It's not that they disagree with the former aim, it's just that they want something more. They want to ensure that the school provides their children with discourse patterns, interactional styles, and spoken and written language codes that will allow them success in the larger society.

It was the lack of attention to this concern that created such a negative outcry in the Black community when well-intentioned White liberal educators introduced "dialect readers." These were seen as a plot to prevent the schools from teaching the linguistic aspects of the culture of power, thus dooming Black children to a permanent outsider caste. As one parent demanded, "My kids know how to be Black—you all teach them how to be successful in the White man's world."

Several Black teachers have said to me recently that as much as they'd like to believe otherwise, they cannot help but conclude that many of the "progressive" educational strategies imposed by liberals upon Black and poor children could only be based on a desire to ensure that the liberals' children get sole access to the dwindling pool of American jobs. Some have added that the liberal educators believe themselves to be operating with good intentions, but that these good intentions are only conscious delusions about their unconscious true motives. One of Black anthropologist John Gwaltney's (1980) informants reflects this perspective with her tongue-in-cheek observation that the biggest difference between Black folks and White folks is that Black folks *know* when they're lying!

Let me try to clarify how this might work in literacy instruction. A few years ago I worked on an analysis of two popular reading programs, Distar and a progressive program that focused on higher-level critical thinking skills. In one of the first lessons of the progressive program, the children are introduced to the names of the letter *m* and *e*. In the same lesson they are then taught the sound made by each of the letters, how to write each of the letters, and that when the two are blended together they produce the word *me*.

As an experienced first-grade teacher, I am convinced that a child needs to be familiar with a significant number of these concepts to be able to assimilate so much new knowledge in one sitting. By contrast, Distar presents the same information in about forty lessons.

I would not argue for the pace of the Distar lessons; such a slow pace would only bore most kids — but what happened in the other lesson is that it merely provided an opportunity for those who already knew the content to exhibit that they knew it, or at most perhaps to build one new concept onto what was already known. This meant that the child who did not come to school already primed with what was to be presented would be labeled as needing "remedial" instruction from day one; indeed, this determination would be made before he or she was ever taught. In fact, Distar was "successful" because it actually *taught* new information to children who had not already acquired it at home. Although the more progressive system was ideal for some children, for others it was a disaster.

I do not advocate a simplistic "basic skills" approach for children outside of the culture of power. It would be (and has been) tragic to operate as if these children were incapable of critical and higher-order thinking and reasoning. Rather, I suggest that schools must provide these children the content that other families from a different cultural orientation provide at home. This does not mean separating children according to family background, but instead, ensuring that each classroom incorporate strategies appropriate for all the children in its confines.

And I do not advocate that it is the school's job to attempt to change the homes of poor and non-White children to match the homes of those in the culture of power. That may indeed be a form of cultural genocide. I have frequently heard schools call poor parents "uncaring" when parents respond to the school's urging, that they change their home life in order to facilitate their children's learning, by saying, "But that's the school's job." What the school personnel fail to understand is that if the parents were members of the culture of power and lived by its rules and codes, then they would transmit those codes to their children. In fact, they transmit another culture that children must learn at home in order to survive in their communities.

*"Child-centered, whole language, and process approaches are needed in order to allow a democratic state of free, autonomous, empowered adults, and because research has shown that children learn best through these methods."*

People of color are, in general, skeptical of research as a determiner of our fates. Academic research has, after all, found us genetically inferior, culturally deprived, and verbally deficient. But beyond that general caveat, and despite my or others' personal preferences, there is little research data supporting the major tenets of process approaches over other forms of literacy instruction, and virtually no evidence that such approaches are more efficacious for children of color (Siddle, 1986).

Although the problem is not necessarily inherent in the method, in some instances adherents of process approaches to writing create situations in which students ultimately find themselves held accountable for knowing a set of rules about which no one has ever directly informed them. Teachers do students no service to suggest, even implicitly, that "product" is not important. In this country, students will be judged on their product regardless of the process they utilized to achieve it. And that product, based as it is on the specific codes of a particular culture, is more readily produced when the directives of how to produce it are made explicit.

If such explicitness is not provided to students, what it feels like to people who are old enough to judge is that there are secrets being kept, that time is being wasted, that the teacher is abdicating his or her duty to teach. A doctoral student in my acquaintance was assigned to a writing class to hone his writing skills. The student was placed in the section led by a White professor who utilized a process approach, consisting primarily of having the students write essays and then assemble into groups to edit each others' papers. That procedure infuriated this particular student. He had many angry encounters with the teacher about what she was doing. In his words:

> I didn't feel she was teaching us anything. She wanted us to correct each others' papers and we were there to learn from her. She didn't teach anything, absolutely nothing.
>
> Maybe they're trying to learn what Black folks knew all the time. We understand how to improvise, how to express ourselves creatively. When I'm in a classroom, I'm not looking for that, I'm looking for structure, the more formal language.
>
> Now my buddy was in [a] Black teacher's class. And that lady was very good. She went through and explained and defined each part of the structure. This [White] teacher didn't get along with that Black teacher. She said that she didn't agree with her methods. But *I* don't think that White teacher *had* any methods.

When I told this gentleman that what the teacher was doing was called a process method of teaching writing, his response was, "Well, at least now I know that she *thought* she was doing *something*. I thought she was just a fool who couldn't teach and didn't want to try."

This sense of being cheated can be so strong that the student may be completely turned off to the educational system. Amanda Branscombe, an accomplished White teacher, recently wrote a letter discussing her work with working-class Black and White students at a community college in Alabama. She had given these students my "Skills and Other Dilemmas" article (Delpit, 1986) to read and discuss, and wrote that her students really understood and identified with what I was saying. To quote her letter:

> One young man said that he had dropped out of high school because he failed the exit exam. He noted that he had then passed the GED without a problem after three weeks of prep. He said that his high school English teacher claimed to use a process approach, but what she really did was hide behind fancy words to give herself permission to do nothing in the classroom.

The students I have spoken of seem to be saying that the teacher has denied them access to herself as the source of knowledge necessary to learn the forms they need to succeed. Again, I tentatively attribute the problem to teachers' resistance to exhibiting power in the classroom. Somehow, to exhibit one's personal power as expert source is viewed as disempowering one's students.

Two qualifiers are necessary, however. The teacher cannot be the only expert in the classroom. To deny students their own expert knowledge *is* to disempower them. Amanda Branscombe, when she was working with Black high school students classified as "slow learners," had the students analyze RAP songs to discover their underlying patterns. The students became the experts in explaining to the teacher the rules for creating a new RAP song. The teacher then used the patterns the students identified as a base to begin an explanation of the structure of grammar, and then of Shakespeare's plays. Both student and teacher are expert at what they know best.

The second qualifier is that merely adopting direct instruction is not the answer. Actual writing for real audiences and real purposes is a vital element in helping students to understand that they have an important voice in their own learning processes. Siddle (1988) examines the results of various kinds of interventions in a primarily process-oriented writing class for Black students. Based on readers' blind assessments, she found that the intervention that produced the most positive changes in the students' writing was a "mini-lesson" consisting of direct instruction about some standard writing convention. But what produced the *second* highest number of positive changes was a subsequent student-centered conference with the teacher. (Peer conferencing in this group of Black students who were not members of the culture of power produced the least number of changes in students' writing. However, the classroom teacher maintained—and I concur—that such activities are necessary to introduce the elements of "real audience" into the task, along with more teacher-directed strategies.)

*"It's really a shame but she (that Black teacher upstairs) seems to be so authoritarian, so focused on skills and so teacher directed. Those poor kids never seem to be allowed to really express their creativity. (And she even yells at them.)"*

This statement directly concerns the display of power and authority in the classroom. One way to understand the difference in perspective between Black teachers and their progressive colleagues on this issue is to explore culturally influenced oral interactions.

In *Ways With Words*, Shirley Brice Heath (1983) quotes the verbal directives given by the middle-class "townspeople" teachers (p. 280):

— "Is this where the scissors belong?"
— "You want to do your best work today."

By contrast, many Black teachers are more likely to say:

— "Put those scissors on that shelf."
— "Put your name on the papers and make sure to get the right answer for each question."

Is one oral style more authoritarian than another?

Other researchers have identified differences in middle-class and working-class speech to children. Snow et al. (1976), for example, report that working-class mothers use more directives to their children than do middle- and upper-class parents. Middle-class parents are likely to give the directive to a child to take his bath as, "Isn't it time for your bath?" Even though the utterance is couched as a question, both child and adult understand it as a directive. The child may respond with "Aw Mom, can't I wait until . . . ," but whether or not negotiation is attempted, both conversants understand the intent of the utterance.

By contrast, a Black mother, in whose house I was recently a guest, said to her eight-year-old son, "Boy, get your rusty behind in that bathtub." Now I happen to know that this woman loves her son as much as any mother, but she would never have posed the directive to her son to take a bath in the form of a question. Were she to ask, "Would you like to take your bath now?" she would not have been issuing a directive but offering a true alternative. Consequently, as Heath suggests, upon entering school the child from such a family may not understand the indirect statement of the teacher as a direct command. Both White and Black working-class children in the communities Heath studied "had difficulty interpreting these indirect requests for adherence to an unstated set of rules" (p. 280).

But those veiled commands are commands nonetheless, representing true power, and with true consequences for disobedience. If veiled commands are ignored, the child will be labeled a behavior problem and possibly officially classified as behavior disordered. In other words, the attempt by the teacher to reduce an exhibition of power by expressing herself in indirect terms may remove the very explicitness that the child needs to understand the rules of the new classroom culture.

A Black elementary school principal in Fairbanks, Alaska, reported to me that she has a lot of difficulty with Black children who are placed in some White teachers' classrooms. The teachers often send the children to the office for disobeying teacher directives. Their parents are frequently called in for conferences. The parents' response to the teacher is usually the same: "They do what I say; if you just *tell* them what to do, they'll do it. I tell them at home that they have to listen to what you say." And so, does not the power still exist? Its veiled nature only makes it more difficult for some children to respond appropriately, but that in no way mitigates its existence.

I don't mean to imply, however, that the only time the Black child disobeys the teacher is when he or she misunderstands the request for certain behavior. There are other factors that may produce such behavior. Black children expect an authority figure to act with authority. When the teacher instead acts as a "chum," the message sent is that this adult has no authority, and the children react accordingly. One reason this is so is that Black people often view issues of power and authority differently than people from mainstream middle-class backgrounds.[3] Many people of color expect authority to be earned by personal efforts and exhibited by personal characteristics. In other words, "the authoritative person gets to be a teacher because she is authoritative." Some members of middle-class cultures, by contrast, expect one to achieve authority by the acquisition of an authoritative role. That is, "the teacher is the authority because she is the teacher."

---

[3] I would like to thank Michelle Foster, who is presently planning a more in-depth treatment of the subject, for her astute clarification of the idea.

In the first instance, because authority is earned, the teacher must consistently prove the characteristics that give her authority. These characteristics may vary across cultures, but in the Black community they tend to cluster around several abilities. The authoritative teacher can control the class through exhibition of personal power; establishes meaningful interpersonal relationships that garner student respect; exhibits a strong belief that all students can learn; establishes a standard of achievement and "pushes" the students to achieve that standard; and holds the attention of the students by incorporating interactional features of Black communicative style in his or her teaching.

By contrast, the teacher whose authority is vested in the role has many more options of behavior at her disposal. For instance, she does not need to express any sense of personal power because her authority does not come from anything she herself does or says. Hence, the power she actually holds may be veiled in such questions/commands as "Would you like to sit down now?" If the children in her class understand authority as she does, it is mutually agreed upon that they are to obey her no matter how indirect, soft-spoken, or unassuming she may be. Her indirectness and soft-spokenness may indeed be, as I suggested earlier, an attempt to reduce the implication of overt power in order to establish a more egalitarian and non-authoritarian classroom atmosphere.

If the children operate under another notion of authority, however, then there is trouble. The Black child may perceive the middle-class teacher as weak, ineffectual, and incapable of taking on the role of being the teacher; therefore, there is no need to follow her directives. In her dissertation, Michelle Foster (1987) quotes one young Black man describing such a teacher:

> She is boring, bo::ing.* She could do something creative. Instead she just stands there. She can't control the class, doesn't know how to control the class. She asked me what she was doing wrong. I told her she just stands there like she's meditating. I told her she could be meditating for all I know. She says that we're supposed to know what to do. I told her I don't know nothin' unless she tells me. She just can't control the class. I hope we don't have her next semester. (pp. 67–68)

But of course the teacher may not view the problem as residing in herself but in the student, and the child may once again become the behavior-disordered Black boy in special education.

What characteristics do Black students attribute to the good teacher? Again, Foster's dissertation provides a quotation that supports my experience with Black students. A young Black man is discussing a former teacher with a group of friends:

> We had fu::n in her class, but she was mean. I can remember she used to say, "Tell me what's in the story, Wayne." She pushed, she used to get on me and push me to know. She made us learn. We had to get in the books. There was this tall guy and he tried to take her on, but she was in charge of that class and she didn't let anyone run her. I still have this book we used in her class. It's a bunch of stories in it. I just read one on Coca-Cola again the other day (p. 68).

To clarify, this student was *proud* of the teacher's "meanness," an attribute he seemed to describe as the ability to run the class and pushing and expecting stu-

---

*Editor's note: The colons [::] refer to elongated vowels.

dents to learn. Now, does the liberal perspective of the negatively authoritarian Black teacher really hold up? I suggest that although all "explicit" Black teachers are not also good teachers, there are different attitudes in different cultural groups about which characteristics make for a good teacher. Thus, it is impossible to create a model for the good teacher without taking issues of culture and community context into account.

And now to the final comment I present for examination:

*"Children have the right to their own language, their own culture. We must fight cultural hegemony and fight the system by insisting that children be allowed to express themselves in their own language style. It is not they, the children, who must change, but the schools. To push children to do anything else is repressive and reactionary."*

A statement such as this originally inspired me to write the "Skills and Other Dilemmas" article. It was first written as a letter to a colleague in response to a situation that had developed in our department. I was teaching a senior-level teacher education course. Students were asked to prepare a written autobiographical document for the class that would also be shared with their placement school prior to their student teaching.

One student, a talented young Native American woman, submitted a paper in which the ideas were lost because of technical problems—from spelling to sentence structure to paragraph structure. Removing her name, I duplicated the paper for a discussion with some faculty members. I had hoped to initiate a discussion about what we could do to ensure that our students did not reach the senior level without getting assistance in technical writing skills when they needed them.

I was amazed at the response. Some faculty implied that the student should never have been allowed into the teacher education program. Others, some of the more progressive minded, suggested that I was attempting to function as gatekeeper by raising the issue and had internalized repressive and disempowering forces of the power elite to suggest that something was wrong with a Native American student just because she had another style of writing. With few exceptions, I found myself alone in arguing against both camps.

No, this student should not have been denied entry to the program. To deny her entry under the notion of upholding standards is to blame the victim for the crime. We cannot justifiably enlist exclusionary standards when the reason this student lacked the skills demanded was poor teaching at best and institutionalized racism at worst.

However, to bring this student into the program and pass her through without attending to obvious deficits in the codes needed for her to function effectively as a teacher is equally criminal—for though we may assuage our own consciences for not participating in victim blaming, she will surely be accused and convicted as soon as she leaves the university. As Native Alaskans were quick to tell me, and as I understood through my own experience in the Black community, not only would she not be hired as a teacher, but those who did not hire her would make the (false) assumption that the university was putting out only incompetent Natives and that they should stop looking seriously at any Native applicants. A White applicant who exhibits problems is an individual with problems. A person of color who exhibits problems immediately becomes a representative of her cultural group.

No, either stance is criminal. The answer is to *accept* students but also to take responsibility to *teach* them. I decided to talk to the student and found out she had recognized that she needed some assistance in the technical aspects of writing soon after she entered the university as a freshman. She had gone to various members of the education faculty and received the same two kinds of responses I met with four years later: faculty members told her either that she should not even attempt to be a teacher, or that it didn't matter and that she shouldn't worry about such trivial issues. In her desperation, she had found a helpful professor in the English Department, but he left the university when she was in her sophomore year.

We sat down together, worked out a plan for attending to specific areas of writing competence, and set up regular meetings. I stressed to her the need to use her own learning process as insight into how best to teach her future students those "skills" that her own schooling had failed to teach her. I gave her some explicit rules to follow in some areas; for others, we devised various kinds of journals that, along with readings about the structure of the language, allowed her to find her own insights into how the language worked. All that happened two years ago, and the young woman is now successfully teaching. What the experience led me to understand is that pretending that gatekeeping points don't exist is to ensure that many students will not pass through them.

Now you may have inferred that I believe that because there is a culture of power, everyone should learn the codes to participate in it, and that is how the world should be. Actually, nothing could be further from the truth. I believe in a diversity of style, and I believe the world will be diminished if cultural diversity is ever obliterated. Further, I believe strongly, as do my liberal colleagues, that each cultural group should have the right to maintain its own language style. When I speak, therefore, of the culture of power, I don't speak of how I wish things to be but of how they are.

I further believe that to act as if power does not exist is to ensure that the power status quo remains the same. To imply to children or adults (but of course the adults won't believe you anyway) that it doesn't matter how you talk or how you write is to ensure their ultimate failure. I prefer to be honest with my students. Tell them that their language and cultural style is unique and wonderful but that there is a political power game that is also being played, and if they want to be in on that game there are certain games that they too must play.

But don't think that I let the onus of change rest entirely with the students. I am also involved in political work both inside and outside of the educational system, and that political work demands that I place myself to influence as many gatekeeping points as possible. And it is there that I agitate for change—pushing gatekeepers to open their doors to a variety of styles and codes. What I'm saying, however, is that I do not believe that political change toward diversity can be effected from the bottom up, as do some of my colleagues. They seem to believe that if we accept and encourage diversity within classrooms of children, then diversity will automatically be accepted at gatekeeping points.

I believe that will never happen. What will happen is that the students who reach the gatekeeping points—like Amanda Branscombe's student who dropped out of high school because he failed his exit exam—will understand that they have been lied to and will react accordingly. No, I am certain that if we are truly to effect societal change, we cannot do so from the bottom up, but we must push and agitate from the top down. And in the meantime, we must take the responsibility to *teach*, to provide for students who do not already possess them, the additional codes of power.[4]

But I also do not believe that we should teach students to passively adopt an alternate code. They must be encouraged to understand the value of the code they already possess as well as to understand the power realities in this country. Otherwise they will be unable to work to change these realities. And how does one do that?

Martha Demientieff, a masterly Native Alaskan teacher of Athabaskan Indian students, tells me that her students, who live in a small, isolated, rural village of less than two hundred people, are not aware that there are different codes of English. She takes their writing and analyzes it for features of what has been referred to by Alaskan linguists as "Village English," and then covers half a bulletin board with words or phrases from the students' writing, which she labels "Our Heritage Language." On the other half of the bulletin board she puts the equivalent statements in "standard English," which she labels "Formal English."

She and the students spend a long time on the "Heritage English" section, savoring the words, discussing the nuances. She tells the students, "That's the way we say things. Doesn't it feel good? Isn't it the absolute best way of getting that idea across?" Then she turns to the other side of the board. She tells the students that there are people, not like those in their village, who judge others by the way they talk or write.

> We listen to the way people talk, not to judge them, but to tell what part of the river they come from. These other people are not like that. They think everybody needs to talk like them. Unlike us, they have a hard time hearing what people say if they don't talk exactly like them. Their way of talking and writing is called "Formal English."
>
> We have to feel a little sorry for them because they have only one way to talk. We're going to learn two ways to say things. Isn't that better? One way will be our Heritage way. The other will be Formal English. Then, when we go to get jobs, we'll be able to talk like those people who only know and can only really listen to one way. Maybe after we get the jobs we can help them to learn how it feels to have another language, like ours, that feels so good. We'll talk like them when we have to, but we'll always know our way is best.

Martha then does all sorts of activities with the notions of Formal and Heritage or informal English. She tells the students,

> In the village, everyone speaks informally most of the time unless there's a potlatch or something. You don't think about it, you don't worry about following any rules—it's sort of like how you eat food at a picnic—nobody pays attention to whether you use your fingers or a fork, and it feels *so* good. Now, Formal English is more like a formal dinner. There are rules to follow about where the knife and fork belong, about where people sit, about how you eat. That can be really nice, too, because it's nice to dress up sometimes.

---

[4] Bernstein (1975) makes a similar point when he proposes that different educational frames cannot be successfully institutionalized in the lower levels of education until there are fundamental changes at the post-secondary levels.

The students then prepare a formal dinner in the class, for which they dress up and set a big table with fancy tablecloths, china, and silverware. They speak only Formal English at this meal. Then they prepare a picnic where only informal English is allowed.

She also contrasts the "wordy" academic way of saying things with the metaphoric style of Athabaskan. The students discuss how book language always uses more words, but in Heritage language, the shorter way of saying something is always better. Students then write papers in the academic way, discussing with Martha and with each other whether they believe they've said enough to sound like a book. Next, they take those papers and try to reduce the meaning to a few sentences. Finally, students further reduce the message to a "saying" brief enough to go on the front of a T-shirt, and the sayings are put on little paper T-shirts that the students cut out and hang throughout the room. Sometimes the students reduce other authors' wordy texts to their essential meanings as well.

The following transcript provides another example. It is from a conversation between a Black teacher and a Southern Black high school student named Joey, who is a speaker of Black English. The teacher believes it very important to discuss openly and honestly the issues of language diversity and power. She has begun the discussion by giving the student a children's book written in Black English to read.

*Teacher:* What do you think about that book?

*Joey:* I think it's nice.

*Teacher:* Why?

*Joey:* I don't know. It just told about a Black family, that's all.

*Teacher:* Was it difficult to read?

*Joey:* No.

*Teacher:* Was the text different from what you have seen in other books?

*Joey:* Yeah. The writing was.

*Teacher:* How?

*Joey:* It use more of a southern-like accent in this book.

*Teacher:* Uhm-hmm. Do you think that's good or bad?

*Joey:* Well, uh, I don't think it's good for people down this a way, cause that's the way they grow up talking anyway. They ought to get the right way to talk.

*Teacher:* Oh. So you think it's wrong to talk like that?

*Joey:* Well . . . [*Laughs*]

*Teacher:* Hard question, huh?

*Joey:* Uhm-hmm, that's a hard question. But I think they shouldn't make books like that.

*Teacher:* Why?

*Joey:* Because they not using the right way to talk and in school they take off for that and li'l chirren grow up talking like that and reading like that so they might think that's right and all the time they getting bad grades in school, talking like that and writing like that.

*Teacher:* Do you think they should be getting bad grades for talking like that?

*Joey:* [*Pauses, answers very slowly*] No . . . No.

*Teacher:* So you don't think that it matters whether you talk one way or another?

*Joey:* No, not long as you understood.

*Teacher:* Uhm-hmm. Well, that's a hard question for me to answer, too. It's, ah, that's a question that's come up in a lot of schools now as to whether they should correct children who speak the way we speak all the time. Cause when we're talking to each other we talk like that even though we might not talk like that when we get into other situations, and who's to say whether it's —

*Joey:* [*Interrupting*] Right or wrong.

*Teacher:* Yeah.

*Joey:* Maybe they ought to come up with another kind of . . . maybe Black English or something. A course in Black English. Maybe Black folks would be good in that cause people talk, I mean Black people talk like that, so . . . but I guess there's a right way and wrong way to talk, you know, not regarding what race. I don't know.

*Teacher:* But who decided what's right or wrong?

*Joey:* Well that's true . . . I guess White people did.

[*Laughter. End of tape.*]

Notice how throughout the conversation Joey's consciousness has been raised by thinking about codes of language. This teacher further advocates having students interview various personnel officers in actual workplaces about their attitudes toward divergent styles in oral and written language. Students begin to understand how arbitrary language standards are, but also how politically charged they are. They compare various pieces written in different styles, discuss the impact of different styles on the message by making translations and back translations across styles, and discuss the history, apparent purpose, and contextual appropriateness of each of the technical writing rules presented by their teacher. *And* they practice writing different forms to different audiences based on rules appropriate for each audience. Such a program not only "teaches" standard linguistic forms, but also explores aspects of power as exhibited through linguistic forms.

Tony Burgess, in a study of secondary writing in England by Britton, Burgess, Martin, McLeod, and Rosen (1975/1977), suggests that we should not teach "iron conventions . . . imposed without rationale or grounding in communicative intent," . . . but "critical and ultimately cultural awarenesses" (p. 54). Courtney Cazden (1987) calls for a two-pronged approach:

1. Continuous opportunities for writers to participate in some authentic bit of the unending conversation . . . thereby becoming part of a vital community of talkers and writers in a particular domain, and

2. Periodic, temporary focus on conventions of form, taught as cultural conventions expected in a particular community. (p. 20)

Just so that there is no confusion about what Cazden means by a focus on conventions of form, or about what I mean by "skills," let me stress that neither of us is speaking of page after page of "skill sheets" creating compound words or identifying nouns and adverbs, but rather about helping students gain a useful knowledge of the conventions of print while engaging in real and useful communicative activities. Kay Rowe Grubis, a junior high school teacher in a multicultural school, makes lists of certain technical rules for her eighth graders' review and then gives them papers from a third grade to "correct." The students not only have to correct other students' work, but also tell them why they have changed or questioned aspects of the writing.

A village teacher, Howard Cloud, teaches his high school students the conventions of formal letter writing and the formulation of careful questions in the context of issues surrounding the amendment of the Alaska Land Claims Settlement Act. Native Alaskan leaders hold differing views on this issue, critical to the future of local sovereignty and land rights. The students compose letters to leaders who reside in different areas of the state seeking their perspectives, set up audioconference calls for interview/debate sessions, and, finally, develop a videotape to present the differing views.

To summarize, I suggest that students must be *taught* the codes needed to participate fully in the mainstream of American life, not by being forced to attend to hollow, inane, decontextualized subskills, but rather within the context of meaningful communicative endeavors; that they must be allowed the resource of the teacher's expert knowledge, while being helped to acknowledge their own "expertness" as well; and that even while students are assisted in learning the culture of power, they must also be helped to learn about the arbitrariness of those codes and about the power relationships they represent.

I am also suggesting that appropriate education for poor children and children of color can only be devised in consultation with adults who share their culture. Black parents, teachers of color, and members of poor communities must be allowed to participate fully in the discussion of what kind of instruction is in their children's best interest. Good liberal intentions are not enough. In an insightful study entitled "Racism without Racists: Institutional Racism in Urban Schools," Massey, Scott, and Dornbusch (1975) found that under the pressures of teaching, and with all intentions of "being nice," teachers had essentially stopped attempting to teach Black children. In their words: "We have shown that oppression can arise out of warmth, friendliness, and concern. Paternalism and a lack of challenging standards are creating a distorted system of evaluation in the schools" (p. 10). Educators must open themselves to, and allow themselves to be affected by, these alternative voices.

In conclusion, I am proposing a resolution for the skills/process debate. In short, the debate is fallacious; the dichotomy is false. The issue is really an illusion created initially not by teachers but by academics whose world view demands the creation of categorical divisions—not for the purpose of better teaching, but for the goal of easier analysis. As I have been reminded by many teachers since the publication of my article, those who are most skillful at educating Black and poor children do not allow themselves to be placed in "skills" or "process" boxes. They understand the need for both approaches, the need to help students to establish their own voices, but to coach those voices to produce notes that will be heard clearly in the larger society.

The dilemma is not really in the debate over instructional methodology, but rather in communicating across cultures and in addressing the more fundamental issue of power, of whose voice gets to be heard in determining what is best for poor children and children of color. Will Black teachers and parents continue to be silenced by the very forces that claim to "give voice" to our children? Such an outcome would be tragic, for both groups truly have something to say to one another. As a result of careful listening to alternative points of view, I have myself come to a viable synthesis of perspectives. But both sides do need to be able to listen, and I contend that it is those with the most power, those in the majority, who must take the greater responsibility for initiating the process.

To do so takes a very special kind of listening, listening that requires not only open eyes and ears, but open hearts and minds. We do not really see through our eyes or hear through our ears, but through our beliefs. To put our beliefs on hold is to cease to exist as ourselves for a moment—and that is not easy. It is painful as well, because it means turning yourself inside out, giving up your own sense of who you are, and being willing to see yourself in the unflattering light of another's angry gaze. It is not easy, but it is the only way to learn what it might feel like to be someone else and the only way to start the dialogue.

There are several guidelines. We must keep the perspective that people are experts on their own lives. There are certainly aspects of the outside world of which they may not be aware, but they can be the only authentic chroniclers of their own experience. We must not be too quick to deny their interpretations, or accuse them of "false consciousness." We must believe that people are rational beings, and therefore always act rationally. We may not understand their rationales, but that in no way militates against the existence of these rationales or reduces our responsibility to attempt to apprehend them. And finally, we must learn to be vulnerable enough to allow our world to turn upside down in order to allow the realities of others to edge themselves into our consciousness. In other words, we must become ethnographers in the true sense.

Teachers are in an ideal position to play this role, to attempt to get all of the issues on the table in order to initiate true dialogue. This can only be done, however, by seeking out those whose perspectives may differ most, by learning to give their words complete attention, by understanding one's own power, even if that power stems merely from being in the majority, by being unafraid to raise questions about discrimination and voicelessness with people of color, and to listen, no, to *hear* what they say. I suggest that the results of such interactions may be the most powerful and empowering coalescence yet seen in the educational realm—for *all* teachers and for *all* the students they teach.

## References

Apple, M. W. (1979). *Ideology and curriculum*. Boston: Routledge & Kegan Paul.
Bernstein, B. (1975). Class and pedagogies: Visible and invisible. In B. Bernstein, *Class, codes, and control* (Vol. 3). Boston: Routledge & Kegan Paul.
Britton, J., Burgess, T., Martin, N., McLeod, A., & Rosen, H. (1975/1977). *The development of writing abilities*. London: Macmillan Education for the Schools Council, and Urbana, IL: National Council of Teachers of English.
Cazden, C. (1987, January). *The myth of autonomous text*. Paper presented at the Third International Conference on Thinking, Hawaii.
Delpit, L. D. (1986). Skills and other dilemmas of a progressive Black educator. *Harvard Educational Review, 56*, (4), 379-385.
Foster, M. (1987). *"It's cookin' now": An ethnographic study of the teaching style of a successful Black teacher in an urban community college*. Unpublished doctoral dissertation, Harvard University.

Gwaltney, J. (1980). *Drylongso*. New York: Vintage Books.

Heath, S. B. (1983). *Ways with words*. Cambridge: Cambridge University Press.

Massey, G. C., Scott, M. V., & Dornbusch, S. M. (1975). Racism without racists: Institutional racism in urban schools. *The Black Scholar, 7*(3), 2-11.

Siddle, E. V. (1986). *A critical assessment of the natural process approach to teaching writing.* Unpublished qualifying paper, Harvard University.

Siddle, E. V. (1988). *The effect of intervention strategies on the revisions ninth graders make in a narrative essay.* Unpublished doctoral dissertation, Harvard University.

Snow, C. E., Arlman-Rup, A., Hassing, Y., Josbe, J., Joosten, J., & Vorster, J. (1976). Mother's speech in three social classes. *Journal of Psycholinguistic Research, 5,* 1-20.

I take full responsibility for all that appears herein; however, aside from those mentioned by name in this text, I would like to thank all of the educators and students around the country who have been so willing to contribute their perspectives to the formulation of these ideas, especially Susan Jones, Catherine Blunt, Dee Stickman, Sandra Gamble, Willard Taylor, Mickey Monteiro, Denise Burden, Evelyn Higbee, Joseph Delpit, Jr., Valerie Montoya, Richard Cohen, and Mary Denise Thompson.

# CHAPTER 17

# Empowering Minority Students: A Framework for Intervention

JIM CUMMINS

During the past twenty years educators in the United States have implemented a series of costly reforms aimed at reversing the pattern of school failure among minority students. These have included compensatory programs at the preschool level, myriad forms of bilingual education programs, the hiring of additional aides and remedial personnel, and the institution of safeguards against discriminatory assessment procedures. Yet the dropout rate among Mexican-American and mainland Puerto Rican students remains between 40 and 50 percent compared to 14 percent for whites and 25 percent for blacks (Jusenius & Duarte, 1982). Similarly, almost a decade after the passage of the nondiscriminatory assessment provision of PL94-142,[1] we find Hispanic students in Texas overrepresented by a factor of 300 percent in the "learning disabilities" category (Ortiz & Yates, 1983).

I have suggested that a major reason previous attempts at educational reform have been unsuccessful is that the relationships between teachers and students and between schools and communities have remained essentially unchanged. The required changes involve *personal redefinitions* of the way classroom teachers interact with the children and communities they serve. In other words, legislative and policy reforms may be necessary conditions for effective change, but they are not sufficient. Implementation of change is dependent upon the extent to which educators, both collectively and individually, redefine their roles with respect to minority students and communities.

The purpose of this paper is to propose a theoretical framework for examining the types of personal and institutional redefinitions that are required to reserve the pattern of minority student failure. The framework is based on a series of hypotheses regarding the nature of minority students' educational difficulties. These hypothe-

From Cummins, Jim, "Empowering Minority Students: A Framework for Intervention," *Harvard Educational Review*, 56:1, pp. 18–36. Copyright © 1986 by the President and Fellows of Harvard College. All rights reserved.

ses, in turn, lead to predictions regarding the probable effectiveness, or ineffectiveness, of various interventions directed at reversing minority students' school failure.

The framework assigns a central role to three inclusive sets of interactions or power relations: (1) the classroom interactions between teachers and students, (2) relationships between schools and minority communities, and (3) the intergroup power relations within the society as a whole. It assumes that the social organization and bureaucratic constraints within the school reflect not only broader policy and societal factors but also the extent to which *individual educators* accept or challenge the social organization of the school in relation to minority students and communities. Thus, this analysis sketches directions for change for policymakers at all levels of the educational hierarchy and, in particular, for those working directly with minority students and communities.

## THE POLICY CONTEXT

Research data from the United States, Canada, and Europe vary on the extent to which minority students experience academic failure (for reviews, see Cummins, 1984; Ogbu, 1978). For example, in the United States, Hispanic (with the exception of some groups of Cuban students), Native American, and black students do poorly in school compared to most groups of Asian-American (and white) students. In Canada, Franco-Ontarian students in English language programs have tended to perform considerably less well academically than immigrant minority groups (Cummins, 1984), while the same pattern characterizes Finnish students in Sweden (Skutnabb-Kangas, 1984).

The major task of theory and policy is to explain the pattern of school success and failure among minority students. This task applies both to students whose home language and culture differ from those of the school and wider society (language minority students) and to students whose home language is a version of English but whose cultural background is significantly different from that of the school and wider society, such as many black and Hispanic students from English language backgrounds. With respect to language-minority students, recent policy changes in the United States have been based on the assumption that a major cause of students' educational difficulty is the switch between the language of the home and the language of the school. Thus, the apparently plausible assumption that students cannot learn in a language they do not understand gave rise in the late sixties and early seventies to bilingual education programs in which students' home language was used in addition to English as an initial medium of school instruction (Schneider, 1976).

Bilingual programs, however, have met with both strong support and vehement opposition. The debate regarding policy has revolved around two intuitively appealing assumptions. Those who favor bilingual education argue that children cannot learn in a language they do not understand, and, therefore, L1 (first language) instruction is necessary to counteract the negative effects of a home/school linguistic mismatch. The opposition contends that bilingual education is illogical in its implication that less English instruction will lead to more English achievement. It makes more sense, the opponents argue, to provide language-minority students with maximum exposure to English.

Despite the apparent plausibility of each assumption, these two conventional wisdoms (the "linguistic mismatch" and "insufficient exposure" hypotheses) are each patently inadequate. The argument that language minority students fail primarily as a result of a home/school language switch is refuted by the success of many minority students whose instruction has been totally through a second language. Similarly, research in Canada has documented the effectiveness of "French immersion programs" in which English background (majority language) students are instructed largely through French in the early grades as a means of developing fluent bilingualism. In spite of the home/school language switch, students' first language (English) skills develop as well as those of students whose instruction has been totally through English. The fact that the first language has high status and is strongly reinforced in the wider society is usually seen as an important factor in the success of these immersion programs.[2]

The opposing "insufficient exposure" hypothesis, however, fares no better with respect to the research evidence. In fact, the results of virtually every bilingual program that has been evaluated during the past 50 years show either no relationship or a negative relationship between amount of school exposure to the majority language and academic achievement in that language (Baker & de Kanter, 1981; Cummins, 1983a, 1984; Skutnabb-Kangas, 1984). Evaluations of immersion programs for majority students show that students perform as well in English academic skills as comparison groups despite considerably less exposure to English in school. Exactly the same result is obtained for minority students. Promotion of the minority language entails no loss in the development of English academic skills. In other words, language minority students instructed through the minority language (for example, Spanish) for all or part of the school day perform as well in English academic skills as comparable students instructed totally through English.

These results have been interpreted in terms of the "interdependence hypothesis," which proposes that to the extent that instruction through a minority language is effective in developing academic proficiency in the minority language, transfer of this proficiency to the majority language will occur given adequate exposure and motivation to learn the majority language (Cummins, 1979, 1983a, 1984). The interdependence hypothesis is supported by a large body of research from bilingual program evaluations, studies of language use in the home, immigrant student language learning, correlational studies of L1–L2 (second language) relationships, and experimental studies of bilingual information processing (for reviews, see Cummins, 1984; McLaughlin, 1985).

It is not surprising that the two conventional wisdoms inadequately account for the research data, since each involves only a one-dimensional linguistic explanation. The variability of minority students' academic performance under different social and educational conditions indicates that many complex, interrelated factors are at work (Ogbu, 1978; Wong-Fillmore, 1983). In particular, sociological and anthropological research suggests that status and power relations between groups are an important part of any comprehensive account of minority students' school failure (Fishman, 1976; Ogbu, 1978; Paulston, 1980). In addition, a variety of factors related to educational quality and cultural mismatch also appear to be important in mediating minority students' academic progress (Wong-Fillmore, 1983). These factors have been integrated into the design of a theoretical framework that suggests the changes required to reverse minority student failure.

## A THEORETICAL FRAMEWORK

The central tenet of the framework is that students from "dominated" societal groups are "empowered" or "disabled" as a direct result of their interactions with educators in the schools. These interactions are mediated by the implicit or explicit role definitions that educators assume in relation to four institutional characteristics of schools. These characteristics reflect the extent to which (1) minority students' language and culture are incorporated into the school program; (2) minority community participation is encouraged as an integral component of children's education; (3) the pedagogy promotes intrinsic motivation on the part of students to use language actively in order to generate their own knowledge; and (4) professionals involved in assessment become advocates for minority students rather than legitimizing the location of the "problem" in the students. For each of these dimensions of school organization the role definitions of educators can be described in terms of a continuum, with one end promoting the empowerment of students and the other contributing to the disabling of students.

The three sets of relationships analyzed in the present framework—majority/minority societal group relations, school/minority community relations, educator/minority student relations—are chosen on the basis of hypotheses regarding the relative ineffectiveness of previous educational reforms and the directions required to reverse minority group school failure. Each of these relationships will be discussed in detail.

## INTERGROUP POWER RELATIONS

When the patterns of minority student school failure are examined from an international perspective, it becomes evident that power and status relations between minority and majority groups exert a major influence on school performance. An example frequently given is the academic failure of Finnish students in Sweden, where they are a low-status group, compared to their success in Australia, where they are regarded as a high-status group (Troike, 1978). Similarly, Ogbu (1978) reports that the outcast Burakumin perform poorly in Japan but as well as other Japanese students in the United States.

Theorists have explained these findings using several constructs. Cummins (1984), for example, discusses the "bicultural ambivalence" (or lack of cultural identification) of students in relation to both the home and school cultures. Ogbu (1978) discusses the "caste" status of minorities that fail academically and ascribes their failure to economic and social discrimination combined with the internalization of the inferior status attributed to them by the dominant group. Feuerstein (1979) attributes academic failure to the disruption of intergenerational transmission processes caused by the alienation of a group from its own culture. In all three conceptions, widespread school failure does not occur in minority groups that are positively oriented towards both their own and the dominant culture, that do not perceive themselves as inferior to the dominant group, and that are not alienated from their own cultural values.

Within the present framework, the *dominant* group controls the institutions and reward systems within society; the *dominated* group (Mullard, 1985) is regarded as inherently inferior by the dominant group and denied access to high-status positions within the institutional structure of the society. As described by Ogbu (1978), the dominated status of a minority group exposes them to conditions that predispose children to school failure even before they come to school. These conditions include limited parental access to economic and educational resources, ambivalence toward cultural transmission and primary language use in the home, and interactional styles that may not prepare students for typical teacher/student interaction patterns in school (Heath, 1983; Wong-Fillmore, 1983). Bicultural ambivalence and less effective cultural transmission among dominated groups are frequently associated with a historical pattern of colonization and subordination by the dominant group. This pattern, for example, characterizes Franco-Ontarian students in Canada, Finns in Sweden, and Hispanic, Native, and black groups in the United States.

Different patterns among other societal groups can clearly be distinguished (Ogbu & Matute-Bianchi, in press). Detailed analysis of patterns of intergroup relations go beyond the scope of this paper. However, it is important to note that the minority groups characterized by widespread school failure tend overwhelmingly to be in a dominated relationship to the majority group.[3]

## Empowerment of Students

Students who are empowered by their school experiences develop the ability, confidence, and motivation to succeed academically. They participate competently in instruction as a result of having developed a confident cultural identity as well as appropriate school-based knowledge and interactional structures (Cummins, 1983b; Tikunoff, 1983). Students who are disempowered or "disabled" by their school experiences do not develop this type of cognitive/academic and social/emotional foundation. Thus, student empowerment is regarded as both a mediating construct influencing academic performance and as an outcome variable itself.[4]

Although conceptually the cognitive/academic and social/emotional (identity-related) factors are distinct, the data suggest that they are extremely difficult to separate in the case of minority students who are "at risk" academically. For example, data from both Sweden and the United States suggest that minority students who immigrate relatively late (about ten years of age) often appear to have better academic prospects that students of similar socioeconomic status born in the host country (Cummins, 1984; Skutnabb-Kangas, 1984). Is this because their L1 cognitive/academic skills on arrival provide a better foundation for L2 cognitive/academic skills acquisition, or alternatively, because they have not experienced devaluation of their identity in the societal institutions, namely schools of the host country, as has been the case of students born in that setting?

Similarly, the most successful bilingual programs appear to be those that emphasize and use the students' L1 (for reviews, see Cummins 1983a, 1984). Is this success due to better promotion of L1 cognitive/academic skills or to the reinforcement of cultural identity provided by an intensive L1 program? By the same token, is the failure of many minority students in English-only immersion programs a function of cognitive/academic difficulties or of students' ambivalence about the value of their cultural identity (Cohen & Swain, 1976)?

These questions are clearly difficult to answer; the point to be made, however, is that for minority students who have traditionally experienced school failure, there is sufficient overlap in the impact of cognitive/academic and identity factors to justify incorporating these two dimensions within the notion of "student empowerment," while recognizing that under some conditions each dimension may be affected in different ways.

### *Schools and Power*

Minority students are disabled or disempowered by schools in very much the same way that their communities are disempowered by interactions with societal institutions. Since equality of opportunity is believed to be a given, it is assumed that individuals are responsible for their own failure and are, therefore, made to feel that they have failed because of their own inferiority, despite the best efforts of dominant-group institutions and individuals to help them (Skutnabb-Kangas, 1984). This analysis implies that minority students will succeed educationally to the extent that the patterns of interaction in school reverse those that prevail in the society at large.

Four structural elements in the organization of schooling contribute to the extent to which minority students are empowered or disabled. As outlined in Figure 7-1, these elements include the incorporation of minority students' culture and language, inclusion of minority communities in the education of their children, pedagogical assumptions and practices operating in the classroom, and the assessment of minority students.

## SOCIETAL CONTEXT

Dominant Group
|
↓
Dominated Group

## SCHOOL CONTEXT

Educator Role Definitions

| | | |
|---|---|---|
| Cultural/Linguistic Incorporation | Additive | — Subtractive |
| Community Participation | Collaborative | — Exclusionary |
| Pedagogy | Reciprocal Interaction-Oriented | — Transmission-Oriented |
| Assessment | Advocacy-Oriented | — Legitimization-Oriented |

Empowered Students    Disabled Students

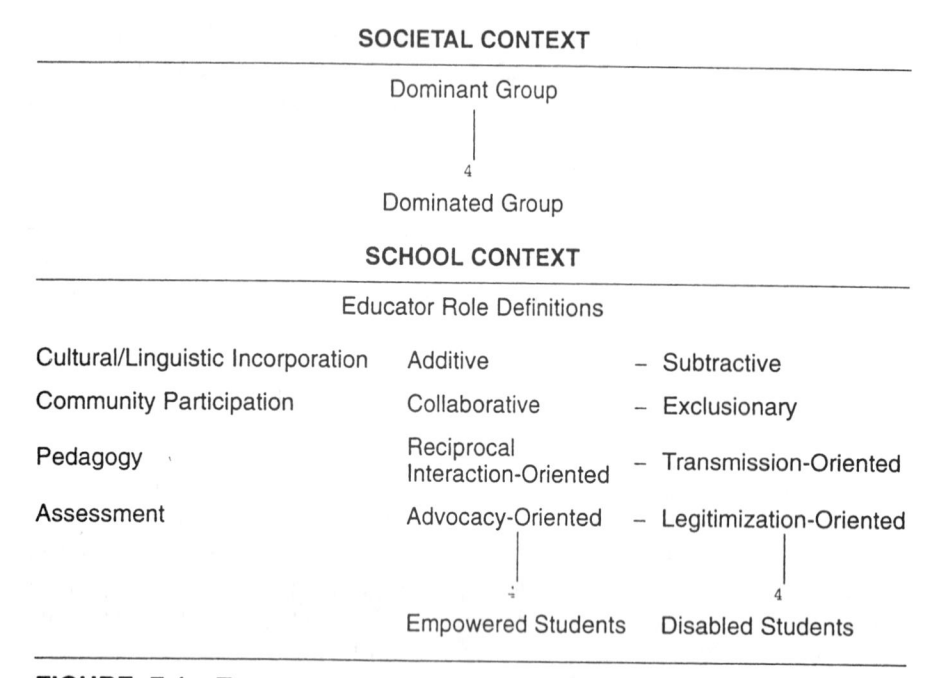

**FIGURE 7-1.** **Empowerment of Minority Students: A Theoretical Framework**

*Cultural/linguistic incorporation.* Considerable research data suggest that, for dominated minorities, the extent to which students' language and culture are incorporated into the school program constitutes a significant predictor of academic success (Campos & Keatinge, 1984; Cummins, 1983a; Rosier & Holm, 1980). As outlined earlier, students' school success appears to reflect both the more solid cognitive/academic foundation developed through intensive L1 instruction and the reinforcement of their cultural identity.

Included under incorporation of minority group cultural features is the adjustment of instructional patterns to take account of culturally conditioned learning styles. The Kamehameha Early Education Program in Hawaii provides strong evidence of the importance of this type of cultural incorporation. When reading instruction was changed to permit students to collaborate in discussing and interpreting texts, dramatic improvements were found in both reading and verbal intellectual abilities (Au & Jordan, 1981).

An important issue to consider at this point is why superficially plausible but patently inadequate assumptions, such as the "insufficient exposure" hypothesis, continue to dominate the policy debate when virtually all the evidence suggests that incorporation of minority students' language and culture into the school program will at least not impede academic progress. In other words, what social function do such arguments serve? Within the context of the present framework, it is suggested that a major reason for the vehement resistance to bilingual programs is that the incorporation of minority languages and cultures into the school program confers status and power (jobs, for example) on the minority group. Consequently, such programs contravene the established pattern of dominant/dominated group relations. Within democratic societies, however, contradictions between the rhetoric of equality and the reality of domination must be obscured. Thus, conventional wisdoms such as the insufficient exposure hypothesis become immune from critical scrutiny, and incompatible evidence is either ignored or dismissed.

Educators' role definitions in relation to the incorporation of minority students' language and culture can be characterized along an "additive-subtractive" dimension.[5] Educators who see their role as adding a second language and cultural affiliation to their students' repertoire are likely to empower students more than those who see their role as replacing or subtracting students' primary language and culture. In addition to the personal and future employment advantages of proficiency in two languages, there is considerable, though not conclusive, evidence that subtle educational advantages result from continued development of both languages among bilingual students. Enhanced metalinguistic development, for example, is frequently found in association with additive bilingualism (Hakuta & Diaz, 1985; McLaughlin, 1984).

It should be noted that an additive orientation does not require the actual teaching of the minority language. In many cases a minority language class may not be possible for reasons such as low concentration of particular groups of minority students. Educators, however, communicate to students and parents in a variety of ways the extent to which the minority language and culture are valued within the context of the school. Even within a monolingual school context, powerful messages can be communicated to students regarding the validity and advantages of language development.

*Community participation.* Students from dominated communities will be empowered in the school context to the extent that the communities themselves are empowered through their interactions with the school. When educators involve minority parents as partners in their children's education, parents appear to develop a sense of efficacy that communicates itself to children, with positive academic consequences.

Although lip service is paid to community involvement through Parent Advisory Committees (PAC)[6] in many education programs, these committees are frequently manipulated through misinformation and intimidation (Curtis, 1984). The result is that parents from dominated groups retain their powerless status, and their internalized inferiority is reinforced. Children's school failure can then be attributed to the combined effects of parental illiteracy and lack of interest in their children's education. In reality, most parents of minority students have high aspirations for their children and want to be involved in promoting their academic progress (Wong-Fillmore, 1983). However, they often do not know how to help their children academically, and they are excluded from participation by the school. In fact, even their interaction through L1 with their children in the home is frequently regarded by educators as contributing to academic difficulties (Cummins, 1984).

Dramatic changes in children's academic progress can be realized when educators take the initiative to change this exclusionary pattern to one of collaboration. The Haringey project in Britain illustrates just how powerful the effects of simple interventions can be (Tizard, Schofield, & Hewison, 1982). In order to assess the effects of parental involvement in the teaching of reading, the researchers established a project in the London borough of Haringey whereby all children in two primary level experimental classes in two different schools read to their parents at home on a regular basis. The reading progress of these children was compared with that of children in two classes in two different schools who were given extra reading instruction in small groups by an experienced and qualified teacher who worked four half-days at each school every week for the two years of the intervention. Both groups were also compared with a control group that received no treatment.

All the schools were in multiethnic areas, and there were many parents who did not read English or use it at home. It was found, nevertheless, to be both feasible and practicable to involve nearly all the parents in educational activities such as listening to their children read, even when the parents were nonliterate and largely non-English-speaking. It was also found that, almost without exception, parents welcomed the project, agreed to hear their children read, and completed a record card showing what had been read.

The researchers report that parental involvement had a pronounced effect on the students' success in school. Children who read to their parents made significantly greater progress in reading than those who did not engage in this type of literacy sharing. Small-group instruction in reading, given by a highly competent specialist, did not produce improvements comparable to those obtained from the collaboration with parents. In contrast to the home collaboration program, the benefits of extra reading instruction were least apparent for initially low-achieving children.

In addition, the collaboration between teachers and parents was effective for children of all initial levels of performance, including those who, at the beginning of the study, were failing in learning to read. Teachers reported that the children showed an increased interest in school learning and were better behaved. Those teachers involved in the home collaboration found the work with parents worthwhile, and they continued to involve parents with subsequent classes after the experiment was concluded. It is interesting to note that teachers of the control classes also adopted the home collaboration program after the two-year experimental period.

The Haringey project is one example of school/community relations; there are others. The essential point, however, is that the teacher's role in such relations can be characterized along a *collaborative-exclusionary* dimension. Teachers operating at the collaborative end of the continuum actively encourage minority parents to participate in promoting their children's academic progress both in the home and through involvement in classroom activities. A collaborative orientation may require a willingness on the part of the teacher to work closely with mother-tongue teachers or aides in order to communicate effectively, in a noncondescending way, with minority parents. Teachers with an exclusionary orientation, on the other hand, tend to regard teaching as *their* job and are likely to view collaboration with minority parents as either irrelevant or detrimental to children's progress.

*Pedagogy.* Several investigators have suggested that many "learning disabilities" are pedagogically induced in that children designated "at risk" frequently receive intensive instruction which confines them to a passive role and induces a form of "learned helplessness" (Beers & Beers, 1980; Coles, 1978; Cummins, 1984). This process is illustrated in a microethnographic study of fourteen reading lessons given to West Indian Creole-speakers of English in Toronto, Canada (Ramphal, 1983). It was found that teachers' constant correction of students' miscues prevented students from focusing on the meaning of what they were reading. Moreover, the constant corrections fostered dependent behavior because students knew that whenever they paused at a word the teacher would automatically pronounce it for them. One student was interrupted so often in one of the lessons that he was able to read only one sentence, consisting of three words, uninterrupted. In contrast to a pattern of classroom interaction which promotes instructional dependence, teaching that empowers will aim to liberate students from instruction by encouraging them to become active generators of their knowledge. As Graves (1983) has demonstrated, this type of active knowledge generation can occur when, for example, children create and publish their own books within the classroom.

Two major pedagogical orientations can be distinguished. These differ in the extent to which the teacher retains exclusive control over the classroom interaction as opposed to sharing some of this control with students. The dominant instructional model in North American schools has been termed a transmission model (Barnes, 1976; Wells, 1982). This model incorporates essentially the same assumptions about teaching and learning that Freire (1970, 1973) has termed a "banking" model of education. This transmission model will be contrasted with a "reciprocal interaction" model of pedagogy.

The basic premise of the transmission model is that the teacher's task is to impart knowledge or skills that she or he possesses to students who do not yet have these skills. This implies that the teacher initiates and controls the interaction, constantly orienting it towards the achievement of instructional objectives. For example, in first- and second-language programs that stress pattern repetition, the teacher presents the materials, models the language patterns, asks questions, and provides feedback to students about the correctness of their response. The curriculum in these types of programs focuses on the internal structure of the language or subject matter. Consequently, it frequently focuses predominantly on surface features of language or literacy such as handwriting, spelling, and decoding, and emphasizes correct recall of content taught by means of highly structured drills and workbook exercises. It has been argued that a transmission model of teaching contravenes central principles of language and literacy acquisition and that a model allowing for reciprocal interaction among students and teachers represents a more appropriate alternative (Cummins, 1984; Wells, 1982).[7]

A central tenet of the reciprocal interaction model is that "talking and writing are means to learning" (Bullock Report, 1975, p. 50). The use of this model in teaching requires a genuine dialogue between student and teacher in both oral and written modalities, guidance and facilitation rather than control of student learning by the teacher, and the encouragement of student/student talk in a collaborative learning context. This model emphasizes the development of higher level cognitive skills rather than just factual recall, and meaningful language use by students rather than the correction of surface forms. Language use and development are consciously integrated with all curricular content rather than taught as isolated subjects, and tasks are presented to students in ways that generate intrinsic rather than extrinsic motivation. In short, pedagogical approaches that empower students encourage them to assume greater control over setting their own learning goals and to collaborate actively with each other in achieving these goals.

The development of a sense of efficacy and inner direction in the classroom is especially important for students from dominated groups whose experiences so often orient them in the opposite direction. Wong-Fillmore (1983) has reported that Hispanic students learned considerably more English in classrooms that provided opportunities for reciprocal interaction with teachers and peers. Ample opportunities for expressive writing appear to be particularly significant in promoting a sense of academic efficacy among minority students (Cummins, Aguilar, Bascunan, Fiorucci, Sanaoui, & Basman, in press). As expressed by Daiute (1985):

> *Children who learn early that writing is not simply an exercise gain a sense of power that gives them confidence to write—and write a lot.... Beginning writers who are confident that they have something to say or that they can find out what they need to know can even overcome some limits of training or development. Writers who don't feel that what they say matters have an additional burden that no skills training can help them overcome.* (pp. 5–6)

The implications for students from dominated groups are obvious. Too often the instruction they receive convinces them that what they have to say is irrelevant or wrong. The failure of this method of instruction is then taken as an indication that the minority student is of low ability, a verdict frequently confirmed by subsequent assessment procedures.

*Assessment.* Historically, assessment has played the role of legitimizing the disabling of minority students. In some cases assessment itself may play the primary role, but more often it has been used to locate the "problem" within the minority student, thereby screening from critical scrutiny the subtractive nature of the school program, the exclusionary orientation of teachers towards minority communities, and transmission models of teaching that inhibit students from active participation in learning.

This process is virtually inevitable when the conceptual base for assessment is purely psychoeducational. If the psychologist's task is to discover the causes of a minority student's academic difficulties and the only tools at his or her disposal are psychological tests (in either L1 or L2), then it is hardly surprising that the child's difficulties will be attributed to psychological dysfunctions. The myth of bilingual handicaps that still influences educational policy was generated in exactly this way during the 1920s and 1930s.

Recent studies suggest that despite the appearance of change brought about by PL94-142, the underlying structure of assessment processes has remained essentially intact. Mehan, Hertweck, and Meihls (in press), for example, report that psychologists continued to test children until they "found" the disability that could be invoked to "explain" the student's apparent academic difficulties. Diagnosis and placement were influenced frequently by factors related to bureaucratic procedures and funding requirements rather than to students' academic performance in the classroom. Rueda and Mercer (1985) have also shown that designation of minority students as "learning disabled" as compared to "language impaired" was strongly influenced by whether a psychologist or a speech pathologist was on the placement committee. In other words, with respect to students' actual behavior, the label was essentially arbitrary. An analysis of more than four hundred psychological assessments of minority students revealed that although no diagnostic conclusions were logically possible in the majority of assessments, psychologists were most reluctant to admit this fact to teachers and parents (Cummins, 1984). In short, the data suggest that the structure within which psychological assessment takes place orients the psychologist to locate the cause of the academic problem within the minority student.

An alternative role definition for psychologists or special educators can be termed an "advocacy" or "delegitimization" role.[8] In this case, their task must be to delegitimize the traditional function of psychological assessment in the educational disabling of minority students by becoming advocates for the child in scrutinizing critically the societal and educational context within which the child has developed (Cazden, 1985). This involves locating the pathology within the societal power relations between dominant and dominated groups, in the reflection of these power relations between school and communities, and in the mental and cultural disabling of minority students that takes place in classrooms. These conditions are a more probable cause of the 300 percent overrepresentation of Texas Hispanic students in the learning disabled category than any intrinsic processing deficit unique to Hispanic children. The training of psychologists and special educators does not prepare them for this advocacy or delegitimization role. From the present perspective, however, it must be emphasized that discriminatory assessment is carried out by well-intentioned individuals who, rather than challenging a socioeducational system that tends to disable minority students, have accepted a role definition and an educational structure that makes discriminatory assessment virtually inevitable.[9]

## EMPOWERING MINORITY STUDENTS: THE CARPINTERIA EXAMPLE

The Spanish-only preschool program of the Carpinteria School District, near Santa Barbara, California, is one of the few programs in the United States that explicitly incorporates the major elements hypothesized in previous sections to empower minority students. Spanish is the exclusive language of instruction, there is a strong community involvement component, and the program is characterized by a coherent philosophy of promoting conceptual development through meaningful linguistic interaction.

The proposal to implement an intensive Spanish-only preschool program in this region was derived from district findings showing that a large majority of the Spanish-speaking students entering kindergarten each year lacked adequate skills to succeed in the kindergarten program. On the School Readiness Inventory, a districtwide screening measure administered to all incoming kindergarten students, Spanish-speaking students tended to average about eight points lower than English-speaking students (approximately 14.5 compared to 23.0, averaged over four years from 1979 to 1982) despite the fact that the test was administered in students' dominant language. A score of 20 or better was viewed by the district as predicting a successful kindergarten year for the child. Prior to the implementation of the experimental program, the Spanish-background children attended a bilingual preschool program—operated either by Head Start or the Community Day Care Center—in which both English and Spanish were used concurrently but with strong emphasis on the development of English skills. According to the district kindergarten teachers, children who had attended these programs often mixed English and Spanish into a "Spanglish."

The major goal of the experimental Spanish-only preschool program was to bring Spanish-dominant children entering kindergarten up to a level of readiness for school similar to that attained by English-speaking children in the community. The project also sought to make parents of the program participants aware of their role as the child's first teacher and to encourage them to provide specific types of experiences for their children in the home.

The preschool program itself involved the integration of language with a large variety of concrete and literacy-related experiences. As summarized in the evaluation report: "The development of language skills in Spanish was foremost in the planning and attention given to every facet of the pre-school day. Language was used constantly for conversing, learning new ideas, concepts and vocabulary, thinking creatively, and problem-solving to give the children the opportunity to develop their language skills in Spanish to as high a degree as possible within the structure of the pre-school day" (Campos & Keatinge, 1984, p. 17).

Participation in the program was on a voluntary basis and students were screened only for age and Spanish-language dominance. Family characteristics of students in the experimental program were typical of other Spanish-speaking families in the community; more than 90 percent were of low socioeconomic status, and the majority worked in agriculture and had an average education level of about sixth grade.

The program proved to be highly successful in developing students' readiness skills, as evidence by the average score of 21.6 obtained by the 1982–83 incoming kindergarten students who had been in the program, compared to the score of 23.2 obtained by English-speaking students. A score of 14.6 was obtained by Spanish-speaking students who experienced the regular bilingual preschool program. In 1983–84 the scores of these groups were 23.3, 23.4, and 16.0, respectively. In other words, the gap between English-background and Spanish-background children in the Spanish-only preschool had disappeared; however, a considerable gap remained for Spanish-background students for whom English was the focus of preschool instruction.

Of special interest is the performance of the experimental program students on the English and Spanish versions of the Bilingual Syntax Measure (BSM), a test or oral syntactic development (Hernandez-Chavez, Burt, & Dulay, 1976). Despite the fact that they experienced an exclusively Spanish preschool program, these students performed better than the other Spanish-speaking students in English (and Spanish) on entry to kindergarten in 1982 and at a similar level in 1983. On entrance to grade one in 1983, the gap had widened considerably, with almost five times as many of the experimental-program students performing at level 5 (fluent English) compared to the other Spanish-background students (47 percent vs. 10 percent) (Campos & Keatinge, 1984).

The evaluation report suggests that

> *although project participants were exposed to less* total *English, they, because of their enhanced first language skill and concept knowledge were better able to comprehend the English they were exposed to. This seems to be borne out by comments made by kindergarten teachers in the District about project participants. They are making comments like, "Project participants appear more aware of what is happening around them in the classroom," "They are able to focus on the task at hand better" and "They demonstrated greater self-confidence in learning situations." All of these traits would tend to enhance the language acquisition process. (Campos & Keatinge, 1984, p. 41)*

Campos and Keatinge (1984) also emphasize the consequences of the preschool program for parental participation in their children's education. They note that, according to the school officials, "the parents of project participants are much more aware of and involved in their child's school experience than non-participant parents of Spanish speakers. This is seen as having a positive impact on the future success of the project participants—the greater the involvement of parents, the greater the chances of success of the child" (p. 41).

The major relevance of these findings for educators and policymakers derives from their demonstration that educational programs *can* succeed in preventing the academic failure experienced by many minority students. The corollary is that failure to provide this type of program constitutes the disabling of minority students by the school system. For example, among the students who did not experience the experimental preschool program, the typical pattern of low levels of academic readiness and limited proficiency in both languages was observed. These are the students who are likely to be referred for psychological assessment early in their school careers. This assessment will typically legitimize the inadequate educational provision by attributing students' difficulties to some vacuous category, such as learning disability. By contrast, students who experienced a preschool program in which (a) their cultural identity was reinforced, (b) there was active collaboration with parents, and (c) meaningful use of language was integrated into every aspect of daily activities were developing high levels of conceptual and linguistic skills in *both* languages.

## CONCLUSION

In this article I have proposed a theoretical framework for examining minority students' academic failure and for predicting the effects of educational interventions. Within this framework the educational failure of minority students is analyzed as a function of the extent to which schools reflect or counteract the power relations that exist within the broader society. Specifically, language-minority students' educational progress is strongly influenced by the extent to which individual educators become advocates for the promotion of students' linguistic talents, actively encourage community participation in developing students' academic and cultural resources, and implement pedagogical approaches that succeed in liberating students from instructional dependence.

The educator/student interactions characteristic of the disabling end of the proposed continua reflect the typical patterns of interaction that dominated societal groups have experienced in relation to dominant groups. The intrinsic value of the group is usually denied, and "objective" evidence is accumulated to demonstrate the group's "inferiority." This inferior status is then used as a justification for excluding the group from activities and occupations that entail societal rewards.

In a similar way, the disabling of students is frequently rationalized on the basis of students' "needs." For example, minority students need maximum exposure to English in both the school and home; thus, parents must be told not to interact with children in the mother tongue. Similarly, minority children need a highly structured drill-oriented program in order to maximize time spent on tasks to compensate for their deficient preschool experiences. Minority students also need a comprehensive diagnostic/prescriptive assessment in order to identify the nature of their "problem" and possible remedial interventions.

This analysis suggests a major reason for the relative lack of success of the various educational bandwagons that have characterized the North American crusade against underachievement during the past twenty years. The individual role definitions of educators and the institutional role definitions of schools have remained largely unchanged despite "new and improved" programs and policies. These programs and policies, despite their cost, have simply added a new veneer to the outward facade of the structure that disables minority students. The lip service paid to initial L1 instruction, community involvement, and nondiscriminatory assessment, together with the emphasis on improved teaching techniques, have succeeded primarily in deflecting attention from the attitudes and orientation of educators who interact on a daily basis with minority students. It is in these interactions that students are disabled. In the absence of individual and collective educator role redefinitions, schools will continue to reproduce, in these interactions, the power relations that characterize the wider society and make minority students' academic failure inevitable.

To educators genuinely concerned about alleviating the educational difficulties of minority students and responding to their needs, this conclusion may appear overly bleak. I believe, however, that it is realistic and optimistic, as directions for change are clearly indicated rather than obscured by the overlay of costly reforms that leave the underlying disabling structure essentially intact. Given the societal commitment to maintaining the dominant/dominated power relationships, we can predict that educational changes threatening this structure will be fiercely resisted. This is in fact the case for each of the four structural dimensions discussed earlier.[10]

In order to reverse the pattern of widespread minority group educational failure, educators and policymakers are faced with both a personal and a political challenge. Personally, they must redefine their roles within the classroom, the community, and the broader society so that these role definitions result in interactions that empower rather than disable students. Politically, they must attempt to persuade colleagues and decisionmakers—such as school boards and the public that elects them—of the importance of redefining institutional goals so that the schools transform society by empowering minority students rather than reflect society by disabling them.

## ENDNOTES

**1.** The Education of All Handicapped Children Act of 1975 (Public Law 94-142) guarantees to all handicapped children in the United States the right to a free public education, to an individualized education program (IEP), to due process, to education in the least segregated environment, and to assessment procedures that are multidimensional and nonculturally discriminatory.

**2.** For a discussion of the implications of Canadian French immersion programs for the education of minority students, see California State Department of Education (1984).

**3.** Ogbu (1978), for example, has distinguished between "caste," "immigrant," and "autonomous" minority groups. Caste groups are similar to what has been termed "dominated" groups in the present framework and are the only category of minority groups that tends to fail academically. Immigrant groups have usually come voluntarily to the host society for economic reasons and, unlike caste minorities, have not internalized negative attributions of the dominant group. Ogbu gives Chinese and Japanese groups as examples of "immigrant" minorities. The cultural resources that permit some minority groups to resist discrimination and internalization of negative attributions are still a matter of debate and speculation (for a recent treatment, see Ogbu & Bianchi, in press). The final category distinguished by Ogbu is that of "autonomous" groups who hold a distinct cultural identity but who are not subordinated economically or politically to the dominant group (for example, Jews and Mormons in the United States).

Failure to take account of these differences among minority groups both in patterns of academic performance and sociohistorical relationships to the dominant group has contributed to the confused state of policymaking with respect to language minority students. The bilingual education policy, for example, has been based on the implicit assumption that the linguistic mismatch hypothesis was valid for all language minority students, and, consequently, the same types of intervention were necessary and appropriate for all students. Clearly, this assumption is open to question.

**4.** There is no contradiction in postulating student empowerment as both a mediating and an outcome variable. For example, cognitive abilities clearly have the same status in that they contribute to students' school success and can also be regarded as an outcome of schooling.

**5.** The terms "additive" and "subtractive" bilingualism were coined by Lambert (1975) to refer to the proficient bilingualism associated with positive cognitive outcomes on the one hand, and the limited bilingualism often associated with negative outcomes on the other.

**6.** PACs were established in some states to provide an institutional structure for minority parent involvement in educational decision making with respect to bilingual programs. In California, for example, a majority of PAC members for any state-funded program was required to be from the program target group. The school plan for use of program funds required signed PAC approval.

**7.** This "reciprocal interaction" model incorporates proposals about the relation between language and learning made by a variety of investigators, most notably in the Bullock Report (1975), and by Barnes (1976), Lindfors (1980), and Wells (1982). Its application with respect to the promotion of literacy conforms closely to psycholinguistic approaches to reading (Goodman & Goodman, 1977; Holdaway, 1979; Smith, 1978) and to the recent emphasis on encouraging expressive writing from the earliest grades (Chomsky, 1981; Giacobbe, 1982; Graves, 1983; Temple, Nathan, & Burris, 1982). Students' microcomputing networks such as the *Computer Chronicles Newswire* (Mehan, Miller-Souviney, & Riel, 1984) represent a particularly promising application of reciprocal interaction model of pedagogy.

**8.** See Mullard (1985) for a detailed discussion of delegitimization strategies in antiracist education.

**9.** Clearly, the presence of processing difficulties that are rooted in neurological causes is not being denied for either monolingual or bilingual children. However, in the case of children from dominated minorities, the proportion of disabilities that are neurological in origin is likely to represent only a small fraction of those that derive from educational and social conditions.

**10.** Although for pedagogy the resistance to sharing control with students goes beyond majority/minority group relations, the same elements are present. If the curriculum is not predetermined and presequenced, and the students are generating their own knowledge in a critical and creative way, then the reproduction of the societal structure cannot be guaranteed—hence the reluctance to liberate students from instructional dependence.

## REFERENCES

Au, K.H., & Jordan, C. (1981). Teaching reading to Hawaiian children: Finding a culturally appropriate solution. In H. Trueba, G.P. Guthrie, & K.H. Au (Eds.) *Culture and the bilingual classroom: Studies in classroom ethnography* (pp. 139–152). Rowley, MA: Newbury House.

Baker, K.A., & de Kanter, A.A. (1981). *Effectiveness of bilingual education: A review of the literature.* Washington, DC: U.S. Department of Education, Office of Planning and Budget.

Barnes, D. (1976). *From communication to curriculum.* New York: Penguin.

Beers, C.S., & Beers, J.W. (1980). Early identification of learning disabilities: Facts and fallacies. *Elementary School Journal,* 81, 67–76.

Bethell, T. (1979, February). Against bilingual education. *Harper's,* pp. 30–33.

Bullock Report. (1975). *A language for life.* [Report of the Committee of Inquiry appointed by the Secretary of State for Education and Science under the Chairmanship of Sir Alan Bullock]. London: HMSO.

California State Department of Education. (1984). *Studies on immersion education: A collection for United States educators.* Sacramento: Author.

Campos, J., & Keatinge, B. (1984). *The Carpinteria preschool program: Title VII second year evaluation report.* Washington, DC: Department of Education.

Cazden, C.B (1985, April). *The ESL teacher as advocate.* Plenary presentation to the TESOL Conference, New York.

Chomsky, C. (1981). Write now, read later. In C. Cazden (Ed.), *Language in Early Childhood Education* (2nd ed., pp. 141–149). Washington, DC: National Association for the Education of Young Children.

Cohen, A.D., & Swain, M. (1976). Bilingual education: The immersion model in the North American context. In J.E. Alatis & K. Twaddell (Eds.), *English as a second language in bilingual education* (pp. 55–64). Washington, DC: TESOL.

Coles, G.S. (1978). The learning disabilities test battery: Empirical and social issues. *Harvard Educational Review,* 48, 313–340.

Cummins, J. (1979). Linguistic interdependence and the educational development of bilingual children. *Review of Educational Research,* 49, 222–251.

Cummins, J. (1983a). *Heritage language education: A literature review.* Toronto: Ministry of Education.

Cummins, J. (1983b). Functional language proficiency in context: Classroom participation as an interactive process. In W.J. Tikunoff (Ed.), *Compatibility of the SBIS features with other research on instruction for LEP students* (pp. 109–131). San Francisco: Far West Laboratory.

Cummins, J. (1984). *Bilingualism and special education: Issues in assessment and pedagogy.* Clevedon, Eng.: Multilingual Matters, and San Diego: College Hill Press.

Cummins, J., Aguilar, M., Bascunan, L., Fiorucci, S., Sanaoui, R., & Basman, S. (in press). *Literacy development in heritage language programs.* Toronto: National Heritage Language Resource Unit.

Curtis, J. (1984). *Bilingual education in Calistoga: Not a happy ending.* Report submitted to the Instituto de Lengua y Cultura, Elmira, NY.

Daiute, C. (1985). *Writing and computers.* Reading, MA: Addison-Wesley.

Feuerstein, R. (1979). *The dynamic assessment of retarded performers: The learning potential assessment device, theory, instrument, and techniques.* Baltimore: University Park Press.

Fishman, J. (1976). *Bilingual education: An international sociological perspective.* Rowley, MA: Newbury House.

Freire, P. (1970). *Pedagogy of the oppressed.* New York: Seabury.

Freire, P. (1973). *Education for critical consciousness.* New York: Seabury.

Giacobbe, M.E. (1982). Who says children can't write the first week?, In R.D. Walshe (Ed.), *Donald Graves in Australia: "Children want to write"* (pp. 99–103). Exeter, NH: Heinemann Educational Books.

Goodman, K.S., & Goodman, Y.M. (1977). Learning about psycholinguistic processes by analyzing oral reading. *Harvard Educational Review,* 47, 317–333.

Graves, D.H. (1983). *Writing: Teachers and children at work.* Exeter, NH: Heinemann Educational Books.

Hakuta, K., & Diaz, R.M. (1985). The relationship between degree of bilingualism and cognitive ability: A critical discussion and some new longitudinal data. In K.E. Nelson (Ed.), *Children's language* (Vol. 5, pp. 319–345). Hillsdale, NJ: Erlbaum.

Heath, S.B. (1983). *Ways with words.* Cambridge: Cambridge University Press.

Hernandez-Chavez, E., Burt, M., & Dulay, H. (1976). *The bilingual syntax measure.* New York: The Psychological Corporation.

Holdaway, D. (1979). *The foundations of literacy.* Sydney, Australia: Ashton Scholastic.

Jusenius, C., & Duarte, V.L. (1982). *Hispanics and jobs: Barriers to progress.* Washington, DC: National Commission for Employment Policy.

Lambert, W.E. (1975). Culture and language as factors in learning and education. In A. Wolfgang (Ed.), *Education of immigrant students* (pp. 55–83). Toronto: O.I.S.E.

Lindfors, J.W. (1980). *Children's language and learning.* (Englewood Cliffs, NJ: Prentice-Hall.

McLaughlin, B. (1984). Early bilingualism: Methodological and theoretical issues. In M. Paradis & Y. Lebrun (Eds.), *Early bilingualism and child development* (pp. 19–46). Lisse: Swets & Zeitlinger.

McLaughlin, B. (1985). *Second language acquisition in childhood: Vol. 2. School-age children.* Hillsdale, NJ: Erlbaum.

Mehan, H., Hertweck, A., & Meihls, J.L. (in press). *Handicapping the handicapped: Decision making in students' educational careers.* Palo Alto: Stanford University.

Mehan, H., Miller-Souviney, B., & Riel, M.M. (1984). Research currents: Knowledge of text editing and control of literacy skills. *Language Arts,* 65, 154–159.

Mullard, C. (1985, January). *The social dynamic of migrant groups: From progressive to transformative policy in education.* Paper presented at the OECD Conference on Educational Policies and the Minority Social Groups, Paris.

Ogbu, J.U. (1978). *Minority education and caste.* New York: Academic Press.

Ogbu, J.U., & Matute-Bianchi, M.E. (in press). Understanding sociocultural factors: Knowledge, identity and school adjustment. In California State Department of Education (Ed.), *Sociocultural factors and minority student achievement.* Sacramento: Author.

Ortiz, A.A., & Yates, J.R. (1983). Incidence of exceptionality among Hispanics: Implications for manpower planning. *NABE Journal,* 7, 41–54.

Paulston, C.B. (1980). *Bilingual education: Theories and issues.* Rowley, MA: Newbury House.

Ramphal, D.K. *An analysis of reading instruction of West Indian Creole-speaking students.* Unpublished doctoral dissertation, Ontario Institute for Studies in Education, 1983.

Rosier, P., & Holm, W. (1980). *The Rock Point experience: A longitudinal study of a Navajo school.* Washington, DC: Center for Applied Linguistics.

Rueda, R., Mercer, J.R. (1985, June). *Predictive analysis of decision making with language-minority handicapped children.* Paper presented at the BUENO Center 3rd Annual Symposium on Bilingual Education, Denver.

Schneider, S.G. (1976). *Revolution, reaction or reform: The 1974 Bilingual Education Act.* New York: Las Americas.

Skutnabb-Kangas, T. (1984). *Bilingualism or not: The education of minorities.* Clevedon, Eng.: Multilingual Matters.

Smith, F. (1978). *Understanding reading* (2nd ed.). New York: Holt, Rinehart & Winston.

Temple, C.A., Nathan, R.G. & Burris, N.A. (1982). *The beginnings of writing.* Boston: Allyn & Bacon.

Tikunoff, W.J. (1983). Five significant bilingual instructional features. In W.J. Tikunoff (Ed.), *Compatibility of the SBIS features with other research on instruction for LEP students* (pp. 5–18). San Francisco: Far West Laboratory.

Tizard, J., Schofield, W.N., & Hewison, J. (1982). Collaboration between teachers and parents in assisting children's reading. *British Journal of Educational Psychology,* 52, 1–15.

Troike, R. (1978). Research evidence for the effectiveness of bilingual education. *NABE Journal,* 3, 13–24.

Wells, G. (1982). Language, learning and the curriculum. In G. Wells, (Ed.). *Language, learning and education* (pp. 205–226). Bristol: Centre for the Study of Language and Communication, University of Bristol.

Wong-Fillmore, L. (1983). The language learner as an individual: Implications of research on individual differences for the ESL teacher. In M.A. Clarke & J. Handscombe (Eds.), *On TESOL '82: Pacific perspectives on language learning and teaching* (pp. 157–171). Washington, DC: TESOL.

# CHAPTER 18

# Social Class and the Hidden Curriculum of Work

JEAN ANYON

Scholars in political economy and the sociology of knowledge have recently argued that public schools in complex industrial societies like our own make available different types of educational experience and curriculum knowledge to students in different social classes. Bowles and Gintis (1976), for example, have argued that students from different social class backgrounds are rewarded for classroom behaviors that correspond to personality traits allegedly rewarded in the different occupational strata—the working classes for docility and obedience, the managerial classes for initiative and personal assertiveness. Basil Bernstein (1977), Pierre Bourdieu (Bourdieu and Passeron 1977), and Michael W. Apple (1979), focusing on school knowledge, have argued that knowledge and skills leading to social power and reward (e.g., medical, legal, managerial) are made available to the advantaged social groups but are withheld from the working classes, to whom a more "practical" curriculum is offered (e.g., manual skills, clerical knowledge). While there has been considerable argumentation of these points regarding education in England, France, and North America, there has been little or no attempt to investigate these ideas empirically in elementary or secondary schools and classrooms in this country.[1]

This article offers tentative empirical support (and qualification) of the above arguments by providing illustrative examples of differences in student work in classrooms in contrasting social class communities. The examples were gathered as part of an ethnographical study of curricular, pedagogical and pupil evaluation practices in five elementary schools. The article attempts a theoretical contribution as well, and assesses student work in the light of a theoretical approach to social class analysis. The organization is as follows: the methodology of the ethnographi-

Reprinted from *Journal of Education*, 162:67–92, 1980, by permission of the publisher and the author.

Jean Anyon is an Associate Professor and Chair of the Education Department of Rutgers University.

cal study is briefly described; a theoretical approach to the definition of social class is offered; income and other characteristics of the parents in each school are provided, and examples from the study that illustrate work tasks and interaction in each school are presented; then the concepts used to define social class are applied to the examples in order to assess the theoretical meaning of classroom events. It will be suggested that there is a "hidden curriculum" in school work that has profound implications for the theory—and consequence—of everyday activity in education.

## METHODOLOGY

The methods used to gather data were classroom observation; interviews of students, teachers, principals, and district administrative staff; and assessment of curriculum and other materials in each classroom and school. All classroom events to be discussed here involve the fifth grade in each school. All schools but one departmentalize at the fifth grade level. Except for that school where only one fifth grade teacher could be observed, all the fifth grade teachers (that is, two or three) were observed as the children moved from subject to subject. In all schools the art, music, and gym teachers were also observed and interviewed. All teachers in the study were described as "good" or "excellent" by their principals. All except one new teacher had taught for more than four years. The fifth grade in each school was observed by the investigator for ten three-hour periods between September 15, 1978 and June 20, 1979.

Before providing the occupations, incomes, and other relevant social characteristics of the parents of the children in each school, I will offer a theoretical approach to defining social class.

## SOCIAL CLASS

One's occupation and income level contribute significantly to one's social class, but they do not define it. Rather, social class is a series of relationships. A person's social class is defined here by the way that person relates to the process in society by which goods, services, and culture are produced.[2] One relates to several aspects of the production process primarily through one's work. One has a relationship to the system of ownership, to other people (at work and in society) and to the content and process of one's own productive activity. One's relationship to all three of these aspects of production determines one's social class; that is, all three relationships are necessary and none is sufficient for determining a person's relation to the process of production in society.

*Ownership Relations.* In a capitalist society, a person has a relation to the system of private ownership of capital. Capital is usually thought of as being derived from physical property. In this sense capital is property which is used to produce profit, interest, or rent in sufficient quantity so that the result can be used to produce more profit, interest, or rent—that is, more capital. Physical capital may be derived from money, stocks, machines, land, or the labor of workers (whose labor, for instance, may produce products that are sold by others for profit). Capital, however, can also be symbolic. It can be the socially legitimated knowledge of how the production process works, its financial, managerial, technical, or other "secrets." Symbolic capital can also be socially legitimated skills—cognitive (e.g., analytical), linguistic, or technical skills that provide the ability to, say, produce the dominant scientific, artistic, and other culture, or to manage the systems of industrial and cultural production. Skillful application of symbolic capital may yield social and cultural power, and perhaps physical capital as well.

The ownership relation that is definitive for social class is one's relation to physical capital. The first such relationship is that of capitalist. To be a member of the capitalist class in the present-day United States, one must participate in the ownership of the apparatus of production in society. The number of such persons is relatively small: while one person in ten owns some stock, for example, a mere 1.6 percent of the population owns 82.2 percent of *all* stock, and the wealthiest one-fifth owns almost all the rest (see New York Stock Exchange, 1975; Smith and Franklin, 1974; Lampman, 1962).

At the opposite pole of this relationship is the worker. To be in the United States working class a person will not ordinarily own physical capital; to the contrary, his or her work will be wage or salaried labor that is either a *source* of profit (i.e., capital) to others, or that makes it possible for others to *realize* profit. Examples of the latter are *white*-collar clerical workers in industry and distribution (office and sales) as well as the wage and salaried workers in the institutions of social and economic legitimation and service (e.g., in state education and welfare institutions).[3] According to the criteria to be developed here, the number of persons who presently comprise the working class in the United States is between 50 percent and 60 percent of the population (see also Wright, 1978; Braverman, 1974; Levison, 1974).

In between the defining relationship of capitalist and worker are the middle classes, whose relationship to the process of production is less clear, and whose relationship may indeed exhibit contradictory characteristics. For example, social service employees have a somewhat contradictory relationship to the process of production because, although their income may be at middle-class levels, some characteristics of their work are working-class (e.g., they may have very little control over their work). Analogously, there are persons at the upper income end of the middle class, such as upper-middle-class professionals, who may own quantities of stocks and will therefore share characteristics of the capitalist class. As the next criterion to be discussed makes clear, however, to be a member of the present-day capitalist in the United States, one must also participate in the social *control* of this capital.

*Relationships Between People.* The second relationship which contributes to one's social class is the relation one has to authority and control at work and in society.[4] One characteristic of most working-class jobs is that there is no built-in mechanism by which the worker can control the content, process or speed of work. Legitimate decision making is vested in personnel supervisors, in middle or upper management, or, as in an increasing number of white-collar working-class (and most middle-class) jobs, by bureaucratic rule and regulation. For upper-middle-class professional groups there is an increased amount of autonomy regarding work. Moreover, in middle- and upper-middle-class positions there is an increasing chance that one's work would also involve supervising the work of others. A capitalist is defined within these relations of control in an enterprise by having a position which participates in the direct control of the entire enterprise. Capitalists do not directly control workers in physical production and do not directly control ideas in the sphere of cultural production. However, more crucial to control, capitalists make the decisions over how resources are used (e.g., where money is invested) and how profit is allocated.

*Relations Between People and Their Work.* The third criterion which contributes to a person's social class is the relationship between that person and his or her own productive activity—the type of activity that constitutes his or her work. A working-class job is often characterized by work that is routine and mechanical and that is a small, fragmented part of a larger process with which workers are not usually acquainted. These working-class jobs are usually blue-collar, manual labor. A few skilled jobs such as plumbing and printing are not mechanical, however, and an increasing number of working-class jobs are *white*-collar. These white-collar jobs, such as clerical work, may involve work that necessitates a measure of planning and decision making, but one still has no built-in control over the content. The work of some middle- and most upper-middle-class managerial and professional groups is likely to involve the need for conceptualization and creativity, with many professional jobs demanding one's full creative capacities. Finally, the work that characterizes the capitalist position is that this work is almost entirely a matter of conceptualization (e.g., planning and laying-out) that has as its object management and control of the enterprise.

One's social class, then, is a result of the relationships one has, largely through one's work, to physical capital and its power, to other people at work and in society, and to one's own productive activity. Social class is a lived, developing process. It is not an abstract category, and it is not a fixed, inherited position (although one's family background is, of course, important). Social class is perceived as a complex of social relations that one develops as one grows up—as one acquires and develops certain bodies of knowledge, skills, abilities, and traits, and as one has contact and opportunity in the world.[5] In sum, social class describes relationships which we as adults have developed, may attempt to maintain, and in which we participate every working day. These relationships in a real sense define our material ties to the world.

An important concern here is whether these relationships are developing in children in schools within particular social class contexts.

## THE SAMPLE OF SCHOOLS

With the above discussion as a theoretical backdrop, the social class designation of each of the five schools will be identified, and the income, occupation, and other relevant available social characteristics of the students and their parents will be described. The first three schools are in a medium-sized city district in northern New Jersey, and the other two are in a nearby New Jersey suburb.

The first two schools I will call *Working-class Schools.* Most of the parents have blue-collar jobs. Less than a third of the fathers are skilled, while the majority are in unskilled or semiskilled jobs. During the period of the study (1978–1979) approximately 15 percent of the fathers were unemployed. The large majority (85 percent) of the families are white. The following occupations are typical: platform, storeroom, and stockroom workers; foundrymen, pipe welders, and boilermakers; semiskilled and unskilled assembly-line operatives; gas station attendants, auto mechanics, maintenance workers, and security guards. Less than 30 percent of the women work, some part-time and some full-time, on assembly lines, in storerooms and stockrooms, as waitresses, barmaids, or sales clerks. Of the fifth grade parents, none of the wives of the skilled workers had jobs. Approximately 15 percent of the families in each school are at or below the federal "poverty" level[6]; most of the rest of the family incomes are at or below $12,000, except some of the skilled workers whose incomes are higher. The incomes of the majority of the families in these two schools (i.e., at or below $12,000) are typical of 38.6 percent of the families in the United States (U.S. Bureau of the Census, 1979, p. 2, table A).

The third school is called the *Middle-class School,* although because of neighborhood residence patterns, the population is a mixture of several social classes. The parents' occupations can be divided into three groups: a small group of blue-collar "rich," who are skilled, well-paid workers such as printers, carpenters, plumbers, and construction workers. The second group is composed of parents in working-class and middle-class white-collar jobs: women in office jobs, technicians, supervisors in industry, and parents employed by the city (such as firemen, policemen, and several of the school's teachers). The third group is composed of occupations such as personnel directors in local firms, accountants, "middle management," and a few small capitalists (owners of shops in the area). The children of several local doctors attend this school. Most family incomes are between $13,000 and $25,000 with a few higher. This income range is typical of 38.9 percent of the families in the United States (U.S. Bureau of the Census, 1979, p. 2, table A).

The fourth school has a parent population that is at the upper income level of the upper middle class, and is predominantly professional. This school will be called the *Affluent Professional School.* Typical jobs are: cardiologist, interior designer, corporate lawyer or engineer, executive in advertising or television. There are some families who are not as affluent as the majority (e.g., the family of the superintendent of the district's schools, and the one or two families in which the fathers are skilled workers). In addition, a few of the families are more affluent than the majority, and can be classified in the capitalist class (e.g., a partner in a prestigious Wall Street stock brokerage firm). Approximately 90 percent of the children in this school are white. Most family incomes are between $40,000 and $80,000. This income span represents approximately 7 percent of the families in the United States.[7]

In the fifth school the majority of the families belong to the capitalist class. This school will be called the *Executive Elite School* because most of the fathers are top executives, (e.g., presidents and vice presidents) in major U.S.-based multinational corporations—for example, ATT, RCA, City Bank, American Express, U.S. Steel. A sizable group of fathers are top executives in financial firms on Wall Street. There are also a number of fathers who list their occupations as "general counsel" to a particular corporation, and these corporations are also among the large multinationals. Many of the mothers do volunteer work in the Junior League, Junior Fortnightly, or other service groups; some are intricately involved in town politics; and some are themselves in well-paid occupations. There are no minority children in the school. Almost all family incomes are over $100,000 with some in the $500,000 range. The incomes in this school represent less than 1 percent of the families in the United States (see Smith and Franklin, 1974).

Since each of the five schools is only one instance of elementary education in a particular social class context, I will not generalize beyond the sample. However, the examples of school work which follow will suggest characteristics of education in each social setting that appear to have theoretical and social significance and to be worth investigation in a larger number of schools.

## SOCIAL CLASS AND SCHOOL WORK

There are obvious similarities among United States schools and classrooms. There are school and classroom rules, teachers who ask questions and attempt to exercise control and who give work and homework. There are textbooks and tests. All of these were found in the five schools. Indeed, there were other curricular similarities as well: all schools and fifth grades used the same math book and series (*Mathematics Around Us,* Scott Foresman, 1978); all fifth grades had at least one boxed set of an individualized reading program available in the room (although the variety and amounts of teaching materials in the classrooms increased as the social class of the school population increased); and, all fifth grade language arts curricula included aspects of grammar, punctuation and capitalization.[8]

This section provides examples of work and work-related activities in each school that bear on the categories used to define social class. Thus, examples will be provided concerning students' relation to capital (e.g., as manifest in any symbolic capital that might be acquired through school work); students' relation to persons and types of authority regarding school work; and students' relation to their own productive activity. The section first offers the investigator's interpretation of what school work is for children in each setting, and then presents events and interactions that illustrate that assessment.

The *Working-class Schools*. In the two working-class schools, work is following the steps of a procedure. The procedure is usually mechanical, involving rote behavior and very little decision making or choice. The teachers rarely explain why the work is being assigned, how it might connect to other assignments, or what the idea is that lies behind the procedure or gives it coherence and perhaps meaning or significance. Available textbooks are not always used, and the teachers often prepare their own dittoes or put work examples on the board. Most of the rules regarding work are designations of what the children are to do; the rules are steps to follow. These steps are told to the children by the teachers and often written on the board. The children are usually told to copy the steps as notes. These notes are to be studied. Work is often evaluated not according to whether it is right or wrong, but according to whether the children followed the right steps.

The following examples illustrate these points. In math, when two-digit division was introduced, the teacher in one school gave a four-minute lecture on what the terms are called (i.e., which number is the divisor, dividend, quotient, and remainder). The children were told to copy these names in their notebooks. Then the teacher told them the steps to follow to do the problems, saying, "This is how you do them." The teacher listed the steps on the board, and they appeared several days later as a chart hung in the middle of the front wall: "Divide; Multiply; Subtract; Bring Down." The children often did examples of two-digit division. When the teacher went over the examples with them, he told them for each problem what the procedure was, rarely asking them to conceptualize or explain it themselves: "3 into 22 is 7; do your subtraction and one is left over." During the week that two-digit division was introduced (or at any other time), the investigator did not observe any discussion of the idea of grouping involved in division, any use of manipulables, or any attempt to relate two-digit division to any other mathematical process. Nor was there any attempt to relate the steps to an actual or possible thought process of the children. The observer did not hear the terms dividend, quotient, etc., used again. The math teacher in the other working-class school followed similar procedures regarding two-digit division, and at one point her class seemed confused. She said, "You're confusing yourselves. You're tensing up. Remember, when you do this, it's the same steps over and over again—and that's the way division always is." Several weeks later, after a test, a group of her children "still didn't get it," and she made no attempt to explain the concept of dividing things into groups, or to give them manipulables for their own investigation. Rather, she went over the steps with them again and told them that they "needed more practice."

In other areas of math, work is also carrying out often unexplained, fragmented procedures. For example, one of the teachers led the children through a series of steps to make a one-inch grid on their paper *without* telling them that they were making a one-inch grid, or that it would be used to study scale. She said, "Take your ruler. Put it across the top. Make a mark at every number. Then move your ruler down to the bottom. No, put it across the bottom. Now make a mark on top of every number. Now draw a line from...." At this point a girl said that she had a faster way to do it and the teacher said, "No, you don't; you don't even know what I'm making yet. Do it this way, or it's wrong." After they had made the lines up and down and across, the teacher told them she wanted them to make a figure by connecting some dots and to measure that, using the scale of one inch equals one mile. Then they were to cut it out. She said, "Don't cut until I check it."

In both working-class schools, work in language arts is mechanics of punctuation (commas, periods, question marks, exclamation points), capitalization, and the four kinds of sentences. One teacher explained to me, "Simple punctuation is all they'll ever use." Regarding punctuation, either a teacher or a ditto stated the rules for where, for example, to put commas. The investigator heard no classroom discussion of the aural context of punctuation (which, of course, is what gives each mark its meaning). Nor did the investigator hear any statement or inference that placing a punctuation mark could be a decision-making process, depending, for example, on one's intended meaning. Rather, the children were told to follow the rules. Language arts did not involve creative writing. There were several writing assignments throughout the year, but in each instance the children were given a ditto, and they wrote answers to questions on the sheet. For example, they wrote their "autobiography" by answering such questions as "Where were you born?" "What is your favorite animal?" on a sheet entitled, "All About Me."

In one of the working-class schools the class had a science period several times a week. On the three occasions observed, the children were not called upon to set up experiments or to give explanations for facts or concepts. Rather, on each occasion the teacher told them in his own words what the book said. The children copied the teacher's sentences from the board. Each day that preceded the day they were to do a science experiment, the teacher told them to copy the directions from the book for the procedure they would carry out the next day, and to study the list at home that night. The day after each experiment, the teacher went over what they had "found" (they did the experiments as a class, and each was actually a class demonstration led by the teacher). Then the teacher wrote what they "found" on the board, and the children copied that in their notebooks. Once or twice a year there are science projects. The project is chosen and assigned by the teacher from a box of three-by-five-inch cards. On the card the teacher has written the question to be answered, the books to use, and how much to write. Explaining the cards to the observer, the teacher said, "It tells them exactly what to do, or they couldn't do it."

Social studies in the working-class schools is also largely mechanical, rote work that was given little explanation or connection to larger contexts. In one school, for example, although there was a book available, social studies work was to copy the teacher's notes from the board. Several times a week for a period of several months, the children copied these notes. The fifth grades in the district were to study U.S. history. The teacher used a booklet she had purchased called "The Fabulous Fifty States." Each day she put information from the booklet in outline form on the board and the children copied it. The type of information did not vary: the name of the state, its abbreviation, state capital, nickname of the state, its main products, main business, and a "Fabulous Fact" (e.g., "Idaho grew 27 billion potatoes in one year. That's enough potatoes for each man, woman and . . ."). As the children finished copying the sentences, the teacher erased them and wrote more. Children would occasionally go to the front to pull down the wall map in order to locate the states they were copying, and the teacher did not dissuade them. But the observer never saw her refer to the map; nor did the observer ever hear her make other than perfunctory remarks concerning the information the children were copying. Occasionally the children colored in a ditto and cut it out to make a stand-up figure (representing, for example, a man roping a cow in the Southwest). These were referred to by the teacher as their social studies "projects."

Rote behavior was often called for in classroom oral work. When going over math and language arts skills sheets, for example, as the teacher asked for the answer to each problem, he fired the questions rapidly, staccato, and the scene reminded the observer of a sergeant drilling recruits: above all, the questions demanded that you stay at attention: "The next one? What do I put here? . . . Here? Give us the next." Or "How many commas in this sentence? Where do I put them . . . The next one?"

The (four) fifth grade teachers observed in the working-class schools attempted to control classroom time and space by making decisions without consulting the children and without explaining the basis for their decisions. The teacher's control thus often seemed capricious. Teachers, for instance, very often ignored the bells to switch classes—deciding among themselves to keep the children after the period was officially over, to continue with the work, or for disciplinary reasons, or so they (the teachers) could stand in the hall and talk. There were no clocks in the rooms in either school, and the children often asked, "What period is this?" "When do we go to gym?" The children had no access to materials. These were handed out by teachers and closely guarded. Things in the room "belonged" to the teacher: "Bob, bring me my garbage can." The teachers continually gave the children orders. Only three times did the investigator hear a teacher in either working-class school preface a directive with an unsarcastic "please," or "let's" or "would you." Instead, the teachers said, "Shut up," "Shut your mouth," "Open your books," "Throw your *gum* away—if you want to rot your teeth, do it on your *own* time." Teachers made every effort to control the movement of the children, and often shouted, "Why are you out of your *seat*??!!" If the children got permission to leave the room they had to take a written pass with the date and time.

The control that the teachers have is less than they would like. It is a result of constant struggle with the children. The children continually resist the teachers' orders and the work itself. They do not directly challenge the teachers' authority or legitimacy, but they make indirect attempts to sabotage and resist the flow of assignments:

*Teacher:* I will put some problems on the board. You are to divide.

*Child:* We got to divide?

*Teacher:* Yes.

*Several children:* (Groan) Not again. Mr. B, we done this yesterday.

*Child:* Do we put the date?

*Teacher:* Yes. I hope we remember we work in silence. You're supposed to do it on white paper. I'll explain it later.

*Child:* Somebody broke my pencil. (Crash—a child falls out of his chair.)

*Child:* (repeats) Mr. B., somebody broke my *pencil!*

*Child:* Are we going to be here all morning?

(Teacher comes to the observer, shakes his head and grimaces, then smiles.)

The children are successful enough in their struggle against work that there are long periods where they are not asked to do any work, but just to sit and be quiet.[9] Very often the work that the teachers assign is "easy," that is, not demanding, and thus receives less resistance. Sometimes a compromise is reached where, although the teachers insist that the children continue to work, there is a constant murmur of talk. The children will be doing arithmetic examples, copying social studies notes, or doing punctuation or other dittoes, and all the while there is muted but spirited conversation—about somebody's broken arm, an afterschool disturbance of the day before, etc. Sometimes the teachers themselves join in the conversation because, as one teacher explained to me, "It's a relief from the routine."

*Middle-class School.* In the middle-class school, work is getting the right answer. If one accumulates enough right answers one gets a good grade. One must follow the directions in order to get the right answers, but the directions often call for some figuring, some choice, some decision making. For example, the children must often figure out by themselves what the directions ask them to do, and how to get the answer: what do you do first, second, and perhaps third? Answers are usually found in books or by listening to the teacher. Answers are usually words, sentences, numbers, or facts and dates; one writes them on paper, and one should be neat. Answers must be in the right order, and one can not make them up.

The following activities are illustrative. Math involves some choice: one may do two-digit division the long way, or the short way, and there are some math problems that can be done "in your head." When the teacher explains how to do two-digit division, there is recognition that a cognitive process is involved; she gives several ways, and says, "I want to make sure you understand what you're doing—so you get it right"; and, when they go over the homework, she asks the *children* to tell how they did the problem and what answer they got.

In social studies the daily work is to read the assigned pages in the textbook and to answer the teacher's questions. The questions are almost always designed to check on whether the students have read the assignment and understood it: who did so-and-so; what happened after that; when did it happen, where, and sometimes, why did it happen? The answers are in the book and in one's understanding of the book; the teacher's hints when one doesn't know the answer are to "read it again," or to look at the picture or at the rest of the paragraph. One is to search for the answer in the "context," in what is given.

Language arts is "simple grammar, what they need for everyday life." The language arts teacher says, "They should learn to speak properly, to write business letters and thank-you letters, and to understand what nouns and verbs and simple subjects are." Here, as well, the actual work is to choose the right answers, to understand what is given. The teacher often says, "Please read the next sentence and then I'll question you about it." One teacher said in some exasperation to a boy who was fooling around in class, "If you don't know the answers to the questions I ask, then you can't stay in this *class!* (pause) You *never* know the answers to the questions I ask, and it's not fair to me—and certainly not to you!"

Most lessons are based on the textbook. This does not involve a critical perspective on what is given there. For example, a critical perspective in social studies is perceived as dangerous by these teachers because it may lead to controversial topics; the parents might complain. The children, however, are often curious, especially in social studies. Their questions are tolerated, and usually answered perfunctorily. But after a few minutes the teacher will say, "All right, we're not going any farther. Please open your social studies workbook." While the teachers spend a lot of time explaining and expanding on what the textbooks say, there is little attempt to analyze how or why things happen, or to give thought to how pieces of a culture, or, say, a system of numbers or elements of a language fit together or can be analyzed. What has happened in the past, and what exists now may not be equitable or fair, but (shrug) that is the way things are, and one does not confront such matters in school. For example, in social studies after a child is called on to read a passage about the pilgrims, the teacher summarizes the paragraph and then says, "So you can see how strict they were about everything." A child asks, "Why?" "Well, because they felt that if you weren't busy you'd get into trouble." Another child asks, "Is it true that they burned women at the stake?" The teacher says, "Yes, if a woman did anything strange, they hanged them. [sic] What would a woman do, do you think, to make them burn them? [sic] See if you can come up with better answers than my other [social studies] class." Several children offer suggestions, to which the teacher nods but does not comment. Then she says, "OK, good," and calls on the next child to read.

Work tasks do not usually request creativity. Serious attention is rarely given in school work to *how* the children develop or express their own feelings and ideas, either linguistically or in graphic form. On the occasions when creativity or self-expression is requested, it is peripheral to the main activity, or it is "enrichment," or "for fun." During a lesson on what similes are, for example, the teacher explains what they are, puts several on the board, gives some other examples herself, and then asks the children if they can "make some up." She calls on three children who give similes, two of which are actually in the book they have open before them. The teacher does not comment on this, and then asks several others to choose similes from the list of phrases in the book. Several do so correctly, and she says, "Oh *good!* You're picking them out! See how *good* we are?" Their homework is to pick out the rest of the similes from the list.

Creativity is not often requested in social studies and science projects, either. Social studies projects, for example, are given with directions to "find information on your topic," and write it up. The children are not supposed to copy, but to "put it in your own words." Although a number of the projects subsequently went beyond the teacher's direction to find information and had quite expressive covers and inside illustrations, the teacher's evaluative comments had to do with the amount of information, whether they had "copied," and if their work was neat.

The style of control of the three fifth grade teachers observed in this school varied from somewhat easygoing to strict, but in contrast to the working-class schools, the teachers' decisions were usually based on external rules and regulations, for example, on criteria that were known or available to the children. Thus, the teachers always honor the bells for changing classes, and they usually evaluate children's work by what is in the textbooks and answer booklets.

There is little excitement in school work for the children, and the assignments are perceived as having little to do with their interests and feelings. As one child said, what you do is "store facts in your head like cold storage—until you need it later for a test, or your job." Thus, doing well is important because there are thought to be *other* likely rewards: a good job, or college.[10]

*Affluent Professional School.* In the affluent professional school, work is creative activity carried out independently. The students are continually asked to express and apply ideas and concepts. Work involves individual thought and expressiveness, expansion and illustration of ideas, and choice of appropriate method and material. (The class is not considered an open classroom, and the principal explained that because of the large number of discipline problems in the fifth grade this year they did not departmentalize. The teacher who agreed to take part in the study said she is "more structured" this year than she usually is.) The products of work in this class are often written stories, editorials and essays, or representations of ideas in mural, graph, or craft form. The products of work should not be like everybody else's and should show individuality. They should exhibit good design, and (this is important), they must also fit empirical reality. Moreover, one's work should attempt to interpret or "make sense" of reality. The relatively few rules to be followed regarding work are usually criteria for, or limits on, individual activity. One's product is usually evaluated for the quality of its expression and for the appropriateness of its conception to the task. In many cases one's own satisfaction with the product is an important criterion for its evaluation. When right answers are called for, as in commercial materials like SRA (Science Research Associates) and math, it is important that the children decide on an answer as a result of thinking about the idea involved in what they're being asked to do. Teacher's hints are to "think about it some more."

The following activities are illustrative. The class takes home a sheet requesting each child's parents to fill in the number of cars they have, the number of television sets, refrigerators, games, or rooms in the house, etc. Each child is to figure the average number of a type of possession owned by the fifth grade. Each child must compile the "data" from all the sheets. A calculator is available in the classroom to do the mechanics of finding the average. Some children decide to send sheets to the fourth grade families for comparison. Their work should be "verified" by a classmate before it is handed in.

Each child and his or her family has made a geoboard. The teacher asks the class to get their geoboards from the side cabinet, to take a handful of rubber bands, and then to listen to what she would like them to do. She says, "I would like you to design a figure and then find the perimeter and area. When you have it, check with your neighbor. After you've done that, please transfer it to graph paper and tomorrow I'll ask you to make up a question about it for someone. When you hand it in, please let me know whose it is, and who verified it. Then I have something else for you to do that's really fun. (pause) Find the average number of chocolate chips in three cookies. I'll give you three cookies, and you'll have to *eat* your way through, I'm afraid!" Then she goes around the room and gives help, suggestions, praise, and admonitions that they are getting noisy. They work sitting, or standing up at their desks, at benches in the back, or on the floor. A child hands the teacher his paper and she comments, "I'm not accepting this paper. Do a better design." To another child she says, "That's fantastic! But you'll never find the area. Why don't you draw a figure inside [the big one] and subtract to get the area?"

The school district requires the fifth grades to study ancient civilizations (in particular, Egypt, Athens, and Sumer.) In this classroom, the emphasis is on illustrating and re-creating the culture of the people of ancient times. The following are typical activities: The children made an 8mm film on Egypt, which one of the parents edited. A girl in the class wrote the script, and the class acted it out. They put the sound on themselves. They read stories of those days. They wrote essays and stories depicting the lives of the people and the societal and occupational divisions. They chose from a list of projects, all of which involved graphic representations of ideas: for example, "Make a mural depicting the division of labor in Egyptian society."

Each child wrote and exchanged a letter in hieroglyphics with a fifth grader in another class, and they also exchanged stories they wrote in cuneiform. They made a scroll and singed the edges so it looked authentic. They each chose an occupation and made an Egyptian plaque representing that occupation, simulating the appropriate Egyptian design. They carved their design on a cylinder of wax, pressed the wax into clay, and then baked the clay. Although one girl did not choose an occupation, but carved instead a series of gods and slaves, the teacher said, "That's all right, Amber, it's beautiful." As they were working the teacher said, "Don't cut into your clay until you're satisfied with your design."

Social studies also involves almost daily presentation by the children of some event from the news. The teacher's questions ask the children to expand what they say, to give more details, and to be more specific. Occasionally she adds some remarks to help them see connections between events.

The emphasis on expressing and illustrating ideas in social studies is accompanied in language arts by an emphasis on creative writing. Each child wrote a rhebus story for a first grader whom they had interviewed to see what kind of story the child liked best. They wrote editorials on pending decisions by the school board, and radio plays, some of which were read over the school intercom from the office, and one of which was performed in the auditorium. There is no language arts textbook because, the teacher said, "The principal wants us to be creative." There is not much grammar, but there is punctuation. One morning when the observer arrived the class was doing a punctuation ditto. The teacher later apologized for using the ditto. "It's just for review," she said. "I don't teach punctuation that way. We use their language." The ditto had three unambiguous rules for where to put commas in a sentence. As the teacher was going around to help the children with the ditto, she repeated several times, "Where you put commas depends on how you say the sentence; it depends on the situation and what you want to say." Several weeks later the observer saw another punctuation activity. The teacher had printed a five-paragraph story on an oak tag and then cut it into phrases. She read the whole story to the class from the book, then passed out the phrases. The group had to decide how the phrases could best be put together again. (They arranged the phrases on the floor.) The point was not to replicate the story, although that was not irrelevant, but to "decide what you think the best way is." Punctuation marks on cardboard pieces were then handed out and the children discussed, and then decided, what mark was best at each place they thought one was needed. At the end of each paragraph the teacher asked, "Are you satisfied with the way the paragraphs are now? Read it to yourself and see how it sounds." Then she read the original story again, and they compared the two.

Describing her goals in science to the investigator, the teacher said, "We use ESS (Elementary Science Study). It's very good because it gives a hands-on experience—so they can make *sense* out of it. It doesn't matter whether it [what they find] is right or wrong. I bring them together and there's value in discussing their ideas."

The products of work in this class are often highly valued by the children and the teacher. In fact, this was the only school in which the investigator was not allowed to take original pieces of the children's work for her files. If the work was small enough, however, and was on paper, the investigator could duplicate it on the copying machine in the office.

The teacher's attempt to control the class involves constant negotiation. She does not give direct orders unless she is angry because the children have been too noisy. Normally, she tries to get them to foresee the consequences of their actions and to decide accordingly. For example, lining them up to go see a play written by the sixth graders, she says, "I presume you're lined up by someone with whom you want to sit. I hope you're lined up by someone you won't get in trouble with." The following two dialogues illustrate the process of negotiation between student and teacher.

*Teacher:* Tom, you're behind in your SRA this marking period.

*Tom:* So what!

*Teacher:* Well, last time you had a hard time catching up.

*Tom:* But I have my [music] lesson at 10:00.

*Teacher:* Well, that doesn't mean you're going to sit here for twenty minutes.

*Tom:* Twenty minutes! OK. (He goes to pick out a SRA booklet and chooses one, puts it back, then takes another, and brings it to her.)

*Teacher:* OK, this is the one you want, right?

*Tom:* Yes.

*Teacher:* OK, I'll put tomorrow's date on it so you can take it home tonight or finish it tomorrow if you want.

*Teacher:* (to a child who is wandering around during reading) Kevin, why don't you do *Reading for Concepts?*

*Kevin:* No, I don't like *Reading for Concepts.*

*Teacher:* Well, what are you going to do?

*Kevin:* (pause) I'm going to work on my DAR. (The DAR had sponsored an essay competition on "Life in the American Colonies.")

One of the few rules governing the children's movement is that no more than three children may be out of the room at once. There is a school rule that anyone can go to the library at any time to get a book. In the fifth grade I observed, they sign their name on the chalkboard and leave. There are no passes. Finally, the children have a fair amount of officially sanctioned say over what happens in the class. For example, they often negotiate what work is to be done. If the teacher wants to move on to the next subject, but the children say they are not ready, they want to work on their present projects some more, she very often lets them do it.

*Executive Elite School.* In the executive elite school, work is developing one's analytical intellectual powers. Children are continually asked to reason through a problem, to produce intellectual products that are both logically sound and of top academic quality. A primary goal of thought is to conceptualize rules by which elements may fit together in systems, and then to apply these rules in solving a problem. School work helps one to achieve, to excel, to prepare for life.

The following are illustrative. The math teacher teaches area and perimeter by having the children derive formulae for each. First she helps them, through discussion at the board, to arrive at $A = W \times L$ as a formula (not *the* formula) for area. After discussing several, she says, "Can anyone make up a formula for perimeter? Can you figure that out yourselves? (pause) Knowing what we know, can we think of a formula?" She works out three children's suggestions at the board, saying to two, "Yes, that's a good one," and then asks the class if they can think of any more. No one volunteers. To prod them, she says, "If you use rules and good reasoning, you get many ways. Chris, can you think up a formula?"

She discusses two-digit division with the children as a decision-making process. Presenting a new type of problem to them, she asks, "What's the *first* decision you'd make if presented with this kind of example? What is the first thing you'd *think?* Craig?" Craig says, "To find my first partial quotient." She responds, "Yes, that would be your first decision. How would you do that?" Craig explains, and then the teacher says, "OK, we'll see how that works for you." The class tries his way. Subsequently, she comments on the merits and shortcomings of several other children's decisions. Later, she tells the investigator that her goals in math are to develop their reasoning and mathematical thinking and that, unfortunately, "there's no *time* for manipulables."

While right answers are important in math, they are not "given" by the book or by the teacher, but may be challenged by the children. Going over some problems in late September the teacher says, "Raise your hand if you do not agree." A child says, "I don't agree with 64." The teacher responds, "OK, there's a question about 64. (to class) Please check it. Owen, they're disagreeing with you. Kristen, they're checking yours." The teacher emphasized this repeatedly during September and October with statements like, "Don't be afraid to say if you disagree. In the last [math] class, somebody disagreed, and they were right. Before you disagree, check yours, and if you still think we're wrong, then we'll check it out." By Thanksgiving, the children did not often speak in terms of right and wrong math problems, but of whether they agreed with the answer that had been given.

There are complicated math mimeos with many word problems. Whenever they go over the examples, they discuss how each child has set up the problem. The children must explain it precisely. On one occasion the teacher said, "I'm more—just as interested in *how* you set up the problem as in what answer you find. If you set up a problem in a good way, the answer is *easy* to find."

Social studies work is most often reading and discussion of concepts and independent research. There are only occasional artistic, expressive, or illustrative projects. Ancient Athens and Sumer are, rather, societies to analyze. The following questions are typical of those which guide the children's independent research: "What mistakes did Pericles make after the war?" "What mistakes did the citizens of Athens make?" "What are the elements of a civilization?" "How did Greece build an economic empire?" "Compare the way Athens chose its leaders with the way we choose ours." Occasionally the children are asked to make up sample questions for their social studies tests. On an occasion when the investigator was present the social studies teacher rejected a child's question by saying, "That's just fact. If I asked you that question on a test, you'd complain it was just memory! Good questions ask for concepts."

In social studies—but also in reading, science, and health—the teachers initiate classroom discussions of current social issues and problems. These discussions occurred on every one of the investigator's visits, and a teacher told me, "These children's opinions are important—it's important that they learn to reason things through." The classroom discussions always struck the observer as quite realistic and analytical, dealing with concrete social issues like the following: "Why do workers strike?" "Is that right or wrong?" "Why do we have inflation, and what can be done to stop it?" "Why do companies put chemicals in food when the natural ingredients are available?" etc. Usually the children did not have to be prodded to give their opinions. In fact, their statements and the interchanges between them struck the observer as quite sophisticated conceptually and verbally, and well-informed. Occasionally the teachers would prod with statements such as, "Even if you don't know [the answers], if you think logically about it, you can figure it out." And "I'm asking you [these] questions to help you think this through."

Language arts emphasizes language as a complex system, one that should be mastered. The children are asked to diagram sentences of complex grammatical construction, to memorize irregular verb conjugations (he lay, he has lain, etc. . . . ), and to use the proper participles, conjunctions, and interjections, in their speech. The teacher (the same one who teaches social studies) told them, "It is not enough to get these right on tests; you must use what you learn [in grammar classes] in your written and oral work. I will grade you on that."

Most writing assignments are either research reports and essays for social studies, or experiment analyses and write-ups for science. There is only an occasional story or other "creative writing" assignment. On the occasion observed by the investigator (the writing of a Halloween story), the points the teacher stressed in preparing the children to write involved the structural aspects of a story rather than the expression of feelings or other ideas. The teacher showed them a filmstrip, "The Seven Parts of a Story," and lectured them on plot development, mood setting, character development, consistency, and the use of a logical or appropriate ending. The stories they subsequently wrote were, in fact, well-structured, but many were also personal and expressive. The teacher's evaluative comments, however, did not refer to the expressiveness or artistry, but were all directed toward whether they had "developed" the story well.

Language arts work also involved a large amount of practice in presentation of the self and in managing situations where the child was expected to be in charge. For example, there was a series of assignments in which each child had to be a "student teacher." The child had to plan a lesson in grammar, outlining, punctuation, or other language arts topic and explain the concept to the class. Each child was to prepare a worksheet or game and a homework assignment as well. After each presentation, the teacher and other children gave a critical appraisal of the "student teacher's" performance. Their criteria were: whether the student spoke clearly; whether the lesson was interesting; whether the student made any mistakes; and whether he or she kept control of the class. On an occasion when a child did not maintain control, the teacher said, "When you're up there, you have authority, and you have to use it. I'll back you up."

The teacher of math and science explained to the observer that she likes the ESS program because "the children can manipulate variables. They generate hypotheses and devise experiments to solve the problem. Then they have to explain what they found."

The executive elite school is the only school where bells do not demarcate the periods of time. The two fifth grade teachers were very strict about changing classes on schedule, however, as specific plans for each session had been made. The teachers attempted to keep tight control over the children during lessons, and the children were sometimes flippant, boisterous, and occasionally rude. However, the children may be brought into line by reminding them that "it is up to you." "You must control yourself," "you are responsible for your work," you must "set your priorities." One teacher told a child, "You are the only driver of your car—and only you can regulate your speed." A new teacher complained to the observer that she had thought "these children" would have more control.

While strict attention to the lesson at hand is required, the teachers make relatively little attempt to regulate the movement of the children at other times. For example, except for the kindergartners, the children in this school do not have to wait for the bell to ring in the morning; they may go to their classroom when they arrive at school. Fifth graders often came early to read, to finish work, or to catch up. After the first two months of school the fifth grade teachers did not line the children up to change classes or to go to gym, etc., but, when the children were ready and quiet, they were told they could go—sometimes without the teachers.

In the classroom, the children could get materials when they needed them and took what they needed from closets and from the teacher's desk. They were in charge of the office at lunchtime. During class they did not have to sign out or ask permission to leave the room; they just got up and left. Because of the pressure to get work done, however, they did not leave the room very often. The teachers were very polite to the children, and the investigator heard no sarcasm, no nasty remarks, and few direct orders. The teachers never called the children "honey," or "dear," but always called them by name. The teachers were expected to be available before school, after school, and for part of their lunch time to provide extra help if needed.

## DISCUSSION AND CONCLUSION

One could attempt to identify physical, educational, cultural, and interpersonal characteristics of the environment of each school that might contribute to an empirical explanation of the events and interactions. For example, the investigator could introduce evidence to show that the following *increased* as the social class of the community increased (with the most marked differences occurring between the two districts): increased variety and abundance of teaching materials in the classroom; increased time reported spent by the teachers on preparation; higher social class background and more prestigious educational institutions attended by teachers and administrators; more stringent board of education requirements regarding teaching methods; more frequent and demanding administrative evaluation of teachers; increased teacher support services such as in-service workshops; increased parent expenditure for school equipment over and above district or government funding; higher expectations of student ability on the part of parents, teachers, and administrators; higher expectations and demands regarding student achievement on the part of teachers, parents, and administrators; more positive attitudes on the part of the teachers as to the probable occupational futures of the children; an increase in the children's acceptance of classroom assignments; increased intersubjectivity between students and teachers; and increased cultural congruence between school and community.

All of these—and other—factors may contribute to the character and scope of classroom events. However, what is of primary concern here is not the immediate causes of classroom activity (although these are in themselves quite important). Rather, the concern is to reflect on the deeper social meaning, the wider theoretical significance, of what happens in each social setting. In an attempt to assess the theoretical meaning of the differences among the schools, the work tasks and milieu in each will be discussed in light of the concepts used to define social class.

What potential relationships to the system of ownership of symbolic and physical capital, to authority and control, and to their own productive activity are being developed in children in each school? What economically relevant knowledge, skills, and predispositions are being transmitted in each classroom, and for what future relationship to the system of production are they appropriate? It is of course true that a student's future relationship to the process of production in society is determined by the combined effects of circumstances beyond elementary schooling. However, by examining elementary school activity in its social class context in the light of our theoretical perspective on social class, we can see certain potential relationships already developing. Moreover, in this structure of developing relationships lies theoretical—and social—significance.

The *working-class* children are developing a potential *conflict* relationship with capital. Their present school work is appropriate preparation for future wage labor that is mechanical and routine. Such work, insofar as it denies the human capacities for creativity and planning, is degrading; moreover, when performed in industry, such work is a source of profit to others. This situation produces industrial conflict over wages, working conditions, and control. However, the children in the working-class schools are not learning to be docile and obedient in the face of present or future degrading conditions or financial exploitation. They are developing abilities and skills of resistance. These methods are highly similar to the "slowdown," subtle sabotage and other modes of indirect resistance carried out by adult workers in the shop, on the department store sales floor, and in some offices.[11] As these types of resistance develop in school, they are highly constrained and limited in their ultimate effectiveness. Just as the children's resistance prevents them from learning socially legitimated knowledge and skills in school and is therefore ultimately debilitating, so is this type of resistance ultimately debilitating in industry. Such resistance in industry does not succeed in producing, nor is it intended to produce, fundamental changes in the relationships of exploitation or control. Thus, the methods of resistance that the working-class children are developing in school are only temporarily, and *potentially,* liberating.

In the *middle-class* school the children are developing somewhat different potential relationships to capital, authority, and work. In this school the work tasks and relationships are appropriate for a future relation to capital that is *bureaucratic.* Their school work is appropriate for white-collar working-class and middle-class jobs in the supportive institutions of United States society. In these jobs one does the paperwork, the technical work, the sales and the social service in the private and state bureaucracies. Such work does not usually demand that one be creative, and one is not often rewarded for critical analysis of the system. One is rewarded, rather, for knowing the answers to the questions one is asked, for knowing where or how to find the answers, and for knowing which form, regulation, technique, or procedure is correct. While such work does not usually satisfy human needs for engagement and self-expression, one's salary can be exchanged for objects or activities that attempt to meet these needs.

In the *affluent professional* school the children are developing a potential relationship to capital that is instrumental and expressive and involves substantial negotiation. In their schooling these children are acquiring *symbolic capital:* they are being given the opportunity to develop skills of linguistic, artistic, and scientific expression and creative elaboration of ideas into concrete form. These skills are those needed to produce, for example, culture (e.g., artistic, intellectual, and scientific ideas and other "products"). Their schooling is developing in these children skills necessary to become society's successful artists, intellectuals, legal, scientific, and technical experts and other professionals. The developing relation of the children in this school to their work is creative and relatively autonomous. Although they do not have control over which ideas they develop or express, the creative act in itself affirms and utilizes the human potential for conceptualization and design that is in many cases valued as intrinsically satisfying.

Professional persons in the cultural institutions of society (in, say, academe, publishing, the nonprint media, the arts, and the legal and state bureaucracies) are in an expressive relationship to the system of ownership in society because the ideas and other products of their work are often an important means by which material relationships of society are given ideological (e.g., artistic, intellectual, legal, and scientific) expression. Through the system of laws, for example, the ownership relations of private property are elaborated and legitimated in legal form; through individualistic and meritocratic theories in psychology and sociology, these individualistic economic relations are provided scientific "rationality" and "sense." The relationship to physical capital of those in society who create what counts as the dominant culture or ideology also involves substantial negotiation. The producers of symbolic capital often do not control the socially available physical capital nor the cultural uses to which it is put. They must therefore negotiate for money for their own projects. However, skillful application of one's cultural capital may ultimately lead to social (for example, state) power and to financial reward.

The *executive elite* school gives its children something that none of the other schools do: knowledge of and practice in manipulating the socially legitimated tools of analysis of systems. The children are given the opportunity to learn and to utilize the intellectually and socially prestigious grammatical, mathematical, and other vocabularies and rules by which elements are arranged. They are given the opportunity to use these skills in the analysis of society and in control situations. Such knowledge and skills are a most important kind of *symbolic capital*. They are necessary for control of a production system. The developing relationship of the children in this school to their work affirms and develops in them the human capacities for analysis and planning and helps to prepare them for work in society that would demand these skills. Their schooling is helping them to develop the abilities necessary for ownership and control of physical capital and the means of production in society.

The foregoing analysis of differences in school work in contrasting social class contexts suggests the following conclusion: the "hidden curriculum" of school work is tacit preparation for relating to the process of production in a particular way. Differing curricular, pedagogical, and pupil evaluation practices emphasize different cognitive and behavioral skills in each social setting and thus contribute to the development in the children of certain potential relationships to physical and symbolic capital, to authority, and to the process of work. School experience, in the sample of schools discussed here, differed qualitatively by social class. These differences may not only contribute to the development in the children in each social class of certain types of economically significant relationships and not others, but would thereby help to *reproduce* this system of relations in society. In the contribution to the reproduction of unequal social relations lies a theoretical meaning, and social consequence, of classroom practice.

The identification of different emphases in classrooms in a sample of contrasting social class contexts implies that further research should be conducted in a large number of schools to investigate the types of work tasks and interactions in each, to see if they differ in the ways discussed here, and to see if similar potential relationships are uncovered. Such research could have as a product the further elucidation of complex but not readily apparent connections between everyday activity in schools and classrooms and the unequal structure of economic relationships in which we work and live.

## ENDNOTES

1. But see, in a related vein, Apple and King (1977) and Rist (1973).

2. The definition of social class delineated here is the author's own, but it relies heavily on her interpretation of the work of Eric Olin Wright (1978), Pierre Bourdieu (Bourdieu and Passeron, 1977) and Raymond Williams (1977).

3. For discussion of schools as agencies of social and economic legitimation see Althusser (1971); see also Anyon (1978; 1979).

4. While relationships of control in society will not be discussed here, it can be said that they roughly parallel the relationships of control in the workplace, which will be the focus of this discussion. That is, working-class and many middle-class persons have less control than members of the upper-middle and capitalist classes do, not only over conditions and processes of their work, but over their nonwork lives as well. In addition, it is true that persons from the middle and capitalist classes, rather than workers, are most often those who fill the positions of state and other power in United States society.

5. Occupations may change their relation to the means of production over time, as the expenditure and ownership of capital change, as technology, skills, and the social relations of work change. For example, some jobs which were middle-class, managerial positions in 1900 and which necessitated conceptual laying-out and planning are now working-class and increasingly mechanical: e.g., quality control in industry, clerical work, and computer programming (see Braverman, 1974).

6. The U.S. Bureau of the Census defines "poverty" for a nonfarm family of four as a yearly income of $6,191 a year or less. U.S. Bureau of the Census, *Statistical Abstract of the United States: 1978* (Washington, D.C.: U.S. Government Printing Office, 1978, p. 465, table 754).

7. This figure is an estimate. According to the Bureau of the Census, only 2.6 percent of families in the United States have money income of $50,000 or over. U.S. Bureau of the Census, *Current Population Reports,* series P-60, no. 118, "Money Income in 1977 of Families and Persons in the United States." (Washington, D.C.: U.S. Government Printing Office, 1979, p. 2, table A). For figures on income at these higher levels, see Smith and Franklin (1974).

8. For other similarities alleged to characterize United States classrooms and schools, but which will not be discussed here, see Dreeben (1968), Jackson (1968), and Sarasan (1971).

9. Indeed, strikingly little teaching occurred in either of the working-class schools; this curtailed the amount that the children were taught. Incidentally, it increased the amount of time that had to be spent by the researcher to collect data on teaching style and interaction.

10. A dominant feeling, expressed directly and indirectly by teachers in this school, was boredom with their work. They did, however, in contrast to the working-class schools, almost always carry out lessons during class times.

11. See, for example, discussions in Levison (1974), Aronowitz (1978), and Benson (1978).

## REFERENCES

Althusser, L. Ideology and ideological state apparatuses. In L. Althusser, *Lenin and philosophy and other essays*. Ben Brewster, Trans. New York: Monthly Review Press, 1971.

Anyon, J. Elementary social studies textbooks and legitimating knowledge. *Theory and Research in Social Education*, 1978, 6, 40–55.

Anyon, J. Ideology and United States history textbooks. *Harvard Educational Review*, 1979, 49, 361–386.

Apple, M.W. *Ideology and curriculum*. Boston: Routledge and Kegan Paul, 1979.

Apple, M.W., & King, N. What do schools teach? *Curriculum Inquiry*, 1977, 6, 341–358.

Aronowitz, S. Marx, Braverman, and the logic of capital. *The Insurgent Sociologist*, 1978, 8, 126–146.

Benson, S. The clerking sisterhood: rationalization and the work culture of saleswomen in American department stores, 1890–1960. *Radical America*, 1978, 12, 41–55.

Bernstein, B. *Class, codes and control, Vol. 3. Towards a theory of educational transmission.* 2nd ed. London: Routledge and Kegan Paul, 1977.

Bourdieu, P. and Passeron, J. *Reproduction in education, society, and culture*. Beverly Hills, Calif.: Sage, 1977.

Bowles, S. & Gintis, H. *Schooling in capitalist America: educational reform and the contradictions of economic life*. New York: Basic Books, 1976.

Braverman, H. *Labor and monopoly capital: the degradation of work in the twentieth century*. New York: Monthly Review Press, 1974.

Dreeben, R. *On what is learned in school*. Reading, Mass.: Addison-Wesley, 1968.

Jackson, P. *Life in classrooms*. Holt, Rinehart & Winston, 1968.

Lampman, R.J. *The share of top wealth-holders in national wealth, 1922–1956:* A study of the National Bureau of Economic Research. Princeton, N.J.: Princeton University Press, 1962.

Levison, A. *The working-class majority*. New York: Penguin Books, 1974.

New York Stock Exchange. *Census*. New York: New York Stock Exchange, 1975.

Rist, R.C. *The urban school: a factory for failure*. Cambridge, Mass.: MIT Press, 1973.

Sarasan, S. *The culture of school and the problem of change*. Boston: Allyn and Bacon, 1971.

Smith, J.D. and Franklin, S. The concentration of personal wealth, 1922–1969. *American Economic Review*, 1974, 64, 162–167.

U.S. Bureau of the Census. *Current population reports.* Series P-60, no. 118. Money income in 1977 of families and persons in the United States. Washington, D.C.: U.S. Government Printing Office, 1979.

U.S. Bureau of the Census. *Statistical abstract of the United States: 1978.* Washington, D.C.: U.S. Government Printing Office, 1978.

Williams, R. *Marxism and literature.* New York: Oxford University Press, 1977.

Wright, E.O. *Class, crisis and the state.* London: New Left Books, 1978.

# CHAPTER 19

## *Challenges for Educators*
### *Lesbian, Gay, and Bisexual Families*

*JAMES T. SEARS*

*Kim and Carolyn, a Boston area lesbian couple, took in Earl, a Black deaf boy, who at the time was five years old. Kim is also deaf, although she can speak and lip-read...Eventually Kim and Carolyn were formally approved as Earl's foster parents by Massachusetts social workers. Several years later the two women adopted Earl....[At age 11] Earl is a child who is different. He is deaf in a hearing world; Black in a predominantly white community; and the son of [white Asian] lesbians in a largely heterosexual culture. (Sands, 1988, pp. 46–47, 50)*

*Since I made the decision seven years ago to become a parent through anonymous donor insemination, the question that others have asked most frequently is, "But how are you going to explain this to your child?"...During breakfast today, in the middle of a discussion about Velcro closings on shoes, Jonathon [her five-year-old son] asked why he has only a mom and some people have a mom and a dad. I explained that there are all kinds of families in the world and gave lots of examples of those he knows: some with, some without kids; some big, some small. We talked about the fact that from the time I was 15, I just had a dad and no mom. I explained that there are no set rules for who family members can be; rather, families are people who love...one another. (Blumenthal, 1990/1991, p. 45)*

A slightly different version of this chapter originally appeared in *The High School Journal,* 77 (1 & 2): 138–156. © 1994 The University of North Carolina Press. Used by permission.

*The seven-year-old daughter [Alicia] asked her father some questions about "Gene" (the lover), and the father answered them honestly, explaining that he loved Gene and he loved Mommy. The daughter did not seem concerned, but shortly afterward she asked her mother, "Do you still love Daddy?" Mother assured her that she did. "Do you love Gene?" the daughter asked. "He's my friend," her mother answered, "but I love your father." (Matteson, 1987, p. 151)*

*Jennifer sits down at the kitchen table to eat her cereal and juice. "What will you be doing at school, today?" asks Patsy, her mother. "Mrs. Thomkins says we will make Christmas trees today." Patsy's husband, Bill, pours another cup of coffee and says: "Well, I guess that means that we won't have to go and chop down a tree this year!" "Oh, no!" Jennifer exclaims. "We're going to make them out of paper. When are we going to get our tree?" "Well," Patsy's mother says, "When Pam's ship returns for Christmas next week. Until then, you and Bill can talk about where we should go this year for our tree." Jennifer finishes her meal, kisses her mother and Patsy's husband goodbye. "Oh, I almost forgot. Where's Bob?" Bob, Bill's lover of five years, sits in the living room reading the morning paper. "I'm out here, Jennifer. Give me a kiss before you go to school."— An Alabama family (circa 1991)*

The traditional American family—to the degree that it ever existed—represents a minority of all households in the United States today (Kamerman & Hayes, 1982). There are three major types of U.S. families: families of first marriage, single-parent families, and families of remarriage. Less than 1 in 4 students come to school from a home occupied by both biological parents. Single-parent households account for about one-quarter of all families in the United States; about 1 of every 2 African-American children (1 of every 4 White children) live with a lone parent (Glick, 1988). If current trends continue, 6 out of 10 children will be part of a single family sometime before they become 18 years of age (Bozett & Hanson, 1991). These single households are generally the product of divorce or separation. Remarried families account for one in six households with nearly six million stepchildren (Glick, 1987).

In recent years, alternative family arrangements have emerged in which either one or both partners are a self-identified lesbian, gay man, or bisexual person (Alpert, 1988; Pollack & Vaughn, 1989; Schulenberg, 1985).[1] Children, like Jennifer, from these alternative marriages may be the product of a prior marriage in which the partner has custody or visiting privileges, or a gay or lesbian couple's decision, like Kim's and Carolyn's, to adopt (Jullion, 1985; Ricketts & Achtenberg, 1987).[2] Other children, like Alicia, may live in a biologically traditional family but have one or both parents who are openly bisexual (Matteson, 1985, 1987). Children, like Jonathon, may also come to school from households of a lesbian or bisexual woman who has elected to bear and raise the child following artificial insemination or the departure of the father (Pies, 1985, 1987). And, of course, the parents of many other children never choose to disclose their bisexuality or homosexuality to their family (Green & Clunis, 1989).

The publications on alternative families, such as *Jenny Lives with Eric and Martin* (Bosche, 1983), *How Would You Feel If Your Dad Was Gay?* (Heron & Maran, 1990), and

*Daddy's Roommate* (Wilhoite, 1990), as well as the controversy surrounding the New York City Public Schools' adoption of the Rainbow Curriculum and the subsequent dismissal of its superintendent, Frank Fernandez, may mean that few of our students will understand the true diversity among the families whose children attend their schools. Deleting lesbian, gay, and bisexual families from the school curriculum, however, does not remove them from the day-to-day realities of school life. If we are to truly serve all of our students, then educators must become more aware of the challenges facing lesbian, gay, and bisexual parents and their children.

## *Challenges Facing Lesbian, Gay, and Bisexual Parents*

*How, the average person wants to know, can a lesbian possibly be a mother? If heterosexual intercourse is the usual prerequisite for maternity, how is it possible for women who by* definition *do not engage in heterosexual behavior to be mothers? If motherhood is a state which requires the expression of nurturance, altruism, and the sacrifice of sexual fulfillment, how can a lesbian, a being thought to be oversexed, narcissistic, and pleasure-oriented, perform the maternal role? How can women who are "masculine," aggressive, and assumed to be confused about their gender be able to behave appropriately within its boundaries, or to assume the quintessentially womanly task of motherhood? If lesbians are women whose lives are organized in terms of the relentless pursuit of clandestine pleasures, if lesbians are women who behave as quasi-men and who have been poorly socialized into their gender roles, then how can they expect to provide adequate models of feminine behavior to their children, to prepare them for their own sexual and parental careers? (Lewin & Lyons, 1982, p. 250)*

Such questions pose challenges to women (and men) who are homosexual but choose parenting. While the assumptions underlying many of these questions are flawed (Sears, 1991a), the coupling of parenthood with homosexuality to form categories of lesbian mothers and gay fathers may appear contradictory. This contradiction, however, is of social not biological origin.

The difficulties confronted by acknowledged lesbian mothers or gay fathers is, in many ways, similar to those faced by single parents and divorced households with the significant exception of the additional burden of wrestling with the social stigma associated with homosexuality. Two of the greatest challenges are securing or maintaining custody of their children and disclosing their homosexuality to their children.

### *Legal Barriers*

In child custody decisions, the judge has a wide leeway within common law to provide for the "best interest of the child" and not to interfere with existing custody arrangements unless there have been "material changes in circumstances" (Achtenburg, 1985; Basile, 1974; Payne, 1977/1978). Although heterosexual mothers have generally not lost custody of their children for unfitness, the sexual orientation of a parent has played a prominent role in both circumstances (Pagelow, 1980; Rivera, 1987).

In general, gay fathers seeking custody face the double burden of being male where the female is presumed more nurturant and of being homosexual where heterosexual is considered normal. Moreover, in those cases involving a son, the court appears more concerned with issues of sexual development than those involving daughters (Miller, 1979b), and in custody disputes involving lesbian mothers, the woman loses 85 percent of those cases that go to trial (Chesler, 1986). A disproportionate number of cases are between the mother and another relative (Hitchens, 1979/1980), and in cases where lesbian mothers are provided custody, the courts have often demanded the absence of same-sex lovers in the household. One lesbian who won provisional custody of her five-year-old son lamented:

*That is unjust! They don't put those kinds of restrictions on a heterosexual mother... for 13 years I'm forbidden to set up a living relationship with a sexual partner of my choice. Sure, I don't have to be celibate—I can sneak out somewhere or I can send my son away—but I want to be free to set up my home with someone I love. It's much better for a child to have more than one parent figure—I can't possibly be available to answer all of my child's needs alone. (Pagelow, 1980, p. 194)*

In deciding whether to award custody, or even visiting privileges, to a homosexual parent or to allow a lesbian or gay couple to adopt a child, judges often base their decisions on other unsubstantiated judicial fears such as "turning" the child into a homosexual, molesting the child, stigmatization of the child, and AIDS (Hitchens, 1979/1980; Payne, 1977/1978; Polikoff, 1987; Rivera, 1987). The willingness of the courts to entertain homosexuality as a factor for denying custody or restricting visiting rights has not escaped the attention of many lesbian mothers who, though themselves not a party to legal action, fear such a possibility (Kirkpatrick, Smith, & Roy, 1981).

Nonbiological parents and lesbians or gay men wishing to adopt also face significant legal hurdles. Six jurisdictions in the United States have ruled in favor of adoptions by same-sex parents (Alaska, Washington, Oregon, California, Minnesota, and the District of Columbia), and although only two states (Massachusetts and Florida) specifically prohibit gay men or lesbians from being foster or adoptive parents, most courts and agencies have allowed sodomy statutes (applicable in 25 states), prejudicial attitudes, or myths and stereotypes to affect their decision. In Minnesota, for example, one lesbian was denied visitation rights to a child she had raised with her former partner, and in Wisconsin, the court refused to enforce a coparenting contract signed by two former lovers. Even in states that have ruled in favor of adoptions, there remains bureaucratic and political resistance and, if approved, joint adoptions by gay men or lesbians are unusual (Achtenberg, 1985; Ricketts & Achtenberg, 1987).

Only recently have educational associations, state departments of education, and school districts developed policies and programs regarding the discrimination and harassment of homosexual students or the inclusion of sexual orientation issues in the school curriculum; little attention has been given to children with a lesbian or gay parent. As I will discuss in the final section of this chapter, these policies and programs will not only have a positive affect on the lesbian, gay, or bisexual student but also on the heterosexual student who comes from such an alternative family structure.

## Disclosure to Children

Some, if not most, of our children from such families have not been told of their parents' sexual identity (Bozett, 1980; Miller, 1979a). In heterosexually coupled families with a gay, lesbian, or bisexual spouse, underlying tensions may create home problems (e.g., marital discord, emotional detachment from the child) that manifest themselves in a child's school behavior or academic achievement (Harris & Turner, 1985/1986; Lewis, 1980; Matteson, 1987). In those families, for example, where gay fathers have not disclosed their sexual identity to their children, Miller (1979b) found "their fathering is of lower quality than the fathering of more overt respondents.... The guilt many of these men experienced over being homosexual manifested itself in over-indulgent behavior.... Data also indicate that respondents living with their wives tended to spend less time with their children" (p. 550). Educators who are aware of this social phenomenon can integrate this knowledge with their classroom assessment while respecting the confidentiality of the family.

Parents often fear the impact of such disclosure on their children. In deciding whether to disclose the parent's sexual identity, the most common parental fears are rejection from the child, inability of the child to understand, and child rejection from peers (Shernoff, 1984, Wyers, 1984, 1987). The difficulties faced by the gay or bisexual partner in "coming out" to a child are well articulated by Matteson (1987) following his analysis of a nonclinical sample of 44 spouses in a mixed-orientation marriage: "Since the beginning, I've been saying, 'next year I'm leaving as soon as the children are bigger.' Now that they are in college, I can't leave because they are my judges. They'd never forgive me for doing this all these years to their mother" (p. 145; quoted from Miller, 1978, p. 217).

The most common time for such disclosure is during a separation or a divorce or when the gay parent elects to enter into a domestic partnership (Bozett, 1981b, Miller, 1978). In the case of still-married bisexual spouses, somewhere between one-third to one-half of their school-age children have been informed (Coleman, 1985; Wolf, 1985). The mean age of gay parental self-disclosure or child discovery ranges from 8 to 11 years of age (Turner, Scadden, & Harris, 1985; Wyers, 1984). According to Bozett (1987b): "The means by which the father discloses takes several forms. For example, with small children the father may disclose indirectly by taking children to a gay social event or by hugging another man in their presence. Both indirect and direct means may be used with older children in which the father also discusses his homosexuality with them" (p. 13).

Studies of gay parents and their children report different findings regarding the child's reaction (Bozett, 1980; Harris & Turner, 1985/1986; Lewis, 1980; Miller, 1979b; Paul, 1986; Pennington, 1987; Turner, Scadden, & Harris, 1985; Wyers, 1987). In her clinical study of 32 children from 28 lesbian-mother families, Pennington (1987) found the differing "children's reactions to mother 'coming out' generally range from 'Please, can't you change, you're ruining my life!' to 'I'm proud of my mom, and if other kids don't like it, then I don't want that kind of person to be my friend'" (p. 66). In his study of 40 gay fathers, Miller (1979b), on the other hand, found all of their children to have reacted more positively than their fathers had anticipated. Further, "children who showed the greatest acceptance were those who, prior to full disclosure, were gradually introduced by their parents to homosexuality through meeting gay family friends, reading about it, and discussing the topic informally with parents" (p. 549). In general, these and other studies (e.g., Gantz, 1983; Lamothe, 1989; Schulenburg, 1985) found the parent-child relationship was ultimately enhanced by such disclosure.

## Challenges Faced by Children with Lesbian, Gay, or Bisexual Parents

*Susan expected her family to be thrilled that she was finally "settling down" after a decade of working as a lawyer. Her mother's first reaction [to Susan's interest in having a baby], however, was "But you're not married!" After Susan explained that she was still lesbian and planned to raise the child with her lover, Susan's mother wondered, "But is it fair to the child? Everyone else will have a father; she'll feel different, she'll be treated badly." (Rohrbaugh, 1989, pp. 51–52)*

In the past, concerns about children growing up in a homosexual household focused on the household as the potential problem. Children were believed to be at a higher risk of developing a gender-inappropriate identity or sex-typed behaviors, acquiring a homosexual orientation, or exhibiting behavioral or psychological problems. While these fears are unjustified, the difficulties of growing up in a lesbian, gay, or bisexual household are linked to the homophobia and heterosexism pervasive in our society and tolerated, if not magnified, in our public schools.

### Impact of Parental Sexual Orientation on Children

As the discussion of gay parenting becomes more public, fears about a child living with a lesbian or gay parent have been expressed. One concern is that the child may become homosexual or experience sexual harassment from either the parent or parental friends. Though persons generally do not identify themselves as gay or lesbian until their late teens or early twenties (Sears, 1991a; Rust, 1993), there is no greater likelihood that a son or daughter of a homosexual parent may declare a homosexual identity than those children from heterosexual households (Bozett, 1981a; 1981b; Gottman, 1990; Green, 1978; Miller, 1979b; Paul, 1986). Further, there is no empirical evidence that such children living with lesbian or gay parents face any greater danger of sexual harassment or molestation than those living with heterosexual parents (Hotvedt & Mandel, 1982; Miller, 1979b).

Another concern is that children living in homosexual families may suffer in gender development or model "inappropriate" sex-role behaviors. Here, research studies present a mixed picture. Some studies have found that homosexual parents, like their heterosexual counterparts, encourage their child's use of sex-typed toys (Golombok, Spencer, & Rutter, 1983; Gottman, 1990; Harris & Turner, 1985/1986; McGuire & Alexander, 1985; Kirkpatrick, Smith, & Roy, 1981; Turner, Scadden, & Harris, 1985); others have reported the opposite finding, including a greater emphasis on paternal nurturance or less preference for traditional sex-typed play (Hotvedt & Mandel, 1982; Scallen, 1981).

In general, studies comparing lesbian or gay men as parents with heterosexual single parents (Bigner & Jacobsen, 1989; Kirkpatrick, Smith, & Roy, 1981; Lewin & Lyons, 1982; Scallen, 1981) portray families that are either similar to the heterosexual norm or that excel in socially desirable ways (e.g., androgynous parenting behaviors, more child-centered fathers). Though the studies cited in this article varied in their methodology and samples, none found homosexuality to be incompatible with fatherhood or motherhood. Further, these studies do not reveal parenting patterns that would be any less positive than those provided by a heterosexual parent (e.g., Bozett, 1985; Golombok, Spencer, & Rutter, 1983; Hoeffer, 1981; Robinson & Skeen, 1982).

In fact, those men who are most open about their homosexuality, compared with other homosexual fathers, display fatherhood traits that many professionals consider to be desirable. These fathers, for example, used corporal punishment less often, expressed a strong commitment to provide a nonsexist and egalitarian home environment, and were less authoritarian (Miller, 1979b). Similar findings were available for lesbian mothers. For example, in comparing Black lesbian with Black heterosexual mothers (Hill, 1981), the lesbians were found to be more tolerant and treated their male and female children in a more sex equitable manner.

Those fathers and mothers who were the most publicly "out" were most likely to provide a supportive home environment. Ironically, given custody or visiting concerns as well as the general level of homophobia in society, those parents who are the most candid may be most vulnerable to denial of their parenting rights and visible targets for anti-gay harassment of themselves and their children.

## *Impact of Homophobia and Heterosexism on Children*

The most commonly experienced problem or fear confronting children, most notably adolescents, from lesbian or gay households is rejection or harassment from peers or the fear that others would assume that they, too, were homosexual (Bigner & Bozett, 1990; Bozett, 1987a; Lewis, 1980; Paul, 1986; Wyers, 1987). An anecdote told to Pennington (1987) by a daughter of a lesbian mother illustrates the genuine acceptance of children *prior* to encountering stereotypes and harassment in school: "When I was around five, my mom and Lois told me they were lesbians. I said good, and thought I want to be just like my mom. Well, when I reached about the fifth grade...I heard kids calling someone a faggot as a swear word, and I thought, "'My God, they're talking about my mom.'" (p. 61).

Based on his study of 16 children with a gay or bisexual father, Paul (1986), as well as others (e.g., Riddle & Arguelles, 1981), found that it was during adolescence that these children had the most difficult time coping with their father's sexuality. An excerpt from a case study, written by a family psychotherapist (Corley, 1990) who worked with the two lesbians, Jane and Marge, and their eight children—a family for more than 10 years—is illustrative. During the next 3 years of therapy, the family began their first open discussions about the special relationship between the two women and the feelings of their children. The therapist continues:

> *Marge's two boys had difficult adjusting to do....By now everyone at their school knew Joe and Tom had two mothers. Both of them had come to their school as the primary parent. The children started to tease them about having "lesbos" for parents. Both of the boys [in their early teens] were rather stout in nature so many fights erupted over the teasing they received. Since Joe and Tom*

*were embarrassed over what the children at school were saying, they usually told the teachers and principal that there was no reason for the fights. When Jane and Marge would question them about the fights, they would equally clam up.... Because of the lack of intervention, the boys continued to get in trouble at school and started to act out in other ways. Although the boys were only average students, they always passed. Now they were bringing home failing marks. Since these were the first failing grades for either of them, Jane and Marge felt the situation would improve. Unfortunately, the grade situation only deteriorated. Several parent conferences were called at school. Although both women showed up at the conferences together, nothing was ever mentioned about the family unit or their relationship. It was not until the family came into therapy that the boys revealed they were having problems. (p. 80)*

A prominent researcher in the study of children of gay fathers, Frederick Bozett (1980) relayed a similar anecdote from a 14-year-old boy whose gay father had made several school visits: "All his jewelry was on. The teachers knew he was gay, and all the kids saw him and figured it out. It was obvious. They started calling me names like 'homoson.' It was awful. I couldn't stand it. I hate him for it. I really do" (p. 178).

According to Bozett (1987a), children generally use one of three "social control strategies" to deal with their parent's homosexuality. The first, *boundary control*, is evidenced in the child's control of the parent's behavior, the child's control of their own behavior vis-á-vis their gay parent, and the child's control of others' contact with the parent. Some of these controls are evidenced in an interview with two adolescent girls, both of whom have lesbian parents:

*Margo:* *I try and hide stuff when people walk in, but probably most of my friends know.*

*Interviewer:* *Do they ever ask you directly?*

*Tania:* *My friends don't. My mother's girlfriend doesn't live with us. My mom keeps stuff out but I make a point of putting it away when someone is going to come over....*

*Margo:* *I used to always walk between my mother and Cheryl. I used to make Cheryl walk at the curb and my mother inside and I'd walk right in the middle....So it wouldn't be really obvious. But it probably was....People say, "Why do they live together?" And you make up all these stories and they don't even fit together....My mother tries to make up stories sometimes, but it doesn't work because they make no sense. "Oh my girlfriend, my brother's ex-wife's sister...." I used to be real embarrassed. One of my girlfriends asked me once and I was really embarrassed. I was like "No! What are you talking about? Where did you get that idea from?" But it turned out that her mother was gay too. (Alpert, 1988, pp. 100–102)*

The second controlling strategy, *nondisclosure*, is evidenced in the child's refusal to share (and in some cases deny) their parent's homosexuality. One lesbian woman, discussing the difficulties she faced in her daughter's denials, commented:

> *When I asked Noelle [now age 13] what she would say if anybody asked her about me she said she would deny it. I was very very hurt. I talked it over with Cathy (a lesbian and a close friend). She said her son...had got into a fight at school about her and had come home really upset.... She told him that she didn't expect him to fight her battles for her.... That was fine by her and that really helped me because I realized I should not expect Noelle to fight my battles either.... I actually did tell my children that if they want to deny it that's fine and I think that helped them because they were caught a bit between loyalties. (Lesbian Mothers Group, 1989, p. 126)*

Some children, however, also employ nondisclosure to protect the parent who might be vulnerable to a child custody challenge or to job discrimination (Paul, 1986).

The third controlling strategy, *disclosure*, is evidenced by a child's selective sharing of this personal information. In Miller's (1979b) study of gay fathers, one 17-year-old son stated, "I don't tell people if they're uptight types or unless I know them well. I've told my close friends and it's cool with them" (p. 548). In Gantz's (1983) study, a 13-year-old child of a household with two lesbians noted, "I've told one person.... We'd go do stuff like shoot pool and all that down in his basement. I just told him, you know, that they were gay.... I didn't know how he'd react. He said he'd keep it a secret, so that made me feel a little better" (p. 68). Another male respondent commented, "You have to be sure they won't tell somebody else. I was worried [about] people knowing [because] I was afraid of what they'd think of me; maybe it would be embarrassing" (Bozett, 1987a, p. 43).

Further, according to Bozett (1987a), there are several factors that influence the degree to which children employ one or more of these strategies. Those children who identify with the father because of their behavior, life-style, values, or beliefs are less likely to use any social control strategy. Those children who view their father's homosexuality as "obtrusive," who are older, or who live with their father are more likely to employ these strategies.

Studies on children from gay families or homosexual mothers and fathers have been conducted within a Euro-American context. Only one study has examined minority homosexual parents (Hill, 1981), and there has been no research directed at minority children of a gay parent. Anecdotal writings by persons of color who are homosexual parents, however, convey some dissimilarities with their Anglo counterparts. For example, Lorde (1987) wrote:

> *Black children of lesbian couples have an advantage because they learn, very early, that oppression comes in many different forms, none of which have anything to do with their own worth.... I remember that for years, in the name-calling at school, boys shouted at Jonathan not—"Your mother's a lesbian"— but rather "Your mother's a nigger." (p. 222)*

Research into the unique difficulties confronting lesbian or gay young adults who must cope with their emerging homosexual identity within the context of a nondominant culture underscores the difficulties of being a minority within a minority and suggests differences that minority children with gay or lesbian parents might confront (Sears, 1991a; Johnson, 1981). Morales (1990) explained:

*What does it mean to be an ethnic minority gay man or lesbian? For ethnic minority gays and lesbians, life is often living in three different communities: the gay/lesbian community, the ethnic minority community, and the predominantly heterosexual white mainstream society. Since these three social groups have norms, expectations, and styles, the minority lesbian or gay man must balance a set of often conflicting challenges and pressures. The multi-minority status makes it difficult for a person to become integrated and assimilated. (p. 220)*

This was evident in my study of young lesbian and gay African-American southerners (Sears, 1991a). Irwin, a working-class Black man, for example, stated: "When you're black in a black society and you're gay it's even harder. Blacks don't want it to be known because they don't want to mimic or imitate white people. They see it as a crutch and they don't want to have to deal with it" (p. 135). Malcolm commented, "If they are going to see you with a man at all, they would rather see you with another black man.... If they think you're gay and you're with a white man, they think that he's your sugar daddy or you're a snow queen" (p. 138). This is also evident in the anecdotal and autobiographical writings by people of color (e.g., Beam, 1986; Moraga & Anzaldua, 1981; Smith, 1983). A Chinese-American (Lim-Hing, 1990/1991), for example, wrote about her family's reactions to her lesbianism:

*The implicit message my family gave me was not so much a condemnation as an embarrassed tolerance inextricably tied to a plea for secrecy.... At the end of my stay [with my father], he asked me if "they" would pick me up at Logan, although he knows Jacquelyn's name. My father's inability to accept my being a lesbian is related to his more traditional values: family first, make money and buy land, don't stand out. (p. 20)*

A Puerto Rican (Vazquez, 1992) expressed his anger at racism encountered within the Anglo gay community: "I won't lay in my own bed with some Euro-American and do Racism 101. Nor do I want to sit down with the cute white boy I'm dating and deconstruct the statement, 'I love sleeping with Puerto Ricans'" (p. 90).

Children from some minority families may have a particularly difficult time coping with the homosexuality of a parent or may choose to cope with the information in a culturally different manner than researchers such as Bozett have found. Whether it is a child "coming out" to his family, a parent disclosing her homosexual orientation to the children, or both revealing this information to their extended family, they do so within different cultural contexts, perhaps facing greater risks than their Euro-American counterparts. Morales (1990) wrote:

*"Coming out" to the family tends to involve both the nuclear and extended family systems. Such a family collective is the major support system for the ethnic persons and is the source of great strength and pride....For minority lesbians and gays coming out to the family not only jeopardizes the intra-family relationships, but also threatens their strong association with their ethnic community. As a result minority gays and lesbians may run the risk of feeling uprooted as an ethnic person. (p. 233)*

Other difficulties faced by both Anglo and minority children of lesbian, gay, and bisexual parents may be the same as children from other families experiencing marital discord or integrating a new adult into the household (Hotvedt & Mandel, 1982; Miller, 1979b; Weeks, Derdeyn, & Langman, 1975). Like children of heterosexual divorces, adolescents generally experience the most difficult period of adjustment during the first year of separation. In one of the first studies of gay fathers and their children, Miller (1979b) found "problems of sexual acting out" in the biographies of 48 daughters and 42 sons. Only

> *two daughters reported premarital pregnancies and abortions; one admitted to engaging in some prostitution. Two interviewed offspring had problems in school, and one had had professional counseling for emotional difficulties. As studies of children of divorced heterosexual parents have revealed similar problems...these concerns may not result so much from the father's homosexuality as from family tensions surrounding marital instability, divorce, and residential relocation. Anger and bitterness toward parents are common to children with disrupted families, and respondents in this study were not immune to such feelings. (p. 547)*

In another study matching separated or divorced lesbian mothers with heterosexual mothers and using a variety of questionnaires, attitudes scales, as well as interviews for both parents and preadolescent children (ages 3 to 11), Hotvedt and Mandel (1982) concluded that there was "no evidence of gender identity conflict, poor peer relationships, or neglect" (p. 285). These findings were extended by Huggins (1989), who examined children's self-esteem through interviews and surveys of 36 adolescents whose head of household was lesbian. Compared with a match-set of heterosexual single female parents, Huggins concluded that "the mother's sexual object choice does not appear to influence negatively the self-esteem of her adolescent children.... The assumption that children of lesbian mothers are socially stigmatized by their mothers' sexual choice is not borne out by this study" (p. 132).

While this study does not imply that these children experienced no difficulties because of the stigma of homosexuality, it does mean that "the development of self-esteem is primarily influenced by the interaction between children and their parents or primary caregivers" (Huggins, 1989, p. 132). For example, one study found that one out of two children of lesbian mothers experienced relationship problems with other people due to the stigma of their mother's sexual identity (Wyers, 1987), and another (Lewis, 1980) concluded: "Although the findings are similar to those...of children of divorce, the particular issue of acceptance of the "crisis" is dissimilar.... Children's initial reaction to divorce was denial of pain; follow-up one year later revealed more open acceptance of the hurt. One reason for this difference may be that children of divorce have community support for their pain; children of lesbians do not" (p. 199).

Of course, parenting by lesbians, gay men, and bisexuals presents society with alternate approaches to family life that can challenge oppressive sexist and heterosexist myths and stereotypes. Sandra Pollack (1989), though acknowledging the legal necessity for demonstrating the sameness between homosexual and heterosexual families, challenges the "underlying assumption that the lesbian mother should be judged on how well she compares to the heterosexual norm." For example, do we really believe that, as a society, we want to foster the continued sex-role education of children?

Pollack has argued that rather than accepting the values associated with the heterosexual family, lesbian and gay parenting affords opportunities to challenge these norms in society and in the upbringing of their children. The "possible benefits of being a child of a lesbian mother" include "the children of lesbians may become aware (perhaps more so than other children) of their responsibility for themselves and their choices" (p. 322). For example, one study (Harris & Turner, 1985/1986) reported that lesbian mothers tended to use their homosexuality in a positive manner through assisting their children to accept their own sexuality, adopt empathetic and tolerant attitudes, and consider other points of view.

Central to the problems faced by children of lesbian and gay parents is the heterosexism and homophobia rampant in today's society. Homophobia—an irrational fear and hatred of homosexuals (Weinberg, 1972)—manifests itself in students' negative attitudes and feelings about homosexuality and the institutionalization of sodomy statutes which deny rights of sexual expression among persons of the same gender, thus restricting the legal definition of marriage and family. Heterosexism—the presumption of superiority and exclusiveness of heterosexual relationships—is evidenced in the assumption that parents of all children are heterosexual or that a heterosexual adult will *prima facie* be a better parent than one who is homosexual.

As two leading researchers on gay parenting stated, "Much ignorance regarding homosexuality is due to the propagation of myths. It is important for educators in many disciplines and at all educational levels to dispel myths, impart facts, and promote values clarification" (Bigner & Bozett, 1990, p. 168). It is at this juncture that educators' concern for the student with a newly identified lesbian or gay parent is married to their concern for the gay or lesbian student and for the heterosexual student harboring intensely homophobic feelings and attitudes. Each of these students can benefit from honest discussion about homosexuality in the school (Sears, 1987, 1991b), the adoption and implementation of anti-harassment guidelines (Sears, 1992d), the portrayal of the contributions and rich history of lesbians, gay men, and bisexuals (Sears, 1983), and the provision of gay-affirmative counseling services (Sears, 1989b).

Based on her interviews with children with lesbian mothers, Lewis (1980) concurred:

> *The children of lesbians seem not to have peer support available to them, since most of these children have either pulled away from their friends altogether or maintained friends but with a sense of their own differentness. Children of lesbians have been taught the same stereotypical myths and prejudices against homosexuals as the rest of society. Better understanding is needed about available family support systems and other systems that should be provided. These might include peer supports as well as educational supports, for example, dissemination of information about homosexuality. (p. 202)*

## *Homosexuality and the Schools*

Though some teachers, administrators, and guidance counselors are reluctant to discuss homosexuality in schools (Sears, 1992a, 1992b), every major professional educational association has adopted resolutions calling upon schools to address this topic. The National Council for the Accreditation of Teacher Education (NCATE) has proposed the inclusion of sexual orientation in its anti-discrimination standard and in its definition of cultural diversity. Some school districts have adopted specific programs and policies, and a variety of recommendations have been made to integrate issues relating to homosexuality in the school curriculum. Educators who assume proactive roles not only benefit lesbian, gay, and bisexual students but are making inroads into the institutionalized homophobia and heterosexism that makes school life more difficult for children from homosexual families.

## *Gay and Lesbian Students and Professional Standards*

Professional educational associations have adopted policies affirming the worth and dignity of lesbians, gay men, and bisexuals, and/or calling for an end to statutes, policies, and practices that effectively condone discrimination and harassment on the basis of sexual identity. Educators, school board members, and parents who have spearheaded these efforts acknowledge the simple social fact that being sexually different in a society of sexual sameness exacts a heavy psychological toll. Struggling to cope with their sexual identity, these students are more likely than other youth to attempt suicide, to abuse drugs or alcohol, and to experience academic problems (Gibson, 1989; Hetrick & Martin, 1987; Martin & Hetrick, 1988; Sears, 1989a; Teague, 1992; Zera, 1992). Other youth coping with their same-sex feelings may not display these symptoms but may excel in schoolwork, extracurricular activities, or sports as a means of hiding their sexual feelings from themselves or others (Sears, 1991a). By hiding, however, their emotional and sexual development languishes (Martin, 1982).

Five states (Massachusetts, New Jersey, Wisconsin, Hawaii, and Minnesota) have adopted some type of antidiscrimination statutes. Massachusetts became the first state to outlaw discrimination against lesbian and gay students in public schools. Wisconsin's statute Section 118.13 reads, in part,"No person may be denied admission to any public school or be denied participation in, be denied the benefits of or be discriminated against in any curricular, extracurricular, pupil services, recreational, or other program or activity because of the person's sex, race...marital or parental status, sexual orientation."

As part of the process of implementing its statute, the Wisconsin Department of Public Instruction issued a 59-page booklet that noted "the board shall adopt instructional and library media materials selection policies stating that instructional materials, texts, and library services reflect the cultural diversity and pluralist nature of American study" and cited lesbian/gay students as one underrepresented group.

Many major educational organizations, such as the National Educational Association, the American Federation of Teachers, and the Association for Supervision and Curriculum Development, have adopted statements affirming the rights of homosexual/bisexual students in K–12 schools and have called on their members to undertake proactive measures to combat the heterosexism and homophobia that are rampant in our nation's schools. For example, the American School Health Association issued a policy statement on gay and lesbian youth in schools that stated, in part: "School personnel should discourage any sexually oriented, deprecating, harassing, and prejudicial statements injurious to students' self-esteem. Every school district should provide access to professional counseling by specially trained personnel for students who may be concerned about sexual orientation."

Finally, the NCATE in its draft of the standards revision has revised one standard as follows: "policies and practices of the unit clearly demonstrate inclusiveness and do not discriminate on the basis of race, ethnicity, language, gender, sexual orientation, religion, age, or disability" (IV.A.54). Further, it has recommended altering its operational definition of "cultural diversity" to include sexual orientation.

## *School Polices and Programs*

Since the late 1980s, the invisibility of homosexuality in education has lessened. Evidence of its being less invisible includes extensive sex education courses in this nation's schools (Haffner, 1990; Sears, 1992c) with some systems including units on homosexuality (Sears, 1991b); the first public funding of a school serving homosexual students, The Harvey Milk School, by the New York City public school system (Friends of Project 10, 1991; Rofes, 1989); the institution of the first gay-affirmative counseling service in a public high school, Project 10 within the Los Angles Unified School District (Rofes, 1989); the election of the nation's first openly gay school board member in San Francisco; and the formation of the Lesbian and Gay Studies special interest group of the American Educational Research Association (Grayson, 1987).

Several school districts have adopted antiharassment guidelines. In 1987, the Cambridge (Massachusetts) public schools included in their policies the following statement:

> *Harassment on the basis of an individual's sexual preference or orientation is prohibited. Words, action or other verbal, written, or physical conduct which ridicules, scorns, mocks, intimidates, or otherwise threatens an individual because of his/her sexual orientation/preference constitutes homophobic harassment when it has the purpose or effect of unreasonably interfering with the work performance or creating an intimidating, hostile, or offensive environment. (Peterkin, 1987)*

More recently, in 1991, the St. Paul school board passed a human rights policy forbidding discrimination on the basis of "sexual or affectional orientation." Several large urban school districts (e.g., New York, Washington, DC, Cincinnati, Los Angeles, Des Moines, San Francisco) have implemented anti-gay and lesbian discrimination policies. Perhaps the most publicized effort to meet the needs of homosexual students has been the funding of a public alternative school for gay and lesbian youth in New York City and the development of counseling services expressly for this target population in Los Angeles. The Harvey Milk School, established in 1985 under the sponsorship of the Hetrick-Martin Institute, serves about 40 students who are unable to function in the conventional school setting (Rofes, 1989). In Los Angeles, Project 10 at Fairfax High School has received international attention for the gay-affirmative services provided by its counseling staff. And, in 1993, the school district, under the auspices of Project 10, hosted the first conference for their high school gay youth at nearby Occidental College.

These policies and programs not only have a positive impact on the gay, lesbian, and bisexual student but on heterosexual students, faculty, and staff who often harbor homophobic feelings or heterosexist attitudes. Thus, these policies and programs can help to create a supportive school climate for heterosexual students who come from lesbian, gay, or bisexual households.

## *Curriculum and Staffing Recommendations*

Elsewhere (Sears, 1987, 1991b, 1992b), I have discussed the importance of integrating issues of homosexuality into the school curriculum. When the issue of homosexuality appears in the school curriculum, the most likely subjects to be targeted are science in the form of human physiology or health in the form of HIV/AIDS prevention (Sears, 1992c). In contrast, I believe, sexuality can serve as a transformative tool for thinking about the construction of one's sexual identities vis-á-vis the interrelationships among language, history, and society (Carlson, 1992; Macanghaill, 1991). As such, sexuality no longer becomes the province of sex educators teaching separate units within physical education or biology but becomes a major strand woven throughout the curriculum (Sears, 1991b).

Educators have long argued that schools ought to be an embryonic environment for engaging young people in the art of democratic living and, in the process, moving society further along its democratic path (Dewey, 1916; Giroux, 1988; Rugg, 1939). In fact, however, the hidden curriculum of school fosters conformity and passivity while seldom encouraging critical thinking, ethical behavior, and civic courage (Giroux, 1988; McLaren, 1991, 1993). Within this environment, controversial ideas and individual differences are seldom welcomed. The discussion of homosexuality, the treatment of lesbian, gay, and bisexual students, and the restrictive definition of family are some of the most glaring examples.

Specific strategies and materials that foster an awareness of homosexuality and homosexual persons already have been proposed or developed (e.g., Friends of Project 10, 1991; Goodman, 1983; Hubbard, 1989; Krysiak, 1987; Lipkin, 1992; Sears, 1983; Wilson, 1984). Educators have been admonished by scholars and activists alike to sit down and talk with bisexual, lesbian, and gay adults to learn first hand about the special problems they faced in school; the importance of lesbian and gay educators as role models for homosexual students has been stressed, as has the need for public school systems to follow the lead of communities such as Berkeley and Cambridge in adopting anti-slur policies and nonharassment guidelines (Griffin, 1992; Hetrick & Martin, 1987; Kissen, 1991; Martin & Hetrick, 1988; Peterkin, 1987; Rofes, 1989; Sears, 1987, 1993; Slater, 1988; Stover, 1992). In some schools, anti-homophobia workshops with heterosexual students and educators have been conducted (Schneider & Tremble, 1986; Stewart, 1984). Professional educators as well as lesbian and gay activists ask, at the very least, for the construction of a nonjudgmental atmosphere in which homosexual-identified students can come to terms with their sexuality, the acquisition by school libraries of biographical books where students can discover the homosexuality of some famous people, and the integration of references to homosexual men and women as well as the topic of homosexuality into the high school curriculum (Jenkins, 1990; Sears, 1983, 1988).

It should be noted that there is no legal justification for systematically barring discussion of homosexuality and the inclusion of the contributions of lesbian, gay, and bisexual artists, politicians, scientists, and athletes from the school curriculum. A United States Court of Appeals ruling that a state statute prohibiting educators and school staff from "advocating, soliciting, or promoting homosexual activity" was unconstitutional was let stand due to a deadlock Supreme Court vote (*National Gay Task Force* v. *Board of Education of the City of Oklahoma*, 1984). Nevertheless, the integration of lesbian, gay, and bisexual topics or persons in the school curriculum appears too radical for many educators. Too few administrators refuse to acquiesce to a scissors and paste mentality of curriculum development in which only the most mundane, least controversial material survives the scrutiny of self-appointed moral vigilantes or the self-censorship of timid school officials (Sears, 1992d; Summerford, 1987; Tabbert, 1988).

In such an Orwellian school world, the curriculum is carefully crafted to omit (without the appearance of omission) the homoerotic imagery in the poetry of Walt Whitman, Sappho, and Langston Hughes or the visual arts of Donatello, Marsden Hartley, and Robert Mapplethorpe, the conflict between racial and sexual identities present in the literature of James Baldwin, Yukio Mishima, and Toni Morrison, or the conflict between the professional and personal lives of computer inventor Alan Turing, sports heroes David Kopay and Martina Navratilova, and political activists Eleanor Roosevelt and Susan B. Anthony. Just as sexuality is extracted from life and compartmentalized into units of sexuality education, so too is bisexuality and homosexuality exorcised from the body politic and tucked away in the curriculum closet.

In each of these areas, educators can play an important role in reducing homophobia and heterosexism. In the process, they can directly counter those litigants who petition courts to deny custody or visitation rights to lesbian or gay parents due to the fear of a "definite possibility of peer ridicule in the future" (Hitchens, 1979/1980, p. 90).

## *Summary and Recommendations*

### *Summary of Research*

Studies on bisexual and homosexual parenting as well as children of lesbians and gay men are far from complete. There are, however, some suggestive findings:

- Children are less accepting when a same-sex parent "comes out" than when a parent of the other gender discloses sexual identity.
- Children of a lesbian or gay parent are no more likely to define themselves as homosexual than children of heterosexual parents, nor are they any more likely to display atypical sex-role preferences.
- Lesbian, gay, and bisexual parents often seek to provide children with a variety of gender role models.
- The earlier the disclosure to the child the fewer problems in the parent/child relationship.
- Children of a lesbian or gay parent follow typical developmental patterns of acquiring sex-role concepts and sex-typed behaviors.

- Children of homosexual parents who have experienced marital turmoil face similar difficulties common to children of divorce.
- Gay fathers may have a more difficult time disclosing their sexuality to their children than lesbian mothers, children of gay fathers are less likely to know of their parents sexual identity, and the coming out process is more difficult for gay fathers with children at home.
- Sons are less accepting when learning their parent is gay than are daughters.
- As children enter adolescence, there is a greater likelihood that they will experience peer harassment about their parents' sexual identity and engage in a variety of self-protective mechanisms.
- Gay fathers are more likely to report their children experiencing difficulty with peer harassment because of the parent's homosexuality.

## *Recommendations for Educators*

In several studies, researchers have noted the important role that educators can play in reducing homophobia and heterosexism that create difficult environments for children of lesbian or gay families to learn and for their parents to visit. Based on these and other writings (e.g., Clay, 1990; Casper & Wickens, 1992), educators should:

- Redesign school paperwork in order to be inclusive. Replace words such as *mother* and *father* with *parent* or *parent 1, parent 2*.
- When establishing associations, such as parent-teacher organizations, develop assistance for single-parent families (e.g., child care) and create or identify a safe space for homosexual parents (e.g., support groups). Encouraging gay parents to share their family status with school officials is important. Based on his extensive research with children of gay fathers, Bozett (1987a) stated:

  > *It is best for school officials to know about the father's homosexuality, especially if the father has child custody. Knowing about the family can alert school personal to problems which may have the home situation as their genesis. Likewise, if the father is known about by school officials, both the father and his lover may participate in school affairs, attend school functions, or the lover may pick the child up at school all without the parents or the child having to make elaborate explanations. (p. 53)*

- Represent family/cultural diversity in classroom materials and books, on bulletin boards, and in everyday teaching practices.
- Ensure that books depicting alternative family patterns are included in school libraries (see following resource section for a few recommendations).
- Sensitize teachers and prepare guidance counselors to work with children as well as their gay parent as they confront issues ranging from the child's need for self-protection to the parent's need of respect for their sexual choices.
- Provide role models of gay or lesbian parents for students. Examples should reflect a multicultural emphasis rather than reinforcing the stereotype of homosexuality existing

*only within the White community. Since some children in every school will identify* themselves as lesbian or gay, it is important for them to have positive parenting role models, should they elect to bear or foster children as adults.
- Inform parents of any sexual harassment or intimidation directed at their child.
- Modify the school's anti-slur and anti-harassment policy to include sexual orientation and equally enforce violations against this policy.
- Interview potential teachers and counselors to ascertain their professional experiences and personal attitudes in working with sexual minorities.
- Revise hiring policies and procedures to enhance the likelihood of recruiting sexual minority faculty.
- Develop and publicize a counseling service for students who wish to discuss issues related to sexual identity.
- Hold a series of informal faculty meetings with gay and lesbian parents and faculty to identify needs and possible solutions.
- Meet with support services personnel (e.g., media specialists, counselors) to determine the adequacy of resource materials available for students and faculty about homosexuality and bisexuality.
- Review and revise accordingly student and faculty school-sanctioned activities that discriminate on the basis of sexual orientation (e.g., Junior ROTC, school dances, job recruitment fairs).
- Review school textbooks for biased or misleading information about lesbians, gays, and bisexuals.
- Review the school curriculum to identify areas within *every* subject matter where relevant information (people, places, events) about lesbians, gay men, and bisexuals can be included.
- Engage teachers and administrators in formal activities that address the cognitive, affective, and behavioral dimension of homophobia.
- Develop prejudice awareness among student leaders through after-school workshops.
- Invite former students and members of the community to address the student body on issues relating to homosexuality.

## *Resources for Educators*

There is a wide selection of books, organizations, and journals appropriate for adults interested in lesbian and gay parents or their children. These include:

Alpert, H. (1988). *We are everywhere: Writings by and about lesbian parents.* Freedom, CA: Crossing Press.

*Boys of Lesbian Mothers.* 935 W. Broadway, Eugene, OR 97402.

Burke, P. (1993). *Family values: Two moms and their son.* New York: Random House.

*Chain of Life.* A newsletter for lesbian and gay adoptees. Box 8081, Berkeley, CA 94707.

Children of Gay/Lesbians. 8306 Wilshire Blvd., Suite 222, Beverly Hills, CA 90211.

*Empathy: An interdisciplinary journal for persons working to end oppression based on sexual identities.* Published twice a year (individuals $15, institutions $20), this 100+ page journal regularly includes essays on alternative family structures and issues relating to lesbian, gay, and bisexual youth. PO Box 5085, Columbia, SC 29250.

*Gay and Lesbian Parents Coalition International.* An advocacy/support group for lesbian and gay parents with a quarterly newsletter. PO Box 50360, Washington, DC 20091.

*Gay Fathers* (1981). Some of their stories, experiences, and advice. Toronto: Author.

*Gay Fathers Coalition.* Box 50360, Washington, DC 20004.

*Gay Parents Support Packet.* National Gay Task Force, 80 Fifth Ave., Room 506, New York, NY 10011.

Jenkins, C. (1990, September 1). *"Being gay: Gay/lesbian characters and concerns in young adult books."* Booklist, 39-41.

Jullion, J. (1985). *Long way home: The odyssey of a lesbian mother and her children.* Pittsburgh, PA: Cleis.

Lewin, E (1993). *Lesbian mothers: Accounts of gender in American culture.*

MacPike, L. (1989). *There's something I've been meaning to tell you.* Tallahassee, FL: Naiad Press.

*Parents and Friends of Lesbians and Gays.* PO Box 27605, Washington, DC 20038-7605.

Pollack, S., & Vaughn, S. (1987). *Politics of the heart: A lesbian parenting anthology.* Ithaca, NY: Firebrand.

Rafkin, L. (1990). *Different mothers: Sons and daughters of lesbians talk about their lives.* Pittsburgh, PA: Cleis.

Schulenburg, J. (1985). *Gay parenting: A complete guide for gay men and lesbians with children.* Garden City, NY: Anchor.

Wolf, V. (1989). "The gay family in literature for young people." *Children's Literature in Education, 20*(1), 51-58.

There is also a growing selection of books appropriate for children and adolescents about gay and lesbian families. These include:

### Children's Books with Lesbian Moms
Newman, L. (1989). *Heather has two mommies.* Boston: Alyson.
Elwin, R., & Paulsee, M. (1990). *Asha's mums.* Toronto: Women's Press.
Willholte, M. (1993). *Belinda's bouquet.* Boston: Alyson.

### Children's Books with Gay Dads
Heron, A., & Maran, M. (1991). *How would you feel if your dad was gay?* Boston: Alyson.
Bosche, S. (1981). *Jenny lives with Eric and Martin.* London: Gay Men's Press.
Willholte, M. (1990). *Daddy's roommate.* Boston: Alyson.

### Children's Books with Lesbian & Gay Families
Willholte, M. (1991). Families: *A coloring book.* Boston: Alyson.
Willholte, M. (1993). *Uncle what-it-is is coming to visit!!* Boston: Alyson.
Valentine, J. (1991). *The duke who outlawed jelly beans and other stories.* Boston: Alyson.

### Adolescent Books with Lesbian & Gay Family Themes
Homes, A. (1990). *Jack.* New York: Vintage
Salat, C. (1993). *Living in secret.* New York: Bantam.
Miller, D. (1992). *Coping when a parent is gay.* New York: Rosen

## Endnotes

1. These real-world vignettes reflect the variety of lesbian, gay, or bisexual families. Although the number of children of lesbian, gay, and bisexual parents is speculative, researchers cite a range of 6 to 14 million children (Bozett, 1987a; Rivera, 1987; Schulenberg, 1985). Empirical data, itself subject to sampling problems, suggests that approximately 1 in 5 lesbians and 1 in 10 gay men have children (Bell & Weinberg, 1978; Jay & Young, 1979) with estimates of upwards of 1.5 million lesbians living with their children (Hoeffer, 1981). Until recently, these children were the result of defunct heterosexual relationships or marriages in which a spouses' homosexuality remains undisclosed (Brown, 1976; Green, 1987; Miller, 1979a).

Studies on lesbian and gay parents and their families have been limited in terms of sample size and methodology. For example, some studies (e.g., Weeks, Derdeyn, & Langman, 1975) have been clinical case studies and others have relied on anecdotal evidence (e.g., Alpert, 1988; Brown, 1976; Mager, 1975); others have studied small (1,040) groups of homosexual parents identified through gayrelated organizations (e.g., Scallen, 1981). Only a few studies have used larger samples with more sophisticated research designs (e.g., Bigner & Jacobsen, 1989; Hotvedt & Mandel, 1982). There have been no ethnographic, longitudinal, or nationwide studies conducted. Further, researchers generally have compared homosexual single parents with single heterosexual parents and, occasionally, homosexual parents living with a domestic partner with remarried heterosexual couples. Due to their incompatibility, no comparisons between homosexual parented households with the "traditional" two-parent heterosexual families have been made. Further, few of these studies present statistical analyses, control for the presence of a male role model in the home, take into account the desire to appear socially acceptable, include a majority of adolescent subjects, or focus on bisexual parents (Gottman, 1990). Finally, only a handful of studies have directly interviewed, surveyed, or observed children raised by a father or mother who is homosexual (Bozett, 1980, 1987b; Green, 1978; Huggins, 1989; Paul, 1986). For a review of much of this literature, see Bozett (1989).

2. One tragedy of failures to challenge successfully state sodomy statutes in the courts and the legislature is the difficulty that lesbians, gay men, or bisexuals have in obtaining child custody or visiting privileges in divorce hearings or approval from adoption agencies even for children whose prospects for adoption are slim, such as an older child or an HIV-infected baby (Hitchens, 1979/1980; Payne, 1978; Ricketts & Achtenberg, 1987; Rivera, 1987).

## References

Achtenburg, R. (1985). *Sexual/ orientation and the law*. New York: Clark-Boardman.

Alpert, H. (1988). *We are everywhere: Writings by and about lesbian parents*. Freedom, CA: Crossing Press.

Basile, R. (1974). "Lesbian mothers and custody and homosexual parents." *Women's Rights Law Reporter, 2,*

Beam, J. (Ed.). (1986). *In the life: A black gay anthology*. Boston: Alyson.

Bell, A., & Weinberg, M. (1978). *Homosexualities*. New York: Simon & Schuster.

Bigner, J., & Bozett, F. (1990). "Parenting by gay fathers." In F. Bozett & M. Sussman (Eds.), *Homosexuality and family relations* (pp. 155–175). New York: Haworth Press.

Bigner, J., & Jacobsen, R. (1989). "Parenting behaviors of homosexual and heterosexual fathers." In F. Bozett (Ed.), *Homosexuality and the family* (pp. 173–186). New York: Haworth Press.

Blumenthal, A. (1990/1991). "Scrambled eggs and seed daddies: Conversations with my son." *Empathy, 2*(2) 45–48.

Bosche, S. (1983). *Jenny lives with Eric and Martin*. London: Gay Men's Press.

Bozett, F. (1980). "Gay fathers: How and why gay fathers disclose their homosexuality to their children." *Family Relations, 29,* 173–179.

Bozett, F. (1981a). "Gay fathers: Evolution of the gay father identity." *American Journal of Orthopsychiatry,* 51, 552–559.

Bozett, F. (1981b) "Gay fathers: Identity conflict resolution through integrative sanctions." *Alternative Lifestyles,* 4, 90–107.

Bozett, F. (1985). "Gay men as fathers." In S. Hanson & F. Bozett (Eds.), *Dimensions of fatherhood* (pp. 327–352). Beverly Hllls, CA: Sage.

Bozett, F. (1987a). "Children of gay fathers." In F. Bozett (Ed.), *Gay and lesbian parents* (pp. 39–57). Westport CT: Praeger.

Bozett, F. (1987b). "Gay fathers." In F. Bozett (Ed.), *Gay and lesbian parents* (pp. 3–22). Westport, CT: Praeger.

Bozett, F. (1989). "Gay fathers: A review of the literature." In F. Bozett (Ed.), *Homosexuality and the family* (pp. 137–162). New York: Haworth Press.

Bozett, F., & Hanson, S. (1991). "Cultural change and the future of fatherhood and families." In F. Bozett & S. Hanson (Eds.), *Fatherhood and families in cultural context* (pp. 263–274). New York: Springer.

Brown, H. (1976). "Married homosexuals." In H. Brown (Ed.), *Familiar faces, hidden lives* (pp. 108–130). New York: Harcourt Brace Jovanovich.

Carlson, D. (1992). "Ideological conflict and change in the sexuality curriculum." In J. Sears (Ed.), *Sexuality and the curriculum* (pp. 34–57). New York: Teachers College Press.

Casper, V., & Wickens, E. (1992). "Gay and lesbian parents: Their children in school." *Teachers College Record,* 94

Chesler, P. (1986). *Mothers on trial: The battle for children and custody.* New York: McGraw-Hill.

Clay, J. (1990). "Working with lesbian and gay parents and their children." *Young Children,* 45(3), 31–35.

Coleman, E. (1985). "Bisexual women in marriages." *Journal of Homosexuality,* 11, 87–100.

Corley, R. (1990). *The final closet.* N. Miami, FL: Editech Press .

Dewey, J. (1916). *Democracy and education: An introduction to the philosophy of education.* New York: Macmillan .

Friends of Project 10 (1991). *Project 10 Handbook: Addressing lesbian and gay issues in our schools* (third edition). Los Angeles, CA: Author. (ERIC Reproduction No. ED 337567).

Gantz, J. (1983). "The Weston/Roberts Family." In J. Gantz (Ed.), *Whose child cries: Children of gay parents talk about their lives* (pp. 49–96). Rolling Hills Estate, CA: Jalmar Press.

Gibson, P. (1989). "Gay male and lesbian youth suicide." *Report of the Secretary's Task Force on Youth Suicide. Volume 3: Prevention and interventions in youth suicide.* Washington, DC: U.S. Department of Health and Human Services.

Giroux, H. (1988). *Teachers as intellectuals: Toward a critical pedagogy of learning.* Boston: Bergin & Garvey.

Glick, P. (1987). *Remarried families, stepfamilies and stepchildren.* Paper presented at the Wingspread Conference on the Remarried Family. Racine, WI.

Glick, P. (1988). "Fifty years of family demography: A record of social change." *Journal of Marriage and the Family,* 50(4), 861–873.

Golombok, S., Spencer, A., & Rutter, M. (1983). "Children in lesbian and single-parent households: Psychosexual and psychiatric appraisal." *Journal of Child Psychology and Psychiatry,* 24, 551–572.

Goodman, J. (1983). "Out of the closet by paying the price." *Interracial Books for Children,* 9(3/4), 13–15.

Gottman, J. (1990). "Children of gay and lesbian parents." In F. Bozett & M. Sussman (Eds.), *Homosexuality and family relations* (pp. 177–196). New York: Haworth Press.

Grayson, D. (1987). "Emerging equity issues related to homosexuality in education." *Peabody Journal of Education,* 64(4), 132–145.

Green, G. (1987, August 28). *Lesbian mothers.* Paper presented at the Annual Convention of the American Psychological Association. (ERIC Reproduction No. ED 297205).

Green, G., & Clunis, D. (1989). "Married lesbians." In E. Rothblum & E. Cole (Eds.), *Lesbianism: Affirming non-traditional roles* (pp. 41–50). New York: Haworth Press.

Green, R. (1978). "Sexual identity of 37 children raised by homosexual or transsexual parents." *American Journal of Psychiatry,* 135(6), 692–697.

Griffin, P. (1992). "From hiding out to coming out: Empowering lesbian and gay educators." In K. Harbeck (Ed.), *Homosexuality and education.* New York: Haworth Press.

Haffner, D. (1990). *Sex education 2000: A call to action.* New York: SIECUS.

Harris, M., & Turner, P. (1985/1986). "Gay and lesbian parents." *Journal of Homosexuality,* 12(2), 101–113.

Heron, A., & Maran, M. (1990). *How would you feel if your dad was gay?* Boston: Alyson.

Hetrick, E., & Martin, A. D. (1987). "Developmental issues and their resolution for gay and lesbian adolescents." *Journal of Homosexuality,* 14(1/2), 25–43.

Hill, M. (1981). "Effects of conscious and unconscious factors on child reacting attitudes of lesbian mothers." Doctoral dissertation, Adelphi University. *Dissertation Abstracts International,* 42 1608B.

Hitchens, D. (1979/1980). "Social attitudes, legal standards, and personal trauma in child custody cases." *Journal of Homosexuality,* 5(1/2), 89–95.

Hoeffer, B. (1981). "Children's acquisition of sex role behavior in lesbian-mother families." *American Journal of Orthopsychiatry,* 51(31), 536–544.

Hotvedt, M., & Mandel, J. (1982). "Children of lesbian mothers." In W. Paul, J. Weinrich, J. Gonsiorek, & M. Hotvedt (Eds.), *Homosexuality: Social, psychological and biological issues* (pp. 275–285). Beverly Hills. CA: Sage.

Hubbard, B. (1989). *Entering adulthood: Living in relationships. A curriculum for grades 9–12.* Santa Cruz CA: Network Publications.

Huggins, S. (1989). "A comparative study of self-esteem of adolescent children of divorced lesbian mothers and divorced heterosexual mothers." In F. Bozett (Ed.), *Homosexuality and the family* (pp. 123–135). New York: Haworth Press.

Jay, K., & Young, A. (1979). *The gay report.* New York: Summit.

Jenkins, C. (1990, September 1). "Being gay: Gay/lesbian characters and concerns in young adult books." *Booklist,* 39–41.

Johnson, J. (1981). *Influence of assimilation on the psychosocial adjustment of black homosexual men.* Unpublished doctoral dissertation, California School of Professional Psychology, Berkeley, CA. *Dissertation Abstracts International* 42, 11, 4620B.

Jullion, J. (1985). *Long way home: The odyssey of a lesbian mother and her children.* Pittsburgh PA: Cleis.

Kamerman, S., & Hayes, C.(1982). "Families that work." In S. Kamerman & C. Hayes (Eds.), *Children in a changing world.* Washington, DC: National Academy Press.

Kirkpatrick, M., Smith, C., & Roy, R. (1981). "Lesbian mothers and their children: A comparative study." *American Journal of Orthopsychiatry,* 51(3), 545–551.

Kissen, R. (1991). *Listening to gay and lesbian teenagers.* Paper presented at the Annual Meeting of the National Council of Teachers of English, Seattle, WA. (ERIC Reproduction No. ED 344220).

Krysiak, G. (1987). "Very silent and gay minority." *School Counselor,* 34(4), 304–307.

Lamothe, D. ( 1989). *Previously heterosexual lesbian mothers who have come out to an adolescent daughter: An exploratory study of the coming out process.* Unpublished doctoral dissertation, Antioch University, Yellow Spring, OH. *Dissertation Abstracts International* 50, 5, 2157B.

Lesbian Mothers Group. (1989). "'A word might slip and that would be it.' Lesbian mothers and their children." In L. Holly (Ed.), *Girls and sexuality* (pp. 122–129). Milton Keynes: Open University.

Lewin, E., & Lyons, T. (1982). "Everything in its place: The coexistence of lesbianism and motherhood." In W. Paul, J. Weinrich, J. Gonsiorek, & M. Hotvedt (Eds.), *Homosexuality: Social, psychological, and biological issues* (pp. 249–273). Beverly Hills, CA: Sage.

Lewis, K. (1980). "Children of lesbians: Their points of view." *Social Work,* 25(3), 198–203.

Lim-Hing, S. (1990/1991). "Dragon ladies, snow queens, and Asian-American dykes: Reflections on race and sexuality." *Empathy, 2* (2), 20–22.

Lipkin, A. (1992). "Project 10: Gay and lesbian students find acceptance in their school community." *Teaching Tolerance, 1* (2), 24–27.

Lorde, A. (1987). "Man child: A black lesbian feminist's response." In S. Pollack & J. Vaughn (Eds.), *Politics of the Heart: A lesbian parenting anthology* (pp. 220–226). Ithaca, NY: Firebrand.

Macanghaill, M. (1991). "Schooling, sexuality and male power: Towards an emancipatory curriculum." *Gender and Education,* 3(3), 291–309.

Mager, D. (1975). "Faggot father." In K. Jay & A. Young (Eds.), *After you're out* (pp. 128–134). New York: Gage.

Martin, A. (1982). "Learning to hide: The socialization of the gay adolescent." In S. Feinstein & J. Looney (Eds.), *Adolescent psychiatry: Developmental and clinical studies* (pp. 52–65). Chicago: University of Chicago Press.

Martin, A., & Hetrick, E. (1988). "The stigmatization of gay and lesbian adolescents." *Journal of Homosexuality,* 15(1–2), 163–185.

Matteson, D. (1985). "Bisexual men in marriages: Is a positive homosexual identity and stable marriage possible?" *Journal of Homosexuality,* 11, 149–173.

Matteson, D. (1987). "The heterosexually married gay and lesbian parent." In F. Bozett (Ed.), *Gay and lesbian parents* (pp. 138–161). Westport, CT: Praeger.

McGuire, M., & Alexander, N. (1985). "Artificial insemination of single women." *Fertility and Sterility,* 43, 182–184.

McLaren, P. (1991). "Critical pedagogy: Constructing an arch of social dreaming and a doorway to hope." *Journal of Education,* 173(1), 9–34.

McLaren, P. (1993). *Schooling as a ritual performance* (second edition). London: Routledge.

Miller, B. (1978). "Adult sexual resocialization: Adjustments toward a stigmatized identity." *Alternative Lifestyles,* 1, 207–234.

Miller, B. (1979a). "Unpromised paternity: The lifestyles of gay fathers." In M. Levin (Ed.), *Gay men: The sociology of male homosexuality* (pp. 239–252). New York: Harper & Row.

Miller, B. (1979b). "Gay fathers and their children." *Family Coordinator,* 28(4), 544–552.

Moraga, C., & Anzaldua, G. (Eds.). (1981). *This bridge called me back: Writings by radical women of color.* Watertown, MA: Persephone Press.

Morales, E. (1990). "Ethnic minority families and minority gays and lesbians." In F. Bozett & M. Sussman (Eds.), *Homosexuality and family relations* (pp. 217–239). New York: Haworth.

*National Gay Task Force* v. *Board of Education of the City of Oklahoma,* State of Oklahoma, 729 Fed.2d 1270 (1984), 33 FEP 1009 (1982).

Pagelow, M. (1980). "Heterosexual and lesbian single mothers: A comparison of problems, coping, and solutions." *Journal of Homosexuality,* 5(3), 189–204.

Paul, J. (1986). "Growing up with a gay, lesbian or bisexual parent: An exploratory study of experiences and perceptions." Unpublished doctoral dissertation, University of California, Berkeley. *Dissertation Abstracts International,* 47, 7, 2756A.

Payne, A. (1977/1978). "Law and the problem patient: Custody and parental rights of homosexual, mentally retarded, mentally ill, and incarcerated patients." *Journal of Family Law,* 16(4), 797–818.

Pennington, S. (1987). "Children of lesbian mothers." F. Bozett (Ed.), *Gay and lesbian parents* (pp. 58–74). New York: Praeger.

Peterkin, R. (1987, June 11). Letter to Administrative Staff: *Anti-harassment guidelines.* Cambridge, MA.

Pies, C. (1985). Considering parenthood. San Francisco, CA: Spinster's Ink.

Pies, C. (1987). *"Considering parenthood:* Psychosocial issues for gay men and lesbians choosing alternative fertilization." In F. Bozett (Ed.), *Gay and lesbian parents* (pp. 165–174). Westport, CT: Praeger.

Polikoff, N. (1987). "Lesbian mothers, lesbian families: Legal obstacles, legal challenges." In S. Pollack & J. Vaughn (Eds.), *Politics of the heart: A lesbian parenting anthology* (pp. 325–332). Ithaca, NY: Firebrand.

Pollack, S. (1989). "Lesbian mothers: A lesbian-feminist perspective on research." In S. Pollack & J. Vaughn (Eds.), *Politics of the heart: A lesbian parenting anthology* (pp. 316–324). Ithaca, NY: Firebrand.

Pollack, S., & Vaughn, J. (Eds.). (1989). *Politics of the heart: A lesbian parenting anthology.* Ithaca, NY: Firebrand.

Ricketts, W., & Achtenberg, R. (1987). "The adoptive and foster gay and lesbian parent." In F. Bozett (Ed.), *Gay and lesbian parents* (pp. 89–111). Westport, CT: Praeger.

Riddle, D., & Arguelles, M. (1981). "Children of gay parents: Homophobia's victims." In I. Stuart & L. Abt (Eds.), *Children of separation and divorce.* New York: Von Nostrand Reinhold.

Rivera, R. (1987). "Legal issues in gay and lesbian parenting." In F. Bozett (Ed.), *Gay and lesbian parents* (pp. 199–227). Westport, CT: Praeger.

Robinson, B., & Skeen, P. (1982). "Sex-role orientation of gay fathers versus gay nonfathers." *Perceptual and Motor Skills,* 55, 1055–1059.

Rofes, E. (1989). "Opening up the classroom closet: Responding to the educational needs of gay and lesbian youth." *Harvard Educational Review,* 59(4), 444–453.

Rohrbaugh, J. (1989). "Choosing children: Psychological issues in lesbian parenting." In E. Rothblum & E. Cole (Eds.), *Lesbianism: Affirming non traditional roles* (pp. 51–64). New York: Haworth.

Rugg, H. (1939). *Democracy and the curriculum: The life and progress of the American school.* New York: Appleton-Century.

Rust, P. (1993). "'Coming Out' in the age of social constructionism: Sexual identity formation among lesbian and bisexual women." *Gender and Society,* 7(1), 50–77.

Sands, A. (1988). "We are family." In H. Alpert (Ed.), *We are everywhere* (pp. 45–51). Freedom, CA: Crossing Press.

Scallen, R. (1981). *An investigation of paternal attitudes and behaviors in homosexual and heterosexual fathers.* Unpublished doctoral dissertation, California School of Professional Psychology, Los Angeles, CA. *Dissertation Abstracts International,* 42, 9, 3809B.

Schneider, M., & Tremble, B. (1986). "Training service providers to work with gay or lesbian adolescents: A workshop." *Journal of Counseling and Development,* 65(2), 98–99.

Schulenberg, J. (1985). *Gay parenting.* New York: Doubleday.

Sears, J. (1983). "Sexuality: Taking off the masks." *Changing Schools,* 11, 12–13.

Sears, J. (1987). "Peering into the well of loneliness: The responsibility of educators to gay and lesbian youth." In Alex Molnar (Ed.), *Social issues and education: Challenge and responsibility* (pp. 79–100). Alexandria, VA: Association for Supervision & Curriculum Development.

Sears, J. (1988). "Growing up gay: Is anyone there to listen?" *American School Counselors Association Newsletter,* 26, 8–9.

Sears, J. (1989a). "The impact of gender and race on growing up lesbian and gay in the South." *NWSA Journal,* 1(3), 422–457.

Sears, J. (1989b). "Counseling sexual minorities: An interview with Virginia Uribe." *Empathy,* 1(2), 1, 8.

Sears, J. (1991a). *Growing up gay in the South: Race, gender, and journeys of the spirit.* New York: Haworth.

Sears, J. (1991b). "Teaching for diversity: Student sexual identities." *Educational Leadership,* 49, 54–57.

Sears, J. (1992a). "Educators, homosexuality, and homosexual students: Are personal feelings related to professional beliefs?" *Journal of Homosexuality,* 29–79.

Sears, J. (1992b). "The impact of culture and ideology on the construction of gender and sexual identities: Developing a critically-based sexuality curriculum." In J. Sears (Ed.), *Sexuality and the curriculum: The politics and practices of sexuality education* (pp. 169–189). New York: Teachers College Press.

Sears, J. (1992c). "Dilemmas and possibilities of sexuality education: Reproducing the body politic." In J. Sears (Ed.), *Sexuality and the curriculum: The politics and practices of sexuality education* (pp. 19–50). New York: Teachers College Press.

Sears, J. (1992d). "Responding to the sexual diversity of faculty and students: An agenda for critically reflective administrators." In C. Capper (Ed.), *The social context of education: Administration in a pluralist society* (pp. 110–172). New York: SUNY Press.

Sears, J. (1993). "Alston and Everetta: Too Risky for School?" In R. Donmoyer & R. Kos (Eds.), *At-risk students* (pp. 153–172). New York: State University of New York Press.

Shernoff, M. (1984). "Family therapy for lesbian and gay clients." *Social Work,* 29(4), 393–396.

Slater, B. (1988). "Essential issues in working with lesbian and gay male youths." *Professional Psychology: Research and Practice,* 19(2), 226–235.

Smith, B. (Ed.). (1983). *Home girls: A black feminist anthology.* New York: Kitchen Table/ Women of Color Press.

Stewart, J. (1984). "What non-gay therapists need to know to work with gay and lesbian clients." *Practice Digest, 7*(1), 28–32.

Stover, D. (1992). "The at-risk kids schools ignore." *Executive Educator, 14*(3), 28–31.

Summerford, S. (1987). "The public library: Offensive by design." *Public Libraries, 26*(2), 60–62.

Tabbert, B. (1988). "Battling over books: Freedom and responsibility are tested." *Emergency Librarian, 16*(1), 9–13.

Teague, J. (1992). "Issues relating to the treatment of adolescent lesbians and homosexuals." *Journal of Mental Health Counseling, 14*(4), 422–439.

Turner, P., Scadden, L., & Harris, M. (1985, March). *Parenting in gay and lesbian families.* Paper presented at the First Annual Future of Parenting Symposium, Chicago, IL.

Vazquez, R. (1992). "(No longer) sleeping with the enemy." *Empathy, 3*(1), 90–91.

Weeks, R., Derdeyn, A., & Langman, M. (1975). "Two cases of children of homosexuals." *Child Psychiatry and Human Development, 6*(1), 26–32.

Weinberg, G. (1972). *Society and the healthy homosexual.* New York: St. Martin's Press.

Wilhoite, M. (1990). *Daddy's roommate.* Boston: Alyson.

Wilson, D. (1984). "The open library." *English Journal, 43*(7), 60–63.

Wolf, T. (1985). "Marriages of bisexual men." *Journal of Homosexuality, 4,* 135–148.

Wyers, N. (1984). *Lesbian and gay spouses and parents: Homosexuality in the family.* Portland, OR: School of Social Work, Portland State University.

Wyers, N. (1987). "Homosexuality in the family: Lesbian and gay spouses." *Social Work, 32*(2), 143–148.

Zera, D. (1992). "Coming of age in a heterosexist world: The development of gay and lesbian adolescents." *Adolescence, 27*(108), 849–854.

**About the Author**

**James T. Sears** is an associate professor in the Department of Educational Leadership and Policies at the University of South Carolina. He is also a senior research associate for the South Carolina Educational Policy Center. Completing graduate degrees at the University of Wisconsin-Madison and at Indiana University, Sears's academic interests are curriculum and sexuality. His books include *Teaching and Thinking About Curriculum: Critical Inquiries* (with J. Dan Marshall) and the critically acclaimed *Growing Up Gay in the South: Race, Gender, and Journeys of the Spirit.* He is currently completing an ethnography that details how persons belonging to various cultural communities within the United States understand sexuality and the implications for sexuality education. Sears's writings have appeared in a variety of scholarly journals and popular magazines and he serves as coeditor of *Teaching Education* and editor of *Empathy.* He holds leadership positions in national organizations, including the Association of Supervision and Curriculum Development and the American Educational Research Association. Additionally, he serves on the editorial boards of the *Journal of Curriculum Theorizing* and the *Journal of Homosexuality.*

# APPENDIX

# Making a Difference through Action Learning: Teaching Study Skills, Learning Strategies, and Self-Advocacy

## Introduction

As a middle- or high-school teacher, one of your major challenges is to balance teaching content (e.g., American government, chemistry, earth science, English, history) with teaching learning strategies and study skills. Teachers are pressured to complete the textbook or cover a set of objectives specified in state or district curriculums, but many students with disabilities and those who are at risk need to be taught how to study and learn more effectively. This appendix describes active learning activities you can integrate into content area classes. The activities are grouped in the following action learning areas:

- effective time management
- organizing your studying
- setting goals, self-monitoring, and self-advocacy
- listening and taking notes
- remembering information
- studying and taking tests

When you teach learning strategies and study skills, keep in mind several general principles or stages of teaching. By using these principles (Deshler et al., 1996), you help ensure that students become proficient in using the skill or strategy and that they generalize its use to different situations.

- *Develop the rationale for learning the study skill or learning strategy.* With students, establish why learning to use the skill or strategy is worthwhile.
- *Analyze the skill or strategy, and if possible determine the steps students can use to develop the skill or strategy.*
- *Develop a memory device, such as an acronym, to help students remember the steps in the skill or strategy.* For editing written work, for example, use COPS—for Capitalization, Organization, Punctuation, and Spelling (Schumaker et al., 1985).
- *Demonstrate or model each step in the skill or strategy. Use "thinking aloud" to model what you are thinking.* It is important to demonstrate not only what you are doing but also what you are thinking. Cue students with a phrase such as, "When I do (describe action), what I am thinking is (describe thinking)."
- *Help students memorize the steps in the skill or strategy.* Use of a memory device can be quite helpful in memorizing the strategy.

- *Provide ample opportunity for students to practice the skills or strategy.* Start by applying the skill or strategy to easy tasks, then to more difficult ones.
- *Cue students to use the skill or strategy.*
- *Throughout the teaching process, discuss when, where, and how the skill or strategy can be used in different situations, such as different classes, tasks, and settings (school and job).* This principle is important for students to generalize the skill or strategy.
- *Have students monitor their success in using the skill or strategy and the way it affects their learning.*

The approach you use to teach study skills and learning strategies can vary. You can present the skill or strategy and its steps, or you can have students develop their own steps in cooperative groups, through class discussion, or independently. Whatever your approach, an important key to success is to use the preceding principles.

**Resources:** For more information about teaching study skills, learning strategies, and self-advocacy, see the following books:

- Bos, C. S., & Vaughn, S. (1998). *Teaching students with learning and behavior problems* (4th ed.). Boston: Allyn & Bacon.
- Bragstad, B. J., & Stumpf, S. M. (1982). *A guidebook for teaching study skills and motivation.* Boston: Allyn & Bacon.
- Bulgren, J., & Scanlon, D. (1997). Instructional routines and learning strategies that promote understanding of content area concepts. *Journal of Adolescent & Adult Literacy, 41,* 292–302.
- Deshler, D. D., Ellis, E. S., & Lenz, B. K. (1996). *Teaching adolescents with learning disabilities* (2nd ed.). Denver: Love.
- Ellis, D. B. (1985). *Becoming a master student* (5th ed.). Rapid City, SD: College Survival, Inc.
- Lenz, B. K., Ellis, E. S., & Scanlon, D. (1996). *Teaching learning strategies to adolescents and adults with learning disabilities.* Austin, TX: Pro-Ed.
- Strichart, S. S., Mangrum, C. T. II, & Iannuzzi, I. (1998). *Teaching study skills and strategies to students with LD, ADD, or special needs* (2nd ed.). Boston: Allyn & Bacon.

# Action Learning Area: Effective Time Management

*Time management* is the organization and monitoring of time so that tasks can be scheduled and completed in an efficient and timely manner. Effective time management includes the following steps:

- identifying the tasks to be completed
- estimating the time needed to complete the tasks
- prioritizing tasks and estimating time
- scheduling the time
- working toward meeting deadlines
- monitoring progress and adjusting deadlines or tasks
- reviewing deadlines after task completion and adjusting schedules and priorities based on past performance

Use the following four activities to teach effective time management.

## Interviewing Others about Time Management

**Objective:** To help students learn the importance of managing their time.

**Grades:** Middle school, high school, and postsecondary classes

**Teaching Procedures:** Have students interview a parent and one other adult they consider a successful manager of time, asking questions such as:

- Describe your schedule or what you do for two typical days during the week and one typical weekend day.
- What strategies do you use to schedule your time so that your tasks get completed?
- What strategies do you use to help you remember what you have to do?
- Do you think that managing your time is important? Why?

Have students work in cooperative groups to compile lists of strategies for scheduling and monitoring schedules. Also have them compile a list of reasons for managing time, such as the following (Bragstad & Stumpf, 1982), making sure that they add their own ideas.

## Why Bother with a Schedule?

- Parents will "get off your back" when you have regular study times.
- Writing down what you have to do gives you less to remember.
- When you give yourself a set amount of time to do an assignment, you concentrate more.
- With a schedule you are less likely to extend your breaks longer than scheduled.
- You feel more satisfied when your are in control of your life and know what you plan to do when.
- Organizing your time helps you come to class prepared.
- Scheduling your time is the smart way to operate if you want to have more time for fun and friends.

**Content Class Integration**: A unit on time management is easily integrated into any class. It can be the first unit of the year in a math class emphasizing time use and computation of time. It can be integrated into an economics class emphasizing how time relates to productivity, or into a life skills class.

## Determining How You Spend Your Time

**Objective**: Students determine how they currently spend their time and how much time it takes to complete usual activities.

**Grades**: Middle school and above

**Teaching Procedures**: Have student groups identify usual activities and estimate the time it takes to complete them. Distribute a schedule form (see Figure A) to students, and have them use the form to keep track of their activities for one week. Also have students list each school assignment and note whether they had "too much time" (+), "the right amount of time" (x), or "too little time" (-) to complete it.

At the end of the week, have student groups review their schedules and compare how much time they spent on different activities such as sleeping, eating, studying, attending class, and so on. Also have students compare their estimates with the actual time it took to complete the activities. Usually students underestimate their time by about 50 percent.

## Planning a Schedule

**Objective**: To have students plan their weekly schedules and develop To-Do lists.

**Grades**: Middle school and above

**Teaching Procedures**: Have students list due dates for assignments, tests, and other important projects. Help them divide complex tasks or projects into smaller tasks and determine the due dates for each smaller task. Next, have students make a To-Do list for each day (refer to Figure A) so that they can see how they need to plan their time, particularly their study time.

Have students plan their weekly schedules, using the following guidelines (Bos & Vaughn, 1998):

- Plan regular study times with at least one-hour blocks.
- Use daytime or early evening for studying, if possible.
- When studying for longer than an hour, plan breaks and stick to the time allowed.
- Determine which assignments you are going to work on.
- For each assignment, take a few minutes to review what you have done and learned, and to plan what you are going to accomplish.
- Work on your more difficult assignments when you are most alert (usually first).
- Distribute your study time for a test instead of cramming for it.
- Plan time for recreational activities.
- Reward yourself by crossing off items on your To-Do list when you complete them.

## Monitoring Your Schedule

**Objective**: To have students monitor their schedules and task completion, and adjust their schedules.

**Grades**: Middle school and above

**Teaching Procedure**: Monitoring task completion is the key to successful use of schedules and To-Do lists. Following are some suggestions for monitoring:

- Have students spend about five minutes during the class period to update their schedules and

## FIGURE A

**Sample Weekly Schedule and To-Do List**

Name: _____         Week of: _____

| Time | Monday | Tuesday | Wednesday | Thursday | Friday | Saturday | Sunday |
|---|---|---|---|---|---|---|---|
| 6 – 7 AM | | | | | | | |
| 7 – 8 AM | | | | | | | |
| 8 – 9 AM | | | | | | | |
| 9 – 10 AM | | | | | | | |
| 10 – 11 AM | | | | | | | |
| 11 – 12 | | | | | | | |
| 12 – 1 PM | | | | | | | |
| 1 – 2 PM | | | | | | | |
| 2 – 3 PM | | | | | | | |
| 3 – 4 PM | | | | | | | |
| 4 – 5 PM | | | | | | | |
| 5 – 6 PM | | | | | | | |
| 6 – 7 PM | | | | | | | |
| 7 – 8 PM | | | | | | | |
| 8 – 9 PM | | | | | | | |
| 9 – 10 PM | | | | | | | |

**To Do-List**

| Monday | Tuesday | Wednesday | Thursday | Friday | Saturday | Sunday |
|---|---|---|---|---|---|---|
| | | | | | | |

Adapted with permission from Bos, C. S., & Vaughn, S. (1998). *Teaching students with learning and behavior problems* (4th ed., p. 308). Boston: Allyn & Bacon.

cross off tasks they have completed. This can be done at the beginning of class when you are taking roll.
- Meet with students, as necessary, to review their schedules and their monitoring.
- Have students adjust their schedules as necessary.

## Action Learning Area: Organizing Your Studying

In addition to organizing and using a schedule, students need to organize their study environment and notebook, and develop positive study habits. The three activities in this section can help students get organized. All the activities can be integrated into a first unit for any content area class.

### Organizing Your Study Environment

**Objective:** To have students assess their study environment at home and modify it to promote studying.

**Grades:** Middle school and above

**Teaching Procedures:** Let parents know that students will be assessing and thinking about modifying their home study environment to promote studying. After students complete a study environment checklist (see Figure B), have them meet in groups to discuss the results and their ideas for modifying their study environments.

Meet with each student individually to summarize the results and to write one to three goals for improving the study environment if warranted. Have students report on their progress toward meeting their goals.

### Shaping Up Your Study Habits

**Objective:** To help students assess their study habits and modify them to promote studying.

**Grades:** Middle school and above

**Teaching Procedures:** Let parents know that students will be assessing and thinking about modifying

---

**FIGURE B**

**Study Environment Checklist**

Name _____ Date _____

Evaluate each statement by checking the column that describes the place where you study.

| Statement | Rarely | Generally | Almost Always |
|---|---|---|---|
| 1. I study in a consistent place. | | | |
| 2. The place I study is quiet. | | | |
| 3. It has good light. | | | |
| 4. There are no visual distractions. | | | |
| 5. There are a comfortable desk/table and a chair. | | | |
| 6. The materials I need are at my desk. | | | |
| 7. The study area is available when I need it. | | | |

Adapted with permission from Strichart, S. S., & Mangrum, C. T. II, (1993). *Teaching study strategies to students with learning disabilities* (p. 356). Boston: Allyn & Bacon.

their study habits to promote studying. After students complete a study habits checklist like the one shown in Figure C, have them meet in groups to discuss the results and their ideas for changing their study habits to promote studying at home.

Next, meet with each student individually to summarize the results and to write from one to three goals for improving study habits. Finally, have students report on their progress toward meeting their goals.

### Organizing Your Notebook

**Objective:** To teach students to organize their notebooks so that materials and information are easy to retrieve and use.

**Grades:** Middle school and above

**Teaching Procedures:** Alert parents that students will be reviewing their notebooks for organization, and send home a list of recommended materials, including the following:

- three-ring notebook, so that pages can be added easily
- supply pouch and school supplies such as pens, pencils, erasers, computer disks, calculator, hole punch, package of file cards, ruler
- labeled dividers—one for each class, plus others labeled "Schedules and Calendar," "Reference Information," "Notebook Dictionary," "Personal Word List,"

---

**FIGURE C**

**Study Habits Checklist**

Name _____ Date _____

Evaluate each statement by checking the column that describes your study habits.

| Statement | Rarely | Generally | Almost Always |
|---|---|---|---|
| 1. I set aside a regular time to study. | | | |
| 2. I do not take calls or allow interruptions during study time. | | | |
| 3. I take short breaks when I get tired, but return to work. | | | |
| 4. I take a few minutes at the beginning to organize my study time. | | | |
| 5. I begin with the hardest assignments. | | | |
| 6. I finish one assignment before going on to the next one. | | | |
| 7. I break long projects down into short tasks and work on the tasks over time. | | | |
| 8. I begin studying for a test at least three days before the test. | | | |
| 9. I have someone I can contact when I get stuck. | | | |
| 10. I write down questions I need to ask the teacher. | | | |

Adapted with permission from Strichart, S. S., & Mangrum, C. T. II, (1993). *Teaching study strategies to students with learning disabilities* (p. 356). Boston: Allyn & Bacon.

"Notebook Paper," "Graph Paper," "Computer Paper"

Have students look at their notebooks to determine how they have organized information for each class, their assignments, schedules, and materials. Work with students to organize their notebooks, using the following suggestions:

- Include a semester calendar, weekly schedules, and To-Do lists in the section on schedules and calendar.
- After the divider for each class, organize materials for that class (starting with class outline or syllabus).
- Date notes and place them in order.
- In the personal word list, alphabetically list frequently misspelled words.

# Action Learning Area: Goal Setting, Self-Monitoring, and Self-Advocacy

One way to get students actively involved in learning is to plan activities in which students learn to set goals, monitor their accomplishments, and advocate for what they want and need. The two activities in this section set the stage for active learning.

## Goal Setting and Self-Monitoring

**Objective:** Students learn to set, plan, and monitor their goals.

**Grades:** Middle school and above

**Teaching Objectives:** Whether you are working on finishing a term paper or saving enough money to buy a car, it is important to set goals, make a plan to accomplish the goals, and monitor your progress. Van Reusen and Bos (1992) developed a strategy that students can use for setting goals and monitoring progress. The strategy uses the acronym *MARKER* (it gives students a *mark* to work toward and is a *marker* of their progress), and includes the following steps:

> Make a list of goals, set the order, set the dates.
> Arrange a plan for each goal and predict your success.
> Run your plan for each goal and adjust if necessary.
> Keep records of your progress.
> Evaluate your progress toward each goal.
> Reward yourself when you reach a goal, and set a new goal.

For each goal, students use a Goal Planning Sheet (see Figure D) to answer the following questions:

- Can I describe my goal?
- What is the reason or purpose for the goal?
- Where am I going to work on and complete this goal?
- How much time do I have to complete the goal?
- What materials do I need to complete the goal?
- Can I divide the goal into steps or parts? If so, in what order should I complete each step or part?
- How am I going to keep records of my progress?
- How will I reward myself for reaching my goal?

Students usually work on one to three goals at one time, keeping progress data on each goal.

**Content Class Integration:** This strategy can be taught as a unit in almost any class, but is particularly appropriate for social studies and life skills classes. When Van Reusen and Bos (1992) used this strategy with middle- and high-school students with learning disabilities and behavior disorders, they found that students accomplished more goals and gained a more informed perspective on their educational and personal goals.

**Resources:** For more information, see:

- Lenz, B. K., Ehren, B. J., & Smiley, L. (1991). A goal attainment approach to improve completion of project-type assignments by adolescents with learning disabilities. *Learning Disabilities Research and Practice, 6,* 166–176.
- Van Reusen, A. K., & Bos, C. S. (1992). *Use of the goal-regulation strategy to improve the goal attainment of students with learning disabilities* (Final Report). Tucson, AZ: University of Arizona.

### FIGURE D

**Goal Planning and Monitoring Sheet**

Name: _____  Class: _____  Date: _____

1. Goal: _____
2. Reason(s) for working on goal: _____
   _____
3. Goal will be worked on at: _____
4. Date to reach goal (due date): _____
5. Materials needed: _____
   _____
6. Steps used to reach the goal: _____
   _____
7. Progress toward the goal: Record in each box the date and progress rating.

   3—Goal reached    2—Good progress made    1—Some progress made    0—No progress made

   | Date / Rating | | | | | |
   |---|---|---|---|---|---|
   | Date / Rating | | | | | |
   | Date / Rating | | | | | |

8. Reward for reaching goal: _____

Adapted from Van Reusen, A. K., & Bos, C. S. (1992). *Use of the goal-regulation strategy to improve the goal attainment of students with learning disabilities* (Final Report). Tucson, AZ: University of Arizona.

## Self-Advocacy

**Objective:** To help students inventory their learning strengths, weaknesses they need to improve, goals, and interests, and then advocate for themselves with key adults (e.g., parents, teachers, counselors).

**Grades:** Middle school and above

**Teaching Procedures:** *Self-advocacy* occurs when individuals effectively communicate and negotiate for their interests, desires, needs, and rights. It involves making informed decisions and taking responsibility for those decisions (Van Reusen et al., 1994). The I PLAN self-advocacy strategy is one way to help students develop their advocacy skills.

During the first (Inventory) step, students (working in instructional groups) develop their own personal inventories. Each student examines the following items:

- strengths
- areas to improve or learn
- goals
- choice for learning or accommodations

## TABLE A

**Components of Education and Transition Inventories**

| | |
|---|---|
| *Strengths* | Reading |
| | Writing |
| | Math |
| | Study Skills |
| | Social Skills |
| | Career & Employment Skills |
| | Independent Living Skills |
| | Leisure & Recreation Skills |
| *Areas to Improve or Learn* | Based on learning strengths and needs |
| *Goals* | Academic |
| | Social |
| | Extracurricular/Recreation |
| | Career/Employment |
| | Independent Living |
| *Choices for Learning* | Helpful Activities |
| | Learning Preferences |
| | Helpful Materials |
| | Testing Preferences |
| *Accommodations* | Changes that need to be made so that student can succeed |

Adapted from Van Reusen, A. K., Bos, C. S., Schumaker, J. B., & Deshler, D. D. (1994). *The self-advocacy strategy for education and transition planning.* Lawrence, KS: Edge Enterprises.

If the emphasis is on career and transition planning, students also think about areas related to jobs and adult life. The major components of an education inventory and a transition inventory are presented in Table A.

The remaining four steps in the strategy focus on the communication skills needed to present the information and advocate with teachers, parents, counselors, and others. These steps are presented, discussed, and then practiced through simulations:

Provide your inventory information.
Listen and respond.
Ask questions.
Name your goals.

Students also learn the following SHARE behaviors to promote positive communication:

Sit up straight.
Have a pleasant tone of voice.
Activate your thinking.

- Tell yourself to pay attention.
- Tell yourself to participate.
- Tell yourself to compare ideas.

Relax

- Don't look uptight.
- Tell yourself to stay calm.

Engage in eye communication.

**Content Class Integration:** This activity can be integrated into most content classes, but is particularly suited for social studies and life skills classes.

**Resources:** For additional information, see *The self-advocacy strategy for education and transition planning,* by A. K. Van Reusen, C. S. Bos, J. B. Schumaker, and D. D. Deshler, published (1994) by Edge Enterprises, Lawrence, Kansas.

# Action Learning Area: Listening and Taking Notes

Listening to lectures, asking questions, and taking notes are skills critical for success in school. Teachers generally are more willing to accommodate students who actively participate in class, and these students tend to be more successful academically (Schumm & Vaughn, 1991). The six activities in this section can be used to promote active listening, note taking, and class participation.

## Creating Rationales for Effective Note Taking

**Objective:** To teach students how to develop rationales for taking notes.

**Grades:** Upper elementary and above

**Teaching Procedures:** On the average, teachers in secondary settings spend at least half their class time presenting information through lectures, and base a significant number of test items on information presented in class discussion and lectures (Putnam et al., 1993). Note taking is one of the most efficient ways to record this information.

Using class discussion or cooperative groups, have students generate a rationale for the importance of taking notes to success in school. If students do not mention the following reasons, make sure that you do:

- Note taking increases attention.
- Note taking requires a deeper level of thinking than just listening, because students must make sense of the information and write the ideas.
- Because students must process information on a deeper level, note taking makes learning and remembering information easier.

With class discussion or cooperative groups, have students create a list of requirements for effective note taking. If the following items are not part of the list, be sure to mention them:

- paying attention
- writing fast and legibly
- using abbreviations
- deciding what to write
- spelling
- making sense of notes after the lecture

Finally, through class discussion or cooperative groups, develop a list of ideas for accommodations for each requirement in the list (e.g., for "spelling," teacher could write difficult words on board, transparency, or handout).

Post the three lists so that students can review them.

**Content Class Integration:** Completing a unit on listening and note taking can be valuable in any content class. Such a unit not only improves students' note taking, but also makes them aware of your style of presenting information.

### Using Listener-Friendly Lectures

**Objective:** To use strategies that make it easier for students to understand and take notes on the information you present during lectures.

**Grades:** Upper elementary and above

**Teaching Procedures:** As you plan your teaching, the following guidelines can make your lectures "*listener-friendly*":

- Use advance organizers.
- Use cue words or phrases to let students know what information is important (e.g., "It is important that you know...," "The key information to remember is...," "In summary...").
- Repeat important information.
- Write important information on board, transparency, and handout.
- Stress key points by varying the tone and quality of your voice.
- Number ideas or points (e.g., first, second, next, then, finally).
- Write technical words or words that are difficult to spell.
- Use a study guide that lists the major concepts, with space for students to add other information.
- Use pictures, diagrams, and semantic maps to show relationships among ideas.
- Provide examples and nonexamples of the concepts you are discussing.
- Ask questions or encourage discussion that requires students to relate the new information to ideas they already know (from their own background or your previous lectures).
- Stop frequently and have students work with partners and discuss what they have learned.
- Allow time at the end of a lecture for students to look over their notes, summarize, and ask questions.

By using these guidelines you will naturally incorporate cues that indicate what information is important.

**Content Class Integration:** Whenever you give a lecture in any content course, make sure it is "listener-friendly."

### Pause Procedure

**Objective:** To give students frequent opportunities to review notes, check for understanding, and ask questions.

**Grades:** Upper elementary and above

**Teaching Procedures:** The pause procedure is a technique that helps students learn more from lectures. During logical breaks in a lecture (approximately every ten minutes), the teacher pauses for two minutes. During that time, pairs of students compare their notes to make certain that key concepts have been recorded. Students also ask each other questions to check for understanding.

At the end of the two minutes, ask students whether they have any questions or concepts that need further discussion or clarification. Then resume lecturing.

**Resources:** For additional information, see the following publications:

- Ruhl, K. L., Hughes, C. A., & Gajar, A. H. (1990). Efficacy of the pause procedure for enhancing learning disabled and nondisabled college students' long- and short-term recall of facts presented through lecture. *Learning Disability Quarterly, 13,* 55–64.
- Ruhl, K. L., Hughes, C. A., & Schloss, P. J. (1987). Using the pause procedure to enhance lecture recall. *Teacher Education and Special Education, 10,* 14–18.

## Teaching Note Taking

**Objective:** To help students evaluate their notes and improve their note-taking strategies.

**Grades:** Middle school and above

**Teaching Procedures:** Teaching note-taking skills to students in your class is a good investment of time and effort. As you teach a content unit you can use the following procedure to evaluate your students' note-taking skills and to introduce and teach alternative ways to take notes:

1. *Have students evaluate the effectiveness of their current note-taking skills.* Give a lecture from the content unit and have students take notes as usual. The next day, give students a quiz. Have them evaluate the completeness, format, and legibility of their notes, as well as their ease of use for review.
2. *Use videotaped lectures to teach students to listen effectively and take notes.* Use a videotape of your lecture so that students can listen and watch for cues you give to note important information. When students notice a cue, stop the videotape and replay it so that all the students can hear and see it.
3. *Control the difficulty of the lectures.* Select the first unit of the year to teach note taking. This unit usually contains simple information that was presented the previous year.
4. *Discuss with students ways to record notes* (i.e., record key ideas, not sentences; use consistent abbreviations; use an outline format; spell a word the way it looks or sounds). As a class, have students develop a set of abbreviations to be posted on a wall chart.
5. *Teach students how to review their notes,* add missing information, and clarify information that is unclear. Have students, working as partners or cooperative groups, use their notes to study for tests. Teach students how to use their notes to create questions and then check to see that they can answer them.
6. *Have students monitor their note taking.* Have them keep track of how often they use their note-taking skills in your class (and others), and record how they are doing on tests and assignments (and the effect of their improved note-taking skills).

**Content Class Integration:** You can integrate teaching how to take notes into any content class. Teaching these skills early in the year improves the atmosphere and student learning throughout the year.

## Using Cues When Listening to Lectures

**Objective:** To help students learn to listen and watch for cues during lectures, and to record important information.

**Grades:** Middle school and above

**Teaching Procedures:** Use the following list of cues to help students learn how to listen and watch for important information:

**Type of Cue**              **Examples**
Organizational Cues
    Today, we will be discussing . . .
    The topic I want to cover today . . .
    There are (number) points I want you to be sure to learn. . . .
    The important relationship is . . .
    The main point of this discussion is . . .

Any statement that signals a number or position (e.g., first, last, next, then)
To review/summarize/recap ...

Emphasis Cues
Verbal     You need to know/understand/remember ...
           This is important/key/basic/critical ...
           Let me repeat this, ...
           Let me check, now do you understand ...
           Any statement repeated.
           Words are emphasized.
           Teacher speaks more slowly, loudly, or with more emphasis.
           Teacher stresses certain words.
           Teacher spells words.
           Teacher asks rhetorical question.
Nonverbal  Information written on overhead or board.
           Information handed out in study guide.
           Teacher emphasizes point by using gestures.

Encourage students to listen and watch for additional cues and add them to the list.

**Content Class Integration:** When integrating a content unit with a unit on note taking, the information presented in this activity can be placed on a handout and posted on a wall chart.

**Resources:** For more information, see:

- Suritsky, S. K., & Hughes, C. A. (1996). Notetaking strategy instruction. In D. D. Deshler, E. S. Ellis, & B. K. Lenz (Authors), *Teaching adolescents with learning disabilities* (2nd ed.), pp. 267–312. Denver: Love.

## Guidelines for Effective Note Taking

**Objective:** To teach students to use a note-taking system that is effective for recording and studying information.

**Grades:** Middle school and above

**Teaching Procedures:** Teach the specifics of note taking, using the following guidelines:

- Use a two- or three-column system for taking notes, with one column for recording key concepts and questions (see Figure E).

---

**FIGURE E**

*Sample Two-Column Note-taking Format*

Date: _____     Page: _____

Topic: _____

| Key Concepts/Questions | Notes |
|---|---|
|  |  |

- Date and number each page of notes, and label the topic.
- Use a modified outline format, leaving space in which to add information when notes are reviewed.
- Write key ideas or phrases. (Paraphrase; do not write complete sentences.)
- Use pictures and diagrams to relate ideas.
- Use consistent abbreviations.
- Record information that the lecturer writes on the board or transparency.
- Underline, highlight, or use asterisks to mark key information.
- If you miss information, draw a blank and fill it in later.
- If you cannot spell a word, spell it the way you think it looks or sounds.
- As soon as possible, review your notes and fill in missing information. Check with your teacher or other students if you have questions.

# Action Learning Area: Remembering Information

Using memory strategies to remember information is critical for success in school. Students, particularly students with disabilities and those who are at risk, often have difficulty memorizing information. Sometimes students do not understand the information, but in other cases students' may not perform well because they have difficulties retrieving information or because they do not use deliberate memory strategies. This section highlights two activities you can use to teach memory strategies.

## Guidelines for Remembering Information

**Objective:** To use general guidelines to increase the amount of information students remember.

**Grades:** Upper elementary and above

**Teaching Procedures:** When you present information, make it easier to remember by following these guidelines:

- Cue students when important information is being presented.
- Activate prior knowledge and help students make connections between old and new knowledge.
- Use visual aids such as semantic maps and diagrams to make the information more memorable.
- Limit the amount of information presented; group related ideas.
- Control the rate at which information is presented.
- Provide time to review, rehearse, and elaborate on the information.
- Teach students how to use and apply memory strategies and devices.
- Provide opportunities for distributed review of information and encourage over learning.

## Generating Acronyms and Acrostics

**Objective:** To teach students to generate acronyms and acrostics that help them remember information.

**Grades:** Middle school and above

**Teaching Procedures:** *Mnemonics* are memory-triggering devices that help us remember and retrieve information by forming associations that do not exist naturally in the content. Two types of mnemonics are acronyms and acrostics. *Acronyms* are words created by joining the first letters of a series of words. Examples are *radar* (radio detecting and ranging), *scuba* (self-contained underwater breathing apparatus), and *laser* (light amplification by stimulated emission of radiation). *Acrostics* are sentences created by words that begin with the first letters of a series of words. A popular example of an acrostic is "Every good boy does fine," which represents the notes on the lines of the treble clef staff: E, G, B, D, F. By teaching students to construct acronyms and acrostics, sharing them in class, and then cueing students to use them when they study and take tests, you help them to learn and retrieve information.

The FIRST-letter mnemonic strategy is one strategy you can teach to help students construct lists of information to memorize and develop an acronym or acrostic for learning and remembering the information. The strategy includes an overall strategy (LISTS) and a substrategy for making the mnemonic device

(FIRST). The steps in the overall strategy include the following:

> *Look for clues.* (In class notes and textbooks, look for lists of information that are important to learn. Name or give a heading to each list.)
> *Investigate the items.* (Decide which items should be included in the list.)
> *Select a mnemonic device, using FIRST.* (Use the FIRST substrategy, explained shortly, to construct a mnemonic.)
> *Transfer the information to a card.* (Write the mnemonic and the list on one side of a card and the name of the list on the other side of the card.)
> *Self-test.* (Study by looking at the name of the list, useing the mnemonic to recall the list.)

To complete the Select step, students use the FIRST substrategy to design an acronym or acrostic:

> Form a word. Using uppercase letters, write the first letter of each word in the list; see whether an acronym—a recognizable word or nonsense word—can be made.
> Insert a letter(s). Insert letter(s) to see whether a word can be made. (Be sure to use lowercase letters so that you know they do not represent an item on the list—BACk, for example.)
> Rearrange the letters. Rearrange the letters to see whether a word can be made.
> Shape a sentence. Using the first letter of each word in the list, try to construct a sentence (an acrostic).
> Try combinations. Try combinations of these above steps to generate the mnemonic.

**Content Class Integration:** This strategy can be taught in any content class but is particularly effective in science and social studies classes in which lists of information are to be learned. The strategy provides a systematic method for students to review text and class notes, construct lists, and develop acronyms and acrostics that help them remember and retrieve information.

**Resources:** For more information, read *The FIRST-letter mnemonic strategy* (Learning Strategies Curriculum), by B. R. Nagel, J. B. Schumaker, and D. D. Deshler, (1986), published by Edge Enterprises, Lawrence, Kansas.

# Action Learning Area: Studying and Taking Tests

Tests are the primary means that teachers use to determine whether students have learned new concepts and can apply them. If your goal in testing is to measure what students have learned (and not test-taking skills), then teaching test-taking strategies as part of the curriculum is important. This section contains five activities for teaching strategies for studying and taking tests.

## Guidelines for Studying for Tests

**Objective:** To help students use general strategies when studying for tests.

**Grades:** Middle school and above

**Teaching Procedures:** Teach the following general guidelines to help students develop positive study habits when studying for tests.

- *Manage your study time.* Keep up with assignments and do daily and weekly reviews. Plan five minutes each day for students to review the material. On Monday, take an extra five minutes and have students review the previous week's material. Use partners, cooperative groups, and whole-class discussion to review.
- *Create study aids.* Create a semantic map, study guide, mnemonic, and other study aids to help students remember key information. Use an ongoing map or study guide that students add to daily.
- *Create flashcards.* Teach students how to create and use flashcards. When students are learning vocabulary, have them put the word on one side and the definition and an example on the other. For other information, have students put the question on one side and the answer on the other. In math or science, have students put a formula on one side and examples of its use on the other. Have students keep index cards in their notebooks and on their desks during

class. Cue students to make a card when they learn about a key concept or idea.
- *Use flashcards to review.* One advantage of flashcards is that each item or piece of information is on a separate card. Have students sort cards into categories, arrange the cards in a semantic map, or review them in random order.
- *Learn about the test.* Rather than telling students about the test, have them learn about it by asking questions. Start the discussion with, "Let's talk about the test. What do you want to ask me?" Use the following checklist to guide the students' questioning:
  - Format of test; types of questions
  - Date of test
  - Time allotted for test
  - Whether books and notes are allowed
  - How much test counts toward the class grade
  - Information covered
  - Teacher's recommendations for how to study
  - Teacher's recommendations for what to study
- *Predict questions.* Show students how they can predict what questions will be asked. Have students predict questions by using what they know about the teacher's testing style, class notes and textbook, and study aids. Two days before a test, have students—working as partners or in cooperative groups—write (and then answer) the questions they think will be on the test.
- *Think positive.* Help students develop a positive attitude by asking the following questions during each day's review:
  - What have you learned today?
  - How does it relate to what you already know?
  - What will you be working on tomorrow?
  - How well have you learned the information?

  Have students rate how well they think they will do on the test and think about what they can do to improve their ratings.
- *Review test-taking strategies and visualize success.* Just before a test, review test-taking strategies and have students visualize themselves being successful as they take the test.

**Content Class Integration:** Guidelines for studying for tests are easily taught in any content class. Students learn not only about effective ways to study in general, but also about your views on developing, studying for, and giving tests.

## Guidelines for Taking Tests

**Objective:** To teach students general strategies for taking tests.

**Grades:** Middle school and above

**Teaching Procedures:** Teach students the following general guidelines for taking tests:
- Bring the necessary materials.
- Be on time and sit where you will not be disturbed.
- Survey the test.
- Read the directions carefully and make sure that you understand them. If not, ask for assistance.
- Schedule your time.
- Be sure you understand the scoring system (i.e., is guessing penalized?).
- If you have memorized specific outlines, formulas, mnemonics, and so on, write that information before you forget it.
- When answering questions, place a mark in the margin next to questions about which you are unsure or that you want to review.
- Avoid changing answers arbitrarily.
- Review your answers and proofread written responses.

## Using a Test-Taking Strategy

**Objective:** To teach students to use a test-taking strategy.

**Grades:** Middle school and above

**Teaching Procedures:** Some students may profit from learning a specific test-taking strategy that they can use when taking objective tests. Introduce the PIRATES strategy, letting students know that its use generally improves test scores by from 10 to 30 percent. Then model the steps in the following strategy.

1. Prepare to succeed.
   Put your name and the word PIRATES on the test.
   Allot time and order the sections.
   Say affirmations.
   Start within two minutes.
2. Inspect the instructions.
   Read instructions carefully.
   Underline what to do and where to respond.
   Notice special requirements.
3. Read, remember, reduce.
   Read the whole question.
   Remember what you studied.
   Reduce your choices.
4. Answer or abandon.
   Answer the question.
   Abandon the question for the moment.
5. Turn back.
6. Estimate your answer.
   Avoid absolutes.
   Choose the longest or most detailed choice.
   Eliminate similar choices.
7. Survey.
   Survey to ensure all questions are answered.
   Switch an answer only if you're sure.

Tell students to repeat the second, third, and fourth steps (i.e., Inspect the instructions; Read, remember, reduce; Answer or abandon) for each section of the test.

Give students the opportunity to learn the mnemonic (PIRATES) and the steps in the strategy, as well as the opportunity for practice. Cue students to use the strategy and discuss when, where, and how it can be used. Have students monitor their success in using the strategy and how it affects their test scores.

**Content Class Integration:** Teaching a test-taking strategy takes time but is worthwhile if you use objective tests as the major way to grade students.

**Resources:** For more information, see the following publications:

- Hughes, C. A., & Schumaker, J. B. (1991). Test-taking strategy instruction for adolescents with learning disabilities. *Exceptionality, 2*, 205–221.

- Hughes, C. A., Schumaker, J. B., Deshler, D. D., & Mercer, C. D. (1988). *The test-taking strategy*. Lawrence, KS: Edge Enterprises.

## Tips for Answering Objective Questions

**Objective:** To teach students tips for answering objective questions.

**Grades:** Middle school and above

**Teaching Procedures:** Discuss the following tips with students and give them a handout. In your discussion, include ideas that you and the students generate. Allow students to use the handout when they answer objective questions.

True–False Questions

- Remember, *everything* in a true statement must be true. One false detail makes it false.
- Look for qualifying words that tend to make statements false, such as: *all, always, everyone, everybody, never, no, none, no one, only.*
- Look for qualifying words that tend to make statements true, such as: *generally, most, often, probably, some, sometimes, usually.*
- Simplify questions that contain double negatives by crossing out both negatives and then determining whether the statement is true or false.
- Don't change an answer unless you have a good reason. Usually your first impression is correct.

Matching Questions

- Read directions carefully. Determine whether each column contains an equal number of items and whether items can be used more than once.
- Read both columns before you start matching, to get a sense of the items.
- Focus on each item in one column and look for its match in the other column.
- If you can use items only once, cross out each item as you use it.

Multiple-Choice Questions

- Determine whether you are penalized for guessing.

- Answer the questions you know, putting a check in the margin next to items you want to return to later.
- Read all possible options, even when you are pretty sure of the right answer.
- See whether multiple options are available (e.g., c. A and B; d. All of the above).
- Minimize the risk of guessing by reading the stem with each option to see which option is most logical.
- Use a process of elimination, crossing out options you know are wrong.
- When you do not know the answer and you are not penalized for guessing, use the following signals to help you select the right option:
  - The longest option is often correct.
  - The most complete answer is often correct.
  - The first time the option "all of the above" or "none of the above" is used, it is usually correct.
  - The option in the middle, particularly if it is the longest, is often correct.
  - Answers with qualifiers such as *generally, probably, sometimes,* and *usually* are frequently correct.

### Completion Questions

- Determine whether more than one word can be put in one blank.
- If blanks are of different lengths, use length as a clue for the length of the answer.
- Read the question to yourself so that you can hear what is being asked.
- If more than one answer comes to mind, write them down; then reread the question with each answer to see which one fits best.
- Makes sure that the answer you provide fits grammatically and logically.

**Content Class Integration:** In any content class, you can teach students to use tips for taking objective tests. You may want to modify the list to better match the type of objective tests you give in your class.

**Resources:** For more information, read J. Lagan's *Reading and study skills* (2nd ed.), 1982, published by McGraw-Hill, New York.

## Using Instruction Cue Words for Answering Essay Questions

**Objective:** To help students learn and apply the meaning of instruction cue words when they answer essay questions.

**Grades:** Middle school and above

**Teaching Procedures:** When you teach strategies for answering essay questions, discuss the meanings of different instruction cue words such as those in Table B on page 506. In your discussion, add other cue words and meanings generated by you and the students. Develop a handout and have students use it when they answer essay questions. Ask students to underline the instruction cue words in each essay question.

**Content Class Integration:** This activity gives students an opportunity to learn how instruction cue words determine what information to include in an answer. For example, as a social studies teacher you can demonstrate how taking one concept, such as *democracy*, and using different instruction cue words (*define* versus *illustrate*) will change the answer.

## TABLE B

**Instruction Cue Words for Answering Essay Questions**

| Cue | Meaning | Cue | Meaning |
| --- | --- | --- | --- |
| Analyze | Break into parts and examine each part. | Interpret | Explain and share your own judgment. |
| Apply | Discuss how the principles would apply to a situation. | Justify | Provide reasons for your statements or conclusion. |
| Compare | Discuss differences and similarities. | List | Provide a numbered list of items or points. |
| Contrast | Discuss differences and similarities, stressing the differences. | Outline | Organize your answer into main points and supporting details. If appropriate, use outline format. |
| Critique | Analyze and evaluate, using criteria. | | |
| Define | Provide a clear, concise statement that explains the concept. | Prove | Provide factual evidence to support your logic or position. |
| Describe | Give a detailed account, listing characteristics, qualities, and components as appropriate. | Relate | Show the connection among ideas. |
| | | Review | Provide a critical summary in which you summarize and present your comments. |
| Diagram | Provide a drawing. | State | Explain precisely. |
| Discuss | Provide an in-depth explanation. Be analytical. | Summarize | Provide a synopsis that does not include your comments. |
| Explain | Give a logical development that discusses reasons or causes. | Trace | Describe the development or progress of the idea. |
| Illustrate | Use examples or, when appropriate, provide a diagram or picture. | | |

**Add your own Instruction Cue Words and definitions!!!**

Adapted from Bos, C. S., & Vaughn, S. (1998). *Teaching students with learning and behavior problems* (4th ed., p. 326). Boston: Allyn & Bacon.

# The Dimensions of Multicultural Education

## Content Integration

Content integration deals with the extent to which teachers use examples and content from a variety of cultures and groups to illustrate key concepts, principles, generalizations, and theories in their subject area or discipline.

## The Knowledge Construction Process

The knowledge construction process relates to the extent to which teachers help students to understand, investigate and determine how the implicit cultural assumptions, frames of reference, perspectives, and biases within a discipline influence the ways in which knowledge is constructed within it.

**Multicultural Education**

## An Equity Pedagogy

An equity pedagogy exists when teachers modify their teaching in ways that will facilitate the academic achievement of students from diverse racial, cultural, and social-class groups. This includes using a variety of teaching styles that are consistent with the wide range of learning styles within various cultural and ethnic groups.

## Prejudice Reduction

This dimension focuses on the characteristic of students' racial attitudes and how they can be modified by teaching methods and materials.

## An Empowering School Culture and Social Structure

Grouping and labeling practices, sports participation, disproportionality in achievement, and the interaction of the staff and the students across ethnic and racial lines are among the components of the school culture that must be examined to create a school culture that empowers students from diverse racial, ethnic, and cultural groups.

Copyright © 1996 by Allyn and Bacon

# INDEX

*AAMR Adaptive Behavior Scale,* 356
Ability grouping, *see* Tracking and ability grouping
Absence seizures (petit mal), 391
Abstract language, 29
Abstract thinking, 28, 351, 422
Academic achievement
   African Americans, 3–4, 405, 459
   Asian Americans, 459
   biased expectations, 59–67
   bilingual education and, 460
   conduct disorders and, 324
   cooperative learning effects on, 249
   cultural disadvantage and, 27–43
   emotional or behavioral disorders and, 336
   gender gap, 5
   genetic differences, 21–27
   Hispanic Americans, 3–4, 405, 459
   language and, 6–7, 37
   learning disability and, 259, 261
   meritocracy theory, 22
   Native Americans, 4, 405
   nonstandard dialects and, 94–95
   poor students, 304
   tests predicting, 26
   tracking based on, 243
Academic benefits, of small groups, 249
Academic failure
   of minority students, 458–475
   *See also* Failure
Academic language, 422
Acceptance, words of, 252
Accidents
   causing traumatic brain injuries, 390
   visual impairment caused by, 375
Accommodations
   attention deficit disorder, 279–284
   communication disorders, 306–315
   diverse students, 428–432
   dual sensory impairments, 350
   emotional or behavioral disorders, 329–336
   hearing loss, 387–389
   learning disabled students, 265–274

   mental retardation or severe disabilities, 351, 359–369
   mental retardation, 345
   physical disabilities and health impairments, 394–398
   visual impairments, 378–383
Acculturation, 410
   assessing, 207–210
   effects, 205–206
   *See also* Assimilation
Accusations, response to, 105
Acquired immunodeficiency syndrome (AIDS), 21, 392, 393
Acronyms, 270, 272, 539
Acrostics, 539
Action learning, 527–543
Active learning, 185–186
Activities
   gender and, 127, 139, 143
   language instruction, 310
Activity levels, 162, 277
Adaptive behavior, 345, 346, 356
Adaptive technology, 242
Additive approach to multicultural curriculum, 413–415
Adjustment problems, conduct disorders and, 324
Administrative positions, gender disparities in, 124
Adult life, transition into, 361
Adult orientation, learning and, 182
Adult register, 301
Advance organizer, 267–268, 269
Affection, display of, 108–109
Affirmative action, 25, 32, 33
Affixes, 299
Affluent professional school, 489–493, 497–498
African American(s)
   AIDS prevalence, 21
   intelligence tests and, 25–26
   pay levels, 25
African American females
   gender bias and, 127
   self confidence, 197
   success in male domain and, 155
African American males
   belief in education, 76

   emotional expression by, 129
   respect for authority, 113
   role models, 30, 31, 41–42
African American students
   achievement and, 3–4, 405, 459
   activity level, 185–186
   aspirations, 39–40
   assessment of, 154, 155, 158–159, 164
   aural learners, 185
   behavior expectations, 61, 62
   belief in education, 76
   belief in genetic differences of, 22, 23
   biased evaluation of, 61–62
   biased treatment of, 64–65
   communication style, 103, 105–106
   community influence, 40
   conflict resolution, 110
   cooperative learning, 192, 193, 194
   cultural characteristics, 409
   cultural deprivation theory and, 27–28
   dialects spoken by, 62, 93, 94, 100, 293, 424, 453
   disability views, 358
   drop out rates, 458
   expression of emotion, 112
   global learners, 161
   high school diplomas and, 77
   language use, 36–37
   locus of control, 41, 199
   motivation to succeed, 188
   nonverbal cues and, 186
   numbers in U.S., 405
   parental substance abuse, 20
   perceptual style, 183–184
   powerlessness of, 57
   prejudices against, 60
   self–concepts, 30, 38, 201
   stimulating environment and, 161
   success avoidance, 156
   suspensions of, 77–78
   time orientation, 196
   tracking and, 60
African American teachers, 65–66, 126
African American Vernacular English, 62, 93, 94, 100, 293, 424, 453

Aggression, 128, 129, 141
  antisocial behavior and, 325
  conduct disorders and, 324
  types of, 325
Agreement, communication of, 114
AIDS, see Acquired immunodefiency syndrome
Alcohol use, during pregnancy, 18, 19–21, 264, 346, 349, 350, 393
Alienation, 76
American Sign Language, 384–385, 389
American society, see Society
Analogous communication, 104
Analytical intellectual powers, 493
Analytic learning, 160, 161, 182, 183–184
Analytic teaching style, 184
Androgynous roles, 141
Anger, expression of, 112
Antidepressants, 327
Antipsychotic medication, 327
Antisocial behavior, 325
Anxiety
  attention deficit disorder and, 283
  medication for, 327
  stuttering and, 294
Anxiety-withdrawal, 326
Anyon, Jean, 478–500
Appreciation, words of, 252
Appreciation approach, dialects and, 99–101
Argumentative instruction, 187
Articulation, 291
  hearing loss and, 387
Articulation disorders, 292–293, 305, 307
Asian(s)
  communication styles, 103, 104
  expression of emotion, 112
  group process and, 109
  respect for authority, 113
Asian Americans, numbers in U.S., 405
Asian American students
  achievement and, 459
  assessment of, 160
  biased evaluation, 63
  cooperative learning by, 192
  expectations of, 61, 408
  learning style, 179, 180, 192
  locus of control, 198
  nonverbal cues and, 186
  parental expectations of, 408
  perceptual style, 183
  risk taking by, 195
  *See also* Southeast Asian American students
Assessment, 153–172
  acculturation, 207–210
  advocacy for minority students and, 461
  biased, 153, 163–172
  communication disorders, 306
  discriminatory, 468–470
  emotional or behavioral disorders, 327–328
  functional, 357, 361
  hearing loss, 386–387
  higher-level functional skills, 351
  language use, 302
  learning characteristics, 206–207
  learning disabilities, 265, 469
  materials and procedures, 163–172
  mental retardation or severe disabilities, 345, 355–357
  physical disabilities and health impairments, 393–394
  self-confidence, 200
  visual impairments, 377–378
Assessors, ethnic background of, 158–159
Assimilation, 9, 70, 204, 205–206, 424. *See also* Acculturation
Assistive listening devices, 387
Assistive technology, 387, 394, 397
Asthma, 389, 393
Attention
  gender and, 125, 140
  hearing loss and, 387
  immaturity and, 326
  learning disabilities and, 263
  mental retardation or severe disabilities and, 351
Attention deficit disorders, 274–284
Audiogram, 384
Auditory discrimination skills, 37
Augmentative communication, 308, 309, 354, 355, 356
Aural learners, 184
Authoritarian parenting, 31
Authoritarian teachers, 64, 447–448
Authoritative style, 448–449
Authority, 447–449
  affluent professional school, 492
  males in positions of, 124
  middle-class schools, 489
  respect for, 112
  social class and, 481
  working-class schools, 487
Autism, 346–348, 353

Balanced bilinguals, 421
Barrier games, 310
Basic interpersonal communication skills (BICS), 90, 422
Basic skills, grouping based on, 249
Basic skills approach, 445
Beckoning, gestures for, 114
Behavior
  adaptive, 345, 346, 356
  antisocial, 325
  attention deficit disorder, 276–277, 278
  autistic, 348
  changing, 331–332, 334
  collaborative, 250
  cultural characteristics influencing, 59, 407
  disadvantaged students, 31
  expectations for, 61, 62
  externalizing, 323
  gender differences, 119–131
  group, 325
  hearing loss and, 387
  internalizing, 323
  mental retardation and, 345, 346
  refugee students, 56
  responsibility for, 106–107
  self-concept and, 38
  self-injurious, 353
  severe disabilities and, 353
  stereotypic, 8, 353
  tracking based on, 75, 243
  verbal directives and, 447–449
Behavioral disorders, *see* Emotional or behavioral disorders
Behavior problems
  attention deficit disorder and, 277
  health care and, 18
  parental substance abuse and, 19, 20
  veiled commands and, 448, 449
  *See also* Emotional or behavioral disorders
Belonging, student's sense of, 366
Bias
  ability grouping, 75
  assessment, 153, 163–172
  gender, 119, 123
  intelligence tests, 356
  resistance to, 69, 71, 76
  teachers exhibiting, 59–67
  *See also* Discrimination; Prejudice
Biased responding, 351
Bicultural ambivalence, 462
Biculturalism, 205, 210

Bidialectalism, 94–99
Bilingual, 248
  balanced, 421
Bilingual education, 89, 90, 403, 459
  goal of, 418
  historical perspectives, 424–428
  maintenance, 430
  successful, 463
  transitional, 430
  two-way, 430
Bilingual Education Act of 1968, 89, 424–426
Bilingualism, 208, 460
  cognitive development and, 421–422
  learning and, 421–422
Biology, gender differences and, 119–121
Biomedical problems, 17, 18–21
Birth, abandonment after, 20
Birth weight, 18
Bisexual families, 502–521
Bisexual students, 145
Black English, *see* African American Vernacular English
Blind, 242
Blindness, 375
Braille, 377, 378
Brain, gender differences and, 120
*Brigance Diagnostic Inventory of Essential Skills,* 351, 352

Calm learning style, 185
Cancer, 393, 398
Capitalist society, 479–480
Career
  gender and, 5, 127
  learning disabilities and, 263, 264
  student aspirations, 30, 39–40
  *See also* Jobs
Cerebral palsy, 391, 393
Ceremonies, 408
Child abuse or neglect
  reporting, 20
  retardation and, 349
  traumatic brain injuries and, 390
Child-centered approach, 445
Child rearing practices, 57
Circles of Friends, 352–353, 366
Civil Rights Act, 426
Civil rights movement, 411
Class notes, *see* Note taking
Classroom
  bilingual, 430
  diversity in, 405–433
  female participation, 126, 193
  partial participation, 364
Classroom discussion, gender differences and, 126
Classroom environment, 368
  hearing loss and, 387–388
  organized, 329–330
  physical disabilities and health impairments, 394–395, 396
  visual impairments and, 376, 380
Classroom management
  biased, 64–65
  gender bias and, 129
  small groups, 249
  whole-class grouping and, 247
Closed captioning (CC), 388
Cognitive ability, research on, 35–36
Cognitive academic language proficiency (CALP), 422
Cognitive academic learning proficiency (CALP), 90
Cognitive development
  bilingualism and, 421–422
  parenting style and, 35–36
Cognitive skills
  educationally disadvantaged students, 28–29, 35–36
  learning disabilities and, 261
  mental retardation and, 345, 351
Cognitive strategies, 268–269
Cognitive styles, 182–188
Collaborative behavior
  females and, 189
  modeling, 250
Collaborative learning, grouping and, 246
Collaborative open-note quizzes, 240
Collective identity, 410
College attendance, bilingual education and, 430
Color, teachers of, 439–441, 447–451, 455
Common underlying proficiency, 421
Communication, 29
  analogous, 104
  augmentative, 308, 309, 354, 355, 356
  between non-White and White educators, 439–441
  context-embedded, 423
  cultural differences, 408
  direct versus indirect, 104
  emotional versus subdued, 103
  formal versus informal, 102–109
  honest, 104–105
  interpersonal skills, 422
  nonverbal, 110–114
  poetic, 104
Communication board, 354, 355, 356, 397
Communication disorders, 291–316
  accommodations for, 306–315
  assessment of, 306
  instructional guidelines, 306–315
  prevalence of, 304–306
Communication skills
  development of, 357
  mental retardation or severe disabilities and, 354
Communication styles, 102–109, 159
Communicatively appropriate education, 89–115
Community
  African American students, 40
  creating connections in, 418–419
  disabled students and, 366
Community college system, 68, 75
Community of learners, 231
Community participation, minority, 461, 465–467, 470, 471–472
Compensatory educational programs, 73
Compensatory skills, 378
Competitive behavior, 156–157
Competitive learning, 182, 191–194, 204, 408
Comprehensible input, 423
Comprehensible output, 423
Comprehension (receptive language), 294, 306, 311, 423
Computer(s)
  augmentative communication and, 309
  availability, 73
  gender and, 5, 125
  helping special learners using, 242
  interactive multimedia, 338–339
  learning disabled using, 273–274, 275
  literacy in using, 4
  visual impairment and, 382
Computer-assisted instruction (CAI), 274, 276, 338
Computer software, gender biases in, 125
Concept(s)
  applying, 489
  bilingualism and, 422
  building on, 445

choice of, in teaching, 235–236
connections among, 295–297, 311–312, 351
labels for, 295
presenting new, 311
teaching to ESL students, 421
working-class schools teaching, 485
Concrete teaching techniques, 32
Concrete thinking processes, 28
Conduct disorders, 277, 324
Confidence, words that show, 252
Conflict resolution, 110, 332–334
Conformity, 128, 140, 181
Consequences, 330, 331
Content bias, in assessment, 164–166, 169, 170
Content instruction, ESL and, 431
Content integration, multicultural education and, 411
Content of language, *see* Language content
Context
  second language acquisition and, 417–419, 421
  teaching language and, 310, 421, 423
Context-embedded communication and instruction, 423
Contextually inappropriate educational approaches, 55–57
Contrastive analysis, 97
Contributions approach to multicultural curriculum, 412
Control, locus of, 198
Controversial issues, discussions about, 109
Convergent thinking processes, 28
Conversation, 302
  culture of power and, 442
  dialects used in, 424
  instructional, 268–269
  learning through, 468
  promoting language through, 312
  second language competence, 422
Cooperative behavior, 156–157
Cooperative learning, 7, 182, 204
  benefits of, 249
  cross-ethnic friendships and, 407
  cultural effects on, 191, 408
  disabled students, 368
  gender and, 142, 193
  groups and, 249–250
Hispanic American students, 409
  learning disabled, 273

results of, 193
self-concept and, 194
test preparation, 240
Corporal punishment, 77
Co-teachers, 404
Course(s)
  planning content, 231
  gender, 127, 139, 143
Course Planning Routine, 230–232
Crack babies, 20
Creativity
  bilingualism and, 422
  gender and, 128, 140
  middle-class schools, 489
Criterion-referenced assessment, 172
Critical thinking skills, reading and, 445
Cross-age pairing, 251
Cross-cultural interactions, 443
Cross-ethnic friendships, 193, 407
Cultural bias, mainstream, 58
Cultural boundaries, crossing, 409–410
Cultural capital, 444
Cultural characteristics, 407–410
Cultural conflicts, resolving, 205–206
Cultural deprivation, 27–43
Cultural dialects, 424
Cultural diversity, 405–415
  accommodations, 428–432
  instructional guidelines, 428–432
  multicultural education and, 410–415
  promoting, 428
  understanding, 406–407
Cultural familial retardation, 23
Cultural heritage, rejecting, 204, 205
Cultural insensitivity, combating, 17
Cultural inversion, 410
Cultural literacy, English and, 90
Culturally inappropriate educational approaches, 57–59
Culturally relevant teaching, 428
Cultural pluralism, promoting, 428
Cultural transmutation, 205
Culture(s)
  articulation and, 293
  collective, 156–157
  deaf, 384–385
  dominant, 38
  empowering school, 411
  incorporating student's, 464–465
  individualistic, 157, 406, 407
  intelligence tests and, 356

macro-, 406–407
maintaining, 9
micro-, 406–407
personal involvement, 180
sensitization to differences, 58
views on disabilities and, 358
Culture of power, 439–456
Culture shock, 55–56
Cummins, Jim, 458–475
Cumulative folders, 207
Curriculum
  assessment bias and, 164–166
  educationally disadvantaged, 34
  gender biases, 124–125
  homosexuality and, 516–517
  incorporating microcultures into, 407
  language development integrated with, 468
  mental retardation or severe disabilities and, 365
  modified by expectations, 59
  multicultural, 412–415
  social class and, 478–500
Curriculum-based assessment, 164

Day care, 33
Daydreaming
  hearing loss and, 387
  immaturity and, 326
Deaf, 384
Deaf–blind, 349
Deaf culture, 384–385
Death, dealing with, 397
Decision making, group processes in, 109
Decoding words, 261, 303
Defiance, expression of, 112
Degrees of Learning, 233–235
Delpit, Lisa D., 439–457
Demand, learning on, 189–191
Dependent learning, 160, 181
Depression, 263, 326, 327
Desegregation, 77
Developmental pathways, conduct disorders and, 324
Developmental period, 345
Developmental problems, birth weight and, 18
Diabetes, 393
*Diagnostic and Statistical Manual of Mental Disorders* (DSM), 323–324
Dialect(s), 89, 92–102
  articulation and, 293
  assessment and, 170–171

defined, 424
  evaluating students based on, 62–63
Dialect readers, 444
Difficulty, avoidance of, 199
Direct communication, 104
Direct instruction, 443–444, 447
Disabilities
  cultural views of, 358
  inclusion movement and, 244
  learning, see Learning disabilities
  multiple, 348, 350
  physical, 389–398
  severe, see Severe disabilities
Disagreement, communication of, 107, 114
Discipline, 31
  gender and, 125, 128–129, 140
  school resegregation and, 77
Discrepancy analysis, 361
Discrimination
  assessment, 468–470
  educational system, 59–60
  sexual orientation and, 146–147, 508, 515
Diseases
  hearing loss caused by, 384
  visual impairment caused by, 375
  See also Health impairments; Physical disabilities
Distar, 443–444, 445
Diverse society, instruction in, 179–211
Diversity
  cultural, see Cultural diversity
  linguistic, 415–432
Divorce, effects of, 512
Down syndrome, 346
Drawing, access to, 397
Dress, 208
  cultural effects on, 408
  culture of power and, 442
Dress codes, 143
Dropouts, 405
  African American, 458
  Hispanic American, 72, 458
  immigrants, 72
  living conditions and, 6
  pay levels, 25
  race and, 4
  sexual orientation and, 145
Drug use, during pregnancy, 18, 19–21, 264, 349, 350, 393
Dual sensory impairments, 349, 350
Dyads, 250–251

Dyscalculia, 260
Dysgraphia, 260
Dyslexia, 260, 261, 264

Echolalia, 376
Ecological inventories, 357
Economic discrimination, academic failure and, 462
Economic reforms, 17
Education
  bilingual, see Bilingual education
  communicatively appropriate, 89–115
  contextually inappropriate approaches, 55–57
  culturally inappropriate approaches, 57–59
  diverse society, 179–211
  gender equity in, 139–150
  holistic approach to, 348
  multicultural, 410–415
  power and, 439–456
  prejudice in system, 59–67
Educational aspirations, of disadvantaged students, 30, 39–40
Educational disadvantage, 27–43
Educational reform, 57–58, 458
Education Amendments Act (Title IX), 143
Effort, words that recognize, 252
Elaboration, promoting language through, 314
Emotion
  discussions about, 108
  expression of, 112, 129
Emotional communication, 103
Emotional environment, appropriate, 330–331
Emotional or behavioral disorders, 321–340
  accommodations, 329–336
  assessment, 327–328
  causes of, 326–327
  cooperative learning and, 250
  definitions, 321
  instructional guidelines, 336–337
  learning disabilities and, 263, 264
  minorities having, 405
  prevalence of, 322
  types and characteristics of, 323–326
Emotional problems
  learning disabilities and, 263
  self-concept and, 38
Empowerment, 71
  gender equity and, 142

  minority students, 458–475
  school culture and, 411
Encouraging words, 251
Energetic learning style, 185
English
  idioms, 298
  standard, 62–63, 92, 93, 94–102
  variations of, 424
English as a Second Language (ESL) instruction, 89, 91
  elements of, 428–430
  goal of, 418
  historical perspectives, 424–428
  techniques, 97
English as a Second Language (ESL) students, 459
  articulation and, 293
  assessment of, 168
  figurative language and, 297
  hearing loss and, 384
  second language acquisition and, 415–432
  syntax and, 300
English-only legislation, 428
English proficiency, 6–7, 33
  grouping based on, 248
English submergence, 91, 168
Environment
  accommodations for disabled students, 368
  classroom, see Classroom environment
  dual sensory impairments and, 350
  emotional, 330–331
  emotional or behavioral disorders and, 326
  IQ and, 25–26
  learning, 185–186
  planning, 228
  second language acquisition, 418–419
  study, 531
Epilepsy, 391, 392
Equal Educational Opportunities Act of 1972, 92–93
Equal opportunity, 22, 33, 92, 463
Equity pedagogy, 411
Essay questions, 543, 544
Ethnic disparities, 3–4
  extrinsic causes of, 55–78
  intrinsic causes of, 17–44
Ethnic heroes, 412
Ethnicity
  assessor's, 158–159

551

gender and career, 5
language use, 36
learning styles, 7
maintaining identity, 9
European American(s), power maintenance and, 67
European American-centric perspective, 38
European American females, success in male domain and, 155
European American students
IQ and, 25–26
locus of control, 198
risk taking, 195
teacher interaction with, 64
European American teachers, 65
Evaluation, biased, 61–63, 125–127
Examples, learning from, 187
Executive elite school, 493–496, 498
Expansion, promoting language through, 314
Expectations of students, 59, 95
biased, 60–64
diversity and, 428
gender and, 122, 125
Experientially-based instruction, 368
Expressive language, *see* Production
External clues, reliance on, 203
Externalizing behaviors, 323
Extrinsic causes of disparities, 55
Extrinsic rewards, 201
Eye contact, 105–106

Fact, discussing matters of, 108
Failure
attributions about, 198
gender and, 127
risk of, 195
of minority students, 458–475
self-image and, 30
Fairness, gender equity and, 139
Families
homosexual, 502–521
physical disabilities and health impaired students, 396
planning for disabled students, 361
traditional, 503
violence in, 327
*See also* Home; Parent(s)
Family values, 407
Fatalistic attitudes, 30, 31
Father absence, 30, 31, 41–42
Federal Education Consolidation and Improvement Act, 34

Feedback, 428
African American students, 66
attention deficit disorder and, 280
biased, 65
gender and, 125–127
learning pairs, 250
Feelings, *see* Emotion
Females
cooperative learning, 193
dependent learning, 181
motivation to succeed, 188–189
nonverbal cues and, 186
reflective style, 183
school experiences, 119–131
self-confidence, 197
sexist education and, 68–69
sexually abused, 326
success in male domain and, 155
Fetal Alcohol Syndrome, 346, 393
Field-independent learning characteristics, 203–204, 206
Field-sensitive learning characteristics, 203–204, 206
Figurative language, 297
Filipino Americans
cooperative learning, 192
learning style, 181
Finger spelling, 384, 386
FIRST-letter mnemonic strategy, 539–540
Flashcards, 540–541
Flexible grouping, 245–247
Fluency, 291
Fluency disorders, 293–294, 305, 307
Food, cultural differences and, 408
Forensic instruction, 187
Formal assessment, 172, 208–210
Formal communication, 102–103
Formal register, 301
Format bias, assessment, 166–167, 170
Form of language, *see* Language form
Foster care, 20
Friends, Circles of, 352–353, 366
Friendship(s)
cross-ethnic, 193, 407
visually impaired students, 377
*See also* Peer(s)
Functional assessment, 357, 361
Functional practice, 368
Functional vision, 375
Funds of knowledge, in home community, 407, 421
Future learning, assessing, 163
Future orientation, 195–196

Gangs, 325
Gay parents, 146, 502–521
Gay students, 145, 514–515
Gender
ability grouping and, 127
attention deficit disorder and, 279
aggression tolerance and, 325
assessment and, 171–172
assessor's, 159
cooperative learning and, 192
defiance of bias, 123
depression and, 326
expression of emotion, 112
field sensitivity, 203
learning disabilities and, 261, 264
learning styles, 7
locus of control, 198
reading disabilities and, 261
risk taking and, 195
speech production and, 292
stereotypes, 204
stuttering and, 293
teacher relationships, 180
*See also* Females; Male(s)
Gender appropriate education, 139–150
Gender disparities, 4–6, 119–131
Gender equity, in education, 139–150
Gender roles, 189
androgyny and, 141
cultural beliefs about, 408
homosexual families, 507–508
rewards for appropriate, 122
textbooks and, 415
General education classes, disabled students in, 359, 366–368
Generalizations, avoiding over-, 8–10
Generalization ability
educationally disadvantaged students, 28
teaching, 351
Genetic differences, inferiority beliefs based on, 21–27
Genetic factors, 17
emotional or behavioral disorders and, 326–327
hearing loss, 384
reading disabilities, 261, 264
Gifted students, 244, 245
Global learners, 161, 183–184
Goals
ability to attain, 200
African American students, 40
assignment completion, 272

cooperative learning, 250
disabled students, 369
future, 195
IEP, 359, 361, 367
learning to set, 533
long-range, 361
positive personal, 334, 335
task analysis, 362
Grade, retention in, 4
Grades
cooperative learning work, 250
tracking based on, 243
Grammar, 29, 37, 95, 97, 424, 488
Group behavior, 325
Group goals, 192
Grouping, 240–252, 368. *See also*
Tracking and ability grouping
Group orientation, learning and, 182
Group processes, 109–110
Group values, 407
Guilt, responses to, 105
Gunshot wounds, 390

Haitian Americans, as aural learners, 185
Hands-on instruction, 368
Hard of hearing, 384, 385
Hawaiian Americans, cooperative learning and, 157, 192
Head injury, 349, 389–390, 393
Head Start, 32, 57, 58, 73
Health care
poor families, 18–19
retardation and, 349
Health impairments, 389–398, 390.
*See also* Disabilities
Hearing impairment
communication disorders with, 305
visual impairment with, 349
Hearing loss, 383–389
Heroes, ethnic, 412
Heterogeneous grouping, 244, 368
High school graduation, 4
outcomes after, 77
pay levels and, 25
Hispanic Americans
AIDS prevalence, 21
belief in genetic differences, 22,
cultural deprivation theory and, 27–28
pay levels, 25
*See also* Mexican Americans
Hispanic American students
achievement and, 3–4, 405, 459

assessment of, 154, 155, 158, 159, 160, 166, 206
aural learners, 185
biased evaluation, 61
biased treatment, 65
communication style, 103, 159
community college and, 75
cooperative learning, 157, 192, 193
cultural characteristics, 409
disability views, 358
dropout rates, 72, 458
global learners, 161
group process, 109
kinship ties, 156
language use, 37
learning style, 179–180, 181
locus of control, 41, 198
motivation to succeed, 188
nonverbal cues and, 186
numbers in U.S., 405
perceptual style, 183
powerlessness, 57
responsibility for mistakes, 106–107
self-concept, 30, 38
stimulation of, 186
subject matter interest, 189–190
teacher relationships, 180
time orientation, 195–196
History, teaching non-European American, 202
HIV, *see* Human immunodeficiency virus
Hmong American students
aural learners, 185
kinship ties, 156
Holidays, 208
Holistic approach to education, 348
Home
changing behavior at, 332
cultural orientation, 445
stimulation in, 161
vocabulary used at, 168
*See also* Families
Home community, of culturally diverse students, 406, 407
Homeless children, 6, 56
Homework
attention deficit disorder and, 280
visually impaired students and, 376
Homogeneous grouping, 243, 244
Homophobia, 508–513
Homosexual parents, 146, 502–521
Homosexual students, 145–149, 514–515
Honest communication, 104–105

Hormones, gender differences and, 119–120
Human immunodeficiency virus (HIV), 21, 349, 392, 393
Hyperactivity, 263, 276, 277, 324

Identity
collective, 410
confident cultural, 462–463
efforts to maintain, 69
gender and, 123
homosexual students, 148
subordinate minorities, 70
Idioms, 297, 298
Illness, hearing loss caused by, 384
Immaturity, 326, 328
Immigrants, 33
involuntary, 70–72
voluntary, 70
Immigrant students
assessment of, 154, 166
contextual problems, 55–56
*See also* Refugee students
Improvement, words that recognize, 252
Impulsivity, 182, 276–277
Inactive learning style, 185
Inattention, 276
Inclusion support teacher, 344
Inclusive learning communities, 351
Inclusive schools, 359
Independent learning, 160, 181
Indirect communication, 104
Individualistic cultures, 157, 182, 406, 407
Individualistic learners, 182, 191–194
Individualized adaptations, 364
Individualized Education Plan (IEP), 228, 359, 361, 367, 378
Individuals with Disabilities Education Act (IDEA), 259, 279, 321, 346–348, 355, 385, 389
Inequality, reproduction of, 65–75
Inferiority
messages about, 38
myths, 70
Inflectional endings, 299
Informal assessment, 172, 208, 210
Informal communication, 102
Informal member checks, 240
Informal register, 301
Information, presenting in multiple ways, 270, 271
Information processing, learning disabilities and, 261

553

Injury, visual impairment caused by, 375
Inner city mothers, substance abuse and, 20
Inner suffering, signs of, 328
Instruction
 English as a Second Language (ESL), 428–430
 hands-on, 368
 one-on-one, 251
 team, 368
Instructional conversations, 268–269
Instructional grouping, 240–252
Instructional guidelines
 attention deficit disorder and, 279–284
 communication disorders, 306–315
 diverse students, 428–432
 emotional or behavioral disorders, 336–337
 hearing loss, 387–389
 mental retardation or severe disabilities, 351, 359–369
 physical disabilities and health impairments, 394–398
 visual impairments, 378–383
Instructional strategies
 culturally disadvantaged and, 32
 educationally disadvantaged and, 34
 learning disabilities and, 265–274
Instructional unit, 232–237
Intellectual functioning, of students with mental retardation or severe disabilities, 345, 350–351
Intelligence, 17
 belief in genetic differences in, 22, 23–27
 expectations about, 61
Intelligence tests, 23, 26–27, 355–356
Interactions
 cross-cultural, 443
 culture of power and, 442, 444
 dominated students, 458–475
Interactive multimedia, 338–339
Interactive planning, 228, 229
Interactive stories, 396–397
Interdependence hypothesis, language and, 460
Interest(s), 202
 grouping based on, 248
 learning pairs based on, 251
 subject matter, 189–191
Internal clues, reliance on, 203
Internalizing behaviors, 323
Interpreters, 169–170, 388–389

Interview, assessing acculturation using, 208
Intrinsic causes of disparities, 17–44
Intrinsic motivation, 190–191, 461
Intuitive learning style, 160, 182
IQ scores, 25, 346

Japanese Americans, communication style of, 159
Jobs
 cultural expectations about, 408
 gender and, 124, 127
 learning disabilities and, 263, 264
 social class and, 481
 visually impaired students, 376
Juvenile delinquency, learning disabilities and, 264

Kinesthetic learning style, 185
Knowledge
 availability of, based on social class, 478–500
 from home community, 407, 421
 teacher as source of, 446–447
 teacher's transmission of, 467–468
Knowledge construction, multicultural education and, 411

Laboratory settings, linguistic research in, 35
Language, 6–7
 academic, 422
 acquisition of second, 415–432
 assessment bias and, 167–171
 codes of, 447–454
 communicatively appropriate education, 89–115
 comprehension, 294, 306, 311, 423
 culture of power and, 444
 figurative, 297
 incorporating student's, 464–465
 interdependence hypothesis, 460
 production, 294, 306, 311, 423
 social, 422
 See also English as a Second Language (ESL); Linguistic diversity
Language arts
 affluent professional school, 491
 executive elite school, 494–495
 middle-class school, 488
 working-class school, 485
Language-based dyslexia, 261
Language content, 294–298, 307, 311, 354

Language development, 100
 facilitating, 308–315
 hearing loss and, 384
 integrated with curriculum content, 468
 mental retardation or severe disabilities and, 354
Language disorders, 294–301
Language elaboration, 314
Language expansion, 314
Language form, 294, 299–301, 307
Language use, 294, 301–302, 307, 311
Latino Americans, see Hispanic Americans
Leaders
 female, 193
 training, 68
Learn, beliefs in ability to, 197–198
Learned helplessness, 181
Learner(s), community of, 231
Learner characteristics, second language acquisition and, 420–421
Learning
 action, 527–543
 bilingualism and, 421–422
 cognitive style and, 182–188
 collaborative, see Collaborative learning
 competitive, 191–194, 204, 408
 cooperative, see Cooperative learning
 degrees of, 233–235
 demonstrating in multiple ways, 270, 271
 environment for, 186
 framework for, 267–268
 gender differences in, 119–131
 individualistic, 191–194
 individualized adaptations and 364
 mental retardation or severe disabilities and, 345, 350–351
 monitoring, 240
 motivational style and, 188–195
 nonstandard dialects and, 94–95
 opportunities for, 337
 relationship style and, 179–182
 relevance and, 189–191
 sensory channels for, 378
 social, 337
 trial and error, 186–187
Learning and developmental process, of second language acquisition, 422–423
Learning characteristics, assessing, 206–207

554

Learning disabilities, 259–274
  accommodations for, 265–274
  assessment of, 265, 469
  attention deficit disorder and, 277
  cooperative learning and, 250
  definitions of, 259–260
  health care and, 18
  instructional techniques, 265–274
  language disorders occurring with, 291, 305
  minorities having, 405
  note taking and, 240
  parental substance abuse and, 19, 20
  pedagogically induced, 467
  prevalence of, 264
  student characteristics, 261–263
  types of, 260
Learning goals, for disabled students, 367
Learning logs, 238
Learning on demand, 189–191
Learning partners in pairs, 250–251, 252
Learning potential
  assessing, 163
  genetic differences, 23, 25
Learning styles, 7
  activity levels and, 185–186
  adult-orientation and, 182
  analytical, 160, 161, 182, 183
  assessment and, 160–162
  aural/visual/verbal, 184
  calm/inactive, 185
  competitive, 182, 191–194, 204, 408
  cooperative, see Cooperative learning
  cultural characteristics influencing, 58, 407, 464
  dependent versus independent, 160, 181
  disabled students, 368
  field-independent, 203–204, 206
  field-sensitive, 203–204, 206
  global, 161, 183–184
  impulsive/spontaneous/intuitive, 160, 182
  kinesthetic/active/energetic, 185–186
  object-oriented, 191
  participatory, 179–180
  passive, 179–180
  people-oriented, 191
  reflective, 160, 182, 183
Learning Style Inventory, 206

Lectures
  listener-friendly, 536
  listening for cues during, 537–538
Legal blindness, 375
Legal issues
  attention deficit disorders, 279
  bilingual education, 424–428
  dialectal differences and, 92–94
  gender and, 143
  homosexual parents, 504–505
  learning disabilities, 259
  limited English proficiency, 89. 91
Leisure, cultural beliefs about, 408
Lesbian parents, 146, 502–521
Lesbian students, 145, 514–515
Lesson planning, 237–240
Lesson Planning Pyramid, 237–240, 247, 360
Lesson Reaction Sheets, 243
Levels of cognitive ability, 22, 23–27
Level system, controlling behavior using, 332
Life Space Intervention (LSI), 335–336
Limited English Proficiency (LEP) students, 6–7, 89–92
  assessment and, 167–170
  separate classes for, 244
  See also English as a Second Language students
Linguistic bias, assessment and, 167–171
Linguistic diversity, 415–432
Linguistic input, 418–419
Linguistic proficiency
  educational disadvantage and, 29–30, 35, 36,–37
  research on, 36–37
Listener-friendly lectures, 536
Listening
  ability in, 299
  for cues during lectures, 537–538
  secondary language acquisition and, 423
Literacy
  direct instruction, 443–444, 447
  need for higher, 264
  physical disabilities and, 395–397
Lithium, 327
Living conditions
  achievements and, 5
  cultural disadvantage and, 33–34
  educational approaches, 55–57
  parental substance abuse, 20
Locus of control, 31, 40–41

Long-range goals, 29
Long-term planning, 230–232
Low vision, 375

Macroculture, 406–407
Maintenance bilingual education, 430
Male(s)
  behavior patterns, 128, 129
  cooperative learning, 193
  feminized, 141
  independent learning, 181
  motivation to succeed, 188
  nonverbal cues, 186
  role models, 30, 31, 41–42
  school experiences, 119–131
  self-confidence, 197
Male domain, 119, 155, 198
Male pronouns, 124
Manic-depression, 327
Materialism, orientation toward, 406
Material reinforcers, 7
Mathematics
  ability grouping, 243
  attention to males, 126
  computer programs, 274
  cooperative learning, 193
  demonstrating learning for, 271
  executive elite school, 493
  functional practice, 368–369
  gender and, 5, 119, 120, 127, 198
  learning disability and, 260
  middle-class schools, 488
  remedial, 4
  working-class schools, 484–485
Matriarchal settings, 31
McGill Action Planning System, 361
Meanings, multiple, 297
Medications
  attention deficit disorder and, 280–284
  emotional or behavioral disorders and, 327
Memory deficits, 351
Memory strategies, 270, 527, 539–540
Mental retardation
  accommodations, 345, 351, 359–369
  assessment, 345, 355–357
  characteristics of students with, 350–355
  definitions, 345–346
  language disorders occurring with, 291, 305
  minorities with, 405
  prevalence of, 349–350

prevention of, 349
types of, 346
Meritocracy theory, 22, 24–25
Metalinguistics, 302–304, 422
Mexican Americans
  lack of progress, 72
  time orientation, 195–196
  See also Hispanic Americans
Microcultures, 406–407
Middle class, 480
  culture, 442
  values, 444
Middle-class schools, 487–489, 497
Middle-class students
  expectations for, 61
  verbal directives and, 448
Migrant students, dropout rate of, 6
Minorities
  empowering students, 458–475
  homosexual parents, 510–511
  types of, 409–410
Mistakes, admission of, 106–107
Mixed-ability grouping, 244–245, 248–249
Mixed-ability small groups, 248–249
Mixed-sex groups, 193
Mnemonic devices, 527, 539–540
Mobility skills, visual impairment and, 378–380
Model(s)
  gender stereotypes, 122
  See also Role models
Modeling
  appropriate behaviors, 337
  cognitive strategies, 268–269
  collaborative behavior, 250
  hearing loss students and, 388
  learning language through, 314
  learning strategies, 527
Morals, learning from, 187
Morphemes, 299
Motivation, 34
  assessment and, 155–158
  disadvantaged students, 30, 39–40
  empowered students, 461, 462
  gender bias, 127
  grouping effects on, 244
  intrinsic, 190–191, 315
  language used for, 315
  meritocracy theory, 22
  techniques, 7
Motivational style, 188–195
Motivational test bias, 154
Motor development, delays in, 353–354

Motor excess, 324
Motor skills, instruction of, 397
Multicultural education, 17, 410–415
Multidisciplinary teams, learning disabled students and, 265
Multimedia, creating community connections using, 418–419
Multiple disabilities, 348, 350
Multiple meanings, 297
Muscular dystrophy, 391–392
Music, 186

Native American students
  achievement, 4, 405
  assessment, 155, 160, 166
  biased treatment, 65
  contextual problems, 56
  cooperative learning, 157
  cultural characteristics, 409
  dialect, 94
  disability views, 359
  high school diploma, 77
  learning style, 181, 184, 408
  locus of control, 41, 199
  parental substance abuse, 20
  perceptual style, 183
  powerlessness, 57
  reflective style, 183
  self-concept, 38, 201
  subject matter interest, 190
  teacher relationship, 180
  time orientation, 196
  visual learners, 184
Natural environment, exploitation of, 406
Needs, sensitivity to others', 106
Neighborhoods, educational disadvantage and, 29
Neo-Marxist perspective, 67–77
Neurological impairment, 18, 390
Neuromuscular diseases, 390, 393
Noise levels, 110
Nonoptical aids, 381–382
Nonstandardized assessment, 172
Nonverbal communication, 110–114
Nonverbal cues, sensitivity to, 186
Norm-referenced assessment, 169, 172
Notebook, organization of, 532–533
Note taking, 240
  effective, 535–536, 538–539
  for hearing loss students, 388–389
  teaching, 537
Nutrition, 18–19

Object-oriented learners, 191
Observation, assessing acculturation using, 208
Omission errors, 292–293
One-on-one instruction, 251
Open admissions, 33
Optical aids, 380
Oral communication
  authoritarian style, 447–448
  dialect and, 171
  language disorders and, 291
Orientation skills, visual impairment and, 378–380
Orthopedic impairment, 389
Other health impairment, 389
Outcomes, 34

Pace
  assessment, 162, 167
  curriculum, 197
  diverse students and, 428
  learning language and, 313–314
Pacific Americans
  communication styles, 104
  expression of emotion, 112
  numbers in U.S., 405
  risk taking, 195
Pacific American students
  assessment, 160
  biased evaluation, 63
  cooperative learning, 192
  expectations for, 61
  learning style, 179–180, 192
  nonverbal cues, 186
Pairs, learning partners in, 250
Parallel talk, 314
Parent(s)
  Asian, 408
  aspirations, 39–40
  assessing assimilation, 210
  culturally diverse students, 406
  disabled students, 369
  educationally disadvantaged students, 28–29
  education programs for, 32
  homosexual, 146, 502–521
  identifying students with disabilities and, 357
  immigrant, 33
  involvement in education, 465–467
  IQ, 25
  language ability and, 35, 37
  participation of minority, 461, 465–467, 470, 471–472
  skills, 29–30

substance abusing, 18, 19–21
training, 33
*See also* Families
Parenting
behavior disorders and, 326
style, 31, 36
Partially deaf, 384
Partially sighted, 375
Partial participation, 364
Participation
female, 126, 193
partial, 364
Participatory learning, 179–180
Passive learning, 179–180
Pause procedure, 536–537
Pay, educational attainment and, 25
Pedagogy
learning disabilities induced by, 467
power and, 439–456
Peer(s), 31
disabled students and, 361, 365
homophobic, 508
note taking for hearing loss students by, 389
physically disabled and health impaired students, 396, 397
planning for disabled students and, 361
Peer orientation, learning and, 182
Peer register, 301
Peer support, 365–366
Peer tutoring, 182, 191, 250–251, 252, 337, 365–366, 389
People-oriented learners, 191
Perceptual style, 183–184
Personal relations, distant versus involved, 180
Person-centered planning, 361
Pervasive developmental disorder, 325–326
Phonemes, 299
Phonology, 299
Phrases, encouraging, 251
Physical contact, 113–114
Physical disabilities, 389–398
Physical stimulation, African American children and, 161
Plan(s), individualized, 251
Planning, 227–240
attention deficit disorder and, 279–280, 282
disabled students and, 360–361
factors that influence, 228
flexible grouping, 246–247

lesson, 237–240
long-term, 230–232
person-centered, 361
physical disabilities and health impairments, 394
types of, 227–228
unit, 232–237
whole-class grouping, 247
PLAN strategy, 534–535
Play materials, 30
Poetic communication, 104
Poor students
achievement, 3–4
aspirations, 40
assessment, 154, 155
belief in genetic differences of, 22, 23
biased evaluation, 61
biased treatment, 65
contextual problems, 56
cooperative learning, 192
cultural deprivation theory and, 27–28
home culture, 445
language and, 36
learning disabilities and, 264
locus of control, 41
motivation to succeed, 188
nonstandard dialects and, 94–95
self-concept and, 30, 38
*See also* Poverty
Positive relationships, 330
Postnatal health care, 18
Poverty, 8
biomedical problems and, 18–21
female-headed families, 41
IQ and, 26
mental health problems and, 326
retardation and, 349
stereotypes and, 205
traditional roles and, 9
Power, 459
intergroup relations, 461–470
maintenance of, 67
pedagogy and, 439–456
standard English and, 101
symbolic capital and, 480
Practice, opportunities for extended, 272
Pragmatics, 301
Praise, 31
African American students, 64
gender differences, 126
learning pairs, 250

Pregnancy, substance use during, 18, 19–21, 264, 346, 349, 350, 393
Prejudice
combating, 17
cultural disadvantage theories and, 32
educational system, 59–60
language use, 37
nonstandard dialects, 96
nonstandard English, 94–95
reducing, 410
Prenatal care, 18, 19, 21
Preplanning, 228, 229
Preschool programs, 33
Spanish-only, 470–472
Present orientation, 195–196
Problem-solving skills, 23, 26, 336, 493
Process approach, 445–446, 455
Production (expressive language), 294, 306, 311, 423
Pronunciation, 95, 97, 171
Psychological assessment, 469
Punctuality, 196–197
Punishment, 331
gender and, 120, 129, 140
language used for, 330

Race
biomedical problems and, 18–21
*See also* Ethnicity; Minorities
Radical pedagogy, 71
Ramirez and Castenada Behavior Rating Scale, 206
Readers, gender and, 124–125, 140
Reading
ability grouping, 243
dialect and, 170
females and, 126, 198
functional practice, 368
hearing loss and, 384
learning pairs and, 251
nonstandard dialects and, 94–95
phonology and, 299
physical disabilities and health impairments and, 396
second language acquisition and, 418–419, 423
visually impaired students and, 377, 378
Reading achievement
auditory discrimination and, 37
tests, 164
Reading disabilities, 260, 261–263
Rebellion, discipline and, 129

Receptive language, *see* Comprehension
Reciprocal interaction model, 468
Recitation, gender differences in, 125
Recognition, difficulty with, 156
Reflective learners, 160, 182, 183
Refractive errors, 375
Refugee students
　assessment of, 154
　contextual problems, 55–56
Regional dialects, 293, 424
Regional differences, creating diversity, 9
Register, 301
Reinforcement
　attention deficit disorder and, 280
　biased, 65
　cooperative, 193
　gender and, 122, 128
　language used for, 315
　small groups, 249
Reinforcers, types of, 7–8
Rejection, risk of, 195
Relationships, social class and, 481
Relationship style, learning and, 179–182
Relevance, subject matter, 189–191
Reliable assessment, 163
Research
　bilingual education, 460
　bilingualism, 421–422
　cultural boundaries, 409–410
　cultural disadvantage and, 35–42
　disabilities, 358–359
　gender disparities, 126
　homosexual parenting, 517–518
　process approaches, 445–446
　structured reproduction, 72
Research-based approach, 7–8
Residual hearing, 384
Resistance, 76
　gender stereotypes, 123
　neo-Marxist perspective, 69–71
　standard English, 98
　working-class schools and, 487
Resource rooms, 244
Respect, communication of, 113
Response style, assessment and, 162
Responsibility
　accepting, 106–107
　gender differences, 198
Restlessness, 277, 324
Rewards
　assignment completion, 272
　attention deficit disorder and, 280
　extrinsic, 201
　types of, 7–8
Risk taking, 161, 195
Rituals, 408
Role models
　disabled students, 366
　homosexual, 148
　male, 30, 31, 41–42
　minority groups, 405
Root words, 299
Rules, 330, 331
Runaways, 6
Rural students
　contextual problems, 56
　dropout rate, 6

Same-ability grouping, 243, 244, 247–248
Same-ability small groups, 247–248
Same-sex groups, 193
Schedules
　attention deficit disorder and, 279
　time management using, 529–531
School(s)
　class-based curriculum in, 478–500
　democratizing influences, 24
　diversity in, 405–433
　financing, 73
　gender disparities and, 124, 130
　homosexuality and, 513–517
　inclusive, 359
　institutional characteristics, 461
　resegregation of, 77–78
　resources, 25
　social organization of, 459
　as social system, 411–412
　vocabulary used at, 168
School culture, empowering, 411
School-level ability grouping, 243
School-related difficulties, 3–10
Science
　affluent professional school, 491–492
　availability of labs, 73
　gender and, 5, 119, 126, 127, 198
　middle-class schools, 489
　remedial, 4
　working-class schools, 485
Sears, James T., 502–521
Secondary language output, 423–424
Second language acquisition, 415–432
Sedentary learning environment, 185–186
Seizure disorders, 391, 392, 393
Self-advocacy, 534–535
Self-concept
　cooperative learning and, 194
　educational disadvantage and, 30, 37–39
　enhancement of, 199–202
　gender and, 198
　native language and, 90
　personal goals and, 334
　research on, 37–39
　withdrawal and, 326
Self-confidence, 197–202, 326
　empowered students, 462
　gender bias, 127
Self-control, promoting, 332–334
Self-criticism, need for, 199
Self-esteem
　attention deficit disorder and, 277
　cooperative learning effects on, 249
　culturally relevant teaching and, 428
　depression and, 326
　dialects and, 100
　educational disadvantage and, 30, 37–39
　empowering school culture and, 411
　enhancement of, 199–202
　gender and, 198
　grouping effects on, 244
　inner suffering and, 328
　learning disabilities and, 263
　learning style and, 181
　multicultural education and, 412
　parental effects on, 512
　personal goals and, 334
　sexual orientation and, 145
　tracking and, 74
　whole-class grouping and, 247
Self-injurious behavior, 353
Self-monitoring, 271
Self-recording, 272
Self-regulation, 271
Self-satisfaction, 328
Self-stimulation, 328
Self-talk, 314
Semantic(s), 295
Semantic feature analysis, 295–296
Sensory channels, 378
Sensory development, delays in, 353
Sensory impairments, 348
　dual, 349, 350

Sequential teaching, 184
Serious emotional disturbance, 321
Severe disabilities
  accommodations, 351, 359–369
  assessment, 355–357
  characteristics of students with, 350–355
  defined, 346
  prevalence of, 350
  speech problems and, 354
  types of, 346–349
Sex education, 140
Sexism, 124–125
Sex roles, see Gender roles
Sexual abuse, 326
Sexual orientation
  of parents, 146, 502–521
  of students, 145–149, 514–515
SHARE strategy, 535
Sheltered English, 89, 91, 428–429
Sight vocabulary, 261
Silent or nonverbal period, 424
Singing, 186
Sit, ability to, 185
Situational factors, in second language acquisition, 417–419
Skills
  maintenance of, 272
  using, 528
Skills-oriented approach to writing, 440–441
Slavery, 70
Small groups, 247–249
Smoking, during pregnancy, 349
Social action approach to multicultural curriculum, 415
Social adjustment, 19
Social benefits, of cooperative learning, 249
Social dialects, 424
Social discrimination, academic failure and, 462
Social experiences, of visually impaired adolescents, 376
Social identity, of subordinate minorities, 70
Socialization, homosexual students and, 148
Socialized-aggression, 325
Social language, 422
Social learning, 337
Social mobility, 406
Social Network Pilot Project, 376–377
Social organization of school, 459
Social protest, activities on, 416

Social skills
  immaturity and, 326
  learning or behavior disorders and, 250
  mental retardation or severe disabilities and, 351–353
Social stratification, grouping effects on, 244
Social studies
  affluent professional school, 490–491
  executive elite school, 494
  middle-class schools, 488
  working-class schools, 486
Social system, school as, 411–412
Societal roles, preparing genders for, 139, 141
Society
  homophobic, 145
  ideals, 67
  reproductive forces of, 67–77
Socioeconomic class/differences, 8
  cultural experiences and, 9
  curriculum and, 478–500
  IQ and, 25
  language use, 36
Socioeconomic disparities, 3–4
  extrinsic causes of, 55–78
  intrinsic causes of, 17–44
Sound, ability to produce, 299
Sound out, sound spell strategy, 299
Southeast Asian American students
  achievement, 3–4
  learning style, 181
Space
  cultural beliefs about, 408
  working-class schools and, 486
Spanish-only program, 470–472
Speaking
  dialect and, 94–101
  secondary language acquisition and, 423–424
Special education
  eligibility for, 355
  physical disabilities or health impairments and, 393
Special education teachers, 265, 359
Special learners
  adaptive technology for, 242
  grouping, 240–252, 368
  planning for, 226–240
Specific learning disabilities, 259
Speech
  hearing loss and, 387
Speech and language pathologists, 307, 354

Speech development
  facilitating, 307–308
  hearing loss and, 384
Speech disorders, 171, 291–294. See also Language disorders
Spelling
  finger, 384, 386
  learning disabilities and, 261–262
  metalinguistics, 303
  phonology and, 299
Spina bifida, 391, 393
Spinal cord injury, 390
Spontaneous learning style, 160, 182
Sports
  gender and, 125, 127, 140, 143
  traumatic brain injuries and, 390
Standardized achievement tests, 164, 172
Standardized assessment, 172
Status, culture and, 408
Status quo, maintenance of, 444, 451
Status relations, school performance and, 461–470
Stereotypes
  assessment and, 154
  avoiding, 8–10, 206
  cultural, 34
  gender, 122, 128, 142, 204
  heterosexist, 512
  reducing, 410, 412
  reproduction of, 69–71
  resistance to, 69–71, 76
Stereotypic behaviors, 353
Stimulant medications
  for attention deficit disorder, 280–284
  for emotional or behavioral disorders, 327
Stimulation
  assessment and, 161
  high versus low, 161
  learning environment, 186
  self-, 328
Stories
  interactive, 396–397
  learning from, 187
Structured English, 89, 91
Structured reproduction, 67–77, 123
Student(s)
  communication styles, 102–109
  expectations of, see Expectations of students
  expenditures on, 73
  homosexual, 145–149, 514–515
  interviews, 208

resistance by, 69–71, 76
school-related problems, 3–10
teacher interaction with, 64
time management, 528–531
Student characteristics
assessment and, 153–162
learning disabilities and, 261–263
second language acquisition and, 420–421
Student outcomes, multicultural education and, 412
Student-related factors, influencing planning, 228
Studying
skills, 527–528, 531–533
for tests, 540–541
Stuttering, 293–294
Substance use, parental, 18, 19–21, 264, 346, 349, 350, 393
Substitution errors, 292
Success, 197–202
attributions about, 198
avoidance of, 156
desire for, 188, 189
preparation for, 17
providing opportunities for, 336
self-confidence about, 197
Suicide, sexual orientation and, 145
Support systems
for disabled students, 359, 394
for mentally retarded, 345, 347, 363
Suspensions, 77
gender and, 5, 119, 129, 140
race and, 4
Symbolic capital, 480, 498
Symbolic rewards, 7
Syntax, 299–301

Task analysis, 362
Teacher(s)
authority, 447–449
biased attitudes, 59–67
biased treatment, 64–65
co-, 404
of color, 439–441, 447–451, 455
communication styles, 102–109
gender biases, 125–127
gender of, 124
as knowledge source, 446–447
knowledge transmission by, 467–468
personal involvement, 180
planning process, 227–240
prejudiced, 59–67
time management for, 232

Teaching
analytic style, 184
argumentative techniques, 187
culturally relevant, 428
direct techniques, 187
sequential style, 184
*See also* Instruction
Teams
teaching, 368
transdisciplinary, 394
Technical bias, assessment and, 163–164
Test(s)
anxiety about, 127, 154
biased, 356
open-note, 240
studying for, 540–541
taking, 154, 541–543
visual impairment and, 382–383
Textbooks
culture of power and, 442
gender and, 125, 140, 143, 415
middle-class schools, 488
visual impairment and, 380
working-class schools, 484
Thinking aloud, 527
Think-Pair-Share method, 240
Time
allocations for learning disabled students, 274
assessment, 167
cultural beliefs about, 408
executive elite school and, 495
orientation, 195–197
study, 540
wait, 183, 313
working-class schools and, 486
Timelines, attention deficit disorder and, 280
Time management
students', 528–531
teachers', 232
Timer, changing behavior using, 334
Token economies, 332
Tonic-clonic seizures (grand mal), 391, 392
Tracking and ability grouping, 242
class-based, 24, 68
culture and, 32
decisions about, 247
educationally disadvantaged and, 24, 34
flexible, 245–247
gender bias in, 127
heterogeneous, 244–245

homogeneous, 243, 249
race and, 24, 60
research on, 73–75
school resegregation and, 77
Transdisciplinary teaming, 394
Transformation
gender stereotypes, 123
neo-Marxist theory and, 69–71
Transformation approach to multi-cultural curriculum, 415
Transitional bilingual education, 430
Translation, of assessment material, 168–169
Trauma, visual impairment caused by, 375
Traumatic brain injury, 389–390, 393
Trial and error, learning by, 186–187
Turn taking, 110
Tutoring, peer, see Peer tutoring
Two-way bilingual education, 430

Unit planning, 232–237
Unit Planning Pyramid, 233–237
United States Department of Education, 28
Unwillingness, communication of, 107
Upper class
culture of, 442
verbal directives and, 448
Use of language, *see* Language use

Valid assessment, 163, 166
Values
cultural differences, 409
family, 407
group, 407
macro- versus microculture, 406–407
middle-class, 444
Verbal directives, 447–448
Verbal learners, 184, 185
Verbal skills, gender differences in, 5, 120
Victim, blaming, 17, 35
Videography, creating community connections, 418–419
Violence
family, 327
traumatic brain injuries and, 390
Vision, deaf students' use of, 384
Visual acuity, 375
Visual clues, 388
Visual field, 375
Visual impairments, 242, 375–383
hearing impairment with, 349
Visual learners, 184

Visual-spatial tasks, gender differences in, 120
Vocabulary, 295
- correcting in school, 95
- disadvantaged students and, 30
- dyslexia and, 261–262
- English as a Second Language students, 421
- hearing loss and, 387
- home, 168
- relationship, 297
- school, 168
- sight, 261
- teaching, 311

Vocal nodules, damaged, 294
Vocation
- aspirations, 39–40
- mental retardation or severe disabilities and, 361
- success in, and standard English, 96, 98
- *See also* Jobs

Vocational education, 34
- attention deficit disorder and, 279
- gender disparities, 5

Vocational Rehabilitation Act of 1973, 279, 389
Voice, 291
Voice disorders, 294, 305, 307

Wait time, 183, 313
"Watch then do" learning, 187
White(s)
- drop out rates, 458
- suspicion of, 158, 159

White cultural frame of reference, 410
Whole-class grouping, 247
Whole language approach, 445
Withdrawal, 326
Within-class same-ability grouping, 243
Word(s)
- acceptance, 252
- appreciation, 251
- confidence, 252
- decoding, 261, 303
- encouraging, 251
- recognizing effort and improvement, 252
- root, 299

Word categories, 295
Word relationships, 295–297
Word retrieval, 313
Work, *see* Career; Jobs
Working class
- curriculum offered to, 478
- dialect, 62
- percent of population, 480
- verbal directives and, 448

Working-class schools, 484–487, 497
Wraparound services, 334
Writing
- access to, 397
- affluent professional school, 489
- culture of power and, 442
- dialect and, 101–102
- executive elite school, 494–495
- functional practice, 368
- learning disabilities and, 260, 270
- learning through, 468
- middle-class schools, 488
- phonology and, 299
- process approaches to, 446
- rules, 454
- secondary language acquisition and, 423–424
- skills-oriented approach to, 440–441
- standard English and, 95
- technical skills, 450
- visual impairment and, 382
- working-class schools, 485